MARRIAGE AND FAMILY

The Quest for Intimacy

FOURTH EDITION

Robert H. Lauer
U.S. International University at San Diego

Jeanette C. Lauer
U.S. International University at San Diego

Boston   Burr Ridge, IL   Dubuque, IA   Madison, WI   New York   San Francisco   St. Louis
Bangkok   Bogotá   Caracas   Lisbon   London   Madrid
Mexico City   Milan   New Delhi   Seoul   Singapore   Sydney   Taipei   Toronto

To
Jeffrey Mathew, Krista Julianne, Benjamin Brindle,
David Christopher, and John Robert,
Who are embarking on the quest

McGraw-Hill Higher Education

A Division of The **McGraw-Hill** Companies

MARRIAGE AND FAMILY: THE QUEST FOR INTIMACY

3 4 5 6 7 8 9 0 DOW/DOW 9 0 9 8 7 6 5 4 3 2 1 0

ISBN 0–07-231572–5

Editorial director: *Phillip A. Butcher*
Sponsoring editor: *Sally Constable*
Developmental editor: *Kate Purcell*
Marketing manager: *Leslie A. Kraham*
Project manager: *Karen Nelson*
Production supervisor: *Michael R. McCormick*
Designer: *Kiera Cunningham*
Cover illustration: © *Roxana Villa, Stock Illustration Source*
Senior photo research coordinator: *Keri Johnson*
Photo researcher: *Connie Gardner*
Associate supplement coordinator: *Carol A. Bielski*
Compositor: *Shepherd Inc.*
Typeface: *10.5/12 Times Roman*
Printer: *R. R. Donnelley & Sons Company*

Library of Congress Cataloging-in-Publication Data

Lauer, Robert H.
   Marriage and family : the quest for intimacy / Robert H. Lauer,
Jeanette C. Lauer.—4th ed.
      p. cm.
   Includes index.
   ISBN 0-07-231572-5 (softcover)
   1. Marriage—United States.   2. Family—United States.   I. Lauer,
Jeanette C.   II. Title.
HQ536.L39   2000
306.8'0973—dc21   99-30977

http://www.mhhe.com

BRIEF CONTENTS

PART ONE

THE CONTEXT OF INTIMACY

1. AMERICAN MYTHS AND DREAMS   3
2. DIVERSITY IN FAMILIES   27
3. GENDER ROLES: FOUNDATION FOR HETEROSEXUAL INTIMACY   59
4. SEXUALITY   81

PART TWO

SEEKING INTIMATE RELATIONSHIPS

5. GETTING TO KNOW SOMEONE ELSE   113
6. GETTING INVOLVED   135
7. FALLING IN LOVE   155
8. SELECTING A LIFE PARTNER   177
9. THE SINGLE OPTION   197

PART THREE

THE INTIMATE COUPLE

10. GETTING MARRIED   221
11. THE CHALLENGE OF COMMUNICATION   241

12. POWER AND CONFLICT IN MARRIAGE   263
13. WORK AND HOME   285

PART FOUR

INTIMACY IN FAMILIES

14. BECOMING A PARENT   311
15. THE FAMILY LIFE CYCLE   337
16. FAMILY LIFE AS MANAGEMENT   363

PART FIVE

CHALLENGES TO INTIMACY

17. FAMILY CRISES   385
18. SEPARATION AND DIVORCE   411
19. REMARRIAGE AND STEPFAMILIES   437

Glossary   459
References   463
Credits   511
Index   513

CONTENTS

Preface   xix

PART ONE

THE CONTEXT OF INTIMACY

1. AMERICAN MYTHS AND DREAMS   3

Learning Objectives   4

Myths About Family Life   4

We've Lost the Extended Family   5

People Marry Because They Love Each Other   5

Having Children Increases Marital Satisfaction 6

A Good Sex Life Is the Best Predictor
of Marital Satisfaction   6

Half of All Marriages End in Divorce   7

The Dangers of Myths   7

Changing Patterns of Intimate Relationships   7

Premarital Sex   8

Out-of-Wedlock Births   8

Living Alone   9

Cohabitation   9

Delayed Marriage   9

COMPARISON
Asian Women Are Marrying
at a Later Age   10

Birth Rates   10

Household Size   10

Employed Mothers   10

Divorce   11

PERSONAL
"It's a Different World"   12

A Concluding Note on Changing Patterns   12

The Family in Utopia   12

The Family in Utopian Writings   13

The Family in Utopian Communities   13

What Works Best?   15

What Do We Want?   15

Changes in Traditional Arrangements   15

PERSPECTIVE
The Utopian Quest for Intimacy   16

In Defense of Marriage and the Family   17

Me or We?   18

'Til Death?   19

INVOLVEMENT
Getting to Know You   19

PERSPECTIVE
A Note on Theory   22

Systems Theory   22

Exchange Theory   22

Symbolic Interaction Theory   23

Conflict Theory   23

Approach of this Book   24

Summary   24

INTERNET CONNECTION
American Myths and Dreams   25

2. DIVERSITY IN FAMILIES   27
   Learning Objectives   28
   The Variability of Family Life   28
      Variations Between Societies   28
      Variations Within Societies   29
      What Is the Family?   30
   The Single-Parent Family   30
      Extent of Single-Parent Families   31
      Challenges of the Single-Parent Family   31
      Challenges of Single Parents   32
   COMPARISON
   Single Parents In Iceland   33
      Challenges of Children of Single Parents   33
      Problems Between Parents and Children   35
      The Successful Single-Parent Family   36
   PERSONAL
   "I Chose to Do It Alone"   37
   Nonwhite Families   38
      The African American Family   38
      The Hispanic Family   44
      The Asian American Family   45
      The Native American Family   46
      The Interracial Family   48
   PERSPECTIVE
   A Slave Family   49
   The Homosexual Family   50
      Problems in Homosexual Families   51
      Intimacy in the Homosexual Family   52
      Long-Term Gay Relationships   53
   INVOLVEMENT
   What Is a Family?   54
   Principles for Enhancing Intimacy   55
   Summary   55
   INTERNET CONNECTION
   Diversity in Families   57

**3. GENDER ROLES: FOUNDATION
   FOR HETEROSEXUAL INTIMACY**   59
   Learning Objectives   60
   Men and Women:
   How Do They Differ?   60
   Men and Women: Some Commonalities   60
      Gender Differences   62
   Sex, Gender, Gender Role,
   and Gender-Role Orientation   65

      Gender Roles   65
   PERSPECTIVE
   Woman's Work   67
      Gender-Role Orientation   67
   Gender Roles: Nature or Nurture?   69
      How Much Is Biological?   69
      The Importance of Nurture   70
      Socialization and Gender-Role Orientation   71
   COMPARISON
   **Inuit Youth Learn to Be Males and
   Females**   73
   Changing Gender Roles and Orientations   74
      Changing Patterns   74
   INVOLVEMENT
   **Gender-Role Development: My
   Personal Journey**   74
      Lingering Traditionalism   75
   Gender-Role Orientation: What Difference
   Does It Make?   75
      Communication   75
      Self-Concept   76
      Mental Health   76
   Gender-Role Orientation and Intimacy   77
   PERSONAL
   "We Worked It Out"   78
   Principles for Enhancing Intimacy   78
   Summary   79
   INTERNET CONNECTION
   **Gender Roles: Foundations of
   Heterosexual Intimacy**   79

4. SEXUALITY   81
   Learning Objectives   82
   The Meaning of Sex   82
      Sex As Physical: The Response Cycle   82
      Sex As Social   84
   INVOLVEMENT
   Sex and Society   87
   Sex and Intimate Relationships   87
   Teenage Sex   88
      Extent of Sex Among Teenagers   88
   PERSONAL
   Sex and the Search for Intimacy   89
      Unwanted Pregnancy and Early Childbearing   89

Contraception   91
  Amount and Kinds of Contraceptive Use   94
  Who Uses Contraceptives?   94
Abortion   95
Premarital Sex   96
  The Double Standard   96
  Changing Attitudes   97
  Changing Behavior   98
Sex in Marriage   99
  Sexual Practices in Marriage   99
  Sexual Satisfaction and Marital Satisfaction 100
  Changes in Marital Sex over the Life Span   100
Extramarital Sex   101
  Why Extramarital Sex?   102
  Some Consequences of Extramarital Sex   102

PERSPECTIVE
The Sexual Needs of Women   103
Sexual Diseases and Dysfunctions   103
  Sexual Diseases   103
  Sexual Dysfunctions   105
  Inhibited Sexual Desire   106
  Safe Sex   106

COMPARISON
Unsafe Sex in Lesotho   107
Principles for Enhancing Intimacy   108
Summary   108

INTERNET CONNECTION
Sexuality   109

PART TWO

SEEKING INTIMATE RELATIONSHIPS

5. GETTING TO KNOW SOMEONE ELSE   113
Learning Objectives   114
We Are Social Creatures   114
  Loneliness   114

PERSONAL
Searching for Intimacy   118
  Fulfillment Through Intimacy   119
The Nature of Intimacy   120
  The Meaning of Intimacy   120

INVOLVEMENT
What Does Intimacy Mean?   121
  Intimacy and Equity   121

INVOLVEMENT
Intimacy As Self-Sustaining   122
Meeting and Getting to Know Others   123
  First Impressions   123

PERSPECTIVE
Getting Acquainted Victorian Style   125
  What Attracts?   125

COMPARISON
Mexican and United States Teens Portray Their Ideals About the Opposite Sex   126
Developing a Relationship   128
  First Stage: Initial Meeting and Awareness 128
  Second Stage: The Selection Process   129
  Third Stage: Developing Intimacy   130
  Fourth Stage: Maintaining or Dissolving the Relationship   132
Principles for Enhancing Intimacy   133
Summary   133

INTERNET CONNECTION
Seeking Intimate Relationships   134

6. GETTING INVOLVED   135
Learning Objectives   136
Dating   136
  Finding People to Date   136
  Selecting a Dating Partner   137

INVOLVEMENT
Changing Patterns of Dating   138
  Functions of Dating   138
  Patterns of Dating   139

COMPARISON
Commitment to Dating Partners in the United States and Taiwan   140
  Dating Problems   141
Moving Beyond Dating   143
  Moving Into a More Permanent Relationship   143
  Engagement   144
Cohabitation   144
  Who Cohabits?   144

PERSPECTIVE
Bundling   145
  Patterns of Cohabitation   146

Cohabitation Compared to Marriage 147
Cohabitation As a Preparation for Marriage 148
Breaking Up 148
Who Breaks Up? 148
Responding to Deterioration 149

PERSONAL
**The Birth, Life, and Death
of a Relationship** 151
Principles for Enhancing Intimacy 152
Summary 152

INTERNET CONNECTION
Getting Involved 153

7. **FALLING IN LOVE** 155
Learning Objectives 156
The Meaning of Love 156
When You Fall in Love 157
The Process of Falling 157

PERSONAL
Falling in Love—Twice 159
How Can You Tell If It's Love? 160
Passionate Versus
Companionate Love 161
The Emergence of Passionate Love 162
The Experience of Passionate Love 163

PERSPECTIVE
Love: A Nineteenth-Century View 165
From Passionate Love to Companionate Love 165
Loving and Liking 166
Rubin's Love Scale 166
Love and Friendship 167
A Triangular Theory of Love 168
Styles of Loving 169
Six Types of Lovers 169

INVOLVEMENT
Love and the Soaps 170
Implications of Differing Styles of Loving 170
Love Threatened—Jealousy 170
Who Is Most Jealous? 171

COMPARISON
**Jealousy Among the Italians, Dutch,
and New Guineans** 172
Situations That Provoke Jealousy 173
Consequences of Jealousy 173
Principles for Enhancing Intimacy 174

Summary 174

INTERNET CONNECTION
Falling in Love 175

8. **SELECTING A LIFE PARTNER** 177
Learning Objectives 178
Is There a Best Way to Select
a Life Partner? 178
What We Expect in a Life Partner 179

COMPARISON
Shirishana-Yanomama Mate Selection 180

INVOLVEMENT
**Dates and Mates: What Do People
Want?** 181
Qualities Desired in a Life Partner 181
Exchange and Equity 182
Narrowing the Field:
Assortative Mating 182
Life Partner Selection As a Filtering Process 182
Age 183
Ethnic Background 184
Race 185
Religion 186
Education 187
Personality 187
And So Forth 188
Why Assortative Mating? 188
Predictors of Marital Satisfaction 190
Timing 190
Equity 190

PERSONAL
Should I Marry My Baby's Father? 192
Communication 192

PERSPECTIVE
Abraham Lincoln Proposes 193
PREPARE: A Multifactor Approach 193
A Final Caveat 194
Principles for Enhancing Intimacy 195
Summary 195

INTERNET CONNECTION
Selecting a Life Partner 196

9. **THE SINGLE OPTION** 197
Learning Objectives 198
How Many Singles? 198
Myths About Singles 198

PERSPECTIVE
The Awfulness of Being Unmarried   200
Why People Are Single   201
  Career   201
  Availability of Sex   203
  Personal Freedom   203
  Desire for Personal Growth   203
  Social Conditions   204
  Family Background   205
  Personal Characteristics   205
Single Life-Styles   205
  Living Arrangements   206
  Sex   206
  Leisure   206
  Family Relations   207
  Singles and Old Age   208
Singles and Loneliness   208

INVOLVEMENT
Observing Singles   209
Singles and Health   209

COMPARISON
Being Single in Japan   210
Intimacy and Life Satisfaction   210
  Intimacy   210
  Life Satisfaction   212

PERSONAL
Single by Choice   214
Principles for Enhancing Intimacy   216
Summary   216

INTERNET CONNECTION
The Single Option   217

PART THREE

THE INTIMATE COUPLE

10. GETTING MARRIED   221
Learning Objectives   222
What Are Your Chances
of Getting Married?   222
  Marital Status of the Population   222
  Who Does, and Doesn't, Marry?   223
Why Do People Marry?   223
  Social Expectations   223

PERSPECTIVE
Dobu Marriage   224
  Social Ideals and Personal Fulfillment   225
  Desire for Children   225
  Marriage As a Practical Solution   226
Types of Marriage   226
  Classified by Alternative Life-Styles   226
  Classified by Structure of the Relationships   226
Expectations   228

COMPARISON
Types of Marriage in Togo   229
  Our Private Contracts   229

INVOLVEMENT
Who Prefers a Traditional Marriage?   230
  Role Expectations   231
  Negotiation: Changing Personal Contracts   232
  *The Marriage Contract:
    Clarifying Expectations*   232
Adjusting to Marriage   233
  His Marriage and Her Marriage   233
  Starting with Two Strikes   234
  Establishing Equity and Consensus   234
  Adjustment and In-Law Relationships   235
First-Year Changes   236

PERSONAL
In-Laws: The Good and the Bad   237
Commitment   237
  The Meaning of Commitment   237
  The Role of Commitment   238
  Building Commitment   238
Principles for Enhancing Intimacy   239
Summary   239

INTERNET CONNECTION
Getting Married   240

**11. THE CHALLENGE OF
COMMUNICATION**   241
Learning Objectives   242
The Nature of Communication   242
  Verbal Communication   242
  Nonverbal Communication   243
Communication As an Interaction Process   244
  A Discussion About Sex   245
  Communication Static   245
  Communicating Feelings   246
Listening   247

Styles of Poor Listening 247
Improving Listening Skills 248

PERSPECTIVE
The Silent Marriage 250
Impediments to Communication 250
Destructive Messages 250
Gender Differences As an Impediment 252
Why Husbands and Wives Don't Talk to Each Other 252

PERSONAL
All the Talk Was Useless 253
Satisfying Communication 254
Communication, Marital Satisfaction, and Intimacy 254
Everyday Conversations 254
Self-Disclosure 255

COMPARISON
Couple Talk in Brisbane and Munich 256
Other Aspects of Communication 256
Improving Communication Skills 258
Rules 258
Practice 258

INVOLVEMENT
Improving Your Communication 259
Principles for Enhancing Intimacy 260
Summary 260

INTERNET CONNECTION
The Challenge of Communication 261

12. **POWER AND CONFLICT IN MARRIAGE** 263
Learning Objectives 264
Power in Marriage 264
The Meaning of Power 264
Why Is Power Important? 266

COMPARISON
The Power of Egyptian Husbands and Wives 267
Sources of Power 268

PERSPECTIVE
Unequal Before the Law 270
Marriage As a Power Struggle 270
Types of Power Interaction 271
Conflict in Marriage 271
The Functions of Conflict 271

What People Fight About 272
Sources of Tension 274
Styles of Conflict 277

INVOLVEMENT
Fighting: From "I Do" 'til Death 278

PERSONAL
Learning How to Fight 280
Good Fighting 280
Maintain Your Perspective 280
Develop Tension Outlets 281
Avoid Festering Resentment 281
Be Sensitive to Timing 281
Communicate Without Ceasing 281
Be Flexible, Willing to Compromise 282
Use Conflict to Attack Problems, Not Your Spouse 282
Keep Loving While You Are Fighting 282
Principles for Enhancing Intimacy 283
Summary 283

INTERNET CONNECTION
Power and Conflict in Marriage 284

13. **WORK AND HOME** 285
Learning Objectives 286
His Work and Her Work 286
Changing Patterns of Working 287
Women in the Labor Force 287
Married Women and Employment 287
Who's Minding the House? 289
Why Do Women Want to Work Outside the Home? 290

PERSPECTIVE
Women's Commitment to Work 291
Dual-Career Families 291
More or Less Equal? 292
Types of Dual-Career Families 293
Challenges of Dual-Career Families 294
Satisfactions of a Dual-Career Family 296

INVOLVEMENT
Exploring the Dual-Career Family 297
Challenges of Dual-Earner Couples 297
Family Work 297
Stress, Intimacy, and Family Life 298

COMPARISON
Work and Divorce in Puerto Rico 301

Role Negotiation   301

Marital Satisfaction   302

PERSONAL

Employed and Married, and Loving Both   304

Work and Well-Being   304

Life Satisfaction   305

Mental and Physical Health   305

Coping Strategies   306

Principles for Enhancing Intimacy   307

Summary   307

INTERNET CONNECTION

Work and Home   308

PART FOUR

INTIMACY IN FAMILIES

---

14. BECOMING A PARENT   311

Learning Objectives   312

Changing Patterns of Childbearing   312

Birth Rates   312

Preferences for Size and Sex   313

To Bear or Not to Bear   315

Why People Want to Have Children   315

The Child-Free Option   316

Involuntary Childlessness   317

PERSPECTIVE

To Be a Parent? The Agonies of the Decision   318

Infertility   318

Coping with Infertility   319

Options for the Infertile   320

Artificial Insemination   321

In Vitro Fertilization   321

Surrogate Mothers   322

Adoption   322

Children and the Quality of Life   324

The Stresses of Raising Children   324

INVOLVEMENT

Problems and Possibilities with Options   325

Children and Marital Satisfaction   326

The Satisfactions of Raising Children   327

Parenting: Her Experience and His Experience   328

Her Experience   328

His Experience   329

COMPARISON

On the Playground in France, Germany, and Italy   330

Parenting and the Well-Being of Children   330

PERSPECTIVE

Advice from a Mother   331

Styles of Parenting   331

Parental Behavior and Children's Adjustment   332

Parental Behavior and Self-Esteem   333

A Final Note: Is Older Better in Parenting?   334

Principles for Enhancing Intimacy   335

Summary   335

INTERNET CONNECTION

Becoming a Parent   336

15. THE FAMILY LIFE CYCLE   337

Learning Objectives   338

The Family Life Cycle   338

The Meaning of the Family Life Cycle   338

What Changes Occur Over the Family Life Cycle?   340

Social Change and the Family Life Cycle   342

PERSPECTIVE

Embarking on a Difficult Road   343

The Newly Married: A Family Without Children   343

The Family with Young Children   344

The Family with Adolescents   345

The Needs of Adolescents   345

Parent-Child Problems   346

Parents' Midlife Concerns   346

Satisfaction at Midlife   348

INVOLVEMENT

Family Rituals   349

The Launching and Empty-Nest Stage   349

The Couple Together Again   350

Grandparenthood   352

PERSONAL

An Empty-Nest High   354

The Aging Family   354

Retirement   354

Marital Relations   355

COMPARISON
**Caring for Elderly Family Members
on Malo**   356
Other Relationships   356
Death of a Spouse   357
Principles for Enhancing Intimacy   359
Summary   359

INTERNET CONNECTION
The Family Life Cycle   361

16. **FAMILY LIFE AS MANAGEMENT**   363
Learning Objectives   364
Money Management   364
The Meaning of Money   364
Money and Family Well-Being   365
When Teenagers Work: Problem or Solution?   367
Financial Planning   368
Minimizing Financial Conflict   370

INVOLVEMENT
Making Your Budget   371

PERSONAL
How I've Handled Our Money   372
Time Management   372
How We Spend Our Time   373
How to Manage Your Time   374
Managing Power and Conflict   375
The Use and Misuse of Power   375

PERSPECTIVE
Wasting Time   376

COMPARISON
**Who Runs the Family? The Case
of Germans and Migrant Turks**   377
Conflict and Family Well-Being   378
Principles for Enhancing Intimacy   380
Summary   380

INTERNET CONNECTION
Family Life as Management   381

PART FIVE

CHALLENGES
TO INTIMACY

17. **FAMILY CRISES**   385
Learning Objectives   386

Sources of Family Crises   386
Stress and Crisis   386
Stressor Events   388
Alcohol Abuse in the Family   391
Extent of Alcohol Abuse   391
Alcohol Abuse and the Quality of Family Life   391

INVOLVEMENT
Self-Help Groups   393
Family Problems and Alcohol Abuse   393
Violence in Families   394
The Extent of Violence   394
Child Abuse   394
Incest   395
Spouse Abuse   396

COMPARISON
Dowry Death in India   398
Parent Abuse   398
Consequences of Abuse   399
Reacting to Crises   400

PERSPECTIVE
Drinking and Fighting   401
Coping Patterns   402
Ineffective Coping Patterns   402
The Foundation of Effective Coping   404
Tools for Effective Coping   405

PERSONAL
"Things Were Terribly Still"   407
Principles for Enhancing Intimacy   408
Summary   408

INTERNET CONNECTION
Family Crisis   410

18. **SEPARATION AND DIVORCE**   411
Learning Objectives   412
Divorce Trends   412
Divorce Rates   412
Changing Grounds for Divorce   413
The Process of Uncoupling   414
Toward Marital Dissolution   415
The Six Stations of Divorce   416
Causes and Correlates of Divorce   417
Sociodemographic Factors   417

INVOLVEMENT
Divorce Court   418
Interpersonal Factors   420

PERSPECTIVE
The Roaring Twenties and Divorce   421

COMPARISON
Divorce, Japanese Style   422

Effects of Divorce on Spouses/Parents   423

Positive Outcomes   423

Health Problems   424

Financial Problems   424

Interaction Between Former Spouses   426

Effects of Divorce on Children   426

Short-Term Effects   426

PERSONAL
"My Whole World Was Lost"   427

Long-Term Effects   428

Gender Differences   430

Child Custody   430

Coping with the Disruption   432

Principles for Enhancing Intimacy   433

Summary   434

INTERNET CONNECTION
Separation and Divorce   435

19. REMARRIAGE AND STEPFAMILIES   437

Learning Objectives   438

Types and Number of Remarriages
and Stepfamilies   438

Types of Remarried Couples   438

*Demographics of Remarriage
and Stepfamilies*   439

Déjà Vu: Dating and Mate

Selection Revisited   440

Why Remarry?   441

Issues in Recoupling   442

The Myths of Remarriage   442

INVOLVEMENT
Toward Remarriage   443

The Challenges of Remarriage   444

The Quality of Remarried Life   445

COMPARISON
Remarrying in Canada and Japan   446

PERSONAL
**"My Husband's First Wife is
Straining My Marriage"**   447

Living in a Stepfamily   447

The Stepfamily Life Cycle   447

The Structure of the Stepfamily   448

Stepparents and Stepchildren   449

PERSPECTIVE
The Unacceptable Stepmother   452

Family Functioning   454

Making It Work   455

Principles for Enhancing Intimacy   456

Summary   456

INTERNET CONNECTION
Remarriage and Stepfamilies   458

Glossary   459
References   463
Credits   511
Index   513

LIST OF FIGURES

1.1 Number of Americans Living Alone

1.2 Birth Rate per 1,000 Population: 1910–1995

1.3 Household Composition: 1970–1997

2.1 Children Living with One Parent, Proportion by Parent's Gender

2.2 Marital Status of the Population, by Race: 1997

3.1 Perceived Versus Actual Differences Between Males and Females

3.2 Intimacy Scores of Boys Versus Girls

3.3 Gender-Role Orientation As One- or Two-Dimensional

4.1 The Sexual Response Cycle

4.2 Reasons for Agreeing to Unwanted Sexual Activity

4.3 Percent Distribution of Women 15–44 Years of Age Using Contraceptive Methods

4.4 Proportion Agreeing That Premarital Sex Is Not Wrong

5.1 Downward Spiral of Loneliness

5.2 Equity and Satisfaction in Relationships

6.1 Dating Activity and Parents' Marriage

7.1 What People Want in Relationships

7.2 Passionate Love Scale

7.3 Types of Lovers

7.4 Love Styles of Those in Love and Not in Love

8.1 Life Partner Selection as a Filtering Process

8.2 Religious Affiliation and Marriage

8.3 Educational Combinations of Married Couples

9.1 Marital Status of the Population

9.2 Labor Force Participation Rates of the Never-Married: 1970 and 1996

9.3 Birth to Unmarried Mothers, by Race and Ethnicity

10.1 Marriage Rates

10.2 Rate Your Marital Preference

10.3 First Choices of Marital Life-Styles of 181 High School Students

11.1 The Communication Process

11.2 Intended and Unintended Communication of Feelings

12.1 Types of Marital Power Relationships

12.2 Areas of Conflict in Intimate Relations

13.1 Civilian Labor Force Participation Rates, by Sex

13.2 Distribution of Married Couples, by Employment Status and Fertility

13.3 What Suffers When Women Work?

14.1 Fertility Rates: 1950–1994

14.2 Number of Children Living with Adoptive Parents

15.1 Some Changes over the Family Life Cycle as Perceived by Wives

15.2 Conflict Styles of Young, Middle-Aged, and Retired Couples

15.3 Proportion Widowed, By Age: 1996

16.1 Worrying About Family Finances

16.2 Percent of Teenagers Who Work: 1970–2000

17.1 Types of Child Maltreatment

17.2 Differing Outcomes of a Family Crisis

18.1 U.S. Divorce Rates: 1950–1995

18.2 Divorce and Religious Activity

19.1 Children Living with Biological, Step, and Adoptive Parents

19.2 Reasons for Remarriage Offered by 205 Men and Women

LIST OF TABLES

1.1 Births to Unmarried Women, by Race: 1960 to 1994

2.1 Percent of People Below the Poverty Level: 1995

2.2 Households by Race, Hispanic Origin, and Type: 1970 and 1997

2.3 Living Arrangements of Children Under 18 Years, by Race and Hispanic Origin: 1996

3.1 Percent of Females Employed in Selected Occupations: 1996

4.1 Methods of Birth Control

4.2 Legal Abortions, by Selected Characteristics

4.3 Reported Cases of Sexually Transmitted Diseases: 1960 to 1995

6.1 Number of Unmarried Couples Living Together: 1970 to 1996

7.1 Responses to Question of Marrying Someone You Do Not Love: 1967 to 1984

7.2 Types of Love

8.1 Most Valued Qualities in a Mate

8.2 Ratio of Males to Females: 1950 to 2000

8.3 Number of Married Couples of Mixed Races and Origins: 1980 to 1996

9.1 Percent Never Married, by Age and Sex: 1970 to 1996

9.2 Types of Singles

9.3 Sex Ratios: 1930 to 1996

10.1 Proportion of the Population Married, by Sex and Age: 1996

10.2 Comparison of Spouses' Expectations About Who Should Perform Marital Roles

10.3 Most Significant In-Law Relationship

11.1 Marital Happiness and Stimulating Exchange of Ideas

11.2 Marital Happiness and Laughing Together

11.3 Marital Happiness and Calm Discussions

12.1 Types of Power in Marriage

12.2 Mean Percentage of Couples Who Identified Problems in 29 Areas of Marriage

13.1 The Female Labor Force: 1940 to 1996

13.2 Marital Status and Labor Force Participation Rates of Women with Children: 1960 to 1996

13.3 Frequency of Work and Family Conflict

13.4 Characteristics of High-Quality and Low-Quality Dual-Career Marriages

14.1 Families, by Number of Own Children Under 18 Years Old: 1970 to 1996

14.2 Social and Economic Characteristics of Women, 15 to 44 Years Old Gave Birth in 1995

15.1 Stages of the Family Life Cycle

15.2 Family Households with Own Children Under Age 18

16.1 Money Income of Households: 1995

16.2 Costs of Selected Items As a Proportion of All Urban Household Expenditures

17.1 Types of Stressor Events

17.2 The 15 Most Severe Family Stressors

18.1 Divorces: 1950 to 1995

18.2 Most Frequent Experiences of 80 Divorced Individuals

19.1 Long-Term Adjustment by Type of Family Background

PREFACE

What do you want out of life? If you are like most Americans, you will probably include happiness in your answer. But where can you find happiness? We have titled this book *The Quest for Intimacy* because we believe your personal happiness is crucially tied up with the quality of your intimate relationships. Our purpose is to provide you not only with a basic understanding of marriage and family life, but to show you how you can apply the knowledge you gain to enrich your life.

In other words, this is not only a text but a practical guide as well. It is both basic and applied social science. The basic part comes in the wealth of information, based on the empirical work of hundreds of researchers. The applied part is found in the principles of intimacy that are specified in each chapter as well as in the "Personal," "Comparison," and "Involvement" inserts. Hopefully, by the time you complete this book, you will have a thorough understanding of marriage and family life today, including the ways in which they bear upon our experiences of intimacy; you will also have an understanding of steps you can take to enhance the quality of your own intimate relationships.

ORGANIZATION OF MARRIAGE AND FAMILY: THE QUEST FOR INTIMACY

We have organized the book to answer a series of questions. What is the context in which intimate relationships occur? What is the meaning of intimate relationships and how do we establish them? What is the nature of intimacy for the married couple? What is the nature of intimacy in the family? What kinds of things threaten our intimate relationships, and how do people cope with those threats?

Part One addresses the context by identifying our beliefs and dreams, the diversity of family life, and the gender roles and sexuality that are integral to intimacy. Part Two explores the meaning of intimate relationships and how we establish them. We discuss the process of getting involved with someone and falling in love. We also note the special case of those who remain single, and how they deal with their intimate relationships.

Part Three looks at the nature of, and problems with, intimacy for the married couple. We discuss such issues as making the transition from singlehood to marriage, communication, conflict, and work. In Part Four, we move to intimacy in the family, to the differences that children make in our intimate lives.

Finally, Part Five is an examination of various threats to our intimate relationships. Family crises, including alcoholism and violence as well as numerous other stressors, put strains on the family. Separation and divorce are one way of dealing with the strains. Those who do get divorced are most likely to remarry at some point, so the final chapter explores the reconstituted family.

SPECIAL FEATURES
OF THE FOURTH EDITION

The World Wide Web has become a tool that can enrich our understanding of marriages and families around the world. The fourth edition takes full advantage of online resources with a new feature called the *Internet Connection* and a *free Making Connections: Family and Relationships Studies on the Internet*. These optional exercises, activities and resources allow students to explore and research topics and issues on the Web, providing students with opportunities to get involved. Additional exercises and resource URLs can be found on the book-specific Web site, **www.mhhe.com/lauer4.** Our thanks to Dr. Susan Hillier, Sonoma State University and Brian Gore, Prometheus Communications for creating the *Internet Connection* end-of-chapter material, book-specific Web site and accompanying booklet, the *Making Connections: Family and Relationships Studies on the Internet* as resources for students and instructors.

We have retained some important pedagogical aids in this edition, including learning objectives and a brief overview at the beginning of each chapter, and a summary at the end. Glossary terms are set in boldface type and defined in the glossary at the end of the book.

In addition, each chapter after the first has four inserts. The "Involvement" section has a project that provides you with some kind of personal involvement in an issue discussed in the chapter. The project is a way of taking the initiative in your own learning; it is a form of self-education. The usefulness of the projects may be enhanced if the entire class participates on a particular project; we give suggestions in most cases on how to do that.

The second type of insert is the "Personal" section. Each of these is an actual experience that has been shared with the authors by someone. We have changed the names, but the people and the circumstances are real. The "Personal" inserts illustrate some principle or principles in the chapters. They should help you grasp the principles better by seeing them at work in a real situation. The "Personal" inserts could also form the basis for some interesting class discussions and analysis.

Third, each chapter has a "Perspective" insert, in which we turn to literature or historical materials, to give an additional perspective on some issue. It is important to see both how some aspects of intimate relations are similar and how other aspects vary across time. People are always tempted to think of a past time when things were so much "better" than they are today. You are likely to decide that some aspects were better and some were worse as you read about past practices and ideas.

Fourth, we have a Comparison. Our understanding is incomplete as long as we know only about our own society. In the "Comparison" insert, we examine some topic in each chapter in terms of what happens in one or more other societies in the world. The materials range from how certain Eskimo children learn to be male and female to how the Japanese divorce. These cross-cultural data reveal both similarities and differences with current American practices. Seeing the similarities makes us feel less alone, more a part of all humankind. Seeing the differences helps us become more tolerant and more appreciative of the rich diversity of humans.

This edition also retains an emphasis on theory, which is important for our understanding as well as giving directives in research. Many students question the usefulness of theory—"just give us the facts" is a frequent request. To show the importance of theory, we have included examples in each chapter of how the theories discussed in chapter 1 aid our understanding of various phenomena. Marginal notations identify where the theoretical explanations are located. To get a better grasp of the various theories and a better sense of how they are useful, the student can thumb through the various chapters and read each section where a theory is explicitly used.

Finally, we have made a number of changes. We have changed some of the inserts to provide newer or more useful information. We have added some new topics, such as body image and Internet romances. We have expanded some materials, including additional materials on cultural and racial/ethnic differences. And we have updated this addition throughout with the latest available information, incorporating the most recent research—more than 300 new references from the professional literature—and utilizing the most recent government data. The new references and government data, in addition to updating our knowledge about intimate relations, provide increasingly more information on racial and ethnic differences in intimate relations. This information, scattered throughout the book, shows how Americans of various racial and ethnic backgrounds have many similar and some dissimilar experiences in their intimate relationships.

SUPPLEMENTARY MATERIALS

The text is accompanied by several supplementary items that will help students better understand the issues involved in intimate relationships, and will help instructors in ensuring that their students achieve this goal.

Each new text is packaged with a free *Making Connections: Family and Relationships Studies on the Internet,* created by Dr. Susan Hillier, of Sonoma State University, Sonoma, California and Brian Gore, Prometheus Communications. This booklet gives readers a basic understanding of the Internet, valuable knowledge on becoming a savvy consumer of web information, and a substantial supply of various Web sites on organizations and careers in sociology.

A *Web site* with additional exercises, self-grading practice tests, and visuals to help you master the material in the text is also available at *www.mhhe.com/Lauer4.*

The *Student Study Guide,* written by Kenrick S. Thompson of Arkansas State University Mountain Home, provides students with material to review and test their comprehension of the text, as well as increase their awareness of the challenges and opportunities of intimacy and marriage. Inside, students will find, for every chapter, a list of key terms highlighted in the text, twenty fill-in-the-blank questions partly based on the terms, and twenty multiple-choice questions with answer keys. The Guide also contains "Personal Journals" which ask students to provide their written thoughts and feelings about various issues relating to intimate relationships, and "Workshops," which give students additional insight into some aspect of the chapter, then ask them to respond in the form of a written exercise.

The *Instructor's Manual,* also by Kenrick Thompson, contains chapter outlines, summaries, lists of electronic teaching aids, and at least four teaching enrichment ideas per chapter. The separate *Test Bank* and *Computerized Test Bank,* contain over 1000 multiple-choice questions that have been thoroughly revised and updated. *PowerPoint* slides are available for presentations.

The *McGraw-Hill Video Library* offers adopters a variety of current videos, suitable for classroom use in conjunction with the topics in the text.

Acknowledgements

We are grateful to Susan Hillier and Brian Gore for creating the informative and stimulating Web exercises at the end of each chapter and for authoring the very valuable *Internet Guide to Families* that accompanies this edition of the text.

We are also grateful to the personnel at McGraw-Hill, who have been most helpful and supportive during the writing of this book, and particularly our editor, Sally Constable. We are grateful to each of our reviewers. Their suggestions have, we believe, enhanced the quality of the book: John Brenner Southwest Virginia Community college; Ramon S. Guerra University of Texas, Pan America; Sandra Caron, University of Maine; Meg Wilkes Karraker, University of St. Thomas; Cynthia Schmiege, University of Idaho; James W. Robinson, Louisiana State University at Eunice; Mark D. Hardt, Montana State University at Billings; Rita Duncan, Tulsa Community College Southeast; Christopher Ezell, Vincennes University, Jaspar campus; Carol Wharton, University of Richmond.

PART ONE

THE CONTEXT OF INTIMACY

Imagine that you have been on a date and your date asks if you had a good time. You have not only had a good time but you also want to pursue the relationship, so you nod, smile, and suggest a good-night kiss. In most cases, the kiss would be an encouragement. But if your date happened to arrive here recently from any of a number of preindustrial societies, the offer of a kiss might be viewed as strange, unhealthy, or even disgusting.

Our quest for intimacy occurs in particular social contexts. We must understand the context in order to establish meaningful relationships. In part one, we examine the context of intimacy in our society. What is happening in the realm of intimate relationships? What effects does our multicultural society have on such relationships? How do sex roles and sexuality bear upon the quest for intimacy? The answers to these questions are crucial for both understanding and pursuing meaningful intimate relationships.

AMERICAN MYTHS
AND DREAMS

Learning Objectives

After reading chapter 1, you should be able to:
1. Recognize and evaluate some myths about family life.
2. Explain the ways in which myths are harmful.
3. Describe the changing patterns of intimate relationships in contemporary society.
4. Discuss utopian ideas of the family.
5. Identify what Americans want in family life in light of the conflicting evidence.
6. Discuss the factors that explain long-term, satisfying marriages.
7. Briefly outline some of the theories used to research and understand family life.

How many families will you live in by the time you reach middle age? It would not be unusual for you to live in at least five or six (Cherlin 1981:1)! You begin life in your parents' home. If your parents divorce and you live with only one of your parents, you then have a second family. A remarriage by that parent brings you into a third family. If, after leaving home, you cohabit with someone, you have a fourth family. If you later marry and have children, you are in your fifth, and if you divorce and remarry, you will be in the sixth family of your life.

Of course, you could live in more or less than six families. Some people spend their lives in only two families—the one into which they were born (their **family of origin**) and the one formed by marriage. Others have experience with more than six. One couple told us that while they were growing up, they had had nine different fathers between them. Clearly, different people have differing experiences of family life.

Given a choice, we would all prefer a happy family life. What would that be like? Leo Tolstoy began his famous novel *Anna Karenina* with the assertion that all happy families are alike, while unhappy families all differ from each other. Tolstoy was wrong. There are both similarities and differences in each kind of family. In the pursuit of a happy family life, we must understand those similarities and differences. We must gain knowledge of what it takes to *enhance the quality of our intimate relationships,* for **intimacy** is one of our fundamental needs and

the source of much of our well-being. Intimacy involves love, affection, caring, and deep attachment to another person. A close, vital relationship with someone—a friend, relative, or spouse—is the basis of personal fulfillment. The major theme of this book, therefore, is understanding and enhancing the quality of our intimate relationships.

In this chapter, we will lay the foundation of our quest for fulfilling, intimate relationships by exploring some of the myths and dreams that exist in society. We will raise the question of whether there can be an ideal form of family. We will observe some of the trends that have been occurring in marriage and family life. And, finally, we will make a few comments about the approach that we will take throughout this book.

MYTHS ABOUT FAMILY LIFE

How much do you know about American families? And, more importantly, *how* do you know what you know? For instance, what was the typical American family in the past? If you think it was composed of happy and healthy children, a wife and mother who kept the home, and a husband and father who was the breadwinner, you have a mistaken image (Coontz 1992). That image reflects little of the reality of family life in America except for the 1950s, when prosperity allowed more families than usual to live well with a single income.

Where do our notions about the family come from? One way we get information is through experience. We know of our own experience and that of our friends and relatives. Another important source of information is the mass media. Consider, for instance, the family life portrayed on television. If you were a foreigner and the only thing you knew about American families came from television programs, how would you describe a typical family?

For example, look at family life on daytime serials, or soap operas (Pingree and Thompson 1990). If you based your knowledge of American families on the soaps, you would say that most are stepfamilies. That is, they include children or grandchildren from earlier marriages or unrelated children who live in the home. The wives and mothers are likely to work, but most are high-paid, high-status professionals or businesswomen. The families are highly unstable, giving the impression at times of a kind of marital musical chairs game. Verbal violence between family members is high, occurring about two-thirds of the time.

Such programs are likely to generate a certain amount of misunderstanding about the nature of family life. The combination of misleading information in the mass media, misinterpretations of correct information, and inferences made from our own limited experiences creates and leads to the acceptance of various **myths**, common beliefs about marriage and family life that are incorrect. Because myths help shape our perceptions, expectations, and hopes, they are important and must be considered carefully. Let us look at a few of those concerning marriage and the family.

We've Lost the Extended Family

The **extended family** refers to a group of three or more generations formed as an outgrowth of the parent-child relationship. Grandparents, parents, and children together comprise an extended family. Was

that a typical family arrangement earlier in American history? Many people think so. But mounting evidence indicates that three generations gathered around a common hearth is a romanticization of the past. It seems that both in America and elsewhere, the **nuclear family** (husband, wife, and any children) has been the most common arrangement since at least the sixteenth century (Laslett 1977).

There are a number of reasons why the extended family has not been common. First, life expectancy in the past was much lower. Infectious diseases claimed the lives of many individuals before they were old enough to be grandparents. Second, children tended to leave home when they married. Like young people today, they preferred to establish their own homes, rather than to live with their parents.

People Marry Because They Love Each Other

Why did you, or will you, get married? Your answer probably includes, or will include, the fact of being

We begin life in our family of origin.

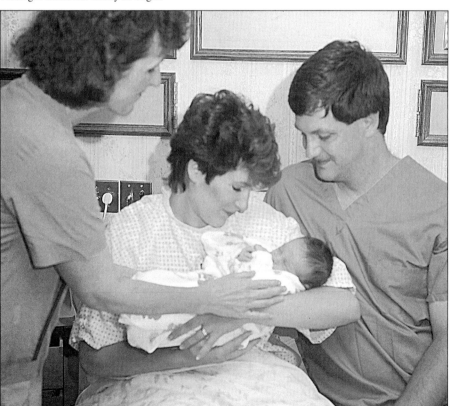

in love. But love, as we will see in chapter 7, is a complex emotion. It is difficult to define. And the feeling we call "love" might really be something different, or at least involve some other emotions. As Lederer and Jackson (1968:42) point out, we all like to think that we marry for love "but by and large the emotion [we] interpret as love is in reality some other emotion—often a strong sex drive, fear, or a hunger for approval."

Lederer (a writer) and Jackson (a therapist) go on to point out that we generally lose all judgment during courtship. We are driven by an "ecstatic paralysis" to mate with someone and reproduce ourselves. We may also wed because parents and other important people expect us to marry, because we are lonely, because we want economic security, or for various other reasons.

It is not that love is absent when people are considering marriage, but it is a myth to believe that love is the only or even the dominant reason that people marry. Love may be the outgrowth as well as the foundation of a good marriage, but many other factors and feelings are involved when we are wrestling with the decision of whether to marry.

Having Children Increases Marital Satisfaction

"Just Molly and me and baby makes three," goes an old song. The outcome is a kind of personal "heaven." Most married people plan on having children, and most expect that those children will enrich their lives. But whatever the effect of children on people's lives as a whole, they clearly do not always increase satisfaction with the marital relationship.

Most studies show that marital satisfaction decreases for one or both spouses during the child-rearing years (Larson 1988:8). The demands of raising children are such that parents often do not have the time or energy for cultivating their own relationship. Children frequently add financial strains. They require a great deal of energy. They may leave one or both parents exhausted and short-tempered. When children eventually grow up and leave home, the parents may find their marital satisfaction increasing again as they enter into a kind of second honeymoon.

This is not to say that children inevitably detract from the quality of one's life or marriage. As we

shall discuss in chapter 14, children have both positive and negative effects. And the effects of children seem to depend on the quality of the marriage in the first place. As Harriman (1986) found, having a good marriage is likely to maximize the benefits and minimize the liabilities of children. Those who have a poor marital relationship, on the other hand, are likely to find that children only add a further strain. Children are generally not the answer to a struggling marriage.

A Good Sex Life Is the Best Predictor of Marital Satisfaction

Tom, a counselor in a university, married when he was twenty-nine. When we talked with him before the wedding, he seemed somewhat ambivalent. He was already having some problems with his fiancée about money and in-laws. He shared very few interests with her. "Why," we asked, "are you marrying her?" "We have a great sex life," he replied. "We're terrific in bed together." One year later, Tom divorced his wife. "Great sex" was not enough to save the marriage.

What about marriages that start off better than Tom's, those in which the couples have shared values, interests, and goals? Is sex the best predictor of satisfaction? Again, the answer is no. The way you communicate with your spouse, the way you solve problems, and the way in which you spend your leisure time are all more important than sex (Snyder 1979). Sexual compatibility and sexual fulfillment are important and desirable, but they are not even essential to a meaningful and satisfying marriage. In a survey of three hundred couples who had long-term (fifteen years or more), satisfying marriages, we found that agreement about sex was not among the top ten reasons people gave for the quality of their marriages (Lauer and Lauer 1986:179–80). One woman who said she was "extremely happy" with her marriage reported very little sexual activity over the past ten years. This was her second marriage. Her first had been "totally sex and little else." Her second husband's health problems contributed to the decline in sexual activity. "So I suppose a kind of trade-off exists here," she said. "I like absolutely everything else about my current marriage."

In other words, you can have a great sex life and an unhappy marriage. You can even have an unfulfilling sex life and a happy marriage. And, as we shall see in chapter 4, some people have both a fulfilling sex life and a happy marriage. But it isn't the sex that is the most important reason for their marital satisfaction.

Half of All Marriages End in Divorce

In the past, more marriages ended because of the death of a spouse than because of divorce. Now the opposite is true. But just how many marriages actually end in divorce? Even professionals sometimes make the claim that half of all marriages will fail. Millions of Americans "know" and believe it, and it causes many of them anxiety as they contemplate marriage.

It is true that the divorce rate is quite high, nearly twice as high in the United States as it is in other industrialized countries (De Vita 1996:30). And it is true that in recent years there has been around one divorce for every two marriages in the United States. In 1995, for example, there were 1.95 million marriages and 973 thousand divorces (U.S. Bureau of the Census 1997:74). But such figures do *not* mean a 50 percent failure rate because there were also more than 57 million couples who had been married before 1995 and who continued to be married in that year. Some of them would eventually divorce, of course, but in that year only about 1.7 percent of married couples divorced.

The point is, predicting failure rates is very complex. Among other things, divorce rates vary considerably between generations. Among some groups, particularly those born in the 1950s, rates may reach 50 percent or more. Yet the ratio of divorces to marriages has tended to decline since 1982. In fact, by 1995 the divorce rate was the lowest it has been since the early 1970s (U.S. Bureau of the Census 1997b:105). One estimate is that about four of ten marriages will eventually end in divorce if recent rates continue (Miller 1993:23). If they continue to decline, of course, the proportion of marriages that eventually fail will also decline.

The Dangers of Myths

There are more myths than those we have discussed. The important point is to recognize that many of the common beliefs about marriage and family living are wrong. Do not take for granted the truth of something simply because a lot of people agree that it is true. Myths are more than simple mistakes. Accepting myths can detract from the quality of your life.

Consider, for example, the myth that people marry only because they are in love. Americans like to think that arranged marriages and marriages of convenience belong to an earlier era or to a less modernized culture and that love is the sole reason people wed today. Yet even in contemporary American society, as we shall see in chapter 8, individuals choose a mate for a variety of factors and not just because they are deeply in love. And even when they marry because of feelings of love, they often find that the feelings are fleeting and question whether they were ever "in love" in the first place.

The experience of Bart, a thirty-year-old businessman who married when he was twenty-three, illustrates this point well. At the time of his wedding, he believed he was "madly in love." But four years later, the "feeling of love" no longer existed. Bart had an affair. His wife found out about it and divorced him. Bart was so upset over the divorce that he went into therapy. There he discovered that his feeling of being "madly in love" was a mix of many different emotions and really wasn't love at all. And he learned that he had gone into the union with very unrealistic expectations about the nature of love and marriage. Like many people, he was certain that being "madly in love" would last a lifetime and didn't realize that these initial feelings needed to be nourished and eventually replaced by something more substantial. Bart has not remarried. He deeply regrets the mistakes he made and fears another relationship. He is somewhat bitter about the myth that led him to this point: "I think I have a better sense of what love means now. I wish someone had drilled that into me ten years ago."

Myths can ruin a good relationship. They blind us to the realities of intimacy. They give us false expectations about the nature of marriage and family life. As such, they are impediments in our quest for well-being.

CHANGING PATTERNS OF INTIMATE RELATIONSHIPS

How do you achieve intimacy before you are married? What does it mean to be a husband or wife?

What does it mean to be a parent? When are you likely to get married? How many, if any, children will you probably have? The answers to such questions vary, depending on when they are asked. Social life, including patterns of intimacy, is dynamic. Young people in their twenties today, for example, may not have yet contemplated marriage at an age when their parents already had two or three children. In this section, we will look at some of the important changes that have been occurring in intimate relationships in recent years. As you understand the dynamic nature of intimate living, you will develop the realistic grounding necessary to enhance the quality of your own life.

Premarital Sex

There has always been premarital sex. Records indicate that even some of our Puritan forebears were pregnant when they were joined in marriage (Demos 1968). But the approval of, and proportion of those engaging in, premarital sex has increased considerably in recent decades. Nearly two-thirds of never-married women aged fifteen through forty-four and 49.5 percent of those aged fifteen through nineteen say that they have had sexual intercourse (Forrest and Singh 1990:208). The proportion varies somewhat by race. For example, among teenagers generally (married and unmarried), 52.4 percent of whites, 48.5 percent of Hispanics, and 60.8 percent of African Americans indicate that they have had sexual relations.

Similarly, among young men, 79 percent of those aged thirteen through nineteen report having had sexual intercourse (Sonenstein, Pleck, and Ku 1991:163). The proportion among men also varies by race, from 75.9 percent of whites to 80.5 percent of Hispanics to 95.8 percent of African Americans.

These proportions may be declining, however. The 1995 National Survey of Family Growth (Abma et al. 1997) found that the percentage of never-married women fifteen through nineteen years of age who had ever had sexual intercourse dropped about five points (from 1990) to 48.1 percent. The percentages go up dramatically, however, with older age groups, to 82.6 percent of those

twenty through twenty-four years of age and 88.6 percent of those twenty-five through twenty-nine years of age. Again, the survey found racial/ethnic differences. Among the fifteen through nineteen year olds, 47.1 percent of whites, 52.0 percent of Hispanics, and 58.3 percent of African Americans had had sexual intercourse.

Out-of-Wedlock Births

The number of babies born to unmarried women has also increased significantly over the past few decades (table 1.1). Since 1960, the proportion of all births that occur out of wedlock has increased enormously, particularly for women in their twenties. Between 1990 and 1994, 53 percent of first births to women fifteen through twenty-nine years of age were either to unmarried women (40 percent) or were conceived before marriage (13 percent) (Bachu 1998). The proportions varied by racial/ethnic group. For black women under thirty years of age, the proportion of first births born or conceived before marriage doubled from 43 percent in 1930 to 1934 to 86 percent in 1990 to 1994. The comparable figures for white women were 15 percent in 1930 to 1934 and 46 percent in 1990 to 1994. And for Hispanics the figures were 30 percent in 1960 to 1969 (the earliest such figures are available) and 55 percent in 1990 to 1994.

TABLE 1.1
Births to Unmarried Women, by Race: 1960 to 1994

Race	1960	1970	1980	1990	1994
Number (1,000)					
White	82	175	320	647	794
Black*	142	224	326	473	448
Percent					
White	36.8	43.9	48.1	55.6	61.6
Black*	63.2	56.1	48.9	40.6	34.8
Births as a Percent of All Births in Racial Group					
White	2.3	5.7	11.0	20.1	25.4
Black*	21.6	34.9	55.2	65.2	70.4

*Figures for 1960 and 1970 are for blacks and other races
Source: U.S. Bureau of the Census, 1988:62 and 1997:79

Living Alone

Increasing numbers of people are living alone. By 1997, 25.4 million Americans, about 59 percent of them women, were living alone (figure 1.1). This represents more than a doubling of the number who were living alone in 1970. People live alone because they are widowed, divorced, separated, or never married. Some of them will eventually marry. Others will opt—willingly or unwillingly—to remain single.

Living alone poses serious questions about fulfilling one's intimate needs. Just because a person lives alone does not mean that he or she can exist without intimate relationships. Rather, it means that the individual must find alternative means of fulfilling his or her needs—a topic that we will explore in chapter 9.

Cohabitation

One way that some people fulfill their intimacy needs without getting married is through **cohabitation,** living with someone in an intimate, sexual relationship without being legally married. By 1996, nearly four million unmarried couples were living together (U.S. Bureau of the Census 1997b:57), more than 7.5 times the number in 1970. About a third of the couples had children living with them; about a fifth were under twenty-five years of age.

Some of those who cohabit will eventually marry. Many of those who opt for cohabitation think it is a way to test their compatibility for marriage, thus beating the odds on the high divorce rate. This is another of the myths that prevail today. We shall see why in chapter 6.

Delayed Marriage

Between 1950 and 1970, half of the females who married did so by the time they were 20.5 years old, and half of males who married did so by the time they were 22.5 years old. In the 1970s, the median age at which people married (that is, the age by which half were married) crept higher. By 1997, it was 26.8 years for men and 25.0 years for women (Lugaila 1998). The figure for women is the highest ever officially recorded in the United States (statistics for this have been kept since 1890).

Most people will eventually marry. But they are delaying marriage. Among whites, marriage is likely to be delayed for those spending part or all of their childhood without a father in the home (Li and Wojtkiewicz 1994). In addition, the availability of sexual relations among singles, the emphasis on personal growth and freedom, the unwillingness to "settle down" before one has many experiences, and fears about commitment and the high divorce rate are factors that may have contributed to the higher age at first marriage.

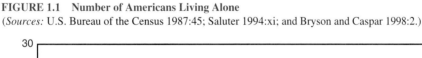

FIGURE 1.1 Number of Americans Living Alone
(*Sources:* U.S. Bureau of the Census 1987:45; Saluter 1994:xi; and Bryson and Caspar 1998:2.)

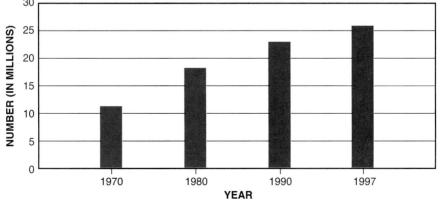

COMPARISON
Asian Women Are Marrying at a Later Age

Delaying marriage until a later age is not unique to women in the United States. In many Asian countries, where women have typically married during, or even before, adolescence, average age at marriage has been increasing. But the average age at first marriage for most Asian women is still considerably lower than it is for women in the United States: 19.2 in Sri Lanka, 18.3 in Malaysia, 12.3 in Bangladesh, 16.0 in Pakistan, and 15.6 in Nepal.

In some countries, there is an interval between the wedding ceremony and the time when a couple begins living together and consummates their marriage through sexual intercourse. In Nepal, for instance, the union is generally not consummated during the first year of marriage. During this time, the young bride is trained to be an accomplished and subservient housewife before she moves in with her in-laws. In other words, she spends a year learning how to make the transition from being a daughter to being a daughter-in-law and wife.

What differentiates those women who marry earlier from those who marry later? In all the countries noted, women with higher levels of education tend to marry at a later age. And closely related to education, women who work in nonagricultural jobs tend to marry later than those engaged in agriculture or those who do not work outside the home. Professional women are particularly likely to marry at a later age. Average age at first marriage will no doubt continue to rise, therefore, in these Asian countries as the educational and occupational levels of women continue to rise (Chowdhury and Trovato 1994; Niraula 1994).

Birth Rates

An increasing number of women are delaying having their first child until their mid or even late thirties. This means that they will likely have fewer children. Moreover, because the capacity for getting pregnant tends to decrease with age, some women are involuntarily childless. Others choose to remain childless (see chapter 14). They do not view children as necessary to a fulfilling life.

As a result of later marriages, delayed first births, and an increasing number of childless marriages, the birth rate has declined considerably (figure 1.2). By 1995, the rate was a little less than half of what it was in 1910. The average number of births to women aged fifteen through forty-four years is about 1.2 (Abma et al. 1997:3), compared to a postwar high of 3.6 in 1955.

Household Size

As would be expected from the increasing number of people living alone and the lower birth rates, the average household size in the country has declined. In 1790, the average household contained 5.8 people. The number reflects not only the tendency to have more children but also may have included boarders, lodgers, and apprentices who lived with the family. By 1960, the average was 3.3 people, and by 1997 the figure was 2.64 (Bryson and Casper 1998).

The changes in average household size are due to changes in the types of households formed (married couple, single parent, nonfamily) as well as in the size of the specific types. The size of specific types of households varies depending on fertility rates. Both changes in types and in size of types account for the decline (Santi 1987). In the early 1970s, average household size went down mainly because of declining fertility rates. In the second half of the 1970s, fertility rates leveled out, but changes in living arrangements (increasing numbers of nonfamily and single-parent households) kept average household size in a continual decline. In the 1980s and 1990s, living arrangements continued to be an important factor in declining household size.

Employed Mothers

Women have been participating in the economy in growing numbers since the 1950s. Census Bureau figures show that the proportion of married women (with a husband in the home) who are employed in-

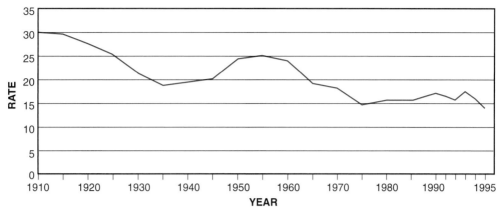

FIGURE 1.2   Birth Rate per 1,000 Population: 1910–1995
(*Source:* U.S. Bureau of the Census 1989:59 and 1997b:79.)

Increasing numbers of married women work outside the home.

creased from 23.8 percent in 1950 to 61.1 percent in 1996 (U.S. Bureau of the Census 1997b:404). The most dramatic increase occurred among women who had children under six years of age. In 1987, for the first time, more than half of the new mothers (those with children under the age of one) stayed in the labor force.

Some mothers are employed out of necessity; their husbands do not earn enough to support the family. Others work outside the home because they want a better lifestyle than they could afford with only one income. And still others define their jobs or careers as important to their own fulfillment. Whatever the reasons, homes with an employed father, a stay-at-home mother, and children are now only a small fraction of all American households.

Divorce

Even though the number of people who divorce is exaggerated in popular belief, it is true that the divorce rate has risen dramatically since 1965. By the

PERSONAL
"It's a Different World"

Patricia is a twenty-five-year-old African American who has been married three years and has a four-month-old son. She shares with us the aspirations and struggles of a woman caught up in the current trend of new mothers who work:

I work as a counselor at a hospital that provides psychological services and treatment for adolescents with emotional problems. I love my work. I love my baby. And I have a good marriage. We've had our problems, of course. There was friction between my husband, Mike, and me when I was pregnant. I was worried about how I was going to have a baby and keep on working. I didn't want to leave my baby with a stranger. And I knew that Mike wasn't too happy with that idea either. But I didn't want to stop working either. Mike just shrugged it off. "Don't worry about it," was all

he would say. I remember getting really angry at him and telling him that he didn't understand how important the issue was to me. He told me that I was just upset because of the pregnancy, that everything would work out all right, and that I would just have to try to calm myself.

I wanted the baby badly. But I was terrified of having to give up my job. It was more than the fact that I love the work. We need the money. We can't make it on Mike's income alone. I remember one day calling my mother on the telephone. She lives five hundred miles away. I tried to persuade her to come and live with us for a while and help take care of the baby. She wouldn't do it. She said she needed to stay with dad. I asked her what she would do if she were in my place. Her reply didn't

encourage me much: "When I had my babies, I stayed home and took care of them. I don't know what to tell you, Patricia. It's a different world you're living in."

Well, when the baby arrived, Mike really surprised me. He arranged for different hours on his job so that he would be home a lot of the time that I was at work. I helped out by cutting back my work days from five to four. Between us, we're able to be with our son most of the time. It isn't easy, but we're managing. The worst part is that Mike and I don't see each other much except on weekends. That's hard on our marriage, but we think we'll be able to change that in a year or two. It's tough right now, but we have a lot of love in our home and a lot of hope for the future.

mid-1970s, the United States had the highest divorce rate in the Western world. After 1981, divorce rates tended to level off and even decline. Since the late 1980s, the rate has been on a slightly downward trend and is now around the level it was in the early 1970s.

A Concluding Note on Changing Patterns

Clearly, there are both long-term trends and short-term fluctuations in patterns of intimate behavior. Making firm conclusions about the future is therefore hazardous. Some experts, for instance, believe that marriage and family patterns will continue to evolve and to diverge from the traditional nuclear family type. They are convinced that we are entering into a new age in which new forms of family are emerging. Others believe that we are

on the verge of a conservative trend that will renew the emphasis on traditional patterns. We will make our own position clear when we discuss what people want. First, however, we want to raise the question of whether there is an ideal pattern.

THE FAMILY IN UTOPIA

Is there an ideal form of family life that will satisfy everyone? Through most of recorded history, humans have attempted to portray and, in some cases, establish an ideal human community, one in which all human needs are fulfilled. Edward Bellamy outlined his ideal community in one of the most famous of American utopian novels, *Looking Backward,* which appeared in 1888. According to Bellamy, Utopia was a place where no man any more has any care for the morrow, either for himself or his children, for the nation guarantees the nurture, education, and comfortable maintenance of every citizen from the cradle to the grave (Bellamy 1960:73).

Utopian writings, like those of Bellamy, give us an author's notion of the ideal way of life and the social arrangements necessary for achieving it. Utopian communities, on the other hand, show us the actual efforts of people to establish their ideal.

In utopia, a number of questions must be answered if all people are to prosper. What is the ideal form of government? What is the ideal way to educate youth? What is the ideal way to provide for the necessities of life—food, clothing, and shelter? And what is the ideal for marriage and family life?

The Family in Utopian Writings

Utopian writers have had varying notions of the ideal form of marriage and the family. Following the views of Plato, some writers have argued that **monogamy** (marriage to one person at a time) and the family should be abolished. Instead, the state regulates childbearing and child-rearing. The rationale for doing away with families is simple—people's first loyalty must be to the state, the source of all benefits. In order to ensure that utopia is not disrupted or destroyed by individualism and selfishness, both private property and the family must be abandoned. A strong indictment of the family is found in Huxley's (1932:25) *Brave New World,* where the family is depicted as the source of virtually all human ills:

> Our Freud had been the first to reveal the appalling dangers of family life. The world was full of fathers—was therefore full of misery; full of mothers—therefore of every kind of perversion from sadism to chastity; full of brothers, sisters, uncles, aunts—full of madness and suicide.

Other utopian writers have not agreed, however. The first book actually to be entitled *Utopia* was written by Sir Thomas More in 1516. More agreed with many of Plato's ideas but differed strongly with his notions about the family. In fact, More virtually left the family of his day intact. In his utopia, the government supervises marriages but does not interfere significantly with family life. Wives obey their husbands, children obey their parents, and the younger serve the older. The nuclear family is maintained. There are communal halls where many families eat together. But, for the most part, More apparently felt that there was little in marriage and the family life of sixteenth-century England that could be improved.

In addition to these two extremes, there are, of course, variations among the utopian writers. For instance, in Bellamy's utopia, the nuclear family continued, but women had a far different position than they had during the Victorian age in which he wrote. Like a man, a woman was employed, and she did not stop working when she married:

> Why on earth should she? Married women have no housekeeping responsibilities . . . and a husband is not a baby that he should be cared for (Bellamy 1960:172).

Like men, women were provided with occupations for which each was best suited. Bellamy did separate the men's "army of industry" from the women's, on the grounds that women were inferior in strength to men and needed somewhat different kinds of work. But women were encouraged to experience it all—marriage, motherhood, and work. And the highest positions in the "feminine army of industry are entrusted only to women who have been both wives and mothers, as they alone fully represent their sex" (Bellamy 1960:175).

The Family in Utopian Communities

Those who have actually established utopian communities, like their literary counterparts, have also given a variety of answers as to the best form of marriage and family life (Lauer and Lauer 1983:56–89). Some groups believed that monogamous marriage and nuclear families would maintain selfishness and threaten the well-being of the community. They therefore forbade marriage and family. Many of the religious groups that eliminated marriage and the family adopted **celibacy.** The Shakers, the largest and longest-lived of all American utopian groups (1774 to the present), have insisted on strict celibacy, growing by conversions rather than procreation. At the high point of their membership in the nineteenth century, the Shakers had communities in various places in the East and

Midwest. Each community governed itself, and each was composed only of people who agreed to live the rest of their lives as celibates. Married couples who joined the group were separated; a husband and wife were not allowed to live in the same house for fear they might yield to temptation. The whole community was regarded as the Shaker's family.

The Shakers and other celibate groups argued that sexual relations lead to a host of social ills. One Shaker writer pointed out that sex means gratification of the individual's passions, and the person who indulges in sex will also strive to satisfy all other passions:

> All contentions and wars have their origin in the selfishness of the flesh—for land, women, or else. Do away with the spirit of MINE, and the dawn of peace begins immediately; happier homes will result, and grinders of the faces of the poor need not tremble because of so-called communists, who are only attempting to equalize the good things of this life unevenly shared by ungodly, unbrotherly monopolists (Anonymous 1878:223–24).

The individual who lives a life of self-indulgence, then, is contributing to all of the misery of the world, from marital quarrels to political corruption to wars between nations.

Not every utopian who abolished the family opted for celibacy, however. Some took part in **group marriage,** a form of marriage in which each member of a group is married to all other opposite-sex persons in that group. One of the more famous communities with group marriage was Oneida, which existed in New York from 1848 to 1881. John Humphrey Noyes, the founder, was a Protestant minister. He believed that his community should be a kingdom of heaven on earth. Jesus had taught that there is no marriage in heaven. Noyes insisted that his earthly utopia follow this same pattern, and as a result, marriage and exclusive arrangements of any sort were not permitted in the Oneida community. However, Noyes claimed that no marriage did not mean no sex. Each member of the Oneida community, therefore, had sexual access to every other member of the opposite sex. In fact, Noyes established a system of record-keeping that prevented any two people from having sexual relations together too frequently. Noyes also instituted a unique system of sexual intercourse, and for some years, conception was closely regulated (Lauer and Lauer 1983:79–82). Children were taken from their mothers when they were infants and reared in the communal nursery. Caretakers taught the children to regard every man in the community as father and every woman as mother. The entire community thus was a single family.

In between the extremes of celibacy and free love, other utopians advocated a more traditional arrangement. Many insisted that sex take place only within monogamous marriage. This is evident even in modern utopian experiments—the communes. Despite a reputation to the contrary, as many as half

The communal dining hall of the Oneida Colony founded by John Humphrey Noyes.

of contemporary communes have monogamous relationships and nuclear families (Zablocki 1980:339). At The Farm, for example, a modern commune in Tennessee, sex is viewed positively and discussed openly. But the group also claims that any kind of promiscuity is wrong. Premarital sex and adultery are both taboo. The nuclear family is valued and protected.

What Works Best?

The utopian experiments, in contrast to the writings, give us an opportunity to inquire into what really works best for humans. You might decide at the outset that the celibate life could never satisfy people. But the Shakers would disagree. They were often effusive in their praise of the celibate life. They claimed that it increased the length and also the fullness of life. They insisted that celibacy was not a sacrifice of present pleasure for future rewards (heaven). Quite the contrary:

> Shakers do not believe in the propriety of making themselves unhappy and miserable in this world for the sake of being happy in the next. A good Shaker is the most thoroughly happy being in existence. Why not? The world, the flesh, and the devil have no attractions for him; he is at peace with God, himself and his neighbor (Basting 1887:203).

Other Shakers wrote similar praise of the celibate way of life. There are, incidentally, a number of modern communes in which celibacy is practiced for either short terms or as a way of life. Celibacy as an ideal is not confined to past generations.

On the other hand, there were many who could not adapt to the celibate life. They left the communities and searched for utopia elsewhere. What of the traditionalists, those who maintained monogamy and the nuclear family? As with the celibates, most had high praise for the arrangement, but even some of them were not satisfied. And those who experimented with group marriage or free love have had more problems with the arrangement than either the celibates or the traditionalists. For a time, group marriage worked well at Oneida, and presently it seems to be working well among the Keristas in San Francisco. In other communities, however, problems abounded. In some cases, individuals who were willing to try, and even ideo-

logically committed to, open relationships found that they could not handle the arrangement. In one rural commune, two teenaged females, one middle-aged man, and two married couples formed a group marriage. The experiment ended abruptly when one of the married men saw his wife with another man, pulled a knife, and dragged her away while shouting, "She belongs to me" (Davidson 1970:95).

So what works best? Obviously, no single arrangement fulfills the needs of every individual. Each arrangement works for some people and frustrates others. On balance, the celibates and the traditionalists have had the fewest problems. But every community has had its malcontents. When only one form is defined as ideal, some people are going to be frustrated. People seem to need a diversity of arrangements from which to choose. And diversity is exactly what is available today. As we shall see in detail, some people are opting for a traditional marriage, some for a nontraditional marriage, some for singlehood, some for single parenthood, and so forth. If the lessons of history are worth anything at all, they teach us to cherish our right to diverse arrangements.

WHAT DO WE WANT?

The utopian experiments suggest that we need a variety of arrangements in marriage and family living in order to satisfy the needs of people. But clearly some of the arrangements will be more attractive than others. Some will meet the needs of more people than will others. What do people want today?

Changes in Traditional Arrangements

If we define a traditional family as one that stays intact except for death and is composed of an employed father (the breadwinner), a stay-at-home mother (the homemaker), and children, then it is clear it is now the choice of a minority of Americans. Most people no longer regard that arrangement as practical. Moreover, the woman's movement and women's experience in the labor force have sensitized women to the value of employment outside the home. The experience of nonfamily living, which an increasing number of young Americans who leave the parental home before marrying have, also contributes to a change in the traditional

PERSPECTIVE
The Utopian Quest for Intimacy

In their quest for the ideal society, utopians concerned themselves with creating an intimate community. Through writings, ideologies, values, and shared experiences, they sought to bind their members together in close relationship. But what of the celibate communities? Today, we often associate intimacy with sex. If this is the case, how did the celibates satisfy their need for intimacy? Did they deny, ignore, or repress the need? Certainly, this was not the case among the Shakers, who claimed that their groups provided people with a truly close and intimate family unlike those in the larger community. The observations of Fredrika Bremer, a mid-nineteenth century visitor to the Shaker community at Canterbury, New Hampshire, support this claim. Here, she describes a game used to teach young girls to love each other and to reinforce the intimacy of the group:

> They placed themselves in a wide circle, each one standing at three or four paces distant from the other. They then began little verses, which, though I can not give literally accurate, were in substance as follows:

> *Must I here alone be standing,*
> *Having none that I can love;*
> *Having none my friend to be,*
> *None who will grow fond of me?*

On this each little girl approached the one nearest to her, and, taking each other's hands, they laid them upon their hearts and sang

> *Nay, my sister, come thou nearer,*
> *And I will to thee be dearer,*
> *Be to thee a faithful friend;*
> *I will share with thee thy sadness;*
> *Thou shalt share with me my gladness!*

With this the children all took hold of hands, and slowly moving round in a circle, repeated the while these last words, or something like them; and in so doing approaching nearer and nearer together, wove their arms round each other like a garland of flowers, then sunk upon their knees singing the while a hymn, the first verse of which was

> *Heavenly Father, we look down in mercy*
> *On this little flock,*
> *United in thy name!*
> *Give us of thy Holy Spirit, etc.*

While singing this hymn, and while still upon their knees, the children all kissed each other, after which they rose up and separated. The beautiful symbolic meaning contained in the whole game, its simplicity, and the beautiful grace with which it was performed; the thought of the difference in the spirit of this game to the bitter reality of many a solitary existence in the great community of the world, affected me deeply; I could not refrain from weeping.

Source: Bremer (1853:575–576).

---

pattern. Using a national sample of young adults, Waite, Goldscheider, and Witsberger (1986) discovered an erosion of traditional family orientation among those who had spent time in nonfamily living. This period of independent living affects personal plans and goals about marriage and family life. In particular, young women who lived independently were more likely to make plans for employment, expect fewer children, be more accepting of employed mothers, and hold nontraditional views of what it means to be a wife and mother in a family. Young men who lived independently also acquired nontraditional views, but the effects were not as dramatic for them as for the women.

Similarly, Glenn (1987) looked at national polls taken between 1969 and 1986 and found that they generally suggested a lessening of allegiance to the family. In particular, there has been an increasing approval of nontraditional, nonfamily roles for women, a decline in the ideal number of children for a family to have, and an increase in sexual permissiveness. Perhaps the most important change in family attitudes observed by Glenn (1992:34) is the "decline in the ideal of marital permanence," as measured by the dramatic increase in the proportion of women who approve of parents who do not get along to split up rather than stay together for the children's sake.

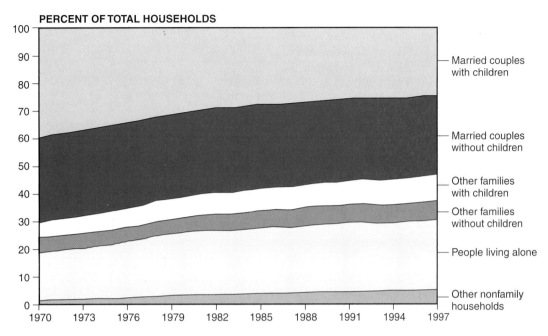

FIGURE 1.3   **Household Composition: 1970–1997**
(Source: Bryson and Casper 1998:1.)

Some people who read about the decline in the number of people opting for a traditional family get anxious about the future not only of the family but of society as well. They believe that the family—especially the traditional arrangement—is the heart of society and if the family disintegrates so will society.

We need to be aware that agonizing words about the death of the family have been with us for centuries:

> The first settlers of New England had sought to create a family unit that would conform strictly to the teachings of the Bible. Within forty years of their arrival in the New World, however, the colonists feared that their families were disintegrating, that parents were growing ever more irresponsible, and that their children were losing respect for authority (Mintz and Kellogg 1988:17).

This does not mean that we should dismiss all warnings about the state of family life today, however. There does seem to be ample reason for concern. Figure 1.3 shows the dramatic change in household composition from 1970 to 1997. Clearly, an increasing number of people are living alone and an increasingly smaller proportion of all households are composed of a father, a mother, and one or more children. By 1996, 3 percent of white children, 9 percent of black children, and 5 percent of Hispanic children lived in a household not headed by a parent (U.S. Bureau of the Census 1997b:66). David Popenoe (1990) has argued that such things as the decline in fertility, the increase in working married mothers, the high divorce rate, increased premarital sexual activity, and delayed age at marriage are not merely signs of family change but of family decline: "It is the individual him- or herself, not the family unit, in whom the main investments are increasingly made" (Popenoe 1990:43).

In Defense of Marriage and the Family

We have not yet seen the whole picture. From 1972 to 1986, the proportion of married people who said they were "very happy" declined, while the proportion of never-married males and widowed females who claimed to be "very happy" increased (Glenn and Weaver 1988). However, even in the 1980s, more married men and women than single,

separated, divorced, or widowed men and women
reported themselves as very happy. Moreover, subsequent surveys showed that the trend of decreasing
differences between the married and never-married
did not continue into the late 1980s (Lee, Seccombe, and Shehan 1991).

The tendency for married people to be happier
and healthier is long-standing. More than 130 studies have reported that both married men and married women are generally happier and less stressed
(as measured by such things as alcoholism rates,
suicide rates, and physical and emotional health)
than are the unmarried (Lauer and Lauer
1986:26–28; Stack and Wasserman 1993 and 1995;
Horwitz, White and Howell-White 1996; Kessler et
al. 1997; Wickrama et al. 1997). The benefits of a
stable marriage for physical and emotional well-
being have also been found in other nations such as
Japan and Great Britain (Kawakami et al. 1995; Murphy, Glaser and Grundy 1997). And a seventeen-
nation study reported that in sixteen of the countries
(Northern Ireland was the only exception) marriage
was significantly related to happiness, and that marriage increases happiness equally among men and
women (Stack and Eshleman 1998). Clearly, a satisfying marital relationship enhances happiness and
is a strong buffer against the negative effects of
stress (Jackson 1992; Barnett 1994).

People continue to put a high value on marriage
and family life. As one research team put it: "There
is no question that the family remains one of the
most significant contributors to individuals' feelings
about the quality of their lives" (Mills, Grasmick,
Morgan, and Wenk 1992:443). Sixty-two percent of
both men and women say their spousal role is satisfying to them, and 93 percent of men and 88 percent of women say they would marry the same person again.[1] Ninety-seven percent of Americans
believe that the world is a better place to live when
families are happy and healthy, and nearly 90 percent indicate that their own family is one of the
most important parts of their lives (Schwartz 1987).
Three out of four Americans believe that having
children is not too limiting on their careers, and
nearly as many agree that mothers of young children should work only if it is financially necessary

Men as well as women place a high value on family life.

(Schwartz 1987). A Gallup poll reported that 95
percent of the respondents identified their family
life as "very" important to them.[2] In contrast, 61
percent identified work and 48 percent named religion as very important. Finally, a series of Gallup
polls from the late 1970s to the early 1990s found
that more than 90 percent of Americans would welcome more emphasis on traditional family ties
(Hugick and Leonard 1991:65).

A *Parents* magazine poll found that parents,
adult children, and in-laws have a good deal of
close contact with each other (Groller 1987). Over
two-thirds of the respondents said they have contact with their parents at least once a week, and
over half said they have contact with in-laws at
least once a week. When the adult children and
parents live in the same area, more than three out
of four have weekly contact or more. Forty-four
percent said they go to their parents for advice on
important matters, and about a fourth said they go
to in-laws. Parents also seek advice from their
adult children.

Me or We?

How can we make sense out of the conflicting evidence? Are Americans moving away from a family
orientation or continuing to affirm that orientation?
We have seen evidence that could suggest that ei-

---

[1]*The American Enterprise,* September/October 1993, p. 91.

[2]*Gallup Report,* no. 307, April 1991, p. 37.

ther position is correct. Our own position is that Americans are caught up in contradictory feelings. These contradictory feelings derive from contrary values with which we are struggling. On the one hand, there is **familism,** a value on family living. Familism leads us to cherish our families, to subordinate our personal desires if necessary for the good of the family group, and to view marriage as that which demands our commitment and fidelity.

On the other hand, we are a nation that values individualism, the well-being of the individual. American individualism has two strains, one of which emphasizes personal achievement (utilitarian individualism) and the other of which emphasizes personal happiness and fulfillment (expressive individualism) (Bellah et al. 1985). Utilitarian individualism emphasizes getting ahead for yourself, while expressive individualism emphasizes fulfillment by doing those things that satisfy you.

Expressive individualism has been particularly strong the past few decades, buttressed by a humanistic psychology that has urged people to search for self-fulfillment above all. There is some evidence that we may be retreating from this strong emphasis on expressive individualism. As we heard one therapist put it, "We've been through the *me* generation and now we're trying to go back to a *we* generation." The contradictory attitudes expressed in various polls and surveys, and the discrepancies between some attitudes and behavior, reflect, we

believe, the fact that Americans are in the midst of a struggle between "me" and "we." It is a difficult struggle. As Bellah et al. (1985:111) point out, our individualistic ideology makes it hard for us to understand why we should even be concerned about giving to each other:

> Now we are all supposed to be conscious primarily of our assertive selves. To reappropriate a language in which we could all, men and women, see that dependence and independence are deeply related, and that we can be independent persons without denying that we need one another, is a task that has only begun.

In sum, we believe that Americans value marriage and family but are struggling between familial and individualistic values. We value and need intimacy, but many are not convinced that marriage and family living are the only ways to fulfill those intimacy needs. Indeed, they are not the only arrangements that will satisfy all people. Thus, we are in a process of making a variety of arrangements legitimate. The majority of people will continue to opt for marriage and family living; a substantial minority will find alternative arrangements.

'TIL DEATH?

For the majority who opt for marriage and family, what are the prospects? To the extent that our expressive individualistic values prevail, people will

INVOLVEMENT
Getting to Know You

Although most Americans agree that the family is a highly important part of their personal lives and well-being, many know little about their extended families. One of the ways we get a better sense of who we are is to know more about the kind of family of which we are a part. In this exercise, therefore, get to know your extended family better. Inquire about members of the family that you both know and don't know—whether grandpar-

ents, cousins, or whatever—and try to get pictures of those people. Ask questions of family members to whom you have access: "Who is or was the most colorful member of this family in your estimation? What is one of the most interesting stories that you know about our family? What did your parents tell you about their parents or other members of the family?"

Summarize your experience by answering the following questions.

What have you learned about your family that you didn't know before? How does that make you feel? What difference does it make in the way you think about yourself?

If the entire class engages in this project, share some of the more colorful stories with each other and discuss as a group both the benefits and the pitfalls of discovering more about our families.

enter and remain in a marriage only so long as it is perceived to be personally beneficial to them. They will then divorce and may seek to fulfill their intimacy needs through another marriage. Indeed, some have raised the question of whether any other pattern is realistic if people are to have their needs fulfilled. That is, can two people maintain a long-term relationship that is not only stable but also satisfying to them both?

Over three decades ago, Levinger (1965) argued that relationships can be described in terms of their stability and satisfaction. Some marriages are high on both (a "full-shell" marriage), some are low on both ("no-shell"), and some have one without the other ("half-shell" marriages are those that are happy but for some reason cannot survive; "empty-shell" marriages are those that last but do not bring satisfaction). All four of these types can still be found. For some, the marriage proves to be unsatisfactory almost from the start. Like the young man who married a woman because of the "great sex" they had, the no-shell marriages break up in a short time (half of all marriages that break up do so within the first seven years).

But are there empty-shell marriages, those that are unsatisfactory yet stable? The answer is yes. In our study of 351 long-term marriages (Lauer and Lauer 1986), the only criterion for being included in the sample was a minimum of fifteen years of marriage. We anticipated that virtually all would have a satisfying union, since people tend not to remain in an unhappy marriage. But in nearly 15 percent (fifty-one) of the couples, one or both of the partners was unhappy to some extent. Why did they stay together? The two major reasons were a sense of duty (religious beliefs or family tradition) and children. A study employing a national sample and looking directly for reasons for stability in unhappy marriages found that those in the more stable unions (as measured by perceived chances for separation or divorce) tended to: be older, be committed to marriage as an institution, and believe that divorce would only further detract from their happiness. Compared to those in less stable marriages, they also had less social activity and less sense of control over their lives (Heaton and Albrecht 1991).

It is the first pattern noted previously, of course, the highly stable *and* satisfying marriage that Levinger called full-shell, that has been the ideal in

modern American life. But can it happen? Can people live together in a vital, meaningful relationship "'til death do us part"? Again, the answer is yes. For some people, marriage is still an experience that enhances their physical and mental health and their general sense of well-being:

> Marriage places more demands on people than friendship, but the rewards are enormous for those who are able to work through the differences and annoyances and maintain a growing relationship. For some, the rewards are so immense that marriage is a watershed in their lives (Lauer and Lauer 1988:86).

What are the ingredients of such a marriage? We asked our happy couples to select from thirty-nine factors those that they regarded as most important in their own experience. In order of the frequency with which they were named, the following are the reasons given by husbands and wives:

Husbands

1. My spouse is my best friend.
2. I like my spouse as a person.
3. Marriage is a long-term commitment.
4. Marriage is sacred.
5. We agree on aims and goals.
6. My spouse has grown more interesting.
7. I want the relationship to succeed.
8. An enduring marriage is important to social stability.
9. We laugh together.
10. I am proud of my spouse's achievement.
11. We agree on a philosophy of life.
12. We agree about our sex life.

Wives

1. My spouse is my best friend.
2. I like my spouse as a person.
3. Marriage is a long-term commitment.
4. Marriage is sacred.
5. We agree on aims and goals.
6. My spouse has grown more interesting.
7. I want the relationship to succeed.
8. We laugh together.
9. We agree on a philosophy of life.
10. We agree on how and how often to show affection.
11. An enduring marriage is important to social stability.
12. We have a stimulating exchange of ideas.

Even though husbands and wives were interviewed or filled out their questionnaires separately, the first seven items are exactly the same! The order varies somewhat after that, but there are no striking differences between husbands and wives. There seems to be considerable consensus on what it takes to forge a union that is both long-lasting and fulfilling to both partners.

A follow-up study of one hundred couples married forty-five years or more found virtually the same results and the same general consensus between men and women (Lauer, Lauer, and Kerr 1990). And other researchers have found similar and compatible characteristics in marriages that last (Fenell 1993; Robinson and Blanton 1993; Sharlin 1996).

Note that the most important factor is liking your spouse, liking the kind of person to whom you are married, appreciating the kind of person that he or she is. Three of the first six factors relate to the individual's perception of the kind of person the spouse is. It is not only a myth but a dangerous myth that people marry each other purely out of love. As one wife, who rated her marriage as "extremely happy," told us:

> I feel that liking a person in marriage is as important as loving that person. I have to like him so I will love him when things aren't so rosy. Friends enjoy each other's company—enjoy doing things together. . . . That's why friendship really ranks high in my reasons for our happy marriage.

A husband summed up the importance of friendship and liking when he said: "Jen is just the best friend I have. I would rather spend time with her, talk with her, be with her than anyone else." And a wife noted that she liked the kind of person her husband was so much that she would want to be friends with him even if she wasn't married to him.

Next to liking and being friends with one's spouse, people talked about the importance of commitment. Couples in unhappy marriages also ranked commitment high, but there was a difference in their commitment. They were committed primarily to the institution of marriage. Once in a particular union, therefore, they were determined to make it last, regardless of how unhappy they were. In other words, they were committed to maintaining a marriage but were not really committed to each other. Couples in happy marriages, on the other hand, are committed to marriage and to their spouses. This involves a determination to work through whatever problems might cause dissatisfaction. As expressed by one wife:

> We've remained married because forty years ago our peer group just did. We worked our way through problems that today we might walk away from. Our marriage is firm and filled with respect and love, but it took time and work. In a marriage today, we might have separated. I'm glad we didn't. I can't emphasize this too strongly. I have two children who are divorced. They are still searching for a magical something that isn't obtainable in the real world. Marriage grows through working out problems and going on. Our marriage took forty years and we are still learning.

There are many other factors that are important, such as humor and the ability to handle conflict constructively. The point is that a long-term and satisfying marriage is not merely a matter of finding just the right person who can make you happy. It is a matter of two people who have some positive factors going for them (such as liking each other and sharing similar values) working together in a committed relationship to achieve a mutually satisfying life. Even in an age of rapid change and high divorce rates, the full-shell marriage can be a reality for those who wish it.

PERSPECTIVE
A Note on Theory

In simplest terms, a theory is an explanation. For example, the myth that people marry simply because they love each other may be based on the theory that love is a dominant emotion in human life, an emotion that we can recognize and one that structures the nature of our relationships. More formally, a theory is a set of logically related propositions that explain some phenomenon (see, for example, Sternberg's triangular theory of love in chapter 7).

Social scientists use theories not only to explain but also to guide research. Consequently, theory is an important part of the study of intimate relationships. There is, however, no single theory that encompasses the field of marriage and the family. In fact, most theoretical perspectives used to study intimate relationships are borrowed from other disciplines (Holman and Burr 1980). In this section, we will briefly describe the more commonly used theories and note a few places in the text where they apply. Because we stress practical application, we will not elaborate on theory in the remaining chapters. For an interesting exercise, try to read through one of the subsequent chapters and see which of the theories seem to apply to the various findings.

SYSTEMS THEORY

A variety of theories fall under the general heading of systems theory, but all share certain assumptions. As applied to intimate relationships, systems theory asserts that the intimate group must be analyzed as a whole; the group has boundaries that distinguish it from other groups. Thus, particular people form the system, and have particular rules and roles that apply to their system. Furthermore, the group is composed of interrelated parts (individuals). That is, the parts are not independent but influence each other and work together in such a way that the system tends to be maintained; outside influences generally cause minimal change. If the system is composed of three or more individuals (as in a family with children), various subsystems may arise (e.g., parent and child may form a coalition against the other parent). Although such subsystems may appear to be threatening, they actually tend to maintain the system. For instance, a woman may only remain in a marriage because she and her child support and protect each other when the alcoholic husband and father becomes abusive.

Family therapists use systems theory. Among the well-known theories of family therapists is that of Murray Bowen (1978), who built his theory on the premise that humans respond primarily at the emotional rather than the cognitive level (Crosby 1991). In this theory, two tasks are important for healthy development. The first is to develop our cognitive functioning so that our behavior is not driven mainly by our emotions. The second is to develop our individuality so that we have separate identities from our family of origin even while remaining members of that family.

These tasks may be complicated by certain family processes, such as the formation of coalitions (subsystems) and the tendency to transmit unhealthy patterns from one generation to another (the system maintaining itself). Thus, what appears to be an individual's problem may be a problem arising out of the family system. In order to help the individual, a therapist should treat the family, for it is the system itself and not merely one of its parts that is not functioning in a healthy way. Bowen's theory is, of course, far more complex than we can discuss here, but see our discussion of the use and misuse of power in chapter 16 for an example of its application.

EXCHANGE THEORY

"You owe me one" is a popular expression of exchange theory, which asserts that we all attempt to keep our costs lower than our rewards in interaction (Nye 1988). *Costs* refers to such things as time, money, emotional or intellectual energy, or anything else that an individual defines as part of his or her investment in a relationship. Similarly, *rewards* include emotional or intellectual gratification, money, a sense of security, or anything else an individual defines as a satisfying outcome of a relationship. If a relationship consistently costs us more than it rewards us, we are likely to avoid the person or break the relationship.

Exchange theory posits a rational assessment of a situation. The individual weighs the pros and cons, the costs and rewards, of a situation. He or she tries to determine if the situation is fair or appealing or worthwhile. To some extent, this happens in selecting a life partner (see the discussion in chapter 8). It

PERSPECTIVE (continued)

happens in the negotiation of responsibilities of dual-career couples (chapter 13). It occurs in many other areas of family life, such as decision making, child-rearing, and division of labor in the home. Exchange theory does not explain all of family life, but it is clearly of value in our efforts to understand.

SYMBOLIC INTERACTION THEORY

Symbolic interactionism views humans primarily as cognitive creatures who are influenced and shaped by their interaction experiences (Lauer and Handel 1983). That is, what happens in interaction is a result not merely of what individuals bring to it but of the interaction itself. Like systems theorists, symbolic interactionists believe that the whole is greater than the sum of its parts. Thus, a young woman who has determined to devote herself to a career rather than marry may find herself changing her mind as she interacts with a particular man. Or a man who is negative about parenthood may find himself becoming enthusiastic and committed as he interacts with his child.

An important concept in symbolic interactionism is **definition of the situation,** which asserts that when we define a situation as real, it has real consequences. That is, our interpretation of a situation is as important as anything that is objectively true about that situation. For example, a man may be very jealous of his girlfriend because he believes she is flirting with other men. In point of fact, she may be completely faithful to her boyfriend.

But if he perceives her to be flirting, there will be real—and perhaps damaging—consequences to the relationship.

Depending on how they define their situation, then, people may be satisfied in a relationship that outsiders view as undesirable or dissatisfied in one that outsiders view as very good. Our discussion of spouse abuse in chapter 17 points out how abused women perceive their situation in a variety of ways that justify staying in the relationship.

Symbolic interactionism can be combined with exchange theory. For example, what is important is not that rewards exceed costs in some objective sense or as assessed by an outside observer but that the people involved in a relationship *perceive* the rewards to exceed the costs (see the discussion of equity in chapter 8).

CONFLICT THEORY

In various parts of this book, we will discuss "his" experience and "her" experience (e.g., of marriage in chapter 10 and of parenting in chapter 14). Conflict theory can be used to understand such diverse experiences or to explain such phenomena as power struggles (chapter 12). According to conflict theory, individuals come to interaction with differing and even contradictory interests, needs, and goals. Because of the contradictions and because the things for which people strive may not be available in sufficient number for all, everyone cannot be satisfied. The individuals therefore struggle with each other, using

whatever resources they have, each striving to realize his or her own interests, needs, and goals.

Some observers believe that men have an inherent advantage in the power struggle of a heterosexual relationship. One resource that is brought to the struggle is money. Typically, men have brought more money than women have into the household, thereby establishing their power over women and having the final say in any decisions that matter to them.

Conflict theory is sometimes presented as an alternative to systems theory. But the two may be combined, for conflict is one way in which a system may be maintained. In some marriages and some families, the glue that holds it all together is ongoing conflict. Without the conflict, there would be no interaction at all between the individuals. And in line with the notion of adaptation of the system, if conflict between some members of the family is resolved, it may break out between others.

The various theories, then, are not necessarily alternatives. Rather, they may be used singly or in combination in order to explain and understand the structure and processes of intimate relationships. Theory can be used to understand all the topics covered in this book. They help you see the utility of theory. We shall at one or more places in each chapter specifically identify the way a particular theory applies, and will note in the margin the theory being used.

APPROACH OF THIS BOOK

We take a multifaceted approach to the study of marriage and family life. First, we believe that the study should be broadbased. Accordingly, we draw on the research of sociologists, historians, social psychologists, family studies experts, psychologists, therapists, and others who have made important contributions to our understanding. Each chapter will have "Perspective," a boxed insert that draws on historical, anthropological, or literary materials to illuminate some topic. With the exception of this one, every chapter will contain "Comparison," a boxed insert that examines beliefs and behavior about intimate behavior in other societies and cultures.

Second, our approach is personal. We will illustrate points throughout the book with materials from our files on people with whom we have worked (including students). In addition, each chapter will have "Personal," a boxed insert that gives a longer personal account related to some topic in the chapter.

Third, we want the book to be practical. Most of the materials have practical implications. But we have found that readers frequently fail to apply the materials to their own lives. As a student told one of us after a lecture, "I didn't think what you were saying was very useful until you asked us to think about it and write down one or two insights that we could use in our own lives. Then I realized that the lecture had some very practical information." To help with the application of material, we are including a number of important principles at the end of each chapter, principles that can be used to enhance the quality of your intimate life.

Finally, we believe that the best learning is participatory. "Involvement," another boxed insert in each chapter, enables you to participate in some way in learning the materials. We hope some of these will become class projects and that the results can be pooled and shared. In any case, the more you engage in your own research, the more you participate in the learning process, the more useful will be your educational experience.

SUMMARY

We learn about family life through our own experience and through the mass media. But some of what we know is mythical. Some of the common myths today include: (1) we've lost the extended family; (2) people marry because they love each other; (3) having children increases marital satisfaction; (4) a good sex life is the best predictor of marital satisfaction; and (5) half of all marriages end in divorce. Such myths are dangerous because they can ruin good relationships.

Patterns of intimate relationships change over time. In recent years, there has been an increase in premarital sex, out-of-wedlock births, the number of people living alone, the number of people cohabiting, age at first marriage, proportion of mothers who work, and the divorce rate. There has been a decline in birth rates and average household size.

Throughout history, people have thought about the ideal form of family life, one that will satisfy everyone. Utopian writers have advocated everything from retaining existing forms of the family to abolishing the nuclear family altogether. In utopian communities, people have tried celibacy, monogamous marriage, and group marriage. No form seems to work well for everyone; all work well for at least some people, supporting our right to diverse arrangements.

What do Americans want? For various reasons, only a minority still choose the traditional arrangement of employed father, stay-at-home mother, and children. There is some evidence that marriage is not as central to our happiness as it once was. However, Americans still seem largely to affirm monogamous marriage, and most indicate satisfaction with their own marriage and family life. One of the problems is that we are caught between our values on familism and individualism. Yet for those who desire a long-term, monogamous relationship, the evidence is that it is still possible and rewarding to those who achieve it.

INTERNET CONNECTION
American Myths and Dreams

Our assumptions about the typical American marriage and family life often contrast sharply with reality. Your text discusses how competing emotional, social, and economic factors lead to increased divorce rates, rates of premarital sex, and out of wedlock births—trends that sharply contrast the idyllic view of the All-American family portrayed on TV. The websites listed below highlight some of the issues touched on in this chapter relating to monogamy and nonmonogamy for married and single people.

www.mhhe.com/lauer4

people who have chosen not to get married, are unable to marry, or are in the process of deciding whether marriage is right for them. The site contains a FAQ page, as well as links to additional print and internet-related resources.

Vaughn-Vaughn.com

http://www.vaughan-vaughan.com/index.html

This website was created by a husband and wife team who experienced the impact of extramarital affairs in their own relationship. The site contains information on married couples who stay in a relationship after an affair has taken place.

Alternatives to Marriage Project

http://www.netspace.org/atmp/homepage.html

The Alternatives to Marriage Project is a national organization that provides resources, advocacy, and support to

1. Review the information at the website in **Articles about Affairs** at **Vaughn-Vaughn.com.** Do you believe extramarital affairs are as common as the research cited at Vaughn-Vaughn indicates? What additional information can you find on the Internet to support or discredit their statistics? How does adultery affect myths about family life? If your partner became involved in an extramarital affair, how would you cope with it?

2. If you were a family therapist using systems theory, how might you use a website like **Alternatives to Marriage?**

3. How is symbolic interaction theory at play in the material on this site? Conflict theory? Exchange theory?

DIVERSITY IN FAMILIES

Learning Objectives

After reading chapter 2, you should be able to:

1. Briefly discuss how families vary across time and between and within societies.
2. Define what a family is.
3. Explain the problems of the single-parent family.
4. Discuss the various ways the single-parent family copes with its problems.
5. Outline the similarities and differences between African American, Hispanic, Asian American, Native American, and white families in American society.
6. Describe life in the contemporary black family.
7. Discuss the strengths as well as the problems of the Hispanic family.
8. Explain how the Asian culture shapes the structure and experience of Asian American families.
9. Identify two factors that affect Native American family life.
10. Understand the difficulties of interracial families and the ways in which they cope with these problems.
11. Describe the similarities and differences between heterosexual and homosexual families in developing lasting intimate relationships.

Imagine that you are an artist and that you have been asked to draw or paint a picture of a family. You may use any setting you like. What would you draw? Whatever the setting, you would probably draw an adult man, an adult woman, and one or more children. And for many of you, these people would probably be white.

But some families are composed of only two people—an adult and a child. Some are composed of nonwhites. Others are racially mixed. And others are composed of two adults of the same sex, with or without children. These various families differ not only by the way they look but also by the way life is carried on within them. To fully understand the family, the context of our first experience of intimacy, we must be familiar with the rich diversity of family life. In this chapter, we will look briefly at how the family varies between and within human societies (we noted in the last chapter some variations in American society when we discussed the utopian groups). Then we will examine some family types that are both similar to and different from

the white, two-parent family: single-parent, non-white (including interracial), and homosexual.

THE VARIABILITY OF FAMILY LIFE

Families vary across time, between societies, and within societies. It would require a number of volumes to fully discuss such variations. In this section, we only want to illustrate the variability by a few examples.

Variations Between Societies

In some ways, people everywhere are alike. People everywhere, for example, need intimate relations and form family units to fulfill some of their intimacy needs. When we talk about variations, then, we are not overlooking the similarities between peoples. Rather, we are stressing the important points that intimacy needs can be fulfilled in diverse ways and diverse kinds of family units can be formed.

The variations between societies underscore the fact that some differ from what we may regard as normal, natural, right, or typical. For example, our ideal is for marriage to be " 'til death do us part." Marco Polo reported a tribe in Asia in which a wife could take another husband if her first husband was away from home for twenty days; the husband could also take another wife if he was staying in a different place (Durant 1954:38).

Another of our ideals is choice—individuals should personally choose the person they marry. In many cultures, both ancient (Greece) and modern (China until recent times), marital partners were chosen by parents, and many brides and grooms did not even see each other before the wedding (Queen, Habenstein, and Quadagno 1985:9).

Finally, the ideal of most Americans is monogamous marriage. We say "most" Americans because the early Mormons, as a part of their belief system, practiced a form of polygamy. **Polygamy** is the marriage of one person to two or more people of the opposite sex. **Polygyny** is the marriage of a man to two or more wives, while **polyandry** is the marriage of a woman to two or more husbands. Although illegal in the United States, a small splinter group of Mormons still practices polygyny in accord with their religious beliefs (Altman and Ginat 1996).

Polygyny has been practiced by more human societies than any other form of marriage. Most preindustrial societies as well as modern Muslim societies allow polygyny. While Americans are prone to see polygyny as a form of female oppression, women who are part of such unions often define them quite differently. Many Mormon wives in the nineteenth century vigorously tried to get the federal government to allow polygyny. A recent study of polygynous wives in the African nation of Cameroon found that the wives most satisfied with the arrangement were junior (newer and younger) wives rather than senior wives, those with more children (a status symbol in the society), and those whose husbands had a higher economic status (Gwanfogbe et al. 1997). For many polygynous wives, it is *their* situation that is the ideal, not the monogamous union that is idealized in American society.

Other variations are based not so much in ideals as in common practices. In our society, at least until recent times, a woman typically assumed the surname of the man she married. Couples establish their own residence, and the family tree is traced through both the husband's and the wife's line. However, anthropologists have discovered a wide range of patterns in other societies. In some societies, for example, the man takes the woman's name. In others, the husband continues to live with his family, rather than with his wife, or couples may alternate residence between the man's and the woman's families. People in some societies trace their line only through the man, while others trace it only through the woman.

There are, in sum, a wide range of practices that people have developed to satisfy their intimacy needs in families. No evidence exists that any particular practice works best for people generally. In fact, one could argue that the diversity of family life is both necessary and desirable if the maximum number of people are to find satisfying family relationships.

Variations Within Societies

Within any particular society, family life varies over time. And in a complex, modern society, it varies between groups at any particular point in time as well. The core of this chapter will explore these variations between groups. Here, we want to illustrate how the family has varied over time by looking at a few aspects of white families in colonial

A "family" can take many different forms.

America (Queen, Habenstein, and Quadagno 1985). You can compare the following materials with what you know about white family life today.

The American colonists generally believed that it was important for every individual to be a part of a household. Single people were not merely encouraged to be married but were stigmatized if they remained single too long. In some cases, they were even penalized; Maryland, for instance, imposed a tax on bachelors.

In spite of the stigma on singlehood, it was not easy to get married. In the early years of the southern colonies, there were about four men for every woman. And in all the colonies, a young man was expected to be financially independent before he married. This meant that he had to have a home on his own land. Once financially secure, he had to secure the permission of the prospective bride's father before he could even begin the courtship.

When a couple was ready to marry, they would make their intention known publicly. This could be done by a posted notice in a public place or the reading of the banns (a public notice, normally given three times) in a public meeting or a church. New Englanders initially regarded marriage as a civil affair. Magistrates, not clergy, performed wedding ceremonies. Not until 1692 were clergymen allowed to perform weddings in Massachusetts. In the southern colonies, except for Maryland, the clergy were required to perform the marriage services.

Because of lack of birth control, marriage was likely to lead quickly to children, and families tended to be large. Seven or more children were not uncommon. Colonial families were not likely to face the issue of an "empty nest" at middle age under such circumstances. Unmarried children could be living at home until the parents were fairly old.

Sexual standards were strict. In New England, unmarried people caught in the act of having intercourse could be fined, whipped, forced to marry, or any combination of the three. Some of the colonies were even stricter in the matter of adultery. Some offenders were required to wear publicly a scarlet letter. Some were whipped or sentenced to time in the pillory. And a few were put to death. The standards were the same in the south, but the penalties were far less severe. Even in the south, however, an offender could be publicly censured and punished.

As in modern America, marriage did not always work out well in the colonies. Divorce was much rarer, however. In the southern colonies, divorce was not legal; unhappy couples might eventually separate, or one or the other spouse might desert. In contrast, since marriage was a civil contract among the early Puritans of New England, the contract could be dissolved by a local court. Adultery, cruelty, and a long period of absence were among the reasons for which a court might grant a divorce. The court also gave the divorcing parties the right to remarry. Desertion was more common than divorce in early New England, leaving some women to raise their children alone.

Clearly, then, the colonial family differed from most families today in a number of important ways. If we had time to trace the family throughout American history, we would discover variations at each time period.

What Is the Family?

Since it has so many variations, what do we mean by a family? One way to define it is to identify those functions that all families fulfill. Four functions identified by anthropologists are sexual relations, reproduction, socialization of children, and economic cooperation. Reiss and Lee (1988:24) have shown that each of these functions, except the socialization of children, is lacking in families in one or more societies in the world. We would go farther and point out that some American families—those that opt to be childless and some homosexual couples—also lack socialization of children as a function.

Our definition of **family,** therefore, is: a group united by marriage, blood, and/or adoption in order to satisfy intimacy needs and/or bear and socialize children. This definition, we believe, applies to the whole range of family types of humankind.

THE SINGLE-PARENT FAMILY

Single-parent families may occur in various ways, including divorce, death of a spouse, and a single person deciding to have or adopt a child without getting married. An increasing number of people, particularly women, have opted for parenthood without marriage in recent years. Some of the women do not want to get married but do want to be a mother. Some may prefer marriage but find themselves in a situation without a prospective husband and with their childbearing years coming to an end. Changing sex roles (chapter 3) and contemporary views on sexuality (chapter 4) make single parenthood an option that is no longer stigmatized, further facilitating the choice.

In the case of divorce, "single-parent" does not mean that the child has no contact with the other parent but that the child lives primarily with one parent. In other cases, contact with the other parent or with the biological parents (in the case of adoption) may not be possible. "Single-parent" also does not mean a permanent arrangement. In fact, using national data Aquilino (1996) found that among children born to unmarried mothers, only one in five spent their entire childhood in a single-parent home and nearly half had grandparents or other relatives living with them during their childhood.

Extent of Single-Parent Families

Single-parent families have increased considerably over the past two decades. By 1996, 28 percent of children lived with one parent, which was nearly double the proportion in 1970. The proportion varies by race: 22 percent for white, 57 percent for

black, and 33 percent for Hispanic children (U.S. Bureau of the Census 1997b:66).

Most of those living with one parent are with a divorced parent, but by 1996 the single-parent home was as likely to involve a never-married as a divorced parent (figure 2.1). Finally, it is important to keep in mind that when we talk about the number of children living in a one-parent home in any year, we are only talking about a fraction of the children who will live with one parent at some point in their lives. Depending on what happens to marriage and divorce rates, as many as half of all children may ultimately spend some time in a one-parent household.

As figure 2.1 shows, the proportion of single-parent families headed by a father has grown considerably. The number of single fathers with children under eighteen increased from 400 thousand in 1970 to 1.7 million by 1995 (Collins 1997b). A growing number of single fathers are young, never married, and have relatively low incomes (Eggebeen, Snyder, and Manning 1996).

Challenges of the Single-Parent Family

What kinds of challenges are you more likely to encounter if you are a single parent or a child in a single-parent family? As we discuss the challenges, keep in mind that these are challenges you are

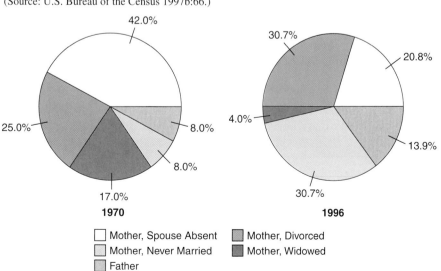

FIGURE 2-1   Children Living with One Parent, Proportion by Parent's Gender
(Source: U.S. Bureau of the Census 1997b:66.)

"more likely" to experience. As we shall see in the next section, "more likely" does not mean a majority; it only means your chances of dealing with certain difficulties are somewhat higher if you live in a one-parent family.

Challenges of Single Parents

Parenthood is challenging and difficult even when there are two parents in the home. With just one parent, the challenges increase greatly. Robert Weiss (1979) pointed out that a basic problem is the inadequacy of resources available to the single parent and the consequent overload. In particular, the single parent is likely to face three kinds of overload: responsibility, task, and emotional.

Responsibility overload may result from having too few financial resources. The problem is especially acute for mothers who are single parents. In fact, much of the disadvantage of single-mother households, including the academic performance of the children, is accounted for by economic disadvantages. And never-married single mothers are likely to suffer more economic problems than those previously married (Thomson, Hanson, and McLanahan 1994; Franklin, Smith, and McMiller 1995). Overall, single-mother households have higher rates of poverty than any other group (table 2.1).

Task overload arises from the fact that one parent must do the work of two parents. If the parent works full-time outside the home as well as takes care of the children and manages the household, he or she is likely to feel overwhelmed by the sheer number of tasks that need to be done. In his study of 1,136 single fathers, Geoffrey Greif (1985) re-

ported that one major source of problems for the men was the conflict between their jobs and their housekeeping duties. Olson and Banyard (1993) found that general parenting tasks such as discipline and getting children to do household tasks were the most frequent sources of stress for low-income single mothers.

Emotional overload can occur when the single parent neglects his or her own needs. Single, employed mothers, for example, spend less time in personal care (including grooming, sleeping, and eating) and in recreation (including watching television and attending social activities) than either the nonemployed single mother or the mother in a two-parent home (Sanik and Mauldin 1986). The single parent may have an intimacy deficit because of the lack of a spouse. The deficit cannot be made up by friends if the parent has little time for anything but his or her job and family work. And the deficit cannot be made up by the children, for they are a responsibility as well as a source of companionship. In addition, the parent needs the intimacy of a peer, the closeness of an adult relationship.

Alone or in combination, the three kinds of overload can result in loneliness, a feeling of hopelessness, or various emotional problems. Anxiety and depression are common problems of single mothers (Propst et al. 1986; Goldberg et al. 1992), who are one of the largest consumers of mental health services.

Emotional problems are more likely to occur among single parents than either those in intact or those in stepparent families. Researchers who compared the three kinds of families reported that the single parents were "more depressed, less satisfied with their family lives, and had more problems with their children than parents in the other family structures" (Fine, Donnelly, and Voydanoff 1986:400). Although there were only a handful of single male parents in their sample, the researchers noted that the men were even more depressed than the women. This is not unexpected in view of the fact that men rely more heavily on a spouse than women do for their emotional support. Greif (1985), incidentally, pointed out that the men who had the hardest time dealing with single parenthood were those whose wives had deserted them.

TABLE 2.1
Percent of People Below the Poverty Level: 1995

	Percent
All people	13.8
People in families	12.3
In white families	9.6
In black families	28.5
In Hispanic families	30.3
In families with female householder, no husband present	36.5

Source: U.S. Bureau of the Census, 1997b:478.

COMPARISON
Single Parents In Iceland

If you are a single parent in the United States, you are likely to deal with more challenges and problems than married parents. How does this compare with single parents in a small nation like Iceland? Juliusdottir (1997) conducted a study of a national random sample of 846 Icelandic parents. A number of interesting findings emerged about Icelandic single parents:

- Ninety-five percent of the single parents are women.
- Nearly a third of the single parents have obtained or are obtaining further education.
- Single mothers on the average work about eight hours a week more than widowed mothers but about the same number of hours a week (approximately forty-three) as married mothers.
- Single parents have a lower average income than married parents, widowed parents, or noncustodial divorced parents—about 74 percent as much as the average of the other three groups.
- Among all parents, visits with grandparents are frequent; about

44 percent of all parents visit grandparents three times a week or more, with single parents visiting somewhat more often than the other three groups.
- When the parents were asked about their health, the single parents complained more about emotional and psychosomatic health problems than did the married parents; the healthiest group was the married parents, followed by never-married single parents, divorced single parents, widowed single parents, and noncustodial divorced parents.

Icelandic single parents show both similarities with and differences from American single parents. Like their American counterparts, the Icelandic single parents are overwhelmingly female, have fewer financial resources, and are likely to have more health problems. Among the health problems cited more often by the Icelandic single parents than by the married parents were insecurity, anxiety attacks, headaches, and fatigue. Inter-

estingly, however, the noncustodial divorced parents had the most severe health problems, complaining about sleeplessness, depression, and pessimism more than the other groups.

The high level of health problems among the noncustodial divorced parents may reflect a grieving process. Family relations in Iceland—as indicated by the high visitation rate—are very strong. The noncustodial divorced parents are not only separated from their ex-spouses and children but also have substantially fewer visits with or calls to grandparents than do the single parents. In a society with a high value on family relations, there are adverse health consequences for those deprived of those relations.

Finally, Icelandic single parents tend to be more involved with family than their American counterparts. This gives them a stronger social support network and helps insulate them from some of the problems faced by their American counterparts.

Challenges of Children of Single Parents

As in the case of the single parent, the child of a single parent, and particularly the male child, is more likely to be depressed (Huntley, Phelps, and Rehm 1986). In the first years after a divorce, the children are also likely to have higher rates of antisocial behavior, aggression, anxiety, and school problems than those in intact families (Fine and Schwebel 1987; Downey 1994; Gringlas and Weinraub 1995). A study reported by the National Center for Health Statistics noted that the prevalence of learning disabilities among children was 5.5 percent in intact families, 7.5 percent in mother-only families, 9.1 percent in mother-stepfather families, and

8.3 percent in other family situations (Zill and Schoenborn 1990). The same study reported the prevalence of emotional and behavioral problems as: 8.3 percent in intact families, 19.1 percent in mother-only families, 23.6 percent in mother-stepfather families, and 22.2 percent in other family situations. Similar results have been found in studies of single-parent children in other nations such as the Netherlands (Garnefski and Diekstra 1997).

The children in single-parent homes have more difficulties within the family as well as within themselves and their outside relationships. Because the bulk of single-parent families are headed by females, it is not surprising that both primary school

Single mothers report more problems with their sons than do married mothers.

children and adolescents in single-parent homes report less support, control, and punishment from their fathers than do other children (Amato 1987). They also report more conflict with siblings, less family cohesion, and more family stress. The sense of cohesion is important. Fewer behavioral problems occur when family members define themselves as part of a cohesive unit (Dreman and Ronen-Eliav 1997).

Why should children in single-parent families feel less cohesion? Cohesion here refers to a sense of emotional bonding that family members have toward each other. One might expect the bond to be stronger with the remaining parent when a divorce or separation has occurred, but it tends not to be. Kennedy (1985) addressed the issue in his study of 631 undergraduate students. He found that the students in single-parent homes not only perceived lower cohesion scores than those in intact families but they also had the highest rates of serious family relationship problems (higher than those in either intact or stepfamilies). Kennedy suggests that the lower cohesion scores may reflect the fact that the students are establishing their independence earlier than the students from intact homes. When children are in the stage of establishing their own separate identities, they typically perceive less family cohesion.

Interestingly, the children may feel greater cohesion if the mother is working (Alessandri 1992).

Mothers who are unemployed are more likely to get depressed, leading to more frequent punishment and increased distress and depression in the children (McLoyd et al. 1994). In such a situation, it is understandable that the children will not sense their home to be very cohesive.

Finally, children in single-parent homes are less likely to achieve higher levels of education, occupation, and income and to maintain stable marriages (Mueller and Cooper 1986; Caspi et al. 1998). McLanahan and Sandefur (1994) found that, compared to those who grew up with both biological parents, teenagers who spend part of their childhood apart from their biological father are twice as likely to drop out of high school, twice as likely to become parents while still in their teens, and one and a half times as likely to be both out of school and without work into their early twenties.

To some extent, these effects reflect the fact that those in single-parent homes are more likely to be in a lower socioeconomic level. But even when we look at those who come from the same socioeconomic levels, the children from the single-parent homes are at a disadvantage. Growing up with two parents appears to increase our level of motivation to achieve. Perhaps the harried single parent simply cannot give the attention to the child's achievements that is necessary to motivate the child to higher and higher levels.

Problems Between Parents and Children

"Anyone who thinks that children are helpless creatures," a weary parent remarked, "should remember that it takes at least two adults to handle one child." Parenting is not an easy responsibility even when there are two in the home. When there is one, relationships with children present even more severe challenges.

Consider some of the problems that can arise when the single parent interacts with the child or children. In a mother-daughter home, there may be more open competition, with the daughter wanting to stay up as late as the mother and measuring her success with boys against her mother's success with men (Bohannan 1985:169–70). The daughter may also lack an appropriate understanding of male-female relationships. As noted family therapist Virginia Satir put it:

> Her attitudes about being female can range all the way from being the servant girl—giving everything, receiving nothing—to feeling she has to do everything herself and be completely independent (1972:172).

Boys seem to present even greater problems than girls. Recently divorced mothers of sons report less control of their children than do mothers of girls or married mothers (Mednick 1987:196). Sons have a harder time adjusting to divorce than do daughters and express some of their anger in disobedience and aggressiveness against the mother. The aggression tends to reach a peak at about a year after the divorce but is still higher after two years than that of boys in intact families.

Some of the problems between mothers and sons arise not from the son's feelings about the situation but from the mother's decisions about how to relate to the son now that the father is absent (Satir 1972:172). A single mother may try to get an older son to assume some of the role responsibilities of the missing father. That distorts both the parent-child relationship and the son's relations with any siblings. If the son feels an obligation to nurture and care for his mother and defend her against her own helplessness, he may not be able to establish his own independence and pursue his own needs for intimate heterosexual relationships. Or he may rebel against the situation and leave home but wrestle for years or even a lifetime with a feeling of

women as enemies. On the other hand, a single mother might tend to "over-mother" the son, who then may form an image of females as dominant and males as nothing.

Most single-parent families are headed by a mother. The single mother, therefore, has been studied far more than the single father. Do single fathers have similar problems with their sons or daughters? We cannot say with certainty. In a small sample, Richards and Schmiege (1993) found that both mothers and fathers identified at least one *significant* problem of being a single parent, but the fathers identified fewer total problems than did the mothers. A larger study, of 912 single-father households, reported that fathers of preadolescent girls reported significantly fewer problems than fathers with boys, with girls and boys, or with adolescent girls (DeMaris and Greif 1992). Finally, a study comparing father-headed with mother-headed single families in Israel found no differences in well-being between the two groups (Fitchen and Cohen 1995). The single fathers were handling the situation as well as the single mothers.

An advantage of single fathers is the likelihood of higher income. In the Richards and Schmiege (1993) research, nearly 80 percent of single mothers but less than 20 percent of single fathers identified money as a problem. Single mothers may also be rewarded less than are fathers by their children (Ambert 1982). The children of single fathers are more likely to express their appreciation than are the children of single mothers. This tendency may reflect the belief that it is the mother's responsibility to care for the children. When the father assumes that responsibility, he is going beyond what is expected of him, and he deserves special praise and appreciation. There is, of course, no reason why the mother should be any more responsible than the father for rearing the children. Nevertheless, as long as people believe this, the single father is likely to continue receiving more rewards in the form of appreciation and admiration than is the single mother.

Finally, dating can be a vexing problem. Unfortunately, the parent may have problems and issues with regard to interpersonal relationships quite apart from the children (see chapters 18 and 19). Those problems and issues may be intensified and added to by the presence of children (Petronio and

Endres 1985/1986). The parent may feel guilty about leaving the child alone to go out on a date. This may cause some resentment toward the child, who consumes so much of the parent's time and energy. The child, in turn, may decide that the parent is considering remarriage and that he or she may have to adapt to a stepparent. In spite of the difficulties of the single-parent home, some children resist the idea of a stepparent. The potential stepparent is defined as an intruder and one who reminds the child again of the pain of the breakup of the family.

Single parents who perceive their children to be less positive about their dating agree that the children react with both anger and resentment toward the dates (Petronio and Endres 1985/1986). Some parents, recognizing the potential problems, delay introducing their dates to their children, though a majority do so immediately or soon after dating someone. Single mothers are more quick to introduce dates to children than are single fathers. This may reflect women's greater concern with relationships and the sense that it is easier for a woman than a man to accept a nurturing relationship with someone else.

The problem of dating is compounded by the fact that the children not only do not like the parent's dates but the dates also may be less than enthusiastic about the children. A survey of eighty-three single parents reported that about two-thirds felt that their dates had at least some reservations about the fact that they had children (Petronio and Endres 1985/1986). If the parent is strongly attracted to a date who dislikes the children and/or who is disliked by the children, the parent may have to struggle with frustration, disappointment, and resentment toward both the date and the children.

The Successful Single-Parent Family

In spite of the challenges and problems we have noted, there are positive things to be said about the single-parent family. Most experts agree that it is not the ideal, though it may be preferable to an intact family with a high level of conflict or other kinds of problems. But when we compare the single-parent with the intact family generally, the picture is not as gloomy as the previous discussion might suggest.

First, Richards and Schmiege (1993) reported that about two-thirds of their single parents said that the parenting became easier for them over time. And while all the single parents in their sample reported at least one significant problem, all but two of the 71 mothers and fathers also identified at least one parenting strength. Some kind of parenting skill, such as being supportive and fostering independence, was the most frequently named strength.

Second, while it is true that children in single-parent homes perceive less cohesion than do those in intact homes, the average level of the perceived cohesion of children in single-parent homes is within the range of normal functioning (Kennedy 1985:123). In other words, "less cohesive" should not be interpreted to mean "chaotic" or "disjointed." While those in single-parent homes are likely to experience less closeness than those in intact homes, this does not mean a serious intimacy deficit. Children living with a mother only report about the same levels of both support and punishment as those living with both parents (Amato 1987).

Moreover, in spite of the greater likelihood of mental health problems, the majority of single parents and their children have fairly high levels of both physical and mental health. In her study of forty-two single parents and their children, however, Hanson (1986) found some sex differences in health status. Single mothers had poorer health than single fathers. But children living with a mother reported higher overall health than those living with a father. Interestingly, boys living with their mothers had the best overall health, while girls living with their fathers had the least. We should note that the sample was small and the health status was based on self-reports of such things as eating and sleeping habits, use of drugs, smoking, self-care, use of preventive health measures, history of illness and accidents, and other indicators of well-being. In part, the results probably reflect the fact that women generally report lower health levels than men. They also reflect some of the interaction problems discussed. Thus, mothers with sole custody of sons reported the lowest levels of mental health.

While it has higher rates of various kinds of problems, the single-parent family is neither intrinsically nor inevitably unhealthy or pathological (Fine, Donnelly, and Voydanoff 1986:401). Studies of single fathers report that most of them feel com-

PERSONAL
"I Chose to Do It Alone"

Most people are not single parents by choice. They become single parents because of separation, divorce, or death, or because of a sexual relationship that for some reason did not result in marriage. Emma is a fifty-year-old teacher who became a single parent by choice, eventually provided her children with a father, but then returned to singlehood again. She regrets none of her decisions:

My experience with raising children has been deeply colored by the fact that I chose to do it alone. My children were not the result of a love relationship gone sour, but of deliberate planning. Having been raised in a highly dysfunctional family, I left home at an early age with a really negative concept of marriage.

After a few years of living on my own, I realized I badly wanted to have children. But I still had a very negative attitude about marriage. To make a long story short, I managed to have two children in the space of sixteen months amidst violent protest from both friends and family. I expected the protest, and I was prepared to deal with it. I knew there would be rough times ahead and that whatever happened, I was going to have to do it entirely alone.

I also knew my children would have to be strong and independent if they were to survive. So as infants, I gave them all the cuddling, stimulation, and nurturing I could, and I found babysitters who did the same. I had to work full-time to support us. So it was important to make what time we had together really count. I did as much as possible with them.

Life was tough, mostly because money was short. But my children seemed secure and well adjusted. Then, when the oldest was eight, I reassessed my situation and soon found myself married to a man who seemed to be what we all needed to make life really complete. Eventually, my "prince" turned out to be a real toad. But he was a good father to my children, and we had a third child. He told me I could stop working and stay home with the children. That was my first mistake. After four years, I got increasingly bored, restless, and irritable. My husband, meanwhile, turned out to be an alcoholic like my father. That awful kind of family life that I was so determined to avoid had developed right under my nose!

When my husband was transferred to another city I stayed behind with the children. I told them we would be on welfare for a while, that I wanted to go back to school and get a degree to teach. They agreed. I went to school days while they were in school and worked nights while

they slept. It wasn't ideal, but we made the most of it. They were understanding, and I began to feel better than I had in years. Eventually, I divorced my husband, got my degree, and improved our financial situation by going back to work.

My children agree that there were times when they felt angry and wished that I was more like the mothers of their friends. But they also feel they grew up stronger, more self-confident and independent than most of the people they see around them. It's been a rough life, but I believe it's been a highly successful one. I am pleased with the way my children are conducting their lives and with the relationships I have with them. My two daughters are married and have their own children. My son is having some problems developing a relationship with a woman, but maybe he will work that out.

If I had it to do all over again, I think the only thing I would change would be to go to school first and then get artificially inseminated. Otherwise, I have no regrets in spite of the painful times. I have discovered quite happily that motherhood does not end when a child leaves home. Being a mother to an adult is quite different from mothering an infant. But it's still mothering.

fortable and competent with their roles (Risman 1986; Nieto 1990). Other studies indicate that both single fathers and single mothers like being parents, feel competent, and are basically satisfied with the parenting experience (Mednick 1987:197).

In spite of the extra demands on their time and energy, single parents also function well at work. Single parents indicate high levels of satisfaction with their work, and they are not absent from work significantly more than others (Burden 1986). In fact, having a job that provides both meaningful work and a predictable source of income enhances the mental health of single mothers (Mednick 1987:192).

Finally, based on in-depth interviews of twenty-six single parents whom professionals had identified as successful, Olson and Haynes (1993) identified a number of factors that contribute to successful single parenthood. The parent must accept the responsibilities and challenges of single parenthood. The parenting role must be given priority. Open communication is essential, as is consistent but nonpunitive discipline. Successful parents are supportive and they foster individuality. At the same time, they maintain a sense of family by creating and maintaining rituals and traditions. Finally they continue to nurture their own needs, knowing that if they neglect those needs they will be less capable of adequately parenting their children.

NONWHITE FAMILIES

Is life any different if you grow up in an African American or Hispanic family, rather than a white family? In some ways, the answer is no. That is, there are many similarities between white American families and those of nonwhites. For example, Hispanic families are as cohesive as those of whites (Vega et al. 1986). And many of the processes are the same, such as the tendency for a greater sharing of family work when the wife is employed outside the home (Ybarra 1982).

Black families are also like white families in many ways. Married African Americans are likely to be happier and healthier than the unmarried (Zollar and Williams 1987; Keith 1997). And marital happiness is the most important determinant of general life happiness (Thomas 1990). African Americans who perceive their family to be close are happier than others (Ellison 1990). Black stepfather families are very similar to white stepfather families in terms of parent and child adjustment (Fine et al. 1992). Using national samples, Heiss (1988) addressed the issue of whether black and white women differ in their values about marriage and the family. There are some differences, he found, but they are trivial in size. Black women, in spite of their higher divorce rates, are not different in terms of their values and attitudes toward divorce. They

also differ little in terms of accepting nontraditional forms of family life. The primary difference Heiss found was in the tendency for black women to be more instrumental than white women in their reasons for marrying and in their goals for marriage. That is, black women were more concerned than white women for such matters as family responsibilities, income, and the quality of life. Given the historic deprivations of blacks, such concerns are understandable.

The African American Family

Many of the special problems and challenges faced by nonwhite families are rooted in their situation in the society. Heiss (1988) found that race is less important than socioeconomic position in explaining variations in family values. The greater proportion of nonwhites in the lower socioeconomic strata contributes to most of the differences in their family life-styles.

The Demographics of African American Families Blacks are the largest of America's racial minorities. About 12 percent of all households in the nation are black households. Seven out of ten black households are family households, the same proportion as for whites. As table 2.2 shows, the proportion of all households that have a family has declined since 1970.

Table 2.2 shows one striking difference between black families on the one hand and white and Hispanic families on the other, namely the lower proportion of black families that are composed of a married couple. Over half of all black family households are single-parent families. And while the proportion of married-couple households has declined for all races, the decline has been sharper for blacks than for others. Blacks are also more likely than those of other races to be never married, widowed, or divorced (figure 2.2).

For black children, these figures mean a greater likelihood of growing up with only one parent. As table 2.3 shows, black children are more than three times as likely as white children and nearly twice as likely as Hispanic children to be living in a single-parent family. Black children are also far more likely to be living with a mother who has never been married. What accounts for such differences?

TABLE 2.2

Households by Race, Hispanic Origin, and Type: 1970 and 1997

Race, Hispanic Origin, and Type	Number (1,000)		Percent Distribution	
	1970	**1997**	**1970**	**1997**
Total households				
Total[1]	63,401	101,018	100	100
White	56,602	85,059	89	84
Black	6,223	12,109	10	12
Hispanic[2]	2,303	8,225	4	8
Family households				
White, total	46,166	58,934	100	100
Married couple	41,029	47,650	89	81
Male householder[3]	1,038	2,944	2	5
Female householder[3]	4,099	8,339	9	14
Black, total	4,856	8,455	100	100
Married couple	3,317	3,851	68	46
Male householder[3]	181	657	4	8
Female householder[3]	1,358	3,947	28	47
Hispanic, total[2]	2,004	6,631	100	100
Married couple	1,615	4,520	81	68
Male householder[3]	82	494	4	7
Female householder[3]	307	1,617	15	24
Nonfamily households				
White, total	10,436	26,125	100	100
Male householder	3,406	11,481	33	44
Female householder	7,030	14,644	67	56
Black, total	1,367	3,654	100	100
Male householder	564	1,669	41	46
Female householder	803	1,985	59	54
Hispanic, total[2]	299	1,593	100	100
Male householder	150	854	50	54
Female householder	148	740	49	46

Source: U.S. Bureau of the Census, 1994:62; Bryson and Casper 1998:2.
[1]Includes other races not shown separately.
[2]Hispanic persons may be of any race.
[3]No spouse present.

To answer the question, we must explore at least briefly the black experience in America, particularly the way in which black families have been affected by American institutions.

Social Institutions and African American Family Life From slavery through segregation to present-day discrimination, African Americans have waged a long battle in the United States for justice and equality. Even after slavery was ended and African Americans had won certain fundamental rights, such as the right to vote, they faced various kinds of pressures to keep them from exercising their rights. Indeed, efforts to keep blacks from voting appeared even in the 1980s (Lauer 1995:306). Politically, then, African Americans have had difficulties exercising the power needed to press their causes and redress their grievances. *Conflict theory* helps us understand their long struggle and its consequences for family life, for much of the segregation and discrimination experienced by African Americans is rooted in the competition between racial groups for economic and political advantage.

Conflict Theory Applied

Various means have been used to keep African Americans economically disadvantaged (Lauer 1995). Economic deprivation, in turn, places great

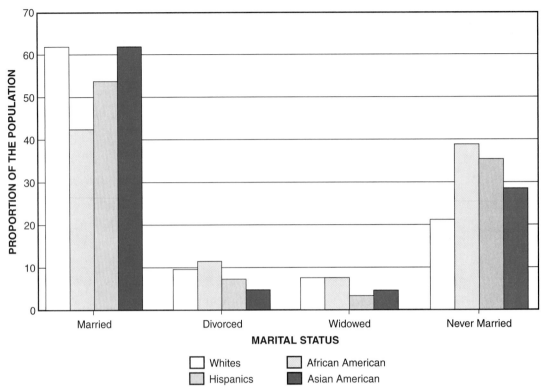

FIGURE 2-2   **Marital Status of the Population, by Race: 1997**
(Source: U.S. Bureau of the Census 1997a and Yax 1998.

strains on family life. The higher rates of divorce and single-parent families among African Americans become more understandable when we realize that black unemployment has tended to double that of whites over the past two decades and that recently the median income of black families is around 60 percent that of whites. Some people mistakenly believe that African Americans have made great strides economically since the civil rights movement of the 1960s. But in 1960, the median income of black families was 55 percent of that of white families, while in 1995 the figure was 60.9 percent. In other words, after thirty-five years of struggle black families still earn less than two-thirds the income of white families (U.S. Bureau of the Census 1997b:469).

You might think that one reason for the income differences is an educational gap. Indeed, blacks are not as likely as whites to graduate from either high school or college. But African Americans are at a disadvantage even when they get the same amount of education (Day and Curry 1998). At every educational level, black income is less than white income, and the disparity actually increases as the educational level goes up.

A number of factors, all of which have some basis in this economic situation, affect marriage rates among African Americans. More young black adults postpone marriage—both first marriages and remarriage after divorce—than young adults of any other race (Glick 1997). Black men and women are both less desirous of marriage than their white counterparts, but the difference between the men is particularly large (South 1993). Because the black male is more likely than the white to be unemployed or, if employed, in a lower income bracket, he is less likely than his white counterpart to be able to offer secure and adequate financial support. Black women, aware of the situation, put more importance than white women on a potential husband being able to offer good financial support (Bulcroft and Bulcroft 1993).

TABLE 2.3
Living Arrangements of Children Under 18 Years, by Race and Hispanic Origin: 1996 (numbers in thousands)

Living Arrangement	Number	Percent Distribution
WHITE		
Children under 18 years	53,944	100.0
Living with		
Two parents	41,609	77.1
One parent	12,335	22.9
Mother only	10,239	19.0
Father only	2,096	3.9
BLACK		
Children under 18 years	10,376	100.0
Living with		
Two parents	3,816	36.8
One parent	6,560	63.2
Mother only	6,056	58.4
Father only	504	4.9
HISPANIC		
Children under 18 years	9,702	100.0
Living with		
Two parents	6,381	65.8
One parent	3,321	34.2
Mother only	2,937	30.2
Father only	384	4.0

Source: U.S. Bureau of the Census 1997b:67.

The situation is compounded by the disproportionate number of African American men who are in jails or prisons, and the higher mortality rate for young black males compared to that of other racial groups. African American women who look for a mate within their race, then, have a smaller pool from which to choose. It is this combination of factors that accounts for the lower rate of marriage and the high proportion of female-headed households among African Americans (Rolison 1992; Fossett and Kiecolt 1993). It may also account for the fact that black women are far more likely than white women to marry men who are markedly older than they are (Shehan et al. 1991).

Those who do marry face some problems that other groups do not, at least not to the same extent. In black marriages, in contrast to white, the wife is likely to be more educated than the husband (Secord and Ghee 1986). African American wives, therefore, provide a greater proportion of income to their families than do white wives. This can cause strain, because one of the factors in marital satisfaction on the part of wives is the perception that the husband is a good provider. It may also help explain the higher rate of depression among black wives than among white wives (Gazmararian, James and Lepkowski 1995).

As the economic problems of the black family diminish, the black husband and father assumes a more active role in family life (McAdoo 1985/ 1986; Hossain and Roopnarine 1993). He becomes more involved with teaching his children and with making child-rearing decisions. Moreover, the black father seems, more than those of other races, to try to socialize daughters to be competent and independent at an early age.

In other words, the fate of the black family, like that of all families, is tied up with its position in the American economy. And its position in the economy, in turn, depends in part on what happens in the government. Various governmental actions in the past, such as school desegregation, voter registration laws, and affirmative action programs have helped many black families. But a political conservatism during the 1980s led to a reversal of some of the gains. For instance, we noted that the ratio of the median family income of blacks to that of whites is now only slightly higher than it was in 1960. It is, however, lower than it was in 1978, when it had risen to a high of 64 percent.

In particular, black families have suffered as a result of attacks on affirmative action and cutbacks in social and income maintenance programs (Crawley 1988). With regard to affirmative action programs, corporations were told that they could no longer require timetables or quotas for minority hiring. With regard to cutbacks, there was supposed to be a "safety net" that would prevent groups already disadvantaged from suffering even more from efforts to control federal spending. But as the figures on median family income illustrate, black families have lost ground economically since the 1980s.

Life in the African American Family If you are African American, then you are more likely than if you are white to grow up in a family that is impoverished, that is disrupted by divorce, or that is headed by a mother who has never married. This means that a greater proportion of African Americans will grow up in homes with less consistent and less involved parenting (McLoyd 1990). Young black girls who grow up in impoverished, single-parent homes may no longer even define childbearing as something that should occur in the context of marriage (Farber 1990). Young black adults, struggling to establish themselves, are likely to contribute more income and receive less from their families than whites (Goldscheider and Goldscheider 1991).

Married women generally who work outside the home tend to feel more overworked than their husbands. Black women, however, are twice as likely as their husbands to feel overworked by household responsibilities (Broman 1988a). And being overworked means a lower satisfaction with family life. When the husband performs most of the household chores, the wife is relieved, but the husband is less satisfied with family life (Broman 1991). African Americans get assistance from other relatives and adult friends (Padgett 1997) in such household tasks as laundry, shopping, and housecleaning. But they do not get as much assistance as do whites. Data from a national survey show that white men and women both give to and receive more help from relatives and friends than do African Americans, Chicanos, or Puerto Ricans (Roschelle 1997).

In his study of a sample of Detroit families, Whyte (1990) found that whites and blacks were similar in terms of division of power and labor in the home. In other ways, however, there were significant differences. In comparison to the white wives, the black wives put more value on a good income and less value on sexual fidelity. The black wives reported less togetherness (in terms of such things as spending free time together, confiding in each other, and having a joint banking account) and, in general, lower marital satisfaction. As Whyte (1990:162) sums it up, the differences "point to a more incomplete 'merger' of the two spouses into the conjugal relationship . . . producing a greater maintenance of separate activities and resources." Broman (1993) also found lower satisfaction among black than white wives. In addition, he reported that blacks are significantly less likely than whites to perceive their marriages as harmonious.

Given such findings, it is not surprising that violence is more prevalent in African American homes. Results from the Second National Family Violence Survey show that 17 percent of wives had at least one violent incident, and seven percent reported severe violence (Hamptom and Gelles 1994). But these figures varied by race, with black wives being 1.2 times more likely to experience minor violence and almost 2.4 times more likely to experience severe violence than white wives.

But such facts should not obscure the strengths and the positive aspects of life in the black family. Most of the problematic aspects we have discussed are rooted in the economic deprivation that African Americans have endured. But black families have strengths and, in fact, advantages over white families in some areas.

A study of urban newlyweds reported that the African Americans reported more disclosure, more positive sexual relationships, and less disagreement than did the whites (Oggins, Veroff, and Leber 1993). Moreover, the decline in marital satisfaction during the child-rearing years may not hold for African Americans. Some research reports that blacks show no decline in life or family satisfaction when they become parents (Broman 1988b). Similarly, though being a single parent is a difficult task, it may not be as difficult for blacks as for whites. While there has not been a great deal of research, some of the findings from small samples include (Fine and Schwebel 1987):

Nonmarried black mothers reported no greater role strain than did their married counterparts.

Black mothers, with or without a husband in the home, perceive their families as being cohesive.

Black students in the fifth and sixth grades had about the same levels of self-esteem whether they came from one-parent or two-parent homes.

The difference between actual and ideal self-concepts was lower for black than for white adolescents from single-parent families (lower differences are considered healthier).

Finally, a survey of a group of white and black single parents reported that the blacks were more positive about parenting and were more certain that their children added satisfaction to their lives (Jacobsen and Bigner 1991). And results from the National Survey of Families and Households show no racial differences among single mothers in parenting behavior or involvement with their children (McKenry and Fine 1993). The survey did find, however, that African American single mothers had higher expectations than did whites for their children to be independent, to control their temper, and to be obedient.

Overall, then, black single parents appear to be more satisfied than are whites with their parenting and may have fewer problems with their children (Fine, McKenry, and Chung 1992). Three factors help account for some of these strengths of black single parents: the greater extended family support among African Americans, the way children are viewed, and a greater acceptance of single parenthood (Fine and Schwebel 1987). With regard to extended family support, blacks report close relations and frequent contact (Hatchett and Jackson 1993; Raley 1995).

Thus, there are likely to be additional resources available to the black single parent. As two anthropologists summed it up, the black family

> consists of a wide-reaching group of relatives involved in relations of exchange and coparenting; and a collective and cooperative spirit prevails (Aschenbrenner and Carr 1980:469).

With regard to the view of children, some researchers have argued that black children are valued regardless of their origin. There has not been a stigma on black children, as sometimes there has been on white children, who are born to an unwed mother. Thus, it is unlikely that a black child would be called illegitimate or treated any differently from any other child because of his or her origin.

Finally, there is a greater acceptance of single parenthood in the black community. There is a larger proportion of such families among African Americans, and those that function well provide a model to others. African Americans, then, are more likely than whites to believe that a single parent can provide a good family environment.

Among black two-parent families, there is likely to be a greater amount of equality than among whites. Interestingly, African Americans tend to be more traditional in their ideology about family life but more egalitarian in practice (Beckett 1976). That is, African Americans are more likely than whites to affirm traditional family roles but are also more likely than whites to actually have an egalitarian relationship. McAdoo (1993) found a high degree of cooperation and shared decision making in

African American couples. For example, a higher proportion of black wives (70.3 percent) than of white wives (56.6 percent) report that their husbands or partners act as childcare providers (John 1996).

In part, the egalitarianism results from the fact that black wives are more likely than white wives to work, and black husbands are more likely than white husbands to approve of their wives working. In fact, black women have a more consistent history of being employed than do white women; both they and their husbands are more likely to expect (not just accept) the wife's employment. Perhaps because of such an expectation, black husbands are more willing than whites to adjust their own schedules in order to help their working wives, such as agreeing to stay home with a sick child or to a wife's overnight absence from home because of work (Beckett 1976).

Finally, African Americans may have some advantage over whites at the time when their children have grown and left home. The empty nest is a problem only for a minority of people, particularly for those women who have focused their lives on their children, and it seems to occur mainly among white women. Neither African American nor Mexican American families seem to be troubled by the empty nest (Borland 1982).

Thus, life in the black family is likely to have certain problematic aspects primarily because of the effects of discrimination and deprivation in American society. But many black families are strong and

Studies of Hispanic families show more egalitarianism than male dominance.

viable and in some areas even have an advantage over white families.

The Hispanic Family

Hispanics (Mexican Americans, Puerto Ricans, and others with Spanish surnames) are the second-largest minority group in the United States, comprising 10.9 percent of the population (Collins 1997c). The Hispanic population is growing rapidly, and may exceed that of non-Hispanic African Americans by 2005. On the average, Hispanics are poorer than whites. They were not as poor as African Americans until the mid-1990s; by 1995, however, the median family income of Hispanics was $24,570, compared to $25,970 for African Americans (U.S. Bureau of the Census 1997b:469). The 1995 poverty rate for Hispanics was 30.3 percent, compared to 8.5 percent for non-Hispanic Whites (Collins 1997c).

As table 2.2 shows, Hispanics are more likely than either African Americans or whites to have a family household; they are less likely than whites but much more likely than African Americans to have a married couple in that household. Hispanics are less likely than whites or African Americans to be divorced (figure 2.2). And they are less supportive, than are whites, of mothers who get divorced (Wagner 1987).

Compared to non-Hispanics, Hispanic men are more likely and Hispanic women less likely to want to marry (South 1993). Hispanic women tend to marry a little later and have more children than do either whites or African Americans. Average Hispanic family size is therefore larger than that of non-Hispanics—3.95 people compared with 3.2 in all families (Collins 1997c).

As with African Americans, Hispanics may have a different experience of marital satisfaction than whites. A study of three generations of Mexican American families reported that men showed a decline in satisfaction during the middle years and then a subsequent rise. This is the same as the pattern for white families. But the Hispanic women had a successively lower marital satisfaction over the three generations. This is a different pattern than occurs among white women (Markides and Hoppe 1985). On the other hand, a study of interaction showed lower levels of conflict among a sample of Mexican American couples than among either white or black couples (Hampson, Beavers, and Hulgus 1990). Also a study of first-generation Mexican Americans found that relationships are more central to the meaning of their lives than is true for whites (Jenerson-Madden, Ebersole, and Romero 1992).

Minority families tend to acquire certain stereotypes. With African Americans, it is the stereotype of the dominant wife and mother. With Hispanics, it is the stereotype of the dominant husband and father. In both popular and professional views, the Hispanic family has been explained on the assumption that the male suffers feelings of inadequacy and inferiority and compensates for his powerlessness in the larger society through *machismo,* or male dominance, in the family (Staples and Mirande 1980:893). The father becomes the unquestioned authority in the family. The wife and children are subservient and passive.

However, research has failed to uncover a pattern of male dominance in the Hispanic family (Staples and Mirande 1980:894). Nearly every study of spousal roles, including those among Hispanic migrant farm families, has shown more egalitarianism than male dominance. The egalitarianism appears in family decision making and other kinds of behavior. Hispanic fathers help their wives with family work, including child care, prefer to have social and recreational activities with their families rather than with other men, and are playful and companionable rather than stern and authoritarian with their children. This egalitarianism creates an improved climate for family well-being. In fact, recent research among a group of intergenerationally linked Puerto Rican families indicated that marital satisfaction is associated with egalitarian spouse roles (Rogler and Procidano 1989).

As with other groups, there is variation within the Hispanic community on the extent of male dominance. In her comparative study of working-class and business/professional Mexican Americans, Williams (1990) argued that while male dominance was less common than it was in the past, husbands, particularly those in the working class, continue to have more power than their wives.

Little recent research is available on parenting in Hispanic families. Delgado-Gaitan (1993) studied ten Mexican American families, and found a strong emphasis on respect and family ties. Martinez (1993) noted more frequent use of punishment by Mexican American mothers, but attributed it to their lower economic level rather than their culture. Mexican American mothers also use more guilt than do black mothers as a way of disciplining their children. In a comparison of a sample of Mexican American and white parents, Lopez and Hamilton (1997) reported that the Mexican American mothers were more likely than the white mothers to include bathing, playing with, and being friends with their children as part of their maternal role.

Finally, as with blacks, Hispanics may have closer bonds than whites with members of the extended family. In his study of Mexican American families, Richard del Castillo (1984) pointed out that bonds of affection and help from a wide array of relatives is one of the most important characteristics of these families. A family might also have co-parents, such as godparents, who offer both emotional and financial support. Aged Hispanics find help from family support networks. Paz (1993) reported that 90 percent of the Hispanic elderly he studied in two Western cities said they had someone whom they trusted and could confide in, and most identified family members as their caregivers. The use of the extended family as a resource allows the Hispanic family, like the black family, to cope with the demands of an often hostile environment and still maintain a meaningful family life. Unfortunately, these extended ties may be weakening. Williams (1990) found that the rituals that formed and cemented the extended ties are no longer doing so. Religious commitment has lessened, particularly among the business/professional group. Baptisms and marriages are no longer attended by large numbers of family members. Only funerals continue to bring large numbers together: some Mexican Americans report that they only see many of their uncles, aunts, and cousins when a death occurs.

The Asian American Family

Comparatively little research has been done on Asian American families. However, Asian Americans are a rapidly growing minority in the United States, numbering about 10 million or 3.7 percent of the population in 1997 (Collins 1997a). The countries of origin include 1.2 million from the

Philippines and about a half million each from China, India, Vietnam, and Korea. More than half of Asian Americans live in the West. They are better off in some ways than other racial groups, including even the white majority. Their educational attainment is the highest in the nation; Asian Americans have a higher proportion than any other group of high-school and college graduates (Day and Curry 1988). In terms of economic well-being, in 1995 Asian and Pacific Islander households had a median income of $40,614 (compared to $35,766 for whites) (Collins 1997a). The poverty rate of 14.6 percent (compared to 11.2 percent of whites), however, shows that there is a higher proportion of Asian Americans at both extremes of the income scale.

Asian American families tended to be larger (an average of 3.8 persons in 1994) than non-Hispanic white families (an average of 3.1 persons in 1994)(Collins 1997a). They have more two-parent families than African Americans and Hispanics—about 80 percent of the children live with two parents. This reflects the fact that they also have lower divorce rates than other groups (figure 2.2).

Asian culture tends to influence Asian American family life (Kitano and Daniels 1988; Ou and McAdoo 1993; Julian, McKenry, and McKelvey 1994; Hamilton 1996). In traditional Asian culture, the individual's needs are subordinated to the group's needs. Thus, Asian Americans are likely to socialize their children into the values of obedience, loyalty, and self-control. Self-control is seen, among other things, in the greater emotional restraint found among Asian American students (Kao, Negata, and Peterson 1997). In addition, Asian Americans instill a high value on education in their children. In particular, a study of Asian Americans from a number of different countries of origin reported three factors that help account for the high level of educational attainment: "(*a*) Children are expected to defer to parental authority without question; (*b*) there is a strong interdependence among family members, both within and beyond the nuclear unit; and (*c*) children are reared to believe that their success in school will affect the honor of their family directly" (Blair and Qian 1998:371).

Traditional Asian culture elevates males over females. The husband is expected to be the breadwinner, while the wife is expected to manage the children and the home. Wives are expected to defer to their husbands' wishes, while children are supposed to defer to both parents' wishes. There is emphasis on extended family obligations; elderly Chinese and Japanese are more likely than whites to live in an extended family household, particularly in an ever-married child's household (Kamo and Zhou 1994).

There are, of course, variations both between and within various Asian American groups in all matters, from educational attainment and financial status to adherence to family traditions. For example, Chinese students perform best academically, and Korean and Southeast Asian students do better than do Japanese and Filipino students (Blair and Qian 1998). As another example, the large number of Vietnamese who came to America after the Vietnam war, like other Asians, lived in male-dominated, extended families. However, the Vietnamese appear to be rapidly adopting such Western patterns as women working outside the home, small family size, and use of day care (Gold 1993).

In some ways, the traditional Vietnamese pattern is strengthened in the United States—they maintain even stronger kin ties out of economic necessity (Kibria 1993/ 1994). But family relations have become more egalitarian. The Vietnamese man encounters problems of earnings and status in the United States. His wife is likely to gain power in the marital relationship. At the same time, parental control over the children tends to diminish, increasing the amount of conflict in the family (Kibria 1993). More quickly than other groups, the Vietnamese find themselves struggling with adapting family style and structure to American ways.

With regard to variations within groups, the Hmong, an ethnic subgroup from Vietnam, have clung more persistently to their traditional pattern, which includes male dominance, early marriage for females, and early and frequent childbearing (Hutchison and McNall 1994). Interestingly, at the same time, the Hmong maintain high educational expectations for their women, which will increase pressures to change the traditional pattern.

An example of intergroup variation among the Chinese are those families who live in Monterey Park, a suburban city in southern California that has been called the "Chinese Beverly Hills," have a life-style that is in stark contrast to that of the masses of Chinese Americans in the Chinatowns of New York, San Francisco, and Los Angeles (Takaki 1989:425f). In Monterey Park, many professionals and business-owners live in expensive homes and drive luxury cars. In the Chinatowns, a significant portion of the people are employed in service occupations at low wages. Many are immigrants who speak little or no English and who must work such long hours to make a living that they have little time or energy to learn English. Thus, they are trapped in an impoverished life-style.

The longer Asian American families are in this country, the more likely they are to be acculturated. Acculturation can be slow because of the tendency for people to cluster together and to provide for themselves a continuing Asian cultural context. For instance, New York's Chinatown has an extensive Chinese-language media, including newspapers, magazines, radio, and television, that can satisfy the family's information and entertainment needs (Lum 1991). Nevertheless, the younger generation will inevitably become Americanized to some extent.

The process already shows up in the second generation. A study of Chinese immigrant families reported that filial piety remains alive but undergoes a change (Lin and Liu 1993). The children of the immigrants continue to provide help and resources to their parents, but they resist parental control over matters having to do with their personal freedom and self-development. Among other things, the children 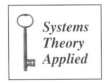 want to make their own choice in marriage. Thus, as *systems theory* emphasizes, the children are struggling with how to establish their own identity while remaining a part of their family, a struggle that is more painful because of the contradiction between American and traditional Chinese values.

Similarly, Chinese American women who are successful occupationally have, like their white counterparts, fewer children than Chinese American women who remain more traditional (Espenshade and Ye 1994). The Asian American family appears to be increasingly less Asian and more American.

The Native American Family

In 1997, there were 2.3 million American Indians, Eskimos, and Aleuts, or about 0.9 percent of the

Systems Theory Applied

Tribal tradition is important in Native American family life.

total U.S. population (Collins 1997d). The median age of Native Americans is low (under 27 years of age, compared to 37.4 years for non-Hispanic whites). They tend to be clustered in the West, with 13 percent residing in Oklahoma. Among their family households, 65 percent are married couples, 27 percent are female-headed, and 9 percent are male-headed (compare these figures with those of other groups in table 2.3). Native Americans have lower rates of educational attainment and higher rates of poverty than do other groups.

Family life among Native Americans is circumscribed by two important factors. One is the high poverty rate. As a consequence, Native American families have some of the same characteristics as people generally who live in poverty, such as higher rates of fertility, alcoholism and drug use, and health problems (Oetting and Beauvais 1990; Yee 1990; Beauvais and Segal 1992; Beauvais 1996). Alcohol abuse in the family increases the chances of child abuse (DeBruyn, Lujan, and May 1992). Adolescents, growing up in a context of comparatively high rates of drug abuse, child abuse, and troubled family life, tend to have higher rates of depression and of thoughts about, and attempts at, suicide (King et al. 1992; Sack et al. 1994).

The severity of these problems is underscored by a survey of 14,000 Native Americans in grades seven through twelve living on reservations in fifteen states.[1] The Native Americans were twice as likely as other teenagers to have attempted suicide (22 percent of the girls and 12 percent of the boys admitted they had tried). Eleven percent said that at least one of their parents was dead; fewer than half lived with both parents. Twenty-two percent of the twelfth-grade girls reported being victims of sexual abuse.

The other important factor in Native American family life is tribal tradition. About three hundred different tribes exist. As Staples (1988:350) points out, we cannot talk about a Native American family: "There are only tribes and family systems, which vary from tribe to tribe." For example, some tribes are **patrilineal** (descent is traced through the male line), while others are **matrilineal** (descent is traced through the female line).

The Hopi, who live mainly in northern Arizona, are an example of a matrilineal group (Queen, Habenstein, and Quadagno 1985). In the traditional Hopi family, one's lineage was traced through one's mother, grandmother, and so on, and the females owned most of the property and directed tribal ceremonies. The husband was considered a guest in his wife's home.

Nevertheless, while acknowledging the tribal variations, we can make some general points about

[1]*Facts on File,* 2 April 1992, p. 235BZ.

Native American families. For example, they select life partners on the basis of romantic love (John 1988); their rate of intermarriage is high, particularly those involving white men and Native American women; and divorce is likely to be a less guilt-ridden and recriminating process than it is among whites (John 1988).

Compared to white families, Native American families are more interdependent (Yee 1990). Greater emphasis is placed on the extended family. In most tribes, parents are not expected to assume total responsibility for child-rearing (American Indian Law Center 1986:124). Consequently, older Native Americans are more likely than either older whites or Hispanics to be involved in child-caring activities (Harris, Begay, and Page 1989). Children may experience "extra love and attention provided by grandmothers or other relatives living with the family or nearby" (American Indian Law Center 1986:123; Bahr, 1994).

The Interracial Family

Although the vast majority of Americans marry within their own racial group, the number of interracial marriages has increased dramatically in recent decades. In 1970, less than 0.5 percent of all marriages were interracial. By 1980 the proportion was 1.3 percent, and by 1996 it was 2.3 percent (U.S. Bureau of the Census 1997b:57). A little over a fourth of interracial marriages are between whites and African Americans. Among Hispanics, over a fourth of all marriages are with non-Hispanics. Public attitudes at one time strongly disapproved of such unions, but in 1991, for the first time, a Gallup poll found a larger proportion of Americans approving (48 percent) rather than disapproving (42 percent) of white-African American marriages (Gallup and Newport 1991:60).

Who is likely to marry someone of another race? A study of intermarriage between whites and Asian Americans reported that a third of the Asian Americans in California were intermarried and that the intermarriages tended to occur between those in the higher socioeconomic levels (Shinagawa and Pang 1988). A study of African American-white intermarriages found regional and gender differences: rates are higher in the West, and more men than women intermarry (Tucker and Mitchell-Kernan

1990). The study also reported that those who intermarry tend to be younger, are more likely to have been previously married, and are more likely to marry someone more distant in age.

Interracial marriages are more fragile than marriages that are racially homogamous (Glick 1988). In some cases, the stability of the marriage depends on which spouse is of which race. For example, marriages with a black husband and white wife are more stable than those with a white husband and black wife. The probability of an interracial marriage lasting depends on a number of factors. As with other marriages, interracial unions are more likely to last when there are children and when the couple marry at a relatively later age (Rankin and Maneker 1987).

Because we are likely to be attracted to those who are like us (the principle of **homogamy,** or marriage between people who are similar in social and demographic characteristics) and because interracial marriages are more likely to fail, why do people marry across racial lines? In essence, their reasons are the same as others (Porterfield 1982). That is, when asked about the motives for their marriages, interracial couples primarily mention love and compatibility (Kouri and Lasswell 1993). Compatibility, of course, suggests a homogamous relationship, and an interracial marriage might seem to be **heterogamous** (between people who are dissimilar in social and demographic characteristics). However, people of different races in our country may have similar values and attitudes, and people may prefer someone of another race who is similar in values and attitudes than someone of their own race who is different in values and attitudes. An in-depth study of twenty-one black-white marriages found that none of the individuals had intended to have an interracial relationship (Rosenblatt, Karis, and Powell 1995). Rather, the two people met and "clicked" with each other and pursued the relationship as individuals rather than as members of particular races.

A few of those in interracial marriages indicate that they are motivated by rebellion against the conventions of society or by an attraction to the opposite sex of another race. While a deeper study of the couples might identify some more subtle forces at work, we have no other answers at present. Some people are so much in love and so compatible with a person of another race that they are willing to assume the risk of lower stability and perhaps go counter to pressures from friends and family in order to enter an interracial union.

The risk of breakup and the pressure to refrain from interracial marriages varies from place to place. In a multicultural setting, interracial marriages may be more common and more acceptable. There may be more support for the couple, enabling them to maintain the union. In some places, children of an interracial union are stigmatized; they may not be fully accepted by either of their parents' races. But they may escape the stigma and its negative psychological consequences in a multicultural setting. For example, children of interracial marriages in Hawaii, where there is general acceptance of such unions, are as well adjusted psychologically as children from marriages within the same race (Johnson and Nagoshi 1986).

Still, there are likely to be some unique problems even when the couples are in a generally accepting environment. McDermott and Fukunaga (1977) reported research with a group of interracial Hawaiian families that sought psychiatric help because of emotional problems with their children. These marriages involved a white-Asian union.

PERSPECTIVE
A Slave Family

Frederick Douglass was born a slave early in the nineteenth century in Maryland. As a young man, he escaped, fled to New York, and became a part of the abolition movement. The following excerpt from one of his autobiographical works illustrates some of the problems of slave family life. Though slavery, segregation, and discrimination have all assaulted the integrity of the black family, the slave experience was especially severe:

My father was a white man. He was admitted to be such by all I ever heard speak of my parentage. The opinion was also whispered that my master was my father; but of the correctness of this opinion, I know nothing; the means of knowing was withheld from me. My mother and I were separated when I was but an infant—before I knew her as my mother. It is a common custom, in the part of Maryland from which I ran away, to part children from their mothers at a very early age. Frequently, before the child has reached its twelfth month, its mother is taken from it, and hired out on some farm a considerable distance off, and the child is placed under the care of an old woman, too old for field labor. For what this separation is done, I do not know, unless it be to hinder the development of the child's affection toward its mother, and to blunt and destroy the natural affection of the mother for the child. This is the inevitable result.

I never saw my mother, to know her as such, more than four or five times in my life; and each of these times was very short in duration, and at night. She was hired by a Mr. Stewart, who lived about twelve miles from my home. She made her journeys to see me in the night, travelling the whole distance on foot, after the performance of her day's work. She was a field hand, and a whipping is the penalty of not being in the field at sunrise, unless a slave has special permission from his or her master to the contrary—a permission which they seldom get, and one that gives to him that gives it the proud name of being a kind master. I do not recollect of ever seeing my mother by the light of day. She was with me in the night. She would lie down with me, and get me to sleep, but long before I waked she was gone. Very little communication ever took place between us. Death soon ended what little we could have while she lived, and with it her hardships and suffering. She died when I was about seven years old, on one of my master's farms, near Lee's Mill. I was not allowed to be present during her illness, at her death, or burial. She was gone long before I knew anything about it. Never having enjoyed, to any considerable extent, her soothing presence, her tender and watchful care, I received the tidings of her death with much the same emotions I should have probably felt at the death of a stranger.

Source: Frederick Douglass, *Narrative of the Life of Frederick Douglass, An American Slave* (Boston: Anti-Slavery Office, 1845), pp. 1–2.

One of the problems the interracial couples had was that of trying to establish consensual parental roles. A number of Asian men married to white women tried to assume the traditional Asian role of male leadership. But some of their white wives "repeatedly competed for this role, undercut their husbands, or attempted to act as co-leader with the husband" (McDermott and Fukunaga 1977:84). In such cases, the husband often either ignored his wife or treated her as one of the children. The reaction of the children tended to be withdrawal and mild depression.

Another problem arising in the interracial families was the differing value systems of the parents. Some cultures value accuracy over creativity, while others have the opposite value. Husbands and wives with differing values put their children into the difficult situation of having to obey contradictory parental expectations.

The troubled families had tried to cope with their differences in various ways. Three coping efforts were dysfunctional. First, some of the families had settled into a kind of cold war where, for the most part, the parents no longer attempted to accommodate their differences but rather each maintained a different and contrary approach in dealing with the children. Second, in other families, there was a "competitive adjustment," where each parent tried to get the other to acknowledge his or her leadership in the family. Finally, some of the families engaged in a "reluctant adjustment" in which the parents withdrew from trying to establish leadership and allowed the children to govern themselves most of the time.

Eventually, the families in this research learned better ways of coping with their differences. *Complementary adjustment* in an interracial family involves letting one parent be the primary leader in the family while the other engages in supplementary functions. For example, one parent makes a decision and the other supports it, encourages the children to support it, and models supportive behavior to the children. In *additive adjustment,* the parents try to take elements from each of their cultures that they both define as desirable and use these in making decisions about family life.

In sum, interracial families face the same problems as others plus some additional problems that are unique. But they can work through their problems and maintain a strong and meaningful family

life. When the family lives in a hostile environment (among people who resist or resent interracial unions), the prospects for long-term stability are not encouraging. In a more accepting atmosphere, the family will still have its unique problems to solve, but it will be better able to do so.

THE HOMOSEXUAL FAMILY

Although many people do not think of homosexual relationships as resulting in a family, it has been estimated that about one of five **gays** and one of three **lesbians** enter a homosexual marriage (Schulenburg 1985). The marriage may or may not be established by a formal ceremony. One male couple, for example, after four months of cohabitation, went to mass and let the service be their private ceremony of commitment (Ammon 1985:112). They used the term *marriage* to describe their relationship. They bought matching rings and verbally agreed to be sexually faithful, to emotionally support each other, and to have equal say in such matters as finances.

Moreover, millions of gays and lesbians have had children. In many cases, the children were born when the individual was part of a heterosexual marriage. Subsequently, the individual "came out," that is, openly acknowledged his or her homosexual preference. Some of these children are being raised in a homosexual family—two men, two women, or some other arrangement. For example, Schulenburg (1985) is a lesbian who is raising a daughter with two gay males, one of whom is the child's father.

Homosexual couples have to work through the same problems as heterosexual couples. They face issues of household division of labor, power, sexual relationships, and money (Blumstein and Schwartz 1983). In addition, like the interracial couple, they face problems arising from being in a socially stigmatized relationship. Gallup polls show that a slight majority of Americans agree that homosexual relationships should be illegal. A 1997 Gallup poll following the disclosure by a popular television comedienne that she was gay reported that 59 percent of the respondents agreed that homosexuality is morally wrong (Saad 1997). Homosexual families, then, must not only deal with the same issues as other families but also with a hostile environment and with some problems that are unique to the homosexual relationship.

Homosexuals want the same things as heterosexual couples in an intimate relationship.

Problems in Homosexual Families

Gay couples have some unique sources of stress that may require them to seek counseling or therapy (George and Behrendt 1987). One is the stereotypical male role. Men in our society are expected to be relatively unemotional, strong, competitive, independent, and in control. If the partners in a gay relationship each attempt to live by the stereotype, they will encounter serious problems. How can they maintain a loving relationship if they are constantly competing with each other? Or if both want to win all the time? Or if both want to be in control?

Another source of stress is the stereotypical sexual role of the male. In our society, men are expected to be sexually active, experienced, and prepared to engage in a sexual relationship at almost any time. This can create performance anxiety, an anxiety that may be intensified by the spread of AIDS and the knowledge that homosexual relationships are particularly vulnerable to AIDS.

Homophobia, the irrational fear of homosexuality, is a third possible source of stress (Cortez 1996). Because our society has viewed homosexuality negatively and because most homosexuals have grown up hearing such derogatory labels as "fag" and "queer," most gays "cannot escape, at least for a period of time, incorporating these negative societal messages into their own self-concepts"

(George and Behrendt 1987:81). One of the partners, therefore, may still be struggling with his self-esteem and his own identity as a homosexual. Furthermore, the partners may feel it necessary to refrain from behavior that is meaningful and acceptable for heterosexual couples, such as public displays of their affection for each other (Brewer 1997).

Finally, there is the stress of sexual dysfunctions. Contrary to the popular image and to the general pattern of the homosexual male, some gays suffer from inhibited sexual desire. The problem intersects with the stereotypical male sex role and with homophobia. That is, a man might have inhibited sexual desire because he is still battling his feelings of guilt or his ambiguity about his sexual orientation. But the inhibited desire intensifies his stress because he also may accept the stereotype of himself as one who is supposed to be a sexually active individual.

Undoubtedly, there are some unique problems for lesbian couples also, but we do not have the research necessary to identify them. However, the Blumstein and Schwartz (1983) study produced a number of findings that suggest that lesbian couples do not have the same kind of problems as either gay or heterosexual couples. For example, they found that in gay and heterosexual couples, income tends to determine which partner will be dominant. But lesbians use income to avoid being dependent on each other, rather than to establish dominance. Heterosexual and gay couples who are disappointed with the amount of money they earn are likely to be less satisfied with their overall relationship; that is not true of lesbians. Lesbians also report somewhat less conflict over money management and income than do other couples.

What about children who are being raised by two adults of the same sex? There is little research on which to base firm conclusions, but what evidence we have indicates that the unique problems are minimal. Homosexual, like heterosexual, parents tend to report few serious problems in child-rearing and generally satisfactory relationships with the children (Harris and Turner 1985/1986; Turner, Scadden, and Harris 1990). Homosexual fathers do not differ from heterosexual fathers in their reported involvement or intimacy level with their children (Bigner and Jacobsen 1989). The children of gay fathers may need help to understand their own feelings about homosexuality, and some experience anger and a sense of isolation (Barret and Robinson 1990:91). But they also report their relationships with their fathers to be honest and open (Barret and Robinson 1990:91).

Gay fathers have more difficulty disclosing their homosexual orientation to their children than do lesbian mothers (Bozett 1989). Once disclosed, however, both gay and lesbian parents say that their children generally have a positive attitude about the homosexuality. O'Connell (1993) studied 11 young adults whose mothers came out as lesbians either before or after divorcing the fathers. She found "profound loyalty and protectiveness" toward the mothers even though the subjects remained sad about the parental breakup.

Homosexual parents do not indicate a preference for their children also to be homosexual. In fact, Javaid (1993) found, in a small sample, that the lesbian mothers preferred their children, and particularly their sons, to marry and procreate. In another study, two researchers compared twenty-five adults raised in lesbian families with twenty-one adults raised by single heterosexual mothers (Golombok and Tasker 1996). They found that while those raised by lesbian mothers were more likely to explore same-sex relationships, the large majority identified themselves as heterosexual when they were young adults (only two women identified themselves as lesbian as young adults). Finally, a survey of fifty-five gay or bisexual men found that more than 90 percent of their sons were heterosexual (Bailey et al. 1995).

As far as the children's well-being generally is concerned, we have some evidence from the comparative study of those raised by lesbian couples and single heterosexual mothers (Tasker and Golombok 1997). The two groups were first studied as adolescents and then again some fifteen years later as young adults. The researchers found no differences between the two groups in their acceptance of their family identity during adolescence. The children raised by lesbian parents, in other words, were not traumatized by their family situation when they were adolescents, particularly those who had close relationships with their mothers and their mothers' partners. Problems did arise for those who were stigmatized by their peers and those who felt that their mothers were too open

about their lesbian identity in front of their friends. By the time they were young adults, however, those raised in lesbian families were more positive about their background than were those raised by single heterosexual mothers.

Intimacy in the Homosexual Family

What do homosexuals want in an intimate relationship? They want the same thing as heterosexuals. Peplau (1981) compared one hundred homosexuals with one hundred heterosexuals and found that the differences between men and women were generally greater than any differences between homosexuals and heterosexuals. Both homosexuals and heterosexuals value such things in an intimate relationship as being able to talk about feelings, being able to laugh together, having a supportive group of friends, and sharing as many activities as possible with one's partner. Whatever their sexual orientation, people expect family life to provide them with a measure of emotional support, love, security, and companionship.

It is more difficult for a homosexual couple to fulfill its intimacy needs, however, because of the hostile environment. As a result, homosexual couples tend to receive more emotional support from friends, including other homosexuals, than they do from their extended families (Kurdek and Schmitt 1987). Homosexual couples, then, are more dependent on friends for support than are other couples. Those with a high degree of emotional support from friends are less psychologically distressed than those who report less emotional support from friends.

Other than a support system, the factors that add to the quality of a homosexual relationship are the same as those for a heterosexual union. Comparing married, heterosexual cohabiting, gay, and lesbian couples, Kurdek and Schmitt (1986) found that the quality of the relationships, regardless of the type of couple, depended on such things as perceived investment in the relationship, few alternatives to the relationship, commitment to the relationship, and shared decision making. There were no differences in the level of love expressed by the various partners, though the heterosexual cohabitors expressed a lower level of liking of the partner than did the others.

Thus, in most respects, the homosexual couple is no different from the heterosexual. In both kinds of relationships, the partners are seeking to fulfill their intimacy needs. And many of the same kinds of factors determine the extent to which those needs are fulfilled.

There are, however, some differences. While both homosexual and heterosexual couples argue about the same issues, Kurdek (1994) found differences in frequency of conflict over particular issues. Heterosexual couples argue more frequently over politics and social issues, while homosexual couples argue more frequently over distrust or lying (about, e.g., previous lovers, which may be especially troublesome because the ex-lovers are still part of their social support network).

Two additional differences that affect intimacy are the greater probability of equality among homosexuals and the way in which fidelity is defined by gays. Equality facilitates intimacy. Women, regardless of their sexual orientation, are more likely than men to value equality (Peplau 1981). But equality in such matters as decision making and sharing of household tasks is more likely between homosexual than heterosexual partners (Peplau and Cochran 1981; Harry 1982; Kurdek 1993). Patterson (1995) studied twenty-six lesbian couples who had at least one child in their home. She found that the partners agreed that they shared household tasks and decision making equally. But biological mothers reported more child care and nonbiological mothers reported more hours in paid work outside the home. In other words, equality doesn't have to involve an equal sharing of every task. In fact, in their study of male homosexual unions, McWhirter and Mattison (1984) identified a development that they called "planned incompetence." One of the partners may "unlearn his own level of competence" in a particular area in order to allow the other to fulfill himself by achieving in that area. In other words, one partner will deliberately minimize his skills in order to allow the other to develop the same skills, so that the two are more equal than before.

With regard to fidelity, gays may opt for either an open or closed relationship. In an open relationship, the partners retain their commitment to each other while allowing occasional outside relationships. In a closed relationship, the partners are expected to be sexually faithful to each other. Those in an open re-

lationship say that monogamy cannot meet all of an individual's needs, interests, and fantasies. They say that an occasional outside contact enhances their enjoyment of their partner and strengthens their bond (Ammon 1985:32). This open arrangement may be the more common one (McWhirter and Mattison 1984:252). Fidelity, then, is defined as emotional commitment rather than sexual exclusivity. Such a definition of fidelity is contrary to that of most het-

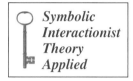

Symbolic Interactionist Theory Applied

erosexuals. But recall that *symbolic interactionist* theory argues that we must understand people's own definitions of the situation. Thus, gay partners who allow for occasional outside sexual activity still feel that they are being faithful to each other.

Long-Term Gay Relationships

The stereotype of the homosexual, particularly the male, is one of promiscuity. Indeed, there is some basis for the stereotype; about half of all white males in one study reported that they had had over five hundred partners (Bell and Weinberg 1978). But many gays, and an even greater proportion of lesbians, try to form stable, monogamous relationships. Riedmann (1995) estimated that 75 percent of lesbians and 50 percent of gay men are in stable, monogamous relationships at any given time.

In an effort to provide a portrait of the development of a long-term gay relationship, two researchers have charted six stages through which a gay couple move over time (McWhirter and Mattison 1984). The first stage is called *blending*. It takes up the first year of the relationship and is characterized by such things as intense feelings, a high degree of sexual activity, and efforts to bond the partners and make the relationship one of equality.

In the second and third years, the couple is in the *nesting* stage. During these years, they try to establish themselves in homemaking and explore the areas of life in which they are compatible. There is, as with heterosexual marriages, some decline in sexual passion. And one or both partners may begin to feel somewhat ambivalent about the relationship.

Years four and five are the *maintaining* stage. The partners reestablish their individuality in the context of togetherness, learn to handle conflict, and begin to establish certain family traditions. Up to this point the partners may not have had many arguments. But in this stage, couples

> generally devise means of neutralizing, resolving or completely avoiding conflict for the present and into the future. Dealing with conflict is a developmental task that can be avoided no longer if the relationship is to continue to grow (McWhirter and Mattison 1984:38).

The *building* stage follows, from years six through ten. In this stage, the partners become increasingly productive in their work, establish their independence as individuals, and come to sense a dependability in the other. In the *releasing* stage, years eleven through twenty, the relationship is usually one of trusting, combining money and possessions, and perhaps taking each other for granted. Finally, the *renewing* stage, twenty or more years together, is characterized by security and a shared history of experiences.

Thus, some gays, contrary to the stereotype, form a lasting relationship with one partner. The bonding in such a relationship occurs in the first three to four years. In an effort to refine our understanding of bonding among gays, Ammon (1985) interviewed thirty couples who had been together a

minimum of five years. He found that the bonding process involves some of the same factors as those in heterosexual couples. Initially, for example, communication is crucial:

> The single most frequent activity reported by every couple was talking. Regardless of any other simultaneous activity such as sex, skiing or sailing, a constant exchange of self-information was consistently reported (Ammon 1985:86).

The couples also reported sharing many activities.

An interesting aspect of a developing gay relationship is what happens when one of the partners was married and fathered children. Ammon found that the fathers in his sample were committed to their children and that the new lover had to accept the children and the fact that the children would make demands on their father's time. The fathers said that if the new lover could not accept the children, the relationship would not last.

Following the working out of some of these issues, the men faced such problems as the development of trust, working out any differences in life-styles, learning to share equally in decision making, and making a long-term commitment to the relationship.

Clearly, then, the development of bonding and commitment to a homosexual relationship can be

INVOLVEMENT
What Is a Family?

Have you ever played the game of word association? For example, when you hear the word *fun,* what is the first word that comes to your mind? How about *happiness? Dating? Marriage?* Jot down your first response to each word.

Now respond to the word *family.* Instead of just one response, however, write down five words that come to mind. Then think about your responses. Why do you think you made these particular associations? Are there any common elements in your choices? Did your responses to *fun, happiness, dating,* and *marriage* have anything to do

with family life? Based on your responses, what is your family like?

How do you think other people would respond to the words? Would they respond differently depending on their family situations or backgrounds? Ask ten others to play the game of word association with you. If possible, select two different groups of five people each, such as five married people and five single parents, or five white and five black married people, or five heterosexuals and five homosexuals. If that isn't possible, get people who come from as many of the groups discussed in this chapter as possible.

Write down their responses. Then compare the two groups or those from differing groups. What kinds of meaning of family life seem to emerge from the words they chose? Do you see any differences between them? If so, how would you explain the differences? If not, why do you think there are no differences?

If the entire class participates in this project, you can specify the groups you want to investigate (perhaps three or four different groups) and pool the results. What conclusions would you now draw about the meaning of *family?*

very similar to that of a heterosexual relationship. Homosexuals have the same intimacy needs and many of the same aspirations for intimate relationships as heterosexuals. A major difference is that homosexuals are following a socially disapproved route, which adds many impediments to their search for intimacy.

PRINCIPLES FOR ENHANCING INTIMACY

Beginning with this chapter, we will briefly note some of the principles that can be derived from materials in the chapter and used to enhance the quality of your own intimate relationships. A major premise of the chapter, of course, is the point that intimate relationships are a necessary part of our well-being. Some of the important principles are:

1. People have always fulfilled many of their intimacy needs within the context of the family. However, today, the family comes in many varieties. And although the nontraditional or nonwhite family may present unique problems, it can be a vital source of satisfaction and well-being to its members.

2. Although nontraditional and nonwhite families encounter a host of obstacles, strong bonds of affection and shared values, interests, and goals help minimize the difficulties and produce a fulfilling relationship.

3. The same factors—love, respect, support, and sharing—are vital in all types of families. These are the bonds in any strong, enduring intimate relationship and thus should be cultivated. It may require extra effort and added determination in a nontraditional family to develop these bonds, but the end result will be worth the struggle.

4. Nonwhite families have special problems, but they also have some special strengths, such as the resource of strong extended-family relationships. Members of these families can tap into the unique strengths and use them to maximize intimacy even in the face of various political and economic disadvantages.

SUMMARY

The number of single-parent families has increased considerably over the past two decades, with more than one of four children living with only one parent. Single parents face the problems of responsibility, task, and emotional overload. The children of single parents are more likely to have both personal and interpersonal difficulties than are children who live with both parents. They perceive their homes as less cohesive, and they are likely to achieve less in education, occupation, and income than those from intact homes.

Boys seem to present more problems than girls for single parents. Single mothers may try to get their older sons to assume the responsibilities of the missing father, or they may go to the opposite extreme and "over-mother" their sons. There is not a great deal of research on single fathers, but children tend to reward single fathers more than single mothers.

Problems may arise when a single parent begins to date. Children may be angry and resentful about the parent dating. The problem may be compounded by the fact that the dates may be less than enthusiastic about the children.

In spite of the problems, most single-parent homes function reasonably well. The majority of single parents and their children have good physical and mental health. Single parents also function well at work.

Nonwhite families are similar to white families in many ways, but they face special problems because of their situation in society. African Americans make up the largest racial minority in the United States. They have a higher rate of single-parent families than either whites or Hispanics. They are also more likely to be single, widowed, or divorced. Black children are far more likely than others to be living with a mother who has never been married.

The problems of the black family must be viewed in the context of centuries of political and economic disadvantages. African Americans have lower incomes and higher rates of unemployment than whites, making the role of provider a more difficult one for the black male. Those African Americans who have fewer economic problems are more like whites in their family life. During the 1980s, however, the economic problems increased again because of various political decisions.

Although African Americans are more likely than whites to have a disadvantaged family situation, the black family tends to have a number of strengths and, in some cases, advantages over white families. Parenthood may not diminish the quality of life for African Americans as it does for whites, and being a single parent may not be as difficult for African Americans as for whites. African Americans tend to be more egalitarian in practice than do whites. And African Americans are not as likely as whites to be distressed by the empty nest.

Hispanics, the second largest racial minority, have a lower median family income than either whites or African Americans. They are more likely than either whites or blacks to have a family household and less likely to be divorced. Hispanic women differ from white women in that they show a progressive decline in marital satisfaction over time. In contrast to popular stereotype, however, Hispanic families are not male-dominated; they tend to be egalitarian. Finally, Hispanics tend to have closer bonds with members of the extended family than do whites.

Asian American families are better off in some ways than those of other races and even the white majority. They have higher educational attainment and higher median income than any other group. The families tend to be large and stable—they have the lowest divorce rate of any group. Influenced by Asian culture, Asian American families tend to subordinate individual needs to group needs and stress such values as obedience, loyalty, and self-control. They also tend to be male-dominated.

Native Americans are one of the most impoverished groups in the nation. Native American family life is circumscribed by the high poverty rate (leading to such things as high rates of fertility, alcoholism, and drug use) but also by tribal traditions (seen in such things as patrilineal versus matrilineal

descent and the importance of the extended family). The rate of intermarriage is high. Like other Americans, Native Americans tend to select life partners on the basis of romantic love.

Interracial families have increased dramatically in recent decades. A little over a fourth of interracial marriages involve white and African American partners. There is a higher rate of divorce in interracial marriages. People are attracted to mates of other races because of such things as love and compatibility. Even in an accepting environment, however, interracial unions face some unique problems. One problem is which parental roles and values to adopt when the husband and wife come from different cultural traditions.

About 20 to 30 percent of gays and lesbians enter a homosexual marriage. Homosexual couples have to work through the same problems as heterosexual couples. In addition, they face problems arising from a hostile environment and from the nature of their relationship. For example, gay couples may be stressed as their relationship is affected by the stereotypical male role (including the male sexual role), by homophobia, or by sexual dysfunctions.

Lesbian couples may not have the same kind of problems as either gay or heterosexual couples. They report less conflict over money management and income and more egalitarianism than other couples.

Homosexual couples trying to raise children report few serious problems and generally satisfying relationships. Children of homosexuals are likely to be heterosexual when they grow up.

In general, homosexuals want the same thing as heterosexuals in an intimate relationship. And the same factors enhance the quality of both homosexual and heterosexual relationships: commitment, shared decision making, and perceived investment in the relationship.

Two ways in which homosexual couples differ from heterosexual are the greater egalitarianism of the former and the way in which fidelity tends to be defined by gays. Gays frequently opt for an open relationship, which allows sexual relations with outsiders. Fidelity is defined as an emotional commitment rather than sexual exclusivity. But gays do form long-term relationships. The process of bonding and commitment in a homosexual relationship is very similar to that in a heterosexual relationship.

INTERNET CONNECTION
Diversity in Families

While most Americans view monogamous marriage as the ideal form of intimate relationships, many cultures presently, as well as throughout history, practice polygamy. While some cultures practice polygamy, it is illegal and generally looked down upon in the United States. Active practice of nonmonogamous behavior is often viewed from the perspective of "alternative lifestyles." The **Polygamy** website is designed as a resource for non-monogamous people of all sexual orientations. Review the information available at this site to answer the questions below.

www.mhhe .com/lauer4

Polygamy.com

http://www.polygamy.com/

This site contains links to resources and organizations on the topic of multiple relationships.

1. In what ways are the views of polygamy and group marriage portrayed at this site based on individualism or famialism?
2. Is polygamy realistic, or utopian?
3. Do you believe you are monogamous? Polygamous? How does your view on this issue effect your feelings on marriage?

GENDER ROLES: FOUNDATION FOR HETEROSEXUAL INTIMACY

Learning Objectives

After reading chapter 3, you should be able to:

1. Describe psychological and social similarities and differences that exist between men and women.
2. Define gender, gender role, and gender-role orientation.
3. Discuss traditional gender roles and their social consequences.
4. Explain the four types of gender-role orientation—masculine, feminine, undifferentiated, and androgynous.
5. Discuss the extent to which gender roles are a product of biology or environment.
6. Describe the functions of the family, school, and media in gender-role development.
7. Evaluate the extent to which people are becoming less traditional in their gender-role orientation.
8. Understand how gender-role orientation affects communication patterns.
9. Explain how attitudes about love, sex, and self are shaped by gender-role orientation.
10. Discuss the relationship between gender-role orientation and mental health.

According to a Harvard physician, Dr. Dudley Sargent, the physique of women has changed. He observed: "Twenty years ago women were the very antithesis of men in physical proportions." But now women have begun looking more like men. "It is to be hoped," said Dr. Sargent, "that women do not grow to be more like men than they are today. . . . The danger of women becoming too mannish is imminent."[1] The doctor also pointed out that men have changed and are in danger of becoming too "effeminate."

Dr. Sargent's remarks were made in 1910. They illustrate the ongoing concern that people have about men being men and women being women. But what does it mean to be a man? What does it mean to be a woman? In this chapter, we will explore this complex issue. We will look at similarities and differences between the sexes. We will explore the meaning of gender roles and the way in which we develop those roles. Finally, we will examine the

consequences of gender roles, including the implications of those roles for intimate relationships.

MEN AND WOMEN: HOW DO THEY DIFFER?

As an interesting exercise, write down five ways you believe that men and women are alike and five ways in which they differ. When you have finished this chapter, look at your list again and see if you want to make any changes in it. Keep in mind that even social scientists do not completely agree on how the two sexes differ and in what ways they are similar.

Men and Women: Some Commonalities

While we will focus more on differences than similarities, we want to underscore the fact that there are some similarities. Both men and women have some of the same fundamental needs: survival, self-esteem, intimacy, and growth. Both need the sense of having some control over their lives. Both need to achieve. Both need recreation. When we talk about the basic needs of humans, neither sex is exempt, even though they may fulfill those needs in somewhat different ways.

In addition, some recent research shows that men and women are similar in areas in which we formerly thought they were different. For example, women have typically been viewed as more emotional than men. But that may only be partly true. Psychologist Anthony Greenwald found that women are no better than men in recalling emotion-laden words.[2] But he also found that women give the words higher ratings on emotional intensity than did men. It may be, therefore, that men and women react to events with similar emotions but that women are prone to describe their reactions in more emotional terms.

Many people also believe that men and women differ in their responses to erotic stimuli. Presumably, men are more aroused than women by such stimuli. However, when researchers measured arousal by physiological changes (rather than self-reports), women and men showed very similar

---

[1]Reported in the *St. Louis Post-Dispatch,* 28 November 1910.

[2]Reported in *Psychology Today,* June 1986, p. 12.

kinds of response (Rubinsky et al. 1987). A third example of supposed difference is in the tendency to cooperate. Women are said to be more cooperative than men in group tasks. But the differences appear to be very small, and gender is not as important as other factors in determining whether someone will be cooperative (Stockard, Van de Kragt, and Dodge 1988).

Finally, women are thought to conform more than men. Even many social scientists have asserted that women are easier to persuade and more prone to comply with group pressures than are men. Indeed, some experimental evidence supported such a position. Yet in a review of all the available evidence, Alice Eagly (1978) argued that the case is not closed on gender differences in conformity. In most settings, Eagly found that women are not more easily influenced than men. In group settings where pressure is exerted on each member to conform, the findings are somewhat mixed. Although most studies do not show any gender differences, about a third did report women to be more conforming in group settings than men. We are not certain about the reasons for these findings. One explanation is that men generally have higher status in our society, and higher-status individuals have more latitude for nonconformity than do lower-status individuals.

The point is that there are similarities, including some that go against the conventional wisdom. Men and women are different, but not as different as some people think (figure 3.1).

FIGURE 3.1   Perceived versus Actual Differences between Males and Females
(From Arnold S. Kahn, *Social Psychology.* Copyright © 1984 Times Mirror Higher Education Group, Inc. All Rights Reserved. Reprinted by permission.)

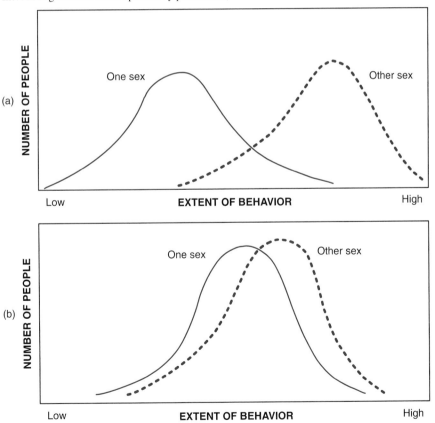

(a) The amount of difference that people often think exists between males and females
(b) The extent of differences actually found for social behaviors

Gender Differences

Men and women differ in numerous ways, including everything from women's longer average life span to their differing attitudes on social issues. In fact, males and females see themselves differently. That is, they tend to have differing self-concepts, with males rating themselves higher on such things as giftedness, power, and invulnerability, and females rating themselves higher on likability and morality (Stake 1992). We will not discuss the obvious physical differences. Instead, we will focus on some of the diverse social and psychological characteristics.

Ability　If you read a poem, a story, or an article, do you think your evaluation of it would be influenced by the name of the author? You probably think not. But studies have shown that when people are led to believe that something is the work of a male, they are likely to rate it higher than do others who believe the work was produced by a female. Among other things, people have rated males higher on essays, paintings, and applications for a job or for study abroad (Kahn 1984:360). Studies have also shown that people believe that males will perform better in virtually all occupations.

In other words, many people believe that males are superior to females in their abilities. This belief begins early in life. Researchers asked a group of 170 children aged eight to twelve years to draw a picture of an intelligent and an ordinary person (Raty and Snellman 1997). The most common portrait of the intelligent person was an adult male. Even people who hold egalitarian beliefs about males and females ascribe certain abilities, such as leadership, more to males than females. A study involving 150 adults with egalitarian beliefs reported that males were more likely than females to be selected as task leaders (Sapp, Harrod, and Zhao 1996).

Despite the beliefs, however, it is not true that male abilities are generally superior to those of females. On intelligence tests, girls evidence superior verbal ability. They score higher than boys on tests that demand an understanding of complex language, creative writing, analogies, fluency, and spelling. Boys, on the other hand, have better spatial and quantitative ability. They score higher on math tests and do better on tasks that require visual

and spatial perception. The reasons for these differences are still debated; some people believe that they are rooted in the brain, while others believe they are a product of socialization.

The notion that men can perform better than women in all occupations is also untrue. One reason some people give for the presumed difference is that women are less involved with the workplace than are men. Some businessmen have been reluctant to promote women into the upper ranks of management because they assume that women are not as committed to their careers as are men. Yet given equivalent kinds of work, women may be more involved than men, and their involvement may increase over time while men's may decline (Lorence 1987). When women are given the same opportunities as men, both their competence and their motivation are equal to men's for most tasks. Again, where superior spatial and visual skills are required, men may be more competent. And where superior verbal skills are required, women may be more competent. Still, either sex can perform well in nearly all kinds of work. The fact that people have not fully accepted this notion, however, may be seen in the extent to which many occupations are still dominated by one sex or the other (table 3.1).

Aggression　It appears universally true that men are more aggressive than women. Anthropologists have reported that violence typically occurs at the hands of men in all societies. The difference appears even in people's dreams. Men in tribal societies are more likely to dream of sexual intercourse, wives, weapons, and animals, while women are more likely to dream of husbands and children, mothers and fathers, and crying (Konner 1982:56). Studies of children in various societies show that boys exhibit a much higher preference for sports as a leisure activity than do girls (Lightbody et al. 1996; Gibbons, Lynn, and Stiles 1997). Boys, that is, prefer a more aggressive kind of activity.

Men are more aggressive by almost any measure. Men commit more violent crimes than women. They are more likely to assault someone. In social psychological experiments, males are typically more aggressive than women in their responses.

However, we need to note that there are different kinds of situations and different kinds of aggres-

TABLE 3.1
Percent of Females Employed in Selected Occupations: 1996

Occupation	Percent Female
All occupations	46.2
Managerial and professional	48.6
Managers, medicine, and health	75.3
Purchasing managers	45.7
Architects	16.7
Engineers	8.5
Math and computer scientists	30.6
Physicians	26.4
Elementary school teachers	83.3
Lawyers and judges	29.0
Librarians	82.7
Technical, sales and administrative support	64.2
Licensed practical nurses	95.3
Electronic technicians	12.7
Insurance sales	40.4
Cashiers	78.1
Secretaries	98.6
Service occupations	59.4
Child care workers	97.1
Firefighting and fire prevention	2.1
Police and detectives	15.8
Waiters and waitresses	77.9
Precision production, craft, repair	9.0
Mechanics and repairers	4.1
Carpenters	1.3
Operators, fabricators, laborers	24.4
Pressing machine operators	76.3
Motor vehicle operators	11.2
Farming, forestry, fishing	19.0
Farm workers	18.8
Forestry and logging	3.5

Source: U.S. Bureau of the Census (1997b:410–12).

Adolescent girls report higher levels of intimacy than do boys, and girls tend to have their highest level with their girlfriends.

sion. In a situation where people are provoked or angered, men are more likely than women to use physical aggression, while women are more likely to use verbal aggression. In situations where there is no provocation, men seem to be consistently more aggressive than women (Kahn 1984:384).

Interaction: Quantity and Quality Females are more relationship-oriented than males. Males tend to value independence more than females, while females value connectedness and intimacy more than males (Lang-Takac and Osterweil 1992).

Even when talking about a best friend, males speak of the relationship in more instrumental terms—how it is useful to them rather than the intrinsic value of relating intimately to someone else (Orosan and Schilling 1992). And when dealing with a troubling situation, women are likely to reach out to others for support while men are more likely to solve the problem on their own (McCall and Struthers 1994).

It is not surprising, then, that in his study of ninety-six college students Reis (1986:95–96) found that females have more interactions with other people per day than do males. He also reported on the quality of the interaction. Interestingly, the quality varied by the gender of the participants. The least meaningful interaction reported was that between two males. Heterosexual and all-female interaction was rated higher in terms of quality and satisfaction than all-male interaction. Even when males interacted with best friends, they did not find the interaction as satisfying as when they interacted with a female.

Why is the quality of interaction rated as better when there is at least one female involved? Females appear to be more skilled than males in maintaining quality interaction because of certain aspects of their conversational style. Women do much of the work in starting and maintaining conversations.

Women have a questioning style that includes a number of characteristics (Kohn 1988:66):

> Women ask more questions than men. One analysis of conversations between professional couples reported that the women asked three times as many questions as the men.
>
> Women have a questioning tone to their statements. The tone asks for confirmation from the listener that the speaker is correct.
>
> Women use more tag questions. Tag questions occur at the end of sentences and encourage the listener to respond. For instance: "This is a beautiful day, isn't it?" and "School gets to be a drag sometimes, don't you think?"
>
> Women are more likely to begin with a question. "Guess what?" and other leading questions are meant to capture the listener's attention.
>
> Women use more qualifiers ("sort of," "maybe," etc.) and intensifiers ("really") than men. The qualifiers and intensifiers give hints to the listener about how to react.

The interpersonal skills of females emerge early in their lives. A study of thirty-eight preschool children found that the girls were more likely than the boys to share play stickers and to negotiate and cooperate with each other (Burford et al. 1996). A survey of over two thousand seventh- through tenth-grade adolescents found that the girls reported higher levels of intimacy than the boys (Blyth and Foster-Clark 1987). The students were asked to rate their relationships with various people who were important to them (friends, parents, siblings, or oth-

ers). Then they indicated to what extent they had an intimate relationship with each of those people. Intimacy was measured by the students' responses to four questions: How much do you go to this person for advice? How much does this person accept you no matter what you do? How much does this person understand what you're really like? How much do you share your inner feelings with this person?

Girls reported higher levels of intimacy overall. In addition, they reported the highest level of intimacy with their same-sex friends (figure 3.2). Boys, in contrast, reported higher levels of intimacy with their parents than with their same-sex friends.

Note that one of the ways that the researchers measured intimacy was the question about self-disclosure of inner feelings. Females continue the pattern of greater self-disclosure into adulthood (Snell et al. 1988). We have noted in earlier chapters that self-disclosure is an essential part of an intimate relationship and that the amount of self-disclosure increases as the relationship intensifies. The greater ease of the female to engage in self-disclosure means that she is more skilled than the male in creating intimacy.

Nonverbal Behavior It has been estimated that anywhere between 50 and 80 percent of the meaning in a conversation is communicated nonverbally. The same words can take on quite different meanings depending on one's facial expression, gestures, voice tone, and inflection. For example, depending on the nonverbal cues, the three words "I love you" could mean sarcasm, indifference (suggesting that the speaker said them only to try to placate the

FIGURE 3.2   Intimacy Scores of Boys versus Girls
(Source: Data from D. A. Blyth and F. S. Foster-Clark, *Sex Roles,* 17:711, 1987.)

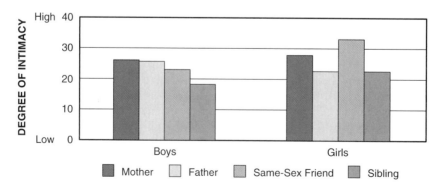

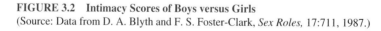

other), disbelief (I love *you*?), true devotion, or a variety of things in between. Nonverbal behavior, then, is a crucial part of intimate relationships.

Conflict Theory Applied

Gender differences exist in nonverbal behavior. Women are more skilled at interpreting nonverbal behavior. *Conflict theorists* explain this as a protective measure. They note that those who are less powerful (women and minorities) have a greater need to know what the more powerful people with whom they interact are really thinking and planning. But women also use somewhat different kinds of nonverbal behavior, and they use both differences in communicating and interpreting nonverbal behavior to enhance their ability to form and maintain intimate relationships. For example, eye contact is an important nonverbal component of intimacy. Researchers who have watched videotapes of people conversing note that pairs of women have more eye contact than do pairs of men (Kahn 1984:366). And women are more likely to maintain eye contact when they are sitting close to each other, while men are more likely to maintain eye contact when farther apart from each other.

From an early age, females seem to use eye contact to communicate intimacy more than do males. And from an early age, females are superior in communicating nonverbal emotional messages. In fact, boys seem to get poorer at sending nonverbal emotional messages as they get older. Overall, then, women's nonverbal behavior suggests that they are warm, friendly, and attentive to others. Men's nonverbal behavior suggests that they have high status and are important and somewhat distant.

Keeping Differences in Perspective   Clearly, not every woman is warm, friendly, and attentive to others. Nor does every man act superior and distant. Similarly, every man is not more aggressive than any woman. There are differences, but the differences refer to averages in whole groups (recall figure 3.1). Thus, it is more accurate to say that more men than women are highly aggressive, rather than to say that men are more aggressive than women. And it is more accurate to say that more women than men are warm, friendly, and attentive to others, than to say that women are warmer, more friendly, and more attentive than men.

The difference in language may seem subtle, but it is an important difference. It helps us keep in mind that there are numerous similarities between the sexes, and that at least some of the differences are relatively small.

SEX, GENDER, GENDER ROLE, AND GENDER-ROLE ORIENTATION

Are you male or female? How much does the answer tell us about your behavior? As the above discussion indicates, it tells us some things, but not a great deal. We need to ask some additional questions of you. What kinds of behavior do you see as appropriate for someone of your sex? And to what extent do you see yourself having both masculine and feminine traits?

The questions refer to the fact that we need to distinguish between sex, gender, gender role, and gender-role orientation. "Sex" is what you are biologically—male or female. But since so much of our behavior is based on social rather than biological factors, we use the term **gender** to refer to males and females as social creatures. **Gender role** refers to the behavior associated with being either male or female. And **gender-role orientation** refers to the conception of yourself as having some combination of masculine and feminine traits.

Many people think that being male or female is a major factor in determining behavior. Indeed, we all do tend to treat people differently by gender. But for many kinds of behavior, gender roles and gender-role orientations are even more important than gender.

Gender Roles

Are men and women equal in American society? One way to answer the question is to ask about gender roles. What kind of behavior do we expect from the two sexes? Traditionally, the differences have been well defined.

Traditional Gender Roles   For the last few decades, researchers have inquired into the stereotypes that people have of men and women. Both men and women tend to agree on the attributes that they believe are typical of each sex. In essence, men are generally held to be strong, independent, successful, courageous, aggressive, and logical. Women are viewed as more gentle, dependent on men for support and protection, nurturing, emotional, and submissive. Traditional roles—men as breadwinners and women as homemakers—reflected these qualities.

Men, then, are expected to be achievement-oriented, dominant, strong, and self-controlled (Harris 1995). Or as one researcher put it, there are four distinct norms that are the basis for the male gender role (Brannon 1976):

1. "No Sissy Stuff." Men must not do anything that might appear to be feminine. A man who engages in an activity that people define as feminine, such as appearing to be too emotional, is something less than a true man.
2. "The Big Wheel." Men need to act in such a way that they are respected and admired. This means that they must be successful in something. Ideally, they should be successful in everything they do, especially in functioning as the breadwinner in the family.
3. "The Sturdy Oak." Men are strong, silent types of humans. They stay calm in the midst of turmoil and difficulty. They face up to crises without showing any weakness and without giving way to emotions. They keep intimate feelings to themselves.
4. "Give 'Em Hell." Men love adventure, risk, danger, violence. A man who refuses to take risks is a dull man.

In contrast, two researchers who developed a measure of traditional versus nontraditional behaviors for women used questions such as the following (Robinson and Follingstad 1985):

> "If trying to get your own way, how likely are you to use tears with a person of the opposite sex within the next year at least once?"

> "How frequently have you pretended to know less than you really knew to protect the ego of a person of the opposite sex during the past year?"

> "How likely are you to wait in the car for a person of the opposite sex to open the door for you during the next year?"

According to their study, the more likely their respondents were to engage in these behaviors, the more traditional they were.

Clearly, the traditional male is someone who is in control of his life, who acts with reason and determination to achieve goals and complete tasks. The traditional female is someone who is dependent on that male, who tries to protect the male from any threats to his ego, and who must resort to emotions, rather than reason, when she tries to influence him.

Consequences of the Traditional Roles   To some extent the traditional roles are stereotypes. That is, few if any people have followed them precisely. But to the extent that people have approximated those roles, certain consequences for a wide range of behavior follow, one of which is illustrated in table 3.1—the tendency to consider certain occupations as more appropriate for one sex than the other.

Numerous additional consequences arise. For instance, three sociologists found a number of correlates among those men who agree more with the traditional male gender role (Thompson, Grisanti, and Pleck 1985). The more traditional men expressed more anxiety about being perceived as a homosexual. They were more favorable toward Type A behavior, such as rapid speaking, preoccupation with one's work, impatience, and a generally aggressive, competitive approach. Type A behavior has been identified as increasing one's risk of coronary heart disease. The more traditional males were also less inclined to disclose intimate matters to females and more desirable of being in control (including making the decisions) in intimate relationships.

Even though our ideas about gender roles have been changing (see PERSPECTIVE), many people still react to others on the basis of those traditional roles. For instance, a man who acts passive and dependent or a woman who insists on pursuing a career in a male-dominated occupation may be defined as maladjusted. Males who behave in a dominant fashion may be rated as more attractive by females (Sadalla, Kenrick, and Vershure 1987). Men who engage in nurturing behavior may be defined as less masculine, less strong, and less likely to be achievers than other men (Draper and Gordon 1986).

PERSPECTIVE
Woman's Work

Some people have argued that the traditional roles do not contradict the notion of equality. The struggle of women to gain rights, such as voting and equal opportunities in the workplace, has proceeded in the face of such arguments as the one below, offered by a nineteenth-century physician in his book on the ethics of marriage:

> Nature clearly indicates that woman was intended to be man's companion and coworker. Nature arranged that woman should be man's equal—not that she should be his equivalent nor that she should do a man's work—that she should bear her fair share of the burdens [of] life, and should have her full share of the compensation.
>
> Broadly considered, Nature arranged that man should be the provider of means of subsistence, and that woman should be the dispenser of these means. [It is true that a woman can do the kind of work that men do.] But without going into the details of man's work and his superiority over woman in it, let us consider woman's work. In the first place, it certainly *is* woman's work, for it cannot be done by a man, however willing a man might be to do it; and, in the second place, it is absolutely necessary, for the world would soon come to an end without it; in the third place, it is a more honorable and important work than man's; and, finally, if woman does her work well and thoroughly, it requires all her time and vitality. So woman is debarred from doing a man's work not because she *cannot* do it, but because her own work is all she can possibly attend to. The key to the question, What is woman's work? is the fact that Nature has imposed on her the most of the burden of reproduction. The rest of woman's work follows naturally, for as she is brought into peculiarly close relations with the human individual at its tenderest age . . . the Creator has endowed woman with a special store of the gentler and finer qualities of mind and heart, and has given her a peculiar adaptability for planning and executing little details connected with the distribution of means of subsistence to the ends of the comfort and happiness of those about her. But in doing this, woman is the homemaker and housekeeper, and this is just what God meant her to be—just this and nothing more.

Source: Pomeroy (1888:125–28).

In an interesting experiment with undergraduates, students were divided into heterosexual pairs and watched a horror movie (Zillmann et al. 1986). Men enjoyed the movie most when they were with a woman who acted distressed and least when they were with a woman who appeared in control. Women enjoyed the movie most when they were with a man who was in control and least when they were with a man who acted distressed. In other words, enjoyment was enhanced by being with someone who acted in accord with the traditional gender roles.

One final example involves housework. Traditionally, the woman was the homemaker and the man was the breadwinner. While the majority of women now work, most of them retain major responsibility for doing the housework (Spain and Bianchi 1996). Whatever people's ideals may be, traditional gender roles continue to influence their behavior.

Gender-Role Orientation

As we pointed out, few if any people have conformed precisely to the traditional roles. Most people have some combination of the qualities or traits of each role. Social scientists call those traits associated with the traditional male role **instrumental** and those associated with the traditional female role **expressive.** Instrumental traits, such as aggressiveness, competitiveness, self-confidence, and logic, enable people to achieve goals. Expressive traits, such as warmth, caring, sensitivity, and nurturance, enable people to establish good interpersonal relationships.

The way to find people's gender-role orientation is to ask them to describe themselves in terms of the various traits. Those who select predominantly instrumental traits are masculine, while those who select predominantly expressive traits are feminine in their orientation. For example, the Personal

Attributes Questionnaire, developed by Spence and Helmreich (1978), asks respondents to rate themselves on a number of traits, such as the following:

Not at all   A . . . B . . . C . . . D . . . E Very
aggressive   aggressive

Not at all   A . . . B . . . C . . . D . . . E Very
emotional   emotional

Very rough A . . . B . . . C . . . D . . . E Very gentle

A strong masculine response would be E on the aggressive scale and A on the emotional and rough/gentle scales. A strong feminine response would be the opposite.

At first, it seems reasonable to assume that masculine and feminine are the two extremes of one dimension. That is, the more masculine you are, the less feminine and vice versa. But social scientists agree that masculinity and femininity are not opposites that exclude each other. Instead of a continuum, with masculine at one end and feminine at the other, gender-role orientation must be understood as two-dimensional (figure 3.3). Thus, an individual can be high on both, low on both, or high on one

FIGURE 3.3   Gender-Role Orientation as One- or Two-Dimensional

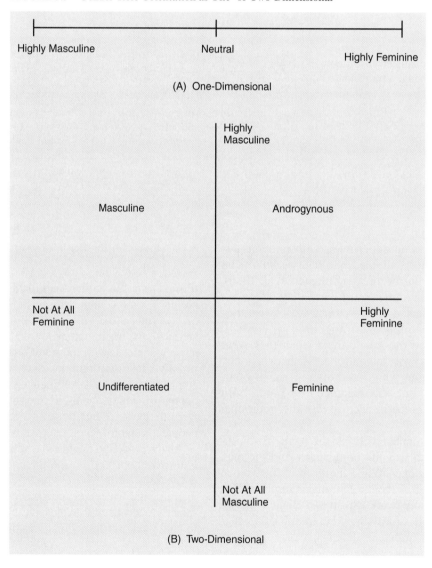

and low on the other dimension. The smallest category, in terms of numbers of people, is the *undifferentiated,* in which an individual sees himself or herself as low on both masculine and feminine traits. You would be undifferentiated if you saw yourself as moderately aggressive (in between "very" and "not at all"), moderately independent, moderately emotional, and so on.

As figure 3.3 indicates, an individual can be aggressive and competitive and independent and also gentle and sensitive. Such people, as figure 3.3 indicates, are called androgynous. **Androgyny** is a term coined by Sandra Bem (1974) to describe those people who possess both masculine, or instrumental, and feminine, or expressive, traits. Bem has argued that androgynous individuals are healthier and more adaptable than others. This makes sense, because they should have a greater range of behaviors available to them to meet diverse demands of differing situations. We shall see to what extent androgyny does facilitate people's functioning.

GENDER ROLES: NATURE OR NURTURE?

One of the controversies surrounding gender roles is whether they reflect human nature. Are women more expressive than men because there is something in their biological makeup that leads them to behave in that way? Or do gender roles reflect socialization, the way in which children are nurtured? Those who stress nature may prefer to use the term *sex* role, which suggests that the differences are innate. We use the term *gender* role because we believe the evidence shows that male-female differences are due more to nurture than nature.

Differences between males and females develop quite early in life. There are certain differences even in infants (girl babies, for example, tend to smile more than boy babies). By the time they are three years old, children think of themselves as male or female (Brown 1995:40) and show definite preferences for toys that are stereotypically appropriate for their own gender (e.g., dolls for girls, trucks for boys) (Martin and Little 1990). By the time children are five and in kindergarten, they clearly assign certain activities and tasks as more appropriate for one gender than another (Bardwell, Cochran, and Walker 1986). They believe, for instance, that women put up drapes and men build houses. These differences tend to continue to intensify throughout the elementary school years (Galambos, Almeida, and Petersen 1990). How can we account for them?

How Much Is Biological?

Sigmund Freud (1949) set forth an influential case for the biological basis of gender roles. Freud's arguments were summed up in his famous idea that *anatomy is destiny.* He argued that girls reach the point in their development when they realize that they are anatomically different from boys. They lack a penis, and therefore they feel severely deprived. This leads to "penis envy." According to Freud, only in the act of conceiving and giving birth to a child can a woman find fulfillment. But she never fully overcomes her penis envy, so that jealousy and envy are more prominent in women than in men. Without going into the details of his theory, we should note that Freud also concluded that women are naturally more passive, submissive, and neurotic than men. All of this results from women's psychological reaction to their physiology.

Those who draw on research about the brain and hormones also stress innate biological differences (Kolata 1983). The differences are used to explain such things as the higher levels of aggression among males, the greater verbal abilities of females, and the greater mathematical, visual, and spatial skills of males. For example, some researchers believe that the higher levels of the hormone testosterone are present during the development of the brain in the male fetus. The higher levels seem to alter the anatomy of the brain, making the right hemisphere dominant. This, in turn, results in the tendency for males to have superior mathematical ability.

The amount of research is too voluminous to examine here. Fortunately, a biologist, Anne Fausto-Sterling (1985), has examined the full range of research, looking in detail at the research on the brain and on sex hormones and its implications for sex differences. She concluded that there are definite limitations in the extent to which we are shaped by biological factors. With respect to brain structure, she noted that genetic factors are important but "extensive development of nervous connections occurs after birth, influenced profoundly by individual experience" (Fausto-Sterling 1985:77). Rather than there being a simple causal relationship between biological factors and human behavior, then, she argued that the mind, body, and culture all interact with each other. No human behavior can be explained solely and completely in either biological or social terms. Behavior is always a function of multiple factors, she asserted, so that we do not know how much of a particular behavior is biological and how much is social.

Behavior, then, has both a biological and social component. For instance, Grossman and Wood (1993) conducted two experiments; in one, females reported more emotional intensity than did males. The researchers manipulated the situation in the second experiment so that males and females reported about the same emotional intensity, but physiological measures showed that the females had a stronger bodily reaction. Both biological and social factors were at work in the emotional experiences.

The Importance of Nurture

Symbolic Interactionist and Systems Theories Applied

Most social scientists argue, with Fausto-Sterling, that nurture is an important part of gender-role behavior. *Symbolic interactionist* and *systems theorists* both stress the importance of roles in shaping human behavior. That is, the way we behave is due more to social expectations involved in the roles we assume than to any genetic or biological imperatives. Some of the evidence for such a position comes from history and from the observation of other cultures. Historically, American men and women have not always behaved in strict accord with what we have called the traditional sex roles. In the American colonies, married and single women functioned as innkeepers, printers, and the head of dame schools. Further, they were actively involved in the economics of their family and social affairs of their community. In the mid-nineteenth century, as the nation industrialized and the middle classes grew, new ideas about proper gender roles developed. Indeed, women's roles narrowed significantly. Women were to be freed from hard work so that they could engage in the more feminine pursuits of music, art, and em-

broidery. Greater emphasis was placed on the proper dress, appearance, and decorative function of women. Increasingly, as men's work took them away from the home, the women's place became the home. They were to create and maintain the home as a refuge for their husband and children in the face of an increasingly impersonal and hostile environment.

Looking at other cultures, we also find deviations from traditional roles in America. In her study of three primitive cultures in New Guinea, Margaret Mead (1969) concluded that the meaning of being male or female is largely a matter of cultural conditioning. Many of the traits we think of as masculine or feminine are "as lightly linked to sex as are the clothing, the manners, and the form of headdress that a society at a given period assigns to either sex" (Mead 1969:260). Among the Tchambuli, for example, the women were in command and were concerned with the practical matters of tribal life, such as fishing and trading. They also took the initiative in mating. The men, in contrast, concerned themselves with their personal appearance, their jewelry, and their rivalries and jealousies in their efforts to get the attention of women.

Finally, there is some evidence from research in developmental psychology that underscores the importance of socialization. According to the stereotype, females are more emotional and more nurturing than males. With regard to emotions, there is evidence that male infants are more emotional than female—laughing, crying, and showing joy and anger more—but parents tend to teach their sons to suppress their emotions from about one year on (Levant and Kopecky 1994). Similarly, girls do not appear to be *naturally* more nurturing than boys (Melson and Fogel 1988). Until about the age of four or five, boys tend to be equally as interested as girls in babies and their care. As they get older and become more aware of their gender identity, boys become less involved and less interested in babies. They *learn* to engage in the traditional less-nurturing male role.

In sum, the evidence we have supports the earlier conclusions of Chafetz (1974:27–28), who drew a number of conclusions about the relative influence of biological and social factors:

1. Most of the traits and behaviors identified as masculine or feminine in a society are not innate. Those defined as masculine in one society may be feminine in another, and vice versa.

2. A few *tendencies* are innately linked to gender, such as the male tendency to greater aggression. But social factors can virtually eliminate the effects of the tendencies.

3. Whatever innate differences exist, they are quantitative rather than qualitative. That is, we cannot say that men are aggressive and women are passive. But, as we stated earlier, more men than women are highly aggressive.

Socialization and Gender-Role Orientation

Since socialization is important in gender-role development, we need to identify the major sources of that socialization. Reflect back on your own experience. How did you learn what it means to be masculine and feminine? Probably, the three most important sources were family, school, and the mass media. And these three sources may have agreed with and reinforced each other.

Consider, for example, the issue of a woman's appearance. The current cultural ideal for American women is to be slender but shapely. Women who perceive their bodies to be heavier than the ideal may succumb to eating disorders in an effort to lose weight. A study of 400 students at Boston College concluded that the numerous eating disorders resulted from the "cult of thinness" that the women followed (Hesse-Biber 1996).

Girls may develop dissatisfaction with their bodies as early as nine years of age (Gardner, Sorter, and Friedman 1997). How does it happen? A study of 152 college women concluded that body image is shaped by three things: experiences of being teased or criticized about their looks during childhood and adolescence; comparing themselves with siblings' appearance; and perceptions about their mothers' appearance, including any tendency to diet

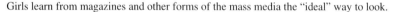

Girls learn from magazines and other forms of the mass media the "ideal" way to look.

and express anxiety about weight or appearance (Rieves and Cash 1996). The pictures of models and glamorous women in the mass media confirm and perpetuate the ideal of thinness. Thus, family, school experiences with peers and teachers, and the mass media combine to teach you what it means to be feminine and masculine.

Family   Our earliest exposure to what it means to be masculine and feminine comes from our parents. We learn from them and tend to model ourselves after them. We learn not only from listening to them but also by observing their attitudes and behavior. This means that children's understandings of gender roles reflect the understandings of their parents (Moen, Erickson and Dempster-McClain 1997).

Parents help their children to differentiate gender roles by treating their male and female children differently. Both fathers and mothers use a greater range and number of emotional terms with their daughters than with their sons (Adams et al. 1995; Garner, Robertson, and Smith 1997). They use different discipline strategies for boys and girls (Leve and Fagot 1997). Parents tend to encourage their children to engage in gender-typed activities (i.e., they encourage boys to pursue such things as math and sports, and girls such things as art and reading) (Eccles, Jacobs, and Harold 1990). Such differential treatment occurs from birth. For instance, in the first two years of life, parents tend to give boys such things as sports equipment, tools, and large and small vehicles of various kinds, while they give girls dolls, child's furniture, and similar toys (Pomerleau et al. 1990). This tendency may or may not be changing (Idle, Wood, and Desmarais 1993). At any rate, parents need to be aware of the implications of their gifts to their children. Even such a seemingly neutral gift as a picture book has an impact, because the books, while becoming less stereotyped, still tend to portray girls as dependent and submissive and boys as independent and creative (Kortenhaus and Demarest 1993; Oskamp, Kaufman and Wolterbeek 1996).

Families also differ in their economic resources. In his study of the effects of economic depression during the 1930s, Elder (1974) found that the extent of deprivation had an impact on the roles adopted by children. Girls from more deprived families were likely to have mothers who had to work to help support the family. The girls had to assume responsibility for housework, and as they matured, they tended to marry early and continue the homemaker role. Boys from more deprived families tended to choose careers earlier in life and to have a more orderly career. Girls from more affluent families were able to obtain more education. By the time they were adults in the 1950s, they tended to be working and to continue working even after marriage. Their education enabled them to depart from the traditional homemaker role assumed by their mothers.

One other factor that affects gender-role socialization is the type of family. Support for nontraditional gender roles is more likely to come from women employed full time outside the home than from women employed part time outside the home. And it is least likely to come from homemakers (Cassidy and Warren 1996). In single-parent families, father-headed families have the most traditional gender attitudes and mother-headed families have the most egalitarian attitudes (Wright and Young 1998).

School   Schools teach equality between the sexes if they group boys and girls together and apply the same standards to both. In practice, however, such equal treatment is absent. Using participant observation, Martin (1998) studied five preschools and found five kinds of practices that differentiate boys from girls. First, parents may send their children to preschool in gendered clothing (61 percent of the girls wore something pink; boys never wore pink). The children observe each other and learn that boys and girls dress in different colors as well as different kinds of clothing. Second, the teachers encouraged girls to behave more formally than boys (girls, e.g., were more likely to be told to "sit on your bottom" during circle while boys might be allowed to squat or be on their knees). Third, teachers were more likely to tell girls than boys to be quiet or to repeat something in a quieter and "nicer" voice. Fourth, teachers gave more directives to girls than to boys about changing their behavior ("talk to her, don't yell, sit here, pick that up, be careful," etc.). Finally, the children taught each other the meaning of being masculine and feminine by engaging in roughhouse (boys) or by trying to be nice (girls). Thus, children in preschool learn the meaning of being male or female both from teachers and their peers.

COMPARISON
Inuit Youth Learn to Be Males and Females

The community of Holman lies some 300 miles north of the Arctic Circle on Victoria Island. A few hundred Eskimos, mostly of the Copper Inuit, live there. Until they settled in Holman during the 1960s, these Inuit Eskimos lived in scattered, isolated hunting and trapping camps. In the camps, males and females had fairly well-defined gender roles that were distinct yet complementary, and both roles were necessary to their joint survival.

What does it now mean to be a male or female Inuit in the more settled and secure community of Holman? As two researchers discovered when they interviewed forty-one Inuit youth between the ages of eleven and nineteen, gender roles have changed, although, as in the past, clear distinctions between the sexes remain. When asked to identify the characteristics of males and females, the youths largely agreed that females are sexy, shy,

clean, quiet, friendly, and nice, while males are bullies, scary, aggressive, dirty, show-offs, and mean. They also agreed that young males, compared to young females, have higher social status, greater freedom to do as they like, fewer household responsibilities, and are indulged more by their parents. The females, nevertheless, preferred their own roles, seeing themselves as more mature and adultlike than the males.

These images of maleness and femaleness are acquired through various socialization techniques. Females are given an increasing number of household chores as they mature. They are treated as adults at a relatively early age. For example, a mother at a community dance told her eleven-year-old daughter that she was running around "like a little kid." The daughter sat down and remained sedate like her parents. In contrast, young sons are given few,

if any, chores. They are sometimes taken by their fathers to learn how to hunt and fish, but only if the youths feel like doing so. Finally, when they are teenagers, Inuit youths do have some opportunities to work and earn money. The females tend to spend all or a portion of what they earn on things that will benefit the family, while the males usually spend everything they earn on themselves.

The gender roles the Inuit youth learn make the transition to adulthood somewhat easier for females. Teenage females have already begun to function as adults, while teenage males engage in largely nonproductive and irresponsible peer group activities. As a result, the males have more behavioral and psychological adjustments to make as they assume the responsibilities of adulthood (Condon and Stern 1993).

The differential treatment of children by teachers tends to continue beyond preschool and even into college (Association of American Colleges 1982). Teachers tend to ask boys more difficult questions. They are more likely to urge boys to try harder if the boys are wrong or unsuccessful at first, implying that the boys have the ability to succeed. They tend to give boys instructions on how to do the work for themselves but take the girls through the work process step by step or even do it for them. Teachers may not intend it, but their behavior can communicate quite different messages to boys and girls about expectations and potential.

The Media   The media generally are influential in shaping our notions of appropriate gender roles. However, we will concentrate on what is perhaps the most influential—television. The National Insti-

tute of Mental Health (1982:54–56) has summed up some of the facts about television programming that can affect gender-role development:

1. In male-female interaction, men are usually more dominant.
2. Men on television are rational, ambitious, smart, competitive, powerful, stable, violent, and tolerant, while the women are sensitive, romantic, attractive, happy, warm, sociable, peaceful, fair, submissive, and timid.
3. For men, the emphasis is on strength, performance, and skill; for women, it is on attractiveness and desirability.
4. Marriage and family are not important to television's men. One study found that for nearly half of the men, it wasn't possible to tell if they were married, a fact that was true for only 11 percent of the women.

It seems that television is more likely than not to support aspects of the traditional roles for men and women. There are, of course, pressures to change, and some evidence of change. But a study of forty MTV videos found that men appeared almost twice as often as women and were significantly more aggressive and dominant, while women were more subservient and likely to be treated as sex objects (Sommers-Flanagan, Sommers-Flanagan, and Davis 1993).

The mass media in other nations may also support traditional ideas about gender roles. An analysis of 106 Australian radio ads concluded that the way men and women were portrayed tended to reflect traditional gender role stereotypes (Hurtz and Durkin 1997).

Women may have come a long way. But there is a long way to go if equality is the goal. The mass media, along with school and family practices, continues to support traditional roles.

CHANGING GENDER ROLES AND ORIENTATIONS

As noted, what we have called the traditional roles emerged in the mid-nineteenth century. Gender roles vary over time and between societies. Gender-role orientations also change over time and may even vary over an individual's life span.

Changing Patterns

Evidence exists that people are becoming less traditional in their attitudes about gender roles (although, as noted earlier, the changes have had little effect on the differential treatment of children). A study of 239 adults found that the subjects believed infant boys and girls as equally capable of acquiring various skills at the same age levels (Paludi and Gullo 1986). Another study reported that female college freshmen from 1969 to 1984 placed increasing emphasis on achievement goals (Fiorentine 1988). Over that period of time, an increasing proportion of the women indicated that they had one or more of the following goals: to become an authority in their field; to be well-off financially; to obtain recognition from colleagues; and to have administrative responsibility.

In essence, those who reject the traditional model tend to affirm more egalitarian roles. They believe that women should have the same opportunities as men and that men can and should engage in some of the traditional female pursuits (such as the nurturing of children). Thus, Hispanic women

---

INVOLVEMENT
Gender-Role Development: My Personal Journey

Write a personal account of your own gender-role development. You can organize your paper along the lines of answers to the following questions:

1. What does it mean to you to be someone of your gender? That is, what kinds of traits and qualities do you have as a male or female?

2. To what extent are you similar and different from your same-sex parent? Describe that parent. If you didn't grow up with a same-sex parent, describe the person who you believe was most influential in shaping your ideas.

3. What messages did you get from your parents about appropriate traits? What kinds of things did they encourage? Discourage?

4. What school experiences do you recall that shaped your development?

5. Who are some of the same-sex people you admire, and some that you dislike, on television? How do you think they influenced you?

6. What is your ideal for someone of your sex? To what extent are you like your ideal?

7. How do you think you will continue to develop? What can you do to further your development along the lines you desire?

If the entire class does this project, it would be useful to have a few males and a few females share their projects. Compare and contrast the male with the female accounts.

who hold to more nontraditional gender roles are more likely than others to delay marriage, go to college, and pursue a career (Cardoza 1991).

With such changes in attitudes, we would expect some changes in gender-role orientations. Evidence exists that orientations are changing, and the change seems to be in the direction of increasing androgyny (Pedersen and Bond 1985). In the study of female freshmen noted in this section, although an increasing proportion affirmed achievement goals, there was no decrease in the value placed on domestic and nurturing goals (Fiorentine 1988). On the other hand, we should not assume that androgyny means nontraditionalism. A study of black women reported that while the majority had androgynous gender-role orientations, they tended to retain traditional beliefs about the female role in the family (Binion 1990).

Lingering Traditionalism

Traditional roles are not dead. Recall the occupational sex ratios (table 3.1), the reactions of people at horror movies, and the fact that women who work still bear the brunt of the responsibility for housework and child-rearing. Women tend to be more egalitarian than men in their views (King and King 1985). But both men and women show some evidence of lingering traditionalism. Using data from a national survey, South and Spitze (1994) looked at time spent on housework in six situations: never married and living with parents, never married and living independently, cohabiting, married, divorced, and widowed. Women spend more time than men on housework in all six situations, and married women spend the most time of all! Moreover, when there is an adult son living at home the woman's time increases, while an adult daughter at home decreases housework time for the parents or woman. And a survey of 139 men reported that those who felt that their earnings alone could enable the family to meet all of its financial obligations if necessary had less marital conflict and less depression than those who felt their earnings were inadequate (Crowley 1998). In other words, many husbands—even if they support their wives having employment outside the home—still want to have the capability to be the sole breadwinner for their family.

Lingering traditionalism is also seen in attitudes. Results from a sample of one hundred middle-school and one hundred college students showed little difference between the younger and older students regarding female gender roles (Mills and Mills 1996). Both groups of students were more likely to pick out a male rather than a female face when asked to identify the "famous" person in a group. And a survey of 3,300 university students found that while both men and women identified an androgynous woman as ideal, men identified a masculine sex-typed man as ideal (Street, Kimmel, and Kromrey 1995). Moreover, while the men tended to view themselves as androgynous, the women viewed themselves as feminine in gender-role orientation. The researchers concluded that little change had occurred in students' gender-role perceptions from a study conducted fifteen years earlier.

Clearly, there is a good deal of traditionalism even while some change is also in evidence. What difference does it make whether gender-role orientations change or remain the same? Let us look at the impact of orientations on our behavior and well-being.

GENDER-ROLE ORIENTATION: WHAT DIFFERENCE DOES IT MAKE?

What difference do you think it would make in your life if you were the opposite sex? Clearly, it would make some significant differences. Important differences depend on your gender-role orientation.

Communication

We have seen that women tend to have a different conversational style than men. There are also differences, however, depending on your gender-role orientation. Individuals of both sexes who have a masculine orientation are likely to talk more in small groups (Jose and McCarthy 1988). Those with a masculine orientation are also more likely to overlap or interrupt the speech of someone else (Drass 1986).

More importantly, gender-role orientation affects such things as our ability to handle conflict and the way in which we will try to influence someone. With regard to conflict, Yelsma and Brown (1985) found gender-role orientation to be more important than sex. They studied ninety-one married couples and found that androgynous and masculine spouses tended to handle conflict more constructively than feminine spouses.

With regard to influence, a variety of tactics can be used. *Manipulation* involves such things as dropping hints, flattering someone, and behaving seductively. *Supplication* includes pleading, crying, and acting helpless. *Bullying* is the use of threats, insults, and ridicule. *Autocracy* refers to such things as insisting and asserting one's authority. *Bargaining* involves reasoning and the willingness to compromise. Finally, *disengagement* is withdrawing in some way (sulking, leaving the scene).

In a study of 235 intimate couples, researchers found that more feminine spouses are more likely to use supplication, while more masculine spouses tend to avoid both supplication and bargaining (Howard, Blumstein, and Schwartz 1986). Supplication is a relatively weak tactic. Thus, those with a feminine orientation are less likely to be influential and more likely to be influenced by a partner.

Self-Concept

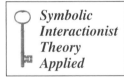

Symbolic Interactionist Theory Applied

Symbolic interactionists define **self-concept** as the totality of the beliefs and attitudes you have about yourself. Your self-concept is important because the way you think about yourself is an integral part of your psychological health. You can't be a healthy individual if you don't think well of yourself and if you don't have a high degree of self-esteem.

Who is likely to have the higher self-esteem? The research consistently indicates that both males and females who are high in masculine traits have higher self-esteem than others. Adolescents who score high on masculinity see themselves as more socially and physically competent and have higher self-esteem scores than those low on masculinity (Cate and Sugawara 1986). Among adult women, masculinity is a better predictor of self-esteem than a woman's educational or occupational achievements (Long 1986).

Four things are important to keep in mind here. First, androgynous as well as masculine people score high on masculinity. The point is that it is the masculinity, rather than the androgyny per se, that makes the difference. Second, masculinity refers to the perception of traits that are associated with the traditional male role, that is, to instrumental traits. Masculinity and femininity are unfortunate choices for terms, because we are not saying that a masculine gender-orientation in a woman means that she is any less of a woman or that she is "mannish." Rather, a masculine orientation for either males or females simply means the possession of such traits as independence, being active rather than passive, competitiveness, and the ability to make decisions. Third, such traits understandably lead to high self-esteem because they are highly valued in American culture. They are the traits that are believed necessary for success in any venture. And fourth, having such traits does not mean that the individual lacks kindness or sensitivity or a willingness to be helpful.

Mental Health

Earlier, some researchers expected psychological health to be highest when there was congruence between gender and gender-role orientation (males would be masculine and females would be feminine in their orientation). Research shows that is not true. Others expected androgynous people to have the best mental health. That also appears to be untrue. Rather, masculinity tends to be associated with such things as high self-esteem, high levels of adjustment, subjective well-being, and less depression and anxiety (Markstrom-Adams 1989; Harris and Schwab 1990; Kleinplatz, McCarrey, and Kateb 1992; Williams and D'Alessandro 1994; Obeidallah, McHale and Silbereisen 1996).

Again, keep in mind the meaning of masculinity here as discussed. It is the instrumental traits that are important. For instance, two psychologists who studied stress and coping reactions among 211 undergraduates also found that a high masculine orientation is an advantage (Nezu and Nezu 1987). The high-masculine subjects had significantly lower levels of depression and anxiety. Compared to low-masculine subjects, they rated their problem-solving ability as more effective; engaged in more active and fewer avoidance methods of coping with stress; and engaged in more problem-focused and less emotion-focused coping styles.

Are, then, the feminine traits a handicap? The answer is no, because androgynous individuals have both the masculine and feminine traits and the same advantages as masculine types in terms of self-concept and mental health. Is there, then, any advantage at all to androgyny? We would say there is. The expressive traits can help with social adjustment by increasing interpersonal skills (Payne 1987). Some researchers continue to find that expressive traits, though to a lesser degree than the instrumental, make some contribution to our mental health (Stoppard and Paisley 1987). In a sample of one hundred elderly subjects, those who were androgynous were significantly more satisfied with life (Dean-Church and Gilroy 1993). Research on the adjustment of women to the death of a spouse reported that androgynous widows had a more positive adjustment than those who were feminine, masculine, or undifferentiated (Solie and Fielder 1987/1988). Finally, a study of 412 French-speaking Canadian women who gave birth found a positive relationship between androgyny on the one hand and self-esteem and satisfaction with social support on the other (Berthiaume et al. 1996). Social support, in turn, lessened the chances of postpartum depression.

GENDER-ROLE ORIENTATION AND INTIMACY

Gender-role orientation may be more important than whether one is male or female in explaining differences in relating to someone intimately. Three researchers surveyed 286 undergraduates and found differences between males and females in their love styles (Bailey, Hendrick, and Hendrick 1987). But they found more and stronger effects for gender-role orientation. Androgynous subjects were more likely and undifferentiated subjects less likely than others to endorse physical and sexual aspects of love. Masculine subjects gave the strongest support and feminine subjects gave the weakest to a view of love as enjoyable and noncommittal. Feminine and androgynous subjects gave strong support to an unselfish love that is concerned with the other's well-being. Masculine and undifferentiated subjects were the most and feminine subjects the least permissive in their sexual attitudes.

Androgynous people tend to be more aware and expressive of love feelings.

Other research underscores the importance of gender-role orientation for intimate love relationships. Androgyny facilitates the development of close friendships (Jones, Bloys, and Wood 1990). It is also associated with the awareness and expression of love feelings and with greater comfort in dating and sexual situations (Ganong and Coleman 1987; Quackenbush 1990).

With such differences, we would expect people to have varying degrees of satisfaction in their relationships depending on their gender-role orientations and the combination of orientations in the couple. Indeed, in a study of 331 couples, Bowen (1987) found that those with the lowest levels of marital adjustment were couples in which the husband was traditional and the wife more modern in gender-role orientation. Lye and Biblarz (1993), using national data, reported that those less satisfied with their marriages are husbands and wives who differ on their attitudes and those with nontraditional attitudes toward family life. Finally, marital satisfaction reflects not just the orientation, but whether that has been a stable or a changing orientation. A study of changing gender roles over an eight-year period found that wives who become less traditional perceive a decline in their marital quality while husbands who become less traditional perceive an increase in marital quality (Amato and Booth 1995).

PERSONAL
"We Worked It Out"

Gender roles and gender-role orientations can change over time both in a society and in an individual's life. Marcie, for example, is a middle-aged woman who began her married life as a traditional wife and mother. She stayed at home and raised her family. When the last of her four children began school, Marcie felt the need to do something more. Because her husband, David, was also traditional in his views, they went through periods of struggle before, as Marcie put it, they finally "worked it out":

I was only thirty-five when my last child started school. The first thought that hit me was that I could now go to college. Maybe I could have a career. I knew I had to do something. At first, David couldn't understand why I was so restless. He argued that the kids still needed me at home. He particularly wanted me to be there when they got home from school. I agreed with this, but I told him that I could take night classes. He was appalled.

Eventually, though, he agreed that one class at night was not unreasonable. But after the first semester, I wanted to take two classes. This made him angry again. I pointed out that I would be an old woman before I ever finished my degree. He said that he and the kids would never see me if I took on more. I suggested that we ask the children how they felt about it. We did, and he was really surprised when they all supported my wishes.

Eventually, I found that I could take a combination of day and night classes and still be home when the children came in from school. Our next struggle was over housework. I told David that I needed his help. He had never done housework. I guess he saw how happy I was working on my degree, so he agreed. But he wouldn't take any initiative. I had to tell him everything to do. And he didn't do things right. Finally, we worked that out. I gave him a list of specific tasks he needed to do each week. He agreed to do them, and I agreed not to complain about the way he did them.

I'm about to graduate now. I have a couple of prospects for jobs. We've already talked about how we can each manage to work and still take care of the children's needs. I'm excited about going to work. I loved being a traditional wife and mom. But now I love the idea of being a working mom. Fortunately, David has changed his views as much as I have. So our marriage and our family are both stronger than ever.

PRINCIPLES FOR ENHANCING INTIMACY

1. Although traditionally many vocations and professions have been closed to them, women should no longer be deterred from pursuing what they most want to do. When women are given the same opportunities as men, they perform as well as men at most tasks.

2. The skills of effective communication and interaction with others can be learned. And because they are more proficient in these skills, women provide appropriate models of behavior for men.

3. If you should choose a behavior or way of life that goes beyond the traditional norms of how a male or female should act, realize that you may encounter criticism. Even though our ideas about sex roles have expanded, many people still react to others on the basis of traditional expectations.

4. An important way to gain self-esteem is to cultivate the traits—such as independence, decisiveness, and competitiveness—that are typically labeled masculine.

5. Those traits—warmth, caring, sensitivity, and nurturance—that are traditionally labeled as female are as appropriate for men as they are for women. These traits help people meet their needs for intimacy. Remember that most of the traits that we generally label as masculine or feminine are not innate but learned.

SUMMARY

Both similarities and differences exist between men and women. Both have some of the same fundamental needs, and both respond to some situations in similar ways. The differences include superior verbal ability of females and superior spatial and quantitative ability of males; a greater proportion of men who are highly aggressive; more interpersonal skills among females; and better ability by females to interpret nonverbal cues.

We need to distinguish between sex (biological males and females), gender (social males and females), gender role (behavior associated with being male or female), and gender-role orientation (conception of the self as having some combination of male and female traits). The traditional gender roles suggest that men are strong, independent, aggressive, and logical, while women are gentle, dependent, nurturing, and emotional. Your gender-role orientation may be masculine (primarily instrumental traits), feminine (primarily expressive traits), androgynous (high on both masculine and feminine traits), or undifferentiated (low on both kinds of traits).

Whether gender roles reflect nature or nurture is a matter of controversy. Evidence from biologists and psychologists as well as cross-cultural studies indicate that most of the traits and behaviors identified as masculine or feminine are not innate, but reflect social factors such as socialization. We have gender-related tendencies, but these can be modified by social factors. Our gender-role orientation is also social, the result of socialization by the family, school, and media.

Gender roles and gender-role orientations change over time. People are becoming less traditional in their attitudes about gender roles. There is some lingering traditionalism, however, that affects both attitudes and behavior.

Gender-role orientations make a difference in various areas of our lives, including the way we communicate, our self-concepts, and our mental health. Androgynous people have a number of advantages over others, although for some things such as mental health it is the masculine component that leads to the advantage. Gender-role orientations also affect intimacy and the extent of satisfaction with intimate relationships.

INTERNET CONNECTION
Gender Roles: Foundations of Heterosexual Intimacy

Gender roles and gender identity play an integral part in the personal and economic socialization of individuals. Cultural perceptions concerning traditional gender roles go far beyond who cooks dinner or cleans the house. Gender inequity in economic occupations and social roles play pivotal roles in global issues like the environment and overpopulation. The United Nations and other organizations have established commissions and task forces on women and gender to address these issues.

www.mhhe
.com/lauer4

Commission on the Status of Women
http://www.un.org/womenwatch/daw/csw/

The Commission on the Status of Women (CSW) was established as a functional commission of the Economic and Social Council to prepare recommendations and reports on promoting women's rights in political, economic, civil, social, and educational fields. The commission also makes recommendations to the council on urgent problems requiring immediate attention in the field of women's rights. The object of the commission is to promote implementation of the principle that men and women shall have equal rights.

UNDP Gender in Development Programm
http://www.undp.org/gender/

This program is designed to facilitate gender equity through UN-initiated research, policies, and programs to achieve gender equality on a global level.

Consult the websites above to answer the following questions:

1. What can you learn about gender, inequality, and economic development from an examination of these two websites. Why is this commission and this program needed?
2. What is "gender mainstreaming"? Why is it needed? How does it help developing countries?
3. How are these organizations within the UN helping to enact changes on a global level?

SEXUALITY

Learning Objectives

After reading chapter 4, you should be able to:

1. Relate the meaning of sex as both a physical and a social phenomenon.
2. Describe the impact of sex on intimate relationships.
3. Discuss the extent of teenage sex and the consequences of early childbearing.
4. Explain the various methods of contraception, the degree to which they are used, and by whom.
5. Outline the role and the practices of sex in marriage.
6. Identify the changing patterns of marital sex.
7. Review the functions and consequences of extramarital sex.
8. Describe the nature and consequences of the major sexually transmitted diseases.
9. Outline the primary types of sexual dysfunction.
10. Summarize the important guidelines for engaging in safe sex.

What is the most intense form of human intimacy? Some people would answer "sex." But sex can be alienating as well as bonding, meaningless as well as exhilarating. Even when it is highly gratifying, sex may not hold a relationship together. Hank got married when he was in his early thirties. When we discussed his impending marriage with him, he told us that he knew it would require a lot of work because he and his future wife had a lot of differences. "What do you have in common?" we asked. The only thing Hank could think of was: "We have great sex together." Hank's marriage was built on little else. Within a year after the marriage, Hank and his wife were divorced. "Great sex" didn't make a lasting marriage.

In this chapter we will look at the meaning of sex and how it affects our relationships. We will examine some of the problems involved with teenage sex, including unwanted pregnancies. We will discuss such issues as contraception, abortion, sexual diseases and dysfunctions, and extramarital sex. And we will see the role of sex in marriage, including long-term marriage.

THE MEANING OF SEX

In our discussion of sex roles, we pointed out that humans are social as well as biological creatures.

For many kinds of behavior, being born a male or female is not as important as the society in which you live and the way in which you think of yourself. Similarly, we shall see that sex, one of the strong drives in humans, is not merely a biological phenomenon. Sexually, we are social as well as biological creatures. We need to examine both aspects of sexuality.

Sex As Physical: The Response Cycle

In the 1960s, William Masters and Virginia Johnson pioneered the investigation of the responses of the body to sexual intercourse. The researchers identified four stages of human sexual response: excitement, plateau, orgasm, and resolution (Masters, Johnson, and Kolodny 1988:80–95). During the response, there are two basic physiological reactions. One involves an increased concentration of blood in bodily tissues in the genitals and the female breasts. The other is increased energy in the nerves and muscles throughout the body.

Excitement, the first stage of arousal, is the result of some kind of physical or psychological stimulation. You can become excited by someone stroking your body, by kissing, by reading erotic literature, by having someone look at you seductively, by remembering a previous sexual experience, by fantasizing about sex, and so on. In the woman, along with various other physiological changes, excitement leads to **vaginal** lubrication, usually within ten to thirty seconds. In the man, similar physiological reactions result in erection of the **penis,** usually within three to eight seconds in young males.

The excitement stage may or may not lead to the next phase. Something may interfere with continued response, such as a telephone ringing, something that the partner says or does, or a thought that suddenly comes into your mind. But if the process continues, you move into the second stage, the *plateau.* As figure 4.1 shows, in the plateau stage there is a continuing high level of arousal, preparing the way for orgasm. The actual length of the plateau varies from individual to individual. For men who have trouble controlling **ejaculation,** the plateau may be extremely short. For women, a brief plateau sometimes precedes an intense orgasm. Others find a longer plateau to be a kind of sexual high that is very satisfying.

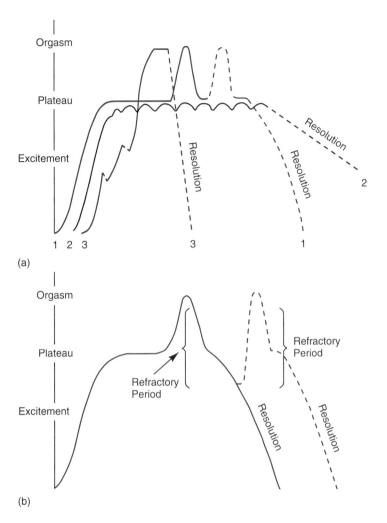

(a) Three types of female response. Pattern 1 is multiple orgasm. Pattern 2 is arousal without orgasm. Pattern 3 involves a number of small declines in excitement and a very rapid resolution.

(b) The typical male pattern of response. The dotted line indicates the possibility of a second orgasm and ejaculation after the refractory period.

FIGURE 4-1　The Sexual Response Cycle
(William H. Masters and Virginia E. Johnson, *Human Sexual Response* (Boston: Little, Brown, 1966), p. 5. Reprinted by permission.)

Both men and women continue to experience physiological changes during the plateau. The woman's vagina becomes increasingly moist and the tissues swell with blood. The portion of the vagina nearest the opening becomes so congested that the penis tends to be gripped because of the reduced size of the vaginal opening. The back part of the vagina opens up and out to accommodate the erect penis. In the male, the penis is fully erect, the **testes** are fluid-swollen, enlarged, and pulled up closer to the body. During the plateau stage, both males and females have increased heart rates, faster breathing, and increased blood pressure.

Orgasm, the third stage, is a discharge of the sexual tension that has been built up and maintained during the plateau. The orgasm takes the least time of any of the stages. Usually it involves muscular contractions and intense physical feelings that occur in the matter of a few seconds and are followed by rapid relaxation. Again, there are physiological changes that occur in both men and women. In both, there is a good deal of involuntary muscular contraction throughout the body. Sometimes the contractions happen in the facial muscles, making the face appear to be frowning or in pain. But normally such an expression reflects a high level of arousal, rather than any pain or displeasure.

Women may have anywhere from three to fifteen muscular contractions during orgasm. These contractions occur in various muscles throughout their bodies. They also have changes in their brain wave patterns. Women may have multiple orgasms if they have continuing stimulation and interest (pattern 1 in figure 4.1). For men, orgasm occurs in two distinct phases. In the first phase, muscular contractions force **semen** through the penis. The man experiences a sense of having gotten to the point where he can no longer control himself; ejaculation is inevitable. In the second phase, additional muscular contractions lead to ejaculation.

Following orgasm, there is a **refractory period** for the male, a time following orgasm in which the individual needs to recover and is incapable of having an additional orgasm or ejaculation. The refractory period may last anywhere from minutes to hours. As the male ages, the refractory period gets longer. For the male, the refractory period is part of the fourth stage, *resolution.* Resolution is a return to a state of being sexually unaroused. In both males and females, the various physiological changes reverse and the individual becomes like he or she was prior to arousal. If the individual has been highly aroused without orgasm having occurred, the resolution will take longer.

Sex As Social

Although sex is one of the basic drives in humans, the expression of sex is still a social phenomenon. That is, we learn how to behave as sexual beings. Despite the notion that sex involves "doing what comes naturally," there is more learned than unlearned sexual activity. Even the meaning of sex is learned, and what you learn depends on when and where you live. In the United States, for instance,

Sex is an important part of intimacy.

the dominant notions about sex from colonial days through the nineteenth to the twentieth centuries changed from "a decorous enjoyment to a morbid suppression to an uneasy liberation" (Lauer and Lauer 1983:20). Nineteenth-century Americans would be shocked by the views of both their forebears and their progeny. And the frank statement of the wife who said "I get irritable when I don't have sex. Sex makes me feel good about myself and my marriage" would not have been made openly in earlier generations. Nor would it be made openly in some societies today. Your views about sex and your sexual activity are shaped by your social context. In American society today, most adults find sexual relations to be a significant aspect of a fulfilled life.

Both gender roles and gender-role orientation affect sexual activity. For example, in our society men are more often the initiators of sexual activity even though women respond positively to initiations as frequently as men do (O'Sullivan and Byers 1992). Men are more permissive than women about casual sex (Oliver and Hyde 1993). Men tend to begin sexual relations at a slightly earlier age (16–17) than do women (17–18) (Seidman and Rieder 1994). And it is more of a stigma for a woman than a man to be sexually promiscuous. In some cases, a woman may resist sex because she doesn't want to appear to be promiscuous (Muehlenhard and Hollabaugh 1988). We should note that this does not mean that a woman really means "yes" even though she says "no." A man should always take a woman's "no" as a serious statement of her desire. If she is only hesitating because she doesn't want to appear promiscuous, it is her responsibility to let that be known, not the man's to assume this.

Gender-role orientations may also influence sexual behavior. Although there has not been much research, one study reported that the masculine gender-role orientation for both men and women was associated with more frequent sexual intercourse (Leary and Snell 1988). Those scoring high on instrumental traits also tended to have more oral sex and more relaxed feelings about sex.

Thus, a variety of factors affect our sexual behavior. There are variations in behavior both within and between societies. Differences in arousal, techniques, and the experience of unwanted sex further underscore the social nature of our sexual behavior.

Variations in Sexual Activity   There is enormous variation in the extent to which people in differing societies and within a particular society are aroused. Levels of sexual activity between societies vary from the extremely low level of the Grand Valley Dani to the unusually high level of the people of Mangaia (both groups are in the South Pacific) (Lauer and Lauer 1983:5–6). The Dani do not begin to have sexual relations until about two years after marriage. Weddings are held only about once each four to six years. The frequency of sexual relations is so low that the population is barely maintained. A couple will abstain from sex for four to six years after the birth of a child. Moreover, there is little extramarital sex, and no evidence of homosexuality or masturbation. The Dani simply seem to have little interest.

By contrast, sex is a principal interest among the Mangaians. Nearly all, both male and female, have considerable premarital experience with a variety of partners. The Mangaians claim that a typical eighteen-year-old male will have, on the average, three orgasms per night each night of the week. A twenty-eight-year-old male will have about two orgasms per night, five to six times each week. In their late forties, males have an orgasm two to three times a week.

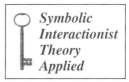

Symbolic Interactionist Theory Applied

From a *symbolic interactionist* point of view, there are no sexual techniques that are inherently more appealing than others. What matters is how people define those techniques. Thus, you probably regard mouth-to-mouth kissing as erotic. The Mangaians did not regard it as such until Westerners influenced them. Most Americans regard foreplay as essential to satisfying sex. In other societies, however, foreplay varies from being virtually absent to consuming even more time than it does among Americans (Ford and Beach 1951:41).

The preferred position for intercourse also varies from one society to another. Among the Trobriand Islanders, the man squats and draws the woman toward him until her legs rest on his hips or his elbows. Islanders maintain that this position gives the man considerable freedom of movement and that it does not inhibit the woman in her movements of response (Malinowski 1932:285).

There are also different preferences within a society. A national survey of Americans reported that receiving oral sex is appealing to about half of men and a third of women (Laumann et al. 1994). The same survey found that 37 percent of men and 19 percent of women like to give oral sex. Clearly, people differ in the sexual behavior that they prefer and in which they are willing to engage.

Such diversity underscores the fact that sexual behavior is learned. What is defined as erotic by some people may be defined as disgusting by others. What is defined as good and pleasurable by some will be defined as evil by others. Social factors are powerful, and they may modify, facilitate, or suppress the expression of the sex drive.

Unwanted Sex   In an ideal world, there would be reciprocal desire between two people. People in love would desire sexual relations with each other at the same time. In the real world, there is a good deal of unwanted sex, sex that occurs when the individual is not aroused and does not want to engage in the activity. It is not always our sex drive that is at work when we have sexual relations.

How many people engage in unwanted sex? It appears that the experience is fairly common and begins early in life. A survey of Los Angeles

Nearly everyone experiences some unwanted sexual activity.

students in grades six through twelve found that 15 percent had some kind of unwanted sexual experience; 39 percent of the experiences occurred when the young person was age twelve or younger (Erickson and Rapkin 1991). Another survey, of 1,149 females in grades seven, nine, and eleven, found that 21 percent admitted some kind of unwanted sexual contact in the past year, and over a third of these said the unwanted contact was forced intercourse (Small and Kerns 1993). Using national data, three researchers found that about a fourth of women who had intercourse at age thirteen or younger reported the experience as nonvoluntary, as did 10 percent of those who were between nineteen and twenty-four years of age at first intercourse (Abma, Driscoll, and Moore 1998). Such forced sex can have long-term adverse consequences for women. A comparison of adolescents who had ex-

FIGURE 4-2   Reasons for Agreeing to Unwanted Sexual Activity
(Source: Data from C. L. Muehlenhard and S. W. Cook, *The Journal of Sex Research,* 24:65, 1988.

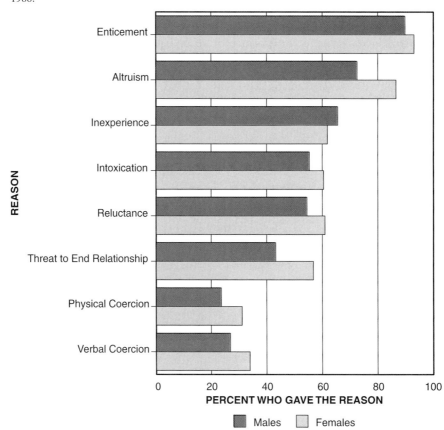

INVOLVEMENT
Sex and Society

As we look at sexual beliefs and practices throughout the world we find both similarities with and differences from our own society. Investigate some kinds of sexual beliefs and/or practices in another society that differ from those in your society (e.g., frequency and/or positions of intercourse, the meaning of sex, attitudes about premarital and/or extramarital sex, what techniques and practices are considered erotic, etc.). Compare them with your society and with your personal values. How do you feel about the beliefs and/or practices of the other society? Do you think that they are more or less preferable to those of your own? Why?

One way to carry on your investigation is through the library. You can check journals, such as the *Journal of Sex Research.* Or you can use the *Social Science Index* or *Psychological Abstracts* to locate appropriate articles. Studies by anthropologists are also excellent sources.

Another way to carry on the investigation is to interview someone from another country. If that person is willing to discuss the topic with you, ask him or her to describe sexual attitudes and/or behavior in some area such as premarital sex or sexual techniques.

If the entire class engages in this project, each student could be responsible for a different society. Discuss the findings in terms of the questions given in the first and second columns.

---

perienced early forced intercourse with those who had not found the former to be more depressed and anxious, lower in self-esteem, and more likely to use drugs and engage in delinquent activities (Lanz 1995).

Interestingly, men also report unwanted sexual activity. In their study of 507 men and 486 women in introductory psychology classes, Muehlenhard and Cook (1988) found that 97.5 percent of the women and 93.5 percent of the men had experienced unwanted sexual activity (kissing, petting, intercourse). More men (62.7 percent) than women (46.3 percent) said that they had experienced unwanted intercourse. What were the reasons they gave for yielding to the pressures? There were many, but the most common was enticement (figure 4.2), some kind of seductive behavior on the part of the other person. The other person may have started taking off his or her clothes, for example, or aroused the enticed person by touching him or her. "Altruism," another common reason, includes such things as knowing the partner wants the activity and engaging in it in order to satisfy the partner's needs even though you are not in the mood. "Inexperience" means agreeing to the activity not from desire but from a sense that you need to have the experience. "Reluctance" refers to being with someone and not knowing anything else to do, wanting to make the other feel attractive, or feeling obligated because the person has spent time and money on you. According to their self-reports, both males and females engage in a certain amount of kissing, petting, and even intercourse for such reasons.

SEX AND INTIMATE RELATIONSHIPS

Human love, according to Erich Fromm (1956), does not reflect a Freudian sexual instinct. Rather, Fromm argued, sexual desire reflects the human need for love and union. In other words, the need for intimacy has primacy over sex. We agree that intimacy is a more fundamental need than the need for sex. The sex drive is strong, and we need to find some outlet for sexual tension. But that tension can be dealt with in ways other than sexual intercourse, if necessary. There are, after all, healthy celibates. You can be celibate and be fulfilled. But you cannot be fulfilled without intimacy.

Sexual relations, then, may be seen as one way to fulfill intimacy needs (Sprecher and McKinney 1983:100–102). Some people have sex simply for the sake of sex. But a number of experts have argued that sex without intimacy, like the casual sex of the one-night stand, is of little or no value (Fromm 1956). At best, casual sex fails to fulfill our intimacy needs. At worst, it leaves us feeling more empty and lonely than we were before the experience. Instead of enhancing the quality of our intimate lives, sex without intimacy can become an impediment to the development of relationships that add to our well-being (Cobliner 1988) (see PERSONAL).

Actually, most people seem to sense the fact that sex needs to be an expression of an intimate relationship. Most Americans, for example, do not approve of **promiscuity,** frequent and indiscriminate sexual relations with many partners. Nor do they want to establish a relationship with someone who has been promiscuous. Most men prefer sexual intercourse within a caring relationship. In fact, a national survey found that 71 percent of men report difficulty having sex without an emotional involvement with the partner (Clements 1994). Similarly, women tend to enjoy intercourse only in the context of both a committed and a caring relationship (McCabe 1987).

Sexual activity is a natural expression of feelings of intimacy. In fact, sex never ages. In most societies, people continue to have sexual relations throughout life. A study of 202 men and women, ages 80 to 102, reported various kinds of sexual activity (Bretschneider and McCoy 1988). Nearly two-thirds of the men and a third of the women were having sexual intercourse, ranging from once a year to once a day. The majority engaged in some kind of caressing and touching. The national survey mentioned above found that men and women in the 55 to 65 age bracket have intercourse an average five times per month (Clements 1994). People are likely to continue sexual intimacy as long as they are healthy and have a partner.

TEENAGE SEX

Pregnancy and sexually transmitted diseases (including AIDS) have been increasing among teenagers, with black teenagers more vulnerable than others to both (Demb 1990). How many teenagers have sex, and at what age do they start? What are some of the consequences of being sexually active as a teenager?

Extent of Sex Among Teenagers

The majority of teenagers become sexually active between the ages of sixteen and nineteen. The proportion declined, however, in the 1995 national survey for the first time in two decades (Abma et al.

Many sexually active teenagers do not use birth control measures.

1997). The survey found that half of women fifteen to nineteen years of age had engaged in sexual intercourse, compared with 55 percent in 1990. The proportion was 29 percent in 1970. The proportion of males also declined, from 60 percent in 1988 to 55 percent in 1995.

The probability of being sexually active varies by a number of factors including racial/ethnic groups. The proportion of fifteen to nineteen year old never-married women who had engaged in sexual relations varied from 47.1 percent of non-Hispanic whites to 52 percent of Hispanics to 58.3 percent of non-Hispanic blacks (Abma et al. 1997). Among all races, adolescents who are sexually active, compared to those who are not, are more likely to rarely attend church, live with only one parent or have a problematic relationship with parents, use drugs (including tobacco and alcohol), and be in the lower socioeconomic strata (Miller and Olson 1988; Holmbeck, Waters, and Brookman 1990; Dorius,

PERSONAL
Sex and the Search for Intimacy

Charles, a young single man, has tried for years to find a fulfilling intimacy solely through sex. He shares with us the conclusions he has reached in his twenty-eighth year:

> While I was in college, I lived on campus for two years. I was really promiscuous. I had sex relations with many women. I thoroughly enjoyed it. I thought of myself as a real stud, and I enjoyed the envy of some of my male friends. In time, my sexual experiences had an unexpected and interesting effect on me. I discovered that my so-called manhood, though sexually fulfilled, lacked a quality of intimacy that became more profound as my need for emotional closeness increased. I had thought that what I—and any real man—needed was a lot of good sex. But the more sex I

had, the more I came to realize that something was missing. I would never have believed it a few years earlier, but one day I admitted to myself that sex wasn't enough. I wanted to have something more with a woman than her body.

Unfortunately, I had gotten the label of being a "player." So it became more and more difficult to develop closeness in a relationship. The women I wanted to go out with had the idea that I was a shallow person only looking for a good time. My reputation was established, and it was keeping me from developing the intimacy that I now yearned for. The only women who were interested were the ones just like me. Or just like I used to be. They didn't even appeal to me anymore.

I couldn't do anything until I moved away. After graduation, I

went to work in another city. I knew I had to change my lifestyle. I decided to play it cool with women. I was still hot to trot. I really missed having sex. But I finally realized that it wasn't going to help me to keep on the way I had been in college. I wanted to make love and please myself and my lover. But more than that, I wanted to emotionally caress a woman and understand her and relate to her. And I wanted her to do that to me as well.

I'm in a kind of limbo right now. I have dated some women, and I am starting to develop a relationship with one that I think may lead to what I need. In any case, I know that I can't let sex be a deterrent to intimacy anymore. I know what I need. And I know that I can't get it in a one-night stand.

Heaton, and Steffen 1993; Whitbeck, Conger, and Kao 1993; Whitbeck, Conger, Simons, and Kao 1993).

Unwanted Pregnancy and Early Childbearing

One of the consequences of teenage sex is a high rate of unwanted pregnancies and giving birth at an early age. Teen birth rates, like teen sex, declined in the 1990s (National Center for Health Statistics 1998). They declined for all racial/ethnic groups and declined dramatically for black teens. Still, around one million teenagers give birth each year, the majority of them unmarried. The pregnancy rate of American teenagers is five times greater than those of other industrialized nations (Nakkab 1997).

Many teenagers give birth to children who are unwanted at the time of conception, in part because of the mother being unmarried. But married people

also bear children who are unwanted at the time of conception. The fact that a child is not wanted at the time of conception does not mean that the child is still unwanted at birth, of course. But we can justly wonder about the well-being of the children who remain unwanted at birth.

Why Pregnancy? Birth control measures are readily available in most communities. Why, then, do so many teenagers get pregnant? First, no contraceptive is foolproof. Failure rates during the first year of use vary from a low of 8 percent for users of the pill to 15 percent for condom users and 25 percent for users of spermicides (Jones and Forrest 1992). Second, the failure to *use* birth control is a significant factor in many teenage pregnancies (Roosa et al. 1997; Trent and Crowder 1997). Birth control measures are readily available, but the sex may be an unplanned response to the strong drive of teenagers. Or the teenagers may be too embarrassed or too poor to purchase birth control measures. Or they may believe that using such things as condoms reduces pleasure.

Third, not all teenagers find the prospect of pregnancy to be unsettling. While the majority of teenage women who become mothers say they did not intend it, about 7.5 percent of the female adolescents in a national survey indicated that they *expected* to bear a child in adolescence out of wedlock (Trent and Crowder 1997). Those more likely to have such an expectation came from families that were Black or Hispanic rather than non-Hispanic white, poor rather than nonpoor, and single-parent rather than two-parent.

Why would they want to get pregnant out of wedlock? Many of them have troubled childhoods. In a small sample of whites and Mexican Americans, half had lost a parent during their childhood years (de Anda, Becerra, and Fielder 1990). A study of 535 young women reported that two-thirds of those who became pregnant had been sexually abused (Boyer and Fine 1992). With such experiences, they may feel isolated and alone and that a baby is the one way to find someone to love. Others may use pregnancy to get attention, to assert their independence from their parents, or, particularly for those in the lower socioeconomic strata, to do something creative in a world of very limited opportunities.

Fourth, certain parental attitudes and behaviors can significantly reduce the likelihood of out-of-wedlock pregnancy (Hanson, Myers, and Ginsburg 1987). Among white girls, the likelihood of pregnancy is less if they feel that they have control over their lives, they have high educational aspirations, and they have concerned parents who teach them to be responsible and talk with them. Among black girls, the likelihood of pregnancy is less if the parents are concerned about them and have high expectations for their educational achievements.

Finally, among both whites and African Americans, the chances of pregnancy are much higher if the girl is going steady and if she has had discipline problems in school. In essence, then, girls who feel good about themselves, have high expectations and aspirations for their lives, and have good relationships with concerned parents are much less likely to get pregnant than others. This is only partly due to a lower amount of sexual activity. It is also due to a greater probability of using birth control.

Some Consequences of Teenage Births   Whether wanted or not, the children of teenagers differ in important ways from other children. And the parents of those children differ from parents who wait at least until their twenties to have children.

Teenagers who give birth during their high school years are far less likely to complete their high school education than are others. A national study pointed out that teenage families with children are more likely to be poor and fatherless. Teenage parents are more likely to suffer from chronic unemployment, to become dependent on public welfare, and to remain dependent longer than those who delay childbearing.[1] When they do get jobs, they are more likely to get low-paying ones. And it is the female who bears the brunt of these negative consequences. Only a minority marry the father. A third or more of the mothers never see the fathers again. Others see the father some but do not marry him and may get little or no support from him.

The news is not all bad. A study of 1,590 inner-city female adolescents by Stiffman, Earls, Robins, Jung, and Kulbok (1987) shows both the negative and the more hopeful findings. The researchers divided the young women into three groups: those who had ever been pregnant, those who were sexually active but never pregnant, and those who were sexually inactive. The girls ranged in age from thirteen to eighteen. The proportion who were sexually inactive declined, and the proportion of those who had ever been pregnant increased with age. Those who lived with both biological parents were more likely than others to be sexually inactive and less likely to have ever been pregnant. The three groups did not differ on measures of physical health. On mental health, however, there were a number of differences. The sexually active who had never been pregnant had the highest rates of conduct disorder and of anxiety. Those who had ever been pregnant were nearly twice as likely as the sexually inactive to have three or more symptoms of conduct disorder. Finally, the sexually active groups

---

[1]*Family Planning Perspectives* 19 (1987):119.

had higher rates of alcohol and drug abuse and depressive symptoms than those who were sexually inactive.

On the more hopeful side, in addition to having equally good physical health, the females who had ever been pregnant had no greater number of current relationship problems or stressful life events than the never-pregnant group. In other words, while those who are sexually inactive had a higher level of well-being than the others, the never-pregnant sexually active group was not manifestly better off in terms of their current life situation than those who had been pregnant.

But will those who had ever been pregnant acquire additional disadvantages as they grow older? A study over a seventeen-year period of three hundred Baltimore women who had been teenage mothers sheds some light on the question (Furstenberg, Brooks-Gunn, and Morgan 1987). The women did have some long-term negative consequences of their early childbearing, including diminished economic mobility and less likelihood of marriage. When they did marry, they had higher rates of breakup. They were more likely than others to become the heads of households, which meant a greater probability of living in poverty. At the same time, the researchers point out that the situation of some of the mothers improved over time. Some had returned to school, and nearly all had at least part-time work. Two-thirds were not on public assistance. And many had fewer children than they had desired or expected in their earlier years. Thus, women are not doomed to poverty and deprivation if they bear children in their teenage years, but the risks are much higher. And those risks involve the children as well as the parents. The consequences for the children are mostly negative. Those consequences begin early, because among teenage mothers, there are higher rates of infant mortality, a greater probability of birth defects, higher rates of mental retardation, and a greater risk of head and spinal injuries to the infant (Bolton 1980:31). Children born to teenage mothers, particularly those who were unplanned, are at greater risk of abuse and neglect (Klerman 1993). And the children have a greater probability of spending their childhood in poverty and of doing poorly in school.

Clearly, little positive can be said for teenage pregnancy and childbearing. Both parents and children are likely to suffer a wide variety of negative consequences. Your chances for maximizing your well-being and the quality of your intimate relationships are much less if you bear children in your teens.

CONTRACEPTION

Contraception, a method of birth control, is the use of devices or techniques to prevent fertilization. When a couple wants to avoid pregnancy, knowledge and use of effective contraception can enhance sexual pleasure and intensify sexual intimacy by removing the fear of conception. Table 4.1 shows the more common methods, how they work, and some of their benefits and limitations. Three relatively new methods are: injections by the drug Depo-Provera (which provides 99 percent effective protection for three months), Norplant (capsules implanted under the skin of a woman's upper arm, giving protection for about five years), and the female condom (which is less effective than the male condom) (Gillis 1993).

People also try a number of other techniques which have little or no use. For example, some people believe that a woman cannot get pregnant the first time she has intercourse and, therefore, no device need be used. That belief has resulted in many pregnancies. Still others try withdrawal (removing the penis from the vagina before ejaculation) or a vaginal douche immediately after intercourse. These were the two most popular methods in the nineteenth century. Neither is reliable. Even if withdrawal occurs before ejaculation, many men have a leakage of seminal fluid prior to ejaculation that can result in pregnancy. And the vaginal douche, ironically, may actually facilitate pregnancy. Rather than flushing out, the douche may force sperm up into the cervix. Moreover, some of the sperm may have already traveled into the cervix, making the douche useless.

Thus, there are both effective and ineffective methods of contraception. Some of the modern methods may not be quite as ineffective or hazardous as the ancient Egyptian mixture that contained crocodile dung, but people continue to use methods that are not effective. In part, this is due to a lack of education. A substantial proportion of adolescents get no formal sexual education in the years

TABLE 4.1
Methods of Birth Control

Popular Name	Description	Effectiveness (pregnancies per 100 women using method for 1 year)	Advantages	Disadvantages
The pill (oral contraceptive; consultation with physician required)	Contains synthetic hormones (estrogens and progestin) to inhibit ovulation. The body reacts as if pregnancy has occurred and so does not release an egg. No egg—no conception. The pills are usually taken for 20 or 21 consecutive days; menstruation begins shortly thereafter.	Combined pills, 2*	Simple to take, removed from sexual act, highly reliable, reversible. Useful side effects: relief of premenstrual tension, reduction in menstrual flow, regularization of menstruation, relief of acne.	Weight gain (5–50 percent of users), breast enlargement and sensitivity; some users have increased headaches, nausea, and spotting. Increased possibility of vein thrombosis (blood clotting) and slight increase in blood pressure. Must be taken regularly. A causal relationship to cancer can neither be established nor refuted.
IUD (intrauterine device; consultation with physician required)	Metal or plastic object that comes in various shapes and is placed within the uterus and left there. Exactly how it works is not known. Hypotheses are that endocrine changes occur, that the fertilized egg cannot implant in the uterine wall because of irritation, that spontaneous abortion is caused.	3–6	Once inserted, user need do nothing more about birth control. High reliability, reversible, relatively inexpensive. Must be checked periodically to see if still in place.	Insertion procedure requires specialist and may be uncomfortable and painful. Uterine cramping, increased menstrual bleeding. Between 4 and 30 percent are expelled in first year after insertion. Occasional perforation of the uterine wall. Occasional pregnancy that is complicated by the presence of the IUD. Associated with pelvic inflammatory disease.
Diaphragm and jelly (consultation with physician required)	Flexible hemispherical rubber dome inserted into the vagina to block entrance to the cervix, thus providing a barrier to sperm. Usually used with spermicidal cream or jelly.	10–16	Can be left in place up to 24 hours. Reliable, harmless, reversible. Can be inserted up to 2 hours before intercourse.	Disliked by many women because it requires self-manipulation of genitals to insert and is messy because of cream. If improperly fitted, it will fail. Must be refitted periodically, especially after pregnancy. Psychological aversion may make its use inconsistent.
Condom	Thin, strong sheath or cover, usually of latex, worn over the penis to prevent sperm from entering the vagina.	7–14	Simple to obtain and use; free of objectionable side effects. Quality control has improved with government regulation. Protection against various sexually transmitted diseases.	Must be applied just before intercourse. Can slip off, especially after ejaculation when penis returns to flaccid state. Occasional rupture. Interferes with sensation and spontaneity.

Popular Name	Description	Effectiveness (pregnancies per 100 women using method for 1 year)	Advantages	Disadvantages
Chemical methods	Numerous products to be inserted into the vagina to block sperm from the uterus and/or to act as a spermicide. Vaginal foams are creams packed under pressure (like foam shaving cream) and inserted with an applicator. Vaginal suppositories are small cone-shaped objects that melt in the vagina; vaginal tablets also melt in the vagina.	13–17 (More effective when used in conjunction with another method, such as the diaphragm.)	Foams appear to be most effective, followed by creams, jellies, suppositories, tablets. Harmless, simple, reversible, easily available.	Minor irritations and temporary burning sensations. Messy. Must be used just before intercourse and reapplied for each act of intercourse.
Sponge	Small sponge that fits over the cervix, blocking and killing sperm.	9–11	Simple to purchase and use. Can be inserted hours before intercourse and left in place up to 24 hours.	Possible health problems, including toxic shock syndrome and vaginitis. Difficult to remove. May make intercourse dry.
Sterilization	Surgical procedure to make an individual sterile.	Less than 1	Safest method. Does not affect sexual drive. No planning or additional steps before intercourse necessary.	May be irreversible. Possibility of postoperative infections for women.
Withdrawal (coitus interruptus)	Man withdraws penis from vagina before ejaculation of semen.	16–18	Simple, costless, requires no other devices.	Requires great control by the male. Possible semen leakage before ejaculation. Possible psychological reaction against necessary control and ejaculation outside the vagina. May severely limit sexual gratification of both partners.
Natural family planning	Abstinence from intercourse during fertile period each month.	10–29	Approved by the Roman Catholic church. Costless, requires no other devices.	Woman's menstrual period must be regular. Demands accurate date keeping and strong self-control. Difficult to determine fertile period exactly.

Note: Individuals vary in their reaction to contraceptive devices. Advantages and disadvantages listed are general ones.

*If taken regularly pregnancy will not occur. If one or more pills are missed, there is a chance of pregnancy. Combination pills contain both estrogen and progesterone.

Source: U.S. Department of Health and Human Services, *Contraceptive Efficacy among Married Woman Aged 15–44 Years.* Publication no. (PHS) 80–1981 (Hyattsville, MD: U.S. National Center for Health Statistics) 1980, and pamphlets published by Planned Parenthood Federation.

when most are becoming sexually active. Of course, not all who receive the information make use of it. An unwanted pregnancy is a painful experience. Today, there is ample information available; no one need get pregnant out of ignorance.

Amount and Kinds of Contraceptive Use

Although few women desire to get pregnant when they first become sexually active, about a fourth use no contraceptive method (Abma et al. 1997:6). This represents a dramatic decrease since 1980, when half used no method. As sexual activity continues, contraceptive use is even more likely. **Sterilization** is the most commonly used method, followed by the oral contraceptive pill (figure 4.3). The pill is the leading method among women under thirty, while sterilization is the leading method for women aged thirty to forty-four years.

Who Uses Contraceptives?

Who is most likely to use some form of contraception? We can distinguish the groups on the basis of age and other characteristics.

Age Differences As the discussion so far indicates, contraceptive use is less likely among younger people who are sexually active. A national survey found that the proportion of women using some contraceptive method was 29.8 percent of those aged fifteen to nineteen, 63.4 percent of those aged twenty to twenty-four, 69.3 percent of those aged twenty-five to twenty-nine, and nearly 73 percent of those in their thirties (Abma et al. 1997:51). Non-Hispanic whites are most likely, and Hispanics are least likely to use contraceptives, with the proportion of African Americans falling in between the other two groups. Part of the reason for the lower rate of use by the young may be what Burger and Burns (1988) called the "illusion of unique invulnerability." They found that undergraduate women who were sexually active tended to view themselves as less likely than other students or other women to become pregnant. This sense of invulnerability is the same thing that leads people into various kinds of self-destructive behavior. For example, many people who smoke or have an unhealthy diet feel that they will escape the negative consequences of their behavior even though others do not.

Similarly, the young woman who adopts the stance of "I just don't think that I will get pregnant" is less likely to use birth control methods . . . and quite likely to get pregnant.

Some younger people, of course, do use contraceptives, and the proportion is increasing. Younger

FIGURE 4-3 Percent Distribution of Women 15–44 Years of Age Using Contraceptive Metehods (Source: Abma, et al. 1997:52.)

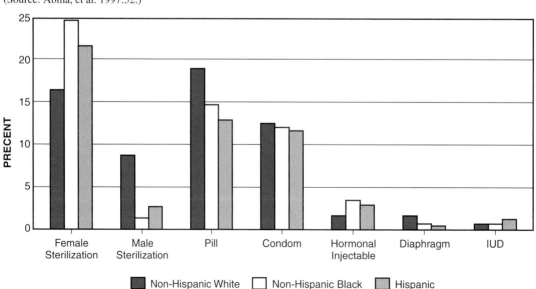

people more likely to use contraceptives are those who have good communication with their parents about sexual matters generally and contraceptives in particular (Kotva and Schneider 1990; Wilson et al. 1994). Peer influence is also important. Those who perceive their peers as using contraceptives are more likely to use them for themselves.

One other important related factor is the age at which the individual first has sexual intercourse. Those who have intercourse early (age sixteen or younger) are less likely than those who begin sexual relations later to know about and use effective methods of contraception (Faulkenberry et al. 1987). The early experimenters are also less likely to use effective contraception at the time of first intercourse.

Other Factors   The proportion of religious women who practice birth control is about the same as for the nonreligious (Goldscheider and Mosher 1991). And the proportion is about the same for Protestants, Catholics, and Jews. However, there are differences in the preferred method; the most frequently used methods are sterilization for Protestants, the pill for Catholics, and diaphragms for Jews.

Religion has another interesting effect. Some religions hold that contraception is wrong. Married people in those religions may refrain from using contraceptives (although many do use them), with resulting large families. Some of the younger, unmarried people, however, may refrain from contraception but not from sexual relations (Studer and Thornton 1987). It is as though they are willing to violate one but not two of their religion's precepts.

Various other factors also affect people's likelihood of using contraceptives. A study of college students reported that use was most strongly associated with partner support for contraception, positive attitudes toward contraception, and high self-esteem (Whitley 1990). And a representative survey of teenagers in four rural Midwestern counties found that those less likely to use contraceptives were those with a low grade point average, frequent alcohol consumption, and low levels of parental monitoring and support (Luster and Small 1994).

ABORTION

Abortion, the expulsion of the fetus from the uterus, is a highly controversial subject. Abortion may be either spontaneous (so-called natural abor-

tion or miscarriage) or induced by some medical or surgical procedure. We include the topic here because induced abortion is used as a method of birth control.

Abortion has been used throughout history to deal with unwanted pregnancies. In the United States, abortion was illegal in most states until the Supreme Court's famous 1973 decision in the *Roe v. Wade* case. That case allowed abortion on demand in the first trimester of the pregnancy. The case was the result of increasing pressures from various groups to give legitimacy to the procedure and protect women from the pain and risks of back-alley abortions. Some women died and many others nearly died from illegal abortions, which could be performed by people who were anything from bookies to midwives.

How many pregnancies end in abortion? Table 4.2 shows that for every ten pregnancies, between two and three are aborted. The number of abortions has tended to decline since about 1980, due possibly to the aging of the population (younger women are most likely to have abortions), fewer abortion services (a result of violence and harassment by pro-life activists), and perhaps some change in attitudes (Sauer 1995). Interestingly, those least supportive of women's right to have abortion on demand are also most likely to have an abortion—young, poor, unmarried or divorced, minority women (Mitchell 1993).

Conflict Theory Applied

Abortion will probably continue to divide the nation into *conflicting camps* for some time. A CBS News/*New York Times* poll found that 60 percent of Americans agreed that *Roe v. Wade* was a good ruling, while 33 percent thought it was bad.[2] At the same time, underscoring the conflicting thoughts and feelings people have, half of the respondents agreed that abortion is the same as murder. Thirty-two percent said that it should be generally available, 45 percent favored stricter limits, and 22 percent wanted to outlaw it altogether.

Abortion poses psychological risks for at least some women. Women who abort may experience the "postabortion syndrome," which includes four components: (1) perceiving the abortion as a

---

[2]Reported in *The San Diego Union-Tribune,* January 17, 1998.

TABLE 4.2
Legal Abortions, by Selected Characteristics

Characteristic	Number (1,000)	Percent Distribution	Abortion Ratio*
Total Legal Abortions	1,529	100	275
Age of woman:			
Less than 15 years	13	1	511
15–19 years old	295	19	370
20–24 years old	526	34	333
25–29 years old	341	22	228
30–34 years old	213	14	192
35–39 years old	110	7	239
40 years old and over	31	2	338
Race of woman:			
White	944	62	229
Black and other	585	38	405
Marital Status of woman:			
Married	257	17	84
Unmarried	1,272	83	508

*Number of abortions per 1,000 abortions and live births.
Source: U.S. Bureau of the Census 1997b:86.

painful, intentional destruction of one's unborn child; (2) negative reexperiencing of the abortion; (3) failure to avoid or deny traumatic recollections of the abortion; and (4) varying negative emotions such as guilt (Speckhard and Rue 1992). Many clinics have both pre- and postprocedure counseling in order to help with such problems. One young woman who had two abortions told us that she is now ready to bear a child: "But I'm having trouble getting pregnant. I'm beginning to feel like I had my children and they died." She was clearly grieving over losses that had occurred some years earlier. Only in a few cases, however, are the problems severe enough to warrant psychiatric care.

PREMARITAL SEX

Most religious traditions link sex with marriage. But premarital sex occurs in all societies. How much occurs in America, and how do Americans feel about it?

The Double Standard

Conflict Theory Applied

As *conflict theory* suggests, men and women have differing interests and their interaction often takes the form of a power struggle. One outcome of the struggle is the double standard, a long-standing fixture of American society that favors male interests. Thus, in terms of premarital sex, this means that boys traditionally were expected to have some experience, while girls were expected to remain virgins until marriage. In his classic study of a small Missouri town, James West (1945:194) captured the essence of the double standard:

> It is expected . . . that most boys will acquire a limited amount of sexual experience before marriage, as they are expected to experiment with drinking and "running around." All these "outlaw traits" are associated with a young man's "sowing his wild oats." It is better if he sows his wild oats outside the community, if possible. . . . A girl who sows any wild oats, at home or abroad, is disgraced, and her parents are disgraced.

Has the double standard changed? To some extent it has. Premarital sexual activity is nearly as acceptable for females as for males. However, in an experimental study, two researchers found that the females were less sexually permissive than the males, and less attracted to permissive males as either a date or a potential marriage partner; the males preferred less permissive females for committed partners but more permissive females for casual dating (Oliver and Sedikides 1992). And in a

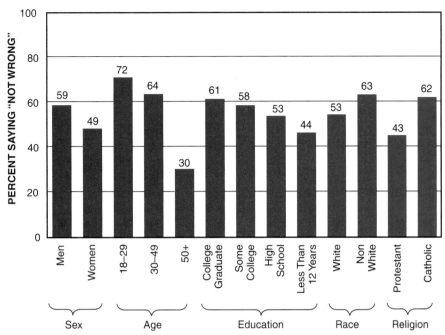

FIGURE 4-4 **Proportion Agreeing that Premarital Sex is not Wrong**
(Source: Data from L. Hugick and J. Leonard, "Sex in America" in *The Gallup Poll Monthly* #313, October 1991, p. 69.

small survey of undergraduates, females reported more social pressure than males to remain a virgin until marriage (Sprecher 1996).

Changing Attitudes

Although the double standard accepted the fact that most boys would have premarital sexual experience, it did not mean that such behavior was considered ideal. Surveys conducted in 1937 and 1959 reported that only 30 percent of the respondents agreed that premarital sex was "all right" for a man and 22 percent agreed that it was "all right" for a woman (Hyde 1986:312). Such attitudes have changed rapidly in the last few decades, however. In Gallup polls, the percentage of respondents who agreed that premarital sex is "not wrong" rose from 21 percent in 1969 to 43 percent in 1973, 52 percent in 1985, and 55 percent in 1997. By 1997, only 39 percent of Americans aged 18 years and older believed that premarital sex is wrong (6 percent didn't have an opinion). The proportion believing that premarital sex is not wrong varies by a number of factors, including sex, age, education, race, and

religion (figure 4.4). Among those who believe that premarital sex is wrong, most give religious or moral reasons; a small proportion cite the risk of AIDS or other diseases (Hugick and Leonard 1991:61).

It is interesting that a majority of Catholics agreed that premarital sex is "not wrong." Officially, the Catholic church continues to teach that premarital relationships are a sin. A 1976 declaration from the Congregation for the Doctrine of the Faith noted that many people now justify premarital sex in cases where people intend to marry and where they have an affection for each other that is like that in the marital state. But even in those cases, sex "is contrary to Christian doctrine which states that every genital act must be within the framework of marriage" (quoted in Hyde 1986:609).

Traditionally, all Christian groups have taught that premarital sex is morally wrong. Whatever the official teachings, however, belief in the immorality of premarital sex has declined among members of all groups except conservative Protestants who attend church often (Petersen and Donnenwerth

1997). Mainline Protestants, Catholics, and conservative Protestants who attend church infrequently have all followed the national trend of increasing acceptance of premarital sex.

Some male-female differences in attitudes exist. Males tend to be more permissive and even expect sex in casual relationships (Wilson and Madora 1990; Cohen and Shotland 1996). Males and females are similar in their attitudes about sex, however, when the couple is in love or engaged. Both tend to approve of sexual relations under such circumstances.

Changing Behavior

Attitudes do not necessarily reflect behavior. That is, because people approve of premarital sex does not mean that they are actually engaging in it. How much premarital sexual behavior actually occurs, and how does the amount now compare with the past?

Extent of Premarital Sex   We pointed out in chapter 1 that the amount of premarital sex has increased considerably in recent decades. In the famous Kinsey studies of the 1940s, the data showed that about a third of all females and 71 percent of all males had premarital sexual relations by the age of 25 (Hyde 1986:306). After the 1960s, the proportions rose dramatically; by the mid-1990s, nearly 70 percent of never-married women aged fifteen to forty-four years reported having had sexual relations (Abma et al. 1997:41). About half of the teenagers had had sexual relations. Those women who refuse to have premarital sex do so for a variety of reasons and handle the pressure in various ways. For instance, a student who had decided to wait for sex until marriage told us:

> I'm up front with the guys I date. I tell them that I don't have hangups. I really look forward to sex. But I just believe that it should wait until marriage. That turns some guys off. At first, I was troubled by some guys that I liked who didn't want to date me anymore because of my attitude. But I decided that if a guy didn't respect me for my stand on sex, we probably shouldn't be together anyway.

Premarital Sex and Equity   Whether sex occurs when dating depends on a number of factors. **Eq-**

Exchange Theory Applied

uity is fairness, in the sense that people are rewarded in proportion to their contributions to something or someone. The idea of equity derives from *exchange theory,* and affirms that, at least in the long run, people need to perceive that they are receiving about as much from the relationship as they are giving to it (Walster, Walster, and Berscheid 1978). Equitable relationships are most likely to be defined as satisfying, and satisfying relationships, in turn, are more likely to involve sex.

Those who are in fairly equitable relationships have the most sexual intercourse (Walster, Walster, and Traupmann 1978). Those who feel either greatly underbenefitted or greatly overbenefitted are more likely to stop before "going all the way." And if they do have sex, they are less likely to do so because both of them want it. The equity of the relationship, then, is an important factor in whether sexual intercourse occurs.

Premarital Sex and Social Background   As in the case of dating patterns, premarital sexual patterns vary depending on background factors. We noted some racial differences in chapter 1. There are also differences based on *religion,* though they are not quite what one would expect. A study of more than 400 singles aged seventeen to twenty-five looked at both church attendance and sexual permissiveness (Jensen, Newell, and Holman 1990). The researchers found that the lowest rates of sexual intercourse occurred among those who were nonpermissive and attended church, but the highest rates occurred among those who were both permissive and attended church every week. In contrast, a survey of young Hispanic women reported that those from intact families who attend church regularly are less likely than other Americans to have premarital sex (Durant, Pendergast, and Seymore 1990). We need more studies before we can draw firm conclusions about the exact relationships between religious activity and premarital sex.

Family background is another factor that causes variation in premarital sexual activity. Styles of parenting as well as the parents' marital status affect the likelihood of engaging in premarital sex. Although young people have more permissive sexual attitudes and behavioral patterns than their parents, children tend to reflect the attitudes of their parents. Thus, mothers with more permissive attitudes are likely to have children who are more sexually active (Small and Luster 1994; Hovell et al. 1994).

In addition to their attitudes, the way that parents discipline their children is important. A study of 2,423 adolescents aged fifteen to eighteen reported that sexual activity was highest among those young people who perceived their parents as having few or no rules or as not being at all strict (Miller et al. 1986). Sexual activity was lowest among those who perceived their parents as moderately strict. Those who reported very strict parents with many rules indicated a level of sexual activity between the other two groups. These results are in accord with others that show that both severe and permissive discipline are likely to lead to more deviant behavior than a moderately strict home environment.

Clearly, both the attitudes of parents and their manner of relating to the child are important factors. This is underscored by the results of a national survey of fifteen- and sixteen-year-olds (Moore, Peterson, and Furstenberg 1986). The researchers found that the daughters of parents with traditional attitudes who talked to them about sex are less likely than others to be sexually active. This study defined parents with more traditional attitudes as those who tended to agree that marriages are better when the husband works and the wife takes care of the home and children, that children are better off if their mothers do not work, and that children develop permanent emotional problems when their parents divorce.

Other important factors related to family background include the behavior of siblings. Older brothers' behavior significantly affects the time of younger siblings' initiation of sexual relations (Widmer 1997). And a study of 455 girls, the majority of them Hispanics and African Americans, reported that those with sexually active sisters and/or an adolescent childbearing sister were more likely to be sexually active (East, Felice, and Morgan 1993).

SEX IN MARRIAGE

Among the things necessary for a successful marriage, how would you rate a good sex life? Most Americans would say it is very important. And it is true that a good sex life can greatly enhance the quality of a couple's intimacy. But what does it mean to have a "good" sex life? Is that measured by frequency of sex? By the number of orgasms? By variety? The relationship between sex and marriage is not a simple one.

Sexual Practices in Marriage

The sex life of married couples has changed considerably over the last few decades. As the famed Kinsey studies reported (Kinsey, Pomeroy, and Martin 1948; Kinsey et al. 1953), in the 1940s, only a minority of married people engaged in oral sex, either **fellatio** or **cunnilingus.** Now, a majority of married people engage in oral sex at least some of the time (Hunt 1974). In addition, married couples now, compared with earlier decades, engage in much more foreplay and try or use a greater number of positions in intercourse (Hunt 1974). These latter changes may reflect an increased concern with the woman's enjoyment and orgasm, both of which tend to be enhanced if more time is given to sexual activity.

How often do married people have sexual relations? Almost 40 percent of married people say they have sex twice a week, compared to 25 percent of singles (Laumann et al. 1994). Frequency varies by such things as age and work (Robinson and Godbey 1998). In general, reported sexual activity is higher among the younger than the older, among those who work forty hours or more a week than those who work fewer hours, and among those identifying themselves as liberals than those identifying themselves as conservatives.

On the average, Americans have sexual relations about once a week (Laumann et al. 1994). Married people tend to have sex more often than the unmarried. However, the "average" can be misleading, because the range of activity is considerable. Some couples never have sex relations while others may have them every day or a number of times each day. It is also important to realize that average does not mean "normal." People sometimes read such statistics and believe that something is wrong with them if they do not follow the average practice. But sexual needs and desires vary widely. There is no "normal" frequency.

Sexual Satisfaction and Marital Satisfaction

How important is sexual satisfaction to marital satisfaction? A number of things can be said. First, it depends on how important sexual satisfaction is to the individual partners. A *Ladies' Home Journal* poll of its readers reported that 55 percent said they could tolerate a sexless union, 11 percent would find it unbearable, and 35 percent said it wouldn't matter that much.[3]

Second, sexual satisfaction involves more than intercourse. A man married twenty-five years told us that he "remembers little about sexual intercourse" in the early years of his marriage. But he does remember "laying at night in my wife's arms. In that way, she was telling me that I was all right. That was very important." Sex, he noted, was not as important as caring and affection. In fact, it is precisely such caring and affection that enables couples to have a satisfying sex life. Once again, we can have intimacy without sex, but we cannot have satisfying sex without intimacy. In other words, sexual satisfaction is likely to be the result of, rather than the cause of, marital satisfaction (Henderson-King and Veroff 1994).

Third, although sexual satisfaction is important, it is less important than other things in the quality of an intimate relationship. A study of 250 couples reported that sexuality is only weakly related to people's perception of the quality of their intimacy (Patton and Waring 1985). More important than sex in intimacy are such things as the ease with which differences are handled, the extent to which the partners express affection, the degree of commitment to the marriage, and the amount of self-disclosure.

Finally, in our study of long-term married couples, we came to three conclusions about the role of sex (Lauer and Lauer 1986:73):

1. A couple can have a meaningful sexual relationship for the duration of their marriage; neither age nor amount of years together necessarily diminishes the quality of sex.
2. Some couples have long-term, satisfying marriages even though one or both has a less-than-ideal sex life.

3. The most important thing in a couple's sexual relationship is agreement about the arrangement.

The last point stresses something we mentioned earlier—there is no such thing as a normal or ideal sex life for all couples. It isn't the kind or frequency of sexual activities that is most important but the extent to which the couple agrees on whatever arrangement they make.

Changes in Marital Sex over the Life Span

Perhaps the most obvious change in sexual activity over the course of a marriage is the decline in frequency. That decline is a function of a number of factors. As people age, their sexual needs and desires change. For most, sex becomes somewhat less urgent. In addition, people come to recognize that other things are as important or more important in their relationships.

Still, sexual activity remains strong and important to many people as they age. And its importance is not merely for physical release. As an eighty-four-year-old woman said: "Sex means more to me than just physical satisfaction. I need to have my husband near to me. I need to hold him and have him hold and hug me." As such needs become increasingly important, the preferred form of sexual activity may change. A study of ninety-nine men and women aged sixty to eighty-five investigated changes in preferred sexual activity over the course of the adult years (Turner and Adams 1988). The researchers found that for forty-seven of their subjects, there was no change. They still preferred the same activity as they did in their earlier years (for forty of the forty-seven, intercourse; for the others, such things as petting and masturbation). Some who had preferred petting in earlier years now preferred intercourse. And some who had preferred intercourse now preferred petting, masturbation, or fantasies.

Health can also alter a couple's sexual pattern. People who must take pain-killing drugs or medication for high blood pressure may find their sexual functioning impaired. Chronic health problems, such as arthritis and diabetes, can diminish sexual desire and activity. A hysterectomy may make intercourse more painful for a woman.

A third factor in changing sexual relations is work. Someone has coined the acronym *DINS* to

---

[3]*Ladies' Home Journal,* February 1993, p. 132.

Sexual activity tends to remain important to people as they age.

refer to those couples who have double income and no sex. Two-career couples may find that they have little energy for sex after work and household chores. Some professionals work weekends as well as long hours during the week. Such schedules do not lend themselves to either intimacy or passionate sexual encounters.

Fourth, the arrival of children may drastically alter a couple's sex life. A survey of nearly six thousand parents reported a marked decline in sexual relations among the couples after the birth of children (Rubenstein 1988). More than a fifth of the couples said they have sexual relations once a month or less, and another third said they have sex between once a week and twice a month. Many new mothers indicated a decline in sexual enjoyment. The most common reasons for the decline in frequency were being tired and lack of desire. Importantly, the same survey found that 40 percent of the

new mothers and 55 percent of new fathers said they were more in love than ever with their spouses.

Finally, our study of long-term marrieds identified three patterns in sexual functioning (Lauer and Lauer 1986). In one pattern, the level and satisfaction with the couple's sex life remained fairly stable over time. A second pattern involved a decline in sexual frequency. Sometimes that was associated with less sexual satisfaction, but in other cases it was not. Third, the sex life of some couples improved over time. In some cases, even the frequency increased. Independently of frequency, however, some couples perceived the quality of their sex life as improving over time. As a woman married forty years told us: "It's better than ever."

EXTRAMARITAL SEX

What do you think about someone who is married having sex with a partner other than his or her spouse? How does that affect marital intimacy? In a 1997 Gallup poll of attitudes about extramarital sex, 79 percent said it is "always" wrong, 11 percent said it is "almost always" wrong, 6 percent said it is wrong "only sometimes," and 3 percent said it is not wrong at all. Most people feel that extramarital sex damages the marital relationship. Nevertheless, a substantial number of people have extramarital sex. One national survey reported that about a fourth of married men and 15 percent of married women admit to ever having an affair (Laumann et al. 1994), while another found that 8.5 percent of men and 4.3 percent of women reported an affair within the past five years (Leigh, Temple, and Trocki 1993).

Clearly, most Americans practice fidelity. Just as clearly, many people engage in extramarital sex who say they do not approve of it. And because only one of the partners in some marriages have the extramarital relationship, a great many couples are affected. Tens of millions of Americans face the problem of a spouse who has been unfaithful. The extent of the unfaithfulness varies, of course. Extramarital sex may involve either an affair or a one-night stand. Affairs may continue on for weeks or even years, with regular or periodic sexual relations. The one-night stand involves a single encounter. Clearly, an affair is much more difficult to maintain than the single encounter.

Why Extramarital Sex?

Many married people fantasize about what it would be like to have sex with someone other than their spouse. But fantasies are not usually enough to motivate someone to have extramarital sex. Those who have such liaisons indicate a variety of reasons. For women, the main motivator seems to be a sense of emotional need. That is, the woman does not feel that all of her emotional needs are being met by her husband. In one survey of married women, 72 percent said that their affair was the result of emotional dissatisfaction with the husband (Grosskopf 1983:195). For men, the motivation is more likely to be a purely sexual one—the desire for variety or for more frequent sex. More than three out of four males attribute their extramarital activity to the strength of their sex drive (Pestrak, Martin, and Martin 1985:110). These gender differences in motivation are reinforced by the reasons that people give for *not* having extramarital sex: a concern about straining the marriage by men and a lack of desire or interest by women (Pestrak, Martin, and Martin 1985:109).

There are other reasons that people give. They may be sexually frustrated (a substantial proportion of women indicate sexual dissatisfaction with their husbands). They may believe that they were seduced. They may use an affair or one-night stand to get revenge against a mate who has cheated or who has angered them. In general, the lower an individual evaluates his or her marriage and the quality of his or her sex life, the more likely that individual is to have extramarital activity (Thompson 1983; Wiederman and Allgeier 1996). In other words, the rate of extramarital sex in the nation is an indicator of marital problems. Extramarital sex causes problems, but it also reflects a troubled relationship.

Some Consequences of Extramarital Sex

On the positive side, some people report that the extramarital experience provided them with a brief but meaningful thrill. But for the most part, extramarital sex doesn't solve people's problems; it only intensifies them.

As a therapist who has dealt with many cases of infidelity notes, most affairs involve "a little bad sex and hours on the telephone" (Pittman 1993:36).

The thrill of engaging in the forbidden turns out to be disappointing.

Those who get involved in extramarital sex because they have "fallen in love" are also likely to be disappointed. "Romantic affairs lead to a great many divorces, suicides, homicides, heart attacks, and strokes, but not to very many successful remarriages" (Pittman 1993:35).

In addition, there is the crisis in the marriage if the extramarital activity is discovered. The betrayed spouse is likely to undergo a time of great trauma. He or she may have trouble concentrating, sleeping, and eating. There may be a preoccupation with the betrayal and an agonizing effort to try to understand it. There may be a feeling of having been victimized to the extent that marital trust is no longer possible. A wife who discovered her husband's extramarital activity told an interviewer that in the week following her discovery, she found herself standing in a department store with no idea why she had come there. She said that she felt "as if the very floor I stood on were moving, waving and buckling underneath me. It was as if I myself, and the world around me, were completely unreal" (Scarf 1987:138).

Various outcomes of infidelity are possible (Charny and Parnass 1995). The harm may be irreparable; the couple may divorce. The marriage may survive but provide a low level of satisfaction and little or no intimacy. And in a few cases, the marriage may survive and improve. If the latter is to occur, the main problems that the couple must work through are the factors in their relationship that might have contributed to the infidelity and the problem of a spouse who was emotionally involved with someone else (having your spouse emotionally involved seems harder to cope with than the purely sexual involvement).

At times, both spouses may be having extramarital activity, sometimes with both knowing this and sometimes not. Even in those cases, the marriage might survive. A professional woman shared the following account with us:

> We have a two-career marriage. We seemed to have less and less time for each other. I got involved in an affair with a man at work. Then one day I discovered that my husband was also having an affair. That made me furious! Suddenly we had to confront the fact that our marriage was on the rocks. We both agreed that we didn't want it to end. We were both hurt, but we

PERSPECTIVE
The Sexual Needs of Women

In the nineteenth and early twentieth centuries, most Americans believed that women did not have the same sexual needs as men. In fact, many argued that normal women had no sexual needs at all. Why, then, would a woman become a prostitute? Dr. William Sanger studied the question. He interviewed prostitutes and was shocked to find that a good number of them said they entered the life because they enjoyed sex. This, he wrote, implied "an innate depravity." He went on to discuss his views of women's sexual drive and needs in contrast to those of men:

The force of desire can neither be denied nor disputed, but still in the bosoms of most females that force exists in a slumbering state until aroused by some outside influences. No woman can understand its power until some positive cause of excitement exists. What is sufficient to awaken the dormant passion is a question that admits innumerable answers.

Acquaintance with the opposite sex, particularly if extended so far as to become a reciprocal affection, will tend to do this . . . so will the excitement of intoxication. But it must be repeated,

and most decidedly, that without these or some other equally stimulating cause, the full force of sexual desire is seldom known to a virtuous woman. . . . In other words, man is the *aggressive* animal, so far as sexual desire is involved. Were it otherwise, and the passions in both sexes equal, illegitimacy and prostitution would be far more rife in our midst than at present.

Source: William W. Sanger, *The History of Prostitution: Its Extent, Causes, and Effects Throughout the World* (New York: Fowlers and Wells, 1850), pp. 488–89.

---

got counseling and worked through the pain. That was three years ago. So far, it's working well. And I intend for that to continue.

SEXUAL DISEASES AND DYSFUNCTIONS

Our examination of sexual diseases and dysfunctions is necessarily brief. But it is important that you at least be familiar with them. Getting, or the fear of getting, a disease can lower or even eliminate the intimacy of sexual relations. You should also be aware of some of the rules of safe sex, our final topic in this chapter.

Sexual Diseases

Sexually transmitted diseases (a term now preferred over *venereal diseases*) have plagued humankind throughout history. Some believe that with the advent of AIDS, the risk is greater than ever, but many people died of sexual diseases before the advent of modern medicines that can cure or control most of those diseases.

Incidence A substantial number of Americans suffer from one or more sexually transmitted dis-

eases. As table 4.3 shows, hundreds of thousands of Americans acquire one of these diseases each year (the numbers refer to the new cases reported each year to the Centers for Disease Control; the table does not include genital herpes because it is not reported to the Centers). There are some racial/ethnic differences in those afflicted by the diseases. Gonorrhea is highest among black female teenagers in poorer urban areas (Rice et al. 1991). Syphilis is more common among non-Hispanic blacks than any other racial/ethnic group and is concentrated in the South (Centers for Disease Control 1998). The racial/ethnic breakdown of new AIDS patients in 1996 was 40 percent non-Hispanic white, 44 percent non-Hispanic black, and 16 percent Hispanic (U.S. Bureau of the Census 1997b:142). Researchers who studied genital herpes, which afflicts millions of Americans, found that it is more common among African Americans and Mexican Americans (Fleming et al. 1997).

Clearly, while some racial/ethnic groups have higher rates of certain diseases, a considerable number of Americans of all races suffer from a sexually transmitted disease at one time or another in their lives. "Suffer" is the appropriate word, because, depending on the particular disease acquired,

TABLE 4.3
Reported Cases of Sexually Transmitted Diseases: 1960 to 1995

Disease	Year					
	1960	1970	1980	1985	1990	1995
Gonorrhea (1,000)	259	600	1004	911	690	393
Syphilis (1,000)	122	91	69	68	134	69
AIDS (1,000)				8	42	72
Chlamydia						478

Source: Adapted from U.S. Bureau of the Census (1989:111) and (1997b:141).

people may experience fear, anger, guilt, and a damaged self-esteem in addition to the physical consequences (Swanson and Chentiz 1993).

Major Types of Sexually Transmitted Diseases   *AIDS,* or acquired immunodeficiency syndrome, is caused by a virus that attacks certain white blood cells, eventually causing the individual's immune system to stop functioning. The individual then falls prey to one infection after another. Even normally mild diseases can prove fatal. Many AIDS patients develop rare cancers or suffer serious brain damage. HIV, the virus that causes AIDS, spreads in a number of ways, including anal or vaginal intercourse with an infected person, blood transfusions, accidental exchange of blood from a contaminated hypodermic needle, and from infected mothers to their infants before or during birth. Up to this point, those most likely to get AIDS have been homosexual and bisexual men, but the incidence among heterosexuals has been increasing. There is no known cure, though some drugs may mitigate the disease or possibly control it.

Gonorrhea is one of the oldest forms of sexual disease. It can be transmitted by any kind of sexual contact, including kissing. In men, gonorrhea causes a thick discharge from the penis and burning while urinating. In women, it has no visible symptoms, but it can damage their fallopian tubes—causing them to become infertile—and also cause lower abdominal pain, nausea, and pain during intercourse. Gonorrhea is treated with penicillin.

Syphilis appeared in Europe in the fifteenth century (Masters, Johnson, and Kolodny 1988:563), killing hundreds of thousands of people. It is transmitted by sexual contact but can also be transmitted

in a blood transfusion or, if a pregnant woman acquires it, to the fetus. The first symptom of syphilis is a sore on some part of the body. The sore usually heals and goes away, but untreated syphilis will go into a second stage involving rash, fever, and pains. If still untreated, it can result in brain damage, heart problems, and, ultimately, death. It also is treated with penicillin.

Genital herpes is caused by a virus. It is transmitted by sexual intercourse and shows up in the form of painful blisters on or in the area of the genitals. The blisters eventually disappear, but they may reappear periodically because the virus continues to live in the human body. Some people suffer repeated seven- to fourteen-day periods of the sores. At the present, there is no cure for genital herpes.

Finally, *chlamydial infections* are caused by a bacterium. Chlamydia usually has no symptoms. It can cause infection of the urethra in males and infections in the reproductive system of females. It can lead to a fatal tubal pregnancy or infertility in women (Wasserheit 1997). If caught early, chlamydia is readily treatable with antibiotics.

Sexually Transmitted Diseases and Sexual Behavior   The possibility of acquiring a sexually transmitted disease has done little in the past to change sexual behavior. An individual's sexual behavior may change once he or she has contracted the disease, of course. But few people have abstained from sexual relations or from a variety of sexual partners out of the fear of disease. It is unclear at this point whether AIDS is changing that. Some studies have reported that, despite having adequate knowledge about AIDS, many young people continue to engage in high-risk sexual behavior (Skurnick et al. 1991; Brown, DiClemente, and

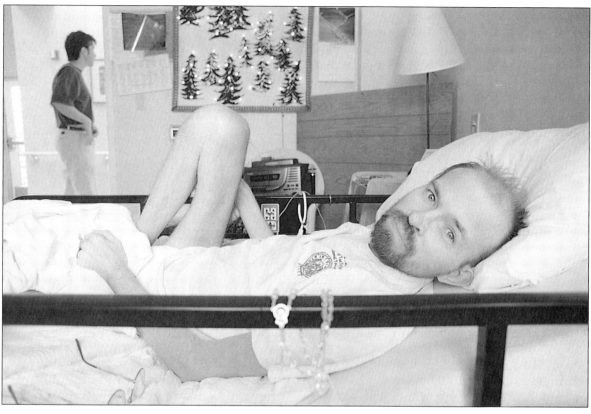

AIDS is now the deadliest of the sexually transmitted diseases and there is no known cure.

Park 1992; Morrison-Beedy 1997). And some who engage in high-risk behavior continue to perceive their own chances of contracting HIV/AIDS as unlikely (Sawyer and Moss 1993; Dolcini et al. 1996). Worse, some of those already infected do not inform a sexual partner of their condition. A study of infected Hispanic men in Los Angeles reported that 45 percent continued to be sexually active and over half of the sexually active had not told one or more partners about the infection (Marks, Richardson, and Maldonado 1991).

Other studies, however, find some changes in behavior, including limiting the number of partners and greater use of condoms (McNally and Mosher 1991; Hugick and Leonard 1991; Clements 1994). The evidence, then, is mixed. Clearly, some people have changed their behavior because of the fear of contracting AIDS. It is too early to know, however, whether there will be long-term changes in the sexual behavior of most Americans.

Sexual Dysfunctions

Famed English author and reformer John Ruskin courted a young woman to whom he wrote such flowery phrases as: "You are like the bright—soft—swelling—lovely fields of a high glacier covered with fresh morning snow" (Rose 1983:54). Ruskin won her heart, and they were married. A few years later, they were divorced because Ruskin could never consummate the union. He was one of many people for whom sex is more of a problem than an experience of intimacy.

Types of Sexual Dysfunctions A **sexual dysfunction** is any impairment of the physical responses in sexual activity. For males, the major sexual dysfunctions have to do with penile *erection* and *ejaculation* (Masters, Johnson, and Kolodny 1988:500). The man may be unable to have or maintain an erection that is firm enough for intercourse.

Or he may ejaculate before the woman is sufficiently aroused for orgasm or even before inserting his penis into her vagina. In a few cases, the man's problem may be the opposite: difficulty ejaculating or even an inability to ejaculate within the vagina.

For women, the main kinds of sexual dysfunction include *vaginismus* (involuntary spasms of the muscles around the vagina, preventing penetration by the penis or making it painful), *anorgasmia* (difficulty reaching or an inability to reach orgasm), and *painful intercourse.*

From 10 percent to 20 percent of sexual dysfunctions have organic causes, such as diabetes, drug abuse, and infections. A variety of psychological and social factors are involved in most cases. The individual may have developed negative sexual attitudes, suffer from anxiety or guilt, feel hostile or alienated from the sexual partner, and so forth. Stress, such as that of unemployment, can affect sexual functioning (Morokoff and Gillilland 1993). Therapy can often help people recapture a satisfying sex life.

Prevalence of Sexual Dysfunctions   Many people have to deal with sexual dysfunction at some point in their lives. Sixteen percent of the respondents in a national survey reported having sexual problems, with **impotence,** the inability to get or sustain an erection, as the most common problem among men and low sex drive as the most common among women (Clements 1994). In 1998, Viagra, a new drug, appeared on the market to help men with erectile problems (Mitka 1998). The drug caused quite a stir, including testimonials from well-known people about its efficacy, conflict over whether HMOs should pay for the drug, and reports of some deaths among men taking medication for coronary artery disease.

Inhibited Sexual Desire

Inhibited sexual desire is a problem but not, strictly speaking, a dysfunction. It does not necessarily involve any physical impairment. It can, however, cause considerable stress. Like sexual dysfunctions, inhibited desire can be rooted in such things as hostility, fear, and anxiety. It may also be the result of the kind of fatigue that two-career couples experience.

In an effort to sort out some of the causes of inhibited desire, a group of social workers studied ninety married women who had come to a sex and marital therapy clinic for help with various sexual problems (Stuart, Hammond, and Pett 1987). Fifty-nine of the women had problems with inhibited desire, while the rest had various dysfunctions though normal desire. Those with inhibited desire, in contrast with the others, perceived their parents to have less affectionate interaction and more negative attitudes toward sex. They were more likely than those with normal desire to have had premarital intercourse. And, most importantly, those with inhibited desire reported far greater dissatisfaction with the quality of the marital relationship, including such factors as trust, commitment, emotional closeness, love, and attractiveness of the spouse. For these women, inhibited desire grew out of poor marital interaction, a conclusion underscored by the fact that most of the women developed the problem gradually after they were married.

We do not know how many people have inhibited sexual desire. Probably anywhere from 20 to 50 percent of people experience it at some point in their lives, some more severely than others. The problem may go away if the couple can outlast it and build or maintain a generally good marital relationship. For some, however, the problem will require therapy.

Safe Sex

The only truly safe sex is no sex. Few people are so concerned about safety that they will opt for celibacy; however, it is helpful to consider some guidelines for maximizing safety:

1. Be careful about whom you allow to be a sexual partner. How well do you know the person and his or her sexual history? Does the person have any signs of infection?
2. Minimize the number of sexual partners you have. Having multiple partners greatly enhances the risk of acquiring a sexually transmitted dis-

ease, including AIDS. The safest sex is between two people who have an exclusive relationship.

3. Discuss health and sexual concerns with the partner before you have sexual relations. It isn't an invasion of privacy to question someone about his or her sexual history when the issue is one of your health and even your life.

4. Use available protection during sexual relations. In particular, experts recommend that males always use a condom, even if the woman is using another birth control device. Condoms do not give absolute protection, but they maximize the safety of sexual intercourse. Experts also recommend that you wash your genitals carefully and thoroughly both before and after sexual relations.

5. Have regular medical checkups. You should be specifically checked for sexually transmitted diseases if you or your partner have sexual relations with more than one person.

6. Know the symptoms of the various diseases. We have briefly noted many of them. But you should be familiar with all the symptoms. Some of the diseases are insidious in that they may appear to go away, only to return in a more advanced and damaging phase.

7. Consult a physician immediately if you have contracted or been exposed to a sexually transmitted disease. You may be embarrassed, but keep in mind that you are dealing with your health, your reproductive capacity, and perhaps even your life.

COMPARISON
Unsafe Sex in Lesotho

Lesotho is an independent kingdom in southern Africa, a region with a high rate of sexually transmitted diseases, including HIV infections. Interviews with about 200 women in Lesotho revealed a considerable amount of knowledge about AIDS. Over 40 percent of the women mentioned the use of condoms as a preventive measure. As in the United States, however, knowledge does not always translate into behavior. Only six of the women said that their partners had ever used condoms, and only two indicated regular usage. The most frequent explanations given by the women for this lack of usage were, first, only a few had actually ever seen a condom because they were not readily available. And second, their husbands or boyfriends objected to the use of condoms. If they suggested to their partners that they use a condom,

some of the women argued, the men would assume that the women were promiscuous or prostitutes.

In point of fact, there is already considerable promiscuity, which enhances the possibility of HIV infection. Eighty-three percent of the women agreed that multiple sexual partners are common. The reason is not prostitution, but the nature of the economy. A large number of the men work in South African mines. That means that they are away from their homes anywhere from a third to 60 percent of their working lives. Because the employment of foreign women is greatly restricted, families tend not to migrate. When the men go alone to the mines, some send part of their wages home. Yet nearly a third of the 80 women whose husbands were working in the mines said they received no money from them.

In these circumstances, multiple sexual partners for the women can mean anything from economic survival to the fulfillment of emotional needs. As one respondent said, the men are always fooling around when they are away so "you do it for the money or just to make your life interesting." If you are faithful to your husband, she pointed out, you wind up spending a lot of time alone.

The combination of multiple partners and sex without the use of condoms leads to a high rate of sexually transmitted diseases in Lesotho. Such diseases account for more than one of every eight visits to health centers. But life circumstances in Lesotho make the continuing practice of "unsafe" sex and, consequently, high rates of sexually transmitted diseases likely to continue (Romero-Daza 1994).

PRINCIPLES FOR ENHANCING INTIMACY

1. Sex is a vital and human function, but it is a very complex one as well. If you want to experience the fullness of your sexual potential, it is important to develop an understanding about the physical and emotional factors that are involved in sex.
2. Sex is not a substitute for intimacy. To be most satisfying, sex needs to be the expression of an intimate relationship, rather than an effort to create intimacy.
3. An unwanted pregnancy is a difficult and painful experience. Knowledge about sexuality and the use of effective contraceptives are the best ways to avoid unwanted pregnancies.
4. Extramarital affairs generally create more problems than they solve for people. In fact, they often cause great personal trauma for the people involved. It is more satisfying to work through the problems in your marriage than to seek escape in an affair.
5. Sexually transmitted diseases pose a significant danger for the sexually active. It is important that you know about the symptoms and consequences of these various diseases as well as the ways you can avoid them.
6. Although sexual dysfunctions are fairly common, they are treatable and need not detract from the quality of an intimate relationship.
7. Sex can be one of the more gratifying of human experiences. But satisfying sex is ultimately responsible sex. Learn the seven guidelines to safe sex and make them a part of your intimate interactions with others.

SUMMARY

Sex is both a physical and a social phenomenon. Physically, sex may be described in terms of the response cycle of excitement, plateau, orgasm, and resolution. As a social phenomenon, sex is a function of learning and of our gender roles and gender-role orientations. The social nature of sex is illustrated by variations in sexual arousal and techniques and by the amount of unwanted sex in which people engage.

Sex is an important part of intimate relationships. The need for intimacy has primacy over the need for sex. Sexual activity is a natural expression of the feeling of intimacy with someone.

The majority of teenagers become sexually active between the ages of sixteen and nineteen. One consequence of teenage sex is a high rate of unwanted pregnancies at an early age. Teenagers get pregnant for a variety of reasons, including a lack of responsible use of birth control measures. Some teenagers may want to get pregnant because of loneliness, alienation from parents, or the need to assert their independence or to do something creative. Concerned parents who talk with their children are less likely to have teenagers who get pregnant.

The consequences of teenage childbearing are mostly negative. The parents are less likely to complete their education and more likely to remain poor. Only a minority of women marry the father, so the woman assumes the child-rearing responsibilities. Some of the mothers will escape poverty, but the risks of a poorer quality of life for them and their children are much higher than they are for those who bear children after their teen years.

Contraception refers to methods of preventing fertilization. Some, such as the rhythm method and withdrawal, are of little use. Others are fairly effective. Only a minority of women use a contraceptive method when they first become sexually active. The pill, condoms, and the diaphragm are common devices. Among married women, there has been a dramatic increase in sterilization since 1965. Contraceptive use is more likely among those who perceive their peers as being users, those who have good communication with their parents, and those who are less religious.

Abortion is a form of birth control for some people. The proportion of legal abortions has risen dramatically since 1973. A slight majority of Americans favor the woman's right to choose whether to have an abortion. There are some psychological risks; many clinics have both pre- and postabortion counseling.

The double standard still exists to some extent with regard to premarital sex, but sexual activity is now nearly as acceptable for females as for males. Over half of Americans believe premarital sex is not wrong. The proportion varies by such things as sex, age, family background, education, and religion. The majority of American women have sexual intercourse before marriage.

The sex life of married people has changed over the past few decades, with an increasing amount of foreplay and variations in technique. The frequency of sex varies considerably among the married. Sexual satisfaction is not essential to marital satisfaction, though most happy couples do have meaningful sex lives. Frequency tends to decline for various reasons, but quality can remain high or even increase as the couple ages.

Although the great majority of Americans disapprove of extramarital sex, a substantial number have at least one extramarital experience. Emotional need tends to motivate women, while men are more likely to have a purely sexual motivation. For the most part, extramarital activity intensifies marital problems.

A substantial number of Americans suffer from one or more sexually transmitted diseases. Gonorrhea, syphilis, genital herpes, chlamydial infections, and AIDS are the most common diseases. Sexual dysfunctions are also common. Men's dysfunctions primarily involve problems of erection and ejaculation. Among women, the main problems are vaginismus, anorgasmia, and painful intercourse. Both men and women may have inhibited sexual desire at some point in their lives.

Widespread concern about disease, particularly AIDS, raises the question of safe sex. While there are no guarantees, a number of steps can be taken to minimize the chances of acquiring a sexually transmitted disease. The safest sex is between two people who have an exclusive relationship.

INTERNET CONNECTION
Sexuality

Your textbook states that teenagers, especially minority teenagers, are among the least likely to make use of contraception when they become sexually active. Religious factors, lack of education, and gender roles all have an impact on teen choices when it comes to premarital sex. Increased rates of teenage pregnancies is often the unwanted outcome of sexual activity that does not involve contraception. But there is another outcome approaching startling proportions: increased risk of transmitting sexual diseases like AIDS.

National Institute of Health

http://www.nih.gov/

The NIH is the U.S. government's most important health issues-related policy and research organization. The website provides access to a considerable amount of policy information, press releases, research findings, and other valuable resources.

www.mhhe
.com/lauer4

United Nations Joint Programm on AIDS

http://www.unaids.org/index.html

As the main advocate for global action on HIV/AIDS, UNAIDS leads, strengthens and supports an expanded response aimed at preventing the transmission of HIV, providing care and support, reducing the vulnerability of individuals and communities to HIV/AIDS, and alleviating the impact of the epidemic.

Each of these websites have local search engines for retrieving specific information on policy and research activities of the organization. Locate these engines, and use them to answer the following questions:

1. How quickly is the rate of HIV transmission increasing among teenagers in the United States and abroad?
2. What cultural, economic, or educational factors account for this?
3. What role can education and contraception play in reducing the rate of HIV infection among teenagers in the United States and abroad?

PART TWO

SEEKING INTIMATE RELATIONSHIPS

The Chinese have a word, *jen,* that refers to a quality of humans that leads them to live in society. In other words, humans by nature seek to live with others. Only unnatural and abnormal people, according to Confucian teachings, live outside of human communities, for it is in society that humans are able to fully develop and realize their potential.

We agree with this ancient Chinese view of our need for relationships. Of course, most of us begin life in the context of family relationships. But sooner or later we begin to establish relationships beyond the family. In part two, we shall look at some of the issues, the alternatives, and the problems that arise as we step outside the family and establish additional intimate relationships. Issues, or points of dispute, include such matters as whether cohabitation is a good preparation for marriage, romantic love can last, and singleness is a healthy option. The issues arise, in part, because we do have so many alternatives—singlehood, sex or celibacy, cohabitation, marriage, and the choice of different possible marriage partners. The alternatives and issues mean that some people face problems, times of doubt, and uncertainty about which choices to make.

GETTING TO KNOW SOMEONE ELSE

Learning Objectives

After reading chapter 5, you should be able to:

1. Define loneliness and aloneness.
2. Distinguish social from emotional loneliness.
3. Explain the symptoms and problems associated with loneliness.
4. Describe the sources of loneliness.
5. Discuss the benefits as well as the perils of intimate relations.
6. Summarize the various dimensions of intimacy.
7. Explain the role of equity in intimate relationships.
8. Discuss the ways that intimate relationships develop.
9. Characterize the various ways in which people are attracted to others.
10. Explain the four stages in the development of an intimate relationship.

Why bother? Everyone who has dated as an adolescent knows the anxiety, uncertainty, and even the anguish of building intimate relationships. A middle-aged man recalled his own time of heartache:

> One of the most agonizing times I remember as a young man was the day my steady girlfriend told me she was breaking up with me. She and I were of different religious backgrounds, and she decided that it was best for us not to see each other anymore. I sat in my car and cried. Then I drove home, weeping off and on the whole way. I just felt crushed and empty.

Why should you go through all that pain? Why not be a loner instead?

In this chapter, we will discuss the problems of the loner, and the values of intimate relationships. We then will explore the factors involved in establishing relationships, the stages we go through in building intimacy, and the nature of intimacy. Finally, we will offer some principles for enhancing the quality of intimacy.

WE ARE SOCIAL CREATURES

Humans, said Aristotle, are social creatures. One of our fundamental needs is to relate to others. John Steinbeck (1962:137–38) noted that, for two successive years, he had spent eight months alone in the Sierra Nevada mountains. After being alone for a while, he found that he stopped whistling, stopped talking to his dogs, and stopped experiencing some of the emotions he had felt at other times. He realized that such emotions are the result of interacting and talking with others and when you have no one around, you become a different kind of creature. It seems that only in relating to others are we fully human.

Loneliness

Despite the fact that we are social beings, nearly everyone is lonely at one time or another. Some people are lonely a good part of the time. We shall define **loneliness** as a feeling of being isolated from desired relationships. We can distinguish between social and emotional loneliness (Weiss 1973; DiTommaso and Spinner 1997). Social loneliness means you have less interpersonal interaction than you desire. Emotional loneliness means you have fewer intimate relationships than you desire. Emotional loneliness can result from a lack of romantic intimacy or family intimacy or both. Contrary to what some believe, elderly people are not the loneliest. They may have more social loneliness, but they have less emotional loneliness than younger people (Larson 1990; Shute and Howitt 1990).

Loneliness in Interaction Loneliness, then, is not the same as aloneness. Most people prefer and benefit from a certain amount of solitude. In fact, adults who spent some of their time alone as adolescents appear to be better adjusted (Larson 1990). As adults, people find a certain amount of solitude useful for such things as contemplation, creativity, recovery from hurt or strenuous activity, and rejuvenation (Pedersen 1997). At the same time, we also want, and require, relationships that fulfill our intimacy needs. But it isn't enough to interact with people, even a lot of people. That may cure social loneliness, but it doesn't necessarily address emotional loneliness. For example, lonely and nonlonely students who kept diaries of their interaction over a two-day period did not differ in the total number of interactions they had (Jones 1982). But the lonely students did have more of their interaction with strangers and casual acquaintances than did the nonlonely students. As Jones noted:

Lonely people may have as much contact and hence social opportunities as do nonlonely people, but may be less satisfied with available relationships . . . satisfaction with contacts is more important than the actual frequency (1982:243).

Emotional loneliness can occur even when you have frequent contact with a particular individual or group of individuals. A young woman who complained of loneliness pointed out that she was a part of a large family but "everyone is busy." And at her work she had some friends that she saw socially on occasions, but, she reported, "I can't say that I feel really close to any of them." Being around the same people on a regular basis is not the equivalent of having intimate relationships with those people. There is even loneliness in some marriages (Stapen 1987). A husband or wife may go through periods of feeling distant from the other, depressed and withdrawn, disconnected from any closeness in the relationship. Fulfilling our intimacy needs is not merely a matter of being in another person's presence, even when we are frequently with that person.

Effects of Loneliness Long-term loneliness has serious negative consequences for people. Lonely people report more health problems (Mahon, Yarcheski, and Yarcheski 1993; Schwartz and Olds 1997). A study of older (sixty to eighty-seven years) Korean immigrants found that those who were lonely were less satisfied with their lives and perceived their health as worse than did those who were less lonely (Kim 1997). In their nationwide survey of loneliness among Americans, Rubenstein and Shaver (1982:201) listed nineteen symptoms and problems associated with being lonely:

1. Feelings of worthlessness.
2. Feeling you just can't go on.
3. Constant worry and anxiety.
4. Irrational fears.
5. Trouble concentrating.
6. Feeling irritable and angry.
7. Feelings of guilt.
8. Crying spells.
9. Feeling tired.
10. Insomnia.
11. Pains in the heart; heart disease.
12. Trouble breathing.
13. Poor appetite.
14. Headaches.
15. Digestive problems.
16. Loss of interest in sex.
17. Being overweight, feeling fat.
18. Suffering from a serious disease.
19. Having a disabling accident.

Many of the symptoms listed above are a part of depression. One of the common findings of social scientists is that lonely people tend to be depressed (Levin and Stokes 1986). If the loneliness is severe, the depression may also be severe and may be associated with thoughts of suicide (Weber, Metha, and Nelsen 1997). Of course, it is possible that the depression occurs first and that depressed people are lonely either because they have isolated themselves from others or that people do not want to associate with them. But while depression no doubt intensifies loneliness, the loneliness occurs first at least among some people (Rich and Scovel 1987).

Clearly, loneliness, which by definition means an inadequate amount of intimacy, leads to an array of other ills. Those ills, in turn, feed back into the loneliness and intensify it. The result is a downward spiral (figure 5.1) that can be difficult to stop.

Sources of Loneliness Some people are lonely for temporary periods because of such things as the breakup of a relationship, a move to a new location, or an accident or illness that confines them to home. But more persistent loneliness may be hard to break out of when it is rooted in certain social and personal factors.

As far as social factors are concerned, loneliness may reflect a failure of **integration** (Rokach and Sharma 1996). That is, the individual may not feel that he or she is a meaningful and significant part of any group. A researcher, for example, found that students who perceived their ideas and interests differed from others were more likely to suffer emotional loneliness (Bell 1993). Such a situation, Emile Durkheim (1933) argued, is inherent in modern society. In more primitive societies, according to Durkheim, people are alike in their ideas, values, and aspirations. The entire society is like a close-knit family. As the population grows, as the society becomes more complex, this familial nature of society inevitably breaks down. Differences increase among the people. The society becomes heterogeneous.

The Downward Spiral

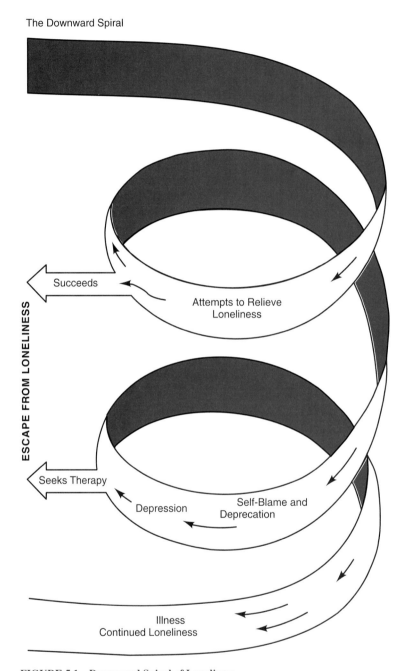

ESCAPE FROM LONELINESS

Succeeds

Attempts to Relieve
Loneliness

Seeks Therapy

Depression

Self-Blame and
Deprecation

Illness
Continued Loneliness

FIGURE 5.1   Downward Spiral of Loneliness
(From Carin Rubenstein and Phillip Shaver, "The Downward Spiral" in *In Search of Intimacy.* Copyright © 1982 Delacorte Press, division of Bantam, Doubleday, Dell Publishing Group, Inc. Reprinted by permission.

As social creatures, we need meaningful relationships in order to be fulfilled.

People are bound together by interdependence, by their need for each other's contributions to the society, rather than by their sense of oneness.

But modern society is no longer an integrated whole; rather, it is a conglomeration of diverse individuals. However, people need to be integrated into some group. Durkheim felt that neither religion nor the family accomplishes this in a modern, industrial society. He predicted that the only source of integration would be occupational organizations.

More recent critics agree that the character of modern society is such that intimate relationships are problematic (and, therefore, loneliness is endemic in the society). We believe that such criticisms have some merit. It would seem that many Americans are yearning for a sense of community. Over half indicate that they would like to live in a small town of fewer than ten thousand people.

> You know that most of those people couldn't stand to actually live in a town that small, where everyone knows everybody else's business. But they have a hankering, a nostalgia, for a face-to-face community (Winkler 1985:8).

Our mobility as well as the nature of our modern society make intimate relationships problematic. It seems all too easy to become a lonely nonentity in the midst of a massive, impersonal urban world. But we must temper the criticism with two points.

First, we have romanticized the preindustrial community. It did not always provide an integrated and satisfying communal life. Anthropological descriptions of some preindustrial communities show them to be filled with suspicion, distrust, and violence. Second, while there may be more loneliness in modern society, there are also more opportunities and more choices. The city enables one to choose one's intimates. You don't have to be friends with the people next door if you choose not to. There are a great many associations and groups of various kinds in most cities that offer people an opportunity to interact with others who have similar interests. The point is that slipping into loneliness is easier in the modern world, and getting out of it into some intimate relationships may require initiative and effort. But the modern world is not structured in a way to squeeze intimacy totally out of human life.

Some individual factors are also involved in loneliness. Stubborn feelings of loneliness may be rooted in certain childhood characteristics and experiences. Low self-esteem is associated with loneliness in adolescents (Inderbitzen-Pisaruk, Clark, and Solano 1992), and the loneliness may continue into adulthood (Olmstead et al. 1991). Those who had a parent die when they were children or lacked warm and supportive parents while growing up, are more likely to suffer from chronic loneliness as adults (Lobdell and Perlman 1986; Murphy 1986/1987).

PERSONAL
Searching for Intimacy

Loneliness is a burden from which most people seek to free themselves. But finding satisfying and lasting intimate relationships is not always easy. Ellie is a forty-year-old woman who married her high school sweetheart at the age of eighteen, then divorced him when she was twenty-one. She is now a high school counselor. Although she lives alone, this does not mean that she suffers from loneliness. At the same time, she is struggling to establish an ongoing intimate relationship:

I have been single now for nineteen years. I can foresee being married in five to eight years. So being single is not a dislike of marriage but a choice. I have used this time to get to know and like myself. And I've gotten to know my parents better as well.

I admit that I was disillusioned after my divorce. I don't remember being against marriage at the time, but I felt an overwhelming lack of trust. And since I had failed at marriage, I lacked self-confidence and found myself being overly cautious. In the long term, though, I learned to be more independent and self-reliant. As I look back, I find that my choices in relationships after my divorce were bad ones. Although most of them lasted from one to four years, I never wanted to marry any of them. I wanted to live with two of them and did with one. But I didn't consider marriage, although two of them asked me.

The first man after my divorce was a tall, good-looking, but uneducated man. I didn't know it at the time, but he was married and had a son. When I found out, I kept going with him because I felt sorry for him. He and his wife had such a bad relationship!

After we had gone together three years, he divorced his wife. I loved the attention he gave me. I thought I was in love. But I wasn't, and I finally told him so. Why did I stay with him so long? I think because it was convenient to have a constant date and satisfying to have a boyfriend. But I learned that he lied a lot and couldn't manage money, and that made me lose respect for him. I couldn't be intimate with him after that. We gradually drifted apart.

The next was Ricardo, who I met while I was studying in Mexico. It was a romantic and passionate relationship. He and his family wanted us to marry. But after a year, I realized that he had a drinking problem. I also realized that I couldn't be happy with a man who was overly dominant and that I didn't want to live far away from my parents. That relationship helped me start my list of "things I know I do not want."

Next I met an artist. He was not very good-looking. In fact, he was short and ugly. But I enjoyed being admired by an artist. And I thought I was in love again. Then I found out that he too was married. For two volatile years we kept seeing each other, with me playing the role of the understanding "other woman." When I got a teaching job in another city, that relationship ended.

Next on my list was Kevin, a wild engineer. Even now when I think of that jerk I have to smile. He was such a mess of truth and lies. I spent four years with him. He was tall and good-looking and had a real zest for life. This really appealed to me. He was not interested in making a commitment of any kind, though. I wanted to live with him, but he said no. Finally, I realized that I wanted a relationship that was more intimate. Since he wasn't interested, we stopped seeing each other.

Soon after, Bill moved in with me. We lived together about nine months. Bill drank too much beer. He had a job when we met, but he was out of work most of the time we lived together. All of this sounds awful, I know. But I learned something from each one. From Bill, I learned that I do want to be close to and share my life with someone. But I know that it has to be the right kind of person. My intimacy needs are currently met by relying and depending on friends and my parents. I'm not lonely. I do enjoy my life. I've made some unwise choices in my selection of men, but they've helped me at least know what I don't want in a relationship.

Lonely adults look back on their childhood and feel that they didn't have enough time with their parents and that they could not trust their parents to give them the support they needed (Rubenstein and Shaver 1982:39). Feeling abandoned and isolated early in life, they never were able to develop the trust in people necessary to form intimate relationships.

Depending on the source of the loneliness, then, it will be more or less difficult to overcome. In either case, however, people need to work at overcoming loneliness, particularly long-term loneliness, because intimate relationships are an essential part of our well-being.

Fulfillment Through Intimacy

A psychotherapist who works with severely mentally disturbed patients in a private hospital told us that she can "mark the beginning of health and recovery in a patient from the time he or she commits to interacting with others." She noted that when patients first come to the hospital, they avoid contact with others, refuse to interact in group therapy settings, and resist making friends with other patients. Disturbed people are unable to relate intimately or even casually to others. Lonely people relate casually but have few or no intimate relationships. Healthy, fulfilled people operate from a base of intimacy.

Our Need for Intimacy   Intimacy is, then, more than merely the icing on the cake of living. It is a fundamental need. We need it from the time we are born. Infants can die if they are deprived of cuddling. As we grow, we tend to expand and alter our sphere of intimacy. Buhrmester and Furman (1987) studied the development of companionship and intimacy among second, fifth, and eighth graders. They had the children rate the importance of companionship and of experiences of intimate disclosure. At all three levels, the children indicated a desire for both companionship and intimacy. But there were some differences in the sources used to fulfill those needs. Parents were more important as a source of companionship for the second- and fifth- than for the eighth-grade students. Same-sex peers were important in all three grades, but they became increasingly important as the children aged. Opposite-sex peers became important as companions for the first time in the eighth grade.

Our need for intimacy continues throughout life. Psychiatrist William Glasser (1984:9–10) argues that the "need to belong" is a part of our genetic makeup:

> As I look inside myself, I find that the need for friends, family, and love—best described as the need to belong—occupies as large a place in my mind as the need to survive. It may not be as immediate as thirst or hunger, but if, over the long pull, I did not have the close, loving family and friends that I almost take for granted, I think that the idea that life is hardly worth living would come occasionally to mind.

Ironically, there is some evidence that intimate relationships have become more important to Americans than they were in the past (Perlman and Fehr 1987:20). We say "ironically" because the trends noted in chapter 1, such as the high rate of divorce and increased number of people living alone, make the fulfillment of intimacy needs more problematic. The struggle of Ellie (see PERSONAL) illustrates the point.

Intimacy and Our Well-Being   We feel the need for intimacy. But do intimate relationships have the expected payoff? Do they bring a satisfaction, a sense of fulfillment to our lives that nothing else can? The answer is yes. And it is important to have those intimate relationships from childhood. A study of 143 children aged eight to twelve years reported that feeling close to mother and to teachers is associated with higher levels of self-esteem (Burnett and Demnar 1996). Childhood friendships are associated with greater emotional strength in adulthood (Flaste 1991). A study of adults found that those who were mentally healthy had, when they were adolescents, good relationships with their peers and positive relationships with adults outside their families (Hightower 1990). A common factor reported by patients seeking outpatient psychotherapy is the failure to develop an intimate relationship (Horowitz 1979). Other researchers have found that the lack of an intimate relationship in marriage is associated with a number of emotional and physical disorders (Waring and Chelune 1983:183).

Two sociologists who examined the relationship between urbanism and a sense of well-being used data from London, England; Los Angeles, California; and Sydney, Australia (Palisi and Canning 1983). They looked at such things as people's age, education, occupation, location and type of home, marital status, and relationships. In all three cities, they found that the best predictor of well-being was the quality of people's social relationships.

Many other studies have shown that our well-being is dependent on "contact with affectively close or intimate partners" (Reis 1984:34). Two psychologists who used a national sample reported that people high in the desire and ability to engage in intimate relations also tend to have better mental health (McAdams and Bryant 1987). The women who scored high said that they are generally happy and basically satisfied with their work and family roles and their leisure time. Men who scored high reported fewer problems of mental and physical health, less drug and alcohol abuse, and less uncertainty about the future.

If, on the one hand, intimacy enhances our sense of well-being, our satisfaction, and our happiness, on the other hand it acts as a buffer when difficulties come. For example, among women who have suffered serious negative life events (such as divorce or death of a loved one), those without a confidant were ten times more likely to become depressed than those who had an intimate with whom to share their problem (Brown and Harris 1978). Intimate relationships moderate the severity of the impact of negative events.

The Perils of Intimacy   Intimate relationships are two-edged swords. When they go well, they enable a person to achieve a higher level of life satisfaction than otherwise possible. When they go badly, however, they are a bitter and painful experience. Parents, friends, and spouses can enrich us. They can also be a point of agony in our lives.

The extent of possible hurt is illustrated by the numbers of those hospitalized for mental illness who have endured some kind of abuse from an intimate. One study of psychiatric patients discharged over an eighteen-month period reported that 43 percent had a history of abuse—physical or sexual or both (Rieker and Carmen 1986). This does not mean, however, that painful intimate relationships inevitably doom people to mental illness. There are those who take painful relationships, work through

them, and emerge as stronger and more mature individuals (Lauer and Lauer 1988:105–16).

The point is that intimate relationships are not a guarantee of well-being. Caution and understanding are necessary tools for establishing helpful relationships. Otherwise, like Ellie, you may make a series of bad choices.

THE NATURE OF INTIMACY

We have briefly defined intimacy as a relationship characterized by mutual commitment, affection, and sharing. We need now to look at the meaning of intimacy in more depth. What happens between two people who have an intimate relationship?

The Meaning of Intimacy

Based on his clinical practice, Erik Erikson (1950: 255) claimed that a central task of the young adult is to establish intimacy:

> the capacity to commit himself to concrete affiliations and partnerships and to develop the ethical strength to abide by such commitments, even though they may call for significant sacrifices and compromises.

Intimate relations exist prior to adulthood, of course, but different tasks are more central at other ages. The young adult, just emerging from adolescence, faces a decision about with whom to be intimate. The choices that are made are crucial to the continued development of the individual.

In Erikson's view, intimacy includes such things between people as openness, sharing, mutual trust, self-abandon, and commitment. Building on the work of Erikson and others, White, Speisman, Jackson, Bartis, and Costos (1986) developed a measure of intimacy that includes five components. One component is an orientation to the other and to the relationship. This involves the extent to which the individual's thinking, feelings, and behavior are focused on the intimate partner and the relationship rather than on his or herself. The second component is caring and concern for the other. The third is sexuality, the degree to which the individual's sexual life emphasizes mutuality rather than personal concerns.

The fourth component is the extent of commitment to the other, and the fifth is the nature or kind of communication with the other. Communication

INVOLVEMENT
What Does Intimacy Mean?

As noted in the text, there are some variations in the meaning of intimacy to people. Conduct your own research into the matter by first taking the following test and then asking six or more other people to take it:

What qualities or characteristics make a relationship an intimate one? Check each one that applies:

caring	understanding
sharing	communication
physical interaction	friendship/ companionship

sexual interaction	trust/faith
openness	commitment
honesty/ sincerity	self-abandon
security	similar interests
love	acceptance
	respect
	mutuality/ reciprocity

Which characteristics are chosen most often? Are any of them omitted altogether? Roscoe, Kennedy, and Pope (1987) found that the five most frequently mentioned characteristics, in order of mention, were:

sharing, physical or sexual interaction, trust/faith, openness, and love.

If the entire class does this project, you can assign people to survey different groups: males, females, adolescents, young adults, older adults, and so on. Tabulate the results from the entire class and see if there are any group differences. Roscoe, Kennedy, and Pope (1987) did find some slight differences between the male and female adolescents they surveyed. What do your results suggest about the quality of intimate relationships today?

---

includes such things as how much an individual reveals to the intimate partner, how much he or she listens, and how often he or she initiates communication.

Other researchers find somewhat similar dimensions to intimacy (Moss and Schwebel 1993). Two hundred and seventy-seven university students were asked to indicate the difference between an intimate and nonintimate relationship (Roscoe, Kennedy, and Pope 1987). The students defined intimate relations in Erikson's terms of openness, sharing, and trust. But they added physical/sexual interaction to Erikson's list, and less than 10 percent of them included his notions of self-abandon and commitment. The divergence from Erikson, the researchers speculate, may be due to the fact that the students have just emerged from adolescence and are just beginning the task of establishing their intimate lives. They may still be uncertain as to whether it is possible to give so much to someone else and still retain their own individuality. Or it may be due to the fact that changes have occurred since Erikson's formulation and that people are less willing to include commitment and self-abandon in their intimate relationships.

In our view, intimacy has somewhat different meanings for various people. But there is a core meaning that is applicable to all people. And we would include affection, sharing (including commu-

nication), and commitment as part of the core of a satisfying intimate relationship.

Intimacy and Equity

Exchange Theory Applied

As noted in the last chapter, *exchange theory* argues that a one-sided intimate relationship will probably not last. For example, research with more than 500 college students showed that those who perceived the relationship to be equitable or felt that they were *slightly* overbenefitted were happier and more contented than others (Walster, Walster, and Traupmann 1978) (figure 5.2). Those who felt they were giving more than they were receiving tended to be angry. Those who believed they were receiving a good deal more than they were giving, on the other hand, tended to feel guilty. Those in equitable relationships also felt more confident about them and were more likely to view them as stable and potentially long-term.

A sense of equity, then, is an important part of a fulfilling intimate relationship. The way that people decide whether equity exists varies by gender and by the type of intimate relationship. Kollock, Blumstein, and Schwartz (1994) compared married and cohabiting couples. They found that, for all but

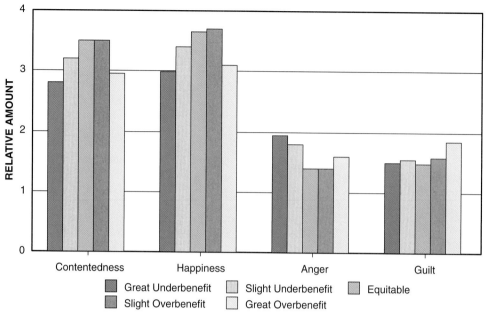

FIGURE 5.2 **Equity and Satisfaction in Relationships**
(*Source:* Data from E. Walster, G. W. Walster, and J.Traupman, *Journal of Personality and Social Psychology,* 36:87, 1978.)

Caring and concern for another is an important aspect of intimacy.

husbands, the more income earned, the more the individual feels that the partner is benefitted. Wives feel themselves benefitted by spending time in the labor force. Husbands who do some housework believe they are more benefitted than do husbands who do little or no housework. The more expressive husbands and wives are, the more they believe their partners are benefitted. The more attractive or better educated female cohabitors are, the more they rate themselves as benefitted. Finally, male cohabitors rate their benefits significantly higher than do female cohabitors. Thus, people use a variety of measures to decide the extent of equity in their relationships.

Intimacy As Self-Sustaining

Just as loneliness tends to generate a downward, self-sustaining cycle (figure 5.1), intimacy tends to generate an upward, self-sustaining cycle. That is, an intimate relationship tends to create certain kinds of behavior, attitudes, and feelings that tend to maintain and even intensify the sense of intimacy. We need to add a word of caution here, however. Intimacy is not self-sustaining in the sense that you will always feel a closeness to the other. We need to distinguish between intimacy as a feeling and intimacy as a behavior. If you are committed to another person and share some of your feelings with that person, you are engaging in intimate behavior even though you may not feel intimate at the moment (perhaps you are angry or agitated or anxious about something). Intimacy as a feeling is "episodic" (Wynne and Wynne 1986). Some intimate behaviors are also episodic. Intimacy, in other words, is not something that is either always increasing and there or decreasing and leaving us. In the normal course of life, our intimate feelings and intimate behaviors wax and wane even while the intimate relationship is developing in a positive way.

MEETING AND GETTING TO KNOW OTHERS

How does the intimate relationship begin? Obviously, it is something that develops over time. There is no instant intimacy. In this section, we will look at some of the factors involved in the process, including factors that we use to select and choose from among those available for an intimate relationship.

First Impressions

First impressions are important, because they may determine whether we shall pursue a relationship. You may decide after the first few moments that another person is or is not the kind of person you want to know better. And, of course, others make similar judgments about you based on their first impressions. It is important to realize that first impressions are not necessarily accurate. Sometimes our first impressions are based on the similarity of a person to someone else we know. Or they grow out of some **stereotype.** For example, you may see a fat man laughing. Is he one of those typical "jolly fat" types? Or does he just happen to be laughing at the time when you see him?

General Appearance   We all tend to make snap judgments about others based on such things as physical appearance and demeanor. A woman wrote

We often use first impressions to decide whether to pursue a relationship.

to an advice columnist because she was concerned about the impression she was making on others. She was a natural blonde, she pointed out, and for much of her life she felt that people hadn't taken her seriously because of the "dumb blonde" stereotype. But then she started wearing glasses, and people began to treat her differently. Glasses are associated with intelligence. She wondered, however, if she would make an even better impression by dyeing her hair, since the blonde hair might cancel out some of the impact of the glasses. The columnist replied that intelligent people do not operate on the assumption that blondes are dumb and people with glasses are intelligent. But the columnist was not totally correct. Many people—even intelligent, informed ones—make judgments about others that are based on such myths. While this does not mean that we should obediently shape our behavior according to the prevailing myths, we do need to be aware that people do react to us on the basis of our appearance.

If we have even a brief interaction with someone, we are likely to form a number of impressions about him or her. In an early, unpublished experiment, an instructor invited a friend, who was unknown to the students, to come into his classroom (Allport 1961:501). The friend was only in the room for about a minute, during which the instructor asked him what he thought of the weather. The man made a few neutral comments, then left. The instructor asked the students to "list your first impressions" of the man. On the average, students listed between five and six different impressions, ranging from such things as quiet and cultivated, to "trying to please," to "nice guy, congenial." Their first impressions included such things as personal traits, physical characteristics, judgments about the man's motivations, ethnic characteristics, speculations about the man's status and role, and the effect he had on them. Obviously, first impressions are often not very reliable, but they are a factor in whether or not we pursue a relationship.

Nonverbal Cues Experts assert that anywhere between 50 and 80 percent of meaning is communicated without words. We communicate meaning not only by what we say but also by a variety of **nonverbal cues**—facial expressions, body positions, gestures, and paralanguage (inflection, rate of

speech, loudness of speaking). Women are generally better than men at picking up nonverbal cues. For example, women usually recognize various emotions from facial expressions. But while men usually recognize happiness in a woman's face, "they pick up on distress just 70 percent of the time. A woman's face has to be really sad for men to see it" (Blum 1998:37).

We expect people's verbal and nonverbal statements to agree with each. Given a contradiction between the two, we tend to believe the nonverbal. For example, if someone says "I love you" but does not look serious or has hesitancy or lack of emotion in the words, you will probably disbelieve or at least question the statement.

Nonverbal cues are an important source of our first impressions. We define the man who slouches as lacking in self-confidence or assertiveness. We define the woman who smiles broadly as a happy person. We use a variety of nonverbal cues rather than a single cue to make judgments about others, of course. In an experiment carried out in a bar, two female associates of the experimenter established eye contact with males (Walsh and Hewitt 1985). In some cases, they made eye contact once and, in other cases, a number of times during a five-minute period. Once eye contact was made, the woman smiled in some cases but not in others. When the woman made repeated eye contact and smiled, the man approached her in 60 percent of the cases. When eye contact was made only once, or when the woman did not smile, approach occurred in less than 20 percent of the cases.

Nonverbal cues are not always interpreted correctly. In particular, males tend to read more sexual content into nonverbal cues (Abbey 1982). A man may define a woman's friendliness as sexual interest. He may hear more sexual innuendos in conversation than are intended. He may see a woman as being seductive or flirtatious when she is just trying to be sociable. Generally, women are more accurate in interpreting nonverbal cues than are men. But whether we interpret them accurately or not, we all attend to them, and we behave on the basis of the way we have defined them.

Opening Lines Verbal cues are also important. Favorable impressions depend on *what* is said as well as *how* it is said. As with the women in the bar,

PERSPECTIVE
Getting Acquainted Victorian Style

The ease or difficulty of establishing a heterosexual relationship varies from time to time and society to society. Such relationships have been more problematic in other times and places than they are in our society today. Samuel Butler's *The Way of All Flesh* is a portrait of Victorian England. Although Theobald, one of the characters in the novel, eventually fell in love and married, the problem of meeting and getting to know women was agonizing for him. This is how Butler describes Theobald's problems:

> Theobald knew nothing about women. The only women he had been thrown in contact with were his sisters, two of whom were always correcting him, and a few school friends whom these had got their father to ask to Elmhurst. These young ladies had either been so shy that they and Theobald had never amalgamated, or they had been supposed to be clever and had said smart things to him. He did not say smart things himself and did not want other people to say them. Besides, they talked about music—and he hated music—or pictures—and he hated pictures—or books and, except the classics, he hated books. And then sometimes he wanted to dance with them, and he did not know how to dance, and did not want to know.
>
> At Mrs. Cowey's parties again he had seen some young ladies and had been introduced to them. He had tried to make himself agreeable, but was always left with the impression that he had not been successful. . . . The result of his experience was that women had never done him any good and he was not accustomed to associate them with any pleasure. . . . As for kissing, he had never kissed a woman in his life except his sister—and my own sisters when we were all small children together. Over and above these kisses, he had until quite lately been required to imprint a solemn, flabby kiss night and morning upon his father's cheek, and this, to the best of my belief, was the extent of Theobald's knowledge in the matter of kissing, at the time of which I am now writing. The result of the foregoing was that he had come to dislike women, as mysterious beings whose ways were not as his ways, nor their thoughts as his thoughts.

Source: Samuel Butler, *The Way of All Flesh* (New York: Signet Classic, 1960), pp. 41–42.

---

nonverbal gestures may gain the attention of another person. They may indicate that you are interested in establishing a relationship. But what then? What do you say to someone you have never met before? What do you use as an opening line?

Three psychologists who asked that question conducted research on male and female preference for opening lines (Kleinke, Meeker, and Staneski 1986). In one of their studies, university students and employees evaluated a number of opening lines used by men to meet women. In another study, university students and employees evaluated opening lines women used to meet men. The researchers compiled their list of opening lines by asking students to record all the ones they could think of.

They grouped the opening lines into three categories. The "direct approach" consisted of such openings as "You look like a warm person" and "Hi. I like you." The "innocuous approach" is illustrated by such lines as "Are you a student?" and "Where are you from?" The "cute-flippant" approach consisted of opening lines like "I'm easy. Are you?" and "Do you fool around?" The subjects agreed that the cute-flippant lines were the least desirable, though the women disliked them more than the men. Women preferred the innocuous approach, while men leaned more toward a direct approach.

What Attracts?

Are you now, or have you been, in an intimate relationship with someone? If so, think about what it was that first attracted you to that person. Was there some kind of "chemistry" that occurred? Was the attraction instantaneous? What were the qualities of the person that appealed to you? Social scientists have been interested in such questions and have

COMPARISON

Mexican and United States Teens Portray Their Ideals About the Opposite Sex

What kind of person of the opposite sex do you prefer? Researchers who asked this question of a group of ninth graders in the United States and another group in Mexico City found both similarities and differences in the adolescents' responses. Both groups were asked to rank ten qualities in the order they valued them and to draw a picture of their ideal. In the rankings, both groups said they preferred someone of the opposite sex who is kind, honest, good-looking, fun, and intelligent. Of ten qualities suggested, "having a lot of money" was the least important to the respondents.

There were some gender differences. Boys emphasized physical attractiveness more than did girls. Girls, on the other hand, stressed personal qualities such as "gentle," "intelligent," and "faithful" more than did boys.

There were also some national differences. Compared to the United States youths, the Mexican teens put less emphasis on physical characteristics when describing their ideal. The United States teens were more likely than Mexicans to emphasize such things as hair and eye color, size of lips, and other physical features on their drawings. The two groups also differed on the

value of intelligence in someone of the opposite sex. While more than half of both groups ranked intelligence as important, the Mexicans ranked the quality significantly higher than did the United States teens.

As this study suggests, there seems to be some consensus among people of various nationalities about what makes a person of the opposite sex attractive. There are also differences. But the one thing that appears consistent is that people generally have little difficulty identifying what they find attractive in the opposite sex (Stiles, Gibbons, and Schnellmann 1990).

found a number of factors involved in interpersonal attraction.

Physical Attractiveness   Beauty may be only skin-deep, but it is an important factor in attraction. It is particularly important in first impressions, when there is little other available information about someone. It diminishes in importance, though it doesn't completely lose its importance, in longer-term relationships or where other information is available. The importance of physical attractiveness is illustrated by an account that Nancy, a female student, shared with us:

Until I was sixteen, I was very unattractive. Actually, I was pretty ugly. I was overweight, wore nerdy glasses, had very bad skin, and my hair was always messy looking. I didn't date anybody until I was sixteen, and even then it was for only a few days. I had been madly in love with a guy that I pursued since I was fourteen. But I wasn't successful. He was the hunk of our class. Everybody liked him and he could have chosen among several girls in my class. So I didn't expect him to go out with me, although I wanted it very much. His rejection reinforced my belief that I was terribly unat-

tractive. And that hurt my self-esteem. It was a vicious cycle. The more my self-esteem went down, the more unattractive I became.

Everything suddenly changed when I was sixteen and a half. I lost weight. I got contact lenses. And I got a haircut that looked good on me. I became a different person. My self-esteem went up just by looking into the mirror. It didn't change my status at school much, but when I went away on vacation, I realized that I had become attractive. Suddenly a number of guys asked me to go out with them, and people seemed generally friendlier than they were before. Just by changing my looks, I changed that whole vicious cycle that had been so painful.

Nancy's experience illustrates some of the findings of research. Attractive persons are more self-accepting, and self-acceptance enhances attractiveness. The more we see ourselves as attractive, the more self-esteem we have at all ages—as children, adolescents, and adults. We also tend to believe that physically attractive people possess socially desirable personality traits, and we expect them to be more successful than those who are less attractive (Berscheid and Walster 1978). When we see someone who is physically attractive to us, we are likely to define that person as more likable, friendly, confident, sensitive, and flexible than someone who is less attractive. Obviously, then, we perceive physically attractive people as more desirable dating partners.

In essence, we tend to operate on the principle that what is beautiful is good. And the meaning of "beautiful" reflects cultural ideals. In our society, "beautiful" for women means shapely but slender. It is not surprising, then, that a survey of 200 female college students found a correlation between body mass index (a measure of weight relative to height) and whether the women were dating and had ever engaged in sexual relations (Wiederman 1998).

Interestingly, when we perceive someone to be physically attractive, we are likely to also attribute a host of other positive qualities to that person. Of course, that initial judgment may change as we get to know the person. But the physically attractive person has an advantage in the quest for intimacy, because more people will desire and seek to know him or her.

Similarity Do opposites attract? That may work for magnets, but for people, it is similarity rather than differences that attract us to each other. At later stages, some differences may enhance an intimate relationship, as we shall discuss in subsequent chapters. Initially, however, we are attracted to people who are like us in their attitudes, their values, and even their personalities; and we are put off by those who are different from us (Neimeyer and Mitchell 1988; Hester 1996). The conclusion reached by Berscheid and Walster (1978:88) more than two decades ago is still valid:

> The answer to the question, "Does attitudinal similarity generate liking?" is a resounding "yes." When we discover that others share our beliefs and attitudes, it is satisfying: we like them. When we discover that others disagree with us, it is unsettling; it's hard to like such persons.

In fact, when we perceive someone to be different, we may communicate with that person in a way that says "I am not available." This was one of the findings of two researchers who wanted to see if couples who developed an intimate relationship

behaved differently with each other from the start than those who only have a casual relationship.[1] The researchers used thirty couples who were dating steadily and paired together sixty people who were strangers to each other. They told some of the pairs of strangers that they were like each other and told others that they were dissimilar. Each pair talked together for ten minutes on a number of selected topics.

After observing all of the couples' discussions, the researchers concluded that the pairs of strangers who believed themselves similar to each other communicated very much like steadily dating couples. On the other hand, those who believed themselves to be dissimilar communicated with each other in a way that said that they were unavailable for an intimate relationship.

Sometimes, it may be nonverbal cues that enable us to decide that the other is similar or dissimilar. Eisenman (1985) raised the question of whether students who were marijuana users would be more attracted to other users even if they didn't know about the drug use. He paired fifty marijuana users with fifty other users on one occasion and then fifty nonusers on another occasion. The students talked with each other for about ten minutes on each occasion, ostensibly to choose a partner for an experiment. The discussion was held in the presence of the experimenter; there was no mention of drug usage. Nevertheless, users tended to choose other users for partners and nonusers tended to choose nonusers. Eisenman noted that this supports the notion that similarity leads to attraction but that we need to investigate the kinds of cues that lead people to choose others who are similar to them.

Incidentally, similarity may be difficult to simulate. An experiment with college students (DePaulo, Stone, and Lassiter 1985) reported that those who tried to feign agreement with an attractive person were not adept at the attempt. If you try to appear to be similar with someone in order to be attractive to that person, your efforts may be obvious.

Why does similarity lead to attraction? Isn't dissimilarity more interesting and exciting? Actually, there are a number of reasons we tend to like those

---

[1]Reported in *Psychology Today,* February 1988, p. 13.

who are similar to us. First, we feel more confident with someone who is like us. That person, we believe, is more likely to reciprocate our feelings than is someone who is very different. Second, those who are similar to us build our self-esteem, because they agree with our attitudes and values, which helps to validate us. All of us need social validation for our attitudes and values. Think, for example, of one of your beliefs about marriage. Do you believe that marriage should be confined to one man and one woman? What if you were the only person in the world to hold such a belief? What if everyone else argued that marriage should involve a man and a number of women or a woman and a number of men. How long would you be able to hold on to your belief?

Third, similarity facilitates the development of intimacy. Sharing thoughts and feelings and ideas is much easier with those who are similar to us, and the sharing is likely to be rewarded (approved) and reciprocated. Those who are very different from us may not understand why we feel the way we do about certain matters or why we believe what we do. Intimacy is more difficult under such circumstances.

Other Factors in Attraction   As in all human behavior, multiple factors are involved in attraction. **Propinquity,** nearness in place, is important. We tend to like people who live near us or who are close to us in some setting (classrooms, workplaces, etc.). A classic study by Festinger, Schachter, and Back (1950) looked at the development of friendships among married students in a new housing project. The researchers asked the subjects to name their three closest friends. They found that next-door neighbors were most frequently named as best friends, followed by those who were only two doors away. Propinquity was the most important factor in determining friendship patterns.

Propinquity may be important because it leads to greater familiarity with those people who are near us. And familiarity is also a factor in attraction. We tend to like people who are familiar to us. Repeated exposure to something or someone can increase our liking, especially if we are neutral or positive initially (Zajonc 1968).

As Nancy's story suggested, self-esteem is also a factor in attraction. We tend to prefer others who have about the same level of self-esteem as we have

(Abloff and Hewitt 1985). We particularly find those with lower self-esteem to be less attractive to us. A different aspect of self-esteem and attraction is that we tend to like people who enhance our own self-esteem. Others enhance our self-esteem when they agree with our ideas, when they compliment us, and when they treat us as special in some sense. For example, you are treated as special and, accordingly, you will tend to be attracted to someone whose expressions of affection are exclusively for you (Kimble and Kardes 1987). A young woman who brushed off the flirtatious behavior of a handsome man as of no consequence explained: "He does that with every woman he meets. It's nothing special for him to flirt with me. I don't intend to be just another one of his long line of conquests."

In sum, many factors other than "chemistry" draw people together and make them attractive to each other. At this point, it would be interesting for you to rethink your own intimate relationship and the qualities you cited earlier that attracted you to him or her.

DEVELOPING A RELATIONSHIP

Once attracted to someone as a friend or potential lover, the relationship develops over time. Again, thinking of an intimate relationship with which you have been involved, can you identify different stages or phases in it? That is, did the relationship at a certain point enter a new stage or phase and become a different kind of relationship than it had been earlier? Social scientists who are interested in the development of relationships have tried to identify such stages or phases. We will use the four-stage model proposed by Carl Backman (1981:239–67).

First Stage: Initial Meeting and Awareness

If we begin at the point when the two intimates have not yet met, we can raise the question of what factors go into any two people getting together. We have already suggested that propinquity is important. But we can go beyond that and raise the question of what determines propinquity. That is, the people who live near you are not there by pure chance. Propinquity and similarity tend to work together. People who are alike tend to live in

Getting together to explore ways in which you are alike or different is an important step in developing relationships.

the same area, have similar leisure interests, and belong to similar kinds of organizations. The probability is, in other words, that those who are around are also similar to you in many ways. In particular, we are likely to grow up in neighborhoods and go to school with people from the same social class. A **social class** is a group of people with similar income, education, and occupational prestige. People in the same class also tend to have similar values and attitudes. Middle-class people tend not to interact much with upper- or lower-class people, at least not in a setting that lends itself to the initiation and development of an intimate relationship.

Thus, there are social factors that lead to clusterings of relatively similar people. Of course, the more mobile you are, the more likely you are to sense dissimilarities with others. Moving from a rural area to the city or from one part of the country

to another part can make you more aware of the differences among people. A Midwestern student who moved to California to go to school said: "I lived in California for three years before I felt like I was no longer in a foreign country." Gradually, the student got involved in some organizations and found people who shared his interests. As he got to know like-minded people, he no longer felt he was in a foreign country.

Second Stage: The Selection Process

Once we are aware of the choices we have, of the variety of relatively similar and dissimilar people with whom we interact, we select those with whom we would like to develop a relationship. We have noted above the important factors in the selection process—first impressions and the various bases for attraction.

But two additional considerations need to be mentioned in the selection process. First, we all operate within the context of the **norms** of our groups. A norm is simply an expected pattern of behavior. Families tend to have norms about the kind of people with whom it is desirable to interact. In fact, many stories and movies, such as Shakespeare's classic tale *Romeo and Juliet* have been based on the problems that arise when people decide to have an intimate relationship with someone who breaks family norms. For any particular family, the norm may dictate against intimate relationships (either friendship or love relationships) with people of other religions, other races, a different social class, or simply with those who have a personality that the family finds offensive.

For example, a male student reported that his father had once asked him not to spend time with a certain neighborhood friend. At first, the father was rather vague about the reasons. But eventually, the student came to understand:

> My friend was different from other kids in our neighborhood. It's hard to say just how he was different. He just didn't like to do the kinds of things other kids did. Actually, he was a little effeminate. I knew he wasn't a homosexual. But my father was afraid he might be. And he was afraid that he would somehow contaminate me if I spent much time with him.

One of Nancy's problems, in addition to her self-acknowledged lack of attractiveness, was that her father didn't want her to date anyone outside of her religion. Nancy said that this increased her difficulties in finding a boyfriend; there just weren't many available Jewish boys around. She was embarrassed to admit that her first date didn't occur until she was sixteen, but she abided by her family's norm.

A second consideration in the selection process is the compromises that we make. We are drawn to others that we consider physically attractive, but we may not try to establish a relationship with the person we regard as the most attractive. Why not? We tend to befriend those who are near us, but we may not want to have a friendship with the lonely person who lives next door. Why not? We are attracted to those who are like us, but we may avoid a certain individual even though that person shares our same political and religious philosophy. Why?

There is no single answer to such questions, but one factor that operates in the selection process is compromise. We compromise with our inclinations or ideals because of other factors. For example, we may not try to establish a relationship with a person who is much more attractive than we are because we assume that the relationship will not endure; that person will find someone equally attractive and abandon us. To be safe, we generally try to establish an intimate relationship with someone we regard as roughly equal to our own attractiveness (Kalick and Hamilton 1986). Or we may not establish an intimate relationship with the person next door because we already have as many such relationships as we can handle. Or we may avoid the person who shares our political and religious philosophy because that person is somewhat obnoxious. Ideals and inclinations frequently have to be compromised in accord with such practical considerations.

Third Stage: Developing Intimacy

Once a relationship begins, certain mechanisms come into play to lead the participants into intimacy. These mechanisms begin almost immediately, but they take on a new intensity and depth in the third stage.

Self-Disclosure   One of the most important mechanisms in the development of intimacy is **self-disclosure,** the honest revealing of oneself to another person. At first, people reveal things about themselves that are relatively safe. As intimacy develops, an increasing amount of private information may be shared. In the early part of the relationship, there tends to be equity in self-disclosure; each person reveals about the same amount of information as he or she is receiving from the other.

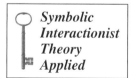

Symbolic Interactionist Theory Applied

This self-disclosure is more than a sharing of information. As stressed by a *symbolic interactionist* point of view, an intimate relationship is created and maintained by ongoing communication in which personal meanings such as values and attitudes are constructed and shared (Duck 1994). That is, the two people are not merely opening up a part of themselves to each other, but are helping shape each other and are growing in their understanding both of themselves and their partner. Self-disclosure links you with another person in a mutually growing process.

Four kinds of things are shared in self-disclosure (Waring and Chelune 1983). First, there is a sharing of emotions. Intimates tell each other how they feel about things. Second, there is a sharing of needs. Intimates reveal what they see as their personal needs in the relationship as well as more general needs. Third, there is a sharing of thoughts, beliefs, attitudes, and even fantasies. "I'm never sure what you're thinking" is as damaging a statement about intimacy as "I'm never sure what you're feeling." Finally, there is a sharing of self-awareness, the way each feels and thinks about himself or herself as a person.

Sharing our feelings, needs, thoughts, and self-awareness with someone else is both a result of intimacy and a creator of greater intimacy. In a study of 231 dating couples, researchers found that the more the partners engaged in self-disclosure to the other, the more they reported love feelings for each other and the closer they regarded themselves to each other (Rubin et al. 1980). Another study, of forty-four nursing students, reported the kind of upward spiral we discussed above: intimacy leads to further self-disclosure, which, in turn, enhances the sense of intimacy (Falk and Wagner 1985). Finally, a study of thirty-eight dating couples over a four-month period revealed that those who were still together had a greater amount of self-disclosure in the initial phases of the relationship than did those who broke up during the period (Berg and McQuinn 1986).

Systems Theory Applied

Because self-disclosure is tied up so closely with the development of intimacy, we tend to disclose ourselves only to a few (we cannot have intimate relations with a great many people) and only to those with whom we expect to have intimacy. Self-disclosure is, after all, a risky process. The more you disclose, the more vulnerable you are to being manipulated, controlled, scorned, and embarrassed. In terms of *systems theory,* we may think of self-disclosure as a "form of

boundary regulation" in which there are two boundaries involved (Derlega et al. 1993:67). One boundary is the dyadic, the boundary within which it is safe to share with one's partner without fear that the information will disrupt the relationship or pass beyond the dyad. The other boundary is the personal boundary, which maintains certain information within the individual. Intimacy development means a progressive shrinking (though not an obliteration) of the personal boundary; in other words, more and more is shared. And because of the risks, that sharing requires trust. We trust the other *not* to react negatively, to support us, and to hold what we say in confidence.

As we disclose ourselves in an intimate relationship, trust tends to grow, enhancing the sense of intimacy. Self-disclosure has a number of other benefits for intimacy. The more the self-disclosure, the greater the level of satisfaction with the relationship (Jorgensen and Gaudy 1980). Self-disclosure can increase the attraction of people toward each other (Archer and Cook 1986). It can enhance the sense of compatibility as partners become increasingly aware of their similarities and at ease with the views of each other. In general, self-disclosure is not all there is to intimacy, but it is a large and essential part of any intimate relationship.

We should note that there are some sex differences in self-disclosure. Among children, girls seem to seek intimate disclosures in their friendships at an earlier age than boys do (Buhrmester and Furman 1987). Among adults, both men and women tend to disclose more to females than to males. Women generally, however, tend to be willing to disclose more than do men. Women, for example, are more willing to talk about their feelings of depression, anxiety, anger, and fear than are men (Snell, Miller, and Belk 1988). Gender-role orientations also make a difference. A survey of 302 undergraduate students found the highest levels of self-disclosure among feminine and androgynous females, followed by (in decreasing levels of self-disclosure) masculine females, masculine males, androgynous males, undifferentiated females, undifferentiated males, and feminine males (Foubert and Sholley 1996). As we saw in chapter 3, gender, gender roles, and gender-role orientations all make a difference in how people behave.

Interdependence and Commitment An increasing sense of interdependence develops during the third stage of intimacy. Each partner is dependent on the other to fulfill some of his or her needs. Each has some power in the relationship, therefore, because of the dependence of the other. But the power may not be equal because of differing amounts of commitment to the relationship. An intimate relationship may be more important to one partner than the other. The one with the most interest in maintaining the relationship is likely to be the most committed to it. And the person who is the most committed can be exploited because that person has the most to lose if the relationship breaks up (Backman 1981:261).

In an ideal situation, issues of power and inequity would not arise. But human life is not ideal. People bring varying amounts of commitment to a relationship. Interdependence seldom if ever means an equal amount of dependence of each partner. And power issues, as we shall see in chapter 12, come into most of our intimate relationships.

In essence, then, interdependence and commitment are both essential elements of a developing intimacy. But they are also problem areas that can lead to the dissolution as well as the maintenance of the relationship.

Fourth Stage: Maintaining or Dissolving the Relationship

In this final stage, processes will be operating that will tend either to maintain or dissolve an intimate relationship. As Backman (1981:262) notes, commitment "is rarely complete, nor is it unchanging." Rather, the extent of commitment tends to reflect the perceived rewards and costs. Whether a friendship, date, or marriage, most of us will reflect at some point on the rewards and costs of the relationship. We will evaluate the relationship in terms of what we think we deserve out of it and the costs in time, money, and energy that are required to maintain it.

Evaluations of costs and rewards can and do change over time, of course. Individuals develop, altering their sense of what they need and what they want. A woman may begin a relationship with a man, for example, with the idea that she only wants some companionship and fun. She may eventually cohabit with him. And she may later decide that she wants to marry this person. Our needs and wants are never static. One of the ironies of an intimate relationship is the fact that those things that fulfill needs at one point in time may become a problem at a later point. For example, the woman who marries a man because he is very careful about spending money may later resent his frugality when they have become financially successful.

Our evaluation of the rewards and costs change also because we observe and compare our relationships with those of other people. Such an evaluation can work in two ways. We may decide that our relationship is costing too much, or we may decide that we are fortunate for having a uniquely rewarding relationship. Observing others may deepen as well as lessen our commitment.

Once a relationship begins to dissolve, many of the processes that built the intimacy work in reverse. For example, intimacy develops as people reward each other in an equitable fashion. A kind of "tit-for-tat" process occurs as rewards are reciprocated in an ongoing fashion. A reverse process, in which there is an "eye for an eye and a tooth for a tooth" on a continuing basis may occur as a relationship dissolves. People begin to punish each other in various ways. And each injury, each slight, each hurt is reciprocated.

Similarly, intimacy grows as people support each other's self-esteem. In dissolution, they may attack each other's self-esteem in various ways. Self-disclosure, the heart of intimacy, may also reverse. The partners may even fear to disclose anything because of the possibility of its being used against them. Trust, interdependence, and commitment all decline as a relationship deteriorates.

"It is sad," a man remarked to us as we watched a joyous and expensive wedding, "to think that they put so much into this and in a few years the marriage might crumble." Intimate relationships do dissolve. Some should. But many continue. People maintain friendships and marriages for the duration of their lives. In either case, such factors as self-disclosure, trust, and commitment are crucial ingredients.

PRINCIPLES FOR ENHANCING INTIMACY

1. If you are lonely, give yourself the assignment of meeting someone new in the next week or two. If you have trouble doing this assignment, get help from a school counselor or from books or articles in the library.

2. Like it or not, people often initially decide on the social desirability of another person by how he or she looks or behaves. The clothes worn, the words spoken, the attitudes assumed become a shorthand method for determining whether you want to get to know someone better or whether that person wants to pursue a relationship with you. Since first impressions are important, therefore, pay attention to your dress, your demeanor, your speech. Make them consistent with the kind of person you are.

3. You are most likely to have an intimate relationship with someone who is similar to you in attitudes and values. Thus, it is important to learn as much as possible about the other person's attitudes and values. Do not think that simply because you have an initial, strong attraction to someone, your feelings of "love" will overcome any differences that exist.

4. Self-esteem is crucial to fulfilling intimate relationships. Anything you do to increase your self-esteem will enhance your relationships and, thereby, your well-being. Books are available to help you build self-esteem. Your self-esteem will also grow to the extent that you associate with people who value you and compliment you on your traits and abilities. Finally, find something that you're good at and pursue that interest; achievement is an integral part of self-esteem.

5. Equity is important to intimacy. You can't build an intimate relationship by giving so much to the other that the other feels overbenefitted. You must both give and receive, so that each of you feels that the relationship is equitable.

6. Self-disclosure is the heart of intimacy. Many people believe they disclose more than they actually do (Stevens, Rice, and Johnson 1986). It is helpful to check with your partner to see if you are disclosing enough about your feelings and thoughts.

7. Intimacy is cyclic. You won't always feel close to your intimate partner. Work through the difficult times, realizing that they are normal and not a sign that the relationship is about to dissolve. In fact, persistence and hard work are essential ingredients in a thriving relationship.

SUMMARY

As social creatures, we need intimate relationships. Without them, we feel lonely. Social loneliness means less interaction than you desire; emotional loneliness is less intimacy than you desire. Long-term loneliness has serious physical and emotional consequences for people. Loneliness results from both social (modern, urban society) and personal (certain childhood experiences) factors.

Intimacy is a fundamental human need. Intimate relationships enhance our well-being, though they can also be a source of deep distress when they do not work out well. Intimacy includes such things as affection, sharing, and commitment. Intimate relationships must be equitable if they are to endure. Intimate relations, like loneliness, tend to be self-sustaining, though feelings of intimacy are episodic.

Intimate relationships develop over time. Initially, first impressions make a difference in whether we will be attracted to someone else. General appearance, nonverbal cues, and opening lines are important in forming first impressions. Those most likely to attract us are people who are physically attractive, who are similar to us in attitudes and values, who are near and familiar to us, and who have about the same level of self-esteem as we have.

There are four stages in the development of an intimate relationship. The first stage is the initial meeting and awareness of someone else. Social factors mean that this is likely to occur with people who are similar to us. The second stage involves the selection process, which involves our group norms and a certain amount of compromise. The third stage is the development of intimacy, a process crucially dependent on self-disclosure and marked by an increasing sense of interdependence and commitment. In the fourth stage, processes are at work to either maintain or dissolve the relationship. Evaluations of costs and rewards are important in the fourth stage.

INTERNET CONNECTION
Seeking Intimate Relationships

www.mhhe
.com/lauer4

The experience of loneliness can have profound effects on individual health and self esteem. Intimacy, while not a cure for loneliness, is a fundamental need that can actually promote healthy personal development and enhance well being. Loneliness, intimacy, and sexuality are interrelated concepts that are subjects of interest at the **Kinsey Institute http://www.indiana.edu/~kinsey/,** publishers of research on Human Sexuality. Use the **Data Archives** hyperlink in the **Reference Resources for Sexology http://www.indiana.edu/~kinsey/reference.html** section of this website to answer the following questions:

1. Enter the key words **loneliness, intimacy** and **attraction** into each of the search engines of data archives linked to this site. What types of research are being done on this subject at the institutes which house these data archives?

2. Examine one set of abstracts or research findings for a key word that interests you. Read the study and briefly describe what you understand of its scope and findings. How does the study help you better understand the challenges and pitfalls associated with human intimacy which are being discussed?

3. Select one of the following sociological theories and describe how it is used in the research findings: systems theory, conflict theory, exchange theory, symbolic interaction.

GETTING INVOLVED

Learning Objectives

After reading chapter 6, you should be able to:
1. Discuss the ways in which individuals find and select a person to date.
2. Explain the functions of dating.
3. Describe the patterns of dating.
4. Identify the factors associated with dating violence.
5. Explain the justifications for date rape.
6. Describe the stages of courtship.
7. Define the role and patterns of cohabitation in courtship.
8. Evaluate the extent to which cohabitation is a preparation for marriage.
9. Discuss the reasons for the breakup of relationships.
10. Describe the ways that people respond when a split occurs.

How would you feel if one of your parents went with you on a date? Or what if it was absolutely necessary to convince your girlfriend's father that you were a suitable mate if you were to have any hope of marrying her? Such things happened earlier in American history. Then, as now, getting involved with someone was a social process. There are norms in every era that govern dating and courtship. The social nature of these practices is underscored by the fact that today we do not date merely in accord with biological needs but also according to social imperatives. That is, it is not sexual maturation alone that determines when we shall start dating. Rather, there are also social pressures and norms that tell us when it is appropriate to enter the world of dating (Dornbusch et al. 1981).

In this chapter, we will examine the processes of dating and courtship. We will study cohabitation, which some social scientists view as a part of the courtship process (because many who cohabit eventually marry). Finally, we will note what happens when a relationship doesn't work out and people go through the painful process of breaking up.

DATING

Getting involved with someone else frequently begins with a date. At least, dating plays a part in the development of a serious relationship; though, as we shall see below, dating has more functions than simply that of finding a potential spouse.

Finding People to Date

Where do you meet people to date? In the past, adults would frequently help to arrange meetings between young people. Before World War I, young people dated regularly only if they planned on getting married. But patterns of dating have changed over time, even over the past few decades (Strouse 1987). For example, in the 1950s and 1960s, young people commonly got together in planned, formal dates. In the 1970s, however, the emphasis began to shift to more casual and spontaneous forms of getting together. Young people gathered at parties, parking lots, and bars. Some even paired off for the evening. But despite the informality and spontaneity, finding dates continues to be one of the problematic aspects of life. For those in school, a classmate is a likely prospect. The workplace is another common source, as are

Holding hands is part of the normative behavior of dating.

various clubs and organizations, mutual friends, and singles' bars.

Once out of school, however, many single adults discover that it is harder to find dates. A survey of singles found that 73 percent of the women and 57 percent of the men agree that it is very difficult to find new people to date (DeWitt 1992:48). The difficulty is underscored by the thousands of dating services now available throughout the nation and the increasing use of personal ads. Dating services may use computer analysis to match people or videotapes to help people choose someone who appeals to them.

Many newspapers now feature large numbers of personal ads in their classified section. The advertisers normally give information on their sex, race, marital status (single or divorced), and interests. People of all ages use the ads, and some become creative in their efforts as the following two examples from a Southwestern newspaper illustrate:

> Catholic widow, 57, 5'5", 128 lbs., healthy, employed, lonely, honest, sincere, would like to meet 58–65-year-old gentleman, healthy, honest, sincere for friend/companion.
>
> Couch potatoes pass this ad! Attractive, single white female, 5'5", 122 lbs., brown/brown, seeking a go-getter, 22 to 31. Must be tender, fun-loving, like dancing, dining out, football and much more. No drugs or diseases, please.

Analyses of these ads show that men tend to seek attractive women and offer financial security, while women tend to seek financial security and offer attractiveness (Willis and Carlson 1993; Cicerello and Sheehan 1995).

Recently people have begun to use the Internet as a way to meet people (Brophy 1997). A number of sites are available where people can place ads or search for possible relationships. Sometimes people meet in chat rooms. A romance can develop through continued meetings in the chat room or by e-mail. Eventually, the couple may decide to telephone each other and/or meet face-to-face. One young woman who met a man on the Internet and married him five months later told us: "As soon as we started e-mailing, we knew we had so much in common that we wanted to meet. And at our first face-to-face meeting he proposed marriage and I accepted."

There are both advantages and disadvantages to meeting someone on the Internet and then pursuing the relationship further. A major disadvantage is that you miss the nonverbal signals that can provide so much information about a person. If you decide to meet face to face, you may find that you have started a relationship with someone who is disturbed or even dangerous; it is important to know how to protect yourself before getting involved on-line (Gwinnell 1998). Another disadvantage is that you may want to pursue a relationship with someone who lives at a great distance from you. We heard an on-line account of a Canadian woman who met and fell in love with a Swedish man via the Internet. They now were engaged and struggling with the logistics of where to live.

On the other hand, it is an advantage that you get to know something about each other before being distracted by physical appearance. As we noted in the last chapter, your feelings about someone, including your evaluation of that person's attractiveness, can change considerably as you get to know the person. Perhaps many potentially fulfilling relationships never develop because there is no initial physical attraction.

One other advantage to Internet meetings is that they provide an opportunity to meet and pursue a relationship with someone when other avenues seem to be closed or less accessible. In a word, many people have found love through Internet meetings. There are even books available to guide people on the proper use of the Internet to locate a potential life partner (see, e.g., Booth and Jung 1998).

Selecting a Dating Partner

As the personal ads indicate, people are selective about whom they date. No matter how anxious an individual is to form a relationship, he or she is not likely to accept just anyone for the sake of having someone. What determines who will be acceptable?

Basically, we use the same criteria noted in the last chapter for what makes people attractive to us (Sprecher and McKinney 1993; Hahn and Blass 1997). Physical attractiveness is one of the most important factors, as illustrated by personal ads and by the fact that it is a primary consideration in the decisions of people who use videodating services.

Physical attractiveness is not the only criterion for selecting a dating partner. Indeed, one's purpose

INVOLVEMENT
Changing Patterns of Dating

As noted in the text, patterns of dating have changed over time. To get a better sense of the changes that have occurred recently, interview three men or three women about their dating experiences. Select one who is under twenty years of age, another between thirty-five and forty, and a third over sixty. In each case, explore the dating experiences of the individual during adolescence. Ask such questions as: Who initiated dates, males or females? What did you typically do on a date? What influence did your parents have over your dates? What did you feel were the purposes of dating? What was one of your most memorable dates?

Compare the results from the three different generations. What did you find that was similar and what was different? If the entire class participates in this project, see if there are gender differences as well as age differences. Did those who interviewed men find different answers to the questions from those who interviewed women?

for dating and one's age both make a difference in the criteria one uses for selecting dates. Nevid (1984) asked 545 undergraduate students to rate various factors in terms of their importance for a purely sexual or a meaningful (long-term) relationship. Males rated physical characteristics more highly than did females for both kinds of relationships. However, attractiveness was rated highly by both males and females for a purely sexual relationship. And for a meaningful relationship, both males and females gave the highest ratings to such qualities as personality, honesty, fidelity, warmth, and sensitivity.

Ironically, then, the things we value for the long-term are not necessarily the criteria used to initiate a relationship with someone. This is particularly true at younger ages. Early adolescents (sixth graders) are more likely to place a higher value on a person's superficial appearance. Late adolescents (college students) are more likely to be concerned about a long-term relationship and are, consequently, more likely to try to find dates who have desirable interpersonal skills and not merely physical appeal (Roscoe, Diana, and Brooks 1987).

Functions of Dating

We have already indicated that people date for differing reasons. We will examine the various functions of dating separately, but keep in mind that a particular date may serve more than one of the following functions and that we date for different reasons at different ages.

Recreation   We all have a need for recreation, for a time when we can relax and have fun. One way to do this is to date. Dating takes us out of the world of work or study and into a world of relating and enjoying. Early and middle adolescents (sixth through eleventh graders) are likely to see dating primarily in terms of recreation. For them, the major purpose of dating is to secure some degree of personal gratification (Roscoe, Diana, and Brooks 1987). For the older individual, however, dating is likely to serve additional purposes.

Intimacy and Companionship   College students recognize recreation as one function of dating, but they emphasize the importance of companionship and intimacy as purposes of dating (Roscoe, Diana, and Brooks 1987). There is some difference between males and females, with males looking for sexual intimacy and females hoping for interpersonal intimacy as a primary objective in dating.

Dating, we should note, is not confined to the young. People date after a divorce or after the death of a spouse. Two researchers who studied dating patterns among those over sixty reported that companionship and intimacy were primary purposes of dating (Bulcroft and O'Connor 1986). Older people date in order to have an emotional and sexual outlet not otherwise available to them. And they do some of the same things on dates as younger people. They go to the movies, go out for pizza, attend dances, and even camp and travel together. Clearly, dating enhances the quality of life for older people.

Mate Selection Mate selection is the most obvious function of dating. We date others in the hope of eventually finding someone to marry. In fact, one of the predictors of stability in a dating relationship is whether the two people believe that there is a chance of marriage (Lloyd, Cate, and Henton 1984).

Status Attainment *Conflict theorists* stress the competition involved in all human relationships. From this perspective, we would expect dating relationships to involve some efforts to enhance one's

Conflict Theory Applied

position in society. And, indeed, one of the findings of the study of older dating couples was that dating enhances the **status,** or prestige, of the female. Dating serves the same purpose for younger people. Those who date during early and middle adolescence are likely to gain prestige. They enhance their status with their peers because they show themselves to be not only more grown up but also desirable individuals. That this is important is illustrated by the young woman who told us of her severe embarrassment in high school because no boy asked her out on a date when most of the other girls her age were already dating.

It is not just dating per se but dating particular people that can enhance status. Among adolescents, for example, the young man who dates a cheerleader or a very popular classmate or the young woman who dates an athlete or prominent classmate gains even more status.

Socialization **Socialization** refers to the process of learning to function effectively in a group. We are not born with the knowledge of how to be a student, an employee, a member of a church, or a member of a family. We learn how to function in the various groups in which we participate. One of the things we have to learn is how to get along with people of the opposite sex, and dating is a way of doing this. The lack of socialization into heterosexual relationships early in life (we interact mostly with same-sex others before puberty) is one of the reasons for the awkwardness of first dating situations. In dating, we begin to learn how to relate more meaningfully to someone of the opposite sex. That means we are learning the skills necessary for a future long-term relationship.

Patterns of Dating

As a social phenomenon, dating differs not only across generations but across societies and among different groups within a particular society as well. In any society, of course, there are norms about dating that are supposed to apply to all groups. Individuals and groups may break these norms, but those who do will probably pay a price. For example, take the issue of who initiates a date in our society. For the most part, men are expected to take the initiative and ask the female for a date (Sprecher and McKinney 1993). Even though the women's movement has rectified some of the inequalities in relationships, it has not eliminated this expectation.

To be sure, many people reject the idea that a woman must wait for a man to ask her out. And many women, including feminists, also insist on sharing the expenses of a date. The acceptability of shared expenses may vary by race, however. Using small samples from a predominantly black and a predominantly white university, two researchers found that the African Americans were more traditional than whites about dating protocol (Ross and Davis 1996).

Sharing expenses is based in part on the belief that the woman who allows a man to assume all of the costs of a date may be under some obligation to provide him with sexual favors in return. In a shared-cost date, the two people are equal and may each decide whether the relationship should include sexual activity. The egalitarian nature of the shared-expense

Shared-cost dating has become more common.

COMPARISON
Commitment to Dating Partners in the United States and Taiwan

Research in the United States has shown that satisfaction with and investment of time and energy in a relationship make it likely that a couple will stay together. Partners are also likely to remain together to the extent that they perceive no alternative relationship that is more attractive than the one they have together. Is this true in other societies? Two researchers addressed that question in their study of 155 undergraduates in North Carolina and 130 Chinese undergraduates in the National Taiwan University. They also examined a number of other factors that might influence commitment levels, including gender-role orientation and the extent to which the relationship is

central (important to the meaning of life) to the individual.

For students in both countries, commitment was higher for those who reported high satisfaction, high perceived investment, and centrality of the relationship. This finding is interesting in light of cultural differences. The researchers had speculated that something like investment would be more important to individualistic Americans than to the more collectively oriented Chinese. But the commitment process was similar for the two groups.

Some differences did exist, however. Higher levels of femininity were associated with satisfaction for the U.S. students but not for the Chinese. And while high levels of

femininity were associated with greater centrality of the relationship for both groups, the linkage was stronger for the Chinese than for the United States students.

In essence, then, the same basic factors were at work among the United States and Chinese undergraduates to secure commitment in their dating relationships. Femininity may have a somewhat different meaning in the two cultures, but both the Chinese and the U.S. students in this study were more committed to their dating partners when they felt high satisfaction, when they perceived a high level of investment in the relationship, and when they reported the relationship as central in their lives (Lin and Rusbult 1995).

date gives a woman more discretion about her behavior. She does not have to feel that she "owes" her date anything sexually. She can ask a man out, share the costs of the evening, and feel free to engage or not engage in sexual activity.

Nevertheless, when male undergraduates were asked about their impressions of women who ask men out, they rated such women as more sexually active and more flexible and agreeable (Muehlenhard and Scardino 1985). Ironically, the woman who believes in equality, who breaks a traditional norm and initiates a date, may find that the man regards her as more sexually interested and available than if he had asked her out.

Although, according to the prevailing social norms, a woman does not generally initiate a date, it is acceptable for her to indicate interest in a man. A variety of verbal and nonverbal cues let a man know of her interest (Muehlenhard et al. 1986). Among some of the more effective verbal cues are compliments, continuation rather than termination of a conversation, giving her telephone number, listening to a man without interrupting him, giving ex-

tended rather than terse answers to questions of the man, and responding to what a man says (laughing at his jokes and commenting on things he says). Nonverbal cues that indicate interest include maintaining eye contact, smiling a lot, leaning toward him, touching him, catching his eye while laughing at someone else's joke, and speaking in an animated way. All of these cues suggest an interest in dating the man. A woman can use all of them with impunity, but if she decides to initiate the date, she faces the possibility of a misinterpretation of her character.

People not only differ in dating patterns because of ideological commitments (such as those of feminists) but also because of differing family backgrounds. For example, how does something like the death of a parent or the divorce of parents affect dating patterns? Three researchers who investigated these questions compared undergraduates from intact homes with those from homes where one parent had died and those from homes where the parents were divorced or permanently separated (Booth, Brinkerhoff, and White 1984). There were

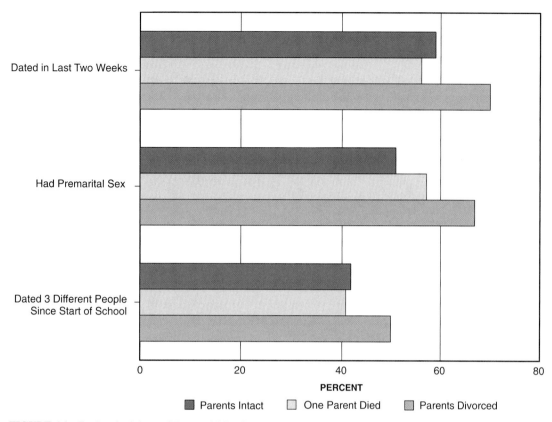

FIGURE 6.1 Dating Activity and Parents' Marriage
(*Source:* Data from A. Booth, D. B. Brinkerhoff, and L. K. White, *Journal of Marriage and the Family,* 46:88, 1984.)

2,538 students in the sample. The researchers discovered a number of differences among the three groups (figure 6.1). In essence, they found that parental divorce increases dating and sexual activity somewhat. The researchers noted that dating activity increased even more if there was a good deal of conflict during and after the divorce and if the parent who had custody of the child remained single. In other words, students who had suffered the most with parental problems had the highest level of dating activity. They also reported less satisfaction with their relationships.

Why are the children of divorced parents likely to have higher levels of dating activity? One possible reason is that they are modeling the activity of their parents, who tend to have high levels of sexual activity and cohabitation. Also those who suffered more through their parents' divorce and report lower satisfaction with their own relationships may be determined not to repeat their parents' mistakes;

consequently, they may be more critical about their own relationships. In any case, the point is that our dating patterns reflect not merely personal preference but also our experiences in varying kinds of families.

Dating patterns also differ among various racial and ethnic groups. Black parents, for example, tend to exert more control over dating, particularly over their female children (Dornbusch et al. 1984). Black females tend to enter the dating world at a somewhat later age than their white counterparts because of this control. Another way in which black patterns differ is the expense-sharing noted above.

Dating Problems

Dating always has its problematic aspects. At the least, there is usually some anxiety about how well things will go and whether one's date will have a good time. But serious problems also arise in dating.

Unfortunately, dating can, and too frequently does, involve violence between the partners.

Violence in Dating   Violence is the use of force to injure or abuse someone. Violent behavior that occurs in dating situations includes pushing, grabbing, shoving, slapping, kicking, biting, hitting with the fist, and date rape (which we will discuss shortly). Men who use violence do so for various reasons, including the belief that violence will enable them to win arguments and control the relationship (Riggs and Caulfield 1997). Thus, men who are dissatisfied with the power they exert in a dating relationship are more likely than others to resort to emotional and/or physical abuse (Ronfeldt, Kimerling, and Arias 1998).

How much violence is there? It is difficult to know because local rather than national samples are used. Moreover, some victims do not report violent incidents. A survey of 140 undergraduates found that 5 percent had been date raped, but none of them had reported the rape to authorities because of embarrassment and feelings of self-blame (Finkelson 1995).

Still, researchers have found a significant amount of violence among all age groups. In a sample of 232 dating high-school students, 59 percent had experienced physical violence at least once, 96 percent had suffered psychological abuse, and 15 percent reported forced sexual activity (Jezl, Molidor, and Wright 1996). Among those college-age and older, about two-thirds to three-fourths reported abusing or receiving abuse in a dating situation (Laner and Thompson 1982; Marshall and Rose 1990).

The rates of violence are about the same for males and females, but females are more likely to

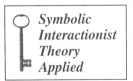

Symbolic Interactionist Theory Applied

receive severe abuse, such as sexual assaults and physical and emotional injuries (Makepeace 1986; Stets and Henderson 1991). Why would women remain in such a relationship? As *symbolic interactionism* stresses, the crucial factor is not the existence of violence, which seldom leads quickly to the end of a relationship (Kasian and Painter 1992). The crucial factor is how the victims define their violent situation. Those in dating situations, like those in an

abusive marriage, may believe they have no better alternative, may blame themselves for provoking the partner, or may believe the abuser's promise that the violent behavior will stop. Some even think that once they marry, the violence will cease. But marital abuse often begins during dating and courtship; marriage will not change a violent man into a gentle husband.

Some aspects of the dating situation encourage and tend to prolong violence between a particular couple (Lloyd 1991). One is the tendency to accept the norm that the male is in control of the relationship and the female is to comply with that control. Another is the way we romanticize relationships—such ideas as "love at first sight" and "love conquers all" may lead some to stay in an abusive relationship on the premise that things will eventually work out.

Violence occurs among all kinds of people. However, those who use violence are more likely to have experienced violence from parents as a child or observed their parents being violent with each other (Marshall and Rose 1990; Smith and Williams 1992; Simons, Lin, and Gordon 1998). Violence in dating is also associated with alcohol and other drug use (Greenwood and Sommer 1991; O'Keefe 1997). Finally, those who have problems with interpersonal relationships generally, or who are prone to jealousy, are more likely to be aggressive in a dating situation (Riggs 1993).

What this all boils down to is that your likelihood of getting into a violent situation increases when you go out with a troubled individual or when your relationship gets more serious. Why should the likelihood increase in a more serious relationship? Perhaps because issues of power and control become more central or because the intensity of the more intimate relationship enhances the intensity of reactions to frustrations and betrayals (Stets and Pirog-Good 1987:245).

Date Rape   Sexual aggression occurs frequently in dating. Sexual aggression refers to any kind of unwanted sexual activity, from kissing to sexual intercourse. In one survey of 635 college students, the researchers found that 77.6 percent of the women and 57.3 percent of the men admitted to having experienced some kind of sexual aggression in the dating situation (Muehlenhard and Linton 1987).

More than one out of four of the women reported a date touching her genitals under her clothes against her will, and more than one out of five said that she had been involved in unwanted sexual intercourse. Although men also are the victims of sexual aggression, it is likely to involve verbal efforts at persuasion or coercion rather than physical force (Fiebert and Tucci 1998). In contrast, forced sexual intercourse is rape, whatever the justification may be. **Rape**—attempted or actual sexual intercourse by the threat or use of force—is one of the most severe forms of dating violence. According to self-reports, as many as 15 to 20 percent of women have been raped on a date (Kiernan and Taylor 1990; Patterson and Kim 1991:128). The consequences of rape are emotional and physical trauma (Shapiro and Chwarz 1997). The trauma may last for years, and impede a woman's ability to relate intimately and/or to have sexual relationships.

Muehlenhard (1988) asked a sample of undergraduates under what circumstances they would justify a man having sex with a woman against her wishes. The students were most likely to justify the act when the woman initiated the date, when she went to the man's apartment, and when the man paid the expenses. The male students were more likely to justify the rape than were the female students and were also more likely to misinterpret certain acts (like going to a man's apartment) as an indication of sexual interest on the part of the woman.

Clearly, one of the problems women encounter in dating situations is the tendency for some men to justify violent behavior, including rape. Men who are more traditional in their gender-role orientation and who oppose feminism are more likely than others to hold attitudes and beliefs supportive of date rape (Truman, Tokar, and Fischer 1996). There are also certain kinds of arrangements and situations that are associated with supportive attitudes. These attitudes begin early in life, as illustrated by a survey of 1,700 sixth- to ninth-graders in Rhode Island.[1] Nearly a fourth of the boys and a sixth of the girls agreed that it was acceptable for a man to force a woman to have sex with him if he has spent money on her (clearly, feminists are correct in claiming that there is frequently an assumption that

the woman owes the man who pays for a date). In addition, 51 percent of the boys and 41 percent of the girls said that a man has the right to force a woman to kiss him if he has spent a lot of money on her. And 65 percent of the boys and 57 percent of the girls in seventh through ninth grades said it is acceptable for a man to force a woman to have sex if they have been dating for more than six months!

MOVING BEYOND DATING

At some point, most people move beyond dating to a more permanent relationship with one person. The initial step may be to decide to go "steady," or to have an understanding that neither one will date anyone else. The ultimate aim is usually marriage, but the process to marriage can take varied forms.

Moving Into a More Permanent Relationship

What factors make it likely that a particular dating relationship will move into something more lasting and exclusive? In brief, they are the same factors that sustain and enhance an intimate relationship in the first place—a sense of equity, the growth of trust, an increasing amount of self-disclosure, and the development of shared attitudes and values. As couples progress to a more permanent relationship they become more alike in attitudes, beliefs, and values (Stephen 1985). They construct a shared and

As a relationship becomes permanent, a couple constructs a unique, shared world of their own.

---

[1] Reported in *San Diego Union,* 3 May 1988.

unique world of their own. They begin to engage in a more intense intimacy than is otherwise possible.

Engagement

Eventually, if the couple is moving toward marriage, they enter the period of engagement. In former times, once people were engaged it was nearly impossible to back out of the marriage. Social disgrace and legal sanctions could be the lot of those who reneged on an engagement. But by the time of Burgess and Wallin's (1953) study of one thousand engaged couples, the researchers found that between a third and a half of the couples had more than one engagement before they were married. Engagement, in other words, is a kind of last testing period before the commitment to marry is finalized.

During the engagement period, a couple has an opportunity to closely examine their relationship. They can get a better picture of how each behaves in a variety of situations, including the somewhat stressful task of planning and executing a wedding. They have an opportunity to interact more closely with future in-laws and to get a sense of the expectations of the fiancé(e) about relationships with future in-laws.

Some couples use the engagement period to enhance the chances of a successful marriage. They may undergo premarital counseling or attend an "engaged couple encounter" seminar. They may read books on typical problems of marriage. Such experiences can help them to more thoroughly and reasonably discuss important topics, such as how they feel and think about their communication with each other, their methods of conflict resolution, their plans for handling their finances, their attitudes about having and rearing children, and so on.

In a sense, then, an engagement is a final countdown period in which potential problem areas can be detected before the union is finalized. This is not to say that every couple uses the engagement period in such a productive way. But judging from the number of people who have more than one engagement, a considerable number of couples use the time for a more intensive examination of their potential for a happy union.

COHABITATION

In the process of moving toward marriage, increasing numbers of couples cohabit (table 6.1). Cohabitation may occur before or after the engagement. That is, some couples decide to get married only after they have cohabited for a time, while others do not cohabit until they have decided to get married.

Cohabitation may now be the most typical path to marriage. (However, we should note that for some people, cohabitation has become an alternative to marriage.) Examination of marriages in an Oregon county found an increase from 13 percent in 1970 to 53 percent in the early 1980s of cohabitation prior to marriage (Gwartney-Gibbs 1986). Thus, the increasing proportion of young people who are unmarried does not necessarily mean an increased number of singles. Rather, young people tend to set up a household at about the same age as they did before marriage rates started to decline, but the household comprises an unmarried couple (although about 40 percent have children in the home) (Bumpass, Sweet, and Cherlin 1991).

Who Cohabits?

Not everyone is equally likely to cohabit. Compared with noncohabitors, cohabitors are likely to have earlier and more sexual experience (Newcomb 1986) and to come from homes broken by divorce (Thornton 1991). They tend to come from less religious families than those who do not cohabit (Thornton, Axinn, and Hill 1992). The most

TABLE 6.1
Number of Unmarried Couples Living Together: 1970 to 1996 (in thousands)

	1970	1980	1990	1996
Number of couples	523	1,589	2,856	3,958
Number with children under 15 years old	196	431	891	1,442

Source: U.S. Bureau of the Census 1994:56 and 1997b:57.

PERSPECTIVE
Bundling

In eighteenth-century colonial America, **bundling**—two people sleeping without undressing on the same bed—was a common practice. Bundling provided a place to sleep for travelers (for whom there was a scarcity of available beds) and for young people who were courting. For example, a young man who visited a young woman during a severe New England winter needed a place to sleep for the night. It would hardly be possible for him, if he traveled any distance at all, to return over the rough, snow-covered roads at night. He would, therefore, bundle with the young woman. This would also give the couple the opportunity to talk and get to know each other better.

Any sexual activity, of course, was forbidden. The couple was not even supposed to embrace. The records of premarital pregnancy and the tirades of preachers testify to the fact that the rules were frequently broken. Eventually, moral opposition led to the demise of the practice. The following is a commentary by an early historian (Stiles 1871:50–53) on the practice and its consequences for the Connecticut colonists, who, pointed out the historian, had multiplied to an "incredible" degree:

> This amazing increase may, indeed, be partly ascribed to a singular custom prevalent among them, commonly known by the name of bundling—a superstitious rite observed by the young people of both sexes, with which

they usually terminated their festivities, and which was kept up with religious strictness by the more bigoted and vulgar part of the community. This ceremony was likewise, in those primitive times, considered as an indispensable preliminary to matrimony. . . . To this sagacious custom do I chiefly attribute the unparalleled increase of the Yankee tribe; for it is a certain fact, well authenticated by court records and parish registers, that wherever the practice of bundling prevailed, there was an amazing number of sturdy brats annually born unto the state.

Hear also that learned divine, the Rev. Samuel Peters, who thus discourseth at length upon the custom of bundling: Notwithstanding the modesty of the females is such that it would be accounted the greatest rudeness for a gentleman to speak before a lady of a garter, knee, or leg, yet it is thought but a piece of civility to ask her to bundle, a custom as old as the first settlement in 1634. It is certainly innocent, virtuous and prudent, or the puritans would not have permitted it to prevail among their offspring. . . . People who are influenced more by lust, than a serious faith in God, ought never to bundle. . . . I am no advocate for temptation; yet must say, that bundling has prevailed 160 years in New England, and, I verily believe, with ten times more chastity than the sitting on a sofa.

Clearly, the historian was appalled by the practice and by the minister's defense of it. Most ministers, however, did not defend the practice. In fact, they took steps to eliminate it. A Massachusetts minister, the Rev. Jason Haven, pastored a church in which bundling and, consequently, premarital pregnancy, was very common. He finally acted:

> Mr. Haven, in a long and memorable discourse, sought out the cause of the growing sin, and suggested the proper remedy. He attributed the frequent recurrence of the fault to the custom then prevalent, of females admitting young men to their beds, who sought their company with intentions of marriage. And he exhorted all to abandon that custom, and no longer expose themselves to temptations which so many were found unable to resist. . . . The females blushed and hung down their heads. The men, too, hung down their heads, and now and then looked out from under their fallen eyebrows, to observe how others supported the attack. If the outward appearance of the assembly was somewhat composed, there was a violent internal agitation in many minds. . . . The custom was abandoned. The sexes learned to cultivate the proper degree of delicacy in their intercourse, and instances of unlawful cohabitation in this town since that time have been extremely rare (Stiles 1871: 78–79).

systematic comparison is provided by Tanfer (1987). Using data from a national survey of twenty- to twenty-nine-year-old never-married women, she found that cohabitors, compared to noncohabitors, tend to:

Have less education (45.9 percent of those with less than twelve years and 22.2 percent of those with more than twelve years of education cohabited).

Have no religion (48 percent, compared with a little over 28 percent of Protestants and Catholics who cohabited).

Not be working (48.4 percent; 27.1 percent worked and 25.3 percent were in school).

Live in large, urban areas (38 percent live in cities of 100,000 or more).

She also noted that rates of cohabitation are much higher in the West (43.6 percent) than in other regions of the country (between 25 and 29 percent).

Cohabitors tend to have distinctive attitudes and values about marriage and various other matters (Clarkberg, Stolzenberg, and Waite 1995). Among other things, compared to noncohabitors they are likely to put a lower value on marriage as a life goal; be less attached to their parents and other kin; put less emphasis on success at work; and highly value using leisure time to pursue their own interests.

While cohabitation is generally associated with younger people, increasing numbers of middle-aged and older people are cohabiting (Chevan 1996). For some of the elderly, cohabitation is a response to poverty—tax laws and other circumstances enable the couple to live more economically unmarried than married.

Patterns of Cohabitation

A little over half of those who cohabit say that one important reason for doing so is that it permits a couple to be sure they are compatible before they marry (Bumpass, Sweet, and Cherlin 1991:920). And about 60 percent of first cohabitations end in marriage (Bumpass and Sweet 1989). In some cases, the relationship leads to marriage when the woman gets pregnant. Racial differences exist in this tendency, however. White cohabiting women are more likely than are African American women

to marry if they get pregnant (Manning 1993). For African American and poorer white women, childbearing is as likely in cohabitation as it is in marriage (Loomis and Landale 1994).

People cohabit for reasons other than as a check on their compatibility. In their attempt to clarify the purpose of cohabitation, Ridley, Peterman, and Avery (1978) identify four types. The *"Linus blanket"* type (based on the popular *Peanuts* cartoon) is a relationship in which one of the partners is highly dependent and/or insecure. Such a person may prefer any kind of relationship to being alone. This relationship is unlikely to endure, because the nondependent partner will probably weary of the endless needs of the other.

In a relationship of *emancipation,* one or both partners use the cohabitation to gain independence from parental values and influence. They may, for instance, come from a sexually repressive home and use cohabitation in order to establish their own sexual values. In any case, the focus tends to be on the relationship with the parents rather than with the partner. The partner tends to be an instrument used for other purposes. A genuine intimate relationship is difficult to develop under such circumstances.

A relationship of *convenience* is the third type. The man generally wants a sexual relationship and someone to care for his home. The woman acquires a sexual relationship, a place to live, and financial care—the same things she would get in a traditional marriage, but without as much security. In this kind of relationship, it is usually the man who is opposed to the idea of marriage.

Finally, there is the *testing* relationship, cohabitation that is a trial marriage. The two partners are committed to each other and may be contemplating marriage. They decide to cohabit as a final testing of their relationship. If it works, they will marry.

These four types are a useful way to categorize cohabiting relationships. But they do not capture the full variety of patterns. They focus on motives, purposes, and styles of relating. We could also categorize relationships according to whether they include children or not. As table 6.1 shows, there were 1,236,000 couples cohabiting in 1993 who had children under the age of fifteen in their home. What difference does having children make in the cohabiting relationship? We don't have research on the relationship between the cohabiting adults, but a five-year study of one hundred families found that divorced mothers who were cohabiting had more maladjusted children than those who had remarried, those who were seriously involved but not living with a new partner, and those who were not involved with a new partner (Isaacs and Leon 1988). It may be that such children know how fragile relationships are and the lack of marital commitment intensifies their sense of insecurity.

Finally, we could discuss differing patterns of relationships among heterosexual and homosexual partners. Some research has been conducted that examines the differences between cohabiting heterosexual, gay, and lesbian couples. In terms of the quality of the relationship, as measured by a scale of marital satisfaction, there is little overall difference among the three types of couples (Kurdek and Schmitt 1986). Rather, all three types of couples seem to go through similar stages of their relationship. In the first year, the *blending stage,* the partners tend to be "head over heels" in love and there is a good deal of sexual activity. In the *nesting stage,* the second and third years, there is a decline in the intensity of their passion, the emergence of some doubts about the relationship, and an emphasis on homemaking and finding compatibility in the relationship. Finally, the *maintaining stage* occurs during the fourth and fifth years. The couple now establishes certain traditions and typical patterns (such as ways of dealing with conflict).

In the research by Kurdek and Schmitt (1986), the stage was more important than the type of couple in determining relationship quality. This does not mean, however, that there were no differences among the couples. In their large-scale study of American couples, Blumstein and Schwartz (1983) looked at the areas of money, work, and sex. They found numerous differences among cohabiting heterosexual, gay, and lesbian couples (as well as married couples). We will give a few examples. With respect to money, they asked couples how often they fought over money management. Lesbians fought less than either gay or heterosexual couples. When asked about the extent to which the couples were relationship-centered or work-centered, 30 percent of the heterosexuals, 27 percent of the gays, and 41 percent of the lesbians said that both partners were relationship-centered. Finally, regarding the frequency of sexual relations, results varied

depending on the number of years the couple had been together. But the lesbians had far less sex than gays or heterosexuals. In fact, 47 percent of lesbians who had been together for ten years or more reported having sex once a month or less (compared to 33 percent of gay couples; data were not available for cohabiting heterosexuals who were together more than ten years).

In sum, cohabitation is not the same experience for everyone. The nature of any individual's experience depends on such things as the motives and purposes of the two partners, the length of time the two have been together, and whether the relationship is heterosexual or homosexual.

Cohabitation Compared to Marriage

For many couples, cohabitation is a testing ground for marriage. How accurate is the test? How much is marriage like cohabitation? Married and cohabiting couples face the same kinds of problems—money, sex, division of labor in the home, and so forth. Nevertheless, just as there are differences among varying kinds of cohabitors, there are differences between the experiences of marriage and cohabitation.

Interestingly, Kurdek and Schmitt (1986) found that the married couples in their sample reported less tension than any of the three kinds of cohabiting couples. A study of communication patterns in married and in cohabiting couples reported that the younger married couples were more communicative and more satisfied than the younger cohabiting couples (Yelsma 1986). Analyses of national surveys find that, compared to those cohabiting, the married report greater happiness, less depression, higher levels of commitment to the relationship, and better relationships with parents (Kurdek 1991; Nock 1995). In particular, those couples who do *not* plan on marrying have a poorer relationship quality than both those who do plan to marry and married couples (Brown and Booth 1996).

On the other hand, Rotkin (1983) studied twenty married and twenty cohabiting graduate student couples and found that the married couples tended to give higher priority than the cohabiting couples to the male's career. This involved the woman's willingness to make her own aspirations and plans secondary in the case of any decisions that affected the male's career. Cohabiting couples who were not planning to marry were more egalitarian, giving equal weight to the career aspirations of both the male and the female.

Finally, the experience of marriage differs in some ways from that of cohabitation in the areas of money, work, and sex. As far as household work is concerned, married women spend significantly more time on housework than do cohabiting women (Shelton and John 1993). Cohabiting women and single, noncohabiting women spend equal amounts of time, suggesting that it is not merely the presence of a man but of a husband that makes a difference in the woman's household responsibilities.

Other differences were noted in the research of Blumstein and Schwartz (1983). With regard to conflict over money management, the researchers found that married couples fight more than the cohabiting couples. Only 23 percent said that they never fight about money management, compared with 31 percent of heterosexual cohabitors, 26 percent of gays, and 31 percent of lesbians. On the question about work, the married couples tended to be more work-centered (rather than relationship-centered) than any of the cohabiting groups. And in the matter of frequency of sex, married couples reported a lower frequency than the heterosexual cohabitors and gays but higher than the lesbians. In another study looking at sexual matters, Forste and Tanfer (1996) found that the rate of infidelity was higher among couples who had cohabited before marriage than those who had not.

The differences noted above are not generally dramatic ones. One could argue, therefore, that cohabitation provides a reasonably good testing ground for marriage. People face the same kinds of problems. They have many of the same kinds of experiences, though with differing degrees of intensity. How well, then, has cohabitation prepared those couples who eventually marry?

Cohabitation As a Preparation for Marriage

One way to test the extent to which cohabitation helps people to have a more satisfying marriage is to compare the experiences of those who cohabited with those who did not. National surveys show that those who cohabit before marriage have a marriage of lesser quality and are more likely to perceive the possibility of divorce than those who do not cohabit (Thomson and Colella 1992; Stets 1993). And the actual divorce rates, both among Americans and Canadians, are higher among those who cohabit before marriage than among those who do not (White 1987/1989; Bumpass and Sweet 1989; DeMaris and Rao 1992).

We can't be sure that these consequences of cohabitation hold for all races. At least among Puerto Ricans who live on the U.S. mainland, cohabitation is more like marriage than two single people living together, in the sense that the women are likely to have children and function as a traditional wife and mother (Landale and Fennelly 1992). At best, then, cohabitation brings no advantage to those who desire marriage. At worst, cohabitors are at some disadvantage for entering marriage or even having a stable and satisfying intimate relationship. Most cohabitations end fairly quickly in either marriage or disruption (Bumpass and Sweet 1989). If the couple marry, they face the prospect of a greater likelihood of breakup than those who did not cohabit. Finally, rates of aggression and abuse are higher among cohabitors (Stets 1991). In spite of the logic of the arrangement, there is little to suggest that cohabitation yields the benefits that people expect from it.

BREAKING UP

Most people experience a number of serious relationships rather than a single one. That means that most will have the painful experience of breaking up. *Painful* is the appropriate word, because most people grieve over the loss of an intimate relationship (Kaczmarek, Backlund, and Biemer 1990). Under what conditions is a breakup likely, and how do people react to a deteriorating relationship?

Who Breaks Up?

On the basis of factors we have discussed that keep a relationship going, we could make some reasonable inferences about when a relationship is likely to break up. If, for instance, there is perceived inequity, the lack of self-disclosure, or the absence of other factors that enhance intimacy, we would expect a relationship not to last.

But there may be other factors as well. Simpson (1987) surveyed 222 undergraduate students about people they were dating. He gathered data about such things as satisfaction with the relationship, closeness, sexual relationships, and perceived ease of finding a different partner. Three months later, he again surveyed the students to see if they were still dating the same person. Those who were still together differed from those who had broken up on five measures. At the time of the first survey, those who stayed together indicated greater satisfaction with the relationship. They had been dating their partner a longer period of time. They had sexual relations with the partner. They had a more difficult time conceiving of a desirable alternative partner. Finally, they tended to have an exclusive relationship. In addition to these factors, couples are less likely to break up when they spend more time together, are of the same race, and perceive social support for their relationship from family and friends (Felmlee, Sprecher, and Bassin 1990).

Responding to Deterioration

People can react in a variety of ways when the quality of a relationship deteriorates. Rusbult (1987) has identified four kinds of responses: exit, voice, loyalty, and neglect. *Exit* refers to a response of withdrawal or threatened withdrawal from the relationship. Those who decide to stop going or living together, to try being "just friends" instead of lovers, or to stop seeing each other altogether have chosen the response of exit. Breaking an intimate relationship, even for the person wanting out of it, is painful. Women tend to cope by confiding in a close friend, while men may try to cope by quickly starting to go out with others (Sorenson et al. 1993).

Voice is the response of facing up to, and trying to talk through, the problems. Discussion, compromise, counseling, and efforts to change oneself or one's partner are ways of dealing with the problems by voice. *Loyalty* is the response of staying with the partner in spite of the problems. Those who opt for loyalty do not try to resolve the problems; they simply try to endure them. They may believe that the situation will improve in time. They may insist that they must have faith in the relationship and the partner.

Finally, *neglect* is a refusal to face the problems and a willingness to let the relationship die. Some examples of behavior that fit the category of neglect are

ignoring the partner or spending less time together, refusing to discuss problems, treating the partner badly emotionally or physically, criticizing the partner for things unrelated to the real problem, "just letting things fall apart," chronically complaining without offering solutions to problems . . . (Rusbult 1987:213).

As Rusbult notes, the terms used may be a little misleading. Voice does not refer only to talking. Rather, voice represents active and constructive reactions. Exit refers to active and destructive behavior. Loyalty is passive, constructive behavior. And neglect is passive, destructive behavior.

Differing personalities will prefer different responses, but there are also other reasons for selecting a response (Rusbult 1987:227–28). Research has shown that people exit when they believe that they have nothing to lose by doing so and that the relationship is not worth saving. A combination of dissatisfaction with the relationship, a sense of minimal investment in the relationship, and a belief that there are good alternatives will make exit a likely response. Exit tends to be used more by younger people in relationships that have been going on for only a short time.

Voice is a response that is appropriate when the relationship is valued but in danger. People who have been satisfied with the relationship and invested themselves in it are more likely to try the response of voice. Females are more likely than males to use voice.

Loyalty is an effort to maintain the status quo. People who have been satisfied with the relationship, feel invested in it, perceive few or no better alternatives, and believe the problems are relatively minor may opt for loyalty. Loyalty tends to be used more by older people who have been in a relationship for a longer period of time. Females are also more likely than males to use loyalty.

Neglect is a destructive response that is used by those who don't know how to mend the relationship and are probably not motivated to do so in any case. Neglect is more common when both satisfaction and investment in the relationship have been low. Males are more likely than females to use neglect.

There may be additional gender differences in reactions to, and methods of coping with, a breakup. Using a small sample of 73 male and 173 female students who had been passionately in

Most people have the painful experience of breaking an intimate relationship.

love, dated, then broke up, three researchers found a number of gender differences (Choo, Levine, and Hatfield 1996). The women were more likely than the men to experience joy or relief immediately after the break-up. As a coping style, the women were more likely than the men to blame their partners while the men were more likely to bury themselves in work or sports.

Although breaking up is difficult, we should beware of a tendency to think that it is always bad for relationships to break up. It is generally always painful, but it is not always bad. There are relationships that are destructive to the individuals involved. They *should* break up. Each case must be judged on its own merits in order to determine whether staying together or breaking up is best for the individuals involved.

PERSONAL
The Birth, Life, and Death of a Relationship

Frank is a graduate student whose account of a relationship illustrates many of the points we made in this chapter and chapter 5. When Frank came face to face with a problem that he believed too great for the relationship to continue, he used the response of exit:

I enjoy working out at a local health spa. One day while running around the track I saw a very physically attractive female. She had an excellent build, a tan, and blond hair. I decided to talk to her as we ran. After chatting a bit, I took a risk and asked her if she would be interested in getting some yogurt. She responded with an enthusiastic "yes."

I was dating a few other women at the time. But I wasn't really interested in developing an intimate relationship with any of them. But I wanted to get more involved. I was ready for an intimate relationship. I thought this beautiful blond woman might be the one.

We hit it off really well from the beginning. I found it easy to talk to her. I felt very comfortable being with her. We both shared things about our families, values, school, work, and other interests. We sat at the table in the yogurt shop for an hour. As we were leaving, I asked her if she would like to go out some night for dinner. Again, she said "yes" enthusiastically. And she gave me a hug. That hug, along with her facial expressions and the way she looked at me told me that she was interested in getting to know me better.

For the next month, we dated three or four times a week. We went to the beach, the mountains, parks, movies, dinner, and sometimes we just went to her place or mine and talked about our lives and our aspirations. I fell head-over-heels in love with her. I bought her clothes, flowers, cards—all kinds of things to let her know how I felt. Being in love with her made me feel more satisfied, more secure, and more peaceful.

It turned out that we had similar political, religious, and social perspectives. And we were in the same graduate program, though at different universities. We had a lot to talk about, and the more we talked the more we realized how much alike we were. The relationship soon became sexual, and that deepened our love for each other. I had truly found the intimate relationship that I had wanted.

After a month, we agreed to date each other exclusively. I felt a growing commitment to her. We only lived about a mile apart, so we began to spend most of our evenings together. It was a natural thing to make the decision to live together. I felt that we had the "chemistry" necessary to make the thing go. And I believed that living together would deepen our commitment and our intimacy.

I moved into her apartment. We then had to figure out the finances. We agreed on a plan for paying specific items like rent and food. Everything seemed to be going well. Then, about a month after I had moved in with her, I found out that she had problems with cocaine. She had somehow kept that part of her life separate from me. I asked her to stop snorting the stuff and to get treatment. She refused. I felt betrayed. I asked her what or who was first in her life. I was stunned when she said it was the cocaine.

I was in agony. I had a lot of beautiful memories already, and we had only known each other for a few months. But as she became more irresponsible with her money and failed to pay specific bills, our relationship deteriorated. Finally, I decided to simply walk away from the relationship. That was tough, because I had really committed myself to her and I expected this to be a long-term relationship. But she had made it clear that I was not her first commitment in life. Maybe I should have tried to stay and help her. But I thought I knew her, and I guess I never really did.

PRINCIPLES FOR ENHANCING INTIMACY

1. If you are dating for purposes of potential mate selection, do not make the mistake of looking for perfection. As Sills (1984) points out, we sometimes sabotage ourselves by limiting our choices. From a field of ten, we only will date the top two. Even if two of the ten are totally unacceptable to us, this still leaves six remaining possibilities whom we also reject. Sills suggests that a mate could probably be found among the six, while a status symbol will be found in those top two.

2. If you are female, support equality in relationships, and are attracted to a certain male, ask him for a date. This is one way to overcome his shyness or to find out quickly whether or not he is interested in you. However, do recognize that some people may label your actions as aggressive, unfeminine, or even as a sexual come-on.

3. Because violence is an all too frequent occurrence in dating, avoid relationships with troubled individuals. And if violence should occur, don't persist in the relationship and do seek the aid and advice of a parent, friend, or counselor.

4. Longer courtships generally result in more satisfying marriages. Get to know the person you plan to marry; that is, find out about his or her values, interests, goals, patterns of behavior, and familial relationships. Every indicator suggests that this will improve your chances for a successful and lasting marriage.

5. Although the breaking up of a relationship is often a painful process, it is also often a necessary and, in the long run, beneficial one.

SUMMARY

Getting involved begins with the dating process. People find dates at school, work, and recreational activities, in singles' bars, and through friends, newspaper ads, and dating services. We select dating partners because we find them attractive in one way or another.

Dating has numerous functions, including recreation, companionship, gaining status, socialization, and mate selection. Every society has norms about dating that regulate such things as who initiates the date. Patterns of dating will differ, however, among various groups in the society. Violence occurs in many dating situations. Three-fourths of women and more than half of men say they have experienced some kind of sexual aggression during a date.

The same factors that enhance an intimate relationship, such as self-disclosure, are at work as a couple moves from dating into a more permanent relationship. If the couple decides to get married, there is likely to be an engagement period, which is a final testing stage of the relationship. Somewhere between a third and a half of people have more than one engagement before marrying.

Cohabitation is a part of the courtship process for some people and an alternative to marriage for others. About half of those who marry have cohabited before marriage. Cohabitors tend to be less religious, less well educated, and living in large, urban areas. Women who cohabit tend not to be employed. There are various types of cohabitation, including the "Linus blanket," emancipation, convenience, and testing relationships. The kind of experience one has in cohabiting depends on such things as the motives involved, the length of time the partners have been together, and whether the relationship is heterosexual or homosexual. Contrary to popular thought, there is no evidence that cohabitation is a good preparation for marriage.

The breakup of a relationship is a common experience. Four ways that people respond to a deteriorating relationship are exit (leaving), voice (confronting and attempting to work through problems), loyalty (sticking it out), and neglect (refusal to admit problems, allowing the relationship to die).

INTERNET CONNECTION
Getting Involved

The prospect of dating presents a number of challenges to the individual wishing to find a suitable partner for a long term relationship. Increasingly the Internet is seen as a viable source for making initial contact with possible partners, as well as finding information about how to meet and date successfully. The websites discussed below highlight some of the challenges and pitfalls associated with dating. Examine them, then answer the questions below.

Youth Resource

http://www.youthresource.com/

This is a website designed for lesbian, gay and transgender teenagers. The site includes many resources including a gallery, chat room, and links to HIV-awareness and political activist sites related to gay and lesbian issues.

GurlTalk: Women on Men Online

http://www.zdnet.com/yil/content/mag/9803/gurltalktoc.html

This site is designed for women to discuss the problems and pitfalls associated with meeting men on line.

www.mhhe.com/lauer4

The Ultimate Girl Meeting Guide

http://meetwomen.com/ultguide.html

This website is designed to sell a book online which claims to show men how to meet women quickly and easily.

1. Based on your examination of the **Youth Resource** website above, what kinds of potential difficulties and dangers do you believe lesbian, gay, and transgendered youth face when confronting the dating issue?

2. Read the section in **Gurl Talk** called **Cynthia Heimel on Online Romance.** Based on this woman's experience, do you think the Internet will increase or decrease someone's ability to meet a suitable dating partner? Is her experience consistent with your experience with meeting people on line or the experiences of your friends?

3. What claims does the **Ultimate Girl Meeting Guide** make about the for-sale material available at its website? To what degree are these claims based on stereotypes concerning men, women, and gender roles? What do you think is the audience for this website?

FALLING IN LOVE

Learning Objectives

After reading chapter 7, you should be able to:

1. Define the meaning of love in terms of the ancient Greek words for love—*storge, philia, eros,* and *agape.*

2. Describe the process of falling in love.

3. Discuss how people can tell whether they're falling in love.

4. Distinguish between passionate and companionate love.

5. Outline the historical development of the concept of passionate love.

6. Explain the measures of passionate love.

7. Describe the process of moving from passionate to companionate love.

8. Distinguish between what it means to love and to like someone.

9. Define the different styles of loving and their implications for relationships.

10. Discuss the causes and consequences of jealousy.

When *Psychology Today* magazine sought readers' views on love and romance, one of the questions asked was, "What do you look for in your relationships with your partner?" (Rubenstein 1983). The most popular response was love (figure 7.1), followed by companionship, and then other things. In another study, 150 college students were asked to choose from a list of items (ranging from basic needs such as food and drink and sleep to realizing their full potential) those things they regarded as most important to their happiness. And they chose falling or staying in love more often than anything else (Pettijohn 1996).

Clearly, love is extremely important to people. In fact, the more deeply you are in love the happier you are likely to be (Willi 1997). But if you look for love, what exactly is it you're seeking? What does it mean to love? We use the term in many different ways, obviously. We say that we love pizza, love our new car, love to ski, love our parents, love our spouses, and so forth.

In this chapter, we will try to bring some clarity to this "love" that people agree is so important in their lives. We will discuss the multifaceted nature of loving another person. We will look at the different ways of loving. And we will examine one of the barriers to a loving relationship—jealousy.

THE MEANING OF LOVE

When we use the same word to express our feelings for food, activities, possessions, and people, it is little wonder that it is difficult to define what we mean by love. When applied to a lover or spouse, the term means, among other things, a deep and passionate affection. But there is more to love than passion. In fact, there is more to love than feelings.

The richness of the term *love* is illustrated by four ancient Greek words that are all translated as love (Lewis 1960). *Storge* (pronounced store-gay) is the kind of love found in the affection between parents and their children. It is, Lewis (1960:54) pointed out, the least discriminating kind of love, because "almost anyone can become an object of affection: the ugly, the stupid, even the exasperating." As such, it is to be cherished, because it is love in spite of the lack of those qualities we discussed earlier as the main factors in attraction.

The second word is *philia* (fill-ee-ah). It is the kind of love that exists between friends. To the Greeks, this was the highest form of love, for philia referred to a warm and close relationship with the characteristics of intimacy we have discussed—sharing, affection, and commitment. It is an intense sharing between two people who have similar perspectives on life.

FIGURE 7.1   What People Want in Relationships
(*Source:* Data from C. Rubenstein, *Psychology Today,* 1983:46.)

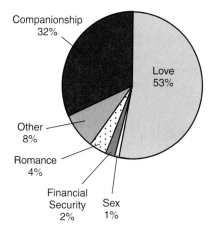

We all need and look for love.

Eros (air-os) is the third love. Eros, from which we get "erotic," is love between men and women. It includes sexual love. Aristotle said that eros makes people long to be in each other's presence. In other words, eros is more than lust. It is more than a desire for sex. It is desire for sex with a particular person. In eros, one is preoccupied with thoughts about the person and the longing to be with the person. As Lewis (1960:150) put it, "it is the very mark of Eros that . . . we had rather share unhappiness with the Beloved than be happy on any other terms."

Finally, there is *agape* (a-gah-pay), a love that is independent of one's feelings for another. To practice agape is to act in behalf of the well-being of someone else, whether you like that person or not. Like storge, agape does not depend on the attractiveness of the other. Rather, it is a love in which we *will* to act beneficially toward another.

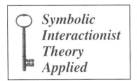 *Symbolic Interactionist Theory Applied*

We will meet these types again as we discuss recent studies of love. Modern research underscores the wisdom in the ancient distinctions. Love, as an old song puts it, is a "many-splendored" rather than a simple thing. Or as *symbolic interactionists* argue, love can mean different things to different people. Hendrick and Hendrick (1992:113) point out that love "is complex, varied, and means different things to different people at different times." To understand the place of love in any individual's life, we must know what love means to that person. Thus, for one person "love" may be primarily a cognitive obsession with someone, while for another person "love" may mean an intense emotional yearning to be with someone, and for still another "love" may mean trying to care for and please someone.

WHEN YOU FALL IN LOVE

When you fall in love, exactly what is it into which you are falling? In terms of the above discussion, most people no doubt have eros in mind. But how do we fall in love? How do we get to the point with someone where we feel intensely and are preoccupied with that person? And how can we tell if it is really love or something else that we feel?

The Process of Falling

In *How to Make a Man Fall in Love with You* (Cabot 1984), the author promises that if a woman follows what she calls "The Love Plan," she will never again have to experience that desperate and helpless waiting for some kind of chemistry to occur with a man. The Love Plan shows the way to make a man, to whom the woman is strongly attracted, fall in love with her.

Whether the book's plan works, we cannot say. It does illustrate, however, the desire of people to have the experience of falling in love. Moreover, the book has an interesting thesis: Falling in love is something more than just a chance event that occurs when two people suddenly realize that there is "chemistry" between them. Indeed, falling in love is, for most of us, a complex process.

The Love-Prone   In the *Psychology Today* survey referred to earlier, Rubenstein (1983:44) reported that a small proportion of people (about 4 percent) say they fall in love over and over again, often "at first sight," and sometimes are in love with several individuals at the same time. These "love-prone" people tend to fall in love for the first time at a comparatively young age (14.5 years, on the average). They believe that sex and chemistry, rather than qualities like trust, are important to an enduring romance. Although they tend to have sex more frequently than others, they report less satisfaction with their love lives. If married, they are more likely to have extramarital affairs and are more apt to believe that their chances of divorce are high.

The Rest of Us   Although some people do experience "love at first sight," including some who are not "love-prone," falling in love is a process for most of us. Ira Reiss (1960) has characterized the development of love in terms of four separate but interrelated processes: rapport, self-revelation, mutual dependency, and intimacy need fulfillment. When two people first meet, they will assess the extent to which they feel comfortable and attracted to each other. Is the other person easy to talk with? Do you like being around that person? Do you seem to have certain attitudes, values, and interests in common? If so, you may quickly develop a **rapport,** a harmonious and comfortable relationship, with someone.

Once rapport is established, you feel relaxed with the other person and the two of you are likely to engage in self-revelation (or, in terms we have used, self-disclosure). We have pointed out that increasing self-disclosure is a characteristic of a developing intimacy. Except for those rare cases of love at first sight, it is difficult for us to feel love for another until there is some mutual knowledge about each other. You may feel strongly attracted to some-

one. You may have sexual desire for someone. But falling in love is more than attraction and sexual desire. It is attraction to and desire for a person with certain qualities, attitudes, and mannerisms.

Self-disclosure not only provides two people with the knowledge about each other that is an essential ingredient to falling in love. It also leads to the next process—mutual dependency. You become mutually dependent because you do things that require the other person to be present:

> One needs the other person as an audience for one's jokes, as a confidant(e) for the expression of one's fears and wishes, as a partner for one's sexual experiences, and so on. Thus, habits of behaving develop that cannot be fulfilled alone, and in this way one becomes dependent on the other person (Reiss and Lee 1988:101).

Finally, then, mutual dependency leads to the fulfillment of our intimacy needs. We all need someone to love, someone in whom we can confide, someone with whom we can share experiences, someone who loves and appreciates us. As such intimacy needs are fulfilled, we are falling in love.

Reiss points out that the four processes are interdependent. If something happens to any one of them, it will adversely affect the development or maintenance of a love relationship. For example, if problems of some sort lead to conflict and a reduction in self-disclosure, mutual dependency and the fulfillment of intimacy needs tend to be reduced also. That leads to a breakdown of rapport, which may in turn depress the amount of self-disclosure. The relationship could go into a downward spiral to break up if something doesn't happen to reverse the process.

His Falling and Her Falling   Although the process described by Reiss applies to both males and females, some gender differences exist in experiences of falling in love. Men and women have somewhat different expectations about love. Typically, women have been more concerned with relationships and men more concerned with work. Thus, women come to a relationship with concerns about emotional closeness and communication, while men are more concerned with practical help and sex (Cancian 1985).

These differences appear in different cultural settings. A study of an ethnically diverse sample of

PERSONAL
Falling in Love—Twice

Laura is a vibrant woman in her late thirties. She talks about falling in and out of love and then back in love again. She also tells about the ways in which her parents influenced her love relationships and her need for intimacy:

My first experience with falling in love came in college. I married my first real love. Prior to that I don't recall having had serious feelings about anyone. Except, of course, for a few infatuations.

My initial attraction to Brian was his understanding and ability to listen and respond to me. I missed this kind of intimacy with my parents. I was never close to either of them. I don't think they know, or ever did know, much about me. Mother was not a good listener, and I didn't talk much with my father. They were close with each other, but I wasn't included. I grew up without learning how to be intimate with another person.

So I was immediately hooked by Brian because he paid attention to me. He looked like a hippie, with his beard and worn jeans. My parents didn't like him, and mother told me I would get bored with him. We were just good friends for several years. Then he went away for a year. He kept in touch through his letters. I lost twenty pounds while he was gone. I really missed him. But I guess the weight loss was good. When he returned, he obviously found me even more attractive than before and started pursuing a love relationship.

Our romance was an adventure. My parents had never been interested in cultural activities. Brian took me to poetry readings, classical concerts, and dinners with fascinating people. We stayed up some nights talking and discussing ideas until dawn. He wrote stories and poetry and shared them with me. We dreamed of him as an English professor in a university some day.

Brian eventually proposed and I accepted. But there was a price to pay. Brian put his dream of being a professor on hold and went into business. We were married soon after. It was wonderful at first. I felt like we were little kids playing house. It was fun to cook, to have friends over, to be together. It was the first time in my life that I could share my thoughts and feelings with someone.

After some years, however, I got restless. There were times that I felt too close to Brian. I shared so much of myself with him that I began to feel the need for space and distance. The intimacy I had longed for was now suffocating me. I didn't share my feelings with Brian, though. I didn't understand what was happening to me, only that I felt closed in. I felt trapped and knew that I had to get out. The intimacy of our relationship seemed more painful to me than the estrangement with which I had grown up. Brian was shocked when I told him. But he finally agreed to a separation and, before the year was over, to a divorce.

I adjusted to being single, I guess. But within a year, a new man entered my life. Kent was divorced. He was sophisticated, traveled to France once a year to buy wine, and owned horses. I truly believed I had found my white knight. This time I fell in love with a beautifully decorated, intriguing package. The only thing missing was the closeness that I had experienced with Brian. My intimacy level with Kent was more like that with my parents. I had all the space I needed. Kent had a family much like mine, so he was also comfortable with less intimacy.

Kent and I lived together for two years, and the experience caused me to reevaluate myself as well as my marriage and relationship with Brian. Frankly, I was confused. I missed him and the intimacy we had shared. Yet I still remembered my feelings of suffocation and of being too close. My confusion led me to several months of counseling, a good deal of soul-searching, and finally to a better understanding of myself. I also began to realize that I still loved Brian and wanted to share my life with him. Fortunately, Brian and I had maintained our friendship, despite the divorce, and gradually our relationship once again became an intimate one. We were remarried two years later—that was over ten years ago. At times it hasn't been easy. I have had to work at keeping the barriers down, and Brian has had to work at allowing me enough space. But this time, it's for keeps!

university students (Anglo-Celtic, Chinese, other Asian, and European) reported that the women generally viewed love as more friendship oriented and less permissive than did men (Dion and Dion 1993). And a study of Mexican American students found that the women gave more importance than did the men to mutual respect (treating each other with special regard or consideration) in love relationships (Castaneda 1993).

Because of their greater concern with relationships, college-age women may fall in love more frequently than do college-age men. But because of concern about the quality of the relationship, women are more cautious. They are likely to compare any potential relationship with alternatives. As a result, men tend to fall in love more quickly than women and women tend to fall out of love more quickly than men (Rubin, Peplau, and Hill 1981). Men try to hang on longer to a deteriorating love relationship (Walster and Walster 1978) and have a harder time adjusting to a broken relationship than do women. Finally, women are more likely than men to break up a romantic relationship.

How Can You Tell If It's Love?

When a student told us that she was "madly in love" with a young man, we asked her how she knew what she felt was really love. She looked startled for a moment, then replied, "You just *know*. You *know* when you're in love." However, others have offered more specific ways of knowing. For example, a group of German undergraduates included among the ways they "knew" they were in love with someone: positive feelings when they were with the person; trust in the other person; and sexual arousal (Lamm and Wiesmann 1997). Actually, it isn't as easy as it might seem to know when we are feeling love or something else. Read Laura's account (PERSONAL) carefully. Was it really love into which she fell when she met Kent?

Misattribution of Arousal   Two social psychologists, Ellen Berscheid and Elaine Walster (1974), have set forth a "two-component" theory of love. The theory is based on the fact that differing emotions can produce similar kinds of physical arousal (such as a pounding heart or sweating). In a classic experiment, Schachter and Singer (1962) injected

volunteer subjects with adrenalin. Among other things, the drug increases heart and breathing rates. The subjects were told that they were testing a new vitamin. Some were told that they would have physical symptoms. Others were told nothing or were led to expect symptoms (such as numbness) that they would not experience. Each group was sent to a waiting room for a twenty-minute period. While there, a confederate of the experimenter acted extremely happy in some cases and angry in others. The confederate's behavior did not affect those who had been correctly informed of what symptoms to expect. But those who had been misinformed or not informed tended to feel the same kind of emotion displayed by the confederate. In other words, exactly the same kind of physical symptoms were defined as happiness by some and anger by others.

Building on the work of Schachter and Singer, Berscheid and Walster (1974) suggested that at least in some cases the feeling of love may be a case of **misattribution of arousal,** attributing the wrong emotion to physical arousal. In other words, there may be times when we believe we feel passionate love because we are aroused and the conditions are such that the conclusion is reasonable. Additional research supports this theory.

In one experiment, men were put into a condition of either high or low arousal by running in place for either two minutes or fifteen seconds (White, Fishbein, and Rutstein 1981). After the exercise, each man watched a videotape of an attractive or unattractive woman he was supposed to meet. After seeing the tape, each man rated the woman's traits and her attractiveness. Those in the high-arousal condition rated the attractive woman more physically attractive, more sexy, and more desirable to date and kiss than those in the low-arousal condition. The unattractive woman received lower ratings from those in the high-arousal than those in the low-arousal condition.

In another experiment, some of the male subjects were aroused by being told that blood would be drawn from them (Gold, Ryckman, and Mosley 1984). Both the aroused and nonaroused subjects were introduced to a woman. In each case, the woman, who was a confederate of the experimenters, displayed dissimilar attitudes from the man. In spite of the fact that attraction is higher toward those with similar attitudes, the aroused males scored higher on measures of liking and love for the woman. They also perceived the woman to be more similar to themselves than did the nonaroused males.

Clearly, then, in some situations we may mistakenly attribute arousal to a feeling of love. It may not be wise to define your feelings as love when you meet someone after just being aroused in some way. Arousal can occur through exercise, drinking, caffeine, stimulating movies, and so forth. Perhaps some of the cases of love at first sight are the result of just such circumstances.

Some Tests of Love   So how can you tell if it's love? Peele and Brodsky (1976) offer some interesting questions to consider. These questions will help you decide if what you are feeling is a loving and healthy relationship or what they call a form of addiction. They point out that some people get into a relationship in order to deal with problems. Such relationships are not really love. Rather, a healthy love should be able to respond positively to most of the following six questions (Peele and Brodsky 1976:83–84):

1. Do you and your lover each believe in your own personal value? That is, do you think well of yourself as a person? Do you have high self-esteem?
2. Has your relationship improved each of you? Are you in some way a better, stronger, more attractive individual? Do you value the relationship because of that improvement?
3. Do you each maintain some separate interests? Do you have meaningful relationships apart from your lover?
4. Is your relationship an integral part of your total life rather than a kind of side interest?
5. Are you each capable of respecting the other's growth and interests without being possessive or jealous?
6. Are you friends? Would you still want to relate to each other even if you weren't lovers?

Such questions take us beyond eros, the passionate kind of love we have been discussing so far. And it may not be possible to answer all of the questions early in a relationship. But neither can you answer the question of whether it's love you feel for someone very early in a relationship. The ultimate test of a loving relationship is time. If it is possible to respond positively to the above questions over a period of time, you will be able to look back and say, "I fell in love."

PASSIONATE VERSUS COMPANIONATE LOVE

If someone had all of the qualities that you desired in another person, would you marry that person if you were not in love with him or her? The question was posed to over 1,000 college students in the mid-1960s, to 246 students in 1976, and to 339 students in 1984. As table 7.1 shows, there were some striking differences between the first (1967) and the other two (1976, 1984) time periods. If the students' attitudes were representative of Americans as a whole, then we can say that in the 1960s, men, but not women, believed that love is necessary for marriage. By the next decade, however, both men and women agreed that love is a precondition of

TABLE 7.1
Responses to Question of Marrying Someone
You Do Not Love: 1967 to 1984

	1967		1976		1984	
	Male	**Female**	**Male**	**Female**	**Male**	**Female**
	Percent					
Yes	11.7	4.0	1.7	4.6	1.7	3.6
No	64.6	24.3	86.2	80.0	85.6	84.9
Undecided	23.7	71.7	12.1	15.4	12.7	11.5

Sources: William M. Kephart, "Some Correlates of Romantic Love" in *Journal of Marriage and the Family,* 29:470–474, 1967; and Jeffrey A. Simpson, et al., "The Association between Romantic Love and Marriage: Kephart (1967) Twice Revisited," in *Personality and Social Psychology Bulletin,* 12:363–372, 1986.

Those passionately in love may have trouble concentrating on other matters.

marriage. The researchers speculate that the change could have occurred because women are no longer as economically dependent on men as they once were. Before women had the educational, legal, and economic means for self-sufficiency, they had to be more pragmatic about marriage. They needed, above all, a man who would be a good provider. Now, both men and women can and do take a romantic approach. Love, not security, is viewed as the foundation for marriage.

What kind of love? The love that most people have in mind when they think of the precondition for an exclusive relationship, living together, or marriage is eros. Such love is sometimes called romantic love, or passionate love. We will use the term **passionate love** and define it as a preoccupation and intense longing for union with a particular other. In contrast, **companionate love** is affection for, and commitment to, someone with whom one is deeply involved. Thus, companionate love is similar to philia.

But does everyone agree that passionate love is necessary for marriage or some other kind of exclusive commitment? And how long can passionate love last? In this section, we will address these questions. Then, we will look a little more closely at the experience of passionate love.

The Emergence of Passionate Love

People have always experienced passionate love, but the notion that passionate love is a precondition for a relationship like marriage is a relatively new idea in human history. In fact, in Greek and Roman mythology love and marriage were not connected with each other. The goddess of marriage was different from the goddess of love. In the past, writers extolled sexual love, and some extolled nonsexual kinds of love, but in neither case was marriage the context. Marriages, throughout most of human history, were contracted for various purposes, such as security, help, and procreation, but not for love.

Then something happened during the twelfth century in Europe. A new ideal about the relationship between men and women emerged, the ideal of "courtly love." At first, the ideal was confined mainly to the aristocracy and spread by troubadours, knights who composed and sang poems. The love they wrote and sang about was something new: it involved a preoccupation with the beloved, a longing for union with the beloved, a proclamation of the lover's undying commitment and loyalty.

No single explanation exists for the sudden appearance and spread of the ideal of passionate love. It may have been due, in part, to the rediscovery of ancient Greek and Roman writings, to a reaction against the brutality of the era, to the shortage of noble women compared to the number of knights, and to antichurch feelings (Reiss and Lee 1988:98). At any rate, sex was placed in a new context, a new kind of relationship between men and women. And while originally the relationship was one that was cultivated outside of marriage, the ideal gradually spread to the premarital state. Romantic liaisons eventually became romantic courtship. The ideals expressed by the twelfth-century troubadours ultimately became the experience expected by young people as the route to marriage.

Romantic, or passionate, love as a precondition of marriage is still not universal. However, romantic love is increasingly the preferred and actual basis for selecting someone as a dating or marriage partner (Hatfield and Rapson 1993).

We should also note that many American observers bemoan rather than applaud this emphasis on passionate love. Some consider it to be an enemy of a lasting marital love, for passionate love cannot be maintained over an indefinite period of time (Lederer and Jackson 1968; Liebowitz 1983). It is frequently an exhilarating experience while it lasts, but the point is that it does not and cannot last indefinitely. The unrealistic expectations of bliss created by our emphasis on passionate love can lead to a considerable amount of "misery, disappointment, and disillusionment" in marriage or long-term relationships (Crosby 1991:20).

The Experience of Passionate Love

How often have you had the experience of passionate love? Not everyone has had such an experience. And among those who do, some experience it only once, while others experience it many times in their lifetime. Often it is a bittersweet experience—the individual may have trouble concentrating on other matters or may be frustrated because of separation from the loved one. Adolescents, those from about twelve or thirteen to twenty-one or twenty-two years of age, are particularly prone to falling into a state of passionate love.

Measuring Passionate Love Passionate love has been compared with the "high" of certain drugs

(amphetamines). But more than feelings are involved. We also think and behave in certain ways when we have passionate love for someone. Hatfield and Sprecher (1986) have developed a scale for measuring these various facets. The scale helps us better understand the nature of passionate love.

In brief, if you are passionately in love with someone, according to the scale, you would tend to: *Think in certain ways,* such as

- Persistently reflect about the other person.
- Idealize his or her qualities (such as kindness and beauty).
- Desire to know and be known by him or her.

Feel in certain ways, such as

- Have sexual desires for him or her.
- Feel bad when things are not going well between the two of you.
- Desire a close and permanent relationship.
- Feel physically aroused by him or her.

Behave in certain ways, such as

- Try to find out how the person feels about you.
- Study the other person.
- Serve and help him or her.

To see the extent to which you are now passionately in love with someone or the extent to which you felt such love for someone in the past, take the short form of the test shown in figure 7.2. Does the scale seem to adequately capture your own experience? Keep in mind that no two people's experience of something is ever precisely the same. Let us look at some research that underscores the point.

Different Kinds of Lovers When you were an infant, you became emotionally attached to your mother or other primary caregiver, and you were distressed if you were separated. Depending on your experiences, you may have developed one of three kinds of attachment styles with your mother—secure, avoidant, or anxious/ambivalent (Johnson 1994). Secure infants will explore and play apart from the mother. They may show distress when left with a stranger, but will soon resume exploring and playing. Security comes from a sense that the mother is sensitive and responsive to their needs. Insecure infants can be either avoidant (are somewhat

Please think of the person whom you love most passionately right now. If you are not in love right now, please think of the last person you loved passionately. If you have never been in love, think of the person whom you came closest to caring for in that way. Keep this person in mind as you complete this section of the questionnaire. (The person you choose should be of the opposite sex if you are heterosexual or of the same sex if you are homosexual.) Try to tell us how you felt at the time when your feelings were most intense.

Mark a number beside each question in accord with the following:

1	2	3	4	5	6	7	8	9

| Not at all true | | | | Moderately true | | | | Definitely true |

____ 1. I would feel despair if _____ left me.

____ 2. Sometimes I feel I can't control my thoughts; they are obsessively on _____.

____ 3. I feel happy when I am doing something to make _____ happy.

____ 4. I would rather be with _____ than anyone else.

____ 5. I'd get jealous if I thought _____ were falling in love with someone else.

____ 6. I yearn to know all about _____.

____ 7. I want _____—physically, emotionally, mentally.

____ 8. I have an endless appetite for affection from _____.

____ 9. For me, _____ is the perfect romantic partner.

____ 10. I sense my body responding when _____ touches me.

____ 11. _____ always seems to be on my mind.

____ 12. I want _____ to know me—my thoughts, my fears, and my hopes.

____ 13. I eagerly look for signs indicating _____'s desire for me.

____ 14. I possess a powerful attraction for _____.

____ 15. I get extremely depressed when things don't go right in my relationship with _____.

FIGURE 7.2 Passionate Love Scale
(Source: From Elaine Hatfield and Susan Sprecher, "Measuring Passionate Love in Intimate Relationshps" in *Journal of Adolescence,* 9:391, December 1986. Copyright © 1986 Academic Press, London, England. Reprinted by permisison.)

detached from mother, showing little preference for her over a stranger) or anxious/ambivalent (tend to cling to the mother and are anxious around new situations or people).

These three styles carry over into adult relationships, for the basic elements of love are the same at any age: "the need to feel that somebody is emotionally there for you, that you can make contact with another person who will respond to you . . ." (Johnson 194:36). The three attachment styles have been found in the love relationships of a nationally representative sample of American adults (Mickelson, Kessler, and Shaver 1997). Most people fell into one of these three styles: 59 percent were secure, 25 percent were avoidant, and 11 percent were anxious/ambivalent (figure 7.3).

With regard to romantic lovers, secure lovers are those who find it fairly easy to get close to others. They feel more trust toward their partners than do those with other styles (Mikulincer 1998). Secure lovers are comfortable depending on others and hav-

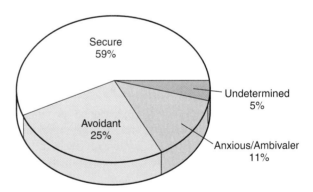

FIGURE 7.3 Types of Lovers
(*Source:* Based on data from Mickelson, Kessler, and Shaver 1997.)

ing others depend on them. They don't worry frequently about a relationship either getting too close or being terminated. They have higher levels of commitment and satisfaction in their relationships than do either of the other two types (Simpson 1990).

PERSPECTIVE
Love: A Nineteenth-Century View

John Cowan, M.D., was the author of a popular marriage manual in the nineteenth century. His views, common during this time, reflect a backing away during the Victorian era from the romantic love ideal. After providing a list of bases for choosing a mate, such as similarities in age, temper, intelligence, and habits, he lectured his readers about love:

> If this mode of mate-choosing is physiologically and psychologically right, as all clear-minded and right-thinking persons will allow, then it must, as a result, dispense with the attribute of love as a preliminary requirement. And so it does. Love, in the popular sense of the term, as applied to the union of the sexes, is a fallacy, and is not only not required, but is an impossibility in the initial requisites to the choice of a wife or husband.
>
> Perfect sexual love comes only of a perfect union—a union of resemblance in mind, soul and body, and this is one reason for my so earnestly advising the employment of the reason in selection; for in and through the intellect you only can choose one who approximates to your standard of character in all its details. The union being consummated, perfect love results as naturally and harmoniously as do all the workings of all other of Nature's laws, and this love, guided by the moral sentiments, through the similarity of [the two people], grows strong, more lasting, pure and holy through the days and months of life's pilgrimage. . . .
>
> A woman marries a man because, as she says (and perhaps believes), she loves him. How? Because her self-esteem prompts her to avoid being an "old maid," and inhabitiveness or love of home, and acquisitiveness or love of money, prompts her to marry the man of her choice. It matters not what may be the man's acquirements as compared with hers, provided he possess money and a home for her. This woman marries through love; but it is a selfish, animal love, and is widely different from the pure and holy love that comes of a perfect union of soul with soul.
>
> A man marries a woman because, as he says (and probably believes) he loves her. How? Because, through his ideality or love for the beautiful, and through his perverted amativeness or love for the gross and sensual, ambition prompts him to marry her. This man marries for love; but it is a love that is as evanescent as the wind, and a miserable help to happiness.

Source: John Cowan, M.D., *The Science of a New Life* (New York: J. S. Olgivie, 1869), pp. 45–47.

Avoidant lovers are somewhat uncomfortable about a close relationship with others; they may even structure their social activities in order to minimize closeness (Tidwell, Reis, and Shaver 1996). They don't trust people and are therefore unwilling to depend on others. Compared with the other two types, they report lower levels of intimacy, enjoyment, and positive emotions, and higher levels of negative emotions in their relationships. They feel that others often want more intimacy than they are willing to provide.

Finally, anxious/ambivalent lovers perceive a reluctance on the part of others to get close to them. They worry about a partner not staying with them or not loving them. They desire to "merge completely" with someone else, a desire that may frighten rather than attract the other person.

From Passionate Love to Companionate Love

As we noted, passionate love cannot last indefinitely. This is fortunate, because the passionate lover might accomplish very little else in his or her life. Gradually, passionate love yields to companionate love as the dominant form of a relationship. The change tends to occur when a relationship has lasted between six and thirty months (Hyde 1986:354). We should note, however, that companionate love exists during the passionate love stage, just as some passionate love can remain during the time when companionate love is dominant. Tucker and Aron (1993) measured the two kinds of love in a small sample of couples and found a decline in the level of passionate love from engagement to marriage, from childlessness to parenthood, and from parenting to the empty nest. But the decline was relatively small; at least a moderate level of passionate love existed at each stage.

What kind of changes occur, then, as companionate love becomes dominant? Among other things, the lovers stop idealizing each other. They notice imperfections. They find things that are annoying. They may experience periods of boredom and irritation. They may begin to question whether they want to remain in the relationship. They may wonder whether the relationship will ultimately be the satisfying experience they had expected and hoped for. In other words, the realities of life set in. The lovers come down from the mountaintop of romantic fantasy and start coping with the vexations of two imperfect humans trying to establish a long-term, meaningful relationship.

We have known students who lament the inevitability of the process. "I would like to live forever in a state of passionate love," one declared with fervor. But such a statement overlooks a number of things. For one, the state of passionate love has its own vexations as we have noted. Second, passionate love consumes time and energy. It may divert us from other things that are important to our growth. And third, the passing of passionate love is not the same as the death of passion. As we shall note below, people in long-term marriages frequently report a passion for each other (including strong sexual desire) that lasts for forty years or more. But the passion in a long-term relationship is episodic rather than continuing. As such, it allows people to engage in other matters with their full attention and faculties.

Companionate love, then, does not mean that a relationship has lost its fire. Rather, it means that two people have found a firm basis for a lasting relationship. And that relationship is likely to have times of passion as well as times of friendship. In a real sense, the transition to companionate love is not a loss but a gain. For companionate love is important for both stability and satisfaction of the relationship. A study of 144 undergraduates reported that those couples experiencing high levels of companionate love had higher quality relationships (Hecht, Marston, and Larkey 1994). The value of companionate love is illustrated in the following excerpt from an account shared with us by a fifty-year-old woman who has been married for over twenty years:

We couldn't get enough of each other during courtship and for the first year of our marriage. But increasingly after that other responsibilities—our professional commitments and then the kids—seemed to intrude on our lovemaking. We often joked about having to make a date for sex. We warned each other about using it or losing it. At times our hit-or-miss love life was a source of real anxiety. But I am happy to report that we have come to terms with the problem. We are more deeply committed to each other than ever before. True, we find ourselves having sex less frequently than we want, but now we don't worry about it. We know each other well, and we are about as intimate as any couple could be.

LOVING AND LIKING

Can you like someone without loving that person? You probably would answer "yes." And can you love someone without liking that person? A lot of people answer "no" to that question. But recall that agape love is independent of feelings for the other, which means that it is possible to love without liking.

Such thoughts raise the question of the relationship between loving and liking. Both the passionate and companionate love styles we have discussed imply that you like as well as love the other. But exactly what does it mean to like someone? Is liking merely a milder form of loving? Are loving and liking similar in some ways? Or are they completely different?

Rubin's Love Scale

One useful way to understanding the relationship between liking and loving is Zick Rubin's (1970) Love Scale. Rubin developed a series of questions that measure both love and liking. The love questions tap into three dimensions of loving: attachment, caring, and intimacy. Attachment refers to the desire to be with and approved by the loved one. Caring is the desire to give to the loved one, and intimacy is close and confidential communication. Two examples of the kind of questions that measure love are: "I would do almost anything for _____" and "If I could never be with _____, I would feel miserable." Clearly, such statements reflect intense emotion.

The measures of liking are less emotional in tone. They reflect the attitudes and feelings we are

Friends enjoy being with each other most of the time.

likely to have for friends. Two examples are: "In my opinion, _____ is an exceptionally mature person" and "I have great confidence in _____'s good judgment." To like someone, then, means to respect, admire, and enjoy being with that person.

In research using the Rubin scales, there is some overlap between loving and liking (Sternberg 1987:338). That is, subjects are likely to score the person they are rating relatively high on both scales or low on both scales. But there is a difference in the scores for friends and those for lovers. Both the love and liking scores tend to be higher for dating partners than for same-sex friends. But whereas the liking score for partners is only slightly higher than that for friends, the love score is considerably higher. In other words, when we love someone, we tend to like that person as well and even more than we like our friends.

Love and Friendship

Keith Davis (1985) has also addressed the question of loving and liking. He put it in terms of the characteristics of love versus those of friendship. There are, he says, eight qualities in friendship. Friends:

1. Enjoy being with each other most of the time.
2. Accept each other as they are.
3. Trust each other to act out of concern for the other's best interest.
4. Respect the judgments of each other.
5. Help and support each other.
6. Share experiences and feelings.
7. Understand each other's feelings and thoughts.
8. Feel at ease with each other, so that the relationship is based on openness and honesty rather than pretense.

The preceding list adds a few dimensions to the respect, admiration, and enjoyment in the Rubin scale. Liking also means a desire to help and a willingness to share. Love includes all of the eight qualities plus two more. Lovers are characterized by a passion cluster and a caring cluster. The passion cluster includes those qualities of passionate love that we have already discussed. The caring cluster includes a willingness to give "to the point of extreme self-sacrifice" and a "championing of each other's interests" to ensure the success of each (Davis 1985:24–25).

In Davis's research, spouses and lovers tended to score higher than friends on all the characteristics. However, friends got slightly higher scores on trust and feeling at ease, and substantially higher scores on acceptance. Apparently lovers and spouses make more efforts to change each other than do friends. And they are more likely to be critical of each other than are friends.

Both friends and lovers enhance our well-being. And they do so in some similar and different ways. To be liked by a friend provides us with some experiences that are desirable. We may or may not like our friends quite as strongly as we like our lovers, but liking and being liked by a friend adds to the quality of our lives.

A TRIANGULAR THEORY OF LOVE

Liking and loving. Passionate love and companionate love. How are they all related? Or are they? Robert J. Sternberg (1987) believes they are. He has developed what he calls a triangular theory of love that shows how various kinds of love are related. His theory asserts that we can understand love best by viewing it in terms of three components. These components can be thought of as the vertices of a triangle. At the top is intimacy. On the left is passion. And on the right is decision/commitment.

Intimacy is a feeling of being connected or bonded to another. Passion is the passionate love we have discussed. The decision/commitment component has two factors. In the short run, there is the factor of deciding that you love someone. In the long run, there is the factor of committing yourself to maintain the love over time. As Sternberg noted, these two factors are separable. That is, you can decide you love someone without committing yourself to maintain that love over an extended period of time. And there are people who are committed who have never consciously decided or admitted their love.

Using these three components, we have a number of different types of love, ranging from the lack of all three (nonlove) to the "consummate love" that involves the presence of all three (table 7.2). Sternberg defined liking as intimacy without either passion or decision/commitment. There is a closeness, a bonding in the experience of liking someone, but there is no passion or long-term commitment.

When you feel highly aroused by someone that you don't know and for whom you have no commitment, you experience *infatuation.* If you for some reason commit yourself to a person without knowing or feeling passion for him or her, your love is an *empty* one. This may occur in some long-term relationships that have become stagnant. The two partners no longer feel much for each other and no longer share a great deal, but for reasons of religion, convenience, or economic and family pressure they stay in the relationship.

In *romantic* love, you feel intimate and passionate but have not yet committed yourself to the other. *Companionate* love has intimacy and commitment but not passion. It is the kind of love that characterizes long-term friendships and some marriages in which the passion has died.

An interesting type that emerges from Sternberg's scheme is *fatuous* love, in which there is passion and commitment but no intimacy. Sternberg (1987:340) said that this is the kind of love that is "sometimes associated with Hollywood and with whirlwind courtships." He called it fatuous because the people make a commitment in the midst of the dizzying experience of passion, rather than in the context of a stabilizing experience of intimacy.

Finally, there is *consummate* love, in which all three components exist. This is the complete love,

TABLE 7.2
Types of Love

Type of Love	Intimacy	Presence of Passion	Decision/Commitment
Nonlove	No	No	No
Liking	Yes	No	No
Infatuation	No	Yes	No
Empty	No	No	Yes
Romantic	Yes	Yes	No
Companionate	Yes	No	Yes
Fatuous	No	Yes	Yes
Consummate	Yes	Yes	Yes

Source: Robert J. Sternberg, "Liking Versus Loving: A Comparative Evaluation of Theories," *Psychological Bulletin,* 102:340. Copyright 1987 by the American Psychological Association. Reprinted by permission.

the love that most of us desire and strive for. The fact that you attain consummate love with someone, unfortunately, does not mean that you will maintain it. But it is attainable, and it is the most rewarding of all love experiences.

Sternberg's typology is very useful for understanding differing kinds of experiences of love. He showed us the complexity of love. For example, we have noted that the idea that there is a transition from passionate to companionate love in long-term relationships is misleading if it is taken to mean that all passion dies. Sternberg's findings agree as reflected in the idea of consummate love in which passion and long-term commitment can coexist. Indeed, we found such love in our study of long-term marriages. Companionate love was the dominant form for some of the couples who had been married fifteen or more years. But others spoke of continuing passion in the relationship. As one woman put it: "We knew that if the passion died we would still have a friendly relationship. Thank God, the passion hasn't died. In fact, it has gotten more intense" (Lauer and Lauer 1986:71).

Applying Sternberg's typology to your own experience can help you better understand the nature of your relationships and why a particular relationship is either rewarding or is in some way falling short of your expectations. Which of the various types of love have you experienced? Which are you experiencing at the present time?

STYLES OF LOVING

Another useful way to understand love is found in the typology of John Alan Lee (1973). Lee used three of the Greek terms we discussed at the beginning of the chapter—*eros, storge,* and *agape.* He added three more—*ludus, mania,* and *pragma*—to get six different styles of loving. Ludus is playful love. Mania is a possessive, dependent love. And pragma is a logical kind of love.

Six Types of Lovers

The *erotic lover* tends to focus on the physical, and particularly the sexual, aspects of the relationship. Erotic lovers may have ideal partners in mind and may fall immediately in love when meeting someone who fits the ideal image.

The *ludic lover* views love as a pleasant pastime, but not something in which to get deeply involved. Ludic lovers have little or no commitment to the other; they tend instead to value highly their autonomy, freedom, privacy, and self-sufficiency (Dion and Dion 1991). They also value variety and are likely to have a larger number of sexual partners than the other types (Hensley 1996).

Storgic lovers have a kind of quiet affection for the other. A storgic relationship tends to develop slowly but to be stable. There is no overwhelming passion, no points of exhilaration. Rather, a storgic love is a slow, perhaps unwitting, process of development.

The *manic lover* combines something of eros and ludus. The manic lover is intensely preoccupied with the beloved, feels intense jealousy, and alternates between ecstasy and despair in the relationship. The manic lover feels the passion of eros but plays the games of ludus as he or she tries to cope with swinging feelings and fear of loss.

A *pragmatic lover* is also a combination to some extent of ludus and storge. The pragmatic lover may take careful stock of the other, including consciously assessing the characteristics of the other. The pragmatic lover tries to find a partner who has a particular set of characteristics that he or she desires in another. To that extent, the pragmatic lover is playing a game. But pragma can also be a stable and growing kind of love.

Finally, the *agapic lover* acts in behalf of the well-being of the other without demanding or perhaps even expecting any benefits in return. Agape is other-focused, patient, and kind. It makes no demands for itself. It seeks only to serve the other. It is the kind of love that psychoanalyst Erich Fromm (1956:22) wrote about: "Love is the active concern for the life and the growth of that which we love."

While we can talk about the six different styles and the corresponding six different types of lovers, in practice we use at least some of each of the styles. But there can be a dominant style. And that can change over time or from one relationship to another. In addition, males generally tend to be more ludic and more erotic than females in their love styles, while females tend to be somewhat more manic, storgic, and pragmatic (Dion and Dion 1985:229). Styles also vary by religious commitment (Hendrick and Hendrick 1987; Montgomery

INVOLVEMENT
Love and the Soaps

Millions of American men and women of all ages watch soap operas on television. What is shown is important, because such programs help shape people's expectations and values about love relationships. Watch one of the programs, such as *Days of Our Lives* or *As the World Turns*. Look at each of the love relationships shown and write up an analysis by addressing the following questions. Use Sternberg's and Lee's typologies of love in your analysis.

1. What kinds of love do family members show each other? How does that square with your ideals?
2. What kinds of heterosexual love relationships exist? To what extent do they agree or disagree with materials in this chapter? How would you evaluate the relationships in terms of your own values?
3. What, if any, kinds of love relationships are missing? Why do you think they are not a part of the program?
4. If the love relationships shown were typical of real life, how would you summarize the nature of love today?

If the entire class participates in this project, have different members watch different programs. Compare the results. Are soap operas giving a consistent portrait of love? If so, why? If not, what are the implications?

and Sorell 1997). Those who define themselves as very religious score higher than others on storge, pragma, and agape and lower on ludus. Those neutral about religion had the highest scores on eros and ludus. There were no differences between the groups on mania scores.

The extent to which you use each of the styles is important. You form your own unique style out of a mixture of the six. But the result is not merely a matter of personal preference. It has serious implications for your well-being and for your relationships.

Implications of Differing Styles of Loving

If you are now in love, to what extent do each of the styles characterize your relationship? And if you are not in love at the present, to what extent have you used each of the styles in past relationships? Clyde Hendrick and Susan Hendrick (1988) raised these questions with more than nine hundred undergraduate students. They measured love styles by the extent of agreement to such statements as "I enjoy playing the 'game of love' with a number of different partners" (ludus) and "It is hard to say exactly where friendship ends and love begins" (storge). They found differences between those who said they were in love and those who said they were not. As figure 7.4 shows, people in love report higher scores on eros and agape and lower scores on ludus than those not in love. There were no significant differences between the two groups on storge, mania, or pragma.

Thus, people in love differ from those not in love. Love styles also affect people's experience of intimacy. In a study of fifty-seven heterosexual couples, Hendrick, Hendrick, and Adler (1988) found eros associated with higher levels of satisfaction for both men and women and ludus associated with lower levels. Clearly, people like passion but dislike games. A survey of 147 undergraduates reported that those with a ludic style were most likely and those with an erotic style were least likely to be lonely (Rotenberg and Korol 1995). Finally, a study of eighty-six couples who were parents of college-age children, reported a positive relationship between marital satisfaction and eros and agape and a negative relationship between satisfaction and ludus (Inman-Amos, Hendrick, and Hendrick 1994). In both studies, the partners tended to be alike in their scores on the various love scales. It seems that we gravitate toward those who are not only similar to us in background, values, and attitudes but also in styles of loving.

LOVE THREATENED—JEALOUSY

A male graduate student told us that one of the more unsettling experiences of his life occurred when he took his girlfriend to a party: "She spent most of the evening talking to and laughing with

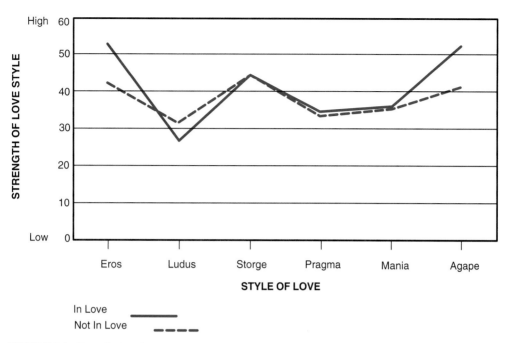

FIGURE 7.4   **Love Styles of Those in Love and Not in Love**
(*Source:* Data from C. Hendrick and S. S. Hendrick, *Journal of Social and Personal Relationships,* 5:175, 1988.)

some guy she met there. I was so mad I could feel myself shaking. It literally made me sick to my stomach." What the student experienced was an intense case of **jealousy,** which is a negative emotional reaction to a real or imagined threat to a love relationship. In the case of the student, the threat was imagined. His girlfriend had met someone who shared her interest in French literature. But she was not romantically attracted to the man. The fact that the threat was imagined, however, did not lessen the intensity of the reaction.

It is interesting to note that prior to the 1970s, popular writers frequently considered a certain amount of jealousy to be normal and even good. Among married people, for example, jealousy could be thought to be evidence of love. A moderate amount of jealousy could cause an individual to examine and realize the value of a relationship, thereby strengthening the bonds (Clanton and Smith 1977). But as the emphasis on personal growth and well-being increased, more and more writers began to see jealousy as evidence of some deficiency in relationships. If jealousy is a deficiency, then perhaps *all* relationships are deficient. Sexual jealousy seems to be universal. It is a signal

that the individual wants to protect his or her relationship. In their study of 103 individuals who ranged in age from twenty-one to sixty-four, Pines and Aronson (1983) reported that all had experienced jealousy at some point in their lives. The frequency and intensity of the experience differed among the subjects. But all had felt jealous, and the nature of the experience was quite similar for all of the subjects.

Who Is Most Jealous?

If the frequency and intensity of jealousy varies, what kind of people get most jealous? Some believe that women are more likely than men to be jealous. But there seem to be few gender differences in the experience of jealousy. Some people, both men and women, have what might be called a jealous personality. Pines and Aronson (1983:124) pointed out that those who were more jealous at the time of their research also tended to report a greater amount of jealousy throughout their lives. This suggests a jealousy component in the personality of some individuals. Unfortunately, their research did not investigate any possible causes. Some psychologists

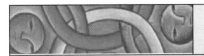

COMPARISON
Jealousy Among the Italians, Dutch, and New Guineans

Jealousy can be a destructive emotion. How you act when you feel jealous, however, depends in part upon your culture. Research on experiences of jealousy among Italian and Dutch students looked at two types of jealousy-evoking situations: one in which a boy- or girlfriend flirted with someone and one in which the boy- or girlfriend was seen passionately kissing someone else.

In the flirting situation, the Italian and Dutch students experienced the same emotions—primarily jealousy—but the Dutch felt relatively helpless while the Italians felt more activated and aroused about it. In the kissing situation, the Italians felt much more jealousy than the Dutch, but both groups felt more anger and sadness than jealousy. In both situations, the Italians were more likely than the Dutch to communicate their feelings of jealousy to their partners.

A study of wife beating in Papua New Guinea shows how jealousy can lead to even more serious consequences than anger and sadness. Researchers interviewed over 2,700 people in rural and urban areas of Papua New Guinea. They found that 67 percent of the rural women and 56 percent of the urban women said their husbands had hit them on one or more occasions. Almost the exact same proportion of husbands admitted that they hit their wives. Rural women said that the main reason for the hitting was a failure to fulfill wifely obligations (such as cooking a meal); urban women named drunkenness as the main reason. Sexual jealousy was the second most common reason given by both urban and rural wives. And sexual jealousy was the most frequent justification given by the rural respondents for hitting a wife with a weapon. Finally, when asked whether it is acceptable for a husband to hit his wife, 66 percent of the rural men, 57 percent of rural women, 47 percent of urban men, and 25 percent of urban women said yes.

In Papua New Guinea, then, sexual jealousy is not only a prominent reason for a husband hitting his wife, but such a reaction is an approved practice by a large number of both men and women. Italians and Dutch are likely to handle their jealousy differently. In any society, of course, jealousy can lead to violence. The point is, each society has its approved and disapproved way to deal with jealousy (Zammuner and Fischer 1995; Morley 1994).

would no doubt look for a problematic relationship with the mother. Freud suggested that jealousy begins early in life when the infant strives for the exclusive love of the mother. The infant who, for whatever reason, feels threatened or thwarted in securing the mother's love may develop problems with jealousy throughout life.

As we might expect, people who are insecure in their love relationships are more likely to feel jealous. Those who feel that they have few alternatives will also tend to be more jealous. Hansen (1985b) studied 220 married people and reported that, regardless of the quality of the marriage, those who saw themselves as having few alternatives to the marriage were more likely to experience jealousy.

People with lower self-esteem have more problems with jealousy. In a *Psychology Today* survey of nearly twenty-five thousand readers, those who reported the most jealousy also had problems with self-esteem (Salovey and Rodin 1985:28). They tended to have a lower opinion of themselves and to see a larger gap than others did between what they are and what they would ideally like to be.

Another interesting finding that emerged from the *Psychology Today* survey was the relationship between marital status and jealousy. Separated and divorced people reported the highest rates of jealousy, followed by cohabiting people. Separated and divorced people were the most likely to look through a lover's personal belongings and listen in on a lover's telephone conversation with someone else. Perhaps the traumatic experience of the disruption of the previous relationship intensified problems with jealousy among the separated and divorced. Cohabiting couples may have problems of jealousy because of the lower levels of commitment to the relationship (compared with that of married people). At any rate, married people seem to have less problem with jealousy than cohabiting, separated, or divorced individuals. And the longer the marriage, the less is jealousy likely to be a problem.

Situations That Provoke Jealousy

Conflict Theory Applied

From the point of view of *conflict theory,* we would expect a fair amount of jealousy. For jealousy can be conceptualized as a reaction to a potential loss in the competition for an intimate relationship. Given the amount of flirting and sexual attraction that occurs in all kinds of situations, jealousy should be fairly common. Indeed, for the person who is intensely jealous virtually anything can arouse feelings of jealousy. Certain situations, however, appear to provoke jealousy in most people. The party situation noted at the beginning of this section is an example. In fact, when readers in the *Psychology Today* survey rated their reactions to different situations, the one that provoked the most intense feelings of jealousy was a party attended by a couple in which one of the partners spends a lot of time with someone else. Basically, any situation in which one partner feels that something is happening that threatens the relationship will provoke jealousy.

One way to think about jealousy-provoking situations is that they violate our expectations for our relationships. Marriage is for most people an exclusive relationship. So is cohabitation. Even dating partners may develop such expectations early in the relationship. Hansen (1985a) studied dating jealousy among more than three hundred students. He found that a significant proportion expected their partners to give up close personal friendships with people of the opposite sex. And most expected sexual exclusiveness from the earliest stages of their relationships. When our expectations are violated, we feel threatened. Jealousy is a sign that we want to protect the relationship.

Consequences of Jealousy

How an individual reacts when feeling jealous depends in part upon attachment style (Sharpsteen and Kirkpatrick 1997). When jealous, anxious lovers are more likely than others to resist expressing anger. Avoidant lovers tend to express anger against and blame the person they feel has intruded into the relationship. Secure lovers are more likely to be angry with the partner but also to try to maintain the relationship.

Nevertheless, when it is too intense and too frequent, jealousy can be destructive. There are, therefore, consequences for personal well-being:

> For most subjects, extreme jealousy was associated with feeling hot, nervous, and shaky; and experiencing fast heartbeat, and emptiness in the stomach. The emotional reactions felt most strongly were anxiety, fear of loss, pain, anger, vulnerability, and hopelessness (Pines and Aronson 1983:131).

In addition, jealousy may lead to a loss of self-esteem (Buunk and Bringle 1987:129; Peretti and Pudowski 1997). When the threat is real, when there is a particular third person involved, the jealous individual is likely to compare himself or herself with the rival. Is the rival inferior or superior? If superior, the rival is an assault on the jealous person's self-esteem. And the assault on self-esteem is particularly strong if the rival is seen as superior in sexual abilities (Buunk and Bringle 1987:130).

Finally, jealousy may lead to the loss of the partner. Ironically, it is the fear of loss that creates jealousy in the first place. When jealousy is too intense and too frequent (and perhaps too frequently imagined rather than real), it becomes a self-fulfilling prophecy. The individual creates the very loss that he or she had feared by distrusting and accusing the partner. In the Pines and Aronson (1983:124) study, the more jealousy the subjects reported at the time, the more relationships they had experienced that had ended because of their jealousy.

PRINCIPLES FOR ENHANCING INTIMACY

1. Although "love at first sight" seems romantic, enduring love needs time to develop. Shared interests, shared confidences, and shared experiences take time to evolve. But the intimacy and love they produce are worth the wait.

2. Don't confuse arousal with love. Remember that such things as vigorous exercise, heavy drinking, or sexy movies can arouse and trick our emotions into thinking that we are in love.

3. To verify your own feelings, use the six indicators of a healthy love found in this chapter to examine your relationships. Remember, however, that a love relationship takes time to develop and that initially it may not measure up to all the indicators.

4. Don't expect passionate love to be unending. It may be the storybook ideal, but it tends to give way to something even better—companionate love. Companionate love maintains the passion but moves beyond the obsessions and irritations of passionate love. Companionate love not only provides you with the intimacy and security that each of us needs; it also frees you to deal with other areas of your life.

5. Because love relationships that are built on friendship seem to be the most satisfying and enduring, it is important to like as well as love a person before you make a commitment. If you feel a strong passion for someone but like nothing about that person, recognize that the relationship is going to have problems and will likely not last.

6. Work at overcoming jealousy; if jealousy is a serious problem, books on it and on self-change are available that can help you overcome it. Jealousy can wreck a relationship. The "green-eyed monster," even if it is a response to a real threat, can cause you to react irrationally and excessively. And, in the process, you may lose the love relationship you are trying to protect.

SUMMARY

The multifaceted meaning of love is illustrated by four ancient Greek words that are all translated as "love." *Storge* is love between parents and children. *Philia* is love between friends. *Eros* involves sexual and romantic love between men and women. *Agape* is a love that is independent of feelings, working in behalf of the well-being of the other.

Falling in love is a complex process. A few people are love-prone, falling in love over and over again and often at first sight. Most people go through a series of phases when falling in love: rapport, self-revelation, mutual dependency, and the fulfillment of intimacy needs. Men fall in love more frequently and quickly than women. Women fall out of love more quickly and are more likely than men to break up a relationship.

It is not easy to know when we are in love. In some cases, we may mistakenly attribute physiological arousal to feelings of love. Tests are available that are more useful than one's own feelings for determining if one is in love.

We may distinguish between passionate love, a preoccupation and intense longing for someone, and companionate love, affection and commitment to someone with whom one is deeply involved. Passionate love is relatively new in human history. It affects our feelings, thoughts, and behavior. Companionate love is a gain rather than a loss in the relationship. It can anchor two people in a lasting and meaningful union.

When we love someone, we tend to like that person as well. In the most meaningful love relationships, the liking is stronger than the liking we have for friends.

Intimacy, passion, and decision/commitment are the three components of Sternberg's triangular theory of love. The most rewarding love has all three. Various other kinds of love have one or two of the three.

John Alan Lee identified six styles of love. Erotic lovers focus on the physical and sexual. Ludic lovers view love as a game. Storgic lovers have a quiet affection for another. Manic lovers have the passion of eros but play the games of ludus. Pragmatic lovers take a rational approach, assessing the other for desirable traits. Agapic lovers act in behalf of the well-being of the other, expecting nothing in return.

Jealousy seems to afflict men and women equally. It may be the result of personality problems and/or may be provoked by certain situations that are defined as threatening to the relationship. Jealousy is destructive when it is too intense and too frequent.

INTERNET CONNECTION
Falling in Love

www.mhhe
.com/lauer4

Your book uses the classic definitions of love established in ancient Greece. Love is identified in terms of storage, philia, eros, and agape, and its process is understood from a decidedly Western cultural framework. Do these perspectives continue to be appropriate in the culturally diverse population of the 21st century? What do nonwestern traditions have to offer, and how do they compare to the classic view?

The Chinese View of Love

http://magazines.sinanet.com/sinorama/199702/article1/english/1html

This online essay briefly describes a Chinese view of love.

1. Read the online essay above. Briefly summarize the view of love expressed in this essay.

2. In what ways are the views in this essay compatible with the classic definitions of love outlined in your textbook? In what ways are they different?

3. Do you believe the traditional Western model used to describe and understand love in our culture still fits? Why or why not?

4. Do you have a jealous personality? The standardized test at this website may help you find the answer.

The Jealousy Test

http://www.queendom.com/jealousy.html

The jealousy test at this website provides three standardized tests for measuring your potential for jealousy.

1. Take the test at the above website. Do you agree with the findings? Why or Why not?

2. Compare and discuss your responses with other students.

SELECTING A LIFE PARTNER

Learning Objectives

After reading chapter 8, you should be able to:
1. Discuss the ways in which people select a life partner.
2. Describe the qualities that people look for in a life partner.
3. Identify the different qualities that men and women value in selecting a life partner.
4. Summarize the process of exchange and role equity in developing a lasting relationship.
5. Define the concepts of assortative mating, homogamy, heterogamy, and hypergamy.
6. Understand the impact of age, ethnicity, race, religion, education, and personality on the selection of a life partner.
7. Discuss how propinquity and attraction affect the choice of a partner.
8. Describe how family traditions and pressures contribute to the selection process.
9. Know the best predictors of marital satisfaction.
10. Understand why long-term satisfaction with the choice of a life partner is ultimately difficult to predict.

Is there a "one and only" for you? Is there a perfect match out there, just waiting to be discovered by you? If you believe such things, you have very romantic and unrealistic notions about love and marriage. For you could have a satisfying long-term relationship with a number of people. This is not to say that you could have a happy relationship with just anyone, however. In this chapter, we will look briefly at some notions of how selecting a life partner should proceed. We will discuss people's expectations for a life partner. We will examine various factors that can narrow the field for you, many of which you might be unaware. Finally, we will look at how you can hedge your bets by being sensitive to the factors that predict marital satisfaction.

IS THERE A BEST WAY TO SELECT A LIFE PARTNER?

Would you be better off selecting your own life partner or having the selection made for you? You may be horrified at the very thought of having a life partner chosen for you, but the practice has been very common throughout human history. Parents or so-called matchmakers may arrange the marriage between two young people who have had little or no contact with each other. In some cases, the matches are arranged while the partners are still children.

For example, matchmakers were the rule in Japan prior to World War II (Murstein 1974:490–92). Young men and women had little contact with each other in school or play. Moreover, the Japanese felt that marriage was too important to be left to the whims of the immature. Parents had to be involved in the process. But families did not deal directly with each other in order to avoid the embarrassment of rejection. Instead, the matchmaker (*nakodo*) acted as a go-between. Sometimes the nakodo would be a friend or relative and sometimes a paid professional. In any case, the nakodo had the job of introducing the families to each other, negotiating the conditions of the marriage, and participating in the wedding ceremony if the match was finalized. The only contact between the two young people, before a formal introduction at which both families would be present, might be a time when the young woman would walk with her mother so that the prospective groom could see what she looked like (from a distance, of course).

In societies with arranged marriages, political and economic considerations are considered far more important than love. Lee and Stone (1980:323) reported that 80 percent of seventy-six nonindustrial societies with arranged marriages have little or no emphasis on romantic love. This is not to say that arranged marriages are loveless; no doubt many couples grow to love each other over the course of the marriage.

While arranged marriages are more common in nonindustrial societies, some of those societies also allow people to choose their own spouses. Lee and Stone (1980) had 114 societies in their total sample. They found that a third allowed people to select their own spouses, and love was generally considered to be an important criterion in the selection.

The ideal in most modern societies is for people to select their own life partners. Presumably, this results in a love match that will bring greater satisfaction to both partners. But to return to the original question, which method is best? If we use stability of the marriage as a criterion, arranged marriages

A sense of humor is one of the qualities we value in others.

are best. If we use satisfaction with the relationship as a criterion, we do not have enough evidence to make a judgment. It is interesting to note that the writers of utopian novels, who have tried to depict their ideal for a society, most frequently have made mate selection a matter of state control (Weiss 1969:142–47). Although some of the utopian writers suggested either individual or parental choice, most either allowed the state to choose or had the state lay down the rules of selection. The purpose of taking the choice out of individual hands, of course, was to ensure the well-being of the total group. For example, people likely to pass on inheritable diseases might not be allowed to marry. The writers believed that such measures would not only enhance the well-being of the society but also maximize happiness within marriage as well.

Few of us are likely to be persuaded that arranged marriages are better than those secured through individual choice. Both kinds have their advantages and their disadvantages. There probably is no best way. But since in our society choosing a life partner is a matter of individual determination, we should at least be aware of the problems and processes involved in the choices we make.

What We Expect in a Life Partner

What do you regard as the qualities in an ideal life partner? More importantly, what qualities do you want in your own life partner? A male undergraduate student offered his list of qualities of an ideal wife:[1]

1. *Intelligence* is easily the most important virtue. . . . I could never be happy and married to a dumbbell.
2. *Character.* I use this term in a general way and subdivide it to make my meaning clear.
   a. *Unselfishness,* in my opinion, is the first requisite to married happiness. I don't mean that I expect a wife to forget herself in bovine devotion to me but I am certain that I have no sympathy for the woman whose first thought is of herself.
   b. *Loyalty* can be the most beautiful of traits. The trials of a man's life can be met with greater courage and left with fewer scars because of the staunch comradeship of a loyal wife.
   c. *Honesty* is of self-evident importance. I refer to absence of deceit and to frankness.
   d. *Sympathy* . . . I know that I can be more successful if my wife has some understanding of me and the difficulties of my work.
   e. *Energy.* Personal laziness is unforgivable.
   f. *Sex purity.*

[1]From Alba Bales, "A Course in Home Economics for College Men" in *Journal of Home Economics,* 21:427–428. Copyright © 1929 American Home Economics Association, Alexandria, VA. Reprinted by permission.

COMPARISON
Shirishana-Yanomama Mate Selection

The Shirishana-Yanomama are a fierce group of Indians who live in northwest Brazil. John Peters, who worked as a missionary among these Indians, is now a sociologist in Canada. He has written about their four types of mate selection. Each involves individual choice, but only by the male:

> The selection of the Yanomama heterosexual partner is done by the male while the female is still quite young. Most betrothals are made when the girl is an infant, or at least before age three. In one case the yet unborn child of a pregnant woman was requested, in the event the baby would be a female. Possibly the unnatural sex ratio of three males for every two females in 1958 contributed to this early selection process among the 120 Shirishana. The sex ratio imbalance practice continued until the mid-seventies, when the sex ratio was much more balanced. By that time some females were betrothed as late as age seven or eight years of age.

Men initiate the betrothal at the time they become hunters of the game in the forest: some time after 15 years of age. . . . The ideal match is a bilateral cross-cousin union. In other words, a male chooses his father's sister's daughter or his mother's brother's daughter. . . .

A second and preferred means of mate selection is sister exchange. Two non-kin single men wish to acquire wives, and have sisters who have not been promised to anyone. They exchange sisters.

As in all other types of mate selection, women in sister exchange betrothals have no influence in the decision. For instance, after about six years of marriage I asked As- why she married Te-. She spontaneously glanced at her brother and said, "Because he wanted his (pointing to her husband) sister." . . .

[The third method is to choose someone in the "wanima relationship," which includes only every second generation of unrelated females. The females chosen may be from one's own or another group of the Yanomama.]

In each of the three ways of mate selection mentioned above, bride payment and service is made.

The fourth and more brutal method to acquire a wife is by means of a raid. A village is attacked, often in revenge for death from a previous surprise attack or a presumed act of witchcraft, or for the single reason to acquire women. Reasons for raiding are not always consistent. Several men might be killed or wounded and available young women between the ages of 6 and 30 are kidnapped. Should the victim have children she usually is forced to flee without them.

Source: John F. Peters, "Yanomama Mate Selection and Marriage," *Journal of Comparative Family Studies,* 18:80–81 (Spring, 1987). *Journal of Comparative Family Studies:* Department of Sociology, University of Calgary, Calgary, Alberta T2N 1N4, Canada. Reprinted by permission.

3. *Disposition.* I refer to buoyancy of nature.
4. *Health.*
5. *Appearance.* My humble wish is that my wife be sufficiently handsome so that no one will pity me. Neatness and taste are far more important than natural beauty.
6. *Education,* in itself, is not especially admirable but it does lead to similarity of taste.
7. *Business ability.* I have seen too many men driven to grayness and imminent insanity by their wives' faulty financial cooperation.
8. *Domesticity.* I still believe in the tradition that a woman's chief function is that of a homemaker if she chooses to marry.

The preceding was written in 1929. Clearly, at least some of our ideals have changed. A list given us by a female student had the following qualities for her ideal husband:

1. Have a strong religious commitment.
2. Be career-oriented with hopes and plans for the future.
3. Be physically attractive, have a healthy body.
4. Come from an emotionally healthy family.
5. Be sexually satisfying.
6. Enjoy being physically active.
7. Be independent.
8. Be committed to the relationship, and want security and trust within the marriage.

INVOLVEMENT
Dates and Mates: What Do People Want?

Have you ever thought about the kind of person you want to marry? What kinds of qualities do you want him or her to possess? How does this compare with the kind of person you prefer to date? Are there differences? Do you think that these findings are typical of your peers as well?

Interview six students. Ask three of them to make a list of the quali-ties they prefer in someone they date. Ask three others to list the qualities they want in someone they marry. Compare the two sets of lists. What similarities and differ-ences are there? What do you see as the implications of your findings for the quality of relationships? Do people look for qualities in dates that are likely to lead to satisfying marriages? How do your lists com-pare with those given in table 8.1?

If the entire class participates in this project, have half the class in-terview males only and the other half females only. Then compare the results along the lines suggested above, but note gender differences in preferences for both dating and mating.

---

9. Be romantic. Bring me flowers and cards. Take me out to dinner. Dance alone with me at home.
10. Be exciting and enjoy change.

How do the two lists compare with your own ideals? What do most Americans want?

Qualities Desired in a Life Partner

Both popular and professional sources have ad-dressed the question of what we look for in a life partner. In a *Family Circle* magazine survey of nearly fifty thousand women, one question asked what things most pleased and displeased them about their husband (Jacoby 1987). The two qualities that most pleased the women were expressing love and func-tioning as a good provider. The qualities that most displeased them were sulking when hurt or angry, easy loss of temper, and lack of communication.

Buss and Barnes's (1986) survey of ninety-two married couples and one hundred unmarried under-graduate students found both differences and simi-larities in the ten most frequently named qualities (table 8.1). The differences suggest that once peo-ple are married, they may value other qualities in their spouse than when they were dating. In other words, some of the qualities you are looking for in a spouse may not be the kinds of things that will be important in a good marital relationship. And some of the qualities you overlook may prove to be quite important for the relationship.

Some gender differences are evident in the re-sults. Among the married couples, women gave greater emphasis than men to such qualities as being

TABLE 8.1
Most Valued Qualities in a Mate

92 Married Couples	100 Unmarried Students
1. Good companion	1. Kind and understanding
2. Considerate	2. Exciting personality
3. Honest	3. Intelligent
4. Affectionate	4. Physically attractive
5. Dependable	5. Healthy
6. Intelligent	6. Easygoing
7. Kind	7. Creative
8. Understanding	8. Wants children
9. Interesting to talk to	9. College graduate
10. Loyal	10. Good earning capacity

From David M. Buss and Michael Barnes, "Preferences in Human Mate Selection," *Journal of Personality and Social Psy-chology,* 50:562, 568. Copyright 1986 by the American Psycho-logical Association. Reprinted by permission.

considerate, dependable, and kind. They also appre-ciated such qualities as being fond of children, well-liked by others, and having a good earning capacity. The husbands gave greater emphasis to such things as being physically attractive and a good cook. Among the unmarried students, males also rated physical attractiveness more important than did fe-males. The females had greater interest than the males in a partner being a college graduate and hav-ing good earning capacity. Data from a national sur-vey of single adults show similar results—youth and physical attractiveness of a mate are more important traits for men than for women, while earning poten-tial of a mate is more important for women than for men (Sprecher, Sullivan, and Hatfield 1994).

The tendency of men and women to place highest value on somewhat different qualities in a life partner seems to be universal. In various societies throughout the world, men tend to look for women who are younger and physically attractive, while women are more concerned with men who have the capacity to be good providers (Feingold 1990; Buss et al. 1990; South 1991; Suman 1992; Waris 1997). Such concerns reflect the male-dominated nature of societies. Females worry about financial security. Males want to display their prizes. Fortunately, people are concerned about other qualities in their life partners as well.

Exchange and Equity

Exchange Theory Applied

If you asked people what they expect in a life partner, they will name the kind of qualities just discussed. They are not likely to say that they also expect someone who will strike a good bargain with them in the relationship. But as *exchange theorists* argue, there is a sense in which we can talk about mate selection as a process of exchange in which people seek equity.

In an exchange relationship, people seek to maximize their rewards and minimize their costs. This does not mean that people seek to take advantage of others, for most of us also believe in equity and are most comfortable in relationships where there is relative equity. But two different relationships could offer equity while also offering differing rewards. For example, a man may propose a traditional marriage to a woman. He offers to be the breadwinner. In return for giving her economic security, he expects her to take care of the home and the children. They will also, of course, provide each other with emotional support and a sexual relationship. The two people might both see this as an equitable arrangement and be willing to engage in the exchange. Another man might offer the same woman an egalitarian marriage. They will both be employed outside the home and share in the responsibilities around the house. This, too, is an equitable arrangement. But depending on the woman's values and aspirations, the rewards are very different. If she values a career for herself, she will define the second proposal as one that is much more rewarding.

Even though we don't consciously think in terms of bargaining and exchange, there are always assumptions about what each mate will give and what each will receive. There are likely to be assumptions about who will handle which tasks in the home. In an era of changing roles, the assumptions of the two partners may be different. The result will be bargaining and negotiation after marriage. As one student told us:

> When I was married, I thought he would do all the repairs around the house and he thought I would do all the cleaning and washing. I had no intention of doing all the housework and he didn't have the faintest idea about how to repair things. But I not only know how, I also love to do this kind of work. We had some arguments about it all. But now we share the housework and cooking. And I do a lot of the repair work.

It is interesting to ponder how many marriages begin with differing expectations on the part of the partners. When those expectations confront reality, the bargaining process begins. The partners must try to clarify the nature of the exchange and bring about consensual equity in the marriage.

NARROWING THE FIELD: ASSORTATIVE MATING

Theoretically, there are millions of people you might marry. Realistically, there are relatively few. The choices for women are even fewer than those for men, because of the sex composition of the population. As table 8.2 shows, after age twenty-four, there is fewer than one male for each female in the United States. That is largely due to the smaller proportion of black males age twenty-five and above. After age forty-four, however, there is fewer than one man per woman for all races. The proportion of men to women changes over time because of such things as war (thus the lower proportion in 1950 than in 1990 for those fourteen to forty-four years of age). Over time, the gap between life expectancy for men and women has also widened (thus the lower proportion of males to females in the older groups).

Life Partner Selection As a Filtering Process

It would, then, be impossible for everyone of marriageable age in the nation to be married at the

TABLE 8.2
Ratio of Males to Females: 1950 to 2000 (number of males per 100 females)

	1950	**1960**	**1970**	**1980**	**1990**	**2000 (projected)**
Age						
Under 14	103.7	103.4	103.9	104.6	104.9	104.8
14–24 years	98.2	98.7	98.7	101.9	104.6	104.1
25–44 years	96.4	95.7	95.5	97.4	98.9	98.9
45–64 years	100.1	95.7	91.6	90.7	92.5	93.8
65 and over	89.6	82.8	72.1	67.6	67.2	70.4

Source: U.S. Bureau of the Census 1994:15 and 1997b:16.

same time. But even if there were equal numbers of men and women, not everyone would be equally desirable. We are selective about choosing a life partner. In particular, we tend to select someone who is like us in various ways. This is the principle of **homogamy,** which refers to marriage between two people who are similar in social and demographic characteristics, such as age, race, ethnicity, and religion. Some social scientists use the term **assortative mating,** which is a broader concept that refers to marriage between two people who are similar on one or more characteristics. In addition to social and demographic characteristics, assortative mating may be based on personality traits, values, attitudes, and various other factors that we shall discuss. Sometimes the term *homogamy* is used to include these other characteristics, but we prefer to restrict it to social and demographic factors.

Assortative mating stresses the fact that mate selection is nonrandom. That is, if we used no such criteria as age or race or any of the others to select a mate, then married partners should have a lot of differences between them. But the similarities are far greater than the differences, and this is true for all societies that have been studied (Buss et al. 1990; Bereczkei 1996). Mate selection is clearly not a random affair.

Some people, of course, do marry in the whirl of romantic infatuation (Lykken and Tellegen 1993). And some marry others who are unlike themselves. **Heterogamy** is marriage between two people who are dissimilar in some social and demographic characteristics. The difference may be along one dimension, such as a fifty-year-old woman who marries a twenty-five-year-old man who is like her in most respects except age. Or the dissimilarities may be more pronounced, such as a black Baptist man who

marries a white Jewish woman who is ten years younger than he is. Sometimes a person will "marry up." **Hypergamy** is marriage with someone who is from a higher socioeconomic background. In other words, hypergamy is a particular kind of heterogamy.

To get a sense of your own perspectives on these ideas, make a list of the qualities of the person you would prefer as a life partner. Write down the person's race, ethnic background, age, nationality, religion, and educational level. Also list any preferences you have in terms of height, weight, other physical characteristics, personality characteristics, and particular attitudes and values. Then make a second list of what you feel you would *accept* (as opposed to prefer) on each of the characteristics. To what extent are you similar to the person you have in mind? To what extent would you accept heterogamy?

Basically, what you have done is put people through a filtering system. In fact, we can think of life partner selection as a kind of filtering process in which we sort out people according to various characteristics (figure 8.1). In the following sections, we will look at some of the more common characteristics that are used.

Age

Age is the most prominent factor along which we sort people out in life partner selection. Men's age, on the average, is about two years older than that of women at the time of marriage. The similarity in age is especially common among younger couples. Those who marry at older ages or those going into a second marriage are more likely to have a larger age gap between the two partners (Buss 1985).

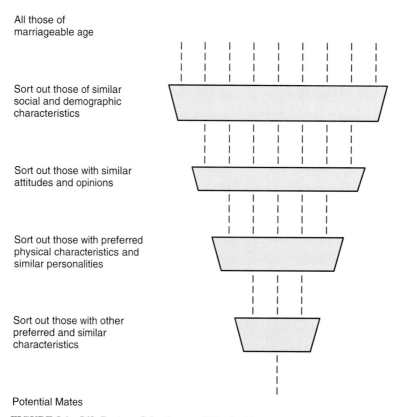

FIGURE 8.1   Life Partner Selection as a Filtering Process

Age homogamy has been increasing since the beginning of the century (Atkinson and Glass 1985; Vera, Berardo, and Vandiver 1990; Qian and Preston 1993). Women have tended more and more to marry men who are within four years of their own age. There has also been a decline in the number of older women who marry younger men.

An examination of age heterogamy in marriage reported that it is more common among people in lower socioeconomic classes (Vera, Berardo, and Berardo 1985). The research also reported that those who are dissimilar in age have no poorer quality marriages than those who are homogamous, contrary to the popular notion that a large age difference is likely to lead to more problems. Whether age heterogamy is associated with lower quality of marriage among higher socio-economic groups or in other societies is an open question. In at least one study of another society—a study of 1,831 middle-aged Hungarians—age homogamy *was* associated with higher marital quality (Bereczkei 1996).

Ethnic Background

Does it matter if your ancestry is Irish or German or Chinese when it comes to getting married? In a small Illinois agricultural community over a fifty-year period, twenty-one out of twenty-three Germans married other Germans and sixteen out of twenty-five Irish married other Irish (Davis-Brown, Salamon, and Surra 1987). Ethnic background is becoming less of a criterion of selection, however. Since World War II, the rate of intermarriage among many ethnic groups has risen considerably. Alba and Golden (1986) examined 27,597 marriages among couples with differing ethnic backgrounds. The couples were not people who had immigrated from other countries but those who had been Americans for at least one or more generations. While the rates were not as high as they were before World War II, there is still a considerable amount of marriage within ethnic groups.

substantial number of those who intermarry, however, are either religiously inactive at the time of marriage or have only one Jewish parent and were never raised as Jews (Judd 1990; Goldberg 1997). From the point of view of Jewish observers, this reduces the rate of intermarriage among Jews.

What are the prospects for a religious intermarriage? Glenn (1982) found that men with religiously homogamous marriages were more likely than those in heterogamous marriages to report being "very happy" with the marriage. Little difference was found between homogamous and heterogamous women. Those least likely to report being very happy with the marriage were religious men and women married to a spouse with no religion (although more than half of those said they were very happy).

Other research shows that religious homogamy tends to increase both satisfaction and stability in marriage (Heaton and Pratt 1990; Dudley and Kosinski 1990; Maneker and Rankin 1993). An exception, however, may be Roman Catholics, for whom heterogamy is not related to marital happiness (Shehan, Bock, and Lee 1990). That is, Catholics report as much happiness whether they are married to other Catholics or to non-Catholics.

Education

Men tend to marry women who are either at or somewhat below their own educational level. Educational homogamy is fairly strong and has increased over time in the United States (Kalmijn 1991b; Mare 1991; Qian and Preston 1993). As figure 8.3 shows, in two-thirds of American marriages, the two partners are at roughly the same educational level. In 18.2 percent of the cases, the husband has a higher educational level, and in the remaining 14.7 percent, the wife has a higher educational level. Less than 1 percent of the marriages involve a large gap, with one partner being a college graduate and the other having failed to complete high school. The importance of educational homogamy is seen in the fact that one of the highest risk groups for divorce is those who are educationally heterogamous (Tzeng 1992). And it is interesting to note that black-white marriages tend to be educationally homogamous (Gadberry and Dodder 1993).

Personality

Some scholars have argued that people marry those who will complement their own personality. That is, we marry people who are different from us but

FIGURE 8.3 **Educational Combinations of Married Couples**
(*Source:* U.S. Bureau of the Census, *Current Population Reports.* Series P-23, No. 150, "Population Profile of the United States: 1984–85" (Washington, DC: Government Printing Office) 1987a:28.)

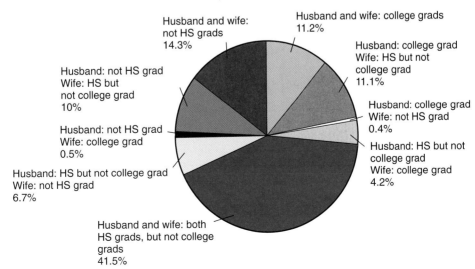

who mesh well with us. Thus, an individual who tends to be volatile might marry someone who is even-keeled, helping the volatile person to maintain more control. But as reasonable as that sounds, the evidence shows that we tend to marry people who are more like than unlike us in personality.

Buss (1985), for example, examined married couples along sixteen personality traits. The traits included such things as tendencies to dominance, extraversion, and quarrelsomeness. He had used self-ratings and ratings by the spouse and an independent observer to minimize the possibility of erroneous results. He found a small but positive correlation between spouses on the personality traits. That is, spouses tend to be more like than unlike each other in their personalities. And as in the case of other variables, those with similar personalities are more likely to have satisfying relationships (Botwin, Buss, and Shackelford 1997).

And So Forth

Our list goes on and on. As Buss (1985:47) points out, the tendency to select a life partner who is similar to you is so strong that one person suggested we use the term *assortative narcissism*. Or as Buss and Barnes (1986) put it:

> The range of characteristics that show positive assortment can only be described as staggering. Couples show assortment for age, race, religion, social status, cognitive abilities, values, interests, attitudes, personality dispositions, drinking, smoking, classes of acts, physical attractiveness, and a host of other physical variables such as height, weight, lung volume, and ear lobe length.

Even the above list does not exhaust all of the factors. We are likely to choose a life partner who shares our sense of humor (Murstein and Brust 1985). That is, we tend to like and love those who find the same things funny as we do. We prefer those with similar leisure interests (Houts, Robins, and Huston 1996), the same love style (Hahn and Blass 1997), and the same attachment style (Quinsey et al. 1996). And those whose first language is something other than English tend to marry within their language group (Stevens and Schoen 1988), particularly those at lower educational levels.

We even may be drawn to people who share some kind of negative characteristic with us. A survey of 586 married couples reported that those with anxiety disorders or alcohol or other drug dependence tended to be mated with those with the same problem (McLeod 1995). Finally, more marriages occur between people whose first name begins with the same letter than we would expect by chance (Kopelman and Lang 1985). Such alliterative homogamy, like some of the others we noted, is less pronounced now than formerly.

In going from age to alliterative homogamy we have gone from the significant to the trivial. Clearly, not all factors are equally important nor equally strong. As Buss (1985:49) sums it up, the strongest factors are age, education, race, religion, and ethnic background. Similar attitudes and opinions are the next strongest, followed by mental ability, socioeconomic status; the physical characteristics of height, weight, eye color; personality traits; number of siblings; and various other characteristics.

Why Assortative Mating?

What factors are at work in assortative mating? Why do we tend to select someone who is like us along so many dimensions? Is it indeed a case of narcissism, or is something else operating in the decision-making process?

Propinquity   As someone has said, even if there is a "one and only" for you, he or she is likely to live within driving distance. Most of us marry someone who is located nearby. The "nearby" may be a neighborhood, a city, a college campus, or a workplace. Thus, we are likely to marry someone of the same age and educational level because many people meet a future spouse in school. We are likely to marry someone of the same religion because many meet at a church or synagogue. Racial and ethnic housing patterns make it more likely that we will interact with, be attracted to, and eventually marry someone within our own racial and ethnic group.

In other words, the various social and demographic factors are powerful because they tend to cluster us with others who are similar to us. And we search for our life partners among those who are near at hand. Thus, in the study of the small Illinois agricultural community, the researchers found that recent shifts toward more heterogamy were the result of a breakdown in ethnic and religious segregation in the community (Davis-Brown, Salamon, and Surra 1987:52). As the everyday contact of diverse people increased, rates of intermarriage also increased.

Attraction   As noted in chapter 5, we tend to be attracted to those who are like us. This is not necessarily the same as narcissism, however. Rather, it may be a case of feeling more comfortable with the familiar. We know how to relate to people who are like us. We have more experience with them, both in the family and among those nearby in neighborhoods, schools, and churches. Many stories and movies have pointed out the discomfort and difficulties people face who try to function in a foreign land or even among people of a different social class in their own country. Such terms as *snobbish, common, uppity, cliquish,* and *rude* sometimes may be rooted in the uncomfortable person's feelings as much as in the behavior of the group. A young woman whose brother acquired great wealth in business told about her own problem with his new set of friends:

> He wanted to fix me up with one of his single friends. I said I'd rather meet this fellow in a group setting. So I went to one of their parties. I thought they were all really snooty. My brother said they liked me a lot. I couldn't believe that at first. But I guess he was right. I just didn't feel comfortable with them. They didn't talk about things that I knew anything about. I still haven't let my brother fix me up. I don't know if I ever will.

Some people cross such social boundaries as class, race, nationality, and ethnicity with relative ease. Others find that they can relate to people who are different, but they are not sufficiently comfortable with them to form an intimate relationship. In other words, the principle of attraction means that we reject those who are dissimilar as much as it means that we choose those who are similar to us. This is not necessarily a judgment about the worth of other people. It may be simply a matter of sorting out people according to how much we feel at ease with them.

Family Traditions and Pressures   We like to think that selecting a life partner is purely a matter

Systems Theory Applied

of personal choice. But there is still the factor of your family's reaction to the selection. As *systems theorists* point out, one of your tasks is to develop your individuality while remaining a part of your family of origin. If your family opposes your individual choice of a life partner, you will be caught in a painful dilemma, as Shakespeare's *Romeo and Juliet* and numerous other works of fiction illustrate. And in point of fact, your family probably does not give you complete freedom to make your own choice. Both male and female students have reported pressure to marry someone of the same race or religion or social status (Prather 1990). It is unlikely that you will completely ignore such pressures. Rather, you may reject some possible life partners before the relationship gets started because you know that your parents would strongly disapprove.

Family traditions and pressures are one reason why matters such as race, religion, and ethnicity are still important. It is in the family that we first learn about the importance of religion, for example. And we also learn about the problems that will attend an interreligious, interracial, or interethnic marriage.

Family traditions and pressures can work in the opposite direction as well. That is, you may be pressured to marry someone about whom you have doubts because all of your family members like and approve of that person. The authors once counseled with a couple who had virtually no interests in common. They came from the same town, had the same socioeconomic background, and were members of the same church. But he had a college degree and she was only a high school graduate. And they were dramatically different in the kinds of things they enjoyed doing, in their beliefs about family finances, in their child-rearing philosophies, and in a variety of attitudes about life. We asked them why they had married in the first place. The man reflected a moment, then said: "I guess because everybody expected us to get married. Both our families thought it was a good match, so we just went along with them." They are now divorced.

When you marry, you do not just marry an individual. You marry into a family. That family, therefore, will have some voice in deciding whether you are an appropriate choice.

PREDICTORS OF MARITAL SATISFACTION

Even if you select someone who is similar to you, it doesn't guarantee that the marriage will be a happy or lasting one. The nineteenth-century philosopher John Stuart Mill was so impressed with the problems of finding a suitable mate that he called marriage a lottery. He said that those who calculate the odds of winding up in a happy union would probably not even take the risk of trying (Rose 1983: 108–9). We do not believe that the odds are that great. But we do agree that there is always a risk and that people should make the effort to minimize the risk of a bad match. One way to do that is to attend to the principle of similarity. That is, the more alike you are on social, demographic, and various other factors, the more likely the marriage will succeed (Whyte 1990:201). But there are other ways, for we know most of the factors that predict a stable and satisfying marriage (Larson and Holman 1994). Among them are:

> Various background factors (characteristics of your family of origin, such as whether your parents were divorced; sociocultural factors, such as age, education, and race; and current situation, such as how much support you have from friends)
>
> Individual traits and behavior (e.g., physical and emotional health, and interpersonal skills)
>
> Couple interactional processes (e.g., homogamy, communication skills, and similarity of values and attitudes)

Here we will look briefly at three of the factors to illustrate how and why they are important.

Timing

By timing we refer to three things: how long a couple has known and dated each other; age at marriage; and general readiness—the sense that one is prepared to commit to marriage. With regard to the first, there are whirlwind romances that lead to marriage after a matter of days or weeks. Although many last and are satisfying unions, the odds are against such marriages. The longer you date someone before marriage, the more likely you are to have a rewarding marriage (Grover et al. 1985).

The second strong predictor of stability and satisfaction is age at marriage. Again, there are some who marry as teenagers and wind up in long-term, happy unions. But it is a great risk. There is also, however, a popular notion that later marriages may be problematic because people get "set in their ways." Robert Bitter (1986) used a national sample of married people to investigate the question of whether late marriages are less stable. His conclusions are fascinating. He found that there is a marriage "squeeze" as people delay getting married until their thirties or forties. That is, there are fewer homogamous choices available. People who marry later, therefore, are more likely to have a heterogamous union. And it is the heterogamy rather than the later age that results in a higher level of instability. If you marry later and have a homogamous union, your chances of breaking up are less than if you married at an earlier age.

Finally, the third aspect of timing—general readiness—means that getting married is not merely a matter of finding the right partner but of being at a point in your life where you feel equipped for the challenges and adventure of marriage. Thus, Holman and Li (1997:141) conclude from their study of 2,508 young adults:

> When a person is older, is financially and educationally in a position to get married, and feels that she or he has support from friends and family for the chosen partner, and when the quality of that couple's relationship is good, then he or she feels ready to marry.

Or as a young man told us, the woman he was dating wanted to get married, and he believed she was the "right" partner for him. But "it's not the right time. I'm just getting started in my career." From the point of view of their compatibility, it was a great match. From the point of view of general readiness, she was ready but he was not. They ended their relationship.

Equity

We have frequently mentioned the importance of perceived equity in a relationship. It is important for marriage as well as other intimate relationships. A study of 162 couples reported that the greater the perceived equity in the relationship, the more that both spouses were satisfied (Davidson 1984). The

Family traditions help shape our sense of who we are and the kind of person we would be comfortable with as a life partner.

point we want to make here is that if you don't feel equity in your relationship now, it is unlikely that you will do so after marriage. In fact, problems of equity may come up after marriage even when they didn't exist before the marriage.

Home responsibilities are one area in which the question of equity may arise. Some couples never discuss matters before marriage that are likely to be sources of conflict afterward: who will take care of the laundry, the cooking, the housecleaning, the finances, and all of the multitude of other things that must be done? It is important that both husband and wife be satisfied with the way these tasks are allocated. Suitor (1991), in fact, found that satisfaction with the division of labor in the home was more important in explaining marital happiness in a national sample than were age, educational attainment, or wife's employment status. The importance of equity continues into later life: wives over 50 years of age who perceive the division of house-

hold tasks to be fair are more likely to report higher levels of marital happiness (Ward 1993). The importance of equity may vary by social class, however. Analysis of a national survey showed that middle-class wives who perceived inequity in the division of household tasks also reported higher levels of marital conflict, but working-class wives reported less conflict when they did most of the traditionally female tasks (Perry-Jenkins and Folk 1994). Working-class wives may not have the same notions as middle-class wives as to what constitutes fairness in a marriage.

Problems of equity may also arise in such areas as emotional support. If one of the partners is always giving and the other always receiving the major part of the support, the giver is likely to grow weary of the inequity. In most cases, the germs of such problems are already evident in the intimate relationship that exists before the marriage. It is wise, therefore, for those contemplating

PERSONAL
Should I Marry My Baby's Father?

Patti is a twenty-six-year-old single mother. The father of the child wanted to marry Patti, but she refused. Her story shows how some of the things that might initially attract us to another person are not sufficient for a long-term relationship. Patti's marriage would have been a heterogamous one. She decided that it wouldn't work:

I guess I am an idealistic person, but I always pictured myself in a wonderful life with a loving spouse with whom I would share things. I was attracted to Paul, my daughter's father, because he was so good looking. I thought that anyone that good looking would have a lot of other good qualities. So I didn't pay attention to some of the warning signs, like the fact that he dressed carelessly and didn't take care of himself very well.

Anyway, we had a whirlwind relationship that quickly involved sex. And I got pregnant. He suggested that we should get married. We weren't even living together yet. I guess the idea of getting married and living with Paul made me think about the kind of relationship we had. I had felt, but hadn't even admitted to myself, that there were some serious problems. We were so different in so many ways. Paul has no interest in reading or learning anything. He can sit for hours and just watch television. He is also not very good at just sitting and talking about things. When I thought about the things we had in common, they didn't seem as important as the things we didn't have in common.

During my pregnancy, I felt physically and emotionally unable to break up with him. I tried a couple of times. But each time, he would talk pleadingly with me, send me flowers and cards, and promise to become more like the person I wanted him to be. I was so afraid of being alone that I agreed to continue the relationship. But I kept putting him off about the mar-

riage. Besides, I needed his help and wanted to share parenthood with him.

For a while, because he didn't want our relationship to end, I thought that being a father might change him. But he wasn't as involved or as enthusiastic as I was about the baby. Finally, I guess I realized that he wouldn't change. It hit me one day that the worst part of each day was the time I spent with Paul. I got tense as soon as I saw him. He had little to say to me; I had to carry on the conversation. One day I just told him that it was over. He tried to persuade me again and sent the usual flowers and cards. But I wouldn't see him again.

I certainly don't regret breaking up with him. He's never tried to see his daughter. She's three now, and I love her dearly. I guess my major problem with her now is trying to decide what I'm going to tell her about her father some day when she asks.

---

marriage to ask to what extent they feel equity in the relationship.

Communication

One of the most important factors in marriage is the pattern of communication. The ability to talk over problems and resolve differences effectively is particularly important. We shall discuss communication in depth in chapter 11 and ways of handling conflict in chapter 12. Here we want to underscore the importance of communication as a predictor of marital success. The way you communicate before marriage is the best indicator of how you are likely to communicate afterward. Indeed, some research has shown that communication patterns prior to

marriage are one of the best predictors of how well the marriage will succeed (Goleman 1985).

Good communication involves not only the ability to discuss problems but also self-disclosure, a sharing of daily events, interesting "small talk," and positive conversation about the spouse (words that convey respect, affection, love, etc.). A study of working couples found that the husband's ability to share his thoughts and feelings and to give his wife emotional support enhanced the wife's marital satisfaction even more than his participation in household and child-care tasks (Erickson 1993). Again, the point is to examine the relationship prior to marriage to see to what extent it is characterized by good communication patterns. As Patti (PERSONAL) said, one of the reasons she decided not to

PERSPECTIVE
Abraham Lincoln Proposes

Selecting a life partner can involve many differing and intense emotions, as Abraham Lincoln discovered the first time he proposed marriage. When he was 29, Lincoln wrote a letter explaining his decision some months earlier to marry a woman he barely knew. She was the sister of a friend. The friend had offered to bring her sister to Kentucky, where Lincoln was living at the time, if he would agree to marry her. Lincoln had seen the sister some three years earlier, "thought her intelligent and agreeable, and saw no good objection to plodding life through hand in hand with her."

When she arrived, however, she looked different than Lincoln remembered. She was larger than he recalled. Her "skin was too full of fat," she lacked teeth, and she had a "weather-beaten appearance in general." But Lincoln had given his word, and he set about preparing himself for the marriage by identifying her good qualities:

"I tried to imagine she was handsome, which, but for her unfortunate corpulency, was actually true . . . I also tried to convince myself, that the mind was much more to be valued than the person; and in this, she was not inferior, as I could discover, to any with whom I had been acquainted. . . . I now spent my time between planning how I might get along through life after my contemplated change of circumstances should have taken place; and how I might procrastinate the evil day for a time. . . .

After I had delayed the matter as long as I thought I could in honor do . . . I mustered my resolution and made the proposal to her direct; but, shocking to re-late, she answered, No. At first I supposed she did it through an affection of modesty. . . . I tried it again and again, but with the same success, or rather with the same want of success. I finally was forced to give it up, at which I very unexpectedly found myself mortified almost beyond endurance . . . and to cap the whole, I then, for the first time, began to suspect that I was really a little in love with her. But let it all go. I'll try and outlive it . . . I have now come to the conclusion never again to think of marrying; and for this reason: I can never be satisfied with any one who would be blockhead enough to have me." (Roy P. Basler, ed., *The Collected Works of Abraham Lincoln* [New Brunswick, N.J.: Rutgers University Press, 1953], pp. 117–119.)

marry Paul was his inability to sustain meaningful conversation with her. Paul seemed to become articulate only when he saw that the relationship was in jeopardy. It is unlikely that he would have easily altered his style after marriage.

Effective communication and similarity, incidentally, tend to go together. For instance, if you have different religious, family, or work values than a potential spouse, you will be handicapped when you try to solve problems in which those values are pertinent (Craddock 1980). Similarity enhances the ease of communicating effectively and of resolving the various kinds of problems that inevitably confront married couples.

PREPARE: A Multifactor Approach

As in the case of assortative mating, a good many other factors go into a satisfying marriage. Problems can arise from a great many things, ranging from dissimilar attitudes to incompatible body clocks (one spouse may be a morning and the other an evening person). Predicting marital satisfaction requires a variety of factors.

But not all factors are equally important. One effort to determine which are the most crucial is PREPARE, an instrument devised by Dr. David Olson and his colleagues to predict marital success among those contemplating marriage. PREPARE was developed in 1977 and validated by David Fournier in 1978 on the basis of one thousand premarital couples and two hundred clergy who had used the instrument. Following this validation, some revisions were made and a second version appeared in 1979. Results from subsequent research are impressive. For example, Fowers and Olson (1986) tested 164 engaged couples, then studied them again three years later. They found that satisfied couples had scored considerably higher on the instrument than those who canceled their engagement or who married and were

Marital satisfaction is enhanced when a couple agrees on how to have fun.

and believe that you and your partner find the same meaning in religion.

The researchers not only measured each partner's score but also looked at the extent to which the partners agreed in each area. The eleven areas are all important in predicting marital satisfaction. In many cases, the important thing is not that you believe a particular way about something but that you and your partner believe the same thing (religious orientation, for example). In other cases, you may believe the same thing, but it can be dysfunctional for a stable, satisfying marriage (for example, both may believe that good marriages are free of conflict).

It is important to keep in mind that no instrument is perfect. You may have serious differences with someone on one or more of the eleven areas prior to marriage. You may continue to have those differences afterward yet have a meaningful and stable relationship. But the odds are not with you. The more agreement you have in these eleven areas, the more likely you are to have a satisfying marriage.

A FINAL CAVEAT

Even with an instrument like PREPARE, it is difficult to predict long-term satisfaction. After all, the researchers only did a three-year follow-up. We don't know if the instrument will also predict much longer relationships. A number of factors make long-term satisfaction difficult to predict prior to marriage. One is that our knowledge of another person is always limited. Even though a good deal of self-disclosure goes on in a relationship, there is usually also a good deal of "putting your best foot forward" during courtship. People may not reveal some of the more problematic aspects of their lives until after the marriage.

Second, everyone changes over time. You may seem to be perfectly compatible with a partner now. But both of you will be different people in ten years. What if you change in ways that make you less compatible? One couple shared with us problems they were having in the tenth year of their marriage that they couldn't have anticipated. The wife had decided to go to college to pursue a degree and a career. Their two children were both in school, and she was not satisfied staying at home. Her husband had not attended college and felt

dissatisfied or who had divorced. They point out that PREPARE scores predicted with 80 to 90 percent accuracy which couples were separated and divorced and which were happily married! Subsequent longitudinal research with nearly 400 couples supports the predictive power of PREPARE scores (Fowers 1996).

PREPARE measures eleven different areas: the extent to which the couple has realistic expectations; personality issues; communication; conflict resolution; management of finances; leisure activities; the sexual relationship; children and marriage; family and friends; equalitarian roles; and religious orientation. For example, the sexual relationship is evaluated by such measures as the extent to which you would be willing to try almost any sexual activity your partner wanted and the extent to which you believe the two of you talk freely about sexual expectations and interests. The religious orientation is evaluated by such measures as the extent to which you feel it is important to pray with your partner threatened by her plans. Moreover, he could not understand her excitement about her classes, her interest in a variety of subjects that meant nothing to him. Eventually he began to ridicule the things she would tell him. She, in turn, stopped talking to him about her interests. Soon, they fell into a pattern of living separate lives while sharing a house and two children. They were different people than when they were first married. And the differences led to less rather than more compatibility.

Our needs as well as our interests change over time. In some cases, something that attracted two people initially becomes a problem as time passes. For example, Janice is a data processor who married Frank because he was strong and assertive. He seemed like the kind of person who would not be defeated by life, and who would always be able to support his family. But after a few years, Frank's strength began to look more like domination to her. He wanted complete control of their finances. Even though she worked, he insisted on giving her an allowance and managing the rest of the budget himself. At the time of their marriage, Janice felt she needed a strong and assertive husband. Some years later, she felt able to care for herself if necessary. Frank's aggressive nature had become a liability because of her changing needs.

Such changes cannot be predicted. We can never be certain, therefore, that a relationship will be lasting and satisfying. But we can increase our odds by attending to the things that we know are part of long-term, satisfying marriages.

PRINCIPLES FOR ENHANCING INTIMACY

1. Although most Americans reject the notion of arranged marriages, it is a good idea to talk over your choice of a prospective life partner with a trusted older or more experienced person. This person should be someone who knows you well and who has your best interests at heart. If he or she has major reservations about your choice, listen and consider the comments carefully.

2. If you haven't selected a life partner as yet or even if you already have someone in mind, take the time to seriously consider what kind of person you want him or her to be. Make a list of those characteristics that you really feel are essential in someone with whom you plan to spend your life, and refer to it often.

3. If you are contemplating marriage in the near future, it is vital to know what your prospective spouse expects from you and from your relationship. Talk about your shared and individual goals, about your respective roles in the marriage, about if and when you are going to have children, and so forth.

4. The old adage says that opposites attract, but it doesn't acknowledge that opposites often produce an unsatisfactory union. The evidence shows that the greater the similarity between you and your spouse, the greater your chances for a happy and enduring marriage.

5. Take time before you marry to get to know your future spouse. A longer courtship gives you a greater opportunity to know more fully your spouse-to-be and to establish the patterns of communication that are so essential to a successful marriage.

SUMMARY

In many societies, marriages have been arranged by parents rather than through the choice of the individuals getting married. Political and economic considerations in those societies are more important than love. In most modern societies, the ideal is for people to select their own life partners.

Most of us know the kinds of things we prefer and those we dislike in a life partner. The unmarried prefer such qualities as kindness, understanding, an exciting personality, intelligence, attractiveness, and good health. Married people have some of the same and some different preferences. Some gender differences also occur in preferences. In addition, people will be more satisfied when they are in a relationship of equity.

While the number of eligible life partners is theoretically enormous, practically, there are only a few for each of us. Because of the sex ratio, women have fewer choices than men. Mate selection is a filtering process. We engage in assortative mating, which means that most people have homogamous rather than heterogamous marriages. Assortative mating takes place along the lines of age, ethnic background, race, religion, education, personality, and a variety of other factors. Assortative mating occurs because of a number of factors, including propinquity, attraction, and family traditions and pressures.

A homogamous marriage doesn't guarantee stability or satisfaction. Homogamous marriages are more likely than heterogamous to last and to be happy, but a number of additional factors enhance your chances. A longer courtship and later age at marriage both increase the probability of a lasting and satisfying union. Other factors include perceived equity, good communication patterns, and the various areas covered in the PREPARE instrument.

Long-term satisfaction is difficult to predict for two reasons. First, our knowledge of someone is always limited. People may not reveal problematic aspects of their lives until after the marriage. Second, our needs and interests change over time. They may change in a way that makes a couple more compatible, but they can also change in a way that makes the couple diverge from each other.

INTERNET CONNECTION
Selecting a Life Partner

Your book outlines some of the statistical challenges facing selection of a life partner. Since there is a higher ratio of women to men, the challenge for women is greater—especially as they head towards midlife and later adulthood. Once you're in a relationship, the qualities that attracted you may not be the ones that solidify a lasting bond. Use the websites listed below to look deeper into these issues.

www.mhhe.com/lauer4

Relationship Preferences

http://WWW.Trinity.Edu/~mkearl/relation.html

This website outlines a 1996 segment of the General Social Survey addressing relationship preferences.

Planetlove

http://www.planet-love.com/

One of the more comprehensive mail order bride websites on the Internet.

Yahoo Personals

http://personals.classifieds.yahoo.com/sanfranciscobayarea/personals/

An Internet-based free personal ad service.

1. How do your relationship values and preferences compare to the findings at the General Social Survey website listed above?

2. Use the terms homogamy, heterogamy and hypergamy to explain the findings presented at the Relationships Preferences site.

3. Examine a mail order bride ad and a Yahoo Personals ad of your choice at the websites listed above. Use the following terms to describe your reaction to the ads you've looked at: propinquity, attraction, family traditions.

4. Is there enough information at the personals website for a potential consumer of the information to recognize the challenges? What does someone have to do if they need more information on the potential partner?

CHAPTER 9

THE SINGLE OPTION

Learning Objectives

After reading chapter 9, you should be able to:

1. Describe the size and composition of the single population today and how it compares with earlier times.
2. Relate and refute the various myths about singles.
3. Explain why individuals remain single.
4. Discuss the life-styles of singles.
5. Compare the way marrieds and singles relate to their families.
6. Characterize how singles deal with the challenges of old age.
7. Examine the impact of being single on health.
8. Describe the ways in which singles meet their intimacy needs.
9. Explain the ways that singles handle the desire for children.
10. Compare the extent to which singles and marrieds are satisfied with their lives.

One well-known producer of frozen foods now has over eighty different offerings that are designed to feed just one person. The food industry, like American business generally, is aware of the growing number of people who are single. Traditionally, our society has operated on the premise that most people will marry. But today an increasing number of people are choosing the single life. Many are delaying marriage, others are choosing not to engage in it at all, and still others who had been married have once again returned to the single life.

Thirty years ago, the majority of Americans believed that there was something wrong with the person who opted for the single life. Even today, people tend to judge the single more severely. Over four hundred college students evaluated the personality traits of married men and women higher than those of the unmarried (Etaugh and Stern 1984). A survey of three thousand singles in various parts of the country reported that over half felt some pressure to marry (Simenauer and Carroll 1982:332). The pressure came from parents, co-workers, dates, and personal feelings. Still, about 45 percent said they never felt any pressure, and the majority of Americans now agree that there is nothing wrong with choosing to be single. In this chapter, we shall look at the extent of singleness and why people opt for it. We will discuss some of the aspects of the single life. And we will see how single people fulfill their needs for intimacy. It should be noted that this is a relatively new and underdeveloped area of study. There are not a great many studies, and those that exist tend to have small samples and focus disproportionately on women. Many of our conclusions, therefore, are tentative.

HOW MANY SINGLES?

As figure 9.1 shows, the proportion of Americans who are unmarried has risen steadily. Moreover, the rise in the unmarried ranks has not been due merely to an increase in divorce. Greater numbers of both males and females are choosing to remain single for longer periods of time and, in some cases, for life (table 9.1). By 1996, 23.3 percent of the population aged eighteen and over (44.9 million Americans) had never been married. An additional 16.5 percent (31.7 million) were divorced or widowed. The figures varied by race and ethnicity. The proportion of those who had never married in 1996 was: 20.7 percent for whites, 38.8 percent for Asian Americans, 39.2 percent for African Americans, and 30.2 percent for Hispanics (U.S. Bureau of the Census 1997a and 1997b:55).

We need to keep the figures in perspective, however. Overall, 26.8 percent of males and 19.9 percent of females had never been married in 1996, figures which are still lower than those around the beginning of the century. In 1910, 33.3 percent of males and 23.3 percent of females were unmarried. In other words, we have not yet reached as high a proportion of singles as existed earlier in the century. Many factors, as we shall discuss, contribute to the decision to remain single. It also may be that marriage patterns follow long-term cycles and that at some point in the future the proportion of the unmarried will drop again. For the foreseeable future, however, it seems that singles will comprise a large and probably increasing proportion of the population.

MYTHS ABOUT SINGLES

Who are the people who are single? As noted in figure 9.1, the unmarried category includes the divorced, the widowed, and the never-married. There

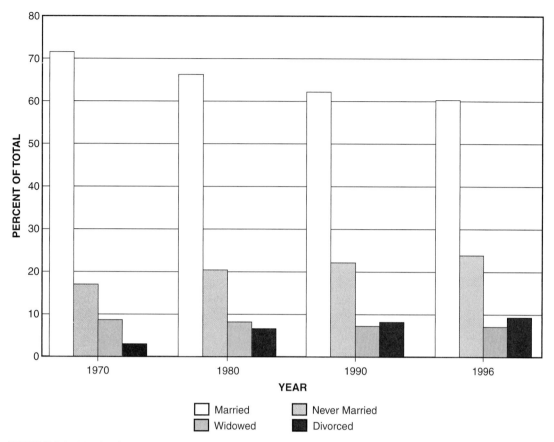

FIGURE 9.1 **Marital Status of the Population**
(*Sources:* U.S. Bureau of the Census 1992:44 and 1997b:55.)

TABLE 9.1

Percent Never Married, by Age and Sex: 1970 to 1996

Age	Male			Female		
	1970	**1980**	**1996**	**1970**	**1980**	**1996**
Total (18 years and above)	18.9	23.8	26.8	13.7	17.1	19.9
20–24 years	54.7	68.8	81.0	35.8	50.2	68.5
25–29 years	19.1	33.1	52.0	10.5	20.9	37.6
30–34 years	9.4	15.9	29.6	6.2	9.5	20.5
35–39 years	7.2	7.8	20.8	5.4	6.2	13.1
40–44 years	6.3	7.1	14.2	4.9	4.8	9.7
45–54 years	7.5	6.1	8.1	4.9	4.7	6.3
55–64 years	7.8	5.3	5.0	6.8	4.5	4.7
65 and over	7.5	4.9	4.0	7.7	5.9	4.1

Source: Saluter 1993:viii and U.S. Bureau of the Census 1997b:56 186.

PERSPECTIVE
The Awfulness of Being Unmarried

In Puritan New England, a stigma was attached to the single state. The Puritans asserted that God had ordained humans to live in societies, "First, of Family, Secondly, Church, Thirdly, Common-wealth" (John Cotton, quoted in Morgan 1944:18). The consequences of this belief for those who were unmarried are illustrated by a nineteenth-century historian (Earle 1893:36–37):

> In the early days of the New England colonies no more embarrassing or hampering condition, no greater temporal ill could befall any adult Puritan than to be unmarried. What could he do, how could he live in that new land without a wife? There were no housekeepers— and he would scarcely have been

allowed to have one if there were. What could a woman do in that new settlement among unbroken forests, uncultivated lands, without a husband? The colonists married early, and they married often. Widowers and widows hastened to join their fortunes and sorrows. The father and mother of Governor Winslow had been widow and widower seven and twelve weeks, respectively, when they joined their families and themselves in mutual benefit, if not in mutual love. At a later day the impatient Governor of New Hampshire married a lady but ten days widowed. Bachelors were rare indeed, and were regarded askance and with intense disfa-

vor by the entire community, were almost in the position of suspected criminals. They were seldom permitted to live alone, or even to choose their residence, but had to find a domicile wherever and with whomsoever the Court assigned. In Hartford [bachelors] had to pay twenty shillings a week to the town for the selfish luxury of solitary living. No colonial law seems to me more arbitrary or more comic than this order issued in the town of Eastham, Mass., in 1695, namely: Every unmarried man in the township shall kill six blackbirds or three crows while he remains single; as a penalty for not doing it, shall not be married until he obeys this order.

is a popular stereotype of the never-married as being either "*swingers*—the beautiful people who are constantly going to parties, who have uncommitted lives and a lot of uncommitted sex" or "*lonely losers*," who are depressed a good deal of the time (Stein 1976:2–3). But most singles fall into neither of those categories. Like other groups who have been subjected to something of a social stigma, singles have had to battle stereotypes and myths.

Cargan and Melko (1982) surveyed four hundred people in Dayton, Ohio, including some married, never-married, divorced, and remarried individuals. They used their data to counter seven myths about the never-married (Cargan and Melko 1982: 193–202):

1. They are still tied to their mothers' apron strings. In fact, the researchers found little difference between the never-married and others in their perceptions of parents and other relatives.

2. They are selfish. Some people believe that singles do not get married simply because they are too centered on themselves, leading lives of self-

indulgence and pursuing self-interests. But Cargan and Melko found that they value friends more highly than do the married and contribute more to community service.

3. They are financially well-off. The married people in the researchers' sample were better off economically than the never-married. Indeed, in the society as a whole, married people are likely to be better off than singles. There are a sufficient number of affluent, single professionals to lend credibility to the myth. But when compared to families, a far greater proportion of singles are in poverty.

4. They are happier. This is a myth held by singles themselves, many of whom tend to think that they are happier than married people. Married people think otherwise. The evidence, as we shall discuss, suggests that marrieds have an advantage in the area of well-being.

5. There are more singles now than ever. As we pointed out, there are far more singles than there were in 1970. But the proportion in 1987 was

not as high as it was in the first four decades of the century.

6. Being and staying single is an acceptable way of life. This is another myth of singles themselves, who like to assert it but don't practice it for the most part. Most singles plan on getting married at some point. In the Cargan and Melko study, most believed that they would be married within about five years.

7. Something is wrong with those who never marry. Evidence also belies this myth. An individual who postpones or even decides against marriage is not suffering from some disorder. Singles have greater problems with loneliness and with maintaining their happiness. But there are advantages as well as disadvantages to their status, and they may decide that the former outweigh the latter.

WHY PEOPLE ARE SINGLE

There is both a voluntary and an involuntary singlehood. That is, some people are single by choice, and some are single because of various barriers to marriage (Frazier et al. 1996). Table 9.2 shows the various types. A study of 217 singles reported that the men desired marriage more than the women and the never-married were more eager to marry than the divorced (Frazier et al. 1996). The study of three thousand Americans found that only a third of men and a fifth of women are single because they prefer the life-style or do not want to be married (Simenauer and Carroll 1982:322). Clearly, millions of Americans choose to be single, some for life and others following a divorce or death of a spouse. Millions of others prefer to marry but for various reasons have not or cannot. Let us look at some of the factors involved in people remaining single.

Career

Increasing proportions of males aged twenty to thirty-four and of females aged sixteen to twenty-four are participating in the labor force (figure 9.2). These, of course, are the years where marriage is most likely. More importantly, an increasing number of males and females define marriage as an impediment to a career and have opted to delay or forgo marriage in order to establish themselves in a career. When asked about their plans for the future, women who anticipate being housewives at age thirty-five are likely to marry in their twenties, but those who foresee a career are likely to delay marriage (Cherlin 1980).

Most single women believe that remaining unmarried will help them in their careers (Rollins 1986). And, in fact, they may be correct. A study of 663 professional women found that length of singlehood is related to career advancement (Houseknecht, Vaughan, and Statham 1987). Those women who remained single tended to have greater occupational attainments than those who married while in, or after completing, graduate school. One reason for this is the fact that women face a different situation than do men who also want both a family and a career. For the male, it has been both a common expectation and common experience to pursue a career while maintaining a family. For a woman, the choice may be more a matter of either/or. As one successful professional woman told us:

> I believe that women have the opportunity to do whatever they want. But you have to make a decision about what you really do want. You can make it in the work world if you are willing to make the necessary sacrifices.

By "necessary sacrifices" she meant forgoing marriage and a family. She herself had never been married.

TABLE 9.2
Types of Singles

	Voluntary	Involuntary
Marital experience	The widowed and divorced who do not want to remarry	The widowed and divorced who want to remarry
No marital experience	The never-married who are postponing or forgoing marriage	The never-married who want to marry

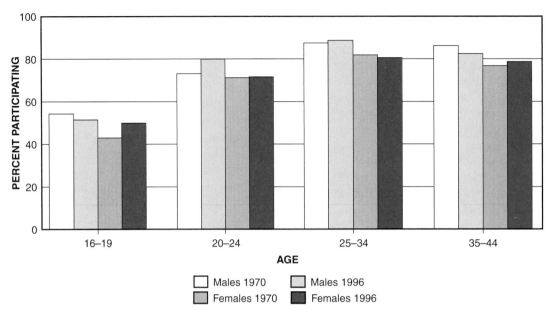

FIGURE 9.2   Labor Force Participation Rates of the Never-Married: 1970 and 1996
(*Source:* U.S. Bureau of the Census 1997b:403.)

The realities of pregnancy and the responsibilities of child care make it difficult for a woman to combine career and family. In addition, she may be expected to make her own career subordinate to that of her husband. If he has an opportunity to advance by moving to a different locale, she may be counted on to follow him even if the move is detrimental to her own career. These and other problems of the employed married woman will be discussed more fully in chapter 13.

It is not surprising, therefore, that the more educated (and, thus, probably the more career-minded) a woman is, the less likely she is to be married at an early age. Glick (1984) reported some statistics from the 1980 census. Among women twenty-five to twenty-nine years of age, 82 percent of those with eleven or fewer years of school were married; in comparison, 62 percent of those with seventeen or more years were married. Moreover, he estimated that about 90 percent of those with a high school education or less would eventually marry, compared to 83 percent of those with seventeen years or more of schooling.

Men as well as women are delaying marriage in order to establish themselves firmly in a career. The following statements illustrate the perspectives of two men who have delayed marriage:

> Since I completed college, achieving success in my profession has been my primary goal. As a result, I've consciously put more effort into my career than I have my social life. I have worked long hours and traveled a lot—both of which, I felt, would be detrimental to a wife and family. Recently, I have begun to think that the time is right. My practice is going extremely well. I have my own home. I honestly think that now I can have both a successful career and a good marriage (thirty-eight-year-old male lawyer).

> I definitely would like to get married. I feel part of me is ready emotionally. The only hindrance is that I haven't carved out my niche professionally. Personal development and finding myself has been my priority as opposed to putting my attention on material things and a career. Now I'm in a transition state, trying to establish myself in a new business. I don't want marriage and a family to take priority over finding the ultimate career for myself. Maybe in six months I'll have it together. And then I'll be ready (thirty-three-year-old male businessman).

In sum, while marriage, a family, and meaningful work are all important to most Americans, many believe that they cannot pursue them simultaneously. They have opted to establish themselves in their career first, before beginning the pursuit of marriage and a family.

Availability of Sex

Sir Thomas More wrote in his *Utopia* that no one would want marriage if sex were available outside marriage. While that overstates the case, it is true that the ready availability of sex is a factor in remaining single. Ironically, as we noted in chapter 4, married people engage in far more sex than do singles. On the other hand, an attraction for singles is the fact that sex with a variety of partners is a possibility. There is no one person to whom one is pledged to be faithful. Some singles regard the freedom and opportunity to have multiple sexual partners as one of the more important attractions of singlehood, although AIDS may be affecting this view. As noted in chapter 4, at least some people have modified their sexual activity to minimize the chances of getting AIDS; unless a cure is found, increasing numbers are likely to do so.

Personal Freedom

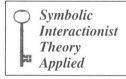

Symbolic Interactionist Theory Applied

What does it mean to be free? We all cherish freedom, but what precisely does it mean? As *symbolic interactionists* emphasize, we need to know how someone defines freedom before we can understand why that person behaves in a certain way in order to maintain his or her freedom. For example, a single thirty-four-year-old professor at a state university defined it this way for us:

> I'm a free man. I can go where I want and do what I want when I want. I don't have to answer to anyone else. I don't have to worry about coming home late or explain to someone why I'm late. I don't have to forgo a trip because I can't afford to take a family. I can pursue new interests without worrying about whether a wife would want to pursue them with me. Frankly, I don't want to have all of my decisions shackled by considerations of other people.

To the extent that you agree with the professor's definition of freedom, you will find more of it in singlehood than in marriage. His statement is probably extreme for the tastes of most people. But he does capture something of what many single people find appealing—the freedom to be spontaneous, to travel, to pursue interests, and to change careers without having to worry about the consequences of those actions for a family. Of course, most single people probably realize that they are engaged in a trade-off between what they define as freedom, independence, and personal growth and the possible loneliness and missed fulfillment that could come from a spouse and children (Dalton 1992). Still, Simenauer and Carroll (1982:347) reported that nearly half of the three thousand singles they studied named mobility and freedom as one of the greatest advantages of their status.

Men seem more concerned than women about retaining their personal freedom. Although the sample was quite small (fifty never-married people), Greenglass (1985) found that nearly three-fourths of the men but only 8 percent of the women regarded marriage as a threat to their freedom.

There is, however, another aspect to freedom that seems to be of concern to women. In her study of fifty single women between the ages of 60 and 101, Simon (1987) reported that most of them had turned down marriage proposals. The most common reason for refusing marriage was a fear of becoming a subordinate creature. "You see, dear," one woman explained, "it's *marriage* I avoid, not men. Why would I ever want to be a wife? . . . A wife is someone's servant. A woman is someone's friend" (Simon 1987:31–32). Another woman compared marriage to a state that is "dangerously close to slavery."

Desire for Personal Growth

The thirty-three-year-old businessman previously quoted pointed out that his first priority had been personal growth. Once he felt he had achieved this, he could establish himself in a career and then think about marriage. His is not an isolated case. Other singles, both men and women, express similar sentiments, emphasizing the need for personal growth before establishing a long-term relationship. In the Simenauer and Carroll study (1982:347), the second most frequently named advantage of singleness was having the time to pursue personal interests (named by 17 percent of the men and 21 percent of the women). One of the differences that Gigy (1980) found between sixty-six never-married and thirty-seven married women was that the former placed a higher value on personal growth and achievement while the latter placed a higher value on relationships. Thus, the never-married were more likely to place high value on such things as competence, economic success, self-improvement, learning new things, and mastering fresh challenges. The married were more likely to place highest value on such things as love and affection, friends, and a happy marriage.

Social Conditions

Social circumstances can also affect your chances of getting married. Both wars and economic depressions tend to result in lower marriage rates and later age at marriage (Trovato 1988). For the generation born around 1910, the Great Depression that began in 1929 left a number of people single who would otherwise have preferred to get married. In some cases, women of marriageable age felt that they had to stay unmarried and go to work both to contribute to their own support and to the survival of their parents and siblings (Allen and Pickett 1987:522). And even if the woman could not find work, she might not find a man who could afford to get married.

In addition to major upheavals, such as wars and depressions, changing sex ratios affect the likelihood of marriage. If the number of men and women were equal, there would be the potential for every person in the society to have a heterosexual, monogamous relationship. But partly because of wars and partly because of differing birth and death rates, the numbers are never quite equal. The **sex ratio,** the number of males per one hundred females, varies from decade to decade (table 9.3).

When the number of males per one hundred females or the number of females per one hundred males gets low, there is a "marriage squeeze." That means that marriage rates will tend to go down (South and Lloyd 1992). As the table shows, before 1940, there were more males than females. Now, there are millions more females than males. The marriage squeeze affected men who wanted to marry prior to 1940. Since then, it has affected females.

The marriage squeeze occurs in many societies, and it tends to have the same kind of consequences.

The marriage squeeze occurs when the number of men and women are unequal.

In his examination of 111 different countries, South (1988) found that when there is an undersupply of women, there is an increase in the marriage and fertility rates for women. There is also a decline in women's average age at marriage, their literacy rate, and the divorce rate. These tendencies are highest in those countries where women tend not to participate in the labor force.

The marriage squeeze in the United States is particularly severe for black women. Young black men have higher mortality rates than white men. They are more likely than white men to be imprisoned or in the military. There is also a higher proportion of homosexuals among black men. Some black men marry white women. Finally, more middle-class black women graduate from college than do black men. The result is that black women at all socioeconomic levels have fewer choices and are more likely than whites to find themselves in a state of involuntary singlehood (Staples 1981). The impor-

TABLE 9.3
Sex Ratios: 1930 to 1996 (number of males per 100 females)

	1930	1940	1950	1960	1970	1980	1990	1996
All ages	102.5	100.7	98.6	97.1	94.8	94.5	95.1	95.8
25–44 years	101.8	98.5	96.4	95.7	95.5	97.4	98.9	99.4

Sources: U.S. Bureau of the Census 1991d:17 and 1997b:16.

tance of the sex ratio for black women is underscored by a Louisiana study that showed that as the sex ratio for African Americans dropped over time, the black marriage rate, number of husband-wife black families, and number of children in the families also dropped (Fossett and Kiecolt 1990).

Family Background

A professional woman who is in her mid-thirties and single said that one of the factors in her decision not to get married before she had established herself in a career was the experience of her parents:

> I've known most of my life that I didn't want to have the same kind of relationship that my parents have. My mother got married because she wanted to get away from her parents, and she needed someone to support her financially. When things didn't work out well, she felt trapped. She felt she couldn't manage economically on her own, especially with the responsibility of her kids. So she just stayed in a bad marriage.

Coming from a home where there has been discord or a disruption may make an individual hesitant to repeat the same kind of mistake. Thus, a study of 134 college females found that those who came from homes where there was discord or where the parents had separated had more negative feelings about marriage (Long 1987).

Personal Characteristics

A number of characteristics such as personality traits and personal attitudes can contribute to whether or not one will remain single. A study of thirty never-married white males in their forties reported that the men valued independence and self-reliance and practiced emotional detachment in their relationships (Waehler 1995). Men also report shyness and the desire to be in multiple relationships as factors in remaining single.

Some people, for various reasons, have a fear of making a commitment to someone else. Eleven percent of the men and 7 percent of the women in Simenauer and Carroll's (1982:321) sample said that they were single because marriage involves too much commitment and responsibility. One therapist who has worked with men who fear commitment wrote:

> These men view personal commitment as being boxed in, being put in a position where they are exposed and vulnerable to their partners. Making plans for the future in such uncertain relationships seems frightening. In contrast, having a sense of future in their careers seems imperative, an integral part of their lives (Freudenberger 1987:46).

Another common reason people give for being single is that they simply haven't found the right person. In most cases, they have been through a series of relationships, but none of them has worked out. No one has quite met the expectations and the standards set by the individual for a suitable life partner. It may be a case of setting standards that are too high. It may be an excuse for avoiding commitment. Or it may be that the individual is a victim of the marriage squeeze or circumstances that have prevented him or her from meeting an appropriate partner.

Finally, although they represent a minority of those who are single, some people simply prefer the single life. They view singlehood as an opportunity to pursue things that they value more than marriage and a family.

SINGLE LIFE-STYLES

If singles are not the swingers or the losers as suggested by popular stereotypes, what kind of life-styles do they have? Work and career are predominant for many singles. What goes on in the rest of their lives?

Living Arrangements

To be single is not necessarily to live alone. In 1995, 53 percent of young adults ages eighteen to twenty-four and 12 percent of those ages twenty-five to thirty-four lived with one or both parents (U.S. Bureau of the Census 1997b:58). Interestingly, for both age groups a greater proportion of males than females lived with parents. In his study of forty-seven older men, Rubinstein (1986) interviewed eleven who had never been married. Nine of them lived with one or both parents until the parents died. Their age at the time of the death of the last parent ranged from thirty-seven to sixty-one.

There are a variety of other living arrangements. Some singles live alone, some share apartments with friends, some cohabit, and an increasing number are buying their own homes. In some cases, singles band together in nonsexual pairs or triads to purchase a home. Such an arrangement may be purely a business one, though it is more likely to occur between those who are friends.

The choice of living arrangement has obvious effects on other aspects of life-style. The single person who lives with his or her parents will have restrictions that the home owner does not have. The single who shares an apartment with a friend will have constraints that the single who lives alone in an apartment does not have. But for financial reasons or personal needs or both, most singles prefer to live with someone.

Sex

The popular image of the single is a young person "on the loose" who is free to engage in numerous sexual relationships. The reality is different, both in terms of amount and satisfaction.

Masters, Johnson, and Kolodny (1988:251) identify a number of common patterns of sexual behavior among single young adults. The *experimenter* seeks to experience the full variety of sexual behavior with as many partners as possible, viewing the world as a "sexual smorgasbord" to be enjoyed fully until he or she settles down. The *seeker* engages in sexual intercourse in order to find an ideal life partner. Living with someone is one way to test out sexual compatibility and, presumably, marital possibilities. The *traditionalist* believes in sexual intercourse only in serious relationships. The traditionalist may have a number of sexual partners before marrying but is likely to have only one partner at a time and rarely or never in a purely casual situation.

In popular myth, the experimenter is one of the most common types of the singles. In actuality, experimenters are a minority of the singles. Moreover, there seems to be an increasing amount of disillusionment with casual sex. Those who experience so-called one-night stands find them less than satisfying in the long run. As a thirty-year-old woman put it:

> You just can't compare the quality of sex with someone you hardly know and feel nothing for with the quality of sex in a caring relationship. Casual sex is just mechanical, one-dimensional release. Sex with someone I care about is warmer and psychologically far more satisfying (in Masters, Johnson, and Kolodny 1988:252).

Cargan and Melko (1982:241) found that singles have less sex than marrieds. Sixty-seven percent of the never-married in their sample had sex once a week or less, compared to only 36 percent of the marrieds. Twelve percent of the never-married and 28 percent of the married had sex three or more times a week. They also reported that the marrieds were more satisfied with their sex lives. Four-fifths of the married but only about half of the singles said they were sexually satisfied.

Leisure

Without family responsibilities, singles should have more opportunities for leisure activities. And those activities can be matters of personal choice rather than ones that will please a spouse or other family member. Singles do in fact tend to go out more than married people. Cargan and Melko (1982:232) found that 31 percent of the never-married, 22 percent of the divorced, but only 8 percent of the married had three or more social outings per week.

Some differences exist between marrieds and singles not only in frequency but also in the kind of activities preferred. Singles prefer movies, nightclubs, and theater more than marrieds. Married people prefer restaurants, visiting relatives, and social clubs somewhat more than singles (Cargan and Melko 1982:85). Interestingly, singles and marrieds watched about the same amount of television. But singles tend to spend more time visiting friends, engaging in hobbies and sports, and being involved in community service.

Family Relations

Systems Theory Applied

In a comparison of singles and marrieds on family relations, the marrieds were much more likely to have warm and stable relationships with their parents (Cargan and Melko 1982:76). Singles are more likely to fight with their parents. It isn't clear why this is so. The proportion of singles who recall growing up with loving and warm parents is close to that of marrieds (60 percent of singles and 64 percent of marrieds). Perhaps the conflict reflects the parents' desire for the single child to marry and some ongoing tension surrounding that issue. It is also possible that at least some singles who recall warm and loving parents actually came from families that had what *systems theorists* call "enmeshed" relationships. That is, they stressed togetherness and solidarity to the point of suppressing individuality on the part of family members. The tension that some singles have with their parents may reflect their ongoing struggle to achieve autonomy. Unfortunately, in an enmeshed family the individual who tries to establish his or her independence will be defined as engaging in betrayal rather than in the quest for personal growth. One aspect of the single's relation with parents seems to particularly affect single women, namely, being entrusted with the care of aging parents. In a study of women born around 1910, Allen and Pickett (1987) found that some felt they had to remain single, live at home, and contribute to the financial care of the family. A common situation was for the last daughter left at home to remain there and care for her widowed mother. As one woman said, "I had to take my mother into consideration. No, I couldn't

Single women frequently assume the care of aging parents.

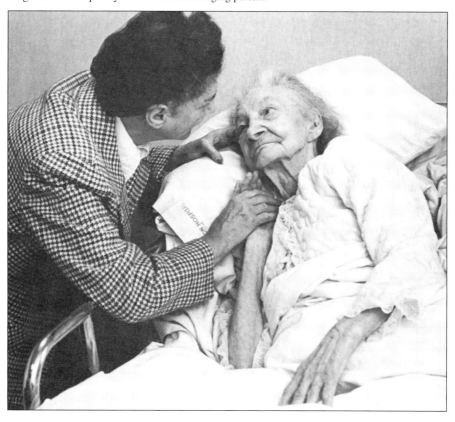

do anything. She had to be my prime concern" (Allen and Pickett 1987:522). Similarly, in her study of fifty never-married women, Simon (1987:60) noted that all but two had partly or totally supported aging parents. The two exceptions came from affluent homes. Women who remain single and whose siblings are married are likely, therefore, to assume the responsibility for the care of aging parents. This is consistent with the traditional sex role for women, who are expected to be the nurturers and caretakers (see the discussion in chapter 3).

Singles and Old Age

When married people retire, they have the option of focusing time and energy on children and grandchildren. What do singles do at this point in their lives? What happens when parents have died or when the individual no longer has the work that may have dominated his or her life?

An analysis of data collected by the U.S. Bureau of the Census showed that retirement tends not to pose such a crisis for the never-married (Keith 1985). The never-married actually adjusted better to retirement than the divorced. On the other hand, there is some degree of isolation among older singles. The data from the Census Bureau showed that about a third of older singles never see neighbors, about 30 percent never see friends, and 21 percent of the men and 14 percent of the women never see relatives (Keith 1986:392). Even larger proportions never talk to neighbors, friends, or relatives on the telephone. To keep the data in perspective, more than half of older singles *do* see friends, relatives, and neighbors. The majority of elderly singles, then, are socially active (Stull and Scarisbrick-Hauser 1989). And for singles of all ages, isolation per se is not so much the problem as is the difference between the amount of social activity one has and the amount one prefers (Keith, Braito, and Breci 1990).

A prime reason for isolation among the men is health problems. Isolated women tend to have less education and to have worked in lower-level occupations. Those who are not isolated engage in a range of activities. The activities vary by gender. Older single men tend to get involved in physical activities such as home maintenance and repairs, walking, exercise, and sports. Older single women

tend to be engaged in hobbies, volunteer work, church activities, and affiliation with relatives (Keith and Nauta 1988).

Older singles also continue to be involved in sexual relationships, including dating and sex (Bulcroft and O'Conner-Roden 1986). To older singles, dating means a committed and long-term relationship. It is analogous to going steady at a younger age. Some of the same feelings also recur. Older people who date report having the symptoms of romantic love, including sweaty palms, the inability to concentrate, and an intense desire for union. What do older people do on dates? Some of the same things that younger people do—get a pizza, go to the movies, and go to dances. They also may go camping together, attend an opera, or fly to another city for a weekend.

As with any other group, older singles are a diverse lot. Some are quite active and satisfied. Others are neither. The older retired single has a different life-style from the older married person, but he or she is not devoid of satisfaction because of the loss of work.

SINGLES AND LONELINESS

We have seen that singles engage in numerous and diverse activities. But involvement in activities does not mean that an individual is no longer lonely and that his or her intimacy needs are being met. Simenauer and Carroll (1982:347) found that over 40 percent of their respondents considered loneliness the greatest disadvantage of singlehood. However, those most likely to feel lonely are in the lower income brackets, which suggests that they may be less able to engage in a variety of stimulating activities. Still, single people report more feelings of loneliness than the married. A survey of eighty-six hundred adults reported that marital status was a stronger predictor of loneliness than income, education, race, or occupation (Page and Cole 1991). Less than 5 percent of the married reported feeling lonely very or fairly often during the preceding year, but 15 percent of never-marrieds and 20 percent of the divorced reported such feelings.

Although most singles are not lonely, your chances of being lonely are much greater if you are single than if you are married. Singles also are more likely than marrieds to define some activities

INVOLVEMENT
Observing Singles

Most communities now have regular activities for single people. Check your newspaper or call local churches to find out what kind of activities are available in your area. Attend one or more group activities. Carefully listen to and observe the people and their activities. Attend to nonverbal as well as verbal behavior. That is, watch the expressions on people's faces. Note if they seem truly involved. Watch for signs of satisfaction or dissatisfaction. If possible, discuss with some of the singles what their interest is in the group and what the group means to them.

Write up an account of your visit or visits. What conclusions would you draw about the life-styles of singles in your area? What functions does the group seem to serve in the lives of the participants (recall, for instance, the functions of dating discussed in chapter 6)? To what extent are singles participating in groups in order to find a possible mate? To what extent do singles seem to get their intimacy needs fulfilled by the group? How would you compare the singles' groups with family activities and with groups of marrieds you have observed?

If the entire class participates in this exercise, have students visit differing kinds of groups. You can include singles' bars or other places where singles tend to hang out. Compare the various groups. Do they have diverse or similar functions for singles? Do different kinds of people attend the differing groups? Why? If all you knew about singleness came from the observations about these groups, to what extent would you find lifelong singlehood appealing?

as lonely experiences. For example, Cargan and Melko (1982:246) found that 46 percent of singles and 34 percent of marrieds thought dining alone to be a lonely activity. And 23 percent of singles but only 15 percent of marrieds said that they were depressed when they were alone. In addition, singles were more likely to indicate that they often have no one with whom to share and discuss things.

Loneliness is more than an uncomfortable feeling. Chronic, intense loneliness may lead to a variety of physical and emotional ills. That is one reason for the higher incidence of such ills among singles.

SINGLES AND HEALTH

In general, as we noted in chapter 1, married people are healthier—both physically and emotionally—than single people. Or perhaps it would be more accurate to say that people in meaningful intimate relationships are healthier than those who lack such relationships, and married people are more likely than single people to be in a meaningful relationship.

Thus, a study of 65 university staff personnel and 243 students found that those in an intimate relationship were healthier than those who were single, and the better the quality of the relationship the

fewer the health problems (McCabe, Cummins, and Romeo 1996). Singles did have somewhat better emotional health than those in troubled relationships. But meaningful relationships guard and enhance well-being. The protection marriage affords is underscored in a study of 141 academic women (Fong and Amatea 1992). The sample included single, single-parent, married, and married-parent women. All of the groups had high levels of career commitment and satisfaction, but the single women reported significantly higher levels of stress symptoms than did the married-parent women.

Married people also have lower rates of emotional problems. Singles tend to suffer more from such things as depression and various personality disorders, a finding that holds true for many different societies (Mastekaasa 1994). It does not appear to be true, however, for African Americans. An analysis of interviews with 18,571 adults concluded that married African Americans do not have a mental health advantage over the never-married, though they do have better mental health than the widowed or divorced/separated (Williams, Takeuchi, and Adair 1992).

There are some gender differences we should note. While the married are healthier than the unmarried, single women are much healthier than single

COMPARISON
Being Single in Japan

In many nations, as we have noted, married people generally enjoy better health than singles. However, singles in Japan may be at even higher risk for health problems and earlier death than people in the United States and in other industrial countries. An examination of mortality patterns in 16 industrialized nations shows that while death rates of singles are higher than those of married people in all the nations (one-and-a-half to two times), the disparity is particularly large in Japan (three times as high). Thus, Japanese singles have a life expectancy which is not only lower than that of the Japanese married but also is lower than that of singles in the industrial nations in this study.

The good news for Japanese singles is that the gap between the life expectancy of singles and the married in Japan has been decreasing, while the gap in the other nations has been increasing. The Japanese gap is still the largest, however.

How can we account for this pattern? Part of the explanation may result from the mate selection process in Japan. As in the United States, about 95 percent of Japanese men and women eventually marry. But unlike the United States, mate selection in Japan has traditionally involved a strong emphasis on the health of a potential spouse. Therefore, anyone with health problems has been at a distinct disadvantage in finding a mate.

Combined with the tendency to avoid poorer people (who also have more health-related problems), then, the emphasis on the health of a potential mate has resulted in a disproportionate number of people with health problems remaining single. Why, then, has the gap between the single and the married been decreasing in recent decades? Because love matches have increasingly replaced the traditional family-arranged marriages (only about a fourth of marriages were arranged by the late 1980s).

The mate selection process is not the only reason for the gap between the health of married and singles in Japan. Unfortunately, we do not know what other factors are operating. But clearly, Japanese singles are, like singles in other nations, at higher risk for ill health and earlier death. And their risk is even higher than is the risk for singles in other nations (Goldman 1993).

---

men. In fact, single men are the unhealthiest of all groups. In part, this may be due to the fact that there is a higher proportion of professionals among single women than among single men. Professional men tend to marry and stay married longer than others. Professional women are more likely than other women to marry late, divorce, or remain single. Professionals also tend to have better health than those in low-paying, blue-collar jobs.

But the gender differences also reflect what Jessie Bernard (1972) called "his" marriage and "her" marriage. Men seem to benefit, in terms of health, more from marriage than do women. The poor health of single men may reflect not only a lack of intimate relations but also the stress of trying to maintain a household by someone who has never been trained in domestic skills (Davis and Strong 1977). Married men have the best health of all. Married women are better off than singles, but they do not benefit in terms of health from marriage as much as men do. In particular, women who are in a traditional role in the home (wife and home-

maker) are especially prone to higher rates of illness (Lauer 1995:484). In other words, it is the restrictive nature of the traditional role that is stressful for women and leads to higher rates of both mental and physical illness among married women than among married men. Nevertheless, married women still have an edge over single women.

INTIMACY AND LIFE SATISFACTION

Much of the preceding indicates that, despite the growing number opting for temporary or permanent singlehood, singles are at a disadvantage in some of the things we highly value. In this section, we will focus on the bottom line: How do singles compare with marrieds in intimacy and life satisfaction?

Intimacy

Recall that while our needs for intimacy differ, all of us require some intimate relationships. How do singles handle their own needs?

Intimate Relationships Singles may fulfill some of their intimacy needs by living with their parents, a friend, or an acquaintance or by cohabiting. Those who live alone have a greater challenge. Whatever the living arrangements, however, singles employ a variety of means to establish relationships with others. There are the more traditional means of meeting people through family, friends, school, and religious groups. And there are the relatively newer methods of singles' bars, groups, ads, and dating services. The popularity of such methods shows that singles are aware of their needs for intimacy and are anxious to establish and maintain intimate relationships.

By establishing a number of relationships, singles in effect may create their own family. A **network family** is a support group of nonkin. One does not live with the network family, but the members are always available to help and support each other in the same way as a family related by blood or marriage.

Friends are particularly important for singles. In essence, a friend is someone whom you like as a person; enjoy being with; feel comfortable and relaxed around; can share thoughts, feelings, cares, and hopes with; and feel free to call on in time of need (Lauer and Lauer 1999b). Close friends provide singles with a number of benefits. Because friendships are intimate relationships, they enhance singles' health. Friends can encourage and support personal growth, help with difficult decisions, and provide various kinds of support and help in difficult times.

In a study of ninety-nine adults living alone in a retirement community, Potts (1997) found that those with high-quality friendships had lower levels of depression. Another study of 796 residents in retirement communities reported that interacting with friends was related to life satisfaction (Hong and Duff 1997).

Of course, friends are important to singles whatever their age. In her study of the lives of never-married women, Simon (1987) pointed out the crucial importance of friendships. The women had pictures of their friends on display in their homes or apartments. They would talk about their friends when discussing such things as work, travel, recreation, and retirement. A common pattern involved having a close, daily, long-term friendship with an-

other person (usually another woman) while also joining a circle of two to five additional friends. The circle might meet once or twice a week, either as a group or in pairs.

The women tended to develop their bonds during their thirties, when it began to appear that they would not marry. They found other women who had made the same choice (or who had the choice forced on them by circumstances) and cemented what would be a long-term relationship. As the friendships developed, the women made long-term plans, including plans about what they would do after retirement. For example, one woman talked about her friend, Maureen, whom she had met in nursing school. They wound up employed in the same hospital and decided to buy a house together:

> Since then we've been like hand and glove. We took all our vacations together and used them to travel all over the world. Her friends were mine and vice versa. When I reached fifty-five, I began to think about retirement. I tried to convince Maureen to enroll in the same retirement community as me for whenever we got too old to be in our house. . . . She took a year to think about it and then agreed (Simon 1987:97).

Thus, the women have a number of close companions, at least some of whom have shared a series of experiences with them. They have established effective network families that provide them with many of the intimate needs of a marriage.

Sexual Intimacy One thing the network family does not provide is the fulfillment of one's sexual needs. Yet sex is an important need. In fact, one study of sixty single women in the thirty-five to sixty-five age group noted that half of the women mentioned the meeting of their sexual needs as a necessary part of a satisfying life (Loewenstein et al. 1981). Some had found fulfillment, and others had not.

We have already pointed out that singles have sex less often than marrieds and report less sexual satisfaction than marrieds. It seems that, at least in terms of the sexual aspect of intimacy, singles are less likely than marrieds to find fulfillment. Even those who choose to be single may find themselves struggling with their sexual needs. According to Laurel Richardson (1986), an increasing number of women who are single by choice or by circumstance are opting for affairs with married men in order to deal with their sexual needs. She found that professional women, those who have opted to give priority to careers, are especially prone to getting involved with married men. Such women have delayed marriage in order to establish themselves in their careers. But when they decide that they are ready to consider marrying, they find a shortage of available men. In order to deal with their need for an intimate, heterosexual relationship, they resorted to an affair.

Unfortunately, the affairs tend to grow difficult and counterproductive over time. As one woman said, her affair drained her energy and ultimately led to her being hurt: "It ended up being very costly to me, to my career and my life in general" (Richardson 1986:27).

Sexual intimacy does not necessarily involve sexual intercourse. In fact, Richardson pointed out that sexual intercourse is not the major activity in the affairs she studied. The subjects did have intercourse, but they also had a good deal of heterosexual closeness, including the sharing and affection that go into intimate relationships. Touching, caressing, admiring, supporting, and caring by someone of the opposite sex is an important part of fulfilling our needs for sexual intimacy. Singles are faced with less likelihood of experiencing such sexual intimacy.

The Question of Children   We will explore the role of children in our intimate needs in chapter 15. Clearly, some people regard children as an important part of their fulfillment. Some people desire the parent-child intimacy whether or not they are married. And at least some women who are childless regret the fact when they are past the childbearing years (Loewenstein et al. 1981).

Victor Callan (1986b) studied forty-two single women who said they wanted to remain childless and sixty who wanted one or more children. He found that those who preferred to be childless tended to be more pessimistic and less loving than the others. Those who preferred either no children or only one child were more concerned about their financial and social independence than those who desired two children. Thus, various factors enter into our desire to have or not have children. As in the case of getting married, one factor is the concern about one's independence and freedom. Inter-

estingly, even some of those women who were more concerned about independence still wanted to have one child.

Increasing numbers of single women are having children. The proportion of births to unmarried mothers varies considerably by race and ethnicity, but it has increased among all groups (figure 9.3). Single women who have children are more likely to be in the lower socioeconomic levels. As such, they are doubly handicapped in their efforts at parenting. Not only do they lack the help of a husband and father, but they also must deal with the problems of a paucity of financial resources. Single mothers are the most impoverished group in the nation. They may fulfill some of their intimacy needs through their children, but the costs in terms of financial and emotional stress are high.

Life Satisfaction

If the pursuit of happiness is one of the fundamental rights of all Americans, how do singles fare? How can we sum it all up in terms of life satisfaction?

Factors in Life Satisfaction   When singles are asked about the factors that go into their life satisfaction, their answers are similar to those of other Americans (Simenauer and Carroll 1982:334–37). Good health is one of the most important factors. Ironically, as just noted, singles are less likely than marrieds to enjoy good health. Other things mentioned by singles include career, personal growth, financial security, love, and social and family life. A good sex life is also important to most singles. The list, of course, comes from all types of singles, including some who hope to marry at some point.

Some research asks singles about their satisfaction with life and then relates that with various factors in their lives. Many of the same factors noted above turn out to be significant. For instance, in their study of sixty single women, Loewenstein et al. (1981) found that life satisfaction was higher among those women who had good health, were not lonely, lived with a female housemate, had many casual friends, and were deeply involved in their work.

A study of male and female never-marrieds focused on the role of social support and loneliness in life satisfaction (Cockrum and White 1985). The re-

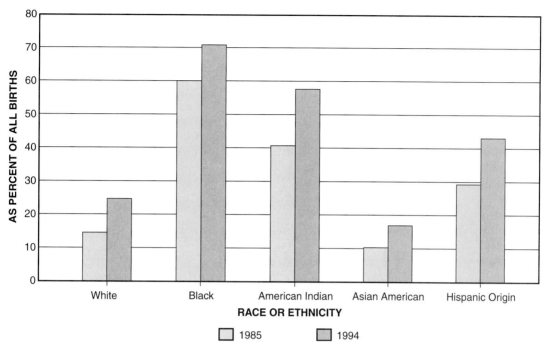

FIGURE 9.3   Births to Unmarried Mothers, by Race and Ethnicity
(*Source:* U.S. Bureau of the Census 1997b:78.)

searchers found that friends were important to both males and females. Visiting friends enabled them to deal with loneliness. There were gender differences, however. For men, life satisfaction depended on having a network of individuals with whom they could share their interests and their values. For women, life satisfaction was higher when they had people with whom they could establish close, emotional bonds. These differences are consistent with the gender patterns we discussed in chapter 3.

How Satisfied Are Singles?   In their interviews with a small sample of never-married and divorced women, Lewis and Moon (1997) found mixed results in terms of life satisfaction. The women identified advantages to being single, including not having to be a caretaker for a man and freedom to do as they pleased. At the same time, they expressed concerns about the lack of intimacy, the lack of children, and growing old alone. On the whole, they were content with being single but also acknowledged a sense of loss in not having a mate or children.

Life satisfaction is high for some singles.

PERSONAL
Single by Choice

Jamie is a thirty-year-old biologist who is single by choice. Because her family and friends all assumed that she would marry and have children, she has struggled with her decision. She talks about her decision, some of the advantages and disadvantages of singlehood, and how she has fulfilled her intimacy needs.

I really like being single. And I'm not single just because I haven't had plenty of opportunities to marry. I've had a number of proposals. In fact, I came within two weeks of walking down the aisle and saying "I do." But in the end, I couldn't go through with it. I just didn't love him the way I felt I should. On paper, we looked like the perfect couple. We both had Ph.D.s, were scientists, loved the outdoors, and enjoyed art, cooking, and travel. He even fit in well with my family. Yet in my most reflective moments, I couldn't

imagine spending the rest of my life with him. In fact, as our wedding approached, I found myself already anticipating with relish his next business trip when I would have time alone—most importantly, time away from him. This, I realized, was no basis for marriage.

Single life has its pluses and minuses. On the plus side, I have greater freedom, flexibility, and independence than my married friends. And I really treasure all three. However, the single life also has its price. For me, it means not having a long-term partner and not having children. I am particularly envious when I see an older couple walking down the street holding hands and know I may never have this.

Sometimes I worry about being single—even more about the fact that I enjoy it so much. I worry about whether I should be looking harder for a husband, and certainly, I am concerned

about the ticking of my biological clock. I also feel pressure from family and friends. Even when they don't say anything, I feel it. I know that they are wondering—when is Jamie going to get married, is there something wrong with her?

I don't think anything is wrong. On the whole, I'm content and happy with almost everything in my life. I have a variety of friends who enrich my life in different ways. They provide me with the intimacy, companionship, and emotional support. I don't feel that I lack any of those vital things. I'm not saying that I'll never marry. However, I don't want to get caught in the trap that ensnares so many women—continually searching for a man and always being frustrated because they haven't found him. I'm not going to wait to start living until I find a man, because that may never happen. I'm living right now.

The researchers did not investigate whether the responses differed by age. Other research has shown that the life satisfaction of singles, like that of marrieds, varies over the course of their lives. For singles, the thirties seem to be one of the more difficult times. Developmental psychologists point out that the thirties are a time of reevaluation of people's lives. "A restless vitality wells up as we approach 30. Almost everyone wants to make some alteration" (Sheehy 1976:198). We look at the decisions we have made in our twenties and question whether they are correct and whether we want to stick with them for the rest of our lives. For singles, the reevaluation includes the single state, the possibility that they may never marry and/or have children, the problem of intimate relationships, and the question of whether a career will be ultimately satisfying. In her study of

thirty-six single men and sixty-three single women, Rollins (1986:123) noted that the only ones who had significantly contemplated suicide were women between the ages of thirty and thirty-nine. After the thirties, however, life satisfaction may improve. Individuals who accept their single status and establish a network family may express high satisfaction with their lives.

Researchers have tried to get at the life satisfaction of people by phrasing questions in a variety of ways. Simenauer and Carroll (1982:351) asked singles whether, on the whole, being single had been a pleasant or unpleasant experience. Twenty-three percent of the men and 12 percent of the women said "it's been wonderful." But overall, about 60 percent of men and slightly more than 50 percent of women indicated that they enjoyed aspects of being

Singles use various kinds of activities to fulfill their intimacy needs.

single, while the others said that they did not enjoy the single life.

Simenauer and Carroll have no sample of marrieds, of course, with which to compare the results. Cargan and Melko (1982:173f) reported the results from both married and singles when people were asked whether they were happy. More than two-thirds of their sample indicated that they were at least moderately happy. But in every age group, including those under thirty, a greater proportion of marrieds than of singles said that they were happy. Interestingly, a greater proportion of marrieds (83 percent) than of singles (75 percent) also agreed that they were getting "a lot of fun out of life."

The same pattern appeared in national surveys reported by Ward (1981:347). A greater proportion of twenty-five- to forty-nine-year-old married people reported themselves as "very happy" (39.4 percent) than did the widowed (20.5 percent), the divorced/separated (16.5 percent), or the never-married (15.5 percent). In the fifty and above age category, the married still led the others (43.2 percent), but the never-married were the next most likely to say they were very happy (26.1 percent), followed by the widowed (23.8 percent), and the divorced/separated (20.3 percent). Clearly, married people are more likely to say they are happy than any of the types of single people. With regard to how exciting people believe their lives are, the situation is a little more complex. In response to the question of whether people found life exciting, pretty routine, or dull, a larger proportion of the never-married (54.4 percent), in the twenty-five to forty-nine age group, said exciting. About 48 percent of the married and 40 percent of the widowed and divorced said that they found life exciting. In the fifty and above age group, however, the married again came out ahead. A little over 41 percent of the married and about a third of the other groups agreed that their lives were exciting.

To sum up, some singles, whether never-married, divorced, or widowed, prefer their life-style and find it satisfying. Yet singles are less likely than the married to perceive themselves as having happy, exciting lives. It may be that the differences are ac-counted for by those who are involuntarily single and are therefore less satisfied with their status. But we have no research to answer the question of whether the involuntary differ from the voluntary singles.

PRINCIPLES FOR ENHANCING INTIMACY

1. If your highest goal as a woman is profes-sional advancement, you are more likely to reach that goal if you remain single. Unfortu-nately, the demands of pregnancy, children, and maintaining a home generally place a far greater burden on the employed woman than on her husband.

2. Although sex is more readily available and is an attractive prospect for many singles, the freedom of the "one-night stand" has its risks—AIDS and other sexually transmitted diseases, physical abuse from a less than well-known lover, lack of intimacy, and even feelings of heightened loneliness when it is over. Your physical and emotional well-being demands that you acknowledge and seek to minimize these risks.

3. If you want to marry and frequently turn po-tential spouses down because they are just not "the right person," you need to ask yourself whether your expectations are too high or whether there is some factor in your personal or familial past that is keeping you from mak-ing a commitment.

4. A single life can be a happy, fulfilled one. An essential ingredient generally is a network of friends with whom you can find satisfactory living arrangements, share social activities and common interests, and, most importantly, develop intimate relations.

5. Marriage can involve giving up some freedom and independence, but the benefits seem to outweigh the possible losses. Every indicator suggests that more married than single people are happy and physically and emotionally healthy.

SUMMARY

The proportion of Americans who are single has risen steadily. The proportion of single people is still lower, however, than it was in the first decades of the century. Singles include the never-married, the divorced, and the widowed. A number of beliefs about singles are myths, such as the idea that sin-gles are selfish, financially well-to-do, and happier than marrieds.

There is both voluntary and involuntary single-hood. A number of factors are involved in people remaining single. Some singles give priority to their careers. Sex is readily available. Some singles be-lieve that marriage would be a threat to their per-sonal freedom. The desire for personal growth may take priority over relationships. Social conditions, such as the sex ratio, may prevent some from mar-rying. Certain family experiences may lead some people to be hesitant about, or even reject, mar-riage. And a number of personality characteristics, such as shyness and fear of commitment, keep some single.

The single life-style includes a diversity of living arrangements, from living with parents to sharing an apartment to living alone. Singles on the whole have less sex than married people. They are likely to engage in more and somewhat different leisure activities than the married. Singles are less likely than marrieds to have warm and stable relationships with their parents. Single women, however, may find themselves caring for their aging parents. A minority of older singles face a problem of isola-tion, which tends to impair their health. Many older singles continue to be involved in sexual relationships, including dating and sexual relations.

Single people have more problems with loneliness and more physical and mental health problems than the married. Singles have various ways to establish and maintain intimate relationships; healthy singles tend to have network families. Sex and children are also problems for singles, who tend to have less access than married people to these sources of intimacy.

Life satisfaction tends to vary through the individual's life, whether married or single. For singles, the thirties seem to be one of the more difficult ages. Many singles prefer their life-style and find it satisfying. But overall, singles are less likely than the married to perceive themselves as having happy and exciting lives.

INTERNET CONNECTION
The Single Option

Evidence presented in your textbook indicates that while a long term partnership benefits health and self esteem, there are also advantages to being single. One thing not yet touched upon is the challenge and opportunity associated with being single and a parent.

www.mhhe
.com/lauer4

Single Parents Online

http://www.singleparents.org/

(SPA) was formed to provide education, resources, friendship and camaraderie, as well as fun activities for single parents and their children.

Parents without Partners

http://www.parentswithoutpartners.org/

PWP provides help in the way of discussions, professional speakers, study groups, publications, and social activities for families and adults.

1. What does this website tell you about the challenges faced by parents who are single?
2. Do you believe that these sites help perpetuate myths concerning being single and being a parent or do they alleviate myths? Explain your answer.
3. Based on your examination of these sites, how do the lifestyle options and choices of the single parent compare to an unmarried person without children?

PART THREE

THE INTIMATE COUPLE

Whatever the attractions of singlehood and cohabitation may be, the fact is that most of us will eventually marry. And marriage means a different experience of intimacy than is likely to occur in other kinds of relationships. Even couples who cohabit tend to report a noticeable change in their relationship after they marry.

In this section, we will look at what is involved in the transition from singlehood to marriage. Then we will examine the challenges that people face as they seek to deepen their intimacy in marriage. What is the role of communication? What is the meaning of conflict, and how and why do couples fight? How will the couple deal with the division of labor both in and outside of the home? These are some of the questions that young adults face when they begin their quest for mature intimacy.

GETTING MARRIED

Learning Objectives

After reading chapter 10, you should be able to:

1. Characterize the marital status of the population.

2. Distinguish between those who do and don't marry and summarize why people marry.

3. Describe the various kinds of marriages.

4. Discuss what people expect from marriage.

5. Explain the role of negotiation and marriage contracts in working through conflicting expectations.

6. Contrast and compare the types of adjustments men and women have to make when they marry.

7. Discuss how teenage, student, and heterogamous marriages begin with certain disadvantages.

8. Describe the process of establishing equity and consensus and adjusting to in-laws.

9. Explain the kinds of changes that are likely to occur during the first year of marriage.

10. Show the importance of commitment in building an enduring and satisfying marriage.

In his description of an ideal society, Sir Thomas More wrote that the Utopians severely punished anyone engaging in premarital sex. The reason, as we pointed out in chapter 9, was that his Utopians believed that if you could have sex outside of marriage no one would ever get married. Apart from the availability of sexual relations, why, he asked, would one put up with all the inconveniences of being married?

There are some people, like the young man we discussed at the beginning of chapter 4, who marry primarily for sexual reasons. But, as we shall see, there are many other reasons for getting married. In spite of Sir Thomas's dire warning, the bulk of Americans marry in the face of readily available sexual relations outside marriage.

In this chapter, in addition to looking at reasons that people marry, we shall look at some different types of marriages and explore our various expectations when we marry. We will see some of the common adjustments that people have to make when they marry, along with changes in the first year of marriage. Finally, we will discuss the meaning of commitment and the way in which it affects the quality of married life.

WHAT ARE YOUR CHANCES OF GETTING MARRIED?

Most Americans want to marry, and most—90 percent or more—will. However, your chances vary depending on a number of factors.

Marital Status of the Population

The **marriage rate,** the proportion of unmarried women aged fifteen and over who get married in a year, fluctuates considerably over time (figure 10.1). Rates have been generally dropping since 1970 in the United States, other Western nations, and Japan (U.S. Bureau of the Census 1997b:834). The lower rates reflect such things as delayed age at first marriage and increasing numbers who remain single for one reason or another. Projections based on these trends suggest that 90 percent of women will marry at some time in their life, down from the 95 percent level that existed during most of the nation's history (Miller 1993:22).

The lower marriage rate, combined with the rates of divorce and widowhood, means that the married proportion of the population in any year has declined over the last few decades. In 1970, 71.7 percent of Americans were married; by 1996, the proportion had declined to 60.3 percent (U.S. Bureau of the Census 1997b:55). People's marital status varies, of course, by such things as sex and age (table 10.1). Men twenty-four and younger and women twenty

TABLE 10.1

Proportion of the Population Married, by Sex and Age: 1996

	Percent	
Age	**Males**	**Females**
Total	62.1	58.6
18 to 19 years old	2.1	7.6
20 to 24 years old	17.8	28.5
25 to 29 years old	43.7	55.9
30 to 34 years old	61.7	69.1
35 to 39 years old	68.6	72.6
40 to 44 years old	71.9	72.6
45 to 54 years old	77.6	73.0
55 to 64 years old	82.4	69.3
65 to 74 years old	79.1	54.8
75 years old and over	69.8	27.4

Source: U.S. Bureau of the Census 1997:55–56.

FIGURE 10.1 **Marriage Rates (rate per 1,000 women, age 15 and over)**
(*Source:* U.S. Bureau of the Census 1975:64 and 1997b:105.)

and younger or seventy-five and older are least likely to be married. Marital status also varies by race, as we saw in chapter 2. Projections from trends suggest that only about three out of four African American women will ever marry, compared to nine out of ten white women (Miller 1993:22).

Who Does, and Doesn't, Marry?

The question of who will and who will not marry is not merely one of preference. We noted in chapter 9 that some people are involuntarily single because of the marriage squeeze. For example, women will have lower rates of marriage when they live in an area where there is a shortage in the number and quality of available men (Lichter et al. 1992). The squeeze has affected women more than men, but Census Bureau projections indicate a reversal occurring throughout the 1990s for people in their twenties. That is, there will be an excess of men to women. It will be men, not women, who will face the greater chance of involuntary singlehood.

For some people, the marriage squeeze is exacerbated by certain social factors and conditions which work further to delay marriage or prevent it altogether. First, the economic independence of increasing numbers of women has decreased the marriage rates for men—women are no longer pressured into marriage in order to survive economically (Lloyd and South 1996). Second, the norm that a man should be somewhat older than a woman he marries limits the choices of both men and women.

Third, the lingering belief among some people that wives should be homemakers leads to lower rates of marriage among those women who hold this belief but who also aspire to a college degree (Barber and Axinn 1998). Finally, the tendency of men to marry women with the same or somewhat less education and for women to marry men with the same or somewhat more education also limits choices. As increasing numbers of women pursue higher education, they will have fewer choices in the marriage market. High-status (as measured by education and occupation) women may forego marriage rather than marry a man who is lower than them in status (Lichter, Anderson, and Hayward 1995).

WHY DO PEOPLE MARRY?

If someone says to you, "I'm going to get married," you are not likely to ask why. You no doubt assume that the two people are in love and want to live together and perhaps have children together. But as we noted in chapter 1, people marry for reasons other than love. In fact, some social scientists believe that the full meaning of love only emerges during the course of a marriage, not prior to marriage. This isn't to say that the two people do not feel that they are in love. However, there are other reasons for getting married.

Social Expectations

The expectation is that you will get married, as illustrated by the fact that there are still some negative

PERSPECTIVE
Dobu Marriage

Marriage customs, including wedding ceremonies, vary considerably. Anthropologist Ruth Benedict studied a number of preindustrial peoples, including the Dobu of the South Pacific. In the passage below, she describes some of the things that happen when the Dobu marry. She found that the Dobuans generally were lawless and treacherous. Four to twenty villages form a unit that is hostile to other such units. But marriage must take place between people from differing units, which means that it may bring together two villages between which there is a great deal of enmity:

> Marriage brings with it no amelioration of hostility. From its beginning the institutions that surround it make for conflict and hard feelings between the two groups. Marriage is set in motion by a hostile act of the mother-in-law. She blocks with her own person the door of her house within which the youth is sleeping with her daughter, and

he is trapped for the public ceremony of betrothal. Before this, since the time of puberty, the boy has slept each night in the houses of unmarried girls. By custom his own house is closed to him. He avoids entanglements for several years by spreading his favours widely and leaving the house well before daylight. When he is trapped at last, it is usually because he has tired of his roaming and has settled upon a more constant companion. He ceases to be so careful about early rising. Nevertheless, he is never thought of as being ready to undertake the indignities of marriage, and the event is forced upon him by the old witch in the doorway, his future mother-in-law. When the villagers, the maternal kin of the girl, see the old woman immobile in her doorway, they gather, and under the stare of the public the two descend and sit on a mat upon the ground. The villagers stare at them for half an hour and gradu-

ally disperse, nothing more; the couple are formally betrothed.

[The betrothal lasts about a year, during which time the boy has to work for his parents-in-law as well as tend to his own garden. There is an exchange of gifts between relatives of the young couple but no friendly mingling.]

The marriage ceremony itself consists in the groom's receiving from his mother-in-law in her village a mouthful of food of her cooking, and the bride's similarly receiving food from her mother-in-law in the village of her husband. . . . From marriage until death the couple live in alternate years in the village of the husband and the village of the wife.

---

attitudes toward people who opt to remain single. All societies have the **institution** of marriage, which is a societal way of regulating heterosexual relationships. Even people in preindustrial societies, such as the Dobu (see PERSPECTIVE), have well-defined rules about people getting married and generally expect that most will marry.

In other words, to say that marriage is a social institution is to point out that there are norms and expectations that govern it. These vary from one society to another, but they serve the same basic functions. Among other things, the institution of marriage prevents heterosexual relationships from deteriorating into chaos (a married person is, at least theoretically, off-limits to others who might be sexually attracted to that person). It provides a nor-

mative way of perpetuating the group, by specifying a context in which sexual relations and the bearing and care of children will occur.

Thus, marriage as an institution is important to the well-being of the total group. Individuals who scorn such an institution are a threat to the group and to its survival. It is understandable, then, that we are raised with the expectation that we will marry. That expectation is communicated to us through family and friends.

If quiet expectations do not motivate an individual, a family may resort to more overt expectations in the form of pressures of various kinds. Parents may pressure their children into marriage because they are embarrassed if the children remain single or because they feel that the children will be happier if married. Unfortunately, sometimes the pressures lead to a marriage that is premature and doomed to failure.

Social Ideals and Personal Fulfillment

We have seen that most Americans still value a monogamous union that results in children and lasts a lifetime. To grow up in a society with that kind of ideal means that you are likely to accept it for your own. It becomes not merely the ideal of most people, as portrayed in stories, television, and family conversations, but your own ideal as well. In other words, through socialization you develop the sense that marriage is the way to fulfill some of your basic needs and to attain the highest reaches of happiness.

Gail Sheehy (1976:145–54) interviewed 115 men who had married in their twenties, asking among other things why they had gotten married. One reason was to "fill some vacancy in themselves." That is, they recognized some quality in which they were deficient and married someone who had that quality. They expected to find fulfillment by a relationship with someone who had the quality (such as vitality or caring) that they lacked. Others married for "safety." They wanted someone on whom they could depend for support.

Desire for Children

As those who are involved with premarital counseling know, most people who get married say that one of the reasons is to have children. They have reached a stage of their lives where they desire to form their own family. As we have seen, some people have children outside of marriage. However, there are many difficulties for those who take that option. If you want to have and raise children, it is a far easier task if you are married.

The desire to have children is one important reason why people want to marry.

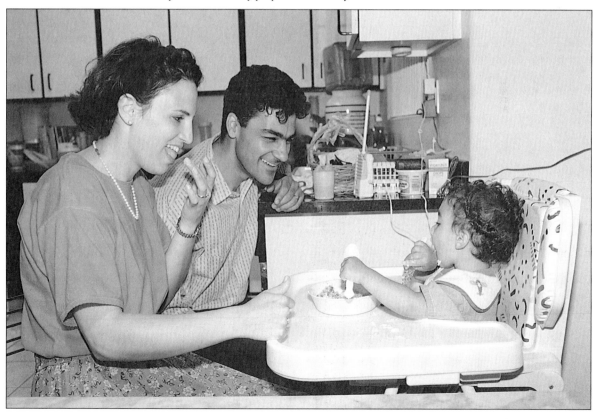

Marriage As a Practical Solution

Some people view marriage as a practical solution to various problems and challenges. Sheehy noted that some of the men she interviewed admitted that they married in order to get away from home. Some married because they believed a wife would help them realize their ambitions, like the physician who needed a helpmate through medical school. Some marry in order to have a steady sex life. Some recognize that singlehood is too lonely and/or difficult for them. Marriage is a practical and acceptable way to deal with these problems.

TYPES OF MARRIAGE

Because people get married for a variety of reasons and because their experiences of marriage are quite diverse, we would expect to find different types of marriage. However, there is no single way to classify marriage by differing types. We could divide them up on the basis of communication styles, amount of conflict, degree of homogamy, or any other basis we choose. Some of the more useful classification schemes, we believe, use alternative life-styles or the nature of the relationship.

Classified by Alternative Life-Styles

Which is most appealing to you, a traditional marriage or some other life-style (figure 10.2)? The traditional marriage is one in which the husband is the breadwinner and major decision maker, the wife is a homemaker, there are children, the spouses have sexual relations only with each other, and the union lasts a lifetime. Three researchers who asked high school students to rate their preferences gave the students a range of alternative life-styles to the traditional marriage just described (Violet, Garland, and Pendleton 1986). The students overwhelmingly gave an equalitarian marriage (one in which husband and wife both are employed and have an equal voice in decisions that are made) as their first choice (figure 10.3).

They defined a working-wife marriage as one where the husband is still the major decision maker even though the wife is employed full- or part-time. Another alternative was the term marriage, an arrangement like a renewable contract in which the

couple contract to get married for a particular period of time, such as five years. If they do not renew the contract, the marriage automatically ends.

The researchers offered the students a number of other life-styles, such as group marriage (in which a number of males and females are all married to each other), swinging (marriage in which both spouses agree that sex with other partners is acceptable), and homosexual marriage. None of the students selected these other life-styles, however.

Other studies have reported the same result. The first choice of both high school and college students is an equalitarian marriage. Whether they will maintain that preference when they are married and begin to live out some of the implications is another matter. We know the meaning of one partner being dominant, but how do you know when there is equity (see "Adjusting to Marriage" in this chapter)?

Classified by Structure of the Relationships

Kantor and Lehr (1975) have divided families into three types of systems. They based their types on the results of thousands of hours of intense observation of the daily lives of nineteen families. We believe that their classification is useful for types of marriages as well as types of families, because they focused on the ways that people relate to each other and to their environment. In essence, they posited three kinds of systems: the closed, the open, and the random. Each type involves a distinctive kind of intimate relationship.

The Closed System   In the closed-type family, stability, obligations, and the maintenance of tradition are emphasized. The tradition may be ethnic, religious, or ideological. Whatever its source, it embodies the ideal of what is right and good and is therefore the ultimate authority for family life.

Intimacy in a closed-type family is likely to be stable but more earnest and sincere than passionate:

> It is expected and natural that members share good feelings with one another. Loyalties based on blood ties are usually honored above those to friends. Affections are deeply rooted in each member's strong and enduring sense of belonging. Feelings of tenderness predominate. Even in times of conflict or separation, fidelity is maintained (Kantor and Lehr 1975:145).

Would you prefer a more traditional or nontraditional kind of marriage? Circle your answer to the statements below, then read the directions beneath the statements on how to score yourself.

1. A wife should respond to her husband's sexual overtures even when she is not interested.

    1. Agree strongly   2. Agree mildly   3. Disagree mildly   4. Disagree strongly

2. In general, the father should have greater authority than the mother in the bringing up of children.

    1. Agree strongly   2. Agree mildly   3. Disagree mildly   4. Disagree strongly

3. Only when the wife works should the husband help with housework.

    1. Agree strongly   2. Agree mildly   3. Disagree mildly   4. Disagree strongly

4. Husbands and wives should be equal partners in planning the family budget.

    4. Agree strongly   3. Agree mildly   2. Disagree mildly   1. Disagree strongly

5. In marriage, the husband should make the major decisions.

    1. Agree strongly   2. Agree mildly   3. Disagree mildly   4. Disagree strongly

6. If both husband and wife agree that sexual fidelity isn't important, there's no reason why both shouldn't have extramarital affairs if they want to.

    4. Agree strongly   3. Agree mildly   2. Disagree mildly   1. Disagree strongly

7. If a child gets sick and the wife works, the husband should be just as willing as she to stay home from work and take care of that child.

    4. Agree strongly   3. Agree mildly   2. Disagree mildly   1. Disagree strongly

8. In general, men should leave the housework to women.

    1. Agree strongly   2. Agree mildly   3. Disagree mildly   4. Disagree strongly

9. Married women should keep their money and spend it as they please.

    4. Agree strongly   3. Agree mildly   2. Disagree mildly   1. Disagree strongly

10. In the family, both of the spouses ought to have as much say on important matters.

    4. Agree strongly   3. Agree mildly   2. Disagree mildly   1. Disagree strongly

Add your total. Note that "agree strongly" is sometimes worth one and sometimes worth four. It is your total score that is important, not whether you agreed or disagreed more often. Your score may vary from 10 to 40. If you score 30 to 40, you are nontraditional. A score of 20 to 30 means you take a middle-of-the-road position. A score of 10 to 20 puts you into the traditional category.

FIGURE 10.2 Rate Your Marital Preference
(Source: Karen Oppenheim Mason, *Sex-Role Attitude Items and Scales from U.S. Sample Surveys* [Rockville, MD: National Institute of Mental Health] 1975:16–19.)

In other words, closed-type family members care deeply about each other, but they are muted in their expression of that caring. They experience intimacy in the context of stable, caring, highly structured relationships.

The Open System Open-type families strive for consensus in ideas and feelings. They are sensitive to the needs of each individual as well as to the well-being of the family unit. They express their emotions more openly and more intensely than do those in the closed system. They encourage each other to be open and honest in their opinions and their feelings. What a person feels is not as important as that person's honesty in expressing the feeling. In other words, it is all right to be angry. It is not all right to be angry and to hide it by pretending not to be angry.

In contrast to the closed system, where people rely on stable affections, those in the open system may search for new emotional experiences. The "emotional mandate is to *share and not withhold*

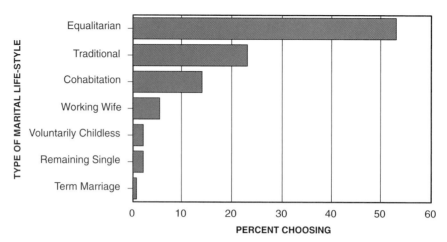

FIGURE 10.3   **First Choices of Marital Life-Styles of 181 High School Students** (*Source:* Data from D. Violet, T. N. Garland, and B. F. Pendleton, *Human Relations,* 39:1060,1986.)

whatever is being felt" (Kantor and Lehr 1975:145). Thus, intimacy in an open system involves an open, experimental, fluid pattern of relationships; intimacy occurs in the context of deeply felt and shared emotional experiences.

The Random System   Random-type families focus on the needs of individual members. Individual members are free to pursue their own interests without being concerned about either the tradition in the closed-type or the consent in the open-type family. There is likely to be a certain amount of caprice, novelty, and humor in the family as the members strive to "raise experience to levels of originality and inspiration" (Kantor and Lehr 1975:146). Members are likely to experience the full range of emotions and to do so with more intensity than those in either the closed- or open-type system. Spontaneity, intensity, and freedom are cherished by family members.

Like those in the open system, random-type members seek new emotional experiences. Unlike those in open systems, however, they do not constrain the search by the consent of other family members. Intimacy occurs at the random intersection of individual explorations rather than in the context of stability or consent, for those in a random system "have faith in the efficacy of creative anarchy" (Kantor and Lehr 1975:147). They abhor coercion. The appropriate way to influence another family member is to inspire him or her to a different pattern of behavior.

Diversity in Relationships   As you read the three kinds of systems, you probably have different reactions to each. Which is most appealing to you? The point is that there are diverse ways of relating to others in the intimacy of marriage and family life, including some that would be modifications of one of the above types. None of these ways is inherently better than others. Different people function better in one or the other system of relationships. Obviously, you are likely to have a more satisfying marriage to the extent that you join with someone who shares your preference.

EXPECTATIONS

When people marry, they have certain expectations about what their marriage will involve. Among other things, they tend to expect that marriage will make them happy and fulfilled, that it will last, and that their spouse will be faithful. Some of these expectations may be unrealistic. If, for instance, you expect that your spouse is always going to make you happy or that your relationship will be invulnerable to infidelity, your expectations are unrealistic.

Yet even if your expectations are all realistic, it doesn't mean that your marriage will be free of problems. You may or may not have the same

COMPARISON
Types of Marriage in Togo

The people of the Moba-Gurma society, who are located in the northern, rural part of the African nation of Togo, live in domestic groups. The groups consist of about nine people on the average and are headed by an older male. Fertility is a central value for the Moba-Gurma people. Thus, a woman's status depends on her ability to bear children and a man's status depends on the number of wives and children he has.

Marriages in this society can be classified by the manner in which a husband obtains a wife. Seven types of marriage are found:

1. *Marriage by exchange* occurs when two heads of domestic groups agree to exchange young women. Such an agreement may arise out of friendship or out of a desire to form an alliance. Nearly a third of marriages occur by this method, which enables all men (including the physically handicapped) to have a wife as long as they have a woman to exchange.

2. *Brideservice marriage* comprises almost 5 percent of the total. In this type, a man who does not have a woman to exchange offers something else. He may, for example, work in the fields of the family from whom he expects to get a wife.

3. *Child betrothal* occurs in a little over one in five marriages. Under this arrangement, the head of the family gives a woman to a man in gratitude for his services (farm work) or as an expression of friendship. Typically, a young daughter is given or an unborn daughter is promised.

4. Nearly a fourth of unions involve *marriage by abduction.* This is a somewhat misleading term, since the woman allows herself to be abducted. She may have been promised to someone else, or she may be already married. But she agrees to meet the man in an arranged place and he "abducts" her. The situation is called abduction in the male-dominated Moba-Gurma society

because they cannot imagine, or acknowledge, a woman doing such a thing of her own volition.

5. About 9 percent of marriages are *leviratic.* The levirate is a common practice in Africa. It requires a man to marry the wife or wives of a deceased brother. If the deceased man had no brother, another male relative is required to marry the widow or widows.

6. *Marriage by reimbursement* also comprises about 9 percent of all unions. This type occurs after a man has obtained a wife through brideservice or child betrothal. Even though the man has paid for his wife under these two methods, he still must give a woman back at some later date to replace the one taken.

7. Finally, a very small number of marriages are *bridewealth* unions, a marriage is formed when a well-to-do man arranges the purchase of a wife. The few men who practice this arrangement tend to use it to get a woman from another ethnic group (Pilon 1994).

---

expectations as the person you marry. You each may have realistic expectations, but they may be incompatible with each other. Unfortunately, sometimes we don't communicate what we expect until after we are married.

Our Private Contracts

Marriage is a contract between two people. It is a legal contract in the sense that the partners can bring each other to court to require performance or to dissolve the relationship. It is a social contract in the sense that family and friends feel that they have a stake in the relationship and the right to intervene or at least to bring pressure to bear on the couple. It

is an interpersonal contract in the sense that the partners agree to commit themselves to each other for the duration of their lives. All of these contracts may result in anguish because the spouses also bring to the marriage their private contracts, which basically involve assumptions that each makes about the nature of the relationship and their mutual obligations. Each partner has a private contract, then, in the sense that each *assumes* that there is agreement about various matters that were never discussed (Lauer and Lauer 1993:54f).

An example of how private contracts result in problems is illustrated in the case of a couple called Bill and Lucille (Sager and Hunt 1979:49–54). Each was involved in a career. They had a two-bedroom

INVOLVEMENT
Who Prefers a Traditional Marriage?

How do you think other people would score on the self-assessment test you took in figure 10.2? Do you think you are typical or different from other people in your attitudes? Make copies of the test and conduct your own research to see how other people feel. One way to do such research is to ask a number of questions about who is most likely to prefer the traditional and who is most likely to prefer the nontraditional union.

For example, do you think that males or females will be more traditional? Will there be differences between older and younger people? Will the more or less educated people prefer a traditional union? Will there be any differences by race?

Decide on which of the questions you would like to try to answer. Of course, you will not have a large enough sample to make a firm conclusion, but if the entire class participates in the project, you could have a sufficient number of responses to be comfortable with your results.

It is important to research only one of the questions. For example, if you are interested primarily in gender differences, try to have an equal number of males and females. Select people who are all of the same race. And select those who are as close as possible in age and education. Otherwise, you can't be sure if any differences you find are due to gender or one of the other factors.

After you score the questionnaires, answer the following questions. Were there any differences between the two groups you studied? If so, which group was the most traditional? How can you account for your results? Did your results turn out differently from what you anticipated? What conclusions would you draw or what are the implications of your findings (assuming that a larger survey of the population would produce similar results)?

apartment. Bill used the second bedroom for a home office, though each knew that eventually it would be a nursery. Lucille intended to have children, but she wanted to wait. She had helped raise some of her younger siblings and was in no hurry to get back into the routine. However, Bill had been an only child and a lonely child. He had envied his peers who had brothers and sisters. He was anxious to have children while he was young enough to do things with them.

Unfortunately, Bill had not talked to Lucille about his feelings. When he suggested they begin their family, she tried to avoid the matter. Eventually, she realized how important it was to him, so she agreed. They had a girl. A year later, Bill wanted to try again. He really wanted a son. Again, Lucille resisted. They were having financial problems, and she wanted to go back to work. In time, she gave in again. They had a son. Bill got a better job, and they bought a home in the suburbs. They seemed to have it all, but they weren't happy. In fact, their marriage was in serious trouble. They needed marriage counseling. And it was all unnecessary. They could have saved "a good bit of time, money, and suffering if they had known right away that each was furious with the other for not living

The private contracts people bring into marriage may trouble the relationship.

up to the terms of *an agreement they never made*" (Sager and Hunt 1979:51).

Bill and Lucille each felt that the other had not lived up to the terms of their agreement. But they never had an agreement. They had two private contracts. They entered marriage with different expectations about children. Lucille had originally expected to keep her job, which was very gratifying to her, and delay having a family. She changed the terms of her contract to allow Bill to fulfill his. She had a daughter and son and became a homemaker. However, with a large mortgage and other debts, Bill became increasingly anxious about money and eventually wanted Lucille to go back to work. He expected her to carry a share of the financial load. Because she gave up her hopes to please her husband, she now expected him to be the breadwinner and support the life-style they had achieved. They both felt that their own expectations were reasonable. Yet they continued to clash because the terms of their private contracts, while changing, were not compatible with each other.

Role Expectations

When private contracts clash, it is frequently over role expectations. Bill originally assumed he would have a more traditional wife who would willingly sacrifice her career to bear and care for their chil-

dren. However, he came to a point where he felt he needed an employed wife. Lucille originally assumed they would have an egalitarian marriage, with each of them working outside of the home. She came to a point where she decided that he could be the family breadwinner.

Symbolic Interactionist Theory Applied

Bill and Lucille are not unique in their problem. The question of the husband role and the wife role is a vexing one in many marriages. It is vexing when, in *symbolic interactionist* terms, we define our own expectations as legitimate and those of our partner as not legitimate when they clash with our own. That defines the situation as one of right and wrong rather than as a difference that needs to be worked out to the mutual satisfaction of the partners.

What, then, are people's expectations about those roles? And do husbands and wives agree? In an effort to answer the questions, Hiller and Philliber (1986) surveyed 489 married couples, inquiring about their expectations with regard to child care, housework, money management, and earning income. With regard to expectations, the researchers found that the couples tended to agree that child care, housework, and money management should be shared (table 10.2). Interestingly, spouses tended to believe that the husband should bear primary responsibility for

TABLE 10.2
Comparison of Spouses' Expectations About Who Should Perform Marital Roles

Expectations for Wife's Traditional Roles:	Child Care	Housework
Agree job should be shared	84%	38%
Agree it is wife's job	2	30
Husband: wife's job/Wife: should share	7	13
Husband: should share/Wife: wife's job	8	20
Total	101%	101%
(N)	(483)	(488)

Expectations for Husband's Traditional Roles:	Money Management	Income Earning
Agree job should be shared	69%	24%
Agree it is husband's job	9	43
Wife: husband's job/Husband: should share	5	9
Wife: should share/Husband: husband's job	17	25
Total	100%	101%
(N)	(487)	(484)

earning the family income. Note that 68 percent of the husbands and 52 percent of the wives agreed that earning income is the husband's job.

Hiller and Philliber investigated various other aspects of expectations about marital roles and drew a number of conclusions. First, spouses do not want to give up their own traditional roles, though they appear to be quite willing to participate in the traditional roles of the opposite sex. Second, spouses correctly perceive their partners' expectations about half the time. Husbands are more accurate than wives. Third, each spouse tends to think that he or she carries more of the burden of household duties than the partner thinks he or she carries. Finally, the researchers note that

> despite the fact that 69 percent of the wives in our sample were working outside the home, the traditional division of labor and dominant role of the male "head-of-household" were still very much in evidence in these marriages (Hiller and Philliber 1986:200).

A good deal of traditionalism in role expectations remains in our society in other ways. A survey of 234 single college students reported that while males and females both expected personal success in life, they differed on their expectations for their future marital partners (Ganong and Coleman 1992). A majority of the females expected their future husbands to be more intelligent, more successful, and make more money than themselves. In contrast, the males tended to expect their future wives to be equal to them in these areas.

Clearly, a sufficient number of discrepancies exist between the expectations of husbands and wives to account for a good deal of discontent and conflict in marriages. Couples who want to avoid problems will find themselves engaging in a process of negotiation about marital roles.

Negotiation: Changing Personal Contracts

Bill and Lucille had problems because neither was aware of the other's private contract, neither discussed the fact that the original contracts had been broken, and neither tried to initiate a process of negotiation to try to clarify and rework expectations. They desperately needed to understand and work with each other's private contract.

Negotiation is a process of working through clashing expectations. In negotiation, the expecta-

tions of each partner are brought out into the open. That is, the private contracts must become joint knowledge. Sometimes the individuals are not even aware of their own private contracts. They only recognize that something the partner has done has frustrated, angered, or disappointed them. Once the differing expectations are acknowledged, then the process of give-and-take can begin as the couple examines their various options and comes to a satisfactory compromise.

Consider the following example of clashing expectations and successful negotiation. A married student told us that she was appalled when she found that her new husband threw his clothes on the floor at night. "I thought that any civilized man would either hang his clothes up or put them in the wash." At first, she picked them up herself. Then she grew angry with him. When she became somewhat cold and distant, he asked her what was bothering her. He was surprised at her response. He expected her, as his wife, to pick up his clothes. His mother had done that. She curtly informed him that she would not be a mother to him.

They soon were able to negotiate a settlement. He agreed that he could change a lifelong habit, and she agreed to remind him and to be patient until he had established a new habit. She became aware of the fact that her private contract included a provision about her husband's neatness and help in keeping the house clean. She was unaware of that until she saw the clothes on the floor. His private contract included the expectation that his wife would behave like his mother in some ways. He, too, was unaware of that until his wife confronted him with her anger.

Not all clashing expectations are negotiated that easily. It is important for couples to recognize the existence of private contracts, the probability of differences in expectations, and the importance of negotiation for working through the differences.

The Marriage Contract: Clarifying Expectations

Instead of waiting until problems arise to clarify and negotiate private contracts, a couple can avoid at least some of the problems of marriage by formulating a marriage contract prior to the wedding. This can be a formal, legal document, such as a prenuptial agreement that is drawn up by a lawyer.

A legal contract, however, may signify a certain lack of trust at the outset of a marriage. Many people are not comfortable with such an arrangement. Moreover, the legal contract will not cover some of the matters in our private contracts that generate problems.

Instead of a legal contract, some couples write informal marriage contracts in order to clarify their expectations (Garrett 1982). These contracts are not legally binding, but they do help the couple to begin their married life with a better understanding of what each expects and, consequently, with less likelihood of friction and conflict over some common issues in marriage. Among other things, Garrett (1982) suggests that you discuss and include the following in your marriage contract:

1. Will the wife use the husband's last name, her own name, or a hyphenated name?
2. What will be the division of labor in the home? Who will do the cooking, cleaning, washing, repairs, and so on?
3. Will you have children? If so, how many and when?
4. Will you use contraception? What kind?
5. If you have children, how will you divide up the child care responsibilities? What kind of discipline will you use?
6. What will you do about housing? Will housing decisions be made in light of the husband's career, the wife's career, or both?
7. Who will be the breadwinner? How will financial decisions be made and who will be responsible for paying bills?
8. What will be your relationships with in-laws? Will you spend part or all of your vacation time with parents or relatives?
9. How much of your leisure will you spend together and how much separately?
10. What are your sexual expectations?
11. How will you change the terms of this contract over the course of your marriage?

The last point is important because no contract should be unalterable. A marriage contract reflects the way you feel at a certain point in time. One or both partners may want to change the terms. The points should always be open to negotiation. Informal contracts are meant to facilitate the ongoing development of intimacy, not bind partners to an inflexible pattern.

Even when both spouses affirm egalitarianism, the wife tends to assume the major responsibility for child care.

ADJUSTING TO MARRIAGE

To get married is to enter a new social world. Even those who have cohabited for a number of years frequently say that their relationship changes when they get married. There are adjustments to be made, whether or not you have lived together prior to marriage. In part, adjustments reflect the differing expectations we discussed above. In part, they reflect the nature of the new social world into which people enter—a world of new responsibilities, new options such as childbearing, and new relationships such as in-laws.

His Marriage and Her Marriage

Conflict Theory Applied

Jessie Bernard (1972) argued that every marriage is really two marriages, his and hers. That is, men and women have substantially different experiences in marriage. Or, in terms of *conflict theory,* men and women have different interests and must to some extent vie with each other to successfully pursue those interests. For example, we all need to have some sense of control over our lives. But when women get married, they tend to have a greater sense of control in terms of increased income but a diminished sense of control in terms of being autonomous (Ross 1991). Given the same income, nonmarried women have a greater sense of control than either married women or men.

Bernard also argued that men derive more from marriage than do women. Research on more than seven thousand married couples reported that men are somewhat more satisfied with their marriages than are women and seem to get greater mental health benefits from marriage than do women (Fowers 1991). It is also true that women have to make more adjustments in marriage than do men.

Why must women make more adjustments? Consider some of the typical things that happen in marriage. A man is less likely than a woman to change his vocation or to drop out of the labor force. He is unlikely to move his residence to accommodate his wife's career, while she may move frequently to accommodate him. In spite of egalitarian attitudes, women still bear the brunt of housekeeping chores in most homes. When children come, women tend to assume the major responsibility for their care.

Furthermore, women are more likely than men to have their private contracts violated. For women, talking things over is an important part of an intimate relationship, and men tend to talk to them in an intimacy-building fashion during courtship (Goleman 1986). But after marriage, the husband may spend less and less time talking with his wife about their relationship. She finds herself deprived of an important facet of her intimacy needs. Worse, she had been led to believe by her husband's behavior that the intimate communication would be a part of their marriage.

Starting with Two Strikes

Adjustment in some marriages is more difficult because they begin at a disadvantage. We have discussed the problems with teenage marriages, for instance. Teenage couples truly begin their married life with two strikes already against them. They fre-

quently face the problem of low income and perhaps of thwarted educational and career hopes at a time in life when they lack the maturity to cope effectively with such things.

Student marriages also begin with some disadvantages, whether the student is married to an employed spouse or another student. There are likely to be problems over the use of time and other strains associated with student marriages (Dyk 1987). The time problems become acute if the student is also employed part- or full-time. School schedules are relatively inflexible. An employed spouse may get weary of always having to accommodate to the demands that professors make on his or her partner. When the employed spouse is the husband and he has more traditional gender-role attitudes, the probability of conflict increases even more (Dyk 1987:330). The strains associated with student marriages arise from the student being so stressed or preoccupied with school work that the marital relationship suffers. Students can get emotionally, intellectually, and physically weary. If the spouse does not understand and fully support the student, marital problems are more likely.

Various other marriages begin at a disadvantage. If the woman is pregnant at the time of marriage, there is the additional adjustment of becoming parents. If the couple is not homogamous, there will be many adjustments to make. The point is that even under the best of circumstances, learning to live intimately with another person requires adjustments. It is unfortunate if the couple begins with disadvantages as well as challenges.

Establishing Equity and Consensus

Exchange Theory Applied

As argued by *exchange theorists,* if you have not worked out a marriage contract, you will have to work on the problems of equity and consensus in such areas as the division of labor around the home, your sex life, your social life, and other matters. A sense of equity is vital to making a satisfying adjustment (Gray-Little, Baucom and Hamby 1996; Huppe and Cyr 1997). A certain amount of consensus is also important. That is, the spouses must agree, or at least perceive that they agree, on various attitudes and behaviors. Couples in long-term, satisfying marriages do not agree on everything, but in our research, 84.4 percent felt that they always or almost always agreed on aims, goals, and things they believed important (Lauer and Lauer 1986:97). A husband put it this way:

> I think the success of our marriage is due in large part to having many common values and that we agree on basically most things that are important in our lives together. This is particularly true for issues related to careers, money, and family life-style.

A relationship based on equity and consensus seems to come rather easily to some couples. Others have a more difficult time. One way those who are struggling can establish equity and consensus is for each spouse to make a list of preferences. For example, in considering the division of labor in the home, the couple can first make a list of the various chores. Then each spouse ranks the chores from most to least desirable. The rankings are compared and the final division of labor negotiated.

Adjustment and In-Law Relationships

A marriage and family therapist told us that he believes as many as 60 percent of all marriages have some tension because of the relationship between the mother-in-law and daughter-in-law. A 1981 Gallup poll reported that 48 percent of Americans believe that living away from in-laws is "very important" to a successful marriage. Popular magazines carry articles regularly that tell people how to deal with in-law problems. In other words, in-laws

are important factors in many marriages. You don't marry an individual. You marry into a family.

In spite of their importance, in-law relationships have been the focus of little research. In some unpublished research, we asked 233 people, with a mean age of 38.3 years and married a mean of 11.4 years, to discuss their in-law relationships. Specifically, we asked which in-law relationship had been the most significant for them, in either a positive or negative sense, and how the in-law relationships had affected their marriage. Only seven said that they didn't regard any of their in-laws as significant (because they lived at too great a distance from them). All of the others acknowledged that an in-law had been significant in some way in their lives.

We found the mother-in-law most likely to be named as the significant in-law relationship (table 10.3). Significant in what sense? Evelyn Duvall (1954:187), in the most recent large-scale study of in-law relationships, reported that 36.8 percent of her respondents named mothers-in-law as the most difficult in-law relationship. We found that about half of those who said their mother-in-law was most significant indicated the relationship was a negative one and half said it was a positive one. Similarly, Arnstein (1985) reported that 48 percent of mother-in-law and daughter-in-law relationships are "good" and 52 percent are "poor." In our research, people defined positive relationships with in-laws as supportive, caring, accepting, warm, and friendly. They described negative relationships as intrusive, domineering, cool, or aloof.

TABLE 10.3
Most Significant In-Law Relationship

	Sex of Respondent		
	Male (N = 88)	**Female** (N = 138)	**Total** (N = 226)
	Percent		
Mother-in-law	39.8	52.2	47.3
Father-in-law	26.1	14.5	19.0
Both mother- and father-in-law	13.6	12.3	12.8
Brother- or sister-in-law	20.5	15.9	17.8
Other	0	5.1	3.1
Total	100.0	100.0	100.0

In terms of adjustment, it is important to note that the in-law relationship is more likely to be a positive than a negative one. Overall, 58 percent of our subjects said their significant relationship was a positive one, while 32 percent defined it as negative. The other 10 percent said that it was mixed, including both positive and negative aspects (such as a mother-in-law who was initially supportive but who became intrusive when the couple had children).

In-laws, then, can help couples in their adjustment. Some in-laws are problems and make adjustment more difficult. However, in-laws are more likely to be resources than problems. The help that in-laws give may be monetary and/or emotional (Goetting 1990). As a young husband told us:

> When I got married, I got, in my father-in-law, the father to whom I could finally talk. He has been invaluable to me over the years. I could never go to my own father with some of the problems I've faced. I can always go to my father-in-law. He's been a security net.

FIRST-YEAR CHANGES

When a young couple returned from their honeymoon, a friend said to them, "Well, it's all downhill from here on." The friend was disillusioned with her marriage, and her disillusionment was rooted in her unrealistic expectations. She had thought of marriage as a kind of endless honeymoon. It isn't. Changes in a couple's relationship begin in the first year of marriage (Huston, McHale, and Crouter 1986). These changes reflect the realities of intimate living in a complex society.

For one thing, the feelings of the spouses change. By the end of the first year, you are likely to feel somewhat less satisfied with the amount of interaction you have with your spouse. You will probably feel less satisfied with the extent to which your spouse initiates activity that pleases you and the frequency with which you have physical intimacy. Wives tend to report less satisfaction in these areas than husbands, both at the beginning of the marriage and at the end of the first year (Huston, McHale, and Crouter 1986:121). It is important to keep in mind that we are *not* saying that people are dissatisfied with their marriages after a year. Most couples still feel positively about their interaction, but they are not as euphoric as they were at the time

of their wedding. The positive feelings are still there, but they have moderated.

Behavior and activities also tend to change. Spouses report a diminished amount of joint household and leisure activities. There tends to be an increase in household and other kinds of work activity and a decrease of about 20 percent in joint leisure activity. The decline in leisure and increase in work activity is particularly strong if the couple has a baby during the first year.

The amount of time spouses spend talking with each other declines slightly. More importantly, there is a significant decline in behavior that reflects affection. Married people report that by the end of the first year, their spouses less frequently engaged in such things as:

Approving and complimenting the partner

Doing or saying something to make the partner laugh

Telling the partner "I love you"

Taking the initiative in sex

Doing something nice for the partner

Showing physical affection and having sexual relations

Discussing their feelings and problems

Talking over things that happened during the day

The number of such activities declined by about 40 percent from their level at the beginning of the marriage (Huston, McHale, and Crouter 1986:123). Again, it is important to underscore the fact that this does not mean that such things were absent, only that they were less frequent after a year. The overall amount of companionship does not change much, but it becomes more instrumental, more task-oriented, and less focused on romance and affection.

In other words, by the end of the first year, couples are well on their way to a realistic mode of living together. Their time and energy are devoted not only to each other but to building careers and perhaps to beginning a family. Our intimacy needs are fundamental, but we also have needs for achievement and for security. Human life is not a honeymoon. Marriage is not a honeymoon. On the other hand, it is important to keep in mind that the exhilaration of the honeymoon can be periodically recaptured in a long-term relationship.

PERSONAL
In-Laws: The Good and the Bad

Henry is sixty-one years old. He has been married for thirty-five years. He has experienced both the good and the bad in in-law relationships. Both his father- and mother-in-law have had an impact on his life and his marriage. He had great admiration for his father-in-law. His mother-in-law is another matter:

My father-in-law is dead now, but he was the most significant in-law I had. He was seventy-three when I met him. His wife was fifty-eight and she supported the family until she retired at sixty-five. He adapted well to the role of taking care of the house. He did the cooking and cleaning, never complained about anything to anyone, and

was always there to talk with me about my problems.

He lived for the first ten years of my marriage. He encouraged me to pursue my goals, and taught me to be compassionate. Every night, he massaged his wife's feet. He had lived through a great deal of poverty and stress, but I never heard him gripe about it and I never heard him curse. He was a kind and gentle man who made me feel welcome into the family and supported me when I was getting my own career going.

My mother-in-law, on the other hand, is still alive and still a problem. She is selfish and thoughtless. Never in the thirty-

five years of our marriage has she offered to help us or anyone that I know of. I can count the number of dinners I have had in her house on one hand. Because of her self-centered behavior and her constant demands on my wife, I have gotten—I still get—very depressed and angry. In the early years of our marriage, we argued a lot about her mother. If it hadn't been for my father-in-law, we would have had a much more difficult time. For about the last five years, we have learned to ignore her self-centered ways. We try to remember that she is very old and we reach out to her even though she will not reciprocate.

COMMITMENT

Why discuss commitment at the end of the chapter on getting married? Doesn't commitment come when a couple is seriously considering marriage? Yes and no. Commitment is certainly a part of the process leading up to marriage. However, even in this process commitment can vary. Surra and Hughes (1997) looked at the commitment to wed among 113 young adults and found two different types. "Relationship-driven commitment" evolved smoothly in a mainly harmonious relationship. "Event-driven commitment" featured sharp increases and decreases in the commitment to wed as a result of such things as episodes of conflict and having different networks of friends.

Commitment, in other words, can vary over time, both in the process leading up to the decision to wed and in the marriage itself. As far as marriage is concerned, there is a reciprocal relationship between commitment and the satisfaction and stability of the union. That is, commitment facilitates satisfaction and stability, and in turn, satisfaction and

stability foster commitment. Commitment is a living part of the marriage, not an insurance policy that is irrevocable.

The Meaning of Commitment

For Americans, commitment in marriage seems to mean three things: promise, dedication, and attachment (Quinn 1982). There is a promise or pledge to engage in something that will include some difficult times (for better or worse, says the traditional marriage vow). There is a dedication to the joint goal of staying together and forming a meaningful family unit. This means there is an attachment between the two people, an emotional attachment that results from joint dedication to their goal. There can also be an element of constraint in the commitment—the fear of the social, financial, and emotional costs of the union breaking up (Adams and Jones 1997). Such constraints, however, are unlikely to maintain a union if the other elements of commitment are lacking.

In essence, then, commitment means "a promise of dedication to a relationship in which there is an emotional attachment to another person who has made the same promise" (Lauer and Lauer 1986:50). It is important to note that the commitment is to the person and not simply to the institution of marriage. One difference between those with long-term satisfying marriages and those that are long-term but unsatisfying is that the former are committed more to the spouse while the latter are committed more to the institution (Lauer and Lauer 1986). Commitment to the institution means that there are family pressures or religious beliefs that make the person unwilling to break the union even though he or she is unhappy with it.

The Role of Commitment

Commitment is a valuable resource in marriage. Those who are committed to their spouses as persons have significantly fewer marriage problems (Swensen and Trahaug 1985). Commitment to the person means that you are determined to work through troubled times. In contrast, commitment to the institution means a willingness to simply endure troubles rather than to work through them. Those who work through problems, rather than endure or wait them out, find the quality of their relationship greatly enhanced.

Commitment also gives the partners a sense of security. A wife told us that she occasionally experienced a "flash of emotion" that could turn into jealousy. Nevertheless, she views that as her own problem and not the fault of her husband, because she knows that they are committed to each other. Neither of them, she said with confidence, would put the marriage into jeopardy. Each has a sense of security with the other.

Commitment has benefits that go beyond enriching the marital relationship. A happy marriage in which there is a firm sense of commitment becomes a strong resource for dealing with the stresses of life. For instance, two researchers studied thousands of Israeli men over a five-year period to try to determine how a particular heart problem, angina pectoris, develops.[1] They found that one of the better predictors of those men who were at high risk was

the answer to the question: "Does your wife show you her love?" Those who answered "no" were more likely to develop the heart disorder. Or as a husband told us: "To know that you have someone that loves you, and on whom you can depend no matter what problems may arise, is really important. It's like having a crutch under a broken leg that you can rely on to support you."

Building Commitment

As we have noted, commitment can change. Married people can act in a way that intensifies the commitment of each to the union or in ways that erode that commitment. One way to build commitment is to make sure that each partner feels a sense of equity in the relationship (Sabatelli and Cecil-Pigo 1985). It is very difficult to maintain commitment to a person if you feel that you are seriously underrewarded, that you are giving far more to the relationship than the other. There are times in any relationship, of course, when one person has to give more, perhaps far more, than the other. But that should balance out over time. Few, if any, people can maintain commitment in the face of long-term inequity.

Commitment also grows as people's satisfaction with their relationship increases. While some decline in the affectional behavior noted is both normal and necessary after the honeymoon period, it is important for the couple to guard romance. The expression of affection is important throughout the marriage. It isn't enough to merely *feel* affectionate. That affection must be *expressed*. There is an old story about a reticent New Englander who said that he loved his wife so much it was all he could do to keep from telling her about it. Men generally have a more difficult time than women in openly expressing affection. But it is the expression, not merely the presence, of affectionate feelings that is necessary for building commitment.

Finally, commitment can be built by planning shared activities that are gratifying to both partners (Lauer and Lauer 1986:62). Sharing times of fun, achievement, or adventure intensifies people's commitment as well as providing them with intimate experiences. The more you have a history of shared, gratifying experiences, the deeper your commitment is likely to become.

---

[1]*New York Times,* 5 June 1988.

PRINCIPLES FOR ENHANCING INTIMACY

1. When, why, and who you marry should be your personal decision. But you need to be aware of the risks involved in marrying too early. Teenage and student marriages face unique difficulties that can place an intolerable burden on the relationship. There are also risks, however, in waiting too long. If you are a female, the chances of marriage after age forty are slim. It is important to be aware of these risks, but do not let them dictate your decision in this important matter.

2. It is important, before your wedding, to talk about the kind of marriage you and your future life partner want. Do you both agree that you want a relationship based on traditional roles or one with equalitarian roles? Do you have "private contracts," assumptions, and expectations that you have not shared with each other? A thorough discussion of these can minimize difficulties after you are married.

3. The first year of marriage generally seems to challenge the popular expectation of "happily ever after." All too frequently, the demands of building a life together change the patterns of interaction and intimacy that characterized your courtship. It is vital, first of all, to understand and prepare to deal with these changes.

Then, it is important to begin a lifelong process of working to maintain the romance and to deepen the intimacy in your relationship.

4. Remember that when you marry you not only gain a spouse but also another family. Learn as much as you can about your future life partner's relationship with his or her family before your wedding. This will not only tell you much about your spouse but also about the kinds of problems you are likely to encounter when you become a member of the family. Recognize potential problem areas, and plan to deal with them in a constructive manner. But keep yourself open to the benefits of an additional family; the benefits will likely outweigh the difficulties.

5. Commitment frightens many people today. Yet it is an essential ingredient in a successful marriage. Commitment to the institution of marriage provides you with the time to work out and grow through the problems that inevitably assault any relationship. Even more important is commitment to your spouse. The goal of this kind of commitment is both the happiness and well-being of your life partner and also a growing and dynamic relationship.

SUMMARY

Although most Americans marry, your chances vary depending on a number of factors. The marriage rate fluctuates over time; only the rates during the 1930s were lower than those in the 1990s. The rates reflect more than preference. Sex ratios and age are factors as well. The longer you wait, the less your chances are of being married.

People marry for various reasons in addition to being in love. One reason is conformity to social expectations. Another reason is the idea that marriage and children are the ideal and most fulfilling state for humans. The desire to have children is a third reason. Finally, some define marriage as a practical solution to various problems and challenges.

We may classify marriages by alternative life-styles or by the nature of the relationship. Among the alternative life-styles are the traditional marriage, the equalitarian marriage, the employed-wife marriage, term marriage, group marriage, swinging, and the homosexual marriage. Marriages classified by the nature of the relationship include the closed-, open-, and random-type systems.

We all have expectations when we marry. Even if we marry with all realistic expectations, we will not have a problem-free relationship. Each partner tends to bring a private contract to the marriage, a set of assumptions about various matters that have not been discussed. When private contracts clash, it is frequently over role expectations. Even in egalitarian marriages, spouses tend not to want to give up their own traditional roles; they are willing, however, to participate in the traditional role of the other.

Negotiation is necessary to work through clashing expectations. In negotiation, private contracts must become joint knowledge. Negotiations can also occur before marriage, as the couple formulates a marriage contract to avoid some problems after they are married.

When you marry you enter a new social world. There are many adjustments to make, even if you have lived together. The adjustments are not the same for both sexes. There is "his" marriage and "her" marriage. Women generally have to make more adjustments than men. Adjustment is more difficult when the marriage begins with disadvantages. Student, teenage, and heterogamous marriages all begin with some disadvantages. One important facet of adjustment is establishing equity and consensus in the relationship. In-laws also require adjustment, though overall they are more likely to be resources than problems.

During the first year of marriage, feelings and patterns of behavior change. Satisfaction tends to decline somewhat. Interaction tends to become more instrumental, more task-oriented, and less focused on romance and affection.

Commitment is not only the basis for marriage but the outcome of a satisfying relationship. Commitment means promise, dedication, and attachment. In stable and satisfying marriages, there is commitment to the spouse as an individual as well as commitment to marriage as an institution. Commitment can be built up by attending to the kinds of things that enhance the quality of the relationship.

INTERNET CONNECTION
Getting Married

Marriage is both a legal and private contract between two individuals. The private aspect of the marriage contract can also involve friends and family who may feel they have a stake in the relationship. Differing expectations regarding roles within a marriage can often lead to challenges and difficulties. As the websites below indicate, informal contracts are not the only way potential partners are choosing to clarify their marriage expectations.

www.mhhe
.com/lauer4

Private Tenaim

The Prenuptial Agreement
http://hillel.stanford.edu/Being_Jewish/tenaim.html

This Hillel Foundation document provides a sample framework for an informal marriage contract or prenuptial agreement.

Prenuptial Agreement
http://home.ptd.net/%7Eclofine/prenupt.htm

This brief online article describes changing trends in the use of prenuptial agreements.

Legal Café: Prenuptial Agreements
http://www.courttv.com/legalcafe/family/prenup/prenup_links.html

This site references some of the many online resources available that discuss prenuptial agreements.

1. What is a prenuptial agreement? Is it a personal contract? A legal contract? How does it differ from a marriage agreement?
2. Examine the prenuptial agreement at the Private Teniam website. To what degree are personal expectations regarding individual values and marriage roles reflected in this document?
3. What can you learn about who is using prenuptial agreements and why they are doing it at the sites listed above? Do you think they are potentially useful? If so, under what circumstances?

THE CHALLENGE OF
COMMUNICATION

Learning Objectives

After reading chapter 11, you should be able to:

1. Describe the different types of nonverbal communication.
2. Explain the functions of nonverbal communication.
3. Show how communication is a process of interaction.
4. Discuss the sources of static and how they interfere with accurate communication.
5. Summarize the difficulties in communicating feelings and the impact that this has on relationships.
6. Describe poor listening and ways to improve listening skills.
7. Characterize the destructive messages and gender differences that impede communication.
8. Identify the ingredients of satisfying communication.
9. Show the ways that satisfying communication contributes to the development of intimacy and marital happiness.
10. Explain how to improve communication skills.

"**W**hen I use a word," said Humpty Dumpty in Lewis Carroll's *Through the Looking-Glass,* "it means just what I choose it to mean—neither more nor less." But Humpty Dumpty was mistaken. We would all like for our words to mean exactly what we choose for them to mean, in the sense that those who hear us understand us perfectly. However, communication is a complicated process. The meaning we convey to others depends on more than our intention.

It is important to understand the complexities of communication. Much of the satisfaction and dissatisfaction of marriage and family life is rooted in the way that people communicate. In this chapter, therefore, we will look at communication as an intricate process that has manifold possibilities for miscommunication. We will discuss the importance of listening as a part of effective communication. We will look at impediments to good communication and the kinds of communication that are satisfying to people. Communication is integrally tied up with marital intimacy and satisfaction, another topic that we will explore. Finally, we will suggest some ways to improve communication between partners.

THE NATURE OF COMMUNICATION

At the outset, we must underscore the point that it is impossible *not* to communicate. Some people use what they call the "silent treatment" as a method of dealing with conflict. The victim of the silent treatment may complain that his or her spouse "won't communicate with me." Still the silent treatment itself is a powerful form of communication, telling the partner that the silent one is angry and unwilling to discuss the problem. We are always communicating to each other, in the sense that our words, our lack of words, and our expressions are interpreted by others to say something about our mood, our feelings, and perhaps about our relationships.

Verbal Communication

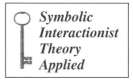
Symbolic Interactionist Theory Applied

When most people use the term *communication,* they probably are thinking of verbal communication, the use of words to convey our ideas to others. All animals engage in communication of some kind. But, as *symbolic interactionists* have shown, humans are symbolic creatures; we create, manipulate, and employ symbols to direct our own behavior and to influence the behavior of others (Lauer and Handel 1983:80). Symbols are shared meanings. Language is a system of these symbols. When we use a particular symbol, such as "love," we engage in a certain amount of shared meaning with others.

Of course, our symbols do not have a standardized and single meaning that is the same for everyone. For instance, if you say "I love you" to someone, you may mean that you feel a deep attachment, that you are sexually attracted to the person, or that you find being with the other person a delightful experience, or some combination of these or other meanings. Also the meaning that the other person imputes to your statement may be different from what you intended. As we shall see in the discussion that follows, we have multiple opportunities to miscommunicate with each other, no matter how precise we try to be with our words.

Nonverbal Communication

"I love you" may not only mean something positive but something negative as well. Depending on the inflection you put on the words, you could give quite contrary meanings to them. They could be put in the form of a question, a surprised reaction to someone's inquiry. They could be stated with sarcasm, indicating not only a lack of love but a degree of contempt for the other. They could be said with an air of indifference, suggesting a failed effort to appease an anxious and unloved inquirer. They could be stated with passion, conveying an intensity of feeling for the other.

Thus, words are only a part of the meaning in communication. Equally important as the words we use is the way in which we express them—the numerous nonverbal cues we use while communicating. It is estimated that anywhere from 50 to 80 percent of the meaning we convey is through the nonverbal part of our communication.

Kinds of Nonverbal Communication   You offer many different kinds of nonverbal cues to others when communicating. One cue is the clothing you wear. If you go out on a date, what you wear may tell the other person something about how you feel or about the kind of person you are. The message is not necessarily what you intend to give. For example, a student told us that she broke up with her boyfriend because he was always so sloppily dressed when they dated. She said that he tried to reconcile with her, insisting that he thought he was being "cool" and casual rather than sloppy. She interpreted his dress as a lack of interest in himself and a lack of respect for her. In spite of his protests, she refused to date him anymore.

Facial expressions and eye behavior are important aspects of nonverbal communication. They are difficult to control, though some people learn to control their facial expressions. They exercise such control in order to mask some kind of emotion they are feeling (Malandro and Barker 1983:21). Eye behavior is even more difficult to control. Our eyes tell others about how we are feeling, how interested we are, how much self-confidence we have, and how trustworthy we are (e.g., no one wants to be known as "shifty-eyed").

Touching is still another important kind of nonverbal behavior. Between lovers, a decline in touching is an important message about feelings. Touching someone while talking to them may indicate affection or remorse. Gripping someone may indicate anger or frustration. It is important to keep in mind that these meanings may be independent of any words that are being said. For example, a man may proclaim "I love you" to a woman while holding her arm in a viselike grip. The woman is likely to define that as threatening rather than an expression of affection.

Finally, all of the cues we give in oral speech apart from the content of the words themselves are one of the most important kinds of nonverbal communication. As illustrated previously by the diverse and contrary meanings that can be given to the phrase "I love you," the tone of voice and the emphasis given to words radically affect the meaning that is communicated. For instance, a woman says to her husband, "How about a movie tonight?" Think of the different meanings he can give to her by responding with the following: "oh, okay" (interpreted by her as willingness but no enthusiasm); "oh *kay*" (interpreted by her as an idea he loves); "*oh* kay" (interpreted by her to mean "we're doing what *you* want to do again"); and "*ohhh* kay" (hesitation in his voice, interpreted by her to mean "I'll do it, but I had something else in mind that I prefer doing").

Functions of Nonverbal Behavior   Nonverbal cues have a number of functions in communication (Malandro and Barker 1983:14–15). First, they *complement* our words. If you say "I love you" and touch or embrace the other, you are reinforcing the meaning of your words. Sometimes people may not really believe what we say, or at least may have doubts, unless we reinforce the words with some kind of nonverbal behavior.

Nonverbal cues may also *contradict* our words. A student told us how happy he was to be married, but the pained look on his face contradicted what he was saying. Eventually, he admitted to some serious problems that he and his new wife were having. At times, the nonverbal rather than the verbal message is more reliable.

Third, nonverbal cues *repeat* the message. Repeating differs from complementing because the latter cannot stand alone. To touch or hug someone may have diverse meanings with the words "I love you." But if two lovers have developed their own special language, such as touching the fingers to the lips as a way of saying "I love you," then they are using a nonverbal cue to repeat the message of love. The message is given without the words. They may be at a party, catch each other's eye, and give the nonverbal signal of love. No words need be spoken.

Fourth, nonverbal cues *regulate* communication. People develop signals to let each other know when they approve of what the other says (such as nodding the head), when they disapprove (a frown), and when they want to interrupt and speak themselves (such as lifting a finger). Such nonverbal cues help to regulate the verbal interaction between them.

Fifth, nonverbal cues may *substitute* for words. A man may ask his wife if she still loves him, and she may respond by smiling and kissing him. Thereby she responds affirmatively though wordlessly. Finally, nonverbal cues may *accent* the verbal message. A pause, an emphasis on a particular word, a touch—all can be used to emphasize a particular point that is being made verbally. "I love you," spoken slowly and with a slight pause between each word may be a way of reassuring a lover who has had doubts about the relationship.

Finally, nonverbal cues trigger attributions. That is, your partner will pick up on nonverbal cues and attribute various motivations and feelings to you. In a study of the interaction of sixty couples, three researchers found that positive cues contributed to satisfaction with the relationship (Manusov, Floyd, and Kerssen-Griep 1997). However, they also noted that the couples tended to notice negative cues more than they did the positive cues.

COMMUNICATION AS AN INTERACTION PROCESS

What you communicate to someone depends not only on what you say and how you say it but also on how the other person interprets what you say and how you say it. Figure 11.1 shows a model of communication as a process of interaction. The sender has certain ideas and feelings that he or she must encode into language. The encoded message is transmitted through the media, the verbal and nonverbal channels we use. The dotted line indicates that part of the process is the sender hearing his or her own words and evaluating them.

Nonverbal cues are an important part of communication. What is this man's nonverbal message about what the woman is saying?

FIGURE 11.1   The Communication Process

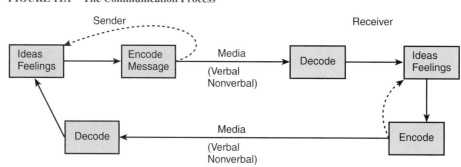

The receiver decodes, or interprets, the message and filters it through his or her ideas and feelings before encoding a reply. At that point, the receiver becomes a sender and the process continues. Let us take a concrete example to underscore the fact that at each phase of the process there can be **static,** interference of some kind with accurate communication.

A Discussion About Sex

Chuck and Linda are a fictitious married couple who are having a discussion about their sexual relationship. Our commentary on their dialogue is enclosed in brackets:

Chuck: I think that women don't have as strong a sexual drive as men. [Chuck desires to have sex more often than Linda. He is upset but isn't sure if he feels anger, frustration, or both. He also wants to avoid offending Linda. He knows she is frequently stressed from dealing with both her career and their family. He encodes his desire into a statement that is a "feeler." He wants to know how she will respond to the idea. Yet when he hears his words, he thinks he might have chosen a better way to start the conversation. He prepares himself to back off if she reacts badly.]

Linda: I don't know why you would say that. [She notices a slight edge to Chuck's voice. She decodes what he has said as a personal complaint. She knows he has wanted sex more often than she has. She isn't sure if that's why he made the statement. If he has, it will open the way to a larger discussion. She feels that he doesn't understand the strain of being both a mother and a career woman. Perhaps if he helped around the house more, she would have more energy. But she, too, doesn't want to offend. Basically, they have a satisfying marriage. She makes her response as terse and neutral as possible.]

Chuck: I just think it's true. [He saw her mouth tighten when she replied. He interprets that as a warning signal that pursuing the topic could lead to an argument. Even though her words suggest that she would not agree that she has a weaker sex drive, her nonverbal cues warn him that this is an emotional topic. He decides to be neutral in his response.]

Linda: Well, I've got too much to do to talk about something silly like that. [Hearing a softening in his voice, she defines him as unwilling to confront the issue directly. This angers her. She decides to force him to cut off the discussion or get to the point. In case he wants to pursue it, she has opened the door to what she regards as the real problem— an inequity in household responsibilities.]

Such conversations can go on endlessly without the couple ever directly discussing the real issue. They communicated, but Linda was never certain what Chuck really wanted to say. And he felt that she was unaware of his feelings about their sex life. Merely because people are talking together does not mean that they are communicating accurately with each other.

Communication Static

Chuck and Linda illustrate some of the manifold ways in which static gets into the communication process. The sender, the media of transmission, and the receiver are all sources of static (Pneuman and Bruehl 1982). Senders may transmit with static because they aren't certain of their own feelings or ideas. Because Chuck was unsure of his own feelings, it was difficult for him to open the conversation in a helpful way. As a result, he sent ambiguous information to Linda. Ambiguous or insufficient information can also result from poor communication habits, such as assuming that one's thoughts or feelings can be inferred accurately without careful communication.

Sender static can also result from certain mannerisms. For instance, a sender who uses "you know" or "uh" repeatedly or who uses exaggerated nonverbal gestures while speaking may so distract the listener that accurate communication is very difficult.

Static occurs in the media when there is a discrepancy between the nonverbal and verbal communication. Chuck and Linda each noticed nonverbal signs that feelings were more intense than the words would indicate. Discrepancies between the verbal and nonverbal leave the hearer somewhat bewildered as to which medium of communication to accept. The man who insists he is not angry when his face is distorted with emotion is sending an ambiguous message. His wife knows that his words do not tell all, but she is not sure if the emotion expressed on his face is anger or something else. Media static may also occur if there are too many distractions in the environment (noisy children, for example, who keep grabbing the attention of one or both parents who are trying to discuss an interpersonal issue).

Receiver static occurs when the listener filters the message through his or her own ideas and feelings—selecting, expanding, and interpreting the words and nonverbal cues to make sense of the message. Chuck interpreted Linda's frequent lack of sexual desire as insufficient passion for him. Linda interpreted Chuck's ambiguity as an unwillingness to confront the issue directly. He never knew that she resented having a disproportionate share of responsibility for the home. She never knew he was sufficiently sensitive to her needs to recognize that she felt stressed over her workload. Each assumed things about the other, because it was important for each to make sense of the situation. Lacking sufficient and accurate information from the other, each interpreted the other in a way that made sense, even though neither reached a satisfying conclusion.

Communicating Feelings

As Chuck and Linda illustrate, when we talk with others we inevitably communicate feelings as well as ideas. Feelings are very important in the marital relationship. The way you think your spouse feels about things may be more crucial to your relationship than what your spouse says. Research has shown that the accurate communication of feelings is as complicated and as subject to distortion as the communication of ideas (Gaelick, Bodenhausen, and Wyer 1985). As figure 11.2 shows, a circular process is involved in the communication of feelings. The feelings you intend to communicate are interpreted by the other and may or may not be perceived correctly. The other person has an affective reaction to his or her perception of your feelings and communicates that to you. You interpret the other's feelings, compare that with what you expected, and have your own affective reaction. You then communicate additional feelings, and the cycle continues.

FIGURE 11.2   Intended and Unintended Communication of Feelings
(*Source:* Data from L. Gaelick, G. V. Bodenhausen, and R. S. Wyer, Jr., *Journal of Personality and Social Psychology,* 49:1248, 1985.)

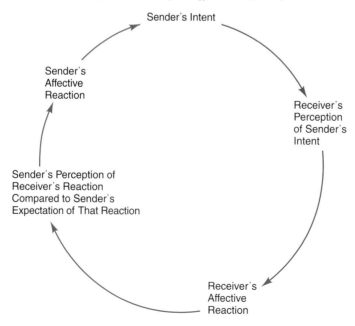

Because of the interpretation that always occurs, the cycle has both intended and unintended communication. Thus, in their study of twenty-nine couples, psychologists Gaelick, Bodenhausen, and Wyer (1985) found that people believe they reciprocate both positive and negative feelings that they perceive from their partners. They had the couples engage in three conversations. One dealt with the events of the day, the second with a conflict they were having, and the third with what they liked best about living together. Although the subjects believed that they generally reciprocated the feeling they perceived their partners to convey and that their partners reciprocated their own expression of emotion, the researchers concluded that, in actuality, they only reciprocated hostility. Among these twenty-nine couples, at least, there was not much accuracy in perceiving the expression of positive emotions.

The researchers also found two interesting gender differences in the communication of feelings. The men tended to distort the messages of their female partners in a negative direction, interpreting the lack of positive feelings as an indication of hostility. The women tended to distort the messages of their male partners in a positive direction, interpreting the lack of hostility as an indication of positive feelings. Clearly, neither feelings nor ideas are easily and accurately communicated to those we love. Effective communication is a complex and difficult task. One thing that is essential is effective listening.

LISTENING

Psychiatrist Karl Menninger (1942:275) once wrote that listening may be even more important than talking: "I believe listening to be one of the most powerful and influential techniques of human intercourse." However, there are various ways we can listen to others, not all of which are helpful to effective communication.

Styles of Poor Listening

A number of styles of listening impede effective communication (Burley-Allen 1982:48–51). Some people habitually listen in one or more of these ways, while others may fall into them on occasion.

The Faker Fakers only pretend to be listening. They may smile while you talk to them. They may nod their heads. They may appear to be intent, but they are either thinking about something else or are so intent on appearing to be listening that they do not hear what you are saying.

Ellen, an undergraduate, broke her engagement because she found that her fiancé consistently faked his listening:

> I realized how little he paid attention to me when I told him one day my doctor wanted me to have another test. He had found some suspicious cells in my cervix. Mike just looked at me and smiled. I really exploded. I was scared to death. He apologized. Said he was worried about an exam. I began probing into some other things I thought we had talked about. He couldn't remember half the things I had told him!

The Dependent Listener Some people primarily want to please the speaker. They are so concerned about whether the speaker has a good impression of them that they are unable to listen and respond appropriately. Dependent listeners may agree excessively with what the speaker says, not because they really agree but because they want to maintain the goodwill of the speaker.

A woman, for example, who is overly dependent on her husband may not listen to what he is saying because she is concerned primarily with pleasing him rather than understanding and helping him. Unfortunately, she does not realize that the relationship she is so desperate to maintain may be jeopardized rather than strengthened by her behavior. By striving to please, dependent listeners are frustrating at best. They may be valued by the individual who only wants someone to support whatever he or she says and does, but they are unable to build fulfilling relationships.

The Interrupter Interrupters never allow the other to finish. They may be afraid that they will forget something important they want to say. Or they may feel that it is necessary to respond to a point as soon as it is made. Or they may simply be more concerned with their own thoughts and feelings than with those of others. In any case, they barrage the other with words rather than offering the other an understanding ear.

Here is how an interrupter might function:

Wife: I really had a rough day today. I thought my boss was going to . . .

Husband: I bet your day wasn't any worse than mine. I couldn't believe the way my clerks were fouling up today. I think I'm going to have to bring them in one by one for some additional training.

Wife: Yeah, those people can drive you up a wall at times. Well, my boss just about went through the ceiling. . . .

Husband: You've got to stop letting him get to you. Just tell him you'll quit if he keeps on.

Wife: I can understand why he got upset. I didn't have the report ready. But he doesn't realize that . . .

Husband: He gets upset at anything. I don't know how you stand working for him.

Note that the interrupting husband never lets his wife completely finish. The wife has no opportunity to talk out her feelings and frustrations. The husband simply breaks in with his own problems or tries to give her a quick-fix solution. He isn't listening, because he is making no effort to fully understand her and the experience of her day.

The Self-Conscious Listener   Some people are concerned primarily with their own status in the eyes of the other rather than with the ideas and feelings of the other. Trying to impress the other person, they don't listen with understanding.

A woman who wants her husband to think of her as intelligent, for example, might be so concerned with that image that she doesn't really listen to him. Instead of trying to understand what he is saying, she will be thinking about how to respond in order to impress him with the quality of her mind. Or she may want to impress him with the fact that she is indispensable to him, that she can help him with any of his problems. Again, instead of listening carefully and trying to understand him, she may be constantly framing her replies in order to appear helpful.

The Intellectual Listener   Intellectual listeners attend only to the words of the other. They make a rational appraisal of what the other has said verbally, but they ignore the nonverbal cues (including the feelings that are communicated nonverbally).

The intellectual listener may develop this style because of the type of work in which he or she engages. Consider the case of Frank, a computer programmer, who had learned to be thoroughly logical and systematic in order to succeed in his work. He tried to apply the same procedure to his marriage, however, and found himself in trouble:

> He was so busy analyzing what was communicated to him, he didn't have time to just be there with the other person. His wife often told him he was a nitpicker. She felt he was overly critical of her and the children because he seldom accepted what she said. He would challenge her thought processes. He spent most of their communication time analyzing what she said as if he had to turn it into a program (Burley-Allen 1982:51).

Frank was a highly intelligent person, but he had to learn how to listen.

Improving Listening Skills

How do you learn to listen? How can you learn to listen so that you understand the other person and the other knows you understand? One thing is to avoid the styles we have described above. Beyond that, Madelyn Burley-Allen (1982:96–98) suggests a number of things you can do to improve your listening skills generally. Some of those particularly appropriate for intimate relationships are:

1. Take the initiative in communication. Unfortunately, we tend to think of listening as a passive activity. But effective listening has to be active. You have to look at your partner and concentrate on what he or she is saying. You need to watch the nonverbal cues and listen to the words carefully and strive to understand exactly what he or she is trying to communicate. It is also helpful to respond to various things with noncommittal remarks such as "I see," "That's interesting," and so on.

2. Resist distractions. The distractions may be in the environment, such as noise in the home, or they may be in your mind, such as preoccupation with some problem or concern. In either case, you must consciously decide to put aside the distractions for a while and focus on what your partner is saying.

3. Control your emotions and your tendency to respond before your partner is finished. We all

Good listening skills can be practiced everywhere, including the home.

have certain "hot buttons," words or ideas that create an emotional reaction in us. At that point we are likely to stop listening and start formulating a reply. Your emotions, in other words, can turn you into an interrupter. It is important to resist that tendency. Hear your partner out completely.

4. Ask questions and rephrase to clarify your partner's meaning. In effective listening, questions are used not to cast suspicion on motives (such as "Are you saying that just to annoy me?") but to get clarification (such as "Are you saying then that you are really hurt because I was late?"). Effective listeners are particularly aware of the value of rephrasing what the other has said. Rephrasing is done to clarify, to check for accuracy, to check for feelings, or simply to show interest and understanding.

For example, a husband says to his wife: "We have blown our budget to bits this month.

You've got to stop spending so much money." She could respond angrily: "What about the money you spend? It's not all my fault." That is likely to start an argument. An effective listening response would rephrase the husband's statement. She might say: "You feel that our budget problems are due mainly to my spending habits?" (clarification); or "You're angry because of the way I spend money" (check for feelings). This provides her husband with the opportunity to respond in a constructive way to their budget difficulties.

5. Make use of the speed of your thoughts by summarizing. We think faster than we can speak. You can make use of this by periodically summarizing what your partner has said. It is important that you not only use your thinking to formulate responses but also to summarize in an effort to understand exactly what your partner is getting at.

PERSPECTIVE
The Silent Marriage

Edith Wharton's classic story *Ethan Frome* relates the unhappy life of a man who lost first his mother and then his wife to silence. The story illustrates the problems of communication and the sterile nature of relationships that lack good communication. Frome's father had died accidentally, and Ethan was left to care for his mother who had become ill after the loss of her husband. She had been a "talker" until his death, but from then on, "the sound of her voice was seldom heard." A cousin, Zeena, came to stay with them and help nurse his mother. After the mother's death, Zeena prepared to return home, but Ethan, dreading the idea of being alone, asked her to stay. They were married. Within a year, Zeena also became sickly. Note in the following excerpt the role that both Ethan

and Zeena played in the deteriorating communication:

Then she too fell silent. Perhaps it was the inevitable effect of life on the farm, or perhaps, as she sometimes said, it was because Ethan "never listened." The charge was not wholly unfounded. When she spoke it was only to complain, and to complain of things not in his power to remedy: and to check a tendency to impatient retort he had first formed the habit of not answering her, and finally of thinking of other things while she talked. Of late, however, since he had had reasons for observing her more closely, her silence had begun to trouble him. He recalled his mother's growing taciturnity, and wondered if Zeena were also turning "queer."

Women did, he knew. Zeena, who had at her fingers' ends the pathological chart of the whole region, had cited many cases of the kind while she was nursing his mother; and he himself knew of certain lonely farmhouses in the neighborhood where stricken creatures pined, and of others where sudden tragedy had come of their presence. At times, looking at Zeena's shut face, he felt the chill of such forebodings. At other times her silence seemed deliberately assumed to conceal far-reaching intentions, mysterious conclusions drawn from suspicions and resentments impossible to guess.

Source: Edith Wharton, *Ethan Frome* (New York: Charles Scribners' Sons, 1911), pp. 77–79.

---

6. Practice. You can enhance your listening skills by practicing with everyone, not merely your intimate partner. The more you try to be an effective listener with people, the more skill you will gain. And, we might add, the more you will enhance the quality of your relationships.

IMPEDIMENTS TO COMMUNICATION

"If people would only learn to communicate." The complaint has been uttered numberless times. The implication is that many of our problems could be solved. Why, then, don't people communicate? As we have seen, it isn't just a matter of not talking. Not many relationships fall into the silent pattern of Ethan and Zeena's (see PERSPECTIVE). But the misunderstandings and speculations that characterized Ethan and Zeena plague even many of those who *are* talking to each other. What happens?

The failure to listen is one obvious impediment to effective communication. In addition, we need to

be aware of certain kinds of destructive messages and of important gender differences in communication patterns.

Destructive Messages

When people communicate effectively, they are able to build intimacy, to share meaningful times together, and to understand each other more fully. Ineffective communication, on the other hand, impedes intimacy and facilitates misunderstanding, feelings of rejection, and conflict. A number of common destructive messages characterize ineffective communication (Liberman et al. 1980; Gottman 1994). Some destructive messages are particularly hazardous to a relationship. Gottman (1994:414) calls four of the most corrosive ways of sending destructive messages the "Four Horsemen of the Apocalypse." They are complain/criticize, contempt, defensiveness, and stonewalling. These four, he notes, are likely to be a sequence, with each one giving way to the next as the communication deteriorates.

For example, a husband begins by complaining that his wife has forgotten to pay a bill again. The complaint becomes a criticism as he adds the point that her neglect makes more work for him. As she tries to defend herself by pointing out that she had an unusually demanding week, he adds insult: "You're just irresponsible. Admit it!" She reacts to his contempt by pointing out ways in which he, too, has failed. He becomes defensive, ignoring her point and listing other ways in which she exhibits irresponsibility. She gets very upset, and demands that he stop attacking her. At that point, he stonewalls her by storming out of the house.

This example makes it clear why the Four Horsemen of the Apocalypse are so destructive to a relationship. There are a number of other ways of communicating that are also hazardous to a good relationship:

Ordering may be occasionally necessary with children, but it is likely to generate such things as fear, anger, resistance, or resentment in an intimate partner. "Stop doing that," "You have to . . . ," and "You must . . ." are the kinds of phrases used in ordering. Ironically, the partner may be quite willing to do what you want but will resist and perhaps refuse simply because you ordered rather than requested. Ordering turns the interaction into a power struggle rather than an opportunity for effective communication between equals.

Threatening tends to generate the same emotions as ordering. It can also lead to passivity or despair. Again, to threaten the other is to engage in a power struggle rather than effective communication.

Moralizing sends a message that the partner should feel guilty or morally inferior or that the partner needs guidance and direction from others. "You ought not . . ." and "You should . . ." are moralizing phrases. Moralizing also can be accomplished nonverbally by a look of disgust or disapproval.

Providing solutions is a parental approach to a relationship. The words may sound like a suggestion, but the nonverbal cues can indicate a kind of parental guidance and even the superiority of the questioner: "Why don't you clean off the table during the commercial?" or "Why don't you balance your checkbook each time you write a check?"

Lecturing is a more forceful way of providing guidance and solutions to problems. "You will have to learn how to keep the house clean if you want to be a good wife." "You will have to be more forceful at work and demand a raise if you are going to be a good father and husband." Lecturing also tends to diminish the self-esteem of the partner and underscore the superiority of the one giving the lecture.

Ridiculing is sometimes used with good intentions (in the mistaken belief that the other person will see how ridiculous his or her behavior or ideas are and change). Sometimes the intentions are not so good (the person who uses ridicule may be demonstrating his or her own superiority over the other). In either case, ridicule will generate more resistance and resentment than change and intimacy. "You're talking like an idiot" and "You're a slob" are examples of ridicule. You can't engage in effective communication with someone who hurls such biting phrases.

Analyzing is the attribution of motives to someone. The world is full of amateur psychoanalysts who tell others why they behave the way they do and why they think and feel as they do. "You're only doing that to hurt me" and "You're only smiling to cover up your hostility" are examples of analyzing. This angers us, because the analyst invades our privacy and suggests motivations that we believe to be wrong. If the analyst is a very powerful and admired person in our lives, we may believe the analysis and lose self-esteem. In either case, effective communication breaks down.

Finally, *interrogating* is another power tactic that conveys a sense of distrust of the other. "Can you give me one good reason why you won't go to the party?" and "You're not telling the truth, are you?" are examples of interrogation. Interrogation is used to coerce information rather than to engage in dialogue.

Conflict Theory Applied

Why do people engage in such destructive messages? In some cases they reflect a *conflict of interests* and the consequent efforts to coerce the partner in order to pursue one's own interests. Criticism of another, for example, can be a way to build up one's own flagging self-esteem. Ordering can be a way of maintaining control in the relationship. And so on. On the other hand, it is important to note that there may be times when some of the messages are appropriate and even necessary. But if they become part of a style of communication or if they are used too frequently or at inappropriate times, they impede effective communication and corrode the relationship.

Gender Differences As an Impediment

In the play *My Fair Lady,* Henry Higgins sings a song of bewilderment in which he asks why a woman can't be more like a man. Higgins doesn't understand women and particularly doesn't understand why they react differently from his male friends. His perplexity symbolizes that of many who run into problems of communication because they do not understand basic gender differences.

Psychiatrist Aaron Beck (1988) has noted some of the important differences in male-male versus female-female communication, such as that men rarely talk about personal matters. Beck wrote that he only learned one of his close male friends was going to be a grandfather when the man's wife told Beck's wife about it. Beck also pointed out that a woman is likely to think her marriage is working as long as she and her husband can keep talking about it; but her husband may think that it is not working if they have to keep talking about it. Beck's observation holds true within the marital relationship as well as between friends. In their study of 120 people who had been married at least twenty years, Mackey and O'Brien (1995) found that a frequent source of tension even of those married many years was husbands' discomfort with talking about their inner thoughts and feelings. And because of their discomfort, husbands often try to control the content and emotional depth of discussions, an effort that is not pleasing to their wives (Ball, Cowan, and Cowan 1995).

Deborah Tannen (1990) has analyzed gender differences in conversational styles in detail. She points out that men approach life as a contest in which each party is striving to "preserve independence and avoid failure" (Tannen 1990:25). Women, by contrast, approach life as a community affair in which the goal is to maintain intimacy and avoid being isolated. In conversations, therefore, men attempt to sustain or gain status, while women strive for relational closeness. As a result, the same

behavior can have very different meanings for men and women. For instance, checking with her partner before making plans may make a woman feel good because her life is intertwined with someone else's. Checking with his partner may make a man feel that he has lost his independence. Men, therefore, are more likely than women to make decisions without consulting their partner.

Tannen discusses various other ways in which men and women differ, differences that lead to misunderstandings and problems. For example, women tend to respond to someone else's trouble with understanding and sympathy; men tend to give advice or try to solve the problem. Women tend to listen and give support; men tend to lecture and give authoritative information and opinions. Women find details about minor daily activities to be a sign of intimacy and caring; men may find such details boring or even irritating.

Finally, research over the past seven decades shows that men and women tend to have somewhat different preferences for topics of conversation. An analysis of the preferences of 253 men and women reported that the most popular topic for both genders was work and money. For men, that choice was followed closely by the topic of leisure activity (including sports). For women, the second most popular topic was equally divided between leisure activity and persons of the opposite sex (Bischoping 1993). In fact, women were almost four times as likely to talk about men as men were to talk about women.

Clearly, not every woman or every man can be characterized in these ways. But it is also clear that gender differences are widespread and fundamental. It is important to understand the differences as a couple tries to build a meaningful intimate relationship.

Why Husbands and Wives Don't Talk to Each Other

"He doesn't talk to me." It's one of the most common complaints. Why does communication sometimes lapse into a kind of silent tolerance? Why do some couples become like Ethan and Zeena (see PERSPECTIVE)? Any of the previously discussed factors may come into play in a marriage. One or both partners may develop a style of sending out destructive messages. There may be a lack of un-

PERSONAL
All the Talk Was Useless

One of the important points in this chapter is that talking together doesn't necessarily mean that effective communication is occurring. Jenny is a nurse who was married for fifteen years to Phil, a psychologist. She was twenty-two and he was thirty when they married. They talked a lot, but it didn't save their marriage. Jenny recalls the relationship with a tinge of sadness in her words:

We were both introspective kinds of people. When I was a child I was lonely and I rarely, if ever, confided totally in another person. Phil also had a difficult childhood. So we were both insecure. The result was that, though we talked a lot, we didn't talk about anything that would threaten our security.

Before we were married, we talked about where we would live and how our careers would go and how our marriage would be a good one. But we didn't discuss things like potential problems or things we liked and didn't like about each other. And we certainly didn't talk about how we would make decisions and who would control the finances. That was unfortunate, because a lot of the troubles we had later on really were the result of a power struggle between us. While we were married, we argued, we discussed, and we hit impasses on many things. We disagreed about our in-laws. I thought he should be more accepting of my parents, and he thought I should feel more warmly toward his parents. We argued about money constantly. We fought about each other's spending habits. We also talked a lot about things we agreed on. We both loved movies, and we discussed them. We told each other about our work and the

things that happened on the job. Phil was supportive when I was stressed at work, and I think I helped him when he was worn down by some of his patients. But the arguments consumed an increasing amount of our conversation as the years went by.

So in the end, all the talk was useless. Because we didn't talk about the really crucial things. We never discussed our own fears and vulnerabilities with each other. We never talked about our differences for what they were—a struggle for control in the relationship. We just fought more and more. The final breakup came within two months of our fifteenth anniversary. We never even discussed the breakup. We didn't talk about the reasons for it. We never talked about how we each felt. We just slipped quietly apart. And the marriage ended.

---

derstanding of gender differences. The result of such things is that conversations become a form of punishment rather than reward. And few of us are willing to engage consistently in behavior that we define as punishing.

For instance, Faye is a homemaker with two preschool children. Her husband, Tom, is an architect. They have a stable marriage of ten years, though they do not converse as readily as they once did. In particular, Faye complains about Tom's reluctance to talk:

I'm hungry for adult conversation and companionship by the time Tom comes home from work. But sometimes it's like I have to yank every word out of him. I feel like he could spend the rest of his life with me without ever initiating a conversation.

Tom is educated, knowledgeable, and interested in a variety of topics from sports to politics. Why doesn't he talk with Faye? Tom told the marriage enrichment group that he and Faye were attending one night: "Sometimes people don't talk to each other because of the way one of them responds." When pressed about what he meant, he said:

Suppose I come home and tell Faye that I'm thinking of starting my own firm, or even of getting out of architecture all together and trying a different career that will be more satisfying to me. Then she tells me that's a dumb idea because I have a wife and two kids to support and a good job and I ought to be thinking about more productive things.

Faye admitted that it sounded like something she would say. She got frightened when he talked about such things. So she would cut him off and ridicule the idea. As a result, Tom had unwittingly fallen into the habit of initiating very little conversation. Tom and Faye are working on improving their communication. They have a basically sound relationship, but effective communication had deteriorated because neither had understood the other, and Tom had chosen the typical male response of lapsing into relative silence.

We should note that while it is true that lack of communication is a common complaint, it is also true that for many couples the quality of communication improves over the course of the marriage. Mackey and O'Brien (1995) reported in their study of lasting marriages that 68 percent of their respondents identified their communication as positive in the third phase of marriage (after the youngest child was at least eighteen years of age), while 44 percent recalled their communication as positive before their children were born. Their respondents also identified the child-rearing years as the most difficult for good marital communication.

SATISFYING COMMUNICATION

If you have a satisfying pattern of communication, will that guarantee a satisfying marriage? The answer is no. Satisfying communication is not sufficient. On the other hand, it *is* necessary. You can't have a satisfying marriage without satisfying communication, even though the latter won't guarantee a happy union. We should note that what is "satisfying" will differ somewhat for various couples. Nevertheless, people who come to therapists with marital problems report a variety of communication problems, including too little conversation, too few things to talk about, too much criticism, and general dissatisfaction with conversations.

What kind of things go into satisfying communication? What makes people happy with the communication pattern of their relationship? Communication is more satisfying to us when we feel understood and when we have agreement with the other (Allen and Thompson 1984). It is likely to be more satisfying with those we regard as good communicators, that is, people who avoid such negative things as insults and complaints and are interested and interesting and comfortable people with whom to talk (Schrader 1990).

Perhaps we can best sum up satisfying communication by looking at the kinds of items in the most frequently used measure of marital communication, the Marital Communication Inventory developed by Bienvenu (1978). This inventory is used by researchers and therapists to study and improve communication. A sampling of items shows that marital communication is more satisfying and effective the more often the spouses:

Discuss the way they will spend their income.

Discuss their work and interests with each other.

Express their feelings to each other.

Avoid saying things that irritate each other.

Have pleasant mealtime conversations.

Listen to each other.

Perceive that they are understood by the other.

Support each other.

Communicate affection and regard.

Avoid the silent treatment.

Confide in each other.

COMMUNICATION, MARITAL SATISFACTION, AND INTIMACY

Satisfying communication facilitates the growth of both marital satisfaction and intimacy. Couples that are satisfied with their relationship, who define their marriage as a happy one, and who indicate high levels of intimacy also report satisfying patterns of communication (Pollock, Die, and Marriott 1990).

Everyday Conversations

We saw that the marriage of Jenny and Phil (see PERSONAL) ended because they never talked about the serious issues in their relationship. We should not conclude that *only* the serious issues are an important part of the communication pattern of a couple, however. Everyday conversations and discussing the events of the day are significant for marital satisfaction (Vangelisti and Banski 1993). Couples who are highly satisfied with their relationship engage in both a greater amount of conversation and a broader range of topics than do those who are less satisfied (Richmond 1995).

In fact, research with thirty-one married couples suggests that everyday conversations may be one of the more important ingredients in a satisfying marriage (Holman and Brock 1986). The researchers tested the couples using the Marital Communication Inventory and a measure of marital satisfaction. They found that marital satisfaction was closely related to empathy in communication, everyday discussions, and the lack of negative kinds of communication (fault-finding, nagging, the silent treatment, etc.). But the strongest of the relationships was that between everyday discussions and overall satisfaction. The researchers concluded that effective listening and speaking skills are important but that

> proficiency in these skills does not make up for easy conversation with a spouse about the events of the day (Holman and Brock 1986:92).

Self-Disclosure

We have seen that self-disclosure comes up repeatedly as an essential factor in an intimate relationship. In marriage, self-disclosure enhances both satisfaction and intimacy. The more that a spouse engages in self-disclosure, the more that both partners are likely to be highly satisfied with the relationship (Hansen and Schuldt 1984; Rosenfeld and Bowen 1991; King 1993; Bogard and Spilka 1996). And self-disclosure accounts for more than half the variation in intimacy among couples (Waring and Chelune 1983).

We never outgrow our need to engage in self-disclosure and to have our partner disclose to us. A study of 120 older couples (average age, 68.9 years; average years married, 42) examined the relationship between self-disclosure of feelings and life satisfaction (Sanders et al. 1987). Husbands were more satisfied with their lives to the extent that they disclosed feelings of pleasure and love to their wives and received love disclosure from their wives. Wives were more satisfied with their lives to the extent that they disclosed feelings of pleasure to their husbands and received disclosure of love and sadness from their husbands. The researchers also investigated disclosure of anger, but it was not related to life satisfaction.

The fact that disclosing love, pleasure, and sadness enhanced satisfaction, while disclosing anger was unrelated to satisfaction, raises the question of what kinds of disclosure contribute to intimacy and

Pleasant mealtime conversations make both communication and the marriage more satisfying.

marital satisfaction. As Fitzpatrick (1988:179) points out:

> No relationship is able to sustain total openness and intimacy over long periods of time. . . . From the beginning, there is a tension between the need to self-disclose and the need to protect the partner from the consequences of such disclosure.

 *Exchange Theory Applied*

Thus, keeping the lines of communication open in a marriage does not mean that there is an indiscriminate and continuous flow of words and feelings between the partners.

For one thing, *exchange theory* suggests that self-disclosure should be equitable (Derlega et al. 1993). A study of troubled versus satisfied marriages reported that there was a relatively equal amount of self-disclosure among the satisfied couples

COMPARISON
Couple Talk in Brisbane and Munich

Troubled couples in many different countries complain about communication problems in their marriage. Skilled communicators are likely to have more satisfying marriages than are those who are less skilled. But specifically what kinds of communication skills are important? And are the same skills important in different countries?

Three researchers attempted to answer the questions by comparing how 81 couples in Brisbane, Australia, and Munich, Germany, communicated during a problem-solving discussion. Forty-nine of the couples were in an unhappy marriage, while thirty-two said they were happily married.

In some ways, the Australians and Germans communicated alike. Compared to the unhappy couples, the happy couples in both countries agreed significantly more often with each other (e.g., "Yes, you're right," "I agree that I started the argument," etc.) and accepted each other (indicated by paraphrasing what the partner said and affirming the partner). The happy couples also made significantly more neutral statements and asked more neutral questions (e.g., "I think we have a problem with the kids," "Would you say that again, please?", etc.). In contrast, unhappy couples in both countries criticized their spouses and disagreed significantly more often than did happy couples. And finally, the happy couples had far more positive, nonverbal interaction (such as smiling at the partner).

But there was an important cross-national difference. German couples, whether happy or unhappy, used significantly more negative responses than did the Australians. In part, this resulted from the fact that the Germans were more likely than the Australians to respond to a partner's negative statement with a negative statement of their own. In terms of the escalation of a negative interchange, the happy German couples were very similar to the unhappy Australian couples!

In other words, there was far more negativity generally in the German than in the Australian couples. In both countries a major problem of couples who defined themselves as unhappy was their inability to terminate negative interaction quickly. Happy couples, in contrast, knew how to either avoid such a process in the first place or to reverse it once it started (Halford, Hahlweg, and Dunne 1990).

(Chelune, Rosenfeld, and Waring 1985). In the troubled marriages, the wives tended to disclose more than the husbands. Secondly, self-disclosure should always be done with discretion. A general rule of thumb is that in a satisfying marriage you can disclose anything to your spouse, but you never disclose everything. Exactly what should and should not be disclosed may vary from one couple to another. It is always appropriate to disclose such things as feelings of pleasure and love. (Perhaps we should say it is imperative to express those feelings. It isn't enough to feel them internally.) Marital satisfaction is enhanced by the *disclosure,* not just the experience, of pleasure and love. It is appropriate to disclose your needs in the relationship, including your sexual needs and desires. In spite of the presumably open sexual nature of our society, many couples still find it difficult to talk freely about sexual matters with each other. It is also appropriate to disclose things that are troubling you or matters of serious concern. Sharing your feelings about a serious illness, for example, can en-

able you to cope better with that illness (Kelley, Lumley, and Leisen 1997). It can also help your partner to understand you better and to give you the support you need.

Self-disclosure, in sum, enhances both your personal and your marital well-being when you and your mate share a substantial part of your lives with each other. But there are always some things that should not be shared. Thus, as long as they can be handled by you in other ways, it is usually better not to disclose those things that you know will hurt or anger your spouse.

Other Aspects of Communication

Certain other aspects of communication are also related to marital satisfaction and intimacy. In their study of 111 married couples, Boyd and Roach (1977) reported a relationship between satisfaction and characteristics of communication. One characteristic of the more satisfied couples was clear and direct messages. That is, they had honest and open communication: "I say what I really think." Second, the satisfied couples reported good listening skills: "I check out and try to clarify what my spouse says so that I am sure that I understand him." Third, the satisfied couples openly expressed respect and esteem for each other.

Finally, in our study of long-term marriages, we found three differences between those in happy, un-happy, and mixed (one partner happy and one un-happy) marriages (tables 11.1, 11.2, and 11.3). Couples in happy marriages tend more frequently to have a stimulating exchange of ideas, to laugh together, and to calmly discuss something. In other words, in happy marriages there are more—and also more stimulating and fun-filled—conversations.

TABLE 11.1
Marital Happiness and Stimulating Exchange of Ideas

Frequency of exchange	Degree of Happiness		
	Both happy	One unhappy	Both unhappy
	Percent		
At least daily	28.3	21.9	18.4
Once or twice a week	47.3	29.7	26.3
Once or twice a month	17.8	28.1	18.4
Less than once a month	6.5	20.3	36.8
	99.9	100.0	99.9
	(N = 505)	(N = 64)	(N = 38)

TABLE 11.2
Marital Happiness and Laughing Together

Frequency of discussions	Degree of Happiness		
	Both happy	One unhappy	Both unhappy
	Percent		
At least daily	72.8	32.8	34.2
Once or twice a week	23.7	37.5	23.7
Once or twice a month	1.8	25.0	26.3
Less than once a month	1.8	4.7	15.8
	100.1	100.0	100.0
	(N = 506)	(N = 64)	(N = 38)

TABLE 11.3
Marital Happiness and Calm Discussions

Frequency of discussions	Degree of Happiness		
	Both happy	One unhappy	Both unhappy
	Percent		
At least daily	61.7	35.9	21.1
Once or twice a week	29.6	28.1	28.9
Once or twice a month	7.3	28.1	18.4
Less than once a month	1.4	7.8	31.6
	100.0	99.9	100.0
	(N = 506)	(N = 64)	(N = 38)

IMPROVING COMMUNICATION SKILLS

There are numerous books, workshops, and courses designed to help people improve their communication skills. Marriage and family therapists spend a good deal of their time helping troubled clients with their communication patterns. In addition, you also can improve your own skills by attending to some basic rules and practicing them at every opportunity.

Rules

All rules for improving communication skills revolve about the goals of making us more effective senders and more effective receivers. Effective senders are those who transmit clear messages and who do so in a nonthreatening way. To transmit a clear message, you need to listen to your own words carefully (figure 11.1) and continue to modify what you say until the message accurately reflects your feelings and ideas. At the same time, the message should be an invitation to dialogue and not an attack. Those who send their messages using some of the destructive styles discussed will threaten their partners in one way or another.

Unfortunately, a clear message sent in a non-threatening manner does not guarantee accurate communication. When you communicate with someone, you are engaging in a process of interaction in which each of you is interpreting the verbal and nonverbal cues of the other. That interpretation may or may not be accurate. It can only be accurate when each of you has learned to be an effective receiver as well as an effective sender. To be an effective receiver means, above all, to be a good listener. Family therapist Virginia Satir (1972:70) pointed out that one of the common communication types she observed was the *distractor*. A distractor is someone who never responds directly to what is said by the other. The distractor tries to avoid the issue by ignoring it and bringing up something more pleasant. For example, a wife may say to her husband, "I was really hurt when you didn't tell me you would be so late." He might respond: "How about taking in a movie tonight?" In doing so, he is not actively listening to her. He has played the role of distractor. You only actively listen when your response indicates that you understand and follow through in the direction suggested by the sender.

Practice

You can improve your own communication skills by attending to the ideas in this chapter when you talk with others. Even when you listen to a lecture, you can hone your skills by using some of the ideas discussed in the section on listening (e.g., summarizing the speaker's points in your mind).

Some couples must go through counseling in order to learn to communicate in a nonthreatening way.

INVOLVEMENT
Improving Your Communication

One way to improve your communication skills is to engage in the exercises suggested in this section. For example, you can use the four ways of communicating offered by Satir and play the game with two other members of your family. After you have each had a chance to play all of the four roles, write down some of your conclusions. What did you learn about communication patterns in your family? With which of the roles did you feel most comfortable? Most uncomfortable? How did the other family members react to the differing roles? What changes would you like to make in your family's pattern of communications on the basis of this experience?

An alternative way to improve communication skills is to observe others and critique their communication pattern on the basis of the materials presented in this chapter. Because it is difficult to observe an actual situation, you can watch a number of episodes of some TV series that deals with marriage and/or family life. Look for such things as effective sending and receiving of messages, static, nonverbal cues, destructive messages, styles of poor listening, and so forth. How would you rate the communication patterns portrayed? What principles of effective communication do they uphold and which ones do they violate?

In addition, certain exercises are specifically designed to improve communication skills. Lederer and Jackson (1968:277–84) suggest a number of exercises, one of which requires intimate partners to acknowledge everything the other says for a two-week period. In fact, they suggest that each acknowledge and in turn have the acknowledgment acknowledged. This should be done no matter how trivial the original statement seems to be. For instance, one of the partners may say, "It is cold today." The other should acknowledge the observation in some way, such as: "Yes, I noticed that it is cold also," or "You're right. It's colder than yesterday." The one who made the original statement could then acknowledge the acknowledgment: "So you noticed it too."

The exercise may seem silly at times. But two points are important. First, it will be done for more serious as well as trivial matters. And second, it is good practice in developing "confirmation" in communication (Montgomery 1981). Confirmation is a way of letting the other know that you are listening and that you understand and accept the feelings of the other.

One further example of a helpful exercise is the communication game suggested by Satir (1972:80–95). In addition to the distractor, Satir identified three other communication types that she found common in her work as a therapist: the *placator* is always agreeable, always trying to please; the *blamer* is always finding fault and acts superior to others; and the *computer* is the ultrarational individual who logically analyzes everything. Most people play one or more of those roles at some time.

Satir suggests playing the game with three people (to represent a family of mother, father, and child), but it also can be played with two as well. Play the game with someone with whom you are intimate. Let us say that it is a spouse or an intimate partner. Decide on a topic of conversation, perhaps a problem you are currently having or plans for a date or vacation. Then each select a way of communicating. For example, you might begin as the blamer and your partner could be the distractor. Discuss the topic for about five minutes or so. Then talk about how each of you felt when you were playing that role.

After the discussion, each partner assumes a second way of communicating, and so on until each has played all four roles. An interesting aspect of this game, Satir noted, is the ease with which people construct an appropriate dialogue. That is because most of us have had practice already at each of the ways of communicating. In the course of playing the game, however, people learn a great deal about themselves and their relationships. You will probably find some of the ways of communicating very repugnant or very difficult for you. Some men react strongly to being a placator, and some women find it very difficult to be a blamer.

The major point is that communication skills are like any other. They can be improved by practice. For those who wish to enhance the quality of their intimate relationships, good communication skills are an imperative.

PRINCIPLES FOR ENHANCING INTIMACY

1. Effective communication is essential to a successful relationship, but it doesn't seem to come naturally or easily. It takes determination and effort. Effective communication requires commitment and hard work for the duration of the relationship.

2. Many people complain that it is the lack of communication that is hurting or even destroying their relationship. It is important to remember, however, that you are always communicating something. Even when you refuse to talk to your partner and give him or her the "silent treatment," you are communicating a powerful message. Unfortunately, what you seem to be saying is that this relationship is not worth talking about. And, not surprisingly, the relationship will be worthless if the silence persists.

3. There is some truth to the old adage "your actions speak louder than your words." For example, your facial expressions, body language, tone of voice, and physical appearance convey a message. At times, it is not the message you intend. Yet to the recipient of the message, nonverbal communication is often a more forceful indicator of your feelings than the words you use. Be open to your partner's readings of your nonverbal cues; you can both learn something about your true feelings.

4. Cultivate the capacity of effective listening. Generally, we master easily the technique of ineffective listening—partial attention, premature conclusions, misunderstood intentions, and so forth. Effective listening, however, involves the need to understand what the other person is really saying and to respond in a way that demonstrates this understanding.

5. Effective communication is not a cure-all for every troubled relationship. At times, effective communication convincingly reveals that the relationship cannot or should not be salvaged. As a necessary ingredient of a vital intimate relationship, however, effective communication is worth the risk.

SUMMARY

It is impossible not to communicate. We communicate nonverbally as well as verbally. Clothing, facial expressions, eye behavior, touching, and various oral cues such as inflection are a part of nonverbal communication. Nonverbal cues may complement, contradict, repeat, regulate, substitute for, or accent our verbal messages.

Communication is an interaction process in which the sender encodes feelings and ideas and transmits them to the receiver who must decode them in the context of his or her own feelings and ideas. Communication static can occur in any part of this process. Feelings as well as ideas are subject to the process of interpretation by each party in the communication.

Listening is a crucial part of communication. Some listening styles impede effective communication, including the faker, the dependent listener, the interrupter, the self-conscious listener, and the intellectual listener. There are various techniques that anyone can use to improve his or her listening skills.

A number of destructive messages are impediments to effective communication. Ordering, threatening, moralizing, providing solutions, lecturing, criticizing, ridiculing, analyzing, interrogating, and withdrawing are forms of destructive messages. These messages may be appropriate and useful at times, but they are destructive when used regularly or at inappropriate times.

It is important to recognize gender differences in communication in order to minimize problems. Women tend to believe the marriage is working as long as they can keep discussing it with their husbands. Men tend to believe the marriage is not working if they have to keep discussing it.

Satisfying communication is crucial to a satisfying marriage, though the former will not guarantee the latter. Communication is satisfying when we feel that we are understood and that the other agrees with us. Marital communication is more satisfying to the extent that the couple discusses both trivial and important matters, avoids irritating each other, and listens to each other.

Satisfying communication facilitates the development of both marital satisfaction and intimacy. Everyday conversations and self-disclosure are particularly important to satisfaction and a deepening intimacy. People in happy marriages have, more frequently than others, a stimulating exchange of ideas, calm discussions, and times of laughing together.

Communication skills can improve by attending to some basic rules and practicing. A good communicator must be both an effective sender and an effective receiver. Various exercises can help make you a more effective communicator.

INTERNET CONNECTION
The Challenge of Communication

Along with differing expectations, differences in communication styles and abilities, such as listening, impact the maintenance of effective, committed relationships. Destructive messages act as impediments to effective communication. In popular psychology, *codependence* is a term often used to describe poorly functioning relationships in which both psychological and communication issues are at play.

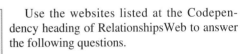

www.mhhe
.com/lauer4

RelationshipsWeb
http://relationshipweb.com/index.shtml

This website is an online "first-aid" resource for all aspects of single and married life.

Use the websites listed at the Codependency heading of RelationshipsWeb to answer the following questions.

1. What is codependency and how does it effect relationships?
2. In what ways might the term *codependency* be useful to understand patterns in relationships? In what ways might the concept impede relationship?
3. What kinds of communication impediments are involved in codependent relationships?
4. How can improvement of communication skills like listening help improve codependent relationships?

CHAPTER 12

POWER AND CONFLICT
IN MARRIAGE

Learning Objectives

After reading chapter 12, you should be able to:
1. Discuss the meaning, measurement, and importance of marital power.
2. Explain the sources of power in light of the resource theory.
3. Analyze the six types of power that can be used in a marriage.
4. Show the ways in which marriage is a power struggle.
5. Define the six types of power interaction in marriage.
6. Discuss the functions of marital conflict.
7. Summarize the primary issues about which couples fight.
8. Describe the sources of marital tension.
9. Outline the common styles of conflict.
10. Relate the principles of "good fighting."

In our fantasies, marriage is a romantic adventure. In reality, marriage is a struggle as well as an adventure. It is a struggle in a number of ways. Consider the explanation of John Ruskin, famed nineteenth-century author and reformer, for the unhappy state of his own union:

> I married her thinking her so young and affectionate that I might influence her as I chose, and make of her just such a wife as I wanted. It appeared that *she* married *me* thinking she could make of me just the *husband she* wanted. I was grieved and disappointed at finding I could not change her, and she was humiliated and irritated at finding she could not change me (quoted in Rose 1983:61).

As Ruskin found to his chagrin, marriage can involve conflict and a struggle for power within the relationship. Power and conflict are a normal part of intimate relationships. They can, however, wreck a relationship. Nonetheless, they need not lead to dissatisfaction in marriage and can, in fact, enhance the quality of the relationship if the partners handle them well.

In this chapter, we will examine those aspects of marriage that *conflict theorists* regard as central to all human interaction—issues of power and conflict. We will look at power in terms of its meaning, importance, sources, and role in the struggles of

marriage. We will also discuss the meaning and role of conflict. We will see the kinds of things that people fight about, the way in which they fight, and some methods of "good fighting."

POWER IN MARRIAGE

Conflict Theory Applied

Who is the head of the house? Who is in control in the marriage? Americans like to think of marriage as a relationship of equals. Yet how equal are marriages? We can only answer the question after we look at power in relationships and at the way in which marriage can become a struggle over power.

The Meaning of Power

What do you actually do when you exert power in a relationship? That is, what does it mean to have interpersonal power? And how can you tell who has the power in a relationship?

Defining Power   A dictionary definition equates power with the possession of such things as authority, influence, and control. Social psychologists like to make a finer distinction:

> Interpersonal power is the ability to get another person to think, feel, or do something they would not have ordinarily done spontaneously. If one possesses the means to affect another, one has *power* vis-à-vis that person. If one uses one's power, it is called *influence*. If one's influence is successful, it is called *control* (Frieze et al. 1978:302).

We will use **power** as defined above, that is, as the ability to get someone to think or feel or act in a way that he or she would not have done spontaneously. It is important to note that this does not imply that the person didn't want to think, feel, or act in that way. Power doesn't necessarily involve coercion. It doesn't necessarily mean that you influence your partner in a way that is contrary to his or her inclination. In other words, we should not think of the use of power as something inherently negative or wrong. Of course, power can be abused and misused. However, it can also be used to enhance the well-being of others, as illustrated by the

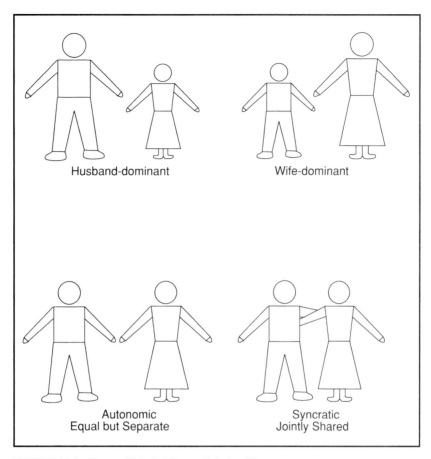

FIGURE 12.1   Types of Marital Power Relationships

work of therapists and the influence of physical fitness experts.

Measuring Power   Think about any marital relationship you know fairly well. Which spouse has the most power? How do you know? Researchers have struggled with these questions but have generally measured marital power on the basis of who makes the major decisions. For example, who has the final say on such matters as buying a house, the kind of car to purchase, the vacation, and the choice of work for either spouse? In a classic study, Blood and Wolfe (1960) used the responses to such questions to identify patterns of power in marriages. They found four different patterns (figure 12.1). The wife-dominant was the least frequent pattern, comprising about 3 percent of the couples. About a fourth were husband-dominant. The rest, the great majority,

were relatively equalitarian in their decision making. There were two types of equalitarian marriages, however. In the "autonomic," the decision making was equal but separate. That is, each spouse had authority over certain areas. In the "syncratic," the spouses shared authority over all decisions.

The methodology of Blood and Wolfe has been criticized on a number of grounds. For one thing, they gave equal weight to all kinds of decisions. But we may question whether the decision about the weekly food budget is as significant as the question of whether and where each spouse works. Another criticism is that they didn't include many important decisions (they used only eight), for example, decisions about sexual matters and the number of children, if any, to have. A third criticism is that they interviewed only the wives in the marriages. What differences might they have found if they also had asked husbands about who made the decisions?

Finally, the work of Blood and Wolfe (and others) has been criticized on the grounds that power involves more than simply who makes the final decisions on specific issues (Safilios-Rothschild 1970). What about the division of labor in the household? What about the way in which conflicts are handled and resolved? What about the ability to use techniques to influence the partner, such as the spouse who makes good sexual relations contingent on the other's behaving in a particular way? The point is that power issues do go beyond such things as who decides which car to buy. Power, whether in a marriage or any other social situation, is difficult to measure. For the sake of clarity, therefore, it is preferable to specify the kind of power we are measuring. In the Blood and Wolfe study, for instance, we could classify the marriages as husband-dominant in eight decision-making areas, wife-dominant in eight decision-making areas, and so forth. Their research may not have measured the full scope of power, but their findings are not trivial.

Why Is Power Important?

A student told us that he didn't believe in power in a marriage. "I wouldn't want to have any power over my wife, and I wouldn't want her to have any power over me. Power contradicts the very meaning of marriage." His ideal was of a totally equal relationship in which power is banished by mutual consent. But that overlooks the point that power is an integral part of human relationships. It also overlooks the point that to be equal does not mean to be powerless.

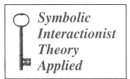
Symbolic Interactionist Theory Applied

In fact, we need power. At a more general level, to have power, to have some sense of control over our lives is important to our mental health. The important point is not whether an outside observer would detect power, but whether people *define their situation* as one in which they have some power. If they feel helpless, they are likely to become depressed and vulnerable to various kinds of physical and mental ills (McLeod 1986).

Those who feel that they have some degree of control over the circumstances of their lives, on the

other hand, are better able to not only cope but to master the various crises of life (Lauer and Lauer 1988). A sense of power is also important in maintaining self-esteem. A study of 90 couples found that those with satisfying marriages divided up decision making so that each spouse had some power in the relationship; that power, in turn, supported the needs of each partner for self-esteem (Beach and Tesser 1993).

There are many matters over which partners might want to exert power and influence each other. They include seemingly trivial things such as picking up clothes or using the remote control and deciding which television programs to watch (Walker 1996). We say "seemingly trivial" because if there is an effort to control many things, it suggests that the couple is locked in a general power struggle of which they may or may not be aware. Such struggles manifest themselves in everything from the seemingly trivial to weightier matters like major purchases or decisions about work. Apart from a fundamental power struggle, however, partners may wish to exert power and influence each other for different reasons: for personal benefit, for the benefit of the partner, or for the smooth functioning of the household and/or the relationship.

Thus, the use of power is inevitable in an intimate relationship. The way the power is used and the perceived balance of power are important to marital satisfaction. Those who perceive power

Marriage is a struggle as well as an adventure.

COMPARISON
The Power of Egyptian Husbands and Wives

In Egypt, the Muslim marriage contract requires a husband to support his wife and a wife to obey her husband. The husband also agrees to a "dower," a substantial sum that must be paid to the wife, usually in installments over a lifetime. If he divorces her, he must pay any balance—a strong deterrent to divorce.

What happens in the case of an abusive relationship? Until relatively recent times, a wife who abandoned an abusive husband and fled to relatives could be returned to her husband by the police upon the husband's request. Her return was justified on the basis that she had pledged obedience to him. Now, however, a judge can declare the request for obedience to be unjustified if there are sufficient grounds for doing so.

Egyptian husbands continue to seek obedience orders in the courts against their wives. Wives who resist the order to return to their husbands generally do so on one of the two grounds—clear evidence of abuse or inadequate provision of a home. What is "inadequate provision of a home"? An adequate home, as one judge outlined it, includes the wife's right to: have quarters that reflect the husband's social standing; refuse to allow members of her husband's family residence in the house; have good neighbors, such that the home is safe; and have a kitchen, bath, and private conveniences that aren't shared with others.

As far as abuse is concerned, a wife who can show either actual or threatened harm from her husband can legally withdraw from him. She can also divorce him, and in fact the most frequent reason for judicial divorce is proven abuse. At the time of the divorce, the husband must pay his wife the balance of the financial obligation he made at the time of their marriage (which could be a substantial amount of money).

Thus, although Muslim marriages are often perceived by Westerners to involve great inequality in power, husbands and wives each have strong obligations and considerable power in Egypt. A husband must support and treat his wife well. As long as he does, she is obligated to remain with him and fulfill her responsibilities as a wife (Fluehr-Lobban and Bardsley-Sirois 1990).

---

inequality are likely to be less satisfied with the marriage (Whisman and Jacobson 1990). One way that the less powerful partner may deal with the inequality is to develop a physical or emotional disorder that forces the more powerful partner to accede to his or her wishes out of consideration for the handicap (Bagarozzi 1990).

On what basis can we say that one partner has more power than the other? Madden (1987) measured power in thirty-seven couples in two ways: according to who made final decisions and according to the extent to which each spouse had control over which tasks he or she did. She found that for both the husbands and the wives, marital satisfaction was related to perceived control over tasks. Who performed which chores around the home was not as important as having a choice. In the most satisfying relationships, the partners believed that each had relatively equal and moderately high control over tasks.

Madden raised the question of why control over decision making was not a factor in satisfaction among her couples. She suggested the possibility that equality in decision making has become the norm so that it is no longer an issue. Mashal's (1985) study is consistent with this line of reasoning. Mashal measured power in terms of decision making, but she also asked the twenty couples in her study about their ideal (that is, who *ideally* should make the decision or who the individual would *prefer* to make the decision). She found that marital satisfaction was positively related to the perception of joint authority and also to congruence between ideal and perceived actual control.

Both studies used samples too small to conclude that couples now are more likely to equally share the authority for making decisions. Still it does seem clear that how you handle power is important to your marital satisfaction. You are more likely to be satisfied with your relationship if you feel that you have some control over it, if there is equity in the use of power, and if the pattern of power accords with your ideals or preferences.

Women's marital power increases when they earn part of the family income.

Sources of Power

Where do we get power? What would give you more power than your partner or your partner more power than you?

Resource Theory   **Resource theory** was formulated by Blood and Wolfe (1960), who argued that the balance of power in a marriage will reflect the relative resources that each partner has. The power over the decision-making process, they said,

> stems primarily from the resources which the individual can provide to meet the needs of his marriage partner and to upgrade his decision-making skills (Blood and Wolfe 1960:44).

Whoever has the most resources will have the most power. For example, one important resource is money. The spouse with the highest income (which normally means the one with the most education and highest-status occupation as well) will probably have the most power in the relationship.

Because money is one of the more important resources, it is understandable that the male generally has had the most power in American family life. To the extent that the husband has been the breadwinner or has been the main contributor to the family's financial resources, he has also assumed the authority to decide how the income will be spent. Thus,

Blumstein and Schwartz (1983:54) found that in a third of those marriages in which the husband earned eight thousand dollars more than the wife, the husband was the more powerful spouse. When the spouses' income was about equal, the husband had more power in only 18 percent of the marriages. Power here refers to the authority to decide how the money shall be spent. Generally, however, the husband's power in money matters spills over into other areas as well.

The relationship between contribution to resources and power does not occur everywhere, but it may be seen in a variety of societies other than the United States. Lee and Petersen (1983) examined the power of wives and the extent to which the wives contributed to food production in 113 nonindustrial societies. They found that the greater the role of wives in food production, the more they tended to have power in the marriage.

There are, of course, important resources other than material ones. For women, educational attainment is typically associated with a greater degree of power in the marital relationship. Thus, a study of wives in Mexico reported that those with higher levels of education were less likely to be victims of violence, more likely to have an equal say in decisions, and more likely to be satisfied with their influence in the decision-making process (Oropesa 1997). It has also been suggested that women can and do use sex to achieve a balance of power with the economically dominant men in their lives (Blumstein and Schwartz 1983:219–21). Historically, sex has been the main commodity that women could withhold or bestow in order to achieve their desires, which often went far beyond personal sexual gratification (Brown 1995).

In addition, emotional support, budgeting skills, the ability to organize and maintain an efficient home, and parenting skills may be important resources. In other words, whatever you have that can help meet the needs of your partner is a resource in your marriage. For example, a female executive told us that she accorded her husband equal authority to make decisions in their marriage because, among other things, "he is such a good father." Although she contributed much more income than he did to the family, she valued his ability to be a good father to her children (he was the stepfather to her children from a previous marriage). His parenting skills were a resource that balanced out her greater financial contribution.

An important nonmaterial resource is a person's interest in maintaining the relationship. Waller (1951) formulated the "principle of least interest," which states that the partner who is least interested in maintaining the relationship has the most power. Consider the situation from the point of view of the one with the most interest. If you are more concerned than your spouse in keeping a marriage going, you are likely to defer to your spouse in various decisions and to strive to please your spouse in diverse matters. In other words, your spouse will have more power in the relationship than you. Even if your spouse does not intentionally exploit the situation, your behavior will be that of a less powerful person interacting with a more powerful person.

It is vital to keep in mind that resources are only resources if they meet the needs of the other. That is, to bring a large income to a marriage may or may not be an important resource. If the partner has a large income of his or her own, money may not be as important as other things. Or if the spouse who earns the income, or most of the income, is abusive or lacks good communication skills or has difficulty expressing affection, the money may be insufficient to hold the marriage together. In other words, we must look at all of the resources each individual has. It is your resource profile, not a particular resource, that will determine your potential power. And it is your resource profile in the context of the needs of your partner that will determine your actual power in the relationship.

Types of Power   Raven, Centers, and Rodrigues (1975) identified six different kinds of power that people can exert in a marriage (table 12.1). Note

TABLE 12.1
Types of Power in Marriage

Type	Reason for Compliance	Example
Coercive	Avoid punishment by spouse	Tired wife agrees to sex to avoid husband's verbal abuse
Reward	Obtain rewards from spouse	Husband becomes less messy as wife praises him for helping keep a clean house
Legitimate	Spouse has the right to ask and you have duty to comply	Husband agrees to share household tasks with working wife because he is committed to equality
Expert	Spouse has special knowledge or expertise	Wife trusts husband's judgment about cars and lets him decide which one to buy
Referent	Identify with, and admire, spouse and want to please him or her	Husband goes to opera and tries to learn more about and enjoy operatic music that wife loves
Informational	Persuaded by spouse that what spouse wants is in your own best interests	Wife votes Democratic even though she is a Republican because husband convinces her that women will benefit more under Democrats

PERSPECTIVE
Unequal Before the Law

Inequities in marital power may be based not only on unequal resources but also on custom and even law. In the nineteenth century, American women had much less power than men in all realms of life, including marriage. Elizabeth Cady Stanton, a prominent feminist, wrote a letter to the *New York Tribune* in 1855 in which she pointed out some of the legal constraints faced by women:

> Now, it must strike every careful thinker that an immense difference rests in the fact that man has made the laws, cunningly and selfishly, for his own purpose. From Coke down to Kent, who can cite one clause of the marriage contract where woman has the advantage?
>
> In entering this compact, the man gives up nothing that he before possessed—he is a man still; while the legal existence of the woman is suspended during marriage, and henceforth she is known but in and through the

husband. She is nameless, purseless, childless—though a woman, an heiress, and a mother.

Blackstone says: "The husband and wife are one, and that one is the husband." Kent says:

> The legal effects of marriage are generally deducible from the principle of common law, by which the husband and wife are regarded as one person, and her legal existence and authority lost or suspended during the continuance of the matrimonial union.
>
> An unmarried woman can make contracts, sue and be sued, enjoy the rights or property, to her inheritance—to her wages—to her person—to her children; but in marriage, she is robbed by law of all and every natural civil right.
>
> The disability of the wife to contract, so as to bind herself, arises not from want of discretion, but because she has entered into an indissoluble connection

by which she is placed under the power and protection of her husband.
> —Kent, vol. 2, p. 127.

If the contract be equal, whence come the terms "marital power"—"marital rights"—"obedience and restraint"—"dominion and control"—"power and protection"—etc., etc.? Many cases are stated, showing the exercise of a most questionable power over the wife, sustained by the courts.

The laws on Divorce are quite as unequal as those of Marriage; yes, far more so. The advantages seem to be all on one side, and the penalties on the other. In case of divorce, if the husband be the guilty party, he still retains the greater part of the property. If the wife be the guilty party, she goes out of the partnership penniless.

Source: Excerpted from Stanton's letter to the *New York Tribune,* May 30, 1855.

---

that the six types represent differing kinds of resources that people have. In their study of 746 subjects, Raven, Centers, and Rodrigues (1975) found that the most common types of power that people perceive their spouses to exert are referent, expert, and legitimate. Women most frequently ascribed referent and expert power to their husbands. Men most frequently ascribed referent power to their wives, with legitimate power coming in a distant second. Of course, the type of power used depends on the situation. A decision about whether to visit a friend or relative is likely to be settled on the basis of legitimate or referent power. A decision about cleaning or repairing something in the home is likely to be settled by legitimate or expert power.

The type of power also varies by how satisfied the individual is with the marriage. Those in less

satisfactory marriages are far more likely to ascribe coercive power to their mates than those in satisfying unions.

MARRIAGE AS A POWER STRUGGLE

A wife says to her husband, "We're going to the movies tonight." He likes to go to the movies and is not even averse to going that night. Still, he doesn't like the way she has put it. She didn't ask whether he wanted to go. She simply informed him that they were going. He responds, therefore: "Not me. You can go if you want, but I'm staying home."

What has happened in this situation illustrates **reactance theory,** which states that when someone tries to force us to engage in a behavior, even though the behavior is consistent with our attitudes, we are likely to resist and may even change our attitudes (Brehm 1966). As stated earlier, we all need to have some control over our lives. At any time, there are a limited number of areas in which we feel we have a choice. We will not take lightly to someone trying to take one of those areas of choice away from us.

Thus, this couple had the beginnings of a power struggle over the choice of how to spend a free evening. It was an unnecessary struggle in that particular case, being spurred on by an unfortunate way of stating a desire. In other cases, the struggle can be more intense. Every marriage has some power struggles. Some are an ongoing struggle for power as long as the marriage lasts.

Types of Power Interaction

There are various ways that spouses can attempt to either exert or avoid power when communicating with each other (Fitzpatrick 1988:116–17). First, a conversation can be either *symmetrical* or *complementary*. In a symmetrical discussion, the two spouses send similar messages, messages designed to control how the relationship is defined. There are, in turn, three types of symmetrical discussions. In *competitive symmetry,* the couple is engaged in a situation of escalating conflict. For example, the husband may say: "I don't want to go out tonight. I've worked hard today." The wife responds: "You never want to go anywhere. I've worked hard, too, but you don't care how I feel about it." Each is trying to control the definition of the situation, and each is doing it in a way that escalates the conflict.

In *neutralized symmetry,* the spouses have respect for each other, and each tries to avoid exerting control. The wife says: "It looks like snow tonight." The husband responds: "If we go out, we better leave early and drive slowly." Each has left the way open for the other to express feelings about going out on a snowy night before they come to a final decision.

In *submissive symmetry,* both spouses try to give control to the other. A husband may say: "How are we going to pay all of our bills this month?" The wife may respond: "Please don't get upset. What do you think we should do?" Neither wants to take control of the situation.

In *complementary interaction,* the two spouses indicate agreement that one is dominant and the other submissive. For example, a husband may say: "Why don't you return this spotted shirt? You're better at that than I am." The wife responds: "Yes, I am. I'll do it." Or a husband may say: "Let's go to the ball game tonight. I don't feel like staying home." The wife responds, "Okay," even though baseball is not her favorite sport.

As the above illustrate, people do not always try to exert power. Sometimes they deliberately refrain from it, trying to relate to the spouse as an equal. Sometimes they try to give the power to the spouse or submit to a spouse who is exercising power. But sometimes both spouses try to take control. And in some marriages, the struggle goes on more or less continuously as every issue becomes a battleground on which to test the relative power of each.

CONFLICT IN MARRIAGE

If a couple is engaged in a power struggle, they are, by definition, having conflict. However, even if they are not in an ongoing power struggle, they will likely have conflict. The lack of conflict is not necessarily the sign of a good marriage. In fact, marriage counselors note that many of the couples who come to them have not been fighting. Some marriages die because the partners no longer care enough about each other to even fight. A healthy marriage, then, has some degree of conflict. The most important thing is how the conflict is handled. Kurdek (1995) studied 155 couples and found marital satisfaction related to styles of dealing with conflict. Other researchers, doing longitudinal research, have concluded that the most powerful predictor of whether a couple will break up or stay together is the way they handle their differences (Markman, Stanley, and Blumberg 1994; Gottman 1994).

The Functions of Conflict

Conflict can have both positive and negative consequences for a marriage. Few people enjoy interpersonal conflict, so it is easier for most of us to think of the negative rather than the positive consequences. The most negative, assuming that one or both partners wants to maintain the marriage, is dissolution. If the marriage is maintained and the conflict continues at a high intensity, spouses might find their self-esteem lowered, their enthusiasm for the marriage dissipating, their differences magnified, and their energy consumed. If there are children in the home, the conflict may lead to a variety of problems: a lowering of the children's self-esteem (Amato 1986); problems of emotional and behavioral adjustment when the conflict leads to divorce, due primarily to poorer mother-child relationships that tend to occur during the process of conflict and divorce (Kline, Johnston, and Tschann 1991); reduced family cohesion and a tendency for the family members to form coalitions (Gehring et al. 1990); and a lower quality of intimate relationships when the children mature (Albers, Doane, and Mintz 1986).

But conflict need not have such deleterious consequences. In fact, people who have some conflict and who handle it well tend to have higher levels of marital adjustment than others (Gottman and Krokoff 1989; Noller et al. 1994). By handling conflict appropriately, they enhance the quality of their relationship and create a more intense sense of intimacy. Their marriage is strengthened rather than threatened by the conflict. Well-managed conflict also has a number of other positive functions:

1. Conflict brings issues out into the open. The couple that engages in good fighting (see the example in #2) will avoid an interpersonal cold war and the resentments that tend to build and corrode the relationship.

2. Conflict helps clarify issues. Jack, a twenty-nine-year-old chemical engineer, is married to Donna, a teacher. He told us about a conflict that helped clarify an issue for them:

> We were on our way back from a ski trip. We've found that our car trips are often ideal times for marital communication. On this trip, Donna brought up the issue of cleaning up the dog's mess in the backyard. Before we got the dog, she had promised she would clean up after it. It was a job I didn't want. But now she was apparently tired of it. I told her I would only consider a change if she would offer me something in return. "Let's negotiate," I said. "If I clean it up, what will you do for me in return?" At that she got really angry. And we argued for most of the way home.
>
> Well, it turned out that she was really upset because she thought I wasn't carrying my share of the work around the house. The dog's mess allowed us to get to the heart of the matter, and we spent the last part of our trip working out an arrangement that made both of us feel better.

3. We can grow through conflict. We grow by striving, not by easing along. Handled properly, conflict will increase your awareness of the kind of person you are and can become (Coser 1956:33).

4. Small conflicts help to defuse more serious conflict. Molehills can become mountains. Ignoring small problems can lead to a buildup of resentment that will eventually explode in a more serious fight.

5. Conflict can create and maintain an equitable balance of power (Coser 1956:133). Two spouses who carry on conflict as equals, each affirming his or her own position and striving to understand the position of the other, demonstrate that each has power in the relationship. In other words, while conflict can be a manifestation of a power struggle, it can also be a means of establishing a power balance. Balanced power means a more satisfying relationship.

What People Fight About

Have you ever had an argument with someone knowing that what you supposedly were fighting about was not the real issue? For instance, we noted previously that although Jack and Donna started arguing over who was going to clean up after the dog, they were really fighting about a larger issue: the division of labor in the home. We need to be careful in conflict, therefore, to distinguish between overt and underlying issues. Sometimes what people initially argue about is the real issue, and sometimes it isn't. Conflict can only be constructive if you learn to focus on the real issue.

What are the issues over which people fight? Blood and Wolfe (1960) found that money issues (both producing and spending income) were the major area of conflict in about a fourth of the marriages they studied. Scanzoni (1970) reported that money issues were the major focus of conflict in 38 percent of marriages. The next most frequently named area of major conflict in both studies was children (discipline, how many to have, and so forth).

Money, children, and other issues such as sex continue to be major issues over which people have conflict. In satisfying marriages, couples argue about these same issues, but the amount of conflict tends to diminish over time. In her survey of 1,152

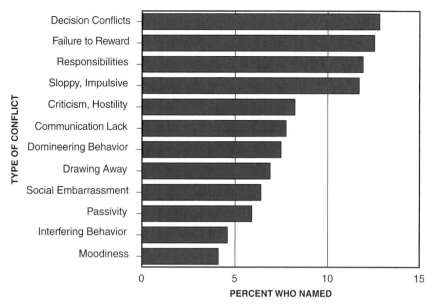

FIGURE 12.2   **Areas of Conflict in Intimate Relations**
(Source: Data from J. D. Cunningham, H. Braiker, and H.H. Kelly, *Psychology of Women Quarterly,* 6:421–422, 1982.)

spouses who have been married fifty or more years, Alford-Cooper (1998:86–7) found that the most common sources of conflict reported were "finances (29 percent), relatives (24 percent), ill health (24 percent), raising the children (21 percent), and the spouse's annoying habits (everything from snoring to alcoholism, 17 percent)."

In addition to these typical major issues, there are countless other topics that are the subject of marital conflict. In an effort to classify the things that people say they fight about into a small number of categories, three researchers asked fifty married and fifty cohabiting couples to describe four problems that occurred in their relationships (Cunningham, Braiker, and Kelley 1982). The spouses ranked the problems in order of their importance to their marriage and their happiness. The researchers were able to put the problems into twelve categories (figure 12.2). *Decision conflicts,* the most frequent of the categories, involves disagreement over such things as what to do, where to live, and allocation of time. *Failure to give attention/reward* includes lack of affection, too little sex, and inadequate appreciation and support. *Division and fulfillment of responsibility* refers to such matters as finances and who does which chores. *Sloppy, impulsive, or careless behavior* involves contrary standards about

neatness, spending money, being punctual, and so forth. These four categories accounted for about half of the problems.

For the most part, men and women—both married and cohabiting individuals—were similar in terms of how frequently they mentioned problems in each category. However, there were a few differences. Males reported *dependence on partner* and *passivity* (partner is too dependent, passive, indecisive, or lacking in motivation and self-confidence) four times as frequently as females and *sloppy, impulsive, or careless behavior* twice as often as females. The most frequent complaint by wives was *failure to give attention/reward.* Three times as many females (half of all the wives) as males reported such failure as a problem.

Finally, what about couples who are in serious trouble, serious enough to be seeing a therapist? What kinds of conflict do therapists see in marriages they counsel? Geiss and O'Leary (1981) have answered the question on the basis of responses from 116 professional therapists. They asked the therapists to estimate the proportion of couples they had seen during the past year who had complaints in each of twenty-nine areas. The results are shown in table 12.2. Communication was a problem for the bulk of the clients, a finding

TABLE 12.2
Mean Percentage of Couples Who Identified Problems
in 29 Areas of Marriage (based on therapists' estimates)

Problem Area	Mean Percentage of Couples	Problem Area	Mean Percentage of Couples
Communication	84	In-laws/relatives	29
Unrealistic expectations of marriage or spouse	56	Conventionality	27
		Jealousy	26
		Employment/job	24
Demonstration of affection	55	Recreation/ leisure time	24
Lack of loving feelings	55	Alcoholism	21
Sex	52	Problems related to previous marriage	20
Power struggles	52		
Decision making/ problem solving	49	Psychosomatic problems	20
Money management/ finances	39	Friends	19
Value conflicts	38	Addictive behavior other than alcoholism	14
Role conflict	38		
Children	37	Personal habits/ appearance	14
Serious individual problems	35	Physical abuse	12
Extramarital affairs	29	Religious differences	10
Household management	29	Health problems physical handicap	9
		Incest	5

Reprinted from Volume 7, Number 4 of *Journal of Marital and Family Therapy.* Copyright 1981 American Association for Marriage and Family Therapy. Reprinted by permission.

corroborated by researchers (Parker and Drummond-Reeves 1993). The therapists also rated communication problems as those that have the most damaging effect on the marital relationship. After communication, the therapists said that the ten most damaging problems are, in order of importance: unrealistic expectations of marriage or the spouse, power struggles, serious individual problems, role conflict, lack of loving feelings, demonstration of affection, alcoholism, extramarital affairs, and sex (Geiss and O'Leary 1981:516).

What, then, do people fight about? In general, everything and anything. But some problems are clearly more common than others, and some are more damaging to the relationship than others. The one problem that stands out as of overriding importance if the marriage is to survive and be healthy is communication. Both spouses must have, or learn, good communication skills or the conflict is likely to be destructive to the marriage.

Sources of Tension

To know what people fight about is not necessarily to know why they fight. As we have pointed out, few people fight because they enjoy conflict. Rather, a number of sources of tension in our lives make conflict inevitable. These sources are at various levels of social life. We are affected not only by our relationships but also by the organizations and the social institutions in which we necessarily function (Garbarino 1982). Accordingly, we will look at social, interpersonal, and personal sources of tension.

Social Sources   Issues about money are a common battleground in marriages. Those issues become more widespread and more acute in times of economic depression. In the years following the Great Depression of 1929, economic problems led to a serious decline in marital quality among working-class and middle-class couples (Liker and Elder 1983). Men who were no longer able to find work to support their families became tense, irritable, and even explosive. In general, tension and conflict increased in families as couples tried to adjust to diminished income. The lack of income led to another source of conflict for those couples forced to move into a parental home—often in cramped quarters. They found themselves facing problems with relatives and having conflict over those problems (Alford-Cooper 1998). We should note that the negative effects of the depression were not nearly so pronounced among those who had a strong marriage before the economic hard times. A strong marriage is a buffer against the stress of social adversity, though even in those marriages the difficult times increased the tension.

Thus, changes in the national economy can have a severe impact on marriage and family life. Financial stress increases the amount of both personal and interpersonal problems. Unemployment, for instance, can lead to mental illness, problems of physical health, depression, and violent behavior in the family, including child abuse (Ulrichson and Hira 1985). Unemployment, unfortunately, is something over which many people have little control. National recessions, depressed local economies, and such things as plant closings confront many people with short- or long-term unemployment. This is likely to mean tension and increased conflict in the marriage.

The economy also brings about adverse consequences in other ways. A high rate of inflation can add to our financial distress. Buying a first home, which is depicted in the media as a joyous event, can actually be extremely stressful (Meyer 1987). Moving to a new home is often disruptive and may create more financial stress than the couple anticipated. In some areas of the country, the price of new housing is so high that young couples despair of ever owning their own home, and some obtain a home only by going into an indebtedness that strains their relationship as well as their pocketbook.

Another social factor that creates tension in marriage is the illusions that prevail in our society. One such illusion is the notion that a marriage can be conflict-free. Whoever first coined that unfortunate phrase "happily ever after" has done a disservice to countless couples who are startled to find out that it

Financial strains can create both personal and marital distress.

can't be done. Starry-eyed young people who have such unrealistic expectations about marriage may find it difficult to cope with even minor disagreements with their spouses.

A second illusion is the belief that whatever problems there are, they will improve with time (Lasswell 1985). "Time heals all wounds" is another poor choice for a principle of life. In point of fact, a significant number of problems do not get better merely because of the passage of time. In a marriage, unless the spouses attend to them, minor problems can escalate into major problems rather than dissipating with time. Half of all serious marital problems arise in the first two years of marriage, but couples who come to marriage counselors have, on the average, been married for seven years.

Other illusions are the various unrealistic expectations we hold about marriage or the meaning of being a husband and a wife. The point here is that these illusions are rooted in our social context. The culture itself gives birth to these expectations through folklore, movies, books, and magazines. In that sense, our culture has not adequately prepared us for the realities of marriage.

Finally, various kinds of change in the society can combine to create tensions in the family. For example, many couples assume that their children will get a college education. Indeed, the job market seems to demand such an education. Yet the cost has soared in recent years. Yearly tuition and living expenses for a student at some private universities equals the total annual family income of a large number of Americans.

Or consider the following combination of changes. Young people are delaying marriage, and when they marry, they often wind up divorced. In addition, the cost of housing has increased dramatically and has made it difficult for young people to obtain a home of their own. The combination of these factors means that a good many adult children are living with their parents, often in less than harmonious circumstances. Also there is a tendency for marital conflict to increase between mother and father as parent-child conflict increases in such homes (Suitor and Pillemer 1987).

Thus, a number of sources of tension in the society come to bear on marriages. The tensions increase the frequency of marital conflict. Sometimes we fight because we are strained by factors that are beyond our control.

Interpersonal and Personal Sources   Of course, conflict also arises from tensions within the relationship and within the individual spouses. Psychiatrist Martin Goldberg (1987) points out six areas of marital interaction that underlie much of the conflict in a marriage. These include the areas of power and control, nurturance, intimacy and privacy, trust, fidelity, and differences in style. Goldberg says that while money, sex, child-rearing, in-laws, decisions about whether to have children, and substance abuse are the most common topics of disagreement, frequently we can understand arguments over such matters better by looking at the possible underlying causes.

First, then, there is the area of *power and control,* which is a matter of "who tells whom what to do and when." This is the area of interaction in

which power struggles occur, though they are often disguised. For instance, arguments about discipline of children may reflect the struggle of two competing philosophies of child-rearing for control of the situation. It becomes more than a matter of disagreement over the appropriate way to discipline; it becomes a matter of who will have the final say in how the children are reared.

Second, there is the area of *nurturance,* which is a matter of "who takes care of whom and how." Ideally, of course, each spouse takes care of the other's needs. When that happens, there is not likely to be conflict arising from this area. But if one of the partners feels neglected, conflict is likely. Goldberg (1987) gives the example of a couple, Ron and Jill, who had a harmonious marriage for the first five years. Ron was an insurance salesman. His job was sufficiently stressful and uncertain so that he needed, and received, Jill's continuing reassurance and emotional support. Then they had a baby. Their relationship began to steadily deteriorate. Jill increasingly focused her nurturing on the baby, and Ron became increasingly hostile and discontented. He began staying out late and drinking to excess. When Jill and Ron fought about his drinking and absence from the home, what was the real issue? Clearly, it was his need for nurturance, which was no longer being fulfilled.

Third, there is the area of *intimacy and privacy,* which involves the amount of interaction versus the amount of aloneness that each partner desires. People who complain that their spouses won't give them "their space," that their spouses tend to "smother" them, or that their spouses are detached and distant all have problems in this area of intimate interaction. If both partners have roughly the same needs for intimacy and privacy, their relationship will be harmonious in this area. If their needs are widely different, they are likely to have serious conflict. A divorced woman told us that she finally left her husband of seven years because she had to have her space:

> Phil is a loving, caring man. But I grew up in a home where we just didn't do a lot of touching and feeling. I was the only child, and I spent a lot of time by myself. I still prefer to spend hours alone. Phil couldn't handle that. And I couldn't handle his wanting to be around me all the time. Even when we were fighting about other things, like going somewhere or whether

to have friends over, the real problem was the difference in how much we wanted to be together and with other people.

Trust is the fourth area of interaction that can give rise to problems. Trust is basic to a marriage. Couples can argue about many things and still have a satisfying marriage if there is a basic foundation of trust. When trust declines or is lacking, the relationship is likely to deteriorate and may sink into a series of severe arguments. If you don't trust your spouse, if you don't have a firm sense that your spouse is honest, supportive, and loyal, you will probably find yourself continually challenging your spouse on a variety of issues. When a spouse isn't trusted, then all sorts of behavior become suspect—being late, going somewhere alone, being with a friend of the opposite sex, mild criticism of your behavior, and so on. The real issue is not the behavior of the spouse but the lack of trust. Thus, a husband says to his wife, "That color of red doesn't look very good on you." In a situation of little trust, she may translate his statement into something like: "He is criticizing me. He finds other women more attractive than he finds me. He doesn't really like me anymore."

The fifth area of interaction involves *fidelity,* which means more than sexual faithfulness: "it can be more precisely defined as general adherence to one's marital vows" (Goldberg 1987:48–49). In other words, it is faithfulness to the expectations that the spouses had for each other when they were married. That means that you can commit infidelity without ever having a sexual relationship with someone else. Goldberg provides the example of Rita and Jeff, who have been married for three turbulent years. When they were married, they wrote their wedding vows and pledged to put each other first above all other people. Each claims that the other has broken the vows. Jeff insists that Rita is spending an inordinate amount of time with her parents, who live a short distance from them. He says that she has given them priority over him. Rita, on the other hand, says that Jeff gives priorities to three of his old friends, with whom he spends a good deal of time at local bars. Neither has been sexually unfaithful to the other, but their marriage is in serious trouble in the area of fidelity.

Finally, there are *differences in style* that underlie many conflicts. Differences in style include diverse preferences for recreation and for order versus clutter. Differences in style also involve diverse ways of thinking and dealing with problems. Some people are more emotional than others. Some are more rational. Some people confront anxiety-provoking situations head on; some shrink from them and try to deny their existence. There are numerous ways in which people differ from each other that can result in conflicts (recall our earlier discussion about the importance of homogamy for a satisfying marriage). The important point for couples is to recognize when these differences in style are the actual issue rather than something else about which they are fighting.

For example, Vern and Sally, two young professionals, fought continually about leisure time. He preferred to stay home and read the paper, plan his investments, and watch television. She preferred to have dinner out and then go dancing or attend a movie. Each thought the other was being obstinate and dull. Neither thought of the problem in terms of differences in style, neither of which was inherently bad or wrong. Neither thought in terms of some compromise that would accord the other a measure of leisure satisfaction until they worked through their problem with a marriage counselor.

These six areas of interaction can be sources of tension in a marriage. When the tension erupts into conflict, the fighting will be most productive if the couple recognizes the underlying issue.

STYLES OF CONFLICT

How do you handle conflict? That is, do you see yourself as basically a "no-holds-barred" type of person, a conflict-avoider, a reasonable individual who will fight only if necessary, or something else? You probably have a dominant style, and you will use that style consistently in various situations of interpersonal conflict (Sternberg and Dobson 1987). Whether the conflict is with a lover, a spouse, a relative, a boss, a co-worker, or a neighbor, we tend to be consistent in our style of fighting.

Social scientists who specialize in interpersonal conflict have identified five different styles (Wilmot and Wilmot 1978). Each of us tends primarily to use one or two of them with which we feel most comfortable. The styles differ in terms of how concerned we are with our own interests versus how

INVOLVEMENT
Fighting: From "I Do" 'til Death

We have listed the major areas of marital conflict in this section. We should point out, however, that the amount of conflict and the things that people fight about vary over the course of a marriage. A man married thirty years told us: "We have arguments from time to time. But we fought more in the first six months of our marriage than we did over the next thirty years."

How much difference is there over time in the frequency of conflict and the kinds of things that people fight about? In this project, you will attempt to answer the question. Interview six people who have been married five years or less, six who have been married fifteen to twenty years, and six who have been married thirty or more years. (You may want to work with two others,

and each of you can interview six people in one of the categories.)

Prepare a questionnaire for your subjects (your instructor can help with this). Tell them that you are researching the amount and kinds of conflict in marriages. Point out that their names will not be on the questionnaire and that you would appreciate a frank response. On the questionnaire, have them record their age, sex, and number of years married. Have them circle their response to the following:

How frequently do you and your spouse have arguments?

1. Never
2. Less than once a month
3. Once or twice a month
4. Once or twice a week
5. Daily

Then let them respond to an open-ended question: What are the issues or topics about which you and your spouse argue?

Tabulate the responses by number of years married. Are there any differences in frequency or in the kinds of things that people say they argue about? What are they? How would you explain the differences or lack of differences? Also note if there are any differences in the responses given by men and women.

If the entire class participates in this project, group all of the responses for each of the three categories (number of years married). The larger number of responses will give you more confidence in answering the above questions.

concerned we are about the interests of the people with whom we are fighting.

One style is *competition,* which involves a high concern for oneself and a low concern for the other. If this is your dominant style, you view conflict as a kind of war. The object is to win the fight, not to be concerned about the other person. A competitive spouse is a dominant spouse, one who has to always be ahead in the struggle for power in the marriage. If both spouses are competitive in their conflict style, the fighting may become vicious and protracted. It is easy for Americans to enter a marriage as competitors, of course, because our culture teaches us to be competitive. We are socialized through the schools and the media to approach life as competitors. Unfortunately, it isn't the best preparation for a marriage.

Avoidance is the second style. If you are an avoider, you have little concern either for your own interests or for the interests of the other. You are mainly concerned about maintaining peace, even if the peace is a hollow or destructive one because dif-

ferences are never resolved. Such peace will be hollow or destructive because the interests of the partners may be thwarted by the lack of conflict. For example, a woman who resents her husband's lack of affection may say nothing because she doesn't want to engage in an argument. She values peace highly. But she is serving neither her own interests nor those of her husband well. Instead, she is putting her marriage into jeopardy. The hazards of avoidance are underscored in research by Crohan (1992), who studied 133 African American and 149 white couples. She found that those couples who believed that conflict should be avoided were less happy over the two-year period of the research than couples who used other styles.

Third, *accommodation* is the opposite of competition. It is a neglect of one's own interests in order to pursue the interests of the other. If you are an accommodator, you may engage in the conflict, but you will always give in to your partner. Unlike the avoider, you do not shrink away from all conflict. But neither can you assert your own interests in the

In school, we learn to be competitive, but competition between spouses can be destructive.

face of those of your partner. Ultimately, you give in because you do not want to offend or deny your partner.

Compromise involves some concern about both one's own interests and the interests of the other. "Some" concern means a moderate amount, enough to seek a solution that is satisfactory to both people but not enough to struggle for an optimal solution. If you are a compromiser, you will assert yourself in conflict, but you will moderate your position when necessary in order to reach an outcome that is acceptable to both yourself and your partner.

Finally, *collaboration* is the opposite of avoidance. It is a high degree of concern both for one's own interests and for the interests of the partner. If you are a collaborator, you will pursue your own interests vigorously while still maintaining a high degree of concern for the interests of your partner. You will not allow your partner to accommodate himself or herself to you. You will not want him or

her even to compromise. You want to continue the struggle until you have an optimal solution, one that is in the best interests of each of you. As may be evident, collaboration is time- and energy-consuming. In some cases, it may not even be possible to collaborate (when one of the spouses strongly prefers to keep things as they are, so that any new arrangement will be a compromise for that spouse). Still, when it is possible, collaboration is the best way to work out conflict in marriage.

We will illustrate the styles with an example. A husband and wife both work. They have two children. For years, the husband has allowed the wife to do the cooking and to assume the major burden of responsibility for the home. He believes that this is appropriate. She resents it. How might she react? If she is an avoider, she will say nothing. She will continue to agonize inwardly and battle with her growing resentment. If she is a competitor, she probably confronted her husband early in their marriage, and insisted that he do his share of work. She may even have tried to get him to do more than would have satisfied her. If she is an accommodator, she might have stood up to him initially but backed down when he insisted that the home was her responsibility. If she is a compromiser, she would have battled with him until they had worked out a division of labor that was acceptable to each. If she is a collaborator, she would have persisted until they not only had an acceptable division of labor, but each was convinced that the solution enhanced their individual and their interpersonal well-being.

Of course, the outcome would depend on the husband's style as well as the wife's. Some combinations, such as two competitors or two avoiders, can be disastrous for a marriage. Some combinations, such as a competitor and an accommodator, may be efficient but not necessarily conducive to maximizing the well-being of both partners. Other combinations, such as two collaborators or a collaborator and a compromiser or two compromisers, are more conducive to a stable and satisfying relationship.

We should note two things here. First, you can change your style. It is important to know what your dominant style is, how you tend to approach interpersonal conflict. But if that style does not help your relationships, you can change it. Second, each of the styles is appropriate at some time or other. There are times when a spouse who is typically,

PERSONAL
Learning How to Fight

Joshua was married three years ago while he was still in graduate school. He and his wife, Kay, each began their marriage with a dominant style of conflict. Both found that they had to change their style if their marriage was to survive and be mutually satisfying. Joshua talks about the way in which they discussed their styles and agreed to change:

Kay and I had a rough way to go for a while. She came from a large family where she learned to handle conflict primarily by avoiding it. I, on the other hand, preferred the "bull-in-the-china-shop" approach. I tended to try to control other people by rational argument, by persuasive charm, or by open hostility. I did whatever it took to win.

It didn't take long for us to realize that our approaches to our differences were very destructive. But it wasn't easy to give them up. We had used them for too many years. We talked about our ways of fighting. I told her that she made me furious by not confronting our differences. I resented it when she would clam up or shut down if she felt threatened. She said that I intimidated and frustrated her by my aggressiveness. She said that sometimes she even felt rage because I was willing to "hit below the belt" if necessary to control things.

We got some books and read what the experts had to say.

Then we talked about whether we could change and learn how to solve our differences by listening, caring, and negotiation. That's what the books told us to do, but neither of us had tried those methods before. We started working on our differing approaches about a year ago. For me, it has mainly been a matter of learning to shut up and listen, *really* listen with compassion and acceptance. I have to learn not to come at our differences like a prize fighter. For her, it has been a matter of becoming more assertive, open, and confident about verbalizing her feelings and her thoughts.

It hasn't been easy. We still break the rules at times. But we're getting better at it. We are learning to fight effectively. Actually, we don't even fight as much anymore. Some of our fights were about the ways we were fighting and not about other things. Now that we're better at handling conflict, we feel a much more intense intimacy. That's something new for me. I always felt good about winning fights before. It's been a kind of a thrill to feel more intimate when we've handled an argument well together. I still feel like a winner, even if I don't get what I wanted.

say, a compromiser should be an accommodator (if the issue is more important to the partner). There are times when it is best to avoid certain conflicts (when one or both spouses are tired or too agitated to be reasonable). No single style is appropriate for every situation, but some are better than others as a dominant style.

GOOD FIGHTING

Androgynous and masculine spouses tend to have a more constructive approach to interpersonal conflict than do feminine or undifferentiated spouses (Yelsma and Brown 1985). However, neither your gender role nor your dominant style can prevent you from learning the principles of good fighting. In our study of long-term marriages, we discovered eight principles that couples in happy marriages use to engage in constructive conflict. Each principle is not necessarily appropriate for every conflict, but the principles comprise a set of tools that can be used to ensure that marital conflict is "good fighting" rather than destructive.

Maintain Your Perspective

There are some things not worth fighting about. "We don't treat everything as a disaster," as one husband put it. People who fight over trivial matters are probably engaging in a power struggle. Couples who have a strong relationship save their energies for the issues that are really important. This means that sometimes one spouse simply accommodates the other or that both spouses recognize that the issue is trivial and decide to avoid it.

Develop Tension Outlets

We noted above that there are tensions in life that can lead to marital conflict. Whether you are a student, a business person, or a homemaker, you probably have a sufficient amount of tension in your life so that you need some kind of outlet for it. Humor, exercise, meditation, and sports are some of the tension outlets that people use. You need to find something that works for you and use it to get rid of some of the tension that otherwise can erupt into conflict in your intimate relationships.

Avoid Festering Resentment

If accommodating your partner means you have maintained your perspective on an issue that is trivial to you, the accommodation is useful. If it means that you are denying your own interests and building resentment, the accommodation is destructive. It is vital to openly confront those things that are important to you and to resolve them. People in long-term, happy marriages do not allow their conflict to continue indefinitely on a hot- or cold-war basis.

Avoiding the buildup of resentment means that each partner must be open and honest about his or her feelings. Spouses should not have to speculate or guess about the feelings of each other. That can lead to misinterpretation and more serious conflict. For example, a man may have a grim look on his face. He has had some serious problems at work and is concerned about job security. But he says nothing. His wife tries to interpret his grimness and decides that he is angry at her for some reason. That makes her angry. He senses this and becomes even moodier, wondering why he can't have some warmth and security at home when his work is so problematic. They speak curtly and coldly with each other. Each resents what the other is doing, but neither has any understanding of what has happened.

Be Sensitive to Timing

Many conflicts that could otherwise have been handled constructively work out badly for a couple simply because they occurred at the wrong time:

> Openly confronting conflict does not necessarily mean immediate attention to an issue. Some people are receptive to problem-solving in the morning and some in the evening. Few if any people can handle conflict well when they are exhausted. In addition, there are times when it is simply inappropriate to raise an issue. The wife who criticizes her husband's appearance just as they are walking into a party, or the husband who angrily tells his wife in front of friends that she neglects his needs both illustrate insensitivity to timing (Lauer and Lauer 1986:125).

Another time at which it is usually best to avoid conflict is when one of the spouses is extremely angry. Conflict can only be constructive to the relationship when both people can function rationally as well as emotionally.

Communicate Without Ceasing

While communication is not a cure-all, it is important not to handle conflict with the silent treatment or by simply hoping that everything will turn out well with the passage of time. Couples who avoid confronting a problem, who rely on the passage of time to dissipate the issue, tend to have a lower quality of intimacy and marriages that are less satisfying (Alford-Cooper 1998:94). In resolving issues, of course, it is the quality of communication and not simply the fact of communication that is important. Recall from the last chapter that listening is a crucial part of effective communication. In conflict, we are particularly prone to want to make our own point rather than to listen carefully to what the other is saying.

In addition, the communication must possess a certain calmness. A study of 130 newlyweds found that those couples in the happiest unions dealt with their problems by discussing them with "gentleness, soothing, and de-escalation of negativity" (Gottman et al. 1998:17). De-escalation of negativity means that if one partner exhibits negative emotions, such as anger, the other tries to de-escalate by not becoming angry in turn. Rather than fueling the process of anger, the partner responds with relative calmness.

De-escalating a process of increasing negative emotion is crucial. The most satisfied couples—however long they have been married—use more affection (see the next point) and less negative emotion to resolve their differences (Carstensen, Gottman and Levenson 1995). It's easy to see why. Anger, for example, can result in verbal aggression, in saying things that one will later regret and that reflect the anger of the moment rather than fundamental feelings. Nearly every one of the three hundred happily married couples in our long-term marriage project advised against arguing when one or both of the spouses is very angry. As one wife of thirty-three years said: "Find something to do until you are both calm, and then talk things out."

Be Flexible, Willing to Compromise

People who are happily married for many years believe in the importance of both accommodation and compromise in conflict. Give in when the issue does not matter that much to you and prepare to compromise when the issue is important to you. Collaboration is desirable but not always practical. Compromise, therefore, is not a surrender and not an acceptance of an inferior solution. Rather, compromise may frequently be the only realistic way to handle differences between two people, each of whom understands both his or her own needs and interests and those of the spouse.

Use Conflict to Attack Problems, Not Your Spouse

This is one of the most important principles. It stresses the fact that a couple needs to approach conflict as a problem-solving rather than a spouse-bashing exercise (Gottman 1994). If you are very angry or frustrated, you may tend to attack your spouse as the cause of your agony. Your energies will better serve your relationship if they are directed toward the problem. Define the conflict as a disagreement, as a problem that must be solved together, rather than as a battle of personalities (Markman, Stanley, and Blumberg 1994). As a husband put it: "We always have good outcomes from our arguments if we remember one simple rule. Namely, that we each must approach our disagreement by saying to the other, 'We have a problem,' rather than 'You are a problem.' "

Keep Loving While You Are Fighting

Marital therapists point out that at times spouses are going to fight unfairly. Exaggerated positions, extreme statements, and some "low blows" are likely to occur at times in any relationship. Nevertheless, the couples in our study insisted that the goal is to keep loving while you are fighting. Loving and fighting may sound like incompatible activities. But two things should be kept in mind. First, in line with the last principle, good fighting involves an attack on a problem rather than on the spouse. And second, the love we are talking about here is agapic love, acting out of concern for the well-being of the other independently of our feelings at the moment. Thus, when you refuse to hurt your partner during conflict (by, e.g., not throwing out cutting remarks that you know will injure him or her), you are continuing to love. To keep the conflict within the bounds of reason, to avoid attacking the spouse, to, as one wife put it, keep in mind the things you like about your spouse even while you are fighting are some of the ways that you can continue to love during conflict.

It is important to keep loving even when you are fighting.

PRINCIPLES FOR ENHANCING INTIMACY

1. Individuals need power; that is, each of us needs some degree of control over our lives. Moreover, this need for power extends into our marriages. There are situations—some critical, others less so—when we need to influence or wield power over our spouse. Power, of course, can be abused. We unfortunately may attempt to dominate or totally control our partner. In a satisfying marriage, however, each spouse has power and shares it on a generally equal basis.

2. Power struggles and conflict in a marriage are not necessarily destructive. In fact, they can be an indication of a healthy and vital relationship and should be treated as such. When a conflict arises, it should be viewed as a shared problem that needs a solution and not as a sign that the relationship is doomed.

3. In order to deal positively with a conflict in marriage, it is essential to identify the true source of the difficulty. If, for example, the problem concerns financial arrangements, then you need to focus on money matters, not on extraneous factors, such as blaming your in-laws for overindulging your spouse or complaining about the tax policies of the federal government. Instead, examine your spending patterns: Are you overextending yourselves financially? Are you trying to buy too large of a house or too expensive of a car too quickly? Are you buying too much on credit? Concentrating on the real nature of your conflict takes insight, determination, and courage. But it is essential to a meaningful resolution of your problems.

4. Effective handling of conflict takes patience and persistence. However, you can build your skills by consulting the experts—books and articles written by professionals in marriage and the family, marriage enrichment seminars, as well as mature and successful couples. Learn the secrets of "good fighting" from them and then consistently apply them in your marriage.

5. People deal with conflict in different ways. In order to deal constructively with problems and power struggles, it is important for you to understand your own as well as your partner's style of handling conflict. You may find that it is essential for you to accommodate, to some extent, your style to that of your partner if solutions are to be found.

SUMMARY

Power is the ability to get someone to think or feel or act in a way that he or she would not have done spontaneously. The use of power is not inherently negative or wrong. It can be used to help as well as to control others. Marital power has typically been measured on the basis of which spouse makes the final decisions. Power is important to both our personal and our marital well-being.

Resource theory asserts that we get power from the resources we bring to a relationship, including income, emotional support, sexual availability, and parenting skills. The principle of least interest says that the partner with the least interest in maintaining the relationship has the most power. Six types of power can be used in marriage: coercive, reward, legitimate, expert, referent, and informational.

Marriage may be analyzed as a power struggle. Spouses attempt to exert or avoid power when communicating with each other. In a symmetrical discussion, the two spouses send similar messages that are designed to control how the relationship is defined. In complementary discussion, the two spouses indicate agreement that one is dominant and the other is submissive.

Like power, conflict can have both positive and negative consequences for a marriage. Among the positive results are that issues are brought into the open and clarified, people may grow through conflict, small conflicts diffuse more serious conflict, and conflict can create and maintain an equitable balance of power.

Money, children, and other issues, such as sex, continue to be major issues over which people have conflict. Therapists report that troubled couples who come to them are most likely to have problems in the areas of communication, unrealistic expectations, showing and feeling love and affection, sex, and power struggles.

A number of sources of tension make marital conflict inevitable. Social sources include the vagaries of the economy, cultural illusions about marriage, and various kinds of social change. Interpersonal and personal sources include such things as issues of power and control, nurturance, intimacy and privacy, trust, fidelity, and differences in style.

Common styles of conflict include competition, avoidance, accommodation, compromise, and collaboration. "Good fighting" occurs when a couple follows certain principles, such as maintaining perspective, developing tension outlets, avoiding festering resentment, being sensitive to timing, continuing to communicate, being willing to compromise, using conflict to attack problems rather than the spouse, and continuing to love the spouse even while fighting.

INTERNET CONNECTION
Power and Conflict in Marriage

Six types of power are described as being at play in marriages: coercive, reward, legitimate, expert, referent, informational. Conflict is an inevitable and potentially productive aspect of long term relationships and marriage. Being able to identify differing styles of conflict can help enhance the ability of partners in coping with conflicts that arise. Many view an individual's ability to recognize and effectively deal with power and conflict styles in relationships as an attribute of emotional intelligence. The following websites introduce the concept of emotional intelligence:

www.mhhe.com/lauer4

Learning about Emotional Intelligence
http://www.6seconds.org/eq/eq.html

Become familiar with the basic concepts of emotional intelligence by reading material in the EQ Fundamentals section of this website. Take the Utne Reader EQ Test, hotlinked to the Journey of 1000 miles section of this website.

1. Using the material at this website or others you can find, try to define emotional intelligence and EQ?
2. What is the relationship of emotional intelligence to aggression and conflict?
3. How can a heightened awareness of emotional intelligence help partners better manage their conflicts?

CHAPTER 13

WORK AND HOME

Learning Objectives

After reading chapter 13, you should be able to:

1. Outline the historical trends in female employment and the impact of these trends on male and female roles.

2. Define the differences between the dual-earner and the dual-career family.

3. Discuss the reasons that some women prefer to work outside the home and others prefer to stay at home.

4. Show the extent to which female employment outside the home has resulted in more egalitarian marriages.

5. Characterize the various types of dual-career families.

6. Understand the problems as well as the satisfactions of dual-career families.

7. Describe the challenges that dual-earner couples face and the extent to which they can achieve marital satisfaction.

8. Explain how dual-earner couples negotiate conflicting role demands.

9. Discuss the effect that working outside the home has on women's physical and emotional health.

10. Relate the various coping strategies that are available to employed women.

In the 1950s, "I Love Lucy" was one of the most popular television shows. A mother who grew up watching and enjoying the show told us: "I won't let my children watch the reruns. I was stunned when I realized how sexist the show was." One of the sexist aspects that angered the woman was the fact that Lucy always wanted to work outside the home, but her husband wouldn't allow it. A decade or so later, the "Bob Newhart Show" was one of the most popular. He was a psychologist and his wife, Emily, was a teacher. They had a two-career marriage. By this time, increasing numbers of women, including wives on television, were working outside the home.

These two shows dramatize the change in attitudes and behavior about work that has occurred in American society. In this chapter, we will look at those changes. We will discuss why women have entered the labor force in large numbers and the impact that employed wives and mothers have on individual and family well-being.

HIS WORK AND HER WORK

Throughout most of human history, the great majority of people lived on farms or in peasant villages. As historian Carl Degler (1980:5) has pointed out, for nearly everyone

> the family was a cooperative economic unit, with children and mother working along with husband, even though usually there was a division of labor by gender. . . . Even those relatively few families which lived and worked in towns acted as cooperative enterprises in their shops, inns, and other businesses. Home and work were close together, and wife and husband participated in both.

This situation changed rapidly and dramatically with the rise of industrialization.

Industrialization meant that some of the things women did in the home, such as making clothes, would increasingly be done in the factory or shop. Women did continue, of course, to cook and clean and nurture their families. But in the emerging industrial economy, paid labor became a primary source of income and the essence of the meaning of *work*. What women did in the home was no longer defined as *work*.

The role of "housewife," or homemaker, developed in this context. It is a role that can be described in terms of four characteristics (Oakley 1974). First, it is allocated almost exclusively to women. Second, it is associated with economic dependence, because the homemaker must lean on her husband for support. Third, it is defined generally as *nonwork*, or at least as not *real* work. This is illustrated by the response often given by some homemakers to the question, "Do you work?" The answer is, "No, I'm just a homemaker." Of course even those who respond in this way recognize that homemaking is every bit as demanding and exhausting as any work outside the home. Indeed, men who spend time taking care of a house and children understand that homemaking is *real* work. Nevertheless, one characteristic of the role of homemaker is the definition of it as nonwork. The fourth characteristic of the role is that it is given priority by women over other roles. Housework and child care are considered the primary responsibilities of the homemaker, responsibilities that must take priority over anything else that a woman might wish to do (such as outside employment or a career). Around 1900, if a married woman was employed, people thought that something was wrong. "Her husband was absent, crippled, or incompetent" (Degler 1980:386).

Since the rise of industrialization, then, there has been a tendency for "his" work to be paid labor outside the home and "her" work to be that of the homemaker. "Her" work has a number of drawbacks that "his" work may not have. The homemaker is relatively isolated in her work and frequently has to cope with the problem of loneliness. If she has children, she may not be lonely, but she feels keenly the need for adult interaction. Housework also tends to be repetitive, boring, and endless.

This is not to say that homemakers all loathe what they do. Many women who have spent the bulk of their lives as homemakers indicate great satisfaction. But clearly a great number of women have not found the role to be adequate to their needs. As we shall see in the next section, over the past few decades women have been opting for employment or career roles in great numbers.

CHANGING PATTERNS OF WORKING

Earlier in our history, some people argued that "his" work and "her" work reflected human nature. That is, they believed that men are programmed for work outside the home and women are programmed for being homemakers. Yet the forces that kept most women in the home in the past were social and cultural, not biological. In recent decades, the situation has changed dramatically.

Women in the Labor Force

At the turn of the century, only about one out of five adult women were in the labor force. By 1940, the rate was still less than a third of the female population. The rate increased during World War II, then fell again after the war was over. In the 1960s and 1970s, however, the proportion of women going into the labor force increased rapidly (table 13.1). Over half of women aged sixteen and above are now in the labor force. We should note that working- and lower-class women have always been more likely than middle-class women to be in the labor force. For example, the famous "Middletown" study found that almost half of working-class wives

TABLE 13.1

The Female Labor Force: 1940 to 1996 (persons 14 years old and over through 1965; 16 years old and older thereafter)

Year	Number (1,000)	Percent of Female Population
1940	13,840	27.4
1950	17,795	31.4
1960	22,516	34.8
1970	31,233	42.6
1980	45,487	51.5
1990	56,829	57.5
1996	61,857	59.3

Source: U.S. Bureau of the Census 1988:373 and 1997b:398.

in Muncie, Indiana, were employed full-time during the early 1920s (Caplow et al. 1982:97).

It is important to keep in mind that the labor force includes part-time and full-time workers and those who are unemployed but looking for work. Interestingly, while the participation of women has been steadily going up, that of men has been steadily going down (figure 13.1). In addition, the proportion of families in which the man is the sole breadwinner has dropped dramatically, from 42 percent in 1960 to 15 percent in the late 1980s (Wilkie 1991). We appear headed toward a labor force equally divided between men and women and toward families in which very few men function as the sole breadwinner. Some people interpret this as part of the "decline" of the family and a deviation from the historic pattern. But as Stephanie Coontz (1997) has pointed out, it was not until the 1920s that the majority of American children lived in a home where the husband was the sole breadwinner, the wife was a homemaker, and the children could attend school rather than work for wages. In other words, the male as sole breadwinner is a deviation, not the norm, in the history of American family life.

Married Women and Employment

The figures in table 13.1 are for all women, whether single, married, separated, divorced, or widowed. Moreover, some of the women are in jobs and some are pursuing careers. These are important distinctions that need to be addressed.

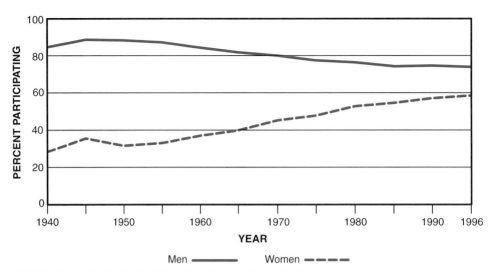

FIGURE 13.1   Civilian Labor Force Participation Rates, by Sex
(*Sources:* U.S. Bureau of the Census 1975:131–32; 1990:378; and 1997b:397.)

TABLE 13.2

**Marital Status and Labor Force Participation Rates[1] of Women with Children: 1960 to 1996
(for women 14 years and older in 1960; thereafter, 16 years and older)**

Year	Total			Children 6 to 17			Children under 6		
	Single	**Married**	**Other**[2]	**Single**	**Married**	**Other**[2]	**Single**	**Married**	**Other**[2]
1960	(NA)	27.6	56.0	(NA)	39.0	65.9	(NA)	18.6	40.5
1970	(NA)	39.7	60.7	(NA)	49.2	66.9	(NA)	30.3	52.2
1980	52.0	54.1	69.4	67.6	61.7	74.6	44.1	45.1	60.3
1990	55.2	66.3	74.2	69.7	73.6	79.7	48.7	58.9	63.6
1996	60.5	70.0	77.0	71.8	76.7	80.6	55.1	62.7	69.2

NA: Not available.[1] Percent of women in each specific category in the labor force.[2] Widowed, divorced, or separated.
Source: U.S. Bureau of the Census 1997b:404.

Marital and Family Status of Employed Women   Table 13.2 shows the labor force participation rates for women with varying marital statuses. Note that the most dramatic increase in participation rates has occurred among married women with children under the age of six—the proportion more than tripled from 1960 to 1996. In fact, 59.1 percent of white mothers and 70.2 percent of black mothers with children one year old or younger are now in the labor force (U.S. Bureau of the Census 1997b:404).

Clearly, women have opted for worker as well as homemaker roles. Again, we need to keep in mind that substantial numbers of married women are not in the labor force. While a slight majority of women with infants prefer to work, a considerable number prefer to stay home and care for their children themselves. The important point is that women have options, and many of them are opting for different roles than those of their mothers and grandmothers.

Jobs and Careers   Some women who work have a job. Others are in a career. We can distinguish between jobs and careers in a number of ways. Careers normally require extensive training—a college education or even graduate school. Careers tend to be more structured in that there is a pattern of mobility people tend to follow. In the university, for instance, you may begin as an instructor and gradually move up to the position of full professor.

The majority of women are in the labor force.

Moving up through the ranks is a common pattern in education, business, government, and social service agencies. Careers may also be pursued by individuals such as therapists. In that case, mobility may involve moving from being an assistant to another therapist, to one's own practice, to the head of one's own clinic. Finally, a career involves commitment. You can frequently take or leave a particular job, but if you are in a career, you probably have a commitment to go as far as you can. You want to get to the top of your field, or as close to the top as possible.

The distinction between job and career leads to the important distinction between a **dual-earner** and **dual-career** family. The dual-earner family is one in which both spouses are involved in paid work, and one or both view the work only as a job. In other words, one of the spouses in the dual-earner family may be pursuing a career, while the other is merely holding down a job. In the dual-career family, on the other hand, both spouses are engaged in careers, which means that both are committed to employment that has a long-term pattern of mobility.

The dual-career family is a type of dual-earner family. In the dual-career family, there is no assumption that either spouse will subordinate his or her career to the interests of the other, and both are committed to combining professional and family roles. As may be clear already, such a family places a lot of demands on the spouses and has a great deal of potential for conflict and stress (see "Problems of Dual-Career Families" later in this chapter). Unfortunately, we do not know how many of the women who work outside the home are holding jobs and how many are involved in a career. In either case, however, a problem arises over who will do the "family work," the housekeeping and child care that formerly were the work of the homemaker.

Who's Minding the House?

With a declining proportion of men in the labor force, a growing emphasis on egalitarian marriages, an increasing number of women who work outside the home and contribute to the support of the family, and a decline in the proportion of Americans who believe that women rather than men should take care of the home (Spain and Bianchi 1996), you would expect a greater sharing by men and women of family work. In point of fact, there is more sharing. Married mothers spend less time on household tasks than they did in the 1960s (Spain and Bianchi 1996). At the same time, the amount of time that men spend in household tasks has increased substantially (Robinson and Godbey 1997).

Husbands are more likely to assume increased responsibility for household tasks when they have high levels of education; have wives with educational levels similar to theirs; have egalitarian attitudes about gender and family roles; are in, along with their wives, professional or managerial occupations; earn about the same, rather than significantly more than, their wives; and have somewhat different work schedules than their wives, so that they are the only parent at home during certain hours of the day or evening (Presser 1994; Brayfield 1995; Harpster and Monk-Turner 1998).

In spite of the progress toward equality, however, wives who work outside the home are still likely to spend substantially more hours than their husbands on housework (Rosenbluth, Steil, and Whitcomb 1998). This inequity occurs in other nations as well. A study of 115 dual-income Canadian couples reported that the mothers in the labor force did twice as many family chores as did their husbands (Huppe and Cyr 1997).

There is also a tendency for men and women to engage in traditional kinds of tasks (Blair and Lichter 1991). Some tasks are shared. But women are more likely to do the cooking, dish washing, housecleaning, laundry, and ironing. And men are more likely to do household repairs and outdoor chores. Those husbands who are willing to assume more of the traditional female tasks tend to be urban, nonwhite, well educated, and egalitarian in their attitudes (Harpster and Monk-Turner 1998).

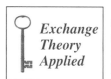 *Exchange Theory Applied*

Thus, while there has been some change, considerable inequity exists when measured by sheer number of hours. We know that a *sense of equity* is important to marital satisfaction. And their husbands' contributions to household tasks are important determinants of women's sense of equity in the relationship (Sanchez 1994). Why, then, isn't there widespread dissatisfaction among employed wives? Interestingly, most women believe the situation to be fair, particularly those who perceive themselves to have fewer alternatives to marriage and less economic resources (Lennon and Rosenfield 1994). In other words, because they have few or no alternatives, they believe that they are getting out of the marriage enough to justify what they are putting into it.

WHY DO WOMEN WANT TO WORK OUTSIDE THE HOME?

The woman who opts for an outside job or career faces the prospect of a good deal less leisure time. She is likely to get some additional help from her husband but not enough to make their total work load equitable. What, then, is the motivation for women to work?

To begin with, we should note that many women who work outside of the home would prefer not to and many who are not employed would prefer to be. According to national polls, about the same proportion of women (61 percent) as men (63 percent) say that their work is very important to them, but over half of women admit they would prefer to stay home and take care of their homes and family if they felt free to do so.[1] One reason that women continue their outside jobs even when they prefer to stay home is that they feel financially constrained. A substantial number of employed women believe they and their families would have a hard time economically if they did not work (Volling and Belsky 1993).

One motivation, then, is economic. Many women are employed in order to maintain a standard of living that they believe is otherwise not possible for them and their families. Whether the woman has a job or a career, she is likely to be more committed to the work to the extent that she perceives her income as necessary for her family's financial security. She may also see her work as necessary to her future security, giving her an independent pension should she become a widow (Uchitelle 1998). Of course, there are costs involved in working, particularly when there are children in the home. One of the largest costs is child care, which can decrease the advantage of the dual-earner family over the single-earner family by as much as 68 percent (Hanson and Ooms 1991). Nevertheless, two incomes do give the dual-earner family advantages both in income and home ownership.

Women, like men, work for a variety of reasons other than an economic one. A poll found that even if women felt they had enough money to live comfortably without working, a majority would either work

---

[1]Reported in *The American Enterprise,* September/October 1992, p. 97 and September/October 1993, p. 94.

PERSPECTIVE
Women's Commitment to Work

Dr. John Cowan, whose views on love we quoted in chapter 7, said many things about male-female relationships that people today would consider archaic and even outrageous. But he was ahead of his time in advocating women's rights to vote, to own, possess, and manage property, and to work. He quotes from a letter by Florence Nightingale, the famous nineteenth-century nurse, who advised women to commit themselves fully to whatever work they undertook:

1. But I would also say to all young ladies who are called to any particular vocation, qualify yourselves for it as a man does for his work. Don't think you can undertake it otherwise. No one should attempt to teach the Greek language until he is master of the language; and this he can become only by hard study. And,

2. If you are called to man's work, do not exact a woman's privileges—the privilege of inaccuracy, of weakness, ye muddleheads. Submit yourselves to the rules of business as men do, by which alone you can make God's business succeed; for He has never said that He will give His success and His blessing to inefficiency—to sketching and unfinished work.

3. It has happened to me more than once to be told by women: 'Yes, but you had personal freedom.' Nothing can well be further from the truth. I question whether God has ever brought any one through more difficulties and contradictions than I have had.

4. But to women I would say, look upon your work, whether it be an accustomed or an unaccustomed work, as upon a trust confided to you. This will keep you alike from discouragement and from presumption, from idleness and from overtaxing yourself.

Cowan then gives his opinion about the effects on women who follow Nightingale's advice to dedicate themselves to their work:

As far as women become self-supporting, they will be emancipated from the bondage of dependence, and be more free in respect to marriage. This relation will not be entered upon to secure a support, as is so often done now, but more from the promptings of affection. The home will not be less sacred and hallowed, but will rest on a more secure basis.

Source: John Cowan, M.D., *The Science of a New Life* (New York: J. S. Ogilvie Publishers, 1869), pp. 384–385.

or volunteer—15 percent would continue working full-time, 33 percent would work part-time, and 20 percent would do volunteer work (Boyle 1995). Obviously, women, like men, reap important benefits from employment, including "the opportunity to develop the instrumental part of themselves and to establish a sense of self apart from a man and children, economic independence, increased self-esteem, and better overall health" (Gilbert 1993:85). It is not surprising, then, that while African American women are more likely than whites to work out of economic necessity, both groups of women increasingly offer reasons other than economic necessity for employment (Herring and Wilson-Sadberry 1993).

Still another reason to work is the power gained (Ross and Mirowsky 1992). We have noted before that power is an important resource to all of us. We each need to feel that we have some control over the circumstances of our lives. Women may work in order to get their own income and thus increase their sense of power. That increased power may make their marriage a more equitable one. It may give a woman a sense of security in case her marriage fails or her husband dies.

Finally, what about the effects of employment on marital and family relations? We will explore these in more detail, but here we want to note that employed women generally do not believe that their marriages or families suffer because of their work outside the home. Whether they are correct is increasingly important, because both partners work in an ever-growing number of marriages (figure 13.2).

DUAL-CAREER FAMILIES

There are more dual-earner families in America than single-earner families. We do not know how many of the dual-earner families are dual-career,

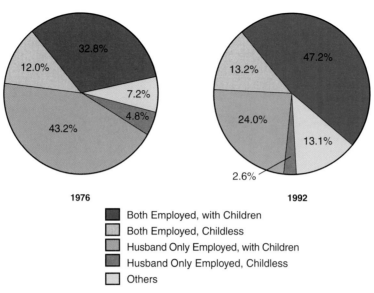

1976   **1992**

- ■ Both Employed, with Children
- Both Employed, Childless
- Husband Only Employed, with Children
- Husband Only Employed, Childless
- □ Others

FIGURE 13.2   Distribution of Married Couples, by Employment Status and Fertility
(*Source:* Amara Bachu, "Fertility of American Women: June 1992" in U.S. Bureau of the Census, *Current Population Reports,* Series P20, No. 470, 1993:xvii.)

but the number is undoubtedly substantial and growing. If you complete your college degree or go on for graduate work, you have a good chance of being a part of a dual-career family. It is important to know the nature of such a family, the problems peculiar to it, and some of the satisfactions that can be gained through it.

More or Less Equal?

We have seen repeatedly that equity is a crucial part of a satisfying, intimate relationship. Researchers have found equity to be related to marital quality in preindustrial as well as modernized societies. In essence, whatever their working status outside the home, women want equity in the marital and family arrangements (Stohs 1995; Hendrix 1997; Rosenbluth, Steil, and Whitcomb 1998). By definition, it would seem that the dual-career family is an equitable relationship. The assumption underlying such an arrangement is that each spouse will be committed both to a career and to the family. Neither spouse will subordinate his or her career to that of the partner. The implication is that because the spouses are equal in their dual commitments, they must take equal responsibility for family work in

order for the arrangement to be viable and satisfying. Indeed, a study of forty-two dual-career couples showed that those who exhibited these characteristics were more satisfied (Ray 1990). That is, those who were most satisfied with their marriages were likely to perceive equality and reciprocity in the sense that each spouse both gave and received support from the other, was involved in the other's career and equally committed to the relationship, and was equally involved in making decisions about work and home.

How many dual-career couples achieve such an equitable arrangement? Most dual-career couples are more equal than other kinds of families in terms of sharing the decision-making power and giving the wife the option of pursuing a career as well as bearing and rearing children (Hertz 1986). Nevertheless, dual-career marriages tend to have something less than full equality. One reason for inequality is differences in income. Money is power in our society. A study of sixty dual-career couples reported that those partners who had the higher income viewed their careers as more important than those of their spouses, were somewhat less involved in child care responsibilities, and had more say in financial decisions (Steil and Weltman 1991).

Inequality may also persist because of the tendency for some aspects of traditional role expectations to persist. Whatever the reasons for the inequality, we should note that inequality in such things as time spent on household tasks is not always defined as inequity by people. In studying marital quality through interviews of forty-one people in dual-career marriages, three researchers found that the respondents gave more importance to such matters as mutual respect, support, commitment, and reciprocity over time than they did to current sharing of household tasks and responsibilities (Rosenbluth, Steil, and Whitcomb 1998). In other words, there does not have to be a 50–50 sharing of household tasks and decision making in order for people to have a sense of equity in the relationship.

Types of Dual-Career Families

While all dual-career families by definition involve a twofold commitment, there are variations in the way that the spouses handle their work and family roles. Moreover, there are differing structural arrangements, perhaps the most radical of which is the commuter marriage.

Three Types of Marital Roles In her study of men in dual-career families, Gilbert (1993) identified three different types of arrangements: the traditional, the participant, and the role-sharing. In the *traditional* dual-career family, the wife simply adds a new role—that of a career woman. She continues to be responsible for the family work. The problems of coordination and time that emerge are problems that she must resolve. This arrangement, of course, violates the principle of equity that underlies the idea of two careers. Nevertheless, it is one pattern that some couples have adopted.

In the *participant* dual-career family, the husband assumes some of the responsibilities of child care. Husband and wife may even share equally the parenting of the children. But the wife still retains the responsibility for housework. As suggested by the studies on time use, this type is fairly common.

Finally, in the *role-sharing* dual-career family, both spouses are actively involved in family work, both child care and household tasks. The role-sharing family implements the principle of equity. The spouses share family power and responsibilities equally as each pursues a meaningful career.

Which of the three patterns is adopted by any particular couple depends on a variety of personal, interpersonal, and social factors. For example, a personal factor may be the attitudes and values of the spouses. If their values are still somewhat traditional, the couple may feel most comfortable with a participant family. An interpersonal factor could be the balance of power in the relationship. If the male has been dominant, he may insist on something less than role-sharing in order to accept his wife's career. She may accede because she has become habituated to his dominance in important decisions. Finally, such things as occupational demands and structures as well as social support systems are examples of social factors. One of the partners may have less flexibility than the other. The wife may be a lawyer and be unable to pursue her career fully without role-sharing. Or the parents of the couple may exert pressure one way or another.

In other words, the type of family arrangement that the couple works out reflects more than their preference. A host of factors come to bear on them as they seek to cope with the difficult task of maintaining two careers and a family. The roles they finally work out may or may not be in accord with their preference, but they may perceive the arrangement as the only one that is viable for them. For example, a university professor who is married to an attorney told us:

> My husband spends many more hours at his office than I do at mine. We didn't have our degrees when we were first married. I knew that he would have long hours as an attorney, but I didn't realize that I would wind up doing more than my share of housework. But I have come to terms with that. I know that if he was the professor and I was the attorney, he would do most of the housework. That's just the way it is.

Commuter Marriages The **commuter marriage** is a dual-career marriage in which the spouses live in different locations and still maintain their dual commitment to work and to family. They do not prefer to live apart, but they don't want to give up their careers or each other. A study of thirty-seven people involved in commuter marriages reported a number of benefits that people see in such an arrangement in addition to being able to continue careers—increased independence, greater self-sufficiency, and an enhanced appreciation for one's partner (Groves and Horm-Wingerd 1991).

Commuter marriages work better if there are no children. Even without children, however, there are unique problems. How do you fulfill your need for intimacy when you are with your spouse less than half the time? Each partner has to learn to live without the emotional support and companionship that normally are expected in marriage (Groves and Horm-Wingerd 1991). According to Gerstel and Gross (1984), some commuter wives say that each reunion with their husbands requires time to reestablish the sense of intimacy. It is not surprising, then, that commuter couples, compared to dual-career couples living together, report more work satisfaction but lower family satisfaction and less satisfaction with life as a whole (Bunker et al. 1992).

For some people, then, the commuter marriage appears to work. We don't have evidence about the long-term consequences of such marriages. Can they survive decades of separation? If they do, what kind of relationship will the couple have when one or both retire? How will they adjust to living together all the time?

Challenges of Dual-Career Families

We have already seen some of the problems of the dual-career family—equity, working out the marital roles, and the special problems of those in a commuter marriage. (We will note a variety of other troublesome areas when we discuss the problems of the dual-earner family generally.) Here we want to look at a number of specific difficulties that are somewhat unusual because of the commitment of both spouses to a career.

Time Management   One of the common complaints of those in dual-career marriages is the lack of time (Kate 1998). There is insufficient time for each spouse to be alone and for them to be together as a couple. The problem is intensified if the couple has children and if one or both have a high need for achievement in their career (Rice 1979:55).

Careful planning and cooperation by all family members are important in order to minimize conflicts over time. Some couples resolve the problem

by following detailed schedules. Others try to depend on the goodwill and good sense of each member of the family, hoping that all of the demands of work and home will be met without the rigid structuring of time. The latter may not succeed. Rice (1979:58) told of one couple that tried to operate without a schedule. The wife said, "We just see what needs doing and do it." But increasingly, things were not being done around the home. Finally, the couple was forced to sit down and write up a schedule, including such details as a half-hour a day for them to be together without the children.

Children   An initial issue is whether to have children because the "presence of children in a dual-career family vastly affects the complexity and viability of this life-style" (Gilbert and Rachlin 1987:19). If the couple opts for children, then they face the question of who will care for them. They probably have the resources to hire outsiders. But because of their own values and attitudes and those of their parents and siblings, they may feel pressure to care for the children themselves and even to revert back to more traditional roles. Couples who have worked out an acceptable arrangement before children face new difficulties once a baby enters the home.

Which parent will be the primary caregiver? Traditionally, that is the responsibility of the mother, and she is still largely responsible, even among dual-career families. Maternity leaves and more flexible schedules for mothers tend to reinforce that traditional responsibility. Of course, it may also be the woman's preference. A study of 391 female managers reported that those who were unemployed or working part-time said they were forgoing full-time employment for the time being because they wanted to spend more time with their preschool children (Rosin and Korabik 1990).

Clearly, the issue of children presents the dual-career couple with difficult decisions. A survey of nearly one thousand professional women found that they tended to make sacrifices in family life or career or both (Olson, Frieze, and Detlefsen 1990). Many of the childless women said they would like to have children. Those who had children reported that they made various kinds of career sacrifices. Interestingly, women in the male-dominated business world reported more difficulty in combining children and career than those in the female-dominated area of library science.

Social practices and pressures thus work against an equal sharing of child-rearing. This may be one reason there are fewer children on the average in dual-career than in more traditional marriages. There is also a tendency in dual-career families for the spouses to postpone childbearing until they have established themselves in their careers.

When the children reach school age, problems of child care are lessened somewhat but not eliminated. Who will stay at home on the days when there is no school? Who will respond if the school calls and says that the child is sick? Again, the burden is likely to fall on the mother. The woman, therefore, is likely to make more career adjustments and sacrifices than the man.

Relationships with Other People   Dual-career couples may deal with time constraints by limiting their activity with other people (Googins 1991). They are likely to engage in leisure and social activities primarily or exclusively with other dual-career people, particularly with those with whom they work. Interacting with colleagues, however, means that the couple runs the risk of overinvestment in career and too little investment in the marital relationship. David Rice (1979:61), a psychiatrist, pointed out that "the greatest problem encountered in the social relationship area relates to the natural forming of close relationships with one's colleagues and resultant spouse jealousy."

Rice (1979:62–63) related the case of Alice and Jeff, who had married while both were in graduate school. They came to a therapist when they were in their late thirties. They were both active in their careers at that time and had two children. Jeff had formed a close relationship with a female colleague who was having problems in her marriage. Jeff and the colleague acknowledged their feelings for each other but decided to just be friends. Jeff, however, felt guilty and talked about the matter with Alice. She seemed to accept the situation easily, particularly because it had not become a sexual relationship. But because her intimacy needs were not being met by Jeff, Alice also became involved in a close friendship with a colleague, a man with whom she worked on several projects. Jeff, like Alice, was able to accept her feelings.

Unfortunately, Jeff and Alice had lost their sense of intimacy with each other. Each had entered an intimate, though nonsexual, relationship at work. With the demands of their careers being heavy and some basic intimacy needs being met by colleagues, their own relationship deteriorated. Dual-career couples have a more severe challenge than others in the area of maintaining their intimate relationship with each other.

The Dual-Career Wife   The wife in a dual-career family is more likely than the husband to bear the brunt of the conflicts between work, spouse, and children. To keep the matter in perspective, however, we should note that women report more stressors from family responsibilities than do men regardless of their outside employment status (Anderson and Leslie 1991). The stress may reflect the fact that mothers with full-time careers, while spending fewer hours in homemaking than full-time homemakers, report the same *range* of household and child-care activities as the full-time homemakers (DeMeis and Perkins 1996). In other words, mothers with careers still try to do all of the tasks that homemakers do even though they may not spend as much time on them. And even though they have careers, they believe they have no choice about the various homemaking tasks in which they engage.

The number of hours a woman works outside the home may make a difference in the experience of conflict and stress, however. In one study, women employed part-time reported about the same amount of role conflict and role overload as those employed full-time; however, the part-timers indicated greater happiness at home and work (Barker 1993). Nevertheless, as a study of one hundred women concluded, most women do not suffer excessive strain from juggling the roles of wife, mother, and worker even when they are employed full-time (Helson, Elliott, and Leigh 1990).

On the other hand, at least some women may try to become the "superwoman"—the perfect mother, the best homemaker, the ideal wife, and the high-achieving career woman. Whatever the motivation for such unrealistic aspirations, the woman who holds them is likely to fall victim to various consequences of stress: depression, anxiety, irritability, and problems with eating and sleeping. One such

Whether employed outside the home or not, women still assume the major responsibility for housework.

woman, Margaret, has an administrative position in health services. She seems to have it all—the career and the family. But one day she told us: "I never thought I'd be saying this. But I'd like to chuck it all—my work, my kids, even my husband. I'm tired. My most prevalent fantasy is to have my own apartment with only myself to take care of." Margaret has reached a point of exhaustion.

Unfortunately, in many cases, husbands expect wives to be "superwomen." Men may support equality in principle, but in practice they still tend to operate from a position of entitlement (Gilbert and Rachlin 1987:15–16). That is, men in our society are socialized to regard themselves as entitled to do whatever is necessary in order to be successful in their work and provide for their family. For many men, success means that they do not have to do housework. A man is entitled to pursue his career without the constraints of time and energy given to family work.

Even in a dual-career family, then, there is a tendency for the husband to decide what is an equitable division of labor in the home, to assume whatever share he has decided is fair, and to expect that everything is all right. He may even expect to receive gratitude from his wife for his willingness to share the household responsibilities. She, on the other hand, even though she is as fully engaged in a career as he is, will get no expressions of gratitude

for doing her share because it is her responsibility in the first place.

Satisfactions of a Dual-Career Family

In spite of the gloomy picture painted previously, there are a number of satisfactions in the dual-career family that make the arrangement worth all the potential problems. Some of these satisfactions are the same as those of the dual-earner family, involving the benefits that accrue to women through work (see "Work and Well-Being" in this chapter). But others are unique or more intense for those in the dual-career family.

Some of the benefits relate to the need for a sense of control over our lives. A woman who has a sense of her own separate identity and a feeling of being independent will be healthier and more satisfied than one who cannot separate herself from her family and who is economically and emotionally dependent on her husband. The other benefits relate to our intimacy needs. The woman who has higher self-esteem, who is emotionally healthy and satisfied, and who is able to be an intellectual companion rather than a servile mate to her husband will likely have a far more meaningful marriage.

But what are the benefits for the husband? Traditionally, he used his career, at least in part, to fulfill

INVOLVEMENT
Exploring the Dual-Career Family

If you have grown up in a dual-career family, reflect on the materials in this section and write up an account of your experiences. How do your experiences compare with the materials presented? Based on your experience, what are the major problems and the greatest rewards and satisfactions in a dual-career family, particularly for the children? What changes in our society would you suggest in order to help dual-career families cope with their challenges?

If you have not grown up in a dual-career family, look through six or so issues of a women's magazine, such as *Working Woman.* Find a number of articles that address the issue of the dual-career family. What are the problems identified in the articles? What are the rewards and satisfactions? How do they compare with the materials in this chapter? Interview a woman who is in a dual-career family. Ask her what she believes to be the most serious problems and the greatest benefits from such an arrangement. Then tell her about the kinds of problems and satisfactions discussed in this chapter. Ask her to comment on them in terms of her own experiences. What kinds of things did she identify as problems and satisfactions? How does her experience compare with the materials in the chapter? If a number of students do this project, let each one choose a different magazine and a different person to interview. Then compare all the results. What are your overall conclusions?

the "good provider role" (Bernard 1981). He had little involvement in the home, but he gave his wife and children a solid financial base. What has a man gained by having his wife also engage in a career? As Gilbert and Rachlin (1987:27) noted:

> The foremost potential benefits of dual-career marriage for the male spouse are freedom from the mantle of total economic responsibility and family dependency and opportunities to involve himself in parenting and to express his inherent needs to nurture and bond.

The husband may also gain a more meaningful marital relationship. If his wife is happier or more fulfilled with a career outside of the home, then this will have a positive impact on their marriage.

There are benefits to the family generally as well. The higher income level will give all family members many options that they would not otherwise have. To the extent that they approach the role-sharing dual-career family, they will have the opportunity to share in an experience of equality that many Americans value but miss. They will also have the opportunity to experience a life-style in which the constraints of traditional gender roles are no longer operative. Also the children may find that they develop a sense of responsibility, independence, and competence earlier in life and more completely because they too must assume a certain share of family work.

In sum, the potential satisfactions and rewards of the dual-career family are great. So are the potential problems. Some dual-career families, therefore, are going to break apart from stress and conflict; however, others are going to be an exciting adventure in growth. We hope that as societal norms and arrangements change, those in dual-career families will get increasing support in their efforts.

CHALLENGES OF DUAL-EARNER COUPLES

For the dual-earner couple generally, as with the dual-career couple in particular, the decision to have both spouses work is a trade-off. That is, there are satisfactions to be gained and certain problems and challenges to be faced. In this section, we will look at the problems and challenges, including the effects on marital satisfaction. In the final section, we will see the payoffs for the individual well-being of the spouses.

Family Work

We have seen that although there is evidence of a greater amount of sharing in the family work by the husbands of employed women, the husband's share is less than equal. In particular, fathers today tend to be more involved in child care tasks than were

There is more sharing of family work when mothers have careers.

previous generations of fathers (Barnett and Rivers 1996). A fourth or more of men with preschoolers and wives who work outside the home provide some care for their children, and nearly a fifth are the major care providers (Casper 1997).

In addition to factors such as education, income, and egalitarian attitudes that we have previously noted, the willingness of men to engage in household tasks depends on their gender-role orientation, as Gunter and Gunter (1990) found in their research on 139 working couples. Women generally performed more household tasks than men, but androgynous and feminine-oriented subjects of both sexes did more tasks than masculine-oriented subjects. Androgynous subjects had less conflict than others over domestic tasks.

The way that a couple comes to terms with the division of labor in the home is important for their marital satisfaction. As we would expect, satisfaction is highest when there is perceived equity. But

what is equity? Husbands and wives both want an equitable arrangement; yet husbands do not want to spend many hours on housework, which suggests that they would prefer equity in the context of lower standards of house care than that preferred by their wives (Benin and Agostinelli 1988). Wives, on the other hand, prefer equality or even something less than an equal share of household work. They are not as satisfied if the husband's share of family work is consumed by child care and traditional male chores as they are if he participates in some traditional female chores (Benin and Agostinelli 1988).

Thus, husbands and wives tend to approach the notion of an equitable division of family work somewhat differently. Because there are no norms to guide them, each couple will have to negotiate the division of labor in the home with a view toward achieving mutual satisfaction.

Stress, Intimacy, and Family Life

Systems Theory Applied

In the dual-career family, we noted, women have more adjustments to make than do men. They tend to carry a larger share of the load of family work. Women who are employed have more hassles of every kind than women who do not work outside the home (Alpert and Culbertson 1987). Unfortunately, these facts may not be fully recognized by husbands and couples may get into what *systems theorists* call circularity. For example, a man complained that his wife was not sufficiently supportive, which caused him to do poorly at his sales job. For him, the problem was simple—she needed to be more supportive so that he could perform better at work. She responded that his performance, which resulted in a lower paycheck, forced her to work more hours at her part-time job. For her, too, the problem was simple—he needed to do a better job so she could work less. The real problem was not simple, but circular. When his commissions were lower, she worried more and spent more hours at her part-time job, which took time and energy away from their marital relationship. Thus, his poor performance caused her stress, which caused her lowered support, which caused his continued poor perfor-

TABLE 13.3
Frequency of Work-Family Conflict

Group (in percent)	Not at All	Not Too Much	Somewhat	A Lot
Total sample	24.3	41.3	24.0	10.4
Employed husbands	25.9	40.4	23.6	10.1
Wife employed	26.7	41.8	21.0	10.5
No children	35.1	37.1	20.3	7.4
Youngest 0–5 years	22.9	41.3	22.9	12.8
Youngest 6–17 years	20.0	46.8	20.7	12.3
Wife not employed	25.0	38.7	26.6	9.7
No children	35.0	38.7	20.0	6.3
Youngest 0–5 years	20.4	32.8	37.1	9.7
Youngest 6–17 years	20.3	45.6	20.9	13.3
Employed wives	22.5	40.5	26.5	10.5
Husband employed	22.9	39.1	27.7	10.4
No children	37.1	33.7	18.5	10.7
Youngest 0–5 years	11.8	40.3	36.1	11.8
Youngest 6–17 years	16.3	43.5	31.0	9.2
Husband not employed	18.6	55.8	14.0	11.6
Employed women in one-parent families	17.0	58.0	13.6	11.4
Youngest 0–5 years	18.6	55.8	9.3	16.3
Youngest 6–17 years	15.6	60.0	17.8	6.7

Source: U.S. Bureau of Labor Statistics, "Conflicts between Work and Family Life" in *Monthly Labor Review*, p. 103.

mance. The problem was circular, and their arguments were endless and fruitless until they recognized the circularity into which they had fallen.

Home Versus the Workplace Stress occurs because of such things as the conflict between the demands of the workplace and the demands of home, and the effect of work fatigue on moods at home (Chan and Margolin 1994). When the conflict occurs, it generates emotional distress which, in turn, adversely affects the quality of the marital relationship (Matthews, Conger, and Wickrama 1996). Women are more likely than men to experience such work-home conflict because there is less flexibility in doing the household tasks they tend to assume (preparing meals, laundry, etc.) than in those their husbands assume (taking care of the car and garden) (Barnett and Shen 1997). There is a tendency for work-home conflict to ease as the children get older (Higgins, Duxbury, and Lee 1994), but the conflict can be serious at any part of the family life cycle.

Both men and women experience these conflicting demands. As table 13.3 shows, employed husbands and employed wives report about the same amount of conflict overall, though employed hus-

bands with nonemployed wives have somewhat less conflict than those whose wives work outside the home.

It may be that one consequence of work-home conflict is that more and more women will spend increasing hours at work in order to escape the demands of home—both the physical demands of the various tasks and the emotional demands of maintaining a meaningful family life. At least that is the conclusion of Hochschild (1997) on the basis of her study of 130 female factory and clerical workers. Hochschild argues that growing numbers of women who work outside the home are fleeing "a world of unresolved quarrels and unwashed laundry for the reliable orderliness, harmony, and managed cheer of work." Whether she obtained valid data from her respondents (were they honest to a researcher who was located in a company office?), and, if so, whether those data apply generally to women (the area where the company was located has a median family income below the national median) remains to be seen by future research.

The Costs of Both Parents Working Stress arises if people perceive that their families are suffering in some way from their employment. Many

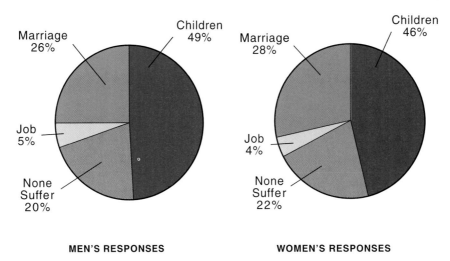

MEN'S RESPONSES   **WOMEN'S RESPONSES**

FIGURE 13.3   **What Suffers When Women Work?**
(*Source:* Data from *Public Opinion,* December/January 1986:31.)

believe that a woman who works outside the home cannot care for her children as well as the woman who is a homemaker. A substantial number of both men and women believe that either the children or the marriage get slighted if the woman is employed (figure 13.3). The belief that children suffer may be greater when there are sons rather than daughters involved (Downey, Jackson, and Powell 1994). Parents tend to believe that sons need more supervision than daughters.

Such concerns raise serious issues. We are dealing, after all, with a situation in which half of all children under the age of six have some kind of nonparental child care on a regular basis, and about a fourth of all children under the age of six spend forty or more hours a week in care (Joesch 1998). Most care, though not all, is related to maternal employment outside the home. If these children are suffering because of nonparental child care, we have a problem of massive proportions.

What, then, does the evidence show? Many studies report no negative consequences for infants and young children when there is warm and close supervision (Greenstein 1993; Youngblut, Loveland-Cherry, and Horan 1993; Parcel and Menaghan 1994). Other research, however, reports that there may be problems in the mother-child bonding for infants younger than two years (Meredith 1986).

A number of studies also examine the impact on adolescents. Most find that maternal employment has no negative consequences for adolescents on such things as cognitive and social competence, emotional well-being, and amount of communication and conflict between mother and child (Armistead, Wierson, and Forehand 1990; Orthner 1990). One study of fifty-two mothers and their adolescent children even found higher self-esteem and less depression among adolescents whose mothers were highly educated and employed (Joebgen and Richards 1990).

Maternal employment may have positive effects on children by encouraging higher levels of educational attainment (Kalmijn 1994; Haveman and Wolfe 1994). This may be particularly true when mothers work in occupations that are complex (such as the professions); these mothers may "create home environments that are more cognitively enriched and more affectively and physically appropriate" than those created by mothers who work in less complex occupations (Parcel and Menaghan 1994:61).

On the other hand, Mueller (1995) examined national data and found that children perform better on achievement tests when mothers are either employed part-time or not employed. And researchers who studied 200 seventh-graders found that daughters, though not sons, reported greater closeness with both parents when the mother was not em-

COMPARISON
Work and Divorce in Puerto Rico

In the United States, when both husband and wife work outside the home, the couple is at greater risk for divorce. The same risk holds for Puerto Rican women who have outside employment. However, the relationship between work and divorce in Puerto Rico is complex. For one thing, the breakup rate is only greater for those women who work for a wage or salary; women who are self-employed or who work in a family business do not have higher rates of divorce than those who are homemakers. Furthermore, even among women who work for a wage or salary, the effect is small if they were already working before they married.

The Puerto Rican women most at risk for divorce, then, are those who begin working outside the home after they are married; their risk is 155 percent higher than that of other women. Those next most likely to divorce are women who were working but who become unemployed while married; their risk is 78 percent higher than that of other women. In other words, the higher divorce rates apply either to those who begin working outside the home after marriage or who were working but lost their jobs after they were married.

It is not clear why the transition from unemployment to employment or vice versa after a woman is married increases marital breakup in Puerto Rico. Over the past two decades, the female labor force has expanded dramatically. At the same time, employment is unstable. Thus, Puerto Rican women tend to go through many cycles of employment and unemployment. Nevertheless, for that change to occur after a woman is married puts a strain on the relationship that increases the chance of divorce. Unlike women in the United States, then, Puerto Rican women do not have to worry about the negative effects of working outside the home on their marriage as much as they need to be concerned about a change in their employment status (Carver and Teachman 1993).

ployed (Paulson, Koman, and Hill 1990). And a study of eighth-graders reported that those who had to care for themselves for eleven hours a week or more because of parental work reported more anger, stress, and family conflict than others (Dwyer 1990). It may be that it is not simply whether both parents work that is crucial but rather the extent to which working parents can still maintain supervision of and activities with their children, a conclusion supported by the fact that children have more behavior problems when their parents work overtime (Parcel and Menaghan 1994).

Finally, to add to the complexity as well as to the controversy, Sugar (1994) studied 253 mothers between the ages of twenty-five and forty-five. Those whose own mothers had worked were more likely to struggle with depression. They also felt less effective as parents, and indicated less satisfaction with their work and with life generally. If Sugar's conclusions are generally valid, they indicate that negative consequences of mothers working may appear mainly when the children become adults and parents themselves.

Role Negotiation

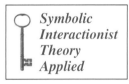

Symbolic Interactionist Theory Applied

Symbolic interactionists talk about *role-making,* the process of working out the nature of particular roles in the course of interaction (Lauer and Handel 1983: 124). "Role-making" suggests that we do not slip easily into ready-made roles, but must work together to construct what our roles will be. That can happen through role negotiation, which has become increasingly common and necessary as the number of dual-earner families has grown. The questions are: Who does what? How can a couple achieve an equitable division of labor? As we might expect, there is little, if any, agreement on the answers. Each couple must negotiate its own compromise about family roles.

Not only is there no social consensus, but specific couples also are likely to disagree. The problems are illustrated by research of eighty-three dual-earner couples who each had at least one preschool child (Chassin et al. 1985). The researchers investigated the perceptions of spousal, parental, and worker roles held by the partners.

They found general agreement on perceptions of worker and husband roles but a considerable amount of disagreement on wife and parental roles. Compared to their husbands, women saw the wife's role as more powerless, more dependent, more child-oriented, and less glamorous. Men viewed the father role as more dependent, more tied-down, and more child-oriented than did the women. Women viewed the mother role as more sensitive, warmer, and less glamorous than did the men.

Generally, the partners saw a lot of overlap between the wife and mother roles. But women rated the employed-woman role as more unfeeling, more independent, more sophisticated and glamorous, and more interesting and tense than the roles of wife and mother. Men rated the employed-woman role as meaner, less good, more independent, more sophisticated, more serious, and colder than the roles of wife and mother.

The researchers also found that women perceived the wife role as less desirable than did the men, suggesting that "the men in this dual-worker sample may underestimate their wives' discontent with the wife role" (Chassin et al. 1985:308). That difference is a potential source of conflict. Another possible source of conflict is the women's lower evaluation than the men's of the father role, suggesting that the wives may undervalue their husbands' contribution to child-rearing. Finally, the overlap between wife and mother and the gap between those roles and the employed woman role indicate conflict between the home and work roles. In particular, women in dual-earner families may see themselves as involved in a " 'trade-off' between the independence, freedom and glamour of the worker role and the sensitivity, warmth and relaxation of the wife and mother roles" (Chassin et al. 1985:308). The wife and mother roles, of course, are more consistent with traditional notions of femininity.

"Whatever works for you" is probably a good rule to follow as partners negotiate such differences. What you settle on as acceptable roles for you and your spouse is not as important as the fact that you settle on something. Agreement about roles is crucial to your marital satisfaction.

Career-oriented women are more satisfied with their lives when they combine work with marriage and family.

Marital Satisfaction

If you are in a dual-earner family, you are at greater risk of separation and divorce (Booth et al. 1984). The risk may be even greater in a dual-career family, because women who are highly committed to a career tend to have lower marital adjustment and satisfaction (Ladewig and McGee 1986). Still, if you successfully negotiate family roles, achieve an equitable division of labor in the home (particularly important for women), and have an equitable sharing of breadwinning (particularly important for men), you have resolved some of the major problems of the dual-earner family and you are likely to have a satisfying marriage (Wilkie, Ferree, and Ratcliff 1998).

Marital satisfaction among dual-earner couples is common. In fact, Smith (1985) examined twenty-seven studies that involved 4,602 subjects and compared those in dual-earner and single-earner families. The studies looked at overall marital adjustment and four specific areas of adjustment: physical (love, affection, sexual relations), companionship (sharing interests, tasks, and activities), communication (self-disclosure, small talk, listening), and tensions and regrets (conflict, willingness to marry same person again). The bulk of studies shows no differences in overall adjustment between dual-earner families and those where the woman is a homemaker. In fact, the majority of studies shows no difference in any of the specific areas. Where a substantial proportion of studies found differences, in the areas of physical relations and companionship, the results tend to favor families with homemakers over the dual-earner families. But it is clear that the majority of couples seem to be working out the problems faced by the dual-earner family (Blair 1993).

The dual-career family, which poses somewhat greater challenges than that of the dual-earner, can also have a high degree of marital satisfaction. Thomas, Albrecht, and White (1984) studied thirty-four dual-career couples and were able to classify fourteen of them as "high quality" and twenty as "low quality." The factors differentiating the two groups are shown in table 13.4. Those in high-quality marriages have addressed successfully the issues of equity and roles and have good patterns of communication and companionship, which suggests that both partners have a high level of commitment to the marriage. Perhaps in the low-quality marriages, one or both partners are giving highest priority to career. Thus, Orbuch and Custer (1995) found that when women define their work as one of the most important aspects of their lives, their husbands

TABLE 13.4
Characteristics of High-Quality and Low-Quality Dual-Career Marriages

High-Quality Marriages	Low-Quality Marriages
Wives	**Wives**
They report little or no difficulty discussing work-related activities, problems, and achievements with their husbands.	They report much difficulty discussing work-related activities, problems, and achievements with their husbands.
They perceive husbands as supportive with child-rearing and household tasks.	They perceive husbands as less supportive with child-rearing and household tasks.
They are satisfied with their work situations.	They are more likely to have made a career shift or change during marriage.
	They are acutely dissatisfied with the level of emotional intimacy in the relationship.
Husbands	**Husbands**
Their support for wives' careers has increased since marriage.	Their support for wives' careers has decreased since marriage.
Their perceptions of wives' role overload and stress levels are similar to what wives report.	Their perceptions of wives' role overload and stress levels are lower than wives report.
Marital Dyad	**Marital Dyad**
They agree husband's career is preeminent.	There is less agreement regarding whose career is preeminent.
They are more likely to be involved in similar career pursuits (similar professions).	They are less likely to be involved in similar career pursuits (similar professions).
They have older children and more jointly share child care responsibilities.	They have younger children and report much stress due to conflict with children's schedules and/or child care arrangements.
They are satisfied with levels of emotional, sexual, intellectual, recreational, and social intimacy within the relationship.	They are dissatisfied with levels of emotional, sexual, intellectual, recreational, and social intimacy within the relationship.

PERSONAL
Employed and Married, and Loving Both

Phyllis is a high-school counselor in her forties. She and Roger have four children. They have had their share of difficult times, but overall, she sees the marriage as a very good one, and believes that working outside the home has enhanced the quality of their family life:

During our twenty-one years of marriage, being happily employed has probably contributed as much to our happiness as anything else. I taught for two years before we married. It was very fulfilling, and the idea of my quitting to be a "good wife" was neither discussed nor considered. Because of my job, I felt a sense of accomplishment, competence, pride, and independence, all of which contributed to my being a very happy person. Roger was just as fortunate in his career choice. He found excitement and challenge in being an architect.

In our twenties, life was amazingly wonderful. Everything was new and thrilling— our jobs, our marriage, our friends, and the babies. We both worked hard and were very conscientious about our jobs. Roger was willing from the beginning to help out a great deal with the children, everything from changing diapers to getting up for middle-of-the-night feedings. We shared chores around the house but with no particular division of labor. Having his help with the mundane, routine aspects of home life endeared him to me greatly and helped me to continue working.

Our jobs were important to both of us because they gave us a sense of our individuality. We have never been suffocated or stifled by each other. Most of the time, we have worked at having enough togetherness to know that we were married. Our careers help us to view each other as competent people and this creates a mutual respect for each other as spouses and as professional people.

During our thirties, however, our professions brought about some frustrations and tensions. Roger had become a licensed architect and opened his own office. I had gone back to college to get my master's degree so that I could change from teaching to counseling. We had two more children, but Roger's work week had gone from fifty to what seemed like ninety hours a week. Time together became scarce. Our relationship became strained. I felt neglected. I was so busy that it took a while, but I gradually realized that I was terribly frustrated and angry. It all came out when we took a vacation. We spent most of the time talking about our situation. We both felt like we needed a vacation after the vacation. But it did help us to make some adjustments. We hired a cleaning lady, planned to spend a number of weekends away from home with just the two of us, and tried to do more things together. We realized that intimacy didn't just happen for us as it did in the first years of our marriage. We now had to put energy and effort into maintaining our intimate relationship.

In our forties, life has quieted down a bit. Roger is somewhat burned out with his work. He's looking for new challenges. I think I am too. So we're talking about what we can do to make our lives more exciting. We've got some ideas and are looking forward to the future.

There's no doubt about it. In spite of the frustrations we've had, the net effect of both of us being employed is that we have been able to maintain a high quality of intimacy during most of our years of marriage.

reacted negatively. African American husbands rated their marriages lower in quality, while white husbands reported higher levels of anxiety. Clearly, husbands are troubled by wives who give top priority to career.

WORK AND WELL-BEING

What would you do if you won a lottery? Would you retire and live happily ever after in glorious leisure? Probably not. Many people who have won lotteries have continued to work. Others have quit their jobs, but they have gone into other kinds of work or have found some way to spend their time. Humans do not generally function well without some kind of meaningful activity to occupy them.

Meaningful work, as Freud once observed, is one of the crucial bases of our well-being. Of course, not everyone who has a job has "meaningful" work. Yet one of the characteristics of Americans in recent decades is the increasing

> concern for work as a source of self-respect and nonmaterial reward—challenge, growth, personal fulfillment, interesting and meaningful work, the opportunity to advance and to accumulate, and the chance to lead a safe, healthy life (Kanter 1978:53).

In other words, more and more Americans are expecting their employment to be fulfilling to them. To what extent can people find such personal fulfillment in a dual-earner family?

Life Satisfaction

The effects of one or both spouses working outside the home on life satisfaction are somewhat different for men and women. Overall, when women are asked about how happy they are, employed women and homemakers report about the same amount of happiness (Benin and Nienstedt 1985). However, for women who are career-oriented, happiness is greater when they are employed full-time than when they are unemployed or employed only part-time (Pietromonaco, Manis, and Markus 1987). For married women who are not career-oriented, being employed or unemployed seems to make no difference in happiness.

The evidence with regard to men is somewhat contradictory. Using national surveys from 1978 to 1983, Benin and Nienstedt (1985) found that husbands of homemakers and husbands of employed wives reported no differences in their happiness. Their overall happiness was greater to the extent that they were happily married and satisfied with their jobs. Also using data from a national survey, however, Stanley, Hunt, and Hunt (1986) reported that men in dual-earner families are less satisfied with their work, their marriages, and their personal lives than are the husbands of homemakers. They also found that the lower satisfaction occurred mainly among younger, highly educated, successful men without children.

The authors speculate that the reason for this may be that the men in the dual-earner families feel deprived when they compare themselves to men who have the full-time services of a homemaker. They may also feel some slight to their manhood for not being the sole support of the family, the good provider. Other research supports the notion

that when husbands of employed wives feel deprived or less adequate as family breadwinners, they may have lower levels of job and life satisfaction (Staines, Pottick, and Fudge 1986).

We may conclude, then, that on the whole men and women in dual-earner families do not differ from those in single-earner families in overall life satisfaction. But women who are career-oriented will have lower satisfaction if they are not employed full-time. And men in dual-earner families who feel that they are deprived or whose self-esteem is threatened by not being the good provider will also have lower satisfaction.

Mental and Physical Health

In a sense, work presents us with one of the dilemmas of human life. On the one hand, work-induced stress is associated with such physical health problems as coronary heart disease, migraines, peptic ulcers, and hypertension (Lauer 1998:397). On the other hand, the stress of being forcibly unemployed can be as serious as the stress of working in undesirable conditions or an unfulfilling job. Unemployment leads to higher rates of suicide, mental illness, and various physical problems (Lauer 1998:401). The way to deal with the dilemma, of course, is to find work that is meaningful and fulfilling.

Having the option to work outside the home is important for wives. Women have higher rates of both physical and mental ailments than do men. For many women, it is the restrictive nature of the traditional role of wife and mother that creates stress and leads to high rates of illness (Lauer 1998:511). Thus, women who are dissatisfied with the homemaker role and not employed have more problems with depression than do other women (Shehan, Burg, and Rexroat 1986; Bromberger and Matthews 1994). Women with meaningful employment, on the other hand, have less psychological distress (Barnett et al. 1993; Barnett and Rivers 1996; Elliott 1996). Moreover, a national survey of women and their physical health reported that the healthiest women are those who are employed and married, followed by those employed and not married, those married but not in the labor force, and finally those unmarried and not in the labor force (Verbrugge and Madans 1985).

On the whole, then, wives who work outside the home are mentally and physically healthier than those who do not. However, other factors bear on the outcome of a wife's employment. One is her preference. As we noted above, some women prefer not to be employed. Using data from a national sample, Ross, Mirowsky, and Huber (1983) found that both spouses are less depressed when the wife's employment status is consistent with their preferences. The researchers also found, incidentally, that employed wives are less depressed when their husbands help with the housework.

Coping Strategies

Given an equitable relationship and agreement about work status, the partners in a dual-earner family will still benefit from using certain coping strategies to deal with various problems. Women in particular must deal with the additional workload that they typically assume. Even if a woman is in an egalitarian marriage, she and her spouse will have to deal with the problems that arise from time constraints.

A study of sixty-nine women in dual-earner families with children reported a number of ways that women handle the problems of time management and self-care (McLaughlin, Cormier, and Cormier 1988). Time-management strategies are those that enable a woman to control her personal and professional time. Self-care strategies are those that enable a woman to care for her physical and emotional well-being. The more women used the strategies, the better their marital adjustment and the lower their levels of distress.

For *time-management,* the coping strategies used, in order of frequency, were:

Do more than one task at a time.

Have contingency plans.

Say "no" to additional time demands.

Break large jobs down into smaller subtasks.

Budget your time so that you are not overwhelmed.

Make a priority list of your tasks.

Ask the family to help.

Leave work in the workplace; don't bring it home.

Make "to-do" lists.

Utilize outside help.

Fifty-five percent of the women said that they never use the last strategy—utilizing outside help. Every other strategy was used at least to some extent by the great bulk of the women.

For *self-care,* the coping strategies used, in order of frequency, were:

Give self permission to be a less-than-perfect housekeeper.

Allow special time for each child.

Eat nutritionally balanced meals.

Engage in family activities.

Give self permission to be a less-than-perfect mother.

Give self permission to be a less-than-perfect wife.

Stress quality rather than quantity time.

Interact with spouse.

Lower standards for housework.

Take time for yourself to do something you enjoy.

Engage in hobby.

Attend social or community group meetings.

Exercise.

Twenty-eight percent of the women said that they never exercised. Every other strategy was used at least to some extent by the great majority of the women.

It is interesting to note that the self-care strategies include giving oneself permission to be less-than-perfect as a housekeeper, wife, and mother. In other words, the women who are coping well have learned to avoid trying to be "superwomen." They know that they cannot be all things to all people. As a result, they are able to work outside the home, enjoy a family, and still maintain their personal well-being.

PRINCIPLES FOR ENHANCING INTIMACY

1. Women today have numerous role options available to them. Women can choose among career, marriage, and motherhood—or any combination of these. They can decide to stay at home or continue to work outside the home after they have children. Increased confusion, however, often accompanies enlarged options as individuals struggle to decide what is the best pattern for their lives. When faced with such choices, it is vital for you to gain an understanding of your needs as well as those of your spouse and to consider carefully your personal and your shared goals.

2. It is very important to negotiate role expectations before marriage. Each person needs to define clearly what role he or she expects to play in the marriage and what the role of the other will be. Then, compromises need to be negotiated. Be aware that the roles you decide on are not etched in stone. The process of negotiation and compromise will be repeated throughout your marriage as circumstances change.

3. Women who decide to combine the responsibilities of job, children, and home must recognize and come to terms with the enormity of their tasks and their own limitations. They can't do everything equally well all of the time. If you choose to assume these roles, you need to make a list of priorities, reduce your expectations, eliminate the less valuable tasks, and seek help when necessary.

4. Research indicates that husbands in dual-earner marriages do not share equally in family work. It is important that housework—including child care—be viewed as "our" work and not just "her" work. Otherwise, the wife may have a sense of inequity.

5. Often because she is not a wage-earner, the work of the homemaker is not highly valued by society or, for that matter, by her husband. If your wife chooses to stop work and stay at home after you have children, you need to support her in this choice and acknowledge the valuable task she is performing. You also need to encourage your wife to see friends, find ways of retaining career ties, and generally maintain interests outside the home. In this way, she will avoid the feelings of isolation that often plague homemakers.

SUMMARY

Since industrialization, "his" work has mainly been to function as a provider and "her" work has been to care for the home. But in the industrial economy, only paid labor has been defined as work. The homemaker has an isolated role that tends to be devalued.

Since the 1960s, women have gone into the labor force in increasing numbers. Most married as well as single women now work outside the home; the most dramatic increase in labor force participation has occurred among married women with children under the age of six. Women may take jobs or enter careers. Those who are employed become part of either a dual-earner or dual-career family. With women employed, men have assumed a larger portion of family work, but women still do the bulk of that work.

Some women prefer not to work outside the home. Those who do may work for economic reasons, for the fulfillment that work brings, or for the power gained. Employed women generally do not believe that their marriages or families suffer because they work.

In some ways, dual-career families are more egalitarian than others. The wife is still likely to do more family work than the husband, and his career is still likely to take priority over hers. Dual-career families may be traditional, participant, or role-sharing. The commuter marriage is a special form of the dual-career family and poses a serious challenge to the maintenance of intimacy for the couple. Some of the other serious problems of dual-career families are: time management; whether to have, and how to raise, children; maintaining relationships with others without jeopardizing the marital relationship; and the special problems of the dual-career wife, who may be tempted to try to become a "super-woman." There are also satisfactions in the dual-career family, enough to make the arrangement worth all the potential problems.

Dual-earner couples face a number of challenges and problems in the areas of family work (who does what in the home?), balancing home and work demands, maintaining intimacy, and satisfactorily negotiating roles. Dual-earner families are at a greater risk of disruption. Yet many couples deal with the difficulties and achieve marital satisfaction.

While the life satisfaction of those in single-earner families is as high as those in dual-earner families, women who are career-oriented will have lower satisfaction if they are not employed, and men who feel deprived or whose self-esteem is threatened will have lower satisfaction if their wives are employed. Women who work outside the home are physically and mentally healthier than those who do not, particularly when the employment is in accord with their preference. An employed woman's adjustment is facilitated when she uses various coping strategies to deal with such problems as time constraints and her need to care for her physical and emotional well-being.

INTERNET CONNECTION
Work and Home

Through a mixture of personal choice and economic necessity the dual earner family has replaced the single earner family as the dominant type of family unit today. Married couples with and without children must adjust to increased stresses coming from competition between career as well as personal goals and responsibilities. The Family and Medical Leave Act signed by President Clinton in 1993 was designed, in part, to alleviate some of the pressures facing dual income families.

National Partnership for Women and Families

http://www.national partnership.org/workandfamily/fmleave/questions_answers.htm

www.mhhe
.com/lauer4

This website provides an overview of the goal and scope of the FMLA as well as online access to the complete text. Use the above website to respond to the following:

1. How, specifically does the FMLA protect families?
2. In what ways do you believe the FMLA can benefit dual income families? Single head of household families?
3. Develop an argument for the value of FMLA. Develop an argument for drastically cutting funds for the program. Critique both arguments.

INTIMACY IN FAMILIES

At some point or other in our lives, we all face the task of establishing meaningful intimate relationships with someone other than a partner. As children, we strive to maintain intimacy with our parents. Once married, most of us will have children. Bringing children into the home poses new challenges and new tasks in our quest for intimacy.

As with the marital relationship, meaningful intimate relationships are not guaranteed simply because a group of people live together in the same house. In some ways, in fact, the challenge of intimacy is more difficult as the family grows.

In this fourth part, then, we will examine family life over the life cycle, including the child-rearing years. We will discuss some of the issues that arise as the family grows, including problems of money, time management, and power and conflict in the family system.

CHAPTER 14

BECOMING A PARENT

Learning Objectives

After reading chapter 14, you should be able to:

1. Discuss the ways in which the birth rate, the ideal number of children, and sex preference have changed over the past few decades.

2. Explain why some people decide to have children and others choose to remain childless.

3. Outline the reasons for infertility.

4. Describe the process that infertile couples go through in coping with the knowledge of their infertility.

5. Discuss the various options that infertile couples have for obtaining a child.

6. Show the stresses involved in raising children and the effect of this stress on marital satisfaction.

7. Compare and contrast men's and women's experience of parenting.

8. Summarize the three primary styles of parenting.

9. Explain the consequences of parental behavior on the well-being of children.

10. Describe the advantages and liabilities of parenting at a later age.

CHANGING PATTERNS OF CHILDBEARING

We saw in chapter 1 that the **birth rate** in the United States has declined considerably during this century. In fact, since the early 1970s, the birth rate has been below the replacement level. That is, if the birth rate continues at this level for an extended period of time, the population will decline unless we have a lowered death rate and/or a sufficient number of immigrants to make up the difference.

Birth Rates

As figure 14.1 shows, the birth rate has fluctuated considerably. The rate declined dramatically from the mid-1950s to the mid-1970s, leveled off and increased somewhat in the late 1980s, and dropped again in the early 1990s. A declining birth rate does not necessarily mean fewer total births; after 1975,

S omeone has said that a new baby is total demand at one end and total irresponsibility at the other. If so, who would want one of those creatures around the house? Actually, most married people do, though most people also want fewer children than did past generations of parents. In this chapter, we shall look at changing patterns of childbearing, why most people want children, and why some do not. We will examine the problem of infertility. We will see how people cope with involuntary childlessness or the loss of a child through death or spontaneous abortion. We will briefly discuss some of the relatively new technologies to help people who would have remained childless in the past.

Children have significant consequences for the quality of our lives. We will discuss those consequences, along with the somewhat different parenting experiences of men and women. Finally, we will explore the consequences of differing parenting styles for the well-being of children.

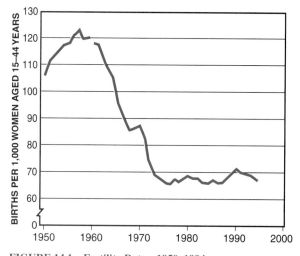

FIGURE 14.1   Fertility Rates: 1950–1994
Note: Beginning with 1959, trend line is based on registered live births; trend line for 1950–59 is based on live births adjusted for underregistration.
(*Source:* U.S. Department of Health and Human Services, 1994:3 and U.S. Bureau of Census 1997b:75.)

the number of live births rose because of the rise in the number of women of childbearing age (the baby boomers). To some extent, the increased birth rate of the late 1980s resulted from increases among both white and black women ages thirty-five to forty-four who had delayed childbearing (Haub 1992). But most of the increase occurred among women under the age of thirty.

In general, birth rates are higher among the poor and minorities than among nonpoor whites. Comparing racial and ethnic groups, Hispanics have the highest rates, followed by African Americans, Asian Americans, and American Indians; whites have the lowest rates (U.S. Bureau of the Census 1997b:20). The dramatic decline after the mid-1950s occurred in all the groups. Thus, while minority birth rates are higher than those of whites, all groups have lower rates than they did in the past. This is reflected in the declining proportion of families of all racial/ethnic groups with three or more children and the increasing proportion with no children (table 14.1). Uniformly, then, Americans are having fewer children.

Table 14.2 shows an overall profile of women who had children in 1995. Note that the birth rate is highest among Hispanics, those who are married, and those who are in the lower socioeconomic strata (as measured by level of income).

Preferences for Size and Sex

One thing that affects the birth rate is the preferred size of one's family, the ideal number of children. That ideal has changed over time. Since the 1930s, the Gallup organization has periodically asked people about the ideal size of a family. In 1936, the

TABLE 14.1
Families, by Number of Own Children Under 18 Years Old: 1970 to 1996

Race, Origin, Year	(1,000)	Number Percent Distribution			
		No Children	One Child	Two Children	Three or More Children
All Families					
1970	51,586	44	18	17	20
1980	59,550	48	21	19	12
1990	66,090	50	21	19	10
1996	69,594	51	20	19	10
White Families					
1970	42,261	45	18	18	19
1980	52,243	49	21	19	11
1990	56,590	53	20	18	9
1996	58,869	52	19	19	9
Black Families					
1970	4,887	39	18	15	29
1980	6,184	38	23	20	18
1990	7,470	41	25	19	14
1996	8,055	43	24	18	14
Hispanic Families[1]					
1970	2,004	30	20	19	31
1980	3,029	31	22	23	23
1990	4,840	37	23	21	19
1996	6,287	36	23	23	18

[1]Hispanic persons may be of any race.
Source: U.S. Bureau of the Census 1994:64 and 1997b:65.

TABLE 14.2

Social and Economic Characteristics of Women, 15 to 44 Years Old, Who Gave Birth in 1995

Characteristic	Number of Women (1,000)	Total Births per 1,000 women
Total	60,225	61.4
Racial/Ethnic Group:		
White	48,603	59.2
Black	8,617	70.6
Hispanic[1]	6,632	79.6
Marital Status:		
Currently married	31,616	86.5
Widowed or divorced	5,762	28.4
Never married	22,846	36.3
Educational Attainment:		
Less than high school	12,629	57.3
High school, 4 years	18,404	67.4
College: 1 or more years	29,192	59.3
Labor Force Status:		
Employed	39,989	46.5
Unemployed	3,287	53.5
Not in labor force	16,949	98.1
Occupation of Employed Women:		
Managerial-professional	11,059	46.2
Technical, sales, admin. support	16,997	48.6
Service workers	7,612	44.0
Farming, forestry, fishing	501	41.0
Precision prod., craft, repair	813	56.6
Operators, fabricators, laborers	3,007	39.5
Family Income:		
Under $10,000	6,957	91.0
$10,000 to $19,999	8,159	64.3
$20,000 to $24,999	4,542	60.6
$25,000 to $29,999	4,364	57.0
$30,000 to $34,999	4,076	60.6
$35,000 to $49,999	9,949	59.1
$50,000 to $74,999	9,720	52.5
$75,000 and over	7,088	53.1

[1]Hispanic persons may be of any race.
Source: U.S. Bureau of the Census 1997b:81.

first year of the survey, two-thirds of Americans said that three or more children is the ideal and the mean number preferred was 3.6; by the late 1990s, 41 percent said that three or more is the ideal and the mean number preferred was 2.5 (Gallup Organization 1997).

These changing preferences for family size are reflected in actual birth rates. Sex preference is also a factor in birth rates. The Gallup poll asked which sex people would prefer if they could only have one child (Gallup Organization 1997). In thirteen of the sixteen nations surveyed, those who expressed a preference were more likely to indicate a boy than a girl. In the United States, 35 percent said a boy, 23 percent said a girl, and 42 percent said they had no preference.

National data show that when there is a preference, it affects birth rates. People who prefer a boy, for instance, may have more children than they initially expected if their first one or two children are girls. And vice versa. Those who have more than one child are likely to want at least one of each sex. Thus, women with different-sex children are more likely to stop childbearing than women with same-sex children, a tendency which is stronger for highly educated than less educated women (Yamaguchi and Ferguson 1995). In other words, if a couple has two children of the same sex, they may have a third child in the hope of having an opposite-sex offspring even though their ideal was two children.

TO BEAR OR NOT TO BEAR

Do you want to have children? Why or why not? Think about the matter a bit before you read the following materials. Reflect on how your own thoughts compare with those of others.

Why People Want to Have Children

As we pointed out in chapter 4, some people who have children do not want them, at least not at the time of conception. As many as one of every ten children born each year were unwanted when they were conceived. On the other hand, in a poll of people forty years or younger, 84 percent said they wanted to have children at some point in their lives (Gallup and Newport 1990). The desire for children is so strong in many couples that both the husband and the wife may grieve for two years or more following a pregnancy loss (Stinson et al. 1992). The wife's grief is likely to be stronger and last longer than the husband's, however.

Why do people want to have children? The reasons are many (Berelson 1979; Gerson 1986; Gallup and Newport 1990). One or more of the following reasons may motivate a particular couple.

Experience of Happiness in a Family   If you grew up in a family that provided you with meaningful experiences, you are likely to want to have your own family. For example, women who perceive their fathers as being warm, affectionate, and helpful and who recall their family life as a happy one are more highly motivated than others to have children (Gerson 1986:58).

We all tend to try to recreate the situations that made us happy in the past. If you associate happiness with family life, therefore, you are likely to want your own family.

Personal Fulfillment   Having children may be perceived as not only adding to our happiness but to

Most couples want to have children.

our fulfillment as humans (Gallup and Newport 1990:8). Some people believe that the experience of having a child is unique, that it adds a dimension to life that is unparalleled by any other. Children enable us to express "life values" (Gerson 1986:59). Friends who have children may convey that impression to you. The mass media may reinforce it through stories of parents who find ultimate joy in the experience of childbirth.

The fulfillment, of course, comes not only at the time of birth but through the child-rearing years. To love and be loved, to share in the growing child's delights of discovery and learning, to shape the life of another, are unique experiences that many people find personally fulfilling. A professional man, deeply involved in his career, said to us: "I can't conceive of my life without my children." Although he is very successful, he finds his children to be an indispensable part of his growth.

Personal and Family Legacy Many if not most of us want to leave our imprint on the world in some way. In addition, there is a desire to carry on the family line. Frequently these desires only awaken as you get older, but at some point you are likely to experience them. Children are the means of satisfying those desires. They are your personal legacy to humanity. And they are the extension of your family line (Berelson 1979).

The importance of this is illustrated by the attorney who told us that she insisted on retaining her maiden name and wanted to have children with that name. "My parents had three girls," she said. "If I don't keep my maiden name and have children by that name, it will die out. And that would deeply hurt my father."

Personal Status In some cultures, having children is a means of achieving high status in the community. Among the ancient Jews, for example, a woman was not considered fully human until she bore a son. In some contemporary societies, women still gain status by bearing children and men gain status (demonstrating their manhood) by fathering children.

For some Americans, having children is also an avenue to higher status. The enhanced status may come from family members, friends, or colleagues. After all, to both achieve in your work and fulfill the responsibilities of parenthood means that you are a very competent person.

Religious Beliefs Those who identify with an organized religion are more likely to want children than those who do not (Gerson 1986:58). Most religions are strongly profamily. Some religions, such as Roman Catholicism and Mormonism, stress theological reasons for people having large families. A couple strongly committed to such a religious faith may feel that they are fulfilling the will of God by having not merely one but many children.

Social Expectations When we ask why people "want" children, we need to recognize that there are

some who have children without necessarily either wanting or not wanting them. That is, they do not think much about the matter in such terms. They believe that everyone who is married should have children as a matter of course because that is normal and typical. In our society, there are in fact many pressures, some subtle and some not-so-subtle, for married people to have children.

While the expectations are changing somewhat, it is still true that married people are expected to have children. No couple, after all, has to explain why they decided to have a baby. But explanations are usually in order if a couple decides not to have children. Moreover, a couple that announces a forthcoming child is likely to be greeted with smiles and congratulations. A couple that declares their intention to remain child-free is likely to be greeted with quizzical looks and perhaps frowns. Clearly, we still expect married people to have children if they can.

The Child-Free Option

In spite of all the reasons for having children, increasing numbers of couples have opted to be child-free. By the mid-1990s, 8.9 percent of American women aged fifteen to forty-four years of age indicated that they expected to have no children (Abma et al. 1997). There are sex differences in the desire for children, however. Among a national sample of those who are child-free, husbands rated the importance of having children higher than did their wives and were more likely to want to have children than were their wives (Seccombe 1991).

The choice is not an easy one for most people. One woman told us: "I have agonized more and cried more about this decision than any I have ever made." But just as there are many reasons why people want to have children, there are also many reasons why they decide to remain child-free (Bernard 1975). For any particular couple, the reasons are likely to include one or more of the following.

Personal Fulfillment Not everyone believes that fulfillment comes best through children. Some people feel that children impede rather than facilitate personal fulfillment (Ramu and Tavuchis 1986). They opt to remain child-free, therefore, in order that they may find fulfillment through their work, their interests, and/or their adult relationships. Children require time and energy that they prefer to put into other pursuits, those they believe more likely to yield personal satisfaction and growth.

Focus on Career People strongly committed to a career, and particularly the dual-career couple, may prefer to remain child-free. As we noted in the last chapter, dual-career couples face some difficult questions when they decide to have children. For some, the questions themselves are reason enough not to have children. Neither the husband nor the wife may be willing to use time and energy for child-rearing tasks.

As this suggests, women who are not career-oriented and those who tend to agree that women should take care of the home and men should be breadwinners are more likely to become mothers and to have more than one child. One researcher found that 38 percent of such traditional women, compared to 14 percent of nontraditional women, have three or more children (Nock 1987). Additionally, nontraditional women are twice as likely as traditional women to have no children.

Economic Costs of Children In addition to time and energy, children cost a great deal of money. Some people feel that the costs are not worth the benefits, that it will cost them more than whatever satisfactions they gain from becoming parents (Callan 1986a). A family with two children in the middle-income range will spend about 40 to 45 percent of its after-tax income on the children.

There are indirect as well as direct costs. Consider the fact that children may narrow the range of economic opportunities parents will have. Women in particular may have to make career compromises if they have children. Men, too, may be constrained in their careers if, for example, a move that would mean career advancement must be deferred because of children's school needs. For example, a child may be one year away from graduating from a primary or secondary school. Or a child may be in a program that is unavailable in the new area. Such opportunity costs are economic as well as personal; the family may lose a considerable amount of potential income.

The costs continue, of course, at least until the children have finished their education. For those who expect their children to get a college education, the costs go up considerably. Taking all the costs—both direct and indirect—into consideration, how much does a child require? One estimate is that the total cost of a middle-class child born in the late 1990s will be $1,455,581 (Longman 1998)!

Focus on the Marriage Some people feel that children will detract from the marital relationship, and they prefer to focus their energies on that relationship (Ramu and Tavuchis 1986). Those in child-free marriages talk about the freedom they have and the continuing romance and sex in their relationships. They feel that they are able to spend more time together and develop a more intimate relationship than would be possible with children. Joan, an artist in her forties, expresses her feelings this way:

> My husband and I have talked about having children many times. But we realized that we were talking about this because other people expected us to have children as much as from our own desires. I guess I would like to have children eventually, but we both have careers and we cherish our marriage. I don't want to sacrifice my marriage to the children. I've seen other people do that. We won't. Our relationship means too much to us.

Doubts About Parenting Skills Clearly, not everyone makes a good parent. Good parenting requires certain skills, and some people question whether they have those skills. They feel that they do not want to be parents unless they can do a good job, and they're not sure they can cope with the demands of parenting. As a graduate student put it: "I would love to be a mother, but I don't think I have the patience to deal with children. I just don't think I would be a good enough mother." Her desire to mother was not stronger than her doubts about her skills, so she opted to remain child-free.

INVOLUNTARY CHILDLESSNESS

If this were a perfect world, those who wanted children would have them, and those who didn't would not. But just as there is a substantial number

PERSPECTIVE
To Be a Parent? The Agonies of the Decision

Lori and Ben are in their late twenties. She is a graduate student in biology, and he is a practicing engineer. Lori talks about their struggle with the question of whether or not to have children. As with many couples, it has not been a settled question for them. Through their years together they have both changed in their attitudes. And although they seem to be in agreement now, the issue continues to trouble them:

I think that both of us would like to have children once I'm finished with school and have gotten my career started. We've made a decision to wait until then. And we think we might have two children. It is interesting that our attitudes have changed over the years. Ben absolutely did *not* want children when we were first married. But I assumed that we would have them anyway after three or four

years. I thought he would probably change his mind.

But as I progressed in college and became more career-oriented, my attitude changed and became like his. I decided that I preferred to pursue my career and not get involved with the hassles of a family. However, by then Ben had changed. He had gotten much more warm-hearted and affectionate with children. When we were first married, he had a kind of dread of them. He felt they were too much responsibility and too much of a burden. I always had a more tender feeling about children, but now I've gotten to feel somewhat more fearful of the vast responsibility that's involved. Maybe that's because we've both finally come to a point where we agree that we will have children. But I'm not sure how it's going to work out with both of us pursuing careers.

Anyway, something really interesting happened this past week. I've always religiously taken my birth-control pills. We've been very responsible. We didn't want any unplanned pregnancy. But a few days ago I accidentally dropped my pill between the kitchen counter and the stove. I got Ben to move the stove away from the wall so I could retrieve it. But we couldn't find it. I would have joyfully popped that peach-colored pill into my mouth even though it had fallen into a thick layer of dust. But it was lost.

I realized that my panic over losing the pill showed that I'm not ready yet for motherhood. I expect to feel differently in a few years. I really do want to have children. And Ben says he is now definitely ready. Life is sure complicated, isn't it?

---

of unwanted pregnancies, there is a substantial number of people who want children but who cannot bear their own.

Infertility

Infertility is usually defined as the inability to conceive after a year of unprotected sexual intercourse. Infertility does not mean that a couple has no children. Sometimes people have one or more children, desire still more, but are unable for various reasons to conceive again.

According to the Centers for Disease Control (1997b), a little over 7 percent of married couples are infertile, a slight decrease from the early 1980s. However, not every woman who wants to have a

baby is married. A national study of all women aged fifteen to forty-four found that 10 percent reported some form of impaired ability to bear children, an increase from the 8 percent figure of the early 1980s (Chandra and Stephen 1998). This means that millions of American couples and American women who want to have a first or an additional child cannot do so. Some will be able to bear with medical assistance. Others will remain infertile.

What causes infertility? Numerous factors are involved. Sustained exposure to environmental factors, such as toxic chemicals, can render an individual sterile. Sexually transmitted diseases can damage a woman's fallopian tubes. Infections from intrauterine contraceptive devices have made some women infertile. Both men and women can suffer from infertility. Let us look briefly at the more common types.[1]

Female infertility can be due to **endometriosis,** a disease in which the tissue that lines the inside of the uterus begins to grow outside as well. The growth may prevent the sperm from meeting the egg in the fallopian tubes. The causes of endometriosis are unknown. It tends to affect women in their twenties and thirties who have not had children. It can frequently be corrected by drugs or surgery.

Various other conditions can also cause blockage of the fallopian tubes, thus preventing conception. Scar tissue from inflammations is a common cause of blocked tubes. The blockage can sometimes be removed through surgery.

A third reason that a woman may be infertile is that she doesn't **ovulate** properly; that is, her body does not release the egg as it should. Drugs may correct this situation.

Finally, a woman's body may, for various reasons, hinder the sperm or even kill it. Again, drug therapy may be effective in resolving the problem. Or the couple may be able to make use of some of the new technologies available.

Male infertility is somewhat less common than female but may also arise from a number of different factors. Males are infertile generally because they have a low sperm count or because their sperm do not swim as fast as they should. Low sperm counts may result from injury, from infection (particularly from having mumps after childhood), exposure to radiation, birth defects, or a variety of other disorders (Masters, Johnson, and Kolodny 1988:144). Sperm production also may be decreased by alcohol and drug use, including some prescription drugs. Finally, environmental pollutants may depress sperm count. Some or all of these factors are probably involved in a substantial drop in sperm counts in the United States and Europe since the 1930s (Schulte 1997). Male infertility can sometimes be treated through drugs or surgery.

In spite of our knowledge of the sources of infertility, there are some cases in which the tests yield nothing. That is, some people seem to have no detectable problem that prevents conception, yet they continue to be unable to conceive. In such cases, they may try some of the technologies described in the "Options for the Infertile" section, though for some couples the expense of such procedures makes them unattainable.

Coping with Infertility

If you strongly desire to have a child but are unable to conceive after a year or more of unprotected sexual relations, you may find yourself struggling to cope with this unexpected situation. Most of us believe that if we want to have children, we can. When we want to and find that we cannot, we are likely to be quite distressed.

A study that compared infertile women with mothers and voluntarily childless wives found that the infertile women reported lower general levels of well-being and rated their lives as less interesting, emptier, and less rewarding than did other women (Callan 1987). Infertility is not simply a biological condition. It deeply affects people. When a couple is unable to conceive, they may experience lowered self-esteem, a diminished sense of control over their lives, and more marital conflict (Abbey, Andrews, and Halman 1992; Slade et al. 1992; Leiblum 1993). In fact, those unable to conceive may experience a process of grief similar to that endured when a loved one dies (Deveraux and Hammerman 1998).

The first stage of the process is *surprise.* People simply do not expect to be infertile, particularly those who are achievement-oriented and think of themselves as capable of dealing adequately with the obstacles of life. Surprise is followed by *denial,* a sense that "this can't happen to me." Then there is *anger,* anger because of the pain and inconvenience of the tests, anger at the pressures from family and friends, anger at the inappropriate comments of people, and perhaps anger at those who seem to have children easily or those who have them but don't want them.

Guilt is the fourth stage. Some people may feel that God is punishing them for their sins. Some find other ways to blame themselves for the condition. *Depression* is a typical fifth part of the process. There is a sense of loss, a sadness, perhaps even a sense of despair. Associated with the sense of loss is *grief.* Those who are infertile grieve because they

---

[1] *U.S. News and World Report,* 5 October 1987, pp. 60–61.

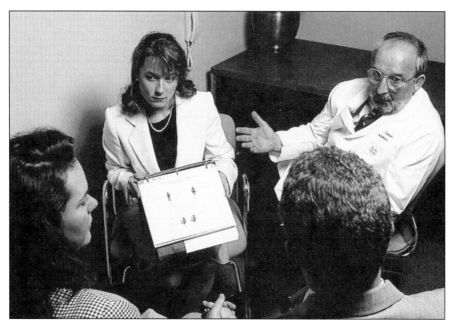

Technology has opened up many new options for those who are infertile.

cannot produce another living being, similar to those who grieve because they have lost a living being. Unfortunately, while those who lose someone through death are expected to grieve openly, that may be more difficult for the infertile. After all, their loss is not of an actual but only a potential person. As such, it may not be viewed as a real and significant loss by many people.

In addition to, and perhaps partly because of, the various negative emotions experienced, the couple is likely to have some problems in their relationship. Sometimes a crisis draws a couple together and enhances their intimacy. The crisis of infertility, at least initially, sometimes strains rather than strengthens the intimate relationship (Sabatelli, Meth, and Gavazzi 1988; Ulbrich, Coyle, and Llabre 1990; Pepe and Byrne 1991). Among other things, there may be diminished marital satisfaction, decreased frequency of and satisfaction with sexual relations, and increased conflict. On the other hand, many couples experience enhanced emotional support from each other. In essence, it seems that infertility calls the meaning and purpose of the marriage into question. The process of reconstructing the meaning and purpose "can place a

considerable strain on the relationship" (Sabatelli, Meth, and Gavazzi 1988: 338).

The final stage of the process is *resolution*. A couple may resolve its situation in a number of ways. Some may accept the fact that they will not have children and get on with their lives. Most will probably first attempt various other ways to have a child. As we shall see in the sections that follow, however, using new technologies or going the route of adoption can be very expensive and frustrating. Many couples do not fully resolve their infertility for years. Those with a strong relationship will ultimately be strengthened for having worked through the crisis; those with weak bonds may break up.

OPTIONS FOR THE INFERTILE

Those who are infertile and who want children, or more children than they already have, can choose from a variety of options. In the mid-1990s, about 15 percent of the women of reproductive age had used some kind of infertility service, including medical advice, tests, drugs, surgery, or other kinds of treatment (Abma et al. 1997). The services can be very expensive, running into tens of thousands of dollars for some couples.

Artificial Insemination

Artificial insemination is the injection of sperm into a woman's vagina. To result in conception, of course, the procedure must be carried out at the time the woman is ovulating (releasing an egg). Artificial insemination uses either the husband's semen (abbreviated AIH) or that of an anonymous donor (abbreviated AID).

AIH is useful when the husband's sperm count is low. The physician can take a larger amount of sperm from several ejaculations. AIH can also be done using fresh semen and inserting it into the vagina at the mouth of the uterus. Only a small portion of the sperm get to that location during intercourse, so the chances of conception are enhanced by the AIH procedure.

If the husband is sterile or his sperm count is exceptionally low, AID may be used (this is also an option for single women who want a child). The couple will normally select a donor from an anonymous list that gives information about health, intelligence, and various physical characteristics. If fresh semen is used, the pregnancy rate with AID is about 75 percent; the rate is around 60 percent when frozen semen from a sperm bank is used (Masters, Johnson, and Kolodny 1988:146).

AID is less acceptable to people than AIH. Some religions view the procedure as morally wrong. Even the courts have occasionally defined it as adultery. Some men feel humiliated; some women are reluctant to have another man be the biological father of their children. One way that a couple may minimize potential problems is to have the physician mix the sperm of the husband with that of a donor so that the couple can't be sure who the natural father is. Generally, however, men whose wives conceive by AID assume the father's role with enthusiasm.

In Vitro Fertilization

If the infertility is due to damaged or blocked fallopian tubes and the condition cannot be corrected, the couple may opt for **in vitro fertilization.** In this procedure, the eggs are removed from the woman's body. Fertility drugs may be used to facilitate the development of healthy eggs and to control the timing of ovulation (Sher et al. 1995). The use of the drugs poses a number of risks, including the possibility of multiple fetuses, various side effects, and ovarian tumors and cancer (National Cancer Institute 1998). The issue of ovarian cancer is debatable, however, because the research is still inconclusive.

Once the eggs are removed from the woman's body, they are fertilized with sperm in a laboratory. The resulting embryo is then implanted in the woman's uterus.

The first case of in vitro fertilization leading to pregnancy and birth of a child occurred in England. In 1978, Louise Brown was born as a result of the work of Doctors Patrick Steptoe and Robert Edwards. The Brown baby was the first success after more than a decade of research and more than thirty failed attempts.

Since 1978, fertility clinics have opened up around the world. Of the tens of thousands of women who have tried to conceive through in vitro fertilization, how many have succeeded? The clinics have varying success rates, but probably average around 20 percent. The success rate depends in part upon a woman's age. In 1995, the success rate was about 25 percent for women aged thirty-four years and younger, but declined rapidly after that (Centers for Disease Control 1997a). The rate was less than 15 percent for women at age forty and zero after the age of forty-six.

Some people are opposed to in vitro fertilization on the grounds that it violates God's way or the "natural" way. Some people also are disturbed by the fact that clinics normally fertilize a number of eggs. The first step in the procedure is to give the woman daily hormone injections to stimulate egg production. Thus, the woman produces a number of eggs, and each is fertilized. Extra fertilized eggs may be discarded (in some the cells are not dividing normally anyway). To some people, this is the same as abortion—in other words, it is a form of murder because they regard the fertilized egg as a human.

For other people, however, procedures such as in vitro fertilization mean that they have the opportunity to become parents. Without the procedure, they would not have children of their own. To deny them the use of the procedure is to deny them the opportunity to have biologically related children.

Surrogate Mothers

When the wife is infertile or incapable of carrying a child, a couple may opt for a surrogate mother. The surrogate mother is a woman who volunteers to carry the baby of the couple and give the infant to them at the time of birth. The arrangement is typically set up with a legal contract. There are at least eight commercial surrogate mother programs in the United States and a number of individuals who handle surrogate contracts on a free-lance basis (Ragone 1994). The total cost ranges from about $30,000 to $45,000 or more.

The surrogate mother may be inseminated with the husband's sperm or, if the husband is also infertile, with the sperm of a donor. If the wife still has functioning ovaries, she can provide an egg, use in vitro fertilization, and have the resulting embryo implanted in the surrogate mother.

As with all the possibilities discussed in this section, the option of a surrogate mother is controversial. In part, each option may present problems because technology has become available before legal and ethical guidelines have been developed to deal with various complications. For instance, two cases during the 1980s illustrate some of the complex and painful problems involved with surrogate motherhood.

The first case occurred in 1983. A Michigan woman gave birth to a deformed baby. A New York man had contracted with her to have a child by AID but rejected it when he discovered it was deformed. He believed that he had firm legal grounds for the rejection because he was not the child's biological father. The surrogate mother didn't want the child, either. Newspaper headlines pointed out that the nation now had an "unclaimed" infant. Eventually, the surrogate mother agreed to keep the child. Future cases may be more difficult if both parties are adamant in their refusal to accept such a child.

The second case occurred in 1986 after Mary Beth Whitehead of New Jersey gave birth to "Baby M." She had contracted with a couple to act as a surrogate mother and had been inseminated with the sperm of the husband. After the girl was born, Whitehead didn't want to give it up. She felt she had a right to keep the child because she was the biological mother. She and her husband fled with the girl to Florida. Ultimately, a New Jersey court awarded the girl to the couple who had contracted for her, honoring the biological father's rights and arguing that Whitehead must honor the contract she had signed.

Adoption

If the above methods fail or a couple objects to using them, adoption is a final option. The number of children living in adoptive families has been decreasing (figure 14.2), because of both the number of unwanted pregnancies that are aborted and the

FIGURE 14.2   Number of children living with adoptive parents
(*Source:* U.S. Bureau of the Census 1994:66.)

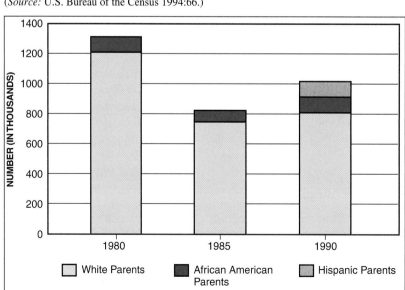

number of single women who choose to keep their babies rather than give them up for adoption (Bachrach, Stolley, and London 1992). The tendency for unmarried women to give up a child for adoption varies by race, however. White women are still more likely than others, although their tendency to relinquish their children has dropped considerably since the 1970s. Black women have always been reluctant to give up their children. Rather than relinquishing the child, unwed adolescent black mothers may opt for shared parenting within the extended family or for placing the child temporarily with someone else (Sandven and Resnick 1990). Finally, relinquishment by Hispanic mothers is almost nonexistent. As a result, the number of adoptions of foreign children has risen dramatically.

A national survey reported that about 3.5 percent of women aged fifteen to forty-four have tried to adopt at some time in their lives (Bachrach, London, and Maza 1991). Black and white women are equally likely to try to adopt. A larger proportion of black women who want to adopt, however, are able to bear children of their own (Bachrach, London, and Maza 1991).

Children may be adopted either through an agency or through a private transaction. Governmental agencies are the least expensive way to adopt a child, because the adoptive parents only pay the legal fees involved. But their requirements are very strict, the time involved is long (usually a minimum of nine months, and it may stretch into years), and the number of children available is small. Private agencies can handle the matter in less time, but they are more expensive.

Instead of going through an agency, some people attempt a private transaction, either through a physician or a lawyer who specializes in private adoptions. Those who use the services of a lawyer may engage in what is called an *open adoption,* which became fairly common in the 1980s. Open adoptions are in sharp contrast to the secretive processes of the past. If you adopted a child through an agency in past years, you would not know the biological parents and they would not know you. The secrecy would, in theory, protect the child, the adoptive parents, and the biological parents. The mother, who was frequently unwed, would not have to bear the stigma of having a child without a husband, and she could get on with her life. The adoptive parents would not have to worry about the mother wanting to have a close relationship with her child at some point in the future. And the child would not be caught between the two sets of parents.

But the secretive procedures so common in the past overlooked one important fact: adopted children generally get to a point where they want to know about their biological parents. They may even insist on their right to have information about their genetic heritage. In many cases, they have won the right to such information and have helped to change the laws. Adopted children who have a reunion with their biological parents and other birth relatives may or may not want to have a close relationship with them (Gladstone and Westhues 1998). But that does not affect either their desire or their right to know their biological family.

An open adoption avoids the problem of the adopted child's desire to know about his or her genetic heritage. The open adoption may involve anything from a minimal exchange of information to extensive contact with the birth mother both before and after the child is born (Grotevant et al. 1994). The following case illustrates extensive contact.

Sandra is a young woman who became pregnant while unmarried. She did not want to have an abortion, but she was financially and emotionally unable to care for a baby. She contacted a lawyer who specialized in open adoptions. The Smiths, a couple in their late thirties, were unable to have children but badly wanted them. They had contacted the same lawyer. The lawyer gave Sandra eight biographies of couples who wanted to adopt; the Smiths were one of the eight.

Sandra was three months pregnant at the time. She selected the Smiths. The lawyer then arranged for a meeting between Sandra and the Smiths. Sandra felt that she had made the right choice. Thereafter, the Smiths and Sandra met on a weekly basis. The Smiths went with Sandra to her Lamaze classes and were present at the birth. The boy is now about six months old. Sandra and the Smiths are friends. The Smiths will tell their son about his mother when he is older. He will have the opportunity to meet her and interact with her. At this point, they are negotiating about the amount of time that Sandra will spend with the boy.

Couples can adopt a child through an agency or a private transaction.

The adoption cost about the same as one through a private agency. Both Sandra and the Smiths are quite happy with the arrangement. This is not to say that there will be no problems in the future, but open adoptions seem to work well for many people. Most couples studied in open adoption situations report being satisfied and confident that the birth mother will not try to reclaim her child (Grotevant et al. 1994).

CHILDREN AND THE QUALITY OF LIFE

The reasons given previously for why people want to have children imply that the children will enhance the quality of life. What does the evidence say?

The Stresses of Raising Children

Clearly, raising children is a demanding and sometimes agonizing task (Bird 1997). Stress, in the form of emotional and physical strain and tension, will be experienced by all parents at some time and by a few a good deal of the time. Evidence of this may be seen in the numerous support groups that have been developed to help parents. Support groups are needed because there is very little formal training available for the task, even though most people agree that raising a child is one of the most important and challenging jobs that one ever undertakes.

Support groups are available to help at virtually every stage of parenting. Both national and local groups exist. Depending on the area where you live, you can find groups that deal with parenting generally or specific aspects of parenting. For example, the La Leche League offers women an opportunity to meet together to learn about breast feeding and to share practical mothering tips. Children are viewed as assets, and the purpose is to enhance the quality of mothering. There are other groups that focus on positive methods of discipline. Toughlove is a support group that provides support to those who have problems with adolescents. Parent education classes also are available in local school districts. They furnish aid in such matters as sex education, communication skills, and helping the child in school. Parents Without Partners is a support group for single parents. Parents Anonymous offers help to those who abuse or who fear they are about to abuse their children. Various other groups offer specialized help and support to those suffering from depression

INVOLVEMENT
Problems and Possibilities with Options

What is your initial reaction to the various options mentioned in this chapter—artificial insemination (do you feel differently about AIH and AID?), in vitro fertilization, surrogate mothers, and adoption? Which would be acceptable to you and which would be unacceptable? Why?

Select one of the options and make some notes about your feelings. Then research it in the popular literature. Use the *Readers' Guide to Periodical Literature* to find articles. Begin with the latest issue available and work back in time until you have found at least ten articles that deal with your option.

How is the option treated in the popular literature? What kinds of legal and ethical problems are posed by that option? What are the effects of the option on people's well-being? What arguments pro and con are offered? How do the attitudes reflected in the popular articles compare with your own feelings? Did anything you read change any of your feelings? If so, how?

If the class participates in this project, set up a debate using the information gathered in this text and the popular sources. Assign some students to take a strong pro position and others to take a strong con position. Discuss such things as the ethical, legal, interpersonal (quality of the couple's intimacy), and personal consequences of the option. Let the class then respond and vote on which option they prefer.

---

after delivery, to mothers of twins, to parents of hyperactive children, and to parents of children with learning disabilities.

The stresses of child-rearing may begin as soon as the infant is brought home. Most people respond to a baby with tenderness, but babies can evoke frustration as well—frustration that affects both mothers and fathers (Barnett, Brennan, and Marshall 1994). For example, a study of over one hundred mothers and fathers of infants three to five months old found a number of sources of stress (Ventura 1987). About a third of the mothers and two-thirds of the fathers described stresses that resulted from their multiple-role demands (the typical problems of the dual-earner family). The effort to meet adequately the demands of work, marriage, and children can be exhausting.

The care of the infant is also stressful:

> The infant's fussy behavior in relation to feeding or soothing techniques was the major stress reported by 35% of mothers and 20% of fathers (Ventura 1987:27).

Mothers said they often felt guilty, helpless, or angry when trying to care for a fussy infant. Fathers felt stress because they didn't know what to do when the infant would not sleep or respond to their attempts to soothe it. Some of the subjects (14 percent of mothers and 11 percent of fathers) also reported being stressed with each other. They had in-

creased marital conflict, less frequent sexual relations, and felt a lack of support from each other since the arrival of the baby.

As the infant grows, there are always "daily hassles" that are stressful to parents (Crnic and Booth 1991). For example, a group of parents of five-year-olds noted such things as: continually cleaning up kids' messes; nagging, whining, or complaining by the children; kids not listening and not obeying without being nagged; kids interrupting adult conversation or interaction; and struggles over going to bed at night (Crnic and Greenberg 1990).

Systems Theory Applied

The bulk of parents agree that the teen years are the most difficult of all (Gallup and Newport 1990:11). But parenting stress can occur at any age. A five-year study of twenty-five hundred Massachusetts women reported that 39 percent identified children as their primary source of stress (Mehren 1988). The stress can get intense when the marriage itself is troubled and one parent enlists a child into a coalition against the other parent. This situation, called *triangulation* by *systems theorists,* only increases the problems of the family and may require therapy in order to help both the child and the marriage (Broderick 1993).

The stress of parenting does not necessarily cease when the children are grown. For instance, when adult children have serious problems in their lives, their parents may get depressed (Pillemer and Suitor 1991). And having an adult child return to live in the home can be more stressful than having a child leave home (Mehren 1988).

The return home of an adult child raises such issues as control (do the parents have any control over the child's schedule, activities, etc.?), division of labor (is the child obligated to help around the house?), differing preferences (which TV program to watch?), and privacy (as one woman said, "We're back to having sex when our son is asleep or out, which isn't very often.").

Children and Marital Satisfaction

In the Massachusetts study (Mehren 1988), some of the couples indicated more marital problems after they had children. Are children, then, hazardous to marriage? Do they inevitably detract from the quality of the marital relationship? We know that first-born children tend to increase the stability of marriages through their preschool years (Waite and Lillard 1991). But does that mean that the marriage is still as satisfying as it was or just that the parents are "hanging in there" for the sake of the children?

Many studies have confirmed the conclusion of Lewis and Spanier (1979) that marital satisfaction declines with the onset of the child-rearing years, then rises again when the children leave home. But some research disputes or modifies that conclusion (Vaillant and Vaillant 1993). Belsky and Kelly (1994) studied 250 new parents during their first postbaby year and found four different patterns: for slightly less than 13 percent, marital satisfaction declined severely; 38 percent experienced a moderate decline; 30 percent reported no change; and 19 percent experienced an improvement. Those with improved marital satisfaction are likely to be more educated, married longer, and have higher levels of income (Belsky and Rovine 1990).

 Conflict Theory Applied

When Belsky and Kelly (1994) sought to identify the cause of decline that occurred in roughly half of the couples, they found the problem was not rooted in stress related to the baby's behavior. Rather, two things are involved in the decline. The first is the fact that the baby brings typical male-female differences into focus. We have

seen that men and women generally have a certain number of *diverse and even contradictory ways of feeling and thinking*. These differences can come into sharp focus when parents are confronted with the important and demanding task of caring for a baby.

The second factor involved in the decline is that some of the mechanisms, which the parents had previously used to deal with their differences, are no longer available to them. For example, disagreement about whose career was more important could be dealt with by simply not talking about it. When the baby comes, the disagreement can no longer be avoided because at least one of the parents may have to put his or her career on the "parent-track." Similarly, differences about the division of labor in the home may have been averted by hiring a housekeeper. When the baby comes, there may be insufficient income for a housekeeper and the couple must confront their differences and work them out.

But there are other factors involved in the decline in marital satisfaction. Researchers who asked thirty-seven couples to keep a diary of time use before and after the birth of a child found that changes in relational patterns affected satisfaction (Monk et al. 1996). The mothers were more likely than the fathers to feel less satisfied with the marriage, mainly because they had so little time to themselves. The fathers were more likely to feel depression than lower satisfaction, mainly because they had less time alone with their wives.

Some babies, of course, are easier to care for than others. Some children seem to be easier to rear than others. The greater the stress of parenting, whatever the age of the children, the more likely the parents feel diminished well-being both personally and in their marriage (Lavee, Sharlin, and Katz 1996).

In sum, there is a tendency for marital satisfaction to decline somewhat after children are born and throughout the child-rearing years, a tendency which holds true not only for whites but for racial and ethnic minorities such as African Americans (Crohan 1996).

We will comment further about marital satisfaction and children in the next chapter, but four points should be made here about those couples who experience a decline in marital satisfaction after the birth of a child.

First, most research has shown that not only couples with children but couples generally report a decline in marital satisfaction during the first two decades (McHale and Huston 1985). A study of changes in ninety-eight couples over the first two and a half years of marriage reported that both the parents and the childless couples tended to report a decline in feelings of love, marital satisfaction, shared activities, and frequency of positive interaction with each other (MacDermid, Huston, and McHale 1990).

Second, to say that satisfaction is lower is not to say that people are dissatisfied. After all, satisfaction is at a peak in the first flush of marriage. If it changes at all, it is most likely to go down. But it does not go down to the point of dissatisfaction for the majority of couples.

Third, at least some of the couples who experience a decline were already having serious problems before the baby came. When an unhappy couple has a child, however, they are less likely to get divorced in the next few years (White, Booth, and Edwards 1986). For at least some couples, then, the transition to parenthood does not mean that a happy marriage becomes an unhappy one, but that an unhappy marriage becomes even more unhappy.

Finally, in some cases marital satisfaction actually goes up after the couple has children. And in the long run, children are likely to contribute to the stability and satisfaction a couple experience. In her study of marriages of fifty-plus years, Alford-Cooper (1998:78) reported that 57 percent of the couples said that their children contributed to the success of their unions and most of the couples "regarded child rearing as one of the happiest, most meaningful experiences of their lives."

The Satisfactions of Raising Children

In spite of the problems and the stresses, most people continue to want children. And the great majority of those who are parents indicate that the experience has given them great satisfaction. This happens even when the parents lack some of the resources we would all prefer to have. Thus, a study of sixty African American mothers with lower-than-average income and education found that they enjoyed being parents and that they were perceived by themselves and their children to be successfully fulfilling their roles (Strom et al. 1990).

In a review of the research literature, Ann Goetting (1986) drew a number of conclusions, including:

Generally, satisfaction with the parental role is very high.

Women report more fulfillment as parents than men, but they also see parenthood as more burdensome and restrictive.

Women are more satisfied with parenthood when they also are able to fulfill whatever aspirations for work or career they have.

Maternal satisfaction is higher to the extent that the woman has the social support of friends.

The satisfaction with parenting may have lifelong benefits. Of course, becoming a parent always involves trade-offs. There are both costs and benefits. Thus, a study of older people in Canada reported that the childless were financially better off and tended to have better health, while parents had more friends and a higher general satisfaction with life (Rempel 1985). Moreover, elderly parents are likely to find their intimacy with their adult children actually increasing over the years (Rossi and Rossi 1990).

The extent to which the bearing and caring of children is satisfying depends on a number of factors. A couple who wants and plans for the child is likely to be more satisfied afterward than one for whom the child is unplanned and/or unwanted. Couples who have a good relationship, including meaningful communication and satisfying experiences of love and affection, are more likely to maintain high marital quality and also to have higher levels of parenting satisfaction (Harriman 1986; Rogers and White 1998). Finally, both marital and parental satisfaction are likely to be higher when the father is more involved with the baby (Goldberg, Michaels, and Lamb 1985; Levy-Skiff 1994).

What about the satisfaction of raising adopted children? The evidence is somewhat mixed. In some cases, such as those who adopted neglected infants from Eastern European countries, the stress of parenting has been severe. The children often exhibited behavioral problems that did not cease after being with their adopted parents in a loving home (Talbot 1998; Mainemer, Gilman, and Ames 1998).

For other situations, the research is sparse and the evidence is not consistent. Drawing on national data, but having only seventy-two adopted children and their adoptive parents in the sample, three researchers found no significant differences between the adopted children and parents and a matched set of biological children and parents on such things as the parents' well-being, parental attitudes toward family life, frequency of the need for discipline, and parental views of the children's adjustment (Borders, Black, and Pasley 1998).

In contrast, many earlier studies have found a higher rate of both emotional and behavioral problems among adopted children (see, e.g., Brodzinsky et al. 1984; Kotsopoulous et al. 1987). More recently, Feigelman (1997) used national data to compare 101 adoptees with those raised in disrupted homes and those raised by both biological parents. Both the adopted children and those from disrupted homes had more problem behaviors during adolescence than did those raised by both biological parents. However, by adulthood, the adoptees were similar to those raised by both biological parents in terms of such things as educational attainment, occupation, and marital stability.

While the issue is important to those millions of couples who are infertile, then, we cannot say with certainty whether adopting a child will be as satisfying an experience as having your own child. Clearly, there are both risks and potential rewards whatever you do.

In sum, while couples are likely to experience some decline in marital satisfaction during the childbearing years, that does not mean that they are dissatisfied with their marriages. Moreover, the amount of decline that occurs depends on a number of factors, including the quality of their relationships before the bearing of children. And the satisfactions of parenting seem, for most people, to outweigh the stresses and problems.

PARENTING: HER EXPERIENCE AND HIS EXPERIENCE

As we have noted, mothers perceive the experience of parenting as more demanding, more constricting, but also more rewarding than do fathers. That suggests that mothers and fathers have somewhat different experiences of being a parent.

Maternal satisfaction is higher for mothers who have support from friends.

Her Experience

"M is for the million things she gave me" begins a parody of an old song about mother. For many mothers, it seems that there are indeed a million things to give. There are also a million things to do. Motherhood is above all a consuming experience. Mothers are expected to be the primary caregivers in our society, even if they are working full-time outside the home (Wilson et al. 1990). That is one of the reasons that, as Jessie Bernard (1974:10) put it, many women "find joy in their children, but they do not like motherhood." Fathers may come and go, but mothers are expected to nurture their children nearly every day, year in and year out.

There is, in fact, an assumption by many people that mothers are far better equipped than fathers to care for the physical and emotional needs of children. "There is something special about mothers," a man told us as he reflected on his own experiences. "They relate to you in a way that no one else in the world ever does." That may be true. Indeed, mothers make a unique contribution to our well-being. In general, mothers are more involved in both getting and giving support, particularly emotional support, than are fathers (Marks and McLanahan 1993). But fathers also make important contributions. It is not fair to women to make them feel that their children will suffer greatly if they are not incessantly there to care for their children's needs.

Nevertheless, it is mothers who give a disproportionate share of themselves to the rearing of the children, including more physical, emotional, and mental work (Walzer 1996). One estimate of the relative amounts of time spent in a typical two-parent, two-child home is that from birth until the child is eighteen the mother will spend between 13,729 and 15,439 hours in childcare while the father will spend between 4,150 and 4,415 hours (Zick and Bryant 1996).

There are a number of negative consequences of this more intense involvement. Compared to fathers, mothers tend to have higher levels of distress and anger, a diminished social network, less discretionary time, and a greater range of tasks (Ross and Van Willigen 1996; Bird 1997; Munch, McPherson, and Smith-Lovin 1997). On the other hand, there are also positive consequences. In the long run, women may receive more psychological benefits from child-rearing than do men (Bird 1997). Children tend to communicate more with and disclose more to their mothers than with their fathers. Mothers, thus, may have a more sustained kind of intimacy with their children. And the overall experience of mothering may enhance a woman's sense of her own worth and help her establish a meaningful identity (McMahon 1995).

Thus, it is not surprising that a survey of twenty-two thousand mothers found that 72 percent said they would have children again (Rosen 1990). And 93 percent said they were as happy or happier as they were before they became mothers.

His Experience

Fatherhood was a relatively neglected topic until recent years. Increasingly, researchers are examining the role of the father and the father's experience of parenting. The research has dispelled the old notion that fathers are not inclined to or capable of nurturing behavior. As Biller (1993) has argued, the father's involvement in the child-rearing process is as important to the child's healthy development as is the mother's involvement.

Shapiro (1987) reported an interesting series of interviews with 227 expectant and recent fathers. Expectant fathers, he pointed out, are in a "double bind." On the one hand, they are expected to be involved. On the other hand, they are not expected to have negative feelings. The woman who is waiting for her first child may feel frightened and apprehensive. That is understandable. The waiting father, on the other hand, is expected to be supportive and to avoid expressing feelings that might upset the mother-to-be.

As a result, Shapiro noted, waiting fathers tend to keep their feelings to themselves. He found that they have seven major fears and concerns about the pregnancy and coming child. Each of the fears and concerns was expressed by at least 40 percent of the men he interviewed. The first was queasiness. The men were concerned about maintaining their composure and being helpful during the birth process. Some feared that they would faint or get sick. Second, the men worried about the increased responsibility, the loss of what seemed like a comparatively free and easy life. Another concern revolved about the medical procedures. The men disliked the dehumanizing atmosphere of examinations and felt that medical personnel regarded them as out of place.

Fourth, more than half of the men were concerned about whether they were truly the child's father. This fear was rooted in a general insecurity surrounding the momentous event rather than in any real doubts about the wife's fidelity. Fifth, the men worried about the possibility of damage or death to the wife and/or the child. The sixth concern involved the marital relationship. The men feared that the child would replace them as the focus of their wife's attention or that the marital relationship would be permanently altered to a less intimate form. Finally, the men became aware of the fragile nature of life and the importance of not dying and leaving the child without their support.

Men who would have turned to their wives with such concerns under other circumstances kept their feelings to themselves. They did not want to make the pregnancy more difficult for their wives than it already was. This is unfortunate. Shapiro found a deeper and more intimate relationship emerged for those men who did share their feelings with their wives.

Although the experience may cause apprehension, attending the birth of a child has positive consequences for fathering. Men who participate in the birth and who have extended contact with their

COMPARISON
On the Playground in France, Germany, and Italy

American fathers and mothers play differently with their children. American mothers' play with their children involves more toys and games, while American fathers' play with their children is more physical. Are there such differences in other countries? A study of mothers and fathers and their children in city playgrounds in France, Germany, and Italy found both gender and cultural differences.

The children in the three countries were similar in their behavior on the playgrounds. But the nature of parent-child interaction depended both on the nationality and on parent gender. French and Italian fathers engaged in more play with their children than did mothers. But

in Germany the mothers played more with their children than did fathers; in fact, German fathers played very little with their children. Overall, French parents played more with their children than either the Italians or Germans.

What do parents do apart from playing? German fathers mainly talked to their children. French and Italian fathers talked and showed affection (by hugging, kissing, smiling, etc.). Among the mothers, all three groups talked to their children, but the French mothers showed affection about as frequently as they played with their children. Overall, the Italians and French interacted with their children more than did the Germans.

Play and affection were closely related. That is, parents who played with their children also tended to express affection. French parents who played with their children also talked more to them.

Finally, some differences were observed depending on the child's gender. French fathers showed and shared objects and toys more with boys than girls, while French mothers and Italian and German fathers showed and shared more with girls than boys.

Thus, a child's experience of parenting depends both upon which parent the child is interacting with and upon the country in which the child lives (Best et al. 1994).

---

infants in the hospital have more interaction with the infants at home and are more involved in caretaking responsibilities (Keller, Hildebrandt, and Richards 1985). Generally, mothers play with their infants more frequently than do fathers, but fathers spend a higher proportion of the time they are with their infants in play (Hanson and Bozett 1987). Fathers engage in more "rough and tumble" kind of play than mothers. Thus, they are both playmates and caretakers with their children. This is an additional source of stimulation and a unique experience for the infant, who attaches to the father as well as to the mother (Ricks 1985).

The extent to which fathers are involved with their children depends, however, on a number of factors. Fathers who are more concerned with adult issues, such as the amount of time they have for various activities, their health, sexual satisfaction, and their own mortality, tend to be less involved with their children, less confident of their parental role, and less likely to use positive child-rearing practices (De Luccie and Davis 1991). Fathers who are satisfied with their marriages are likely to be more involved with their children (Harris and Mor-

gan 1991). When the children are in the preadolescent and adolescent stages, fathers tend to be much more involved with their sons than their daughters (Starrels 1994). Finally, in case of divorce, noncustodial fathers are more likely than mothers to lose some involvement with their children (Rossi and Rossi 1990). Noncustodial fathers also feel less competent and less satisfied in their roles (Minton and Pasley 1996).

PARENTING AND THE WELL-BEING OF CHILDREN

If you feel good about yourself and are doing well in life, you probably grew up in a home with one or two warm, loving parents. Parents are not the only influences in your life, but the way they relate to you is very important for your well-being. Adults who perceive the relationship with their parents as having been warm and loving while they were growing up tend to be less neurotic, more open to experience, more agreeable, more conscientious, and less likely to suffer from various physical ailments (including heart disease, hypertension, ul-

PERSPECTIVE
Advice from a Mother

Motherhood is an ongoing concern for one's child. When John Quincy Adams was eleven, he went with his father to Europe in search of support for the American Revolution. John Quincy's mother, Abigail, wrote him a letter in June 1778 to express her concerns and give him advice. Clearly, she felt that her husband was committed to the role of father and involved in caring for the needs of the growing son:

My Dear Son
'Tis almost four months since you left your native land . . . you may be assured you have constantly been upon my heart and mind. It is a very difficult task, my dear son, for a tender parent to bring her mind to part with a child of your years, going to a distant land; nor could I have acquiesced in such a separation under any other care than that of the most excellent parent and guardian who accompanied you. . . .
The most amiable and most useful disposition in a young

mind is diffidence of itself; and this should lead you to seek advice and instruction from him who is your natural guardian and will always counsel and direct you in the best manner, both for your present and future happiness. You are in possession of a natural good understanding, and of spirits unbroken by adversity and untamed with care. Improve your understanding by acquiring useful knowledge and virtue, such as will render you an ornament to society, an honor to your country, and a blessing to your parents. Great learning and superior abilities, should you ever possess them, will be of little value and small estimation, unless virtue, honor, truth, and integrity are added to them. Adhere to those religious sentiments and principles which were early instilled into your mind, and remember that you are accountable to your Maker for all your words and actions.

Let me enjoin it upon you to attend constantly and steadfastly to the precepts and instructions of your father, as you value the happiness of your mother and your own welfare. His care and attention to you render many things unnecessary for me to write, which I might otherwise do; but the inadvertency and heedlessness of youth require line upon line and precept upon precept, and, when enforced by the joint efforts of both parents, these will, I hope, have a due influence upon your conduct; for, dear as you are to me, I would much rather you should have found your grave in the ocean you have crossed, or that any untimely death should crop you in your infant years, than see you an immoral, profligate, or graceless child. . . .

Source: Charles Francis Adams, *Familiar Letters of John Adams and His Wife Abigail Adams, During the Revolution* (New York: Hurt and Houghton, 1876), pp. 334–336.

---

cers, and alcoholism) than those who do not perceive the relationship as warm and loving (McCrae and Costa 1988; Russek and Schwartz 1997). The way that our parents relate to us tends to set the tone of our future lives.

Styles of Parenting

Many good books are available on appropriate and healthy parenting techniques. Here we will briefly look at three basic approaches to parenting that can have quite different effects on the children (Baumrind 1967).

In **authoritarian parenting,** the approach is to exercise maximum control and to expect unquestioning obedience. Children may perceive such parents as rejecting and as refusing to give them any autonomy. Parent-child interaction is not the give-and-take of a developing relationship but the giving of orders by a superior to a subordinate. In case of infraction of the rules, discipline is likely to be both severe and physical.

In **authoritative parenting,** the approach is to put boundaries on acceptable behavior within a warm, accepting context. Children are likely to perceive such an atmosphere as one that encourages their autonomy, controls their behavior moderately, and allows them to express their opinions and develop their own decision-making ability. Parent-child interaction is generally characterized by affection, a certain amount of give-and-take, but relatively clear expectations for the children's behavior.

Finally, in **permissive parenting,** the approach is to minimize any control. Children are encouraged to make their own decisions and develop their independence with few or no parental constraints or guidance. Parent-child interaction may consist of parental acceptance and approval of whatever the children decide to do.

Parental Behavior and Children's Adjustment

Different styles of parenting have very different consequences. Interestingly, children who perceive their parents as permissive also rate them as less accepting and warm than those who perceive their parents as authoritative (Johnson, Shulman, and Collins 1991). Those who perceive their parents as authoritarian tend to have lower self-esteem and school achievement than those who perceive their parents as authoritative (Bronstein et al. 1996).

In general, an authoritative parenting style seems to produce the most responsible and well-adjusted children. Children from authoritarian homes tend to be less well-adjusted and to have problems of trusting others, while those from permissive homes may lack self-control and the ability to adapt well to situations in which others have authority over them. In contrast, those from authoritative homes report a higher quality of family life, do better academically, are more self-reliant, have less anxiety and depression, are less likely to get involved in delinquent behavior, and have better moral reasoning capability (Steinberg et al. 1991; Boyes and Allen 1993; Hein and Lewko 1994; Bronstein et al. 1996). And these results hold true for all races, all family types, and at all socioeconomic levels (Steinberg et al. 1991). The positive outcomes also occur whether the discipline used is physical or some kind of nonphysical punishment (Simons, Johnson, and Conger 1994).

One reason for the positive outcomes of authoritative parenting is that adolescents who report their parents as authoritative are likely to be involved with peers who refrain from drug use and other behavior that is contrary to adult norms (Durbin et al. 1993). In other words, adolescents from authoritative homes tend to choose friends who prefer generally to conform to their parents' expectations for behavior.

The importance of parental behavior in children's adjustment begins early in life and involves both mother and father. Infants as young as five months are more at ease in social situations when they have been cared for and played with by their fathers (Parke and Sawin 1977). When fathers are substantially engaged in the care of their children, those children exhibit more intellectual competence, more empathy, higher levels of self-control and self-esteem, and a greater degree of social competence than do those children with less father involvement (Lamb 1997). A study of adolescents found that the father's acceptance was the most important predictor of the child's effective functioning outside the home (Forehand and Nousianinen 1993). And a study involving a national sample of 471 young adults reported that closeness to fathers made an important contribution to the respondents' happiness, life satisfaction, and emotional health (Amato 1994).

Similarly, mothers' interaction with their infants is important to the children's adjustment. In particular, mother-infant attachment is related to the infant's sense of competence (Sroufe 1978). Attachment refers to the amount of intimacy and closeness between a mother and child. A strong attachment means that the child feels comfortable and secure with its mother. As young as eighteen months, infants who are strongly attached to their mothers stand out in a social situation. Compared with those who are insecurely attached, they are (Sroufe 1978:56):

> More sympathetic to distress in others.
>
> More involved in social activities.
>
> Less hesitant with other children.
>
> More of a leader with peers.
>
> More likely to be sought out by other children.
>
> More likely to suggest activities.
>
> Less likely to withdraw from excitement and commotion.

Both parents continue to be important to the child's development and adjustment throughout life. The best situation is for the child to grow up with both biological parents. Adolescents who live with both biological parents report more warmth, less conflict, and more authoritative parenting than those in either single-parent or stepfamilies (Kurdek and Fine 1993).

Intimacy with father as well as mother is important to an adolescent's well-being.

Parental Behavior and Self-Esteem

If you are well-adjusted, of course, you are most likely to have high self-esteem, the evaluation of yourself as someone of worth. But self-esteem is important for all aspects of your life, not just your adjustment to social situations. And a number of researchers have specifically looked at the kind of parental behavior that is related to the development of self-esteem.

A pioneering study of the development of self-esteem was done by Morris Rosenberg (1965), who examined more than five thousand high school students in New York. Among his findings were:

Adolescents with close relationships with their fathers are more likely to have high self-esteem than those with more distant relationships.

Only children have higher self-esteem than children with siblings (only children are likely to have a closer relationship with their parents).

Parental interest in the adolescent, such as knowing the adolescent's friends, being concerned about grades, and conversing with the child during meals, is correlated with higher self-esteem.

Two years after Rosenberg's study, Coopersmith (1967) reported the results of an eight-year project. Again, parents were found to be important, with parental warmth, respectful treatment of children, and expressions of concern for the child's well-being all related to self-esteem.

Subsequent studies continue to affirm the importance of parental warmth, communication, and acceptance (e.g., Litovsky and Dusek 1985; Barber, Chadwick, and Oerter 1992; Roberts and Bengtson 1993; Roberts and Bengtson 1996). However, boys and girls respond to somewhat different aspects of parenting. Using a sample of 128 families, Gecas and Schwalbe (1986) found that boys' self-esteem is particularly sensitive to the control/autonomy aspect of the father's behavior. Control/autonomy refers to the extent to which parents attempt to limit the child's autonomy and direct his or her activities. The more the boy perceived his father trying to exercise such control, the higher his self-esteem. It would seem that boys want their fathers to be interested and involved with their lives.

For girls, on the other hand, self-esteem is more sensitive to parental support and participation. Support includes such things as affection, helping, and expressing approval. Parental participation involves spending time with the children and sharing in their activities. Girls' self-esteem is higher to the extent that they perceive their mothers and fathers giving them support and their fathers participating with them.

As in the case of adjustment, the father's involvement with their children during adolescence is somewhat more important to self-esteem than is the mother's. Such findings underscore the importance of recent tendencies in which fathers are more involved with their children than were fathers in the past.

A Final Note: Is Older Better in Parenting?

It is difficult for a teenager to be a competent parent because the teenaged parent is, in many ways, a child raising a child. Fortunately, as we have seen, the tendency to delay childbearing means that fewer children are likely to be raised by very young parents. But can the delaying of parenthood be carried too far? Are there also negative consequences from becoming a parent when you are older? Such questions took on new meaning in 1996 when a sixty-three-year-old woman, who had lied about her age, used in vitro fertilization to become pregnant and give birth to her first child (Kalb 1997).

There is not much research to answer the question of whether there are negative consequences from being older when you become a parent. A study that compared 84 "late" (mean age of thirty-five), 138 "on-time" (mean age of twenty-nine), and 82 "early" (mean age of twenty-four) fathers found that the "late" fathers tended to be more highly involved with their children and to have more positive feelings about parenting (Cooney et al. 1993). An assessment of sixty-nine families in which the first child came after the age of thirty-five concluded that most of the parents "were more satisfied, less stressed, and reported better functioning than their nondelaying counterparts" (Garrison et al. 1997:288). The researchers suggest that those who delay childbearing may be better prepared and more adaptable to the demands than those who have their children early.

The most intensive study was that of sociologist Monica Morris (1988), who addressed the questions by looking at a sample of adults who were "last-chance children"; that is, they were the children of women who waited until their late thirties or early forties to have them. The results were mixed. Some of the subjects reported a variety of problems. Indeed, it is not difficult to imagine that life would be different if you were born to a forty-two-year-old woman and a sixty-one-year-old man. A man who was such a child said that he didn't have a childhood. His parents never bought him toys. They dressed him up instead of letting him play in jeans in the park. He never played baseball with his father or had the rough-and-tumble activities that his friends had with their parents. He feels as if he didn't even have a real relationship with them. They both died when he was in his teens, long before he was old enough to have an adult conversation with them.

The fear of one or both parents dying was expressed by a number of the subjects in Morris's study. The subjects also talked, like the man above, about what they missed. And they mentioned embarrassing incidents, like being taken for the grandchildren of their parents.

But some also believed that having older parents was a positive experience. In fact, the sample of twenty-two was almost evenly divided on whether the experience was positive or negative. Those who perceived it to be positive reflected on such things as the wisdom and stability of their parents, qualities that helped them to feel more comfortable and secure. Nevertheless, only two of them strongly endorsed the idea of having their own children at an advanced age.

Increasing numbers of children are born to women who are thirty-five or older. Older parents will have to recognize some of the problems, anxieties, and embarrassments their children are likely to face and will have to take steps to minimize them. Older parents have much to offer children in the way of security and stability. But they will have to work a little harder to make sure that their children do not miss out on important things that their peers have and that their children do not endure added anxieties and embarrassments because of their parents' older age.

PRINCIPLES FOR ENHANCING INTIMACY

1. To have or not to have children is a serious decision. It is a decision with which each spouse needs to feel comfortable. Therefore, the best time to begin discussion about this decision is before you marry. People sometimes marry with the assumption that their spouse wants a family of two or three or more children. When the matter then comes up for serious debate, they are often surprised that their assumptions were not correct. In fact, they may find that their partner wants no children at all. It is best not to make assumptions about this important matter. Talk it out and arrive at an understanding before the wedding.

2. Flexibility is a requirement in a successful marriage; certainly, this is true where decisions about parenting are concerned, because people do change their minds. Even people who are most adamant about not having children sometimes, when they mature, reverse their decision. Similarly, even the individual most enthusiastic about eventually becoming a parent may change his or her mind in light of new personal or professional commitments. Couples, thus, need not only to begin discussing this important matter be-

fore their wedding but also continue to do so afterward.

3. Becoming a parent is a demanding, lifelong commitment and must be entered into seriously. A baby radically changes your life. The responsibilities are tremendous—a new life is completely dependent on you. You will not be able to go and come as freely as when there were just the two of you. But keep in mind that the responsibilities are balanced by the joys and satisfactions of parenthood.

4. Child-rearing patterns are changing with the erosion of traditional roles and the increase in the number of dual-career couples. Today fathers as well as mothers are involved in nurturing and caring for their children. This is a fortunate change and should be encouraged, for fathers make a unique contribution to the development of their children.

5. If you want to have a baby and seem unable to conceive, don't give up hope. Many options are available for infertile couples today. Patience and determination are required to find a workable solution. However, also be aware that the search for a solution will likely be expensive, and your spouse may be unwilling to consider some of the options available.

SUMMARY

Birth rates have declined and are now below replacement level. The decline has occurred among the poor as well as the rich and minorities as well as whites. The decline mirrors a lower ideal family size reported by Americans.

Among the reasons that people want to have children are the experience of happiness in a family, personal fulfillment, personal and family legacy, personal status, religious beliefs, and social expectations. Among the reasons for remaining child-free are personal fulfillment, a focus on career, the economic costs of children, a focus on the marriage, and doubts about parenting skills.

Many married couples are infertile. Infertility results from a variety of causes, including environ-

mental toxins and sexually transmitted diseases. Among women, common causes of infertility are endometriosis, other conditions that cause blockage of the fallopian tubes, improper ovulation, and a bodily reaction against sperm. Among men, infertility is somewhat less common but is generally due to a low sperm count or to the sperm not swimming as fast as they should. Infections, injuries, exposure to radiation, excessive drug and alcohol use, and birth defects are among the causes of low sperm counts.

Those who discover that they are infertile may go through a process similar to what we experience because of loss through death. The process is characterized by surprise, denial, anger, guilt, depression, and grief. The infertile couple may also experience marital strain.

There are technologies that can help many of the infertile. Artificial insemination, in vitro fertilization, and surrogate mothers are alternative ways to have a baby. These methods are expensive and may pose some legal and psychological problems. Adoption is also available, though the number of couples wanting to adopt is far greater than the number of children available. In recent years, open adoptions have become more common.

Raising children is stressful, as illustrated by the number of support groups available to help parents. The stress begins as soon as the child is brought home. Marital problems may increase, and marital satisfaction will probably go down during the child-rearing years; but the satisfactions are such that most parents indicate they would go through the process again. Whether an adopted child yields the same satisfaction as one's own child is unclear from the existing evidence.

The experience of parenting is somewhat different for men and women. Women tend to find joy in their children but not in the tasks of motherhood. Women tend to be more involved than men in the lives of their children. Men, however, are equally capable of nurturing behavior. Expectant fathers have many anxieties that they tend not to share with others. Men spend a higher proportion of time in play with children than do mothers. They are playmates as well as caretakers.

Three basic styles of parenting are the authoritarian, the authoritative, and the permissive. Authoritarian parents exercise maximum control and provide minimal warmth. Authoritative parents provide warmth in the context of clear expectations. Permissive parents provide little or no guidance or rules. Authoritative parenting tends to produce the most well-adjusted children.

Parental behavior is important for the child's adjustment. Both parents must relate warmly and intimately with the child for maximal adjustment and for the child's self-esteem.

Those who become parents somewhat later have much to offer children in the way of stability and security. But they also confront unique problems. They and their children will have to deal with a number of problems, anxieties, and embarrassments arising from their age.

INTERNET CONNECTION
Becoming a Parent

Your textbook mentions the slight increase in rates of infertility in American couples as detected by Center for Disease Control studies. It also alludes to the possibility of higher rates of infertility, since the studies cited only addressed married couples. How are environmental factors at play in this increased percentage? Are other factors, such as age, at play as well?

www.mhhe.com/lauer4

CHIP Online
http://chid.nih.gov/

The Combined Health Information Base is an excellent tool for locating research material, policy assessments and many other resources at the Centers for Disease Control Prevention and the National Institutes of Health

Environmental Causes of Infertility
http://www.chem-tox.com/infertility/

This site presents the argument that many basic household products are responsible for male and female infertility.

1. What attributes of male and female infertility are presented at the Environmental Causes of Infertility website? What statistical sources are cited as the basis for their claims? Do you believe the argument for what they claim is convincing?

2. Use the search engines at the CHIP website to find the latest statistics on infertility. What is the rate of increase for women? What is the rate of increase for men?

3. What kind of research is being done on infertility at the CDC and NIH? How many studies on environmental causes such as chemicals, radiation, tobacco, or drugs can you find? How many studies on male infertility? How many studies on female infertility?

4. Based on your findings, do you think enough is being done to learn more about the causes of infertility? What more should be done?

CHAPTER 15

THE FAMILY LIFE CYCLE

Learning Objectives

After reading chapter 15, you should be able to:

1. Outline the stages of the family life cycle.

2. Summarize the types of changes that take place in each stage of the cycle.

3. Show the effect of social changes on the family life cycle.

4. Discuss the strengths and tasks of the newly married couple.

5. Describe the challenges facing the family with young children.

6. Analyze the strains and stresses as well as the satisfactions experienced by parents and children in the family with adolescents.

7. Explain how the empty-nest stage can be a time of renewal and enrichment for both the marriage and the family.

8. Describe the various types of grandparents and their functions.

9. Discuss the shift of roles in the aging family.

10. Summarize the challenges of retirement, sex, children, and death in the aging family.

"Y ou aren't the person I married." Usually this statement indicates dissatisfaction, but it could be made by every husband and wife in the nation. We change continuously throughout our lives, and our relationships change as well. In some cases, people change without conscious effort. In other cases, people may deliberately initiate change in order to improve their marital relationship (Brillinger 1985). For instance, they may try to improve their communication skills or work on certain unrealistic attitudes or expectations. At any rate, once the change has occurred, spouses are no longer the same as at the time of their wedding.

In other words, if we ask how satisfied people are with their marriages, if we inquire into communication patterns or styles and kinds of conflict or any one of numerous aspects of family life, the answer will differ somewhat depending on how long the people have been married. In this chapter, we will look at family life as a process, as a set of relationships that inevitably changes over time. They change in terms of such things as interaction patterns, feelings about each other, division of labor in the home, and expectations about behavior. There are, of course, continuities as well as changes, but it is the changes that we shall focus on here. Change is crucial to intimacy; depending on how the individuals change, intimacy in the family can be weakened or strengthened. People can grow apart as they change, or they can grow closer together. We will examine changing relationships in terms of the family life cycle. And we will look at some of the particular challenges, problems, and satisfactions that people face at differing points in the family life cycle.

THE FAMILY LIFE CYCLE

The notion of a life cycle can be applied to all of life, including nonhuman life. From stars to forests, from humans to insects, from nations to organizations, we find identifiable life cycles. That is, we can trace the process from birth to death. And a family, like a star or forest, is different at varying points along the process.

The Meaning of the Family Life Cycle

What is the difference between a family composed of a couple with an infant versus a couple with an adolescent? As it happens, the difference can be dramatic in terms of the experiences of the people involved. There are differing challenges and differing problems. These considerations are the focus of the study of the family life cycle.

In the 1950s, Evelyn Duvall (1977:179) offered a widely used model of the family life cycle, which consisted of eight stages and the various critical tasks facing people in each of these stages. The stages range from the newly married couple, through the childbearing years, to the "aging family members" stage in which the original couple are grandparents or in which one of the spouses dies.

A more recent formulation is that of Carter and McGoldrick (1989), who identified six stages, each of which focuses on at least two generations (table 15.1). The six stages they identify are points at which family members enter or leave the system. These stages include (1) the unattached young adult, (2) the newly married couple, (3) the family with young children, (4) the family with adolescents, (5) the launching and moving on, and (6) the family in later life. Carter and McGoldrick discussed the

TABLE 15.1
Stages of the Family Life Cycle

Family Life Cycle Stage	Emotional Process of Transistion: Key Principles	Second-Order Changes in Family Status Required to Proceed Developmentally
(1) Between Families: The Unattached Young Adult	Accepting parent-offspring separation	(a) Differentiation of self in relation to family of origin (b) Development of intimate peer relationships (c) Establishment of self in work
(2) The Joining of Families through Marriage: The Newly Married Couple	Commitment to new system	(a) Formation of marital system (b) Realignment of relationships with extended families and friends to include spouse
(3) The Family with Young Children	Accepting new members into the system	(a) Adjusting marital system to make space for child(ren) (b) Taking on parenting roles (c) Realignment of relationships with extended family to include parenting and grandparenting roles
(4) The Family with Adolescents	Increasing flexibility of family boundaries	(a) Shifting of parent-child relationships to permit adolescent to move in and out of system (b) Refocus on midlife marital and career issues (c) Beginning shift toward concerns for older generation
(5) Launching Children and Moving On	Accepting a multitude of exits from and entries into the family system	(a) Renegotiation of marital system as a dyad (b) Development of adult relationships between grown children and parents (c) Realignment of relationships to include in-laws and grandchildren (d) Dealing with disabilities and death of parents (grandparents)
(6) The Family in Later Life	Accepting the shifting of generational roles	(a) Maintaining own and/or couple functioning and interests in face of physiological decline: exploration of new familial and social role options (b) Support for a more central role for middle generation (c) Making room in the system for the wisdom and experience of the elderly: supporting the older generation without overfunctioning for them (d) Dealing with loss of spouse, siblings, and other peers and preparation for own death. Life review and integration

ways in which families must alter their attitudes and relationships in order to adapt to the varying stages.

For instance, in the family with an unattached young adult, there is the challenge of accepting the parent-child separation that must occur. Three changes are necessary for that challenge to be successfully met. First, each family member must view the young adult as an individual, someone with a life of his or her own that is separate from that of the family. Second, the young adult must develop close relationships with his or her peers. And third, the young adult must become established in some kind of work or a career.

What Changes Occur over the Family Life Cycle?

It is not merely the challenges and problems that change from one stage of the family life cycle to another. Our relationships with each other also change. Based on their study of nearly two hundred married women, Anderson, Russell, and Schumm (1983) found variations over the family life cycle in a number of important areas of marital interaction (figure 15.1). "Regard" refers to the amount of positive regard the women believe their husbands have for them. "Discussion" is the amount of time the spouses spend talking to each other. "Empathy" refers to the amount of empathic understanding that the wives perceive their husbands to have for them. As many other studies have found, marital satisfaction tends to be lowest during the childbearing years. Perceived empathy follows a similar pattern. The level of regard is cyclic. Discussion and self-disclosure decline somewhat, but for a couple married twenty to thirty years or more, the decline is not significant for the quality of the relationship (because satisfaction goes up).

Figure 15.1 suggests that younger and older couples are more alike in some ways than couples in their middle years. Another piece of research that supports that notion looked at the way that couples handle conflict (Zietlow and Sillars 1988). The researchers divided the couples into three groups: young, middle-aged, and retired. They looked at the extent to which the couples used various communication styles in conflict (figure 15.2). *Denial* is a

FIGURE 15.1   Some Changes over the Family Life Cycle as Perceived by Wives
(*Source:* From Stephen A. Anderson, et al., "Perceived Marital Quality and Family Life-Cycle Categories: A Further Analysis" in *Journal of Marriage and the Family,* 45:133. Copyrighted 1983 by the National Council on Family Relations, 3989 Central Avenue, NE, Suite 550, Minneapaolis, MN 55421. Reprinted by perrmission.)

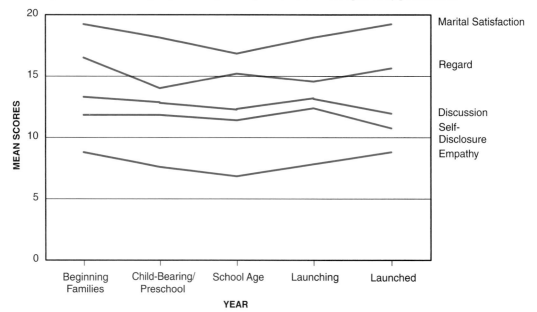

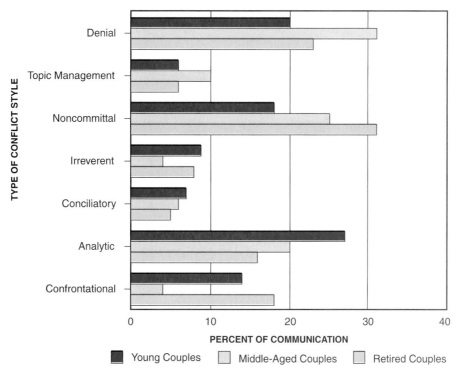

FIGURE 15.2   Conflict Styles of Young, Middle-Aged, and Retired Couples
(*Source:* Data from P. H. Zietlow and A. L. Sillars, *Journal of Social and Personal Relationships,* 5:236, 1988.)

Family life is a succession of different stages.

refusal to acknowledge the disagreement. *Topic management* is an effort to avoid certain topics or to shift to a different topic. *Noncommittal* remarks include such things as questions like "what do you think?" and general statements like "everyone gets mad at times." *Irreverent* remarks include joking (e.g., "maybe we should just burn the house down instead of cleaning it"). *Analytic* remarks are efforts to get clarification. *Confrontational* remarks include criticism of the other person, rejection of statements the other has made, hostile statements, and ultimatums. Finally, *conciliatory* remarks are statements of support for the other, concessions, and the acceptance of personal responsibility for the problem.

As figure 15.2 shows, young and retired couples use about the same proportion of denial, topic management, irreverent remarks, confrontational remarks, and conciliatory remarks. Both are much more likely to be confrontational than are middle-aged couples, who are much more likely to use denial than either of the others.

Thus, some of the changes that occur over the family life cycle are cyclical and some are more linear. That is, some changes are like marital satisfaction, which has its ups and downs through the family life cycle. Others are like self-disclosure, which tends to decline over the life cycle. But whatever characteristic of family life you are interested in, it is likely to be somewhat different in the various stages of the family life cycle.

Social Change and the Family Life Cycle

Your experiences in passing through the family life cycle will depend on a number of things, including various kinds of change that occur in society. During this century, for example, a number of changes have affected the prevalence, timing, and sequence of some important transitions (Hagestad 1988).

First, there is the experience of the death of one's parents or of a child. Improved nutrition and health care have made a dramatic difference in **death rates.** At the turn of the century, more than half of children faced the death of a parent or a sibling before the age of fifteen. Currently the figure is less than 10 percent. Now you may not have to cope with the death of a parent until you are in the fourth, fifth, or sixth stage of the family life cycle (Hagestad 1988).

Similarly, parents are far less likely to face the death of a child. In 1900, parents had a better than even chance of experiencing the death of a child. Now the chances are less than five in a hundred. The rate of infant deaths presently is less than half of what it was even as late as 1970.

Another change involves grandparenthood. Because of increased life expectancy, more people today have the experience of being a grandparent. About three-fourths of people over the age of sixty-five are grandparents, and as many as half of them will become great-grandparents as well (Shanas 1980). Some people, especially women, will even experience being both a grandchild and a grandparent at the same time.

However, fewer women today are both the mother of a small child and a grandmother as well. Women are completing their childbearing at an earlier age than they did in the past. There is now more likely to be a sequence than an overlapping of roles.

A third change relates to marital disruption and remarriage. A widespread belief exists that marital disruption is far more prevalent than it was in the past. However, an analysis of the probability of disruption shows that it was as likely in 1900 as it is presently (Hagestad 1988:407). Under conditions in 1900, people's marriages were likely to be disrupted by death within forty years. Presently, the rate of disruption remains about the same. But the major source of disruption differs. Since 1974, marriages are more likely to be disrupted by divorce than by death.

There are differing consequences to disruption by divorce than by death. In discussing the consequences with people who have experienced one or both, the authors found that many insist that it is more difficult to adjust to divorce than it is to death. If, then, the rate of disruption is about the same, the experience is not.

The incidence of remarriage is also affected (Hagestad 1988:408). The death of a spouse may put one person into the marriage market; divorce may put two. But after the age of forty, males are more likely than females to remarry. In fact, remarriage rates are three times higher for males. In part this is due to the sex ratio and in part to the tendency of men to marry women younger than themselves. The net effect is that a man is likely to spend the last part of his life with a wife, while a woman

PERSPECTIVE
Embarking on a Difficult Road

The following is taken from a popular nineteenth-century woman's magazine. It is a rather dreary picture of the first two stages of the family life cycle. While it does not reflect the experience of every nineteenth-century woman, it was at least common enough to warrant publication. You need only read this account to realize how much the situation has changed for women who marry. As we have noted in previous chapters, women are still likely to benefit less from marriage than are men, but at least they are not likely to face such a difficult road as described in the following:

Kind reader, it is no fancy sketch that I am going to give you. It is drawn from life in all its reality; and in every city, village, country-town, and neighborhood, its truthfulness will be recognized. It is the every-day life of woman. . . .

A young man arrives at an age when he thinks it time for him to get married, and settle down. He has a respectable education, and wants a woman who is his equal. He looks about him, and makes a choice. She is a girl well educated, reared by careful parents, and is, in the truest sense, a lady. She is intelligent, loves books, possesses a refined and delicate taste, and is, in all points, well fitted to be the mistress of a cheerful, happy home.

She becomes his wife; is industrious, and ambitious to do as much as she can toward a living. Maybe they are not very well off as to the things of this world, and both are equally ambitious to accumulate a comfortable property; and the husband soon becomes avaricious enough to allow the woman of his love to become his most devoted drudge. Her life is thenceforth one of the most unremitting toil. It is nothing but cook and bake, wash dishes, thrash among pots and kettles, wash and iron, churn, pick up chips, draw water, and a thousand other things "too tedious to mention."

The result is, the husband soon owns the house he lives in, and something besides; takes his ease when he chooses, reads and improves his mind, and becomes important in the community. But the cares of his faded, broken-down wife know no relaxation. The family enlarges, and she, poor woman, has enough to do without finding time to increase her stock of knowledge, or to watch the progress of the minds of her children. . . . The only wonder is, that the mother does not sink within this circle of everlasting drudgery, which deprives her of the privilege of relaxation for a day. . . .

Thus, many a woman breaks and sinks beneath the wear and tear of the frame and the affections . . . cares eat away at her heart; the day presses on her with new toils; the night comes, and they are unfulfilled; she lies down in weariness, and rises with uncertainty; her smiles become languid and few, and her husband wonders at the gloominess of his home. When he married, he thought the chosen of his heart his equal in intelligence, but now she is far his inferior.

Source: "Every-Day Life of Woman," *Ladies' Repository,* October 1851, pp. 365–66.

is more likely to spend the last part of her life alone or in an institution.

THE NEWLY MARRIED: A FAMILY WITHOUT CHILDREN

You will recall that we considered the first stage of the family life cycle in chapter 9 in our discussion of the single adult. The second stage of the family life cycle occurs when a couple marries. What are the characteristics of this stage in the family cycle, and what are the important challenges a couple faces as they establish a marital system?

The newly married couple tends to have certain family strengths that are at a very high level (Olson and McCubbin 1983:100). In particular, the couple is likely to agree that, among other things, they:

Disclose their feelings.

Do not worry about a great many things.

Trust and confide in each other.

Feel a sense of loyalty to each other.

Share similar beliefs and values.

Have respect for, and pride in, each other.

Do not have a great many conflicts.

To the extent that the above is true for a couple, they have a strong foundation for beginning their life together. They have a high level of communication, are comfortable sharing intimate matters, and find self-disclosure relatively easy.

One of the important tasks facing the newly married couple is that of forming their own marital system (Wallerstein 1994). That is, when you marry, you have to decide on a whole range of matters for your own newly formed family. Will you openly show both positive and negative feelings? Will you each take responsibility for your own actions? Will you deal openly with problems? Will you resolve normal conflicts without causing each other undue stress? If and when you have children, will you freely admit to them when you are wrong? Will you allow them to express views different from yours? Will you consciously strive to maintain a warm and supportive atmosphere in the home? And so on.

In building a marital system, a couple will likely model their relationship after one or the other of their families of origin. As you think about your own family of origin, would the answers to the above questions be "yes"? Using such questions to measure experiences in families of origin, Wilcoxon and Hovestadt (1985) found that the more spouses agreed on their answers (that is, the more similar their family-of-origin experiences), the more likely they were to have a satisfying relationship. In such cases, as the researchers pointed out, "the 'struggle' may not take the form of 'yours or mine' in terms of spouses modeling their respective families of origin" (Wilcoxon and Hovestadt 1985:170). In other words, when you and your spouse have similar perceptions of your families of origin, you do not have to choose between opposing models of family life.

Of course, you may choose to reject the model of your family of origin, though this is probably the exception rather than the rule. It may be difficult to know or to agree on what kind of model to use as a substitute. In such cases, it is easy to fall back on what is familiar. Nevertheless, there are couples who consciously opt for a different model when they are uncomfortable with that of their families of origin. As, for instance, a husband told us:

My wife and I both came from families where our parents argued loudly and vociferously with each other. We both disliked that, and we decided that we would not do this. We have very few arguments but when we do disagree, we make a strong effort to talk about things calmly and get the matter settled as quickly as possible.

The spouses had similar experiences in their family of origin, but each had agreed to find an alternative way in their marriage.

In any case, a central task at this stage is to establish your own marital system, your own way of relating and dealing with the various problems and processes of family life. You will probably model some of your patterns on those of your family of origin. You should be aware, however, that some of those patterns may not work well for you and that unless you consciously decide to do otherwise, you will follow them even though they are not effective for your family.

In establishing your own marital system, you also will have to deal with the dilemma of "fusion and closeness" (McGoldrick 1980). In our quest for intimacy, we try to get close to another person. This effort can be carried to an extreme, so that the couple is no longer two separate individuals in an intimate relationship but almost one fused being. For example, the spouses may always feel the same thing in every situation, may be unwilling to engage in activities without the other, may be unable to make separate and contrary judgments about things, and so forth. Fusion in a relationship will lead sooner or later to difficulties and even to a loss of intimacy in the relationship. Another central task of the newly married couple, then, is to form an intimate union without a loss of individual identity.

THE FAMILY WITH YOUNG CHILDREN

In the third stage of the family life cycle, the couple commits itself to an additional person and to changes in the family system. Spouses face the challenge of the new roles of mother and father as well as those of husband and wife. Initially, they may find great joy in the birth of their child. However, as we saw in the last chapter, the "blessed event" has its problems as well as its blessings. The family strengths we mentioned previously tend to remain high at this stage (Olson and McCubbin 1983:100), but the couple is likely to rate its marital communication as lower. And marital satisfaction starts to decline. Interestingly, husbands of home-makers are least likely to be "very happy" with the marriage when there are preschool children in the home, while husbands of employed wives are least likely to be "very happy" when the children reach school age (Benin and Nienstedt 1985:982). Again, this does not mean that they are unhappy, but only that they are less happy than at other stages. It is probable that the increased attention and energy that the wife gives to the children and the increas-ing demand by employed wives for husbands to share in the family work account for the lower satisfaction.

The same factors are involved in the declining marital satisfaction of wives at this stage. That is, they are consumed with the endless tasks of parent-hood. They may be frustrated with their husbands' reluctance to share the family work. And they may have little time or energy for working at their inti-mate relationships with their husbands.

Another factor that strains marital satisfaction at this stage is the extent of perceived agreement be-tween the spouses. White (1987) looked at eight is-sues in family life: preferred family size, how chil-dren should be disciplined, whether to spend leisure time with friends or family, equality in financial contributions to the family, equal sharing of house-hold chores, perceived equity in the relationship, whether a wife should have an abortion without the husband's consent, and whether a mother with small children should enter the labor force.

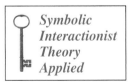

Symbolic Interactionist Theory Applied

While the wives in White's sample tended to see more overall agreement in this stage than they did in the previous one (newly married), the husbands' perceptions of agreement dropped sharply. Actually, when comparing the responses of husbands and wives, it was clear that the couples' agreement on the eight issues went up. But whether the husbands *defined the agreement as going up* is as important as whether it actually went up. In point of fact, the husbands perceived a much lower level of agree-ment and, consequently, they reported a lower level of marital satisfaction.

We noted in the last chapter that marital satisfac-tion increases for some couples in the child-rearing years. This is likely to be true for those with strong

marriages before the children come and with those who engage in certain helpful kinds of behavior. "Helpful" behavior includes such things as establish-ing meaningful family rituals and maintaining a high level of involvement in child-rearing on the part of the father (Levy-Skiff 1994; Fiese et al. 1993).

THE FAMILY WITH ADOLESCENTS

As the children grow older, the couple faces the challenge of allowing their children to form their own independent identities, move beyond the nu-clear family, and establish a wider range of intimate relationships. Meanwhile, the couple will also face its own midlife concerns with regard to the mar-riage and the spouses' careers. This fourth stage, then, may be an agitated clash of two turbulent processes.

The Needs of Adolescents

Adolescents undergo important physical, intellec-tual, and "social definitional" changes (Steinberg 1987:80–81). Physically, adolescents change in size and appearance, develop the capacity to engage in sexual relations, and reproduce. Intellectually, the adolescent develops the capacity to think more logi-cally and more abstractly. This means that the fam-ily now has "an additional person who can think and reason in complex, adult-like ways" (Steinberg 1987:81). The "social definitional" changes refer to the changed expectations about rights and responsi-bilities that people have for the adolescent as he or she emerges into adulthood. These new expecta-tions give the adolescent a different position both in the family and in the larger society.

At adolescence, then, parents and children must work out a new system. Adolescents prefer more egalitarian relationships with their parents, and be-cause of the above changes, they have a basis for advancing that preference. Whereas children may obey simply on the basis of a parental "because I say so," adolescents are likely to be dissatisfied with such statements. Adolescents want to deal with parental expectations on the basis of reason, fair-ness, and mutual respect.

Adolescents also need increasing autonomy and independence. They are striving to establish their own identity, to find out what kind of persons they are. They need to test their abilities and explore their future options. In the process, they may shift their focus from family to friends and peers. It isn't that they reject the family but that they find the perspectives of those outside the family to be an important part of their quest for their own identity.

Parent-Child Problems

Conflict Theory Applied

Because *conflict arises out of opposing needs and interests,* the unique needs of adolescents make this stage one of increasing conflict. Ultimately, how families manage the conflict depends upon the quality of family life before adolescence. Families that are warm and supportive will generally keep the conflict at minimal or moderate levels and parent-adolescent relationships will gradually improve, while families with hostile, coercive atmospheres will generally have intense conflict that tends to worsen (Rueter and Conger 1995).

What do adolescents and their parents fight about? The most frequent sources of conflict, according to a national survey, are everyday matters such as helping around the house, family relations, school, and dress (Barber 1994). Contrary to some popular notions, drug use and sex are seldom the issues of the conflict. And these conclusions hold true for African Americans and Hispanics as well as for whites.

Maintaining good communication between parents and children is particularly important in adolescence. A study of 339 high-school students found that those students who perceived good communication with their parents reported lower rates of delinquency and less serious kinds of delinquency (Clark and Shields 1997). Unfortunately, communication problems tend to be more serious during adolescence than at other stages (Olson and McCubbin 1983:221). Parents may complain that they don't understand their children, who, in turn, complain that they don't understand their parents. Mothers perceive more satisfying communication with adolescents than do fathers. Mothers particularly see the parent-child communication as more open. Adolescents themselves agree with that assessment, perceiving better and more open communication with their mothers than with their fathers.

Parents also report stress from increased financial problems. Children become increasingly expensive as they age. By the time of adolescence, the costs of food, clothing, medical care, automobiles, education, and so on are at a peak for many families. In fact, parents feel that most of their stress during stage four comes from the financial strains they face (Olson and McCubbin 1983:228).

Adolescents see most of their stress arising from daily hassles with parents. They report increasing arguments about household chores, increased pressure to achieve (either academically or in sports), hassles about using the family car and doing things with the family, and arguments over their selection of friends and social activities.

Adolescents are not oblivious to the problems of their parents, incidentally. They also feel some of the stress that their parents experience because of problems with family finances. Carrie, a graduate student, told us that her adolescence was strained more by her parents' problems than her own:

> My parents fought a lot. And they had problems with money most of the time. My main stress was the fact that I felt responsible for helping them solve their problems and for making everything "all right" in our family. I went to work early to try to pay for my own things and relieve my parents of that much worry. And I either tried to mediate their arguments or console my mother after they fought. I guess I didn't have time to rebel or to worry much about myself. I was too busy being a family therapist.

Parents' Midlife Concerns

At the same time that parents are dealing with their adolescents, they often have to contend with other family and personal concerns. Most parents of adolescents are at an age that is a critical time in adult development. They are also likely to experience the problems of the "sandwich generation," those caught between responsibilities for their adolescent children and their own aging parents. And they are far more likely than they were in earlier years of their lives to have other relatives and friends who need some kind of help. As a result, more than one out of every seven adults, including more than one out of five women aged thirty-five to sixty-four, cares for a friend or relative in any given year (Marks 1996). Moreover, many Americans are employed while caring for an

Those in the "sandwich generation" have responsibilities for both their children and their aging parents.

impaired parent; such a situation is stressful and the stress increases with the amount of time the caregiving requires (Starrels et al. 1997). If this caregiving is combined with the challenges of dealing with adolescent children, the stress may be even greater.

In addition to responsibilities for their children and their parents, the couple in stage four faces marital and personal challenges. Midlife is a time when people become increasingly concerned about their own aging process. They face issues of their appearance, physical competency, and health. The importance of health to an individual's quality of life increases significantly around the age of thirty-five (Steinberg 1987:82). It isn't that health actually tends to deteriorate at that age but that people become aware of its importance and get more concerned about it.

At midlife, a change also occurs in the way that people view life. They begin to think in terms of how much time they have left rather than how much has already occurred. Possibilities for change seem limited. For example, they may feel that they no longer have options for a career change and that they are bound to continue in whatever career they have until retirement. There may be a yearning for some new excitement or new direction, but there appear to be few if any opportunities to fulfill these desires. In some cases, their marriage may appear to be stale and a handicap to further growth and/or

excitement in life. One or both partners may seriously think about the possibility of separation or divorce in order to pursue new relationships.

Perhaps the above sounds familiar. It is a description of some of the things that happen to people who wrestle with the so-called midlife crisis. Not everyone has a midlife crisis, but everyone faces a set of challenges and concerns at midlife. For men, Levinson and his associates (1978) have identified four fundamental concerns. First is the concern with mortality. A man comes to realize that his life is limited. Increasingly, he becomes aware that some day he will die. He must come to terms with the fact that he is growing older and learn to find some value in that process. Unfortunately, some men resist the process vigorously, using dress, cosmetics, exercise, diet, new relationships and behavior patterns, and perhaps even plastic surgery in an effort to stay young-looking. Advertisements, of course, play on this desire and offer a wide variety of products and services to maintain a youthful appearance.

A second concern involves destructive and creative tendencies. Destruction, including death, is a part of men's experience. But a man:

> is eager to affirm life for himself and for the generations to come. He wants to be more creative. The creative impulse is not merely to "make" something. It is to bring something into being, to give birth, to generate life. A song, a painting, even a spoon or toy, if made in a spirit of creation . . . has a being of its own and will enrich the lives of those who are engaged with it (Levinson et al. 1978:222).

The hunger to be creative, to give the world some legacy, adds to the restlessness of men at midlife.

Third, men need to recognize and develop both the masculine and feminine aspects of their nature. Up to midlife, for example, a man may focus his energies on being a "true" man, on doing, making, and having. But at midlife, he may begin to explore the feminine side of his nature. In other words, gender-role orientations may shift at midlife and become more androgynous.

Part of the male shift in gender-role orientation is an increasing concern for family and interpersonal relationships (as opposed to a consuming involvement in career). Many men become more nurturant, more expressive, and more invested in their relationships than they were in the past. As a result, the well-being of men at midlife tends to be dependent more on the quality of their intimate relationships than on their financial attainments (McKenry, Arnold, Julian, and Kuo 1987).

The fourth concern is the need to be attached to and separate from the social environment. Attachment means involvement with the environment, including the feelings a man has, and the way in which he interacts with it. When he is attached to the environment, his thoughts are focused on it. Separateness, on the other hand, does not mean that he is not involved with people or activities but that his thoughts are focused within—on his own imagination and fantasies. Separateness helps him grow. When he is too separate, he is in danger of losing touch with reality. When he is too attached, he is in danger of neglecting his personal growth.

In early adulthood, Levinson and his associates point out, a man is more prone to attachment than separateness. During his twenties and thirties, a man is consumed with making his way in the world and successfully pursuing his work. At midlife, it becomes important to attain a more equal balance between separateness and attachment. A man must address such questions as what he really wants, what is really important to him, and how he wants to live in the future.

Although Levinson's work focused on men, women also deal with midlife issues. Women tend to reach the midlife crisis point sooner than men, usually around the age of thirty-five (Sheehy and Brehony 1996). At that point, a woman may feel that she faces her last opportunity to accomplish certain things in her life. She may also experience important changes, such as her last child going to school and the prospective end of her childbearing years. With the tasks of mothering requiring less of her time, a woman may begin to focus more attention on her own needs and development.

Satisfaction at Midlife

Obviously, the intersection of the turmoil of adolescence with the parental crisis of midlife creates a fertile climate for considerable family strain and for diminished satisfaction with life (Steinberg and Silverberg 1987). In fact, stage four tends to be the most stressful of all (Olson and McCubbin 1983:219).

But we do not want to paint a totally bleak picture. In spite of the strains, we should point out that intense conflict between parents and their adolescent children is not inevitable (Steinberg 1987:78). Most adolescents, in fact, note positive relationships with their parents. A national sample of children reported considerable satisfaction with family life (Roper and Keller 1988). Even though some of the children included (ages eight to seventeen) were not adolescents, the results were impressive. Fully 93 percent said they were happy with the amount of love shown by their parents, and 79 percent were happy about the amount of time their parents spent with them. Three-fourths even said they were happy about the amount of work they had to do around the house. In another study, 335 adolescents reported more harmony than discord in their families (Richardson et al. 1984). Their conflict tended to focus on issues of freedom and responsibility. Nevertheless, most of the children perceived their parents as fair and relatively lenient in their discipline.

When families do have conflict, it may partly be due to a lack of **rites of passage** (Quinn, Newfield, and Protinsky 1985; Broderick 1993:203–5). A rite of passage marks a significant time of change in an individual's life. In many preindustrial cultures, the transition to adulthood is marked by a rite of passage. For example, an adolescent male may undergo some kind of physical test, such as a period of isolation and beating by adult men, that marks the end of childhood and his entry into the world of adults. We may find these rites of passage unappealing because they involve varying degrees of anxiety and pain. Still, they clearly indicated when an individual passed from childhood to adulthood.

In our society, there are some markers of this transition. For example, attaining the age when you can get a driver's license may be a rite of passage, but it depends on how it is handled in a family. In some families, the new right may be granted with reluctance or not at all. Or it may be treated as little more than the result of living a certain number of years rather than as a significant accomplishment. To be effective, a rite of passage should treat the event as an achievement that brings with it higher status and greater responsibility and privileges.

Thus, one of the ways that families can deal with conflicts and problems is to institute rites of passage. Consider the following case of a single

INVOLVEMENT
Family Rituals

In this chapter, we have noted the importance of rites of passage in family life. Family rituals are also an important tool in creating family solidarity and providing family members with meaningful experiences of interaction. Unlike rites of passage, rituals occur frequently and regularly. How many rituals do you observe in your family? How are they observed? What were some of the most meaningful rituals to you in your family of origin? How many of them do you, or do you plan to, use in your own nuclear family?

When thinking of rituals, consider what your family did on holidays, on certain special days, and regularly as a part of family life. For example:

Holidays would include:
New Year's Eve
Labor Day
Memorial Day
Thanksgiving
Easter or Passover
Christmas
Mother's and Father's Day
Hanukkah
Independence Day

Special days include:
birthdays
anniversaries
confirmation or Bar Mitzvah or
    Bas Mitzvah
graduation
weddings
baptism

vacations
Other rituals might include:
mealtime activities
family recreation activities
bedtime rituals
family religious activities

Talk to someone of another race or another ethnic background about the rituals in his or her family. How do they compare with yours? Are there different rituals for boys and girls? If so, how would you evaluate that practice?

If the entire class participates in this project, have a number of people describe the rituals that were most meaningful to their family. Then discuss which of the rituals the class members would like to incorporate in their own families.

mother and her adolescent daughter (Quinn, Newfield, and Protinsky 1985:106–7). Mrs. Ward, the mother, was a widow raising her fifteen-year-old daughter, Diane, alone. Diane's father was killed when she was four. Her uncle served as a kind of surrogate father to her, but he was killed in a military accident when she was nine. Mrs. Ward didn't realize how traumatic each of these losses was for Diane. She didn't take Diane's grieving seriously. She tried to take over both parental roles by being a strict disciplinarian and maintaining total control.

But maintaining control meant that Diane's attempts to grow up were thwarted. Her mother defined any efforts on Diane's part to act like an adult as premature. Their conflict culminated in Diane's attempted suicide. At the time of the attempt, Diane had just graduated from junior high after a three-year struggle with her math courses and a number of behavioral problems at school. The therapist suggested a rite of passage. He said it was time for the family to move to a new stage of their lives. He helped them plan a party to celebrate Diane's

school achievements and her entrance into senior high. The party would also allow them each to meet new people. Following the party, Diane and her mother began to make significant progress.

A party as a formal recognition is, of course, only one way that a family can institute its own rites of passage. The point is that there is great value to all members of the family to have some kind of ceremony that carries with it recognition by both parents and children that a new phase has been reached and that this new phase means that the adolescent has achieved something significant and is now endowed with a higher status and new privileges and responsibilities. Such rites of passage may occur profitably a number of times during the adolescent years.

THE LAUNCHING AND EMPTY-NEST STAGE

In stage five, the couple must deal with the children moving out and being on their own. This can be a

Systems Theory Applied

problem for both the children and the parents (Lauer and Lauer 1999b). Family therapists stress the *need for "differentiation,"* the need for each member of the family to be an autonomous individual as well as an integral part of an intimate group (Bowen 1978). As we noted previously in our discussion of the problem of fusion in a newly married couple, a fulfilling intimate relationship is a relationship of interdependence, not of merging and loss of individuality. Fusion can occur between children and parents as well as between spouses. At some point, then, it is important that the children pursue their individual lives by leaving the home. The children seem to sense this to a somewhat greater extent than their parents; a study of high school seniors found that they were more likely than their parents to expect they would establish their own residences before getting married (Goldscheider and Goldscheider 1993). In fact, an independent residence before marriage has become a sign of adult status for young adults.

The age at which a young adult leaves the parental home depends on a number of factors, including the quality of the parent-child relationship, the child's employment status, the parents' marital status, and the status of the child's intimate relationships (engaged or planning to cohabit, e.g.) (Goldscheider 1997). Because increasing numbers of adult children are leaving the parental home for nonmarital reasons, a substantial number return to the parental home for varying periods of time, creating a new set of challenges for both parents and children (Lauer and Lauer 1999b).

When the children leave, the parent-child relationship changes (Lauer and Lauer 1999b). Generally, the relationship is likely to become closer, more supportive, and less conflicted (Aquilino 1997). Moreover, in their interviews with more than a thousand people in upstate New York, Logan and Spitze (1996) found that adult children and their parents engage in a great deal of care for each other, with the parents tending to give more help in the form of household tasks to their adult children than they receive. The situation only reverses when the parents become ill or infirm, and the children become their parents' caregivers. Clearly, family ties are likely to remain strong throughout the family life cycle.

In addition to their relationship with their children, an empty-nest couple faces a number of other changes. The couple must come to terms with its own marital relationship and the meaning of that relationship for the future. Those who reach the empty nest at a relatively early point (between twenty and thirty years of marriage) have an increased risk of divorce, while those who have been married for more than thirty years have a lower likelihood of breakup (Heidemann, Suhomlinova, and O'Rand 1998). Those who stay together may want to make some alterations in their relationship such as renegotiating their roles. They may have to adjust to the marriage of their children, including the addition of in-laws into the family system. They may find themselves in the new role of grandparent. And they may face the problem of their own parents becoming disabled or dying.

We should note that at least some couples never experience, or have little time to experience, the empty nest. As table 15.2 shows, after age forty-five there is a dramatic decline in the number of households with children under the age of eighteen. But 8 percent of couples in which the head of the house is fifty-five to sixty-four years of age and 1 percent of those sixty-five and older still have children under eighteen living at home. For single mothers, the figures are the same, but for single fathers they are even higher—19 percent of those fifty-five to sixty-four years of age and 4 percent of those sixty-five and older have children under eighteen in their homes.

The Couple Together Again

It may be difficult for a couple when the children leave home. A psychology professor put it this way:

> Two of the most painful times I remember are when our oldest child announced he was leaving home to go to college and when our youngest did the same. With the oldest, it meant that the family was beginning to break up. With the youngest, it meant a loss of a special kind of parenting that I valued, that day-to-day involvement with the kids.

Some men find it painful for the children to leave. Those who have poor marital relationships are likely to find the empty nest disagreeable (Lauer and Lauer 1999b). Also, men who have been very work-minded may be well established in their

TABLE 15.2
Family Households with Own Children Under Age 18, 1995

Family Type	Total	Age of Householder					
		15–24 Years	25–34 Years	35–44 Years	45–54 Years	55–64 Years	65+ Years
Number (1,000)							
Family households with children	34,296	1,969	10,763	14,922	5,752	743	147
Married couple	25,241	899	7,528	11,383	4,712	602	118
Male householder[1]	1,440	106	466	556	243	53	16
Female householder[1]	7,615	963	2,769	2,983	798	88	13
Percent Distribution							
Family households with children	100	100	100	100	100	100	100
Married couple	74	46	70	76	82	81	80
Male householder[1]	4	5	4	4	4	7	11
Female householder[1]	22	49	26	20	14	12	9
Households with Children, As a Percent of All Family Households, by Type							
Family households with children, total	49	64	76	86	42	8	1
Married couple	47	55	73	82	42	8	1
Male householder[1]	45	33	59	65	44	19	4
Female householder[1]	61	86	93	85	39	8	1

[1]No spouse present.
Source: U.S. Bureau of the Census 1997b:66.

careers and now would like to devote more time to their children. But the children are leaving, and the men are left with the disappointment of a relationship that can never be.

Women who have invested themselves totally, or nearly so, in child-rearing will also find the empty nest painful (Bart 1971). The woman who had little other than motherhood to occupy herself during the earlier stages may find this stage a deeply painful one. She may have fulfilled her intimacy needs in her relationships with her children. She even may feel somewhat estranged from her husband because she has neglected the marriage. And even if there is no estrangement, she may find that her husband is too involved with work or his career to take the place of the children in her life. She desperately needs new challenges, new tasks, new intimate relationships, but she may be at a loss as to where to find them.

But how many women, or men for that matter, come to the empty-nest stage and find it empty of meaning as well as of children? Certainly not the majority. To the contrary, most people, both men

and women, report that it is a time of increased marital satisfaction and renewal for their marriage (Lauer and Lauer 1999b). A combination of reduced parental and work responsibilities as people age leads to enhanced marital satisfaction (Orbuch et al. 1996).

For most people, then, stage five represents a time of increasing marital satisfaction and renewed family strength (Levenson, Carstensen, and Gottman 1993). Husbands perceive a sharp increase in agreement on various issues at this stage (White 1987). Wives begin to spend less time in housework (Rexroat and Shehan 1987). There may be a sexual renewal in the marriage as the couple realizes that they can express themselves sexually in a more relaxed and private way. There may be a sense of new freedom—fewer responsibilities, less financial strain, less family work. The marriage may become more egalitarian than it was during the child-rearing years. And whatever grief is involved in the children leaving may be more than compensated by pride in their achievements and the satisfactions of having parented them.

When the last child leaves home, a couple must come to terms with their marital relationship for the future.

Overall, then, the empty nest is likely to be a stage that is gratifying and filled with a new zest for living. The psychologist quoted previously had more to say: "What I discovered, however, was that just being with my wife again was great. We're having a ball! I love my children dearly, and I can't imagine being without them, but life has never been any better than it is now."

Grandparenthood

Increasing numbers of people are experiencing the grandparent role. Some people become grandparents as early as their forties. Among those sixty-five and older, nearly three-fourths are grandparents (Barranti 1985). Although the pride of grandparents is legendary in our society, including everything from pins to bumper stickers that say "ask me about my grandchildren" or "happiness is being a grandparent," not everyone welcomes the role. Some grandparents resist the implication of their own aging. Some do not want to get involved in the child care aspects that are frequently expected of them. But for the most part, grandparenting is a positive experience in people's lives (Kivett 1991).

Types of Grandparents Grandparents relate in differing ways to their grandchildren, depending in part on the kind of relationship the grandparents had with their own grandparents (King and Elder 1997). In their study of seventy sets of middle-class grandparents, Neugarten and Weinstein (1968) found that most expressed satisfaction and comfort with the role. About a third had some difficulty adjusting to it, mainly because of such things as resentment over baby-sitting. The researchers identified five different types of grandparent: the formal, the fun seeker, the surrogate parent, the reservoir of family wisdom, and the distant figure.

The *formal* grandparent has definite ideas of the role and clearly distinguishes it from the parental role. Formal grandparents may occasionally indulge the child and do some baby-sitting, but they basically let child care duties remain in the hands of the parents. They show constant interest in the grandchild but do not offer advice on parenting. The *fun seeker* establishes an informal, playful relationship with the grandchild, joining the child in play almost like a playmate.

The *surrogate parent* assumes the responsibilities of child care. Increasing numbers of grandparents are functioning as surrogate parents to some degree, including growing numbers who have total responsibility for childcare. In 1997, grandparents maintained 2.4 million American families, representing 7 percent of all families with children under eighteen (U.S. Bureau of the Census 1998). A disproportionate number of the children were racial/ethnic minorities; of all children living with grandparents, 42 percent were non-Hispanic white, 36 percent were non-Hispanic African American, 17 percent were Hispanic, and 5 percent were Asian, Pacific Islander, American Indian, or Alaska Native.

In nearly half the grandparent-maintained families, the mother is present, and in others the father or both parents may be present. In about a third, there are no parents. Among the factors leading grandparents to assume some or all of the responsibility for parenting are parents who work, divorce, separation, illness, addiction, and death (Jendrek 1994). Grandparents who function as surrogate parents experience changes in their life styles, their relationships with friends and family, and their own marital relationship (Jendrek 1993). They may also suffer various physical and emotional problems from the stress of parenting their grandchildren (Gilbert 1998).

The *reservoir of family wisdom* is a grandfather who acts as a source of special skills and resources for the grandchild. Both the parents and the grandchildren are subordinate to this grandparent. Everyone defers to his judgment. This role, incidentally, seems to be rare. Finally, the *distant figure* is the grandparent who has kindly but rare contact with the child. The distant figure may be separated by distance or by choice. In any case, contact is infrequent and brief.

From the grandchild's perspective, grandparents play some similar and some differing roles (Kornhaber and Woodward 1981). Based on a sample of three hundred grandchildren, ages five to eighteen, the researchers identified five roles: historian, mentor, role model, wizard, and nurturer/great parent. Any one grandparent, of course, can fulfill one or more of the roles.

The *historian* provides a cultural and family sense of history. The *mentor* gives wisdom and guidance in the art of living. The *role model* provides an appropriate model for future roles of the grandchild, including that of grandparent. The *wizard* tells fascinating stories and exercises the grandchild's imagination. The *nurturer/great parent* is a basic role that gives the child a greater support system than he or she would otherwise have.

What Grandparents Do for Us   As the preceding suggests, the idea of grandparenthood as being simply pleasure without responsibility grossly underestimates the role that grandparents play in our lives. Parents may find grandparents helpful in providing various kinds of support, including practical help in child-rearing and giving the grandchildren a sense of their heritage (J. Thomas 1990). We should note that this can be a delicate role to play for grandparents, since the line between support and interference is not always clear. When the behavior is de-

fined as interference rather than support, there is likely to be conflict between parents and grandparents (J. Thomas 1990).

Conflict may also arise in the grandparent-grandchild relationship (J. Thomas 1990), but grandparents are more likely to provide important benefits to the growing child. Research on grandchildren of all ages has uncovered a considerable amount of information about the influence of grandparents (Barranti 1985).

Adolescents report a number of ways that grandparents influence their development (Barranti 1985:347). Grandparents help them to get a sense of their own identity by linking them up with their heritage. Grandparents help adolescents to understand their own parents better and may function as confidants for the adolescents when the latter are unwilling for some reason to talk with their parents about a matter. Adolescents tend to view grandparents in warm, comfortable, and supportive terms. When they have such a relationship with grandparents, they are likely to develop more positive attitudes toward older people and also about their own aging.

When asked about the relationship with their grandparents, young adults agree that it is very important to them. They get a certain amount of emotional gratification from it. A survey of 391 young adult grandchildren (mean age of 19.1 years) reported the following reasons as important factors in feeling close to grandparents: enjoying their personalities; enjoying shared activities with them; experiencing their appreciation, attention, and support; and relating to them as a model, teacher, adviser, and source of inspiration (Kennedy 1991). Another study, of 171 Canadian undergraduates, looked at the relationship the young people had with grandparents with whom they were close and not as close (Boon and Brussoni 1996). The students indicated that the grandparents with whom they were close were influential in their lives, that they had frequent contact with those grandparents and shared a number of activities with them, and that all of these experiences were important to them.

In sum, while the grandparent-grandchild relationship is not as intense as the parent-child, it is a unique and potentially highly gratifying relationship that is important in the lives of both grandparents and grandchildren. It is a form of intimacy that enhances the quality of life.

PERSONAL
An Empty-Nest High

Mark is a building contractor who has been married twenty-six years. A year ago, the last of his four children left home for college. Mark and his wife, Jeri, are devoted parents and have had a close family life. How would they deal with the empty nest? Mark tells us:

We've always had a great time as a family. I must admit that I had mixed feelings when my first kid—my oldest daughter—got married. I had to battle the feeling that an intruder had come and disrupted our family. But at least we still had three other kids. Then marriage and college finally got to all of them. When my youngest girl left for college, my wife and I went with her to help her get settled in the dormitory. We both cried most of the way back home. Our nest was depressingly empty.

At first, I tried to deal with it by increasing my workload. Jeri works with me in the business and she also has been active in the League of Women Voters and our church. She got even more active in the first few months of our empty nest.

That caused some problems. Instead of growing closer together and supporting each other, we were becoming strangers. We irritated each other. We weren't happy with our nest being empty, but neither of us was helping the other to cope with it.

I don't know how long we might have gone on that way. But one day Jeri said to me, "Mark, we're heading for serious trouble." That shocked me. I knew it, but I didn't want to admit it. And I didn't know she felt the same way. We talked about it. We agreed that we needed to get back to work on our marriage. We knew some other couples who talked about how much they were enjoying themselves since their kids were gone. Why couldn't we?

We decided that we would stop burying our sadness in work and start exploring this new stage of life. So we started doing things together. We took a few weekend trips. We almost shocked ourselves when we took off from the office one afternoon and went home, made love, went out to dinner, and took in a show. That was it! I suddenly realized what a great life we have. It still feels a little strange to come home and not have anyone there, or for things to be so quiet at night. But I want to tell you that we're on a second honeymoon. We're learning things about each other and exploring things together and just thoroughly enjoying ourselves.

I guess the thing is that life just isn't as serious as it was when the kids were at home. I don't worry about things. Even when the kids were grown, Jeri and I both worried if they were out real late or if they were going to a party where everyone was drinking a lot or even if they didn't seem to be eating properly. We don't even think about those things now. We're just having fun.

THE AGING FAMILY

In the aging family, there is a shift of roles. The middle generation, the children of the aging couple, take on a more central role in the family. The aging couple must cope with various challenges and problems, including retirement, the death of friends and siblings, and their own physical decline. Eventually, one of the spouses is likely to face the challenge of living alone. But this stage, like every other, has its satisfactions as well as its problems.

Retirement

Retirement can be a critical time for a couple. For those who have been career-oriented, retirement means the loss of one of the more important roles in life. And people are likely to feel stressed as they adjust to the role changes and to building a new identity for themselves (Johnston 1990). In part, the way that people adjust to retirement depends on whether they retired voluntarily. Those who are forced to retire because of age or other factors may have a difficult time adjusting. This can place a strain on the marriage. A depressed man, for example, sitting around the house all day can create considerable frustration and tension.

Even if one spouse adjusts well to retirement, problems may arise if the new roles are not worked out satisfactorily. For example, the wife of a retired business executive had to get help for serious depression (Walsh 1980:201). It turned out that her

Many older couples find retirement an opportunity to pursue their interests.

husband was adjusting well to his retirement, but he did so by becoming a gourmet cook and taking over many of her responsibilities as homemaker. His wife lost her long-time, major role in the home and was unable to adjust to the situation.

For the most part, however, it is involuntary retirement that is most likely to be stressful. Those who desire to retire and make plans for their life following retirement are not likely to be adversely affected by it. A survey of retired men reported that over half said that retirement was better than they had expected and that they were "very happy" with it (Brody 1985). Only 17 percent said that retirement was worse than they had expected, and only 6 percent said that they were "somewhat unhappy" or "very unhappy" with it.

Recognizing that people have differing values and needs with regard to work, the U.S. Congress ended mandatory retirement for most workers in 1986. However, many people opt to retire in their sixties, and some opt for an even earlier retirement to pursue a new career or other kinds of interests. Less than

10 percent choose to continue working in the same career after the age of sixty-five (Brody 1985).

Marital Relations

A couple in the sixth stage is more likely to be oriented maritally than parentally. That is, spouses are likely to focus more of their time and energy on their relationship with each other than on that with their children and grandchildren. Their marriage is likely to be more egalitarian as the husband increases his share of the housework, particularly once he is retired (Rexroat and Shehan 1987).

The couple may continue to have an active and meaningful sex life during this stage, particularly when the marital relationship generally is a good one (Hawton, Gath, and Day 1994). Comedians and popular beliefs reinforce the notion that sexuality vanishes from our lives at some point in the aging process. Butler and Lewis (1981) point out five myths about sex and aging: older people do not have sexual desires; even if they have some desire, they cannot physically engage in sexual relations anymore; sex may be hazardous to the health of the aged; older people are physically unattractive and therefore are not sexually desirable; and, finally, even the thought of sexual activity among the elderly is shameful and perverse. Many people accept one or more of these myths.

In contrast to the jokes and the myths, sex may be an important part of the aging couple's marital relationship. For couples with long-standing problems, of course, age can be an excuse for ceasing sexual activity. But there are no inherent physiological reasons for sex to stop. Actually, the majority of married people over the age of seventy report having sex, sometimes as often as twice a week or more.

In general, then, how much satisfaction is there with marriage at this stage? For most couples, it tends to be high, higher in fact than at any stage since the couple was first married. There are, however, some variations by age. Gilford (1984) found that satisfaction was highest among those in the sixty-three- to sixty-nine-year age group (she measured satisfaction in terms of the amount of positive interaction and negative sentiment expressed by couples). Those between fifty-five and sixty-two and those between seventy and ninety had somewhat lower levels of satisfaction. She speculated that the reason for the higher levels among those

COMPARISON
Caring for Elderly Family Members on Malo

One of the problems facing all societies is the care of the aged. Responsibility for this care generally falls to the family. In the United States, this responsibility is frequently assigned to nursing homes. Malo is an island in the South Pacific whose inhabitants are relatively poor by United States' standards. When family members become old and incapable of fully caring for themselves, the people assume caregiving—but not quite like we do in the United States.

As in the United States, people on Malo are considered in need of caregiving when they clearly cannot be self-sufficient. But who assumes the caregiving responsibility? The Maloese have a saying that "men

stay on the land and women leave it." That is, when a woman marries she is expected to move to her husband's village and become a part of his land. Her sons will belong to that land, but her daughters will marry onto other lands.

The spouse is responsible for caring for his or her aged partner. If the spouse dies, caregiving is assumed by daughters-in-law and, only if necessary, by daughters. Men do not get involved in this caregiving. In fact, a man is not supposed to touch his mother and thus cannot take care of her. Nor is a man supposed to care for his sister, brother, father's father, or various other family members. The man's responsibility is generally

only for his wife. The reason for this arrangement, which the Maloese take very seriously, is the belief that certain embodiments of males and females are very different and are not supposed to come into contact with each other.

Even though they have clearly defined rules, the Maloese can experience conflict when dealing with the elderly. A daughter's first obligation, for instance, is to her husband's family. But she is likely still to have emotional ties to her own parents and other relatives. No society yet, including Malo, has provided a system for care of elderly family members that relieves people of having to make difficult choices (Rubinstein 1994).

---

sixty-three to sixty-nine was that it is the "honeymoon" stage after retirement that allows the spouses to enjoy such resources as "leisure time, inclination to spend it together and with adult children, good health, and adequate income with which to enhance marital lifestyle and negotiate marital happiness" (Gilford 1984:331).

Other Relationships

Although the aging couple is more maritally than parentally oriented, family relationships are still very important. The great majority of adults over sixty-five lives with someone else, primarily with spouses or other relatives. The great majority also lives within a short distance of at least one child. The elderly prefer to maintain their own homes rather than live with their children, but they are likely to have frequent contact with children and to maintain intimate ties. This relationship has been called "intimacy at a distance" (Walsh 1980:198).

For example, in her study of 124 couples in their sixties, Joan Aldous (1987) found that the couples

were involved in "a web of associational and functional activities" with their adult children. Some kind of contact occurred between the parents and their children on the average of more than once a week. Contact includes letters, telephone calls, visits, celebrating holidays and birthdays, and engaging in common recreational and religious activities. During the year preceding the study, there was also a good deal of "functional" activity, such as gifts, loans, provision of transportation, child care, and help with other kinds of family work. Overall, on a scale of 1 (not satisfied) to 5 (very satisfied), the parents rated their relationships with their children at 4.6 and the children rated the relationships at 4.5.

Still, conflict between parents and adult children can continue into later life. Three researchers asked a sample of fifty-five parents in their sixties and seventies to talk about angry confrontations between themselves and their children (Fisher, Reid, and Melendez 1989). Anger of the parents toward the children was most likely to involve the adult child's breaking of family rules about behavior (not keeping appointments, getting drunk, etc.) or failing to live up to role expectations (not being a good citizen, being lazy, etc.). Children's anger toward parents was most likely to involve lack of agreement over values or opinions or the failure of the parent to provide needed help (baby-sitting, financial assistance, etc.).

Strains can also occur when adult children move back into the parental home. This problem is growing because the proportion of families with children aged eighteen and older living at home is also increasing. An adult child may move into the parent home because of divorce, work and/or financial difficulties, or an inability to afford to maintain his or her own home.

A study of thirty-nine parents with adult children living at home found that most do not want the arrangement to continue on an indefinite basis (Clemens and Axelson 1985). The two most common sources of conflict in the homes were disagreements about the adult child's times of coming and going and the issue of cleaning and maintaining the house. About four out of ten of the parents said that they had serious conflicts with at least one of their resident children.

Data from a national survey showed that the majority of parents were highly satisfied with having their adult children living with them (Aquilino and Supple 1991). Satisfaction, however, was inversely related to the level of parent-child conflict; as conflict increased, satisfaction went down. Factors that tended to increase the conflict and/or decrease satisfaction with the arrangement included: children's financial dependency and unemployment; return of a child because of divorce or separation; and return of a child with grandchildren.

Other relationships are also important at this stage of the family life cycle. Social support is important to us at every stage of life. In this sixth stage, men tend to rely on their wives as their main source of support. Women, in contrast, tend to have a larger network and to find support from friends as well as other family members (Antonucci and Akiyama 1987). Both men and women who have living brothers and sisters are likely to develop a new perspective toward them. Older adults generally indicate feelings of greater closeness and compatibility with siblings than do younger adults (Goetting 1986). Older adults are more likely to reminisce with siblings than with their children about earlier experiences and relationships. Such reminiscence can be important in validating one's life and maintaining one's self-esteem.

Death of a Spouse

At nearly every age level, women are far more likely than men to face the death of a spouse (figure 15.3). Although men are likely to have a harder time adjusting to the death of a spouse than are women (because older men tend to lean more heavily than do women on their spouses for support and intimacy), the death of a spouse is always traumatic and typically entails a time of emotional and physical distress. Distress is diminished though not eliminated by a helpful social support network (Miller et al. 1998).

There are various reasons for the distress. For one thing, there is the loss of intimacy. A relationship which for most married people is the most intimate relationship of all has been severed. There is also a loss of identity. One is no longer a husband or a wife, role has occupied a major portion of one's life. What will take the place of that role? The problem is intensified because there tends to be a somewhat negative connotation to the term *widow* or *widower.*

The remaining spouse also must deal with the varied physical and emotional consequences of bereavement (Parkes 1985). Typically, the individual goes through a period of confusion, which includes some lapse of memory, difficulty in concentrating, and wandering thoughts. There is likely to be an intense feeling of loneliness, even for those who have children. We heard a woman try to console her newly widowed friend by reminding the friend, "At least you have your children." The widow replied: "It's not the same as your mate. It's just not the same." Eventually, the children may help assuage the grief and provide a source of support and renewed interest in life. But the remaining spouse typically has to wrestle with difficult periods of loneliness. And depression tends to accompany the loneliness. On top of all this may be practical worries as well—financial concerns or who will do some of the chores that the spouse formerly handled.

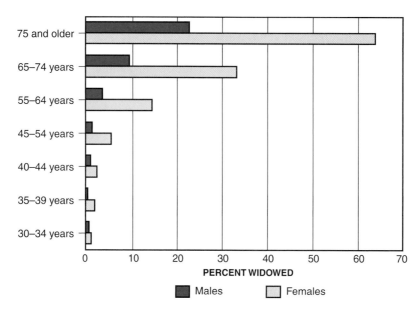

FIGURE 15.3   Proportion Widowed, by Age: 1996
(*Source:* U.S. bureau of the Census 1997b:56.)

Eventually, the surviving spouse is likely to work through his or her grief and begin to pursue a new life. There are ways to facilitate the process, to make it less painful. A study of seventy-five widows, ages sixty to ninety, reported that those who were more successful in resolving their grief had discussed a number of important matters with their spouses, family, or friends prior to the spouse's death (Hansson and Remondet 1987). Specifically, they had talked about finances, family reactions, their own feelings, how their lives might change, and how their friendships might be affected. Discussion with the spouse was possible because most widows (and widowers) have some period of warning. Of course, such discussion requires the spouses to continue to engage in self-disclosure to the very end and not engage in a game of pretending that the dying spouse will recover. Those widows who had discussed the issues not only resolved their grief

more quickly but were better adjusted some years later and reported better physical and emotional health than the others.

Many individuals get on with their lives by dating and eventually marrying again. A study of 249 widows and 101 widowers concluded that those who were either in a new romance or remarried twenty-five months after the spouse's death were emotionally healthier than those who were still uninvolved with someone new (Schneider et al. 1996). The chances for widows to remarry, especially those who are older, is less than that for widowers. Those who do remarry tend to have higher morale than those who do not. The main reasons men give for remarrying are for companionship and to be cared for; the main reasons women give for remarrying are for companionship and love (Jacobs and Vinick 1981). The quest for intimacy never ends.

PRINCIPLES FOR ENHANCING INTIMACY

1. Change is inevitable in our family relationships. Yet we are often surprised and generally resist change when it occurs. And unfortunately, many intimate relationships are strained beyond repair by the onslaught of change. It is vital, therefore, that you understand and prepare for the alterations that typically occur during the family life cycle. Anticipating some of the challenges at each stage of the process will help you to cope when they actually take place.

2. At every stage of life, there are opportunities for personal as well as family growth. Growth comes from taking responsibility for yourself, opening yourself to others and to new experiences, taking advantage of available resources, and persevering in the face of difficulties. If we affirm personal growth, our capacity for genuine intimacy with others will increase.

3. One of the major tasks facing newly married couples is to develop their own family system. This is not an easy job. For example, couples are often uncertain and anxious about how and when to establish holiday traditions that are theirs and separate from those of their families of origin. In order to accomplish this most effectively, the couple needs to discuss the matter thoroughly, come to an understanding of what they want, and then gradually introduce these plans to their families.

4. Children can affect the marriage relationship of their parents at various stages in the family life cycle. They bring joy and pain, fun and responsibility. They also can consume much of the attention of one or both of their parents. Unless the parents are vigilant, their relationship to each other can suffer from neglect. Thus, spouses need to always reserve time for themselves as a couple, work at their marriage, and prepare for the time when the two of them are alone together once again.

5. If these are difficult times, remember there's hope. If you are experiencing problems and frustrations in a particular stage of your family life cycle, it is useful to remember that this time will pass. And if you confront the difficulties and work through them, your family system eventually will be stronger.

SUMMARY

The idea of the family life cycle is based on the notion that families, like everything else, go through a process from birth through growth to decline and death. A useful way of conceptualizing the family life cycle is to look at ways that families must alter their attitudes and relationships in order to adapt to each stage. Six stages are:

1. The young unattached adult.
2. The newly married couple.
3. The family with young children.
4. The family with adolescents.
5. The stage of launching children and moving on.
6. The family in later life.

Both cyclical and linear changes of many kinds occur over these stages, including marital satisfaction, empathy, discussion, and regard.

Our experiences in passing through the family life cycle are affected by social changes. Some important changes in recent times are the lowered likelihood of experiencing the death of one's parents or of a child, the increased likelihood of being a grandparent, and the increased likelihood of facing marital disruption because of divorce rather than death, which also means a greater proportion of people who will experience remarriage.

The newly married couple tends to have a high level of certain family strengths, including self-disclosure, loyalty, trust, and respect. One of the couple's important tasks is forming its own marital system. In doing so, spouses will have to follow or reject the models of their parents. In setting up their marital system, they must deal with the issue of closeness versus fusion, striving to build intimacy while retaining their individual identities.

The couple with young children faces the challenge of taking on the roles of mother and father as well as husband and wife and of enlarging the family system to include other people. Marital satisfaction is likely to be lower at this stage.

The family with adolescents faces the challenge of allowing the children to form their own independent identities and move beyond the nuclear family. At the same time, spouses may be facing their own midlife concerns with regard to marriage and careers. Adolescents are undergoing important physical, intellectual, and social definitional changes that will lead to new expectations about responsibilities. They need increasing autonomy and independence. As a result, considerable strain in the family is likely at this stage. Communication and discipline problems with adolescent children and financial problems for the family are common. Adolescents themselves see most of their stress arising from daily hassles with parents.

The parents of adolescents may be further stressed by their own midlife concerns and by being caught between responsibilities for their children and their own aging parents. Midlife is a time when people become increasingly concerned about their own aging. They begin to change the way that they view life, thinking in terms of how much time is left and how many doors of opportunities are closed. Levinson and his associates have identified four fundamental concerns of men at midlife: mortality, destructive and creative possibilities, balancing masculine versus feminine qualities, and coming to terms with attachment to and separation from the social environment. Women usually reach the midlife crisis point earlier than men and may begin to focus more attention on their own needs and growth.

In spite of the strains, most adolescents report positive relationships with their parents. They see their parents as fair and relatively lenient with them.

One way to minimize conflict is to institute rites of passage, which tend not to occur in our society.

In the launching and empty-nest stage, the couple must deal with the children moving out. They must come to terms again with their marital relationship and its future. Women are more likely than men to find the empty nest painful because they tend to invest themselves more in the child-rearing process. But the majority of people report the empty nest as a time of increased marital satisfaction and renewed family strength.

Grandparenthood is likely to occur in the fifth stage. There are different kinds of grandparents, including the formal, the fun seeker, the surrogate parent, the reservoir of family wisdom, and the distant figure. Grandchildren perceive their grandparents to play a variety of roles, including the historian, the mentor, the role model, the wizard, and the nurturer/great parent. The grandparent-grandchild relationship can be highly gratifying for both generations.

The aging family involves a shift of roles, with the middle generation taking on a more central place in the family. Retirement occurs at this stage. People may adjust well to, or even welcome, retirement when it is voluntary. Marital problems can arise if the new roles are not worked out satisfactorily.

Couples in the sixth stage tend to be maritally rather than parentally oriented. The marriage is likely to become more egalitarian. The couple may continue to have an active and meaningful sex life. And marital satisfaction is likely to be at its highest point since the couple's early years together. Family relationships are still important. Contact with children tends to be frequent. Strains may result if adult children move back into the home, however.

Women are far more likely than men to experience the death of a spouse. Both men and women whose spouses die face a difficult period of adjustment. There is a loss of identity and a variety of physical and emotional consequences of bereavement. Those who talk over various matters with the dying spouse make a better adjustment to the death than do others. Many will eventually remarry, although widows are less likely to do so than are widowers. Companionship is one of the most common reasons that both men and women remarry after the death of a spouse.

INTERNET CONNECTION
The Family Life Cycle

This chapter of your text outlines and describes the transition phases and challenges associated with married and unmarried families. Many of the issues discussed in this text are related to the aging process and its effect within families. How can the resources below be of assistance to you in better understanding the aging family?

www.mhhe
.com/lauer4

Administration on Aging
http://www.aoa.dhhs.gov/

A comprehensive and easy-to-use website on aging in America. You can find handy research and layperson-oriented links to valuable online resources here.

Pacer Program
http://www.pacer.org/tindex.html

This is the website of an interesting and innovative non-profit program with focus on children, education, the family, and disability based in Minnesota.

1. Describe the scope of resources available at the Administration on Aging web site. How can this site be of assistance to a parent? A grandparent? A grandchild? What research can you find on aging issues in the family here? What can you find at this site that might be of assistance to minority or low-income families? To people with limited English comprehension?

2. Describe the Pacer program. What projects are they engaged in? Describe the goals and functions of the Pacer Projects dealing with parents, grandparents and minorities and children.

3. What resources could you use at the Administration on Aging web site to better explain, understand, and evaluate the Pacer programs? Explain in detail.

FAMILY LIFE
AS MANAGEMENT

Learning Objectives

After reading chapter 16, you should be able to:

1. Define the meaning of money in contemporary society.
2. Show how financial conditions contribute to satisfaction or dissatisfaction within a marriage and a family.
3. Discuss the benefits and problems of teenagers working to increase the family income.
4. Outline the techniques of financial planning and how these contribute to the well-being of the family.
5. Explain the essentials of making and adhering to a budget.
6. Describe the various ways to minimize financial conflict in the family.
7. Discuss the importance of time management for the well-being of a marriage and family.
8. Show how people typically spend their time.
9. Explain some of the useful techniques for managing your time.
10. Describe the types and consequences of power struggles that occur in families.

A harried young father told us: "When I got married, I was prepared to be a husband, a worker, and a father. I didn't know I would also have to be a diplomat, a mediator, and a manager." He had discovered that family life rarely flows smoothly without careful attention and management. Indeed, if you don't take care of this part of your life, you may find that the family seems to impede rather than fulfill your intimacy needs.

In this chapter, we will look at three interrelated aspects of family life as management. First, we will discuss handling the family's finances. Then we will explore the problems of time management. Finally, we will examine the management of power and conflict in the family (as opposed to our focus on power and conflict in the marital relationship in chapter 12). The way in which the three are interrelated can be illustrated simply: an individual might pursue money as part of the quest for power, but the pursuit of money puts restraints on the individual's time, which may lead to tension and conflict in the family. We will consider each area of management separately, but it is important to keep in mind the ways in which they are interrelated.

MONEY MANAGEMENT

In considering money management, you should keep in mind a fundamental rule of human life, as expressed by a therapist: "Everyone worries about money, and no one seems satisfied with how much they have and how they use it" (Madanes 1994:1). The quest of many people for more and more income is seductive. You may believe that if you only had *x* more dollars, you would be satisfied and your money troubles would be over. But as a professional writer told us:

> I remember when I was a young man, struggling to make it, I heard of a man who made $10,000 a year. I thought that if I could only make that much, I would be satisfied forever. Now I pay much more than that in taxes each year. And I still don't have quite enough.

The Meaning of Money

Why are we so anxious to earn more and more money? Clearly, money brings many desirable benefits, including increased options and greater security. We learn early in life that by passing coins and bills to the right people at the right place, we can get many pleasurable things. Some people are so impressed by this power of money to get desirable things that they come to see it as a way to solve all of their problems (Mason 1992). We may also learn some negative aspects of money, such as associating money with anxiety when our parents worry and argue over it. Money, then, has both positive and negative meanings for us, meanings that will vary depending on our experiences in our families of origin.

Whatever the experiences in our families of origin, money has certain meanings in the culture that affect us. Generally, money means success and status. Most Americans agree that income is a measure of a family's success (Rubenstein 1981:34). The parents who provide well for their family in monetary terms are considered successful. People who are poorer than their neighbors may feel embarrassed. They may try to hide their lack of money behind a facade of spending. They may get themselves into financial difficulties by trying to provide their children with the same advantages as their neighbor's children.

Success, of course, means that we also gain status and approval from others. For example, a resident of a rapidly growing town explained that, in contrast with the past, people were now judged by their income. Formerly, people had status in this community because of their behavior and skills at their work. But as the community grew, it was no longer possible to know everyone on a personal basis. Now, "we don't know people, but we do know money." And the more money, the more the status.

Money also means freedom in our culture. It is the freedom to opt for one's preferred life-style. We have frequently asked people what they would do if they won a million dollars in a lottery, and their answer usually involves some shift in life-style. Money would, above all, give them the freedom to choose a new house or car, a changed pattern of work or career, travel, and so on.

In addition to success and freedom, money means power to most Americans, the power to affect the behavior of others. In a positive way, some people use money to help others, to support charities or causes that enhance the quality of life. In a negative way, money can be used to influence people or to force them to conform to one's will. People use money (spending it, withholding it, or judging others by how they spend it) to, among other things: prevent a spouse from breaking up a marriage; buy their freedom from a marriage they don't like; assess how much their parents or a spouse truly likes them; punish a spouse or a child; and discriminate among their children, rewarding the obedient and punishing the disobedient or, wittingly or unwittingly, showing which child is their favorite (Millman 1991).

Thus, money can be used in contrary ways—to manipulate or help others. It can be a source of comfort or of anxiety. It can facilitate a meaningful family life or create intense conflict. In any case, it is a significant factor in family well-being.

Money and Family Well-Being

How important is money in our lives? Public opinion polls report that Americans rank relations with family and friends, religious faith, and contributing to a better world far above monetary success.[1] The polls also report, however, that about six in ten Americans state they are not earning enough money to maintain their preferred standard of living.

Financial Well-Being and Satisfaction It may be true that money cannot buy happiness. But the fact is that the higher the income bracket, the greater the proportion of people who say that they are happy and satisfied with their lives (Curtin 1980). The same relationship between income and people's perception of their well-being was found among people in fifty-five nations (Diener, Diener, and Diener 1995). In contrast, when people have financial strains, they are more likely to be depressed and to experience a lowered quality of intimacy in their marriage (Vinokur, Price, and Caplan 1996).

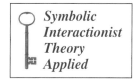 *Symbolic Interactionist Theory Applied*

How you define your financial situation is as important as actual income level. Thus, a study of 150 African American spouses reported that perceived financial adequacy was even more important to marital satisfaction than objective measures of income, education, and occupation (Clark-Nicolas and Gray-Little 1991). Thus, life and family satisfaction are not only a matter of income but also of aspirations and perceptions of fairness and security.

Financial Problems Assume that you are married and that you have one child. How much income do you need in order to live comfortably? Now look at table 16.1. How many Americans are living with less than you feel is necessary? Whatever you think you need, your chances of getting it depend on such things as your age, race or ethnic origin, and the kind of family or household to which you belong. Note in table 16.1, for example, that those in the highest income bracket are more likely to be middle-aged, white, and married couples. Those in the lowest income bracket are more likely to be young, African American or Hispanic, living alone or without a spouse.

How many people have financial worries? Again, we can't tell that simply from the income brackets.

---

[1]Reported in *The American Enterprise,* November/December 1994, p.98.

TABLE 16.1
Money Income of Households, 1995

Percent Distribution

Characteristic	Number of Households (1,000)	Under $10,000	$10,000–$24,999	$25,000–$49,999	$50,000–$74,999	$75,000 and Over	Median Income ($)
Total	99,627	12.2	24.7	31.2	17.1	14.8	34,076
Age of Householder:							
15 to 24 years	5,282	21.9	37.0	31.1	7.8	2.2	20,979
25 to 34 years	19,225	10.1	23.2	38.3	18.0	10.4	34,701
35 to 44 years	23,226	7.0	17.9	33.0	23.5	18.6	43,465
45 to 54 years	18,008	7.6	15.1	29.4	21.9	26.0	48,058
55 to 64 years	12,401	11.8	21.1	29.8	17.7	19.6	38,077
65 years and over	21,486	21.6	40.3	25.1	7.3	5.7	19,096
White	84,511	10.6	24.0	31.6	17.9	15.9	35,766
Black	11,577	24.0	30.4	28.2	11.2	6.2	22,393
Hispanic	7,939	19.9	33.7	28.7	11.6	6.1	22,860
Size of Household:							
One person	24,900	28.1	37.2	25.1	6.2	3.4	17,063
Two persons	32,526	7.3	25.3	35.0	17.3	15.0	35,700
Three persons	16,724	7.8	18.6	32.4	21.8	19.3	42,244
Four persons	15,118	5.4	13.9	31.2	25.4	24.1	49,531
Five persons	6,631	6.8	16.4	31.2	23.0	22.6	45,710
Six persons	2,357	5.9	19.2	29.9	24.9	20.2	44,263
Seven or more persons	1,372	6.6	22.0	36.7	19.4	15.2	39,013
Type of Household:							
Family households	69,594	7.0	20.5	32.9	20.7	18.9	41,224
Married-couple	53,567	3.2	16.8	33.1	23.8	23.0	47,129
Male householder, wife absent	3,513	8.3	27.4	37.2	16.4	10.7	33,534
Female householder, husband absent	12,514	22.5	34.1	30.8	8.8	3.8	21,348
Nonfamily households	30,033	24.5	34.4	27.1	8.7	5.4	19,929
Male householder	13,348	17.0	30.9	32.3	11.6	8.2	20,023
Female householder	16,685	30.5	37.1	23.0	6.4	3.1	15,892

Note: Persons of Hispanic origin can be of any race.
Source: U.S. Bureau of the Census 1997b:466.

A Gallup poll reported that 15 percent of Americans say they worry about family finances "all the time" and another 16 percent worry "most of the time."[2] Broken down by income, even some of those in the highest bracket said that they worry all the time about finances (figure 16.1).

Worry may be one of the lesser consequences of financial problems, which also contribute to stress, a lowered sense of well-being and security, problems at school or work, and tension and conflict in the family. The family conflict reflects the fact that children also experience the stress of financial problems. In such situations, children may develop depression, and engage in more impulsive and antisocial behavior (Takeuchi, Williams, and Adair 1991; Conger et al. 1994).

Thus, money problems affect both our personal well-being and the quality of our interpersonal relationships. In fact, when the economy falters and the unemployment rate goes up, the number of divorces is likely to increase (South 1985). Some marriages are apparently unable to survive the intense stress of unemployment.

[2]*Gallup Report* no. 256–257, January/February 1987, pp. 13–14.

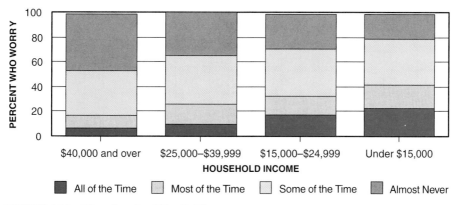

FIGURE 16.1   Worrying about Family Finances
(*Source:* Data from T*he Gallup Poll Monthly,* #256–257, January/February 1987:14.)

Bankruptcy   When a family gets deeply into debt, cannot meet living expenses, and cannot reach an agreement with the creditors outside of court, they may file for bankruptcy. More than three hundred thousand cases of bankruptcy are filed each year in the United States, and most of them are nonbusiness. The typical bankrupt is a male under the age of forty, married, a blue-collar worker, and with more than an average number of dependents (Hira and Mugenda 1987:60).

How does bankruptcy affect a family? Some people have feelings of guilt and stigma, but most believe that they have not lost any social standing as a result of the action. Hira and Mugenda (1987) studied forty families who had filed for bankruptcy in Iowa. They looked at the factors that led to the bankruptcy and the effects on family life. The people identified personal, employment, and financial problems as the causes of bankruptcy. Personal problems included marital disruption, a death in the family, and drug, alcohol, or gambling habits. Employment problems involved loss of hours or a job or layoff because of illness or an accident. The main financial problem was the overuse of credit.

After the bankruptcy, two-thirds of the couples reported that they had changed their money management procedures. Some started budgeting for the first time. Most were more cautious about buying on credit. With regard to family life, it is interesting to note that nearly half of those who were married said that the quality of their marriage improved after the bankruptcy. They viewed the process as

one that gave them a fresh start. They were finally free from the financial pressures that had caused a strain in the marriage.

When Teenagers Work: Problem or Solution?

More than half of all teenagers ages sixteen to nineteen are in the labor force (figure 16.2). A considerable number of younger teens also work part-time or at odd jobs. In some families, teenagers who work can help ease financial problems. But there are potential problems as well as benefits.

On the plus side, the working teenager may learn valuable skills, financial responsibility, time management, and the gratification of sharing in family support. Most working teens do not actually give their earnings to the parents, but they are likely to take over some financial obligations, such as the cost of their clothing (Greenberger et al. 1980). Some teenagers who work part-time find that their grades in school improve because they are forced to be better managers of their time.

On the negative side, grades may go down for those who cannot handle the demands of both work and school. They may spend their income for immediate personal gratification, buying such things as cars and stereos rather than saving for long-range goals. And they may use their work as an excuse to get out of household chores, thus causing other family members to assume a greater share of the work.

Whether the consequences are negative or positive depends on a number of factors (Williams and

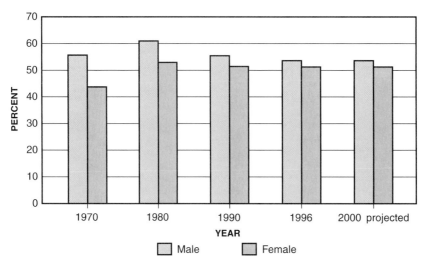

FIGURE 16.2   Percent of Teenagers (16–19) Who Work: 1970–2000
(*Sources:* U.S. Bureau of the Census 1994:395 and 1997b:397.)

Prohofsky 1986). Teenagers reported satisfaction with family life was less the:

> More hours they worked during the school year.
>
> More they enjoyed their work.
>
> Larger the proportion of their earnings they kept for themselves.

The greater involvement in work tends to be combined with less involvement in school and family and, therefore, with more conflict between parents and teens. Thus, a national survey found that working teens have more disagreements with parents about their independence, less parental knowledge and supervision of their activities, and, with increasing hours of work, larger efforts by parents to control their spending patterns (Manning 1990).

Financial Planning

Who should handle the finances in the family? Should it be done by the husband, the wife, both, or the entire family? Should a couple have separate or joint checking accounts? Who makes the final decision about how to allocate the available money? These are a few of the questions that can raise tempers and cause conflict in families. They are a part of the important task of financial planning.

How to Plan   A financial plan is "the complete map of your personal finances, including assets like a house, investments, insurance, and retirement funds, for the purpose of achieving specific goals" (Thomsett 1987:3). The plan must also include whatever steps you need to take to achieve your goals. There are differing ways to make up an overall plan. If you expect to be in the higher income brackets, you should consider using the services of a professional financial planner. But the planner will still want to know your goals.

One way to establish goals in a financial plan is to write down possible major purchases and expenses and then answer certain questions about each one (Donoghue 1987:23–24). You may want to include a house or condominium, education (including your own and that of your spouse and children), automobiles, home improvements and renovations, furniture, expenses of a hobby, home electronics, vacations, recreational expenses (including a recreational vehicle or boat), childrens' weddings, and other items that you feel are important. For each one, you need to decide jointly such things as whether you want it or, if you already have it, whether you want to replace or improve it. If you decide to incur the expense, when will you make the purchase—immediately, in one to five years, five to ten years, or later? Then estimate the probable down payment and costs. You also need to decide at what age you would like to have your major purchases, such as a home, paid off and at what age you plan to retire. An overall plan must

A majority of teenagers work; the consequences for family life may be either positive or negative.

provide for a comfortable retirement as well as solvency during the working years.

There are also important choices to make when you purchase property as a married person. You can decide to be tenants in common, which allows you to leave your share of the property to whomever you choose. You can be joint tenants, which means that the survivor automatically inherits the deceased tenant's share of the property. Or you may be tenants by the entirety, which provides special protection against the joint property being seized by the creditors of one of the tenants. A lawyer or financial planner can help you decide which of these is best for you.

In addition to your goals, you need to list your assets. You must consider how much risk you want to take in investments (generally, the less the risk the lower the rate of return). You also must keep in mind the problem of inflation, which can wreck carefully laid plans based on the current situation. As a result of inflation, people often have to postpone plans to buy a home, return to school, or retire.

Once you have agreed on your goals, your assets, and your attitudes about risk, you can map out a strategy. You can decide on major purchases and when to buy them. You can determine how much you need to save and invest. Such planning requires a considerable amount of skill and work. But planning makes it less likely that a family will face problems that millions of Americans endure every

year—family tension and conflict, bankruptcy, or an impoverished retirement.

Making a Budget   An important part of the long-range financial plan is the monthly family budget. As noted above, many couples that file for bankruptcy have not had budgets. Your budget, of course, will reflect your long-range plan and show you what must be done in the present in order to achieve your goals.

In simplest terms, a budget requires a listing of all income and expenses. Under income, list take-home pay plus any dividends, interest, or other resources. Total your monthly income. Under expenses, include both fixed expenses and estimates of variable expenses. Fixed expenses are stable, or fairly so, over a long period of time. Variable expenses fluctuate more from month to month. Also, you have more control over variable expenses, in the sense that you can take steps to reduce or increase them. An example of a variable expense is the utility bill. A good way to get an estimate is to add up bills for a twelve-month period and get the average. Common expenses are as follows:

Fixed Expenses

Mortgage or rent.

Loan payments for money borrowed or major purchases such as appliances and automobiles.

Insurance premiums, including life, property, health, and automobile.

Child, house, or yard expenses.

Taxes on property and automobile.

Variable Expenses

Gifts to charities or churches.

Utilities.

Telephone.

Food.

Recreation and vacations.

Household expenses (cable TV, small appliances, repairs, maintenance, etc.).

Special occasions (birthdays and holidays).

Clothing.

Automobile gasoline and maintenance.

Medical and dental care.

TABLE 16.2

Costs of Selected Items As a Proportion of All Household Expenditures

Food and tobacco	16.1%
Clothing, accessories, and jewelry	6.5
Personal care	1.4
Housing	15.1
Household operation (furniture, utilities)	11.3
Medical care	17.9
Transportation	11.3
Recreation	8.2
Education and research	2.2
Religious and welfare activities	2.8
Personal business and other expenditures	7.6

Source: U.S. Bureau of the Census 1997b:454.

Personal care (barber, beautician).

Pocket money (for each member of the family to spend on his or her personal wants and needs).

Savings and investments to meet long-range goals.

Budgets will vary from family to family, and within the same family over the life cycle. For example, food expenditures increase 2.4 percent when a child is born, another 29.8 percent when the oldest child reaches school age, another 8.6 percent by the time the oldest child is eighteen or older, then decrease 29 percent when the couple reaches the empty-nest stage (Ambry 1993). Table 16.2 shows, on the average, the proportion of all expenses consumed by various items during the year.

We hope that when you develop a budget, your income will be sufficient to cover all expenses. If it isn't, you can take some measures that may help (Donoghue 1987:15): (1) stop using credit cards until the balance is substantially reduced or paid off completely; (2) check loan rates and consider refinancing some or all of your debts at a lower rate; (3) cut back small things in the list of variable expenses, such as the amount of utilities used and the number of telephone calls made; (4) reduce self-indulgent items in the budget until you can afford them (such as eating out or going on expensive vacations).

Neither long-range planning nor budgets will guarantee freedom from financial problems. People need to be alert to danger signals that may require alterations in the budget and/or long-range plan-

ning. Danger signals include such things as news of inflation, an unexpected pregnancy, the use of savings to pay monthly bills that were budgeted to come out of monthly income, and an increasing use of credit and an increasingly large balance on credit cards.

Finally, it is important to keep in mind that budgets are meant to be our servants, not our masters. A young mother complained rather bitterly about her husband: "We didn't even go out on our anniversary. He said we just couldn't afford it. We have to save for our future. But I'm not sure we're going to have a future together." When they wring all the pleasure out of a relationship, budgets are our oppressors. When they work properly, they enhance the quality of our intimate relationships because they help us avoid tensions and conflict over money and give us both pleasure for today and hope for tomorrow.

Minimizing Financial Conflict

Conflict Theory Applied

No matter how compatible a couple may be, spouses will have some *diverse interests and needs.* And since money is *one of the important but scarce resources for meeting those interests and needs,* money issues are likely to be one of the more frequent reasons for arguments. But there are ways to minimize financial conflict. First, we have to recognize some indicators of a problematic situation. In particular, your financial management probably needs attention and revision if one or more family members:

Are reluctant to bring up the subject of money.

Are secretive with expenditures.

Are not trusted with money.

Feel cheated by the family budget.

Have a private cache of money.

Clearly, communication about money matters is important for sound financial management. One important matter that should be discussed is the meaning of money that the husband and wife learned in their families of origin. Perhaps a husband is tight-fisted because his father made him feel guilty whenever he spent money. Perhaps a wife maintains

INVOLVEMENT
Making Your Budget

Assume you have just gotten married. Make up a budget. Include both fixed and variable expenses. Set your income at what you expect to make when you graduate. When you have completed the budget, compute the percentage that each expenditure is of your total expenses. Compare your figures with those in table 16.2. How does your budget compare with the national figures? How do you explain the differences?

Now show your budget to two or three married couples and ask them to criticize it. Ask them to give you alternative figures for any that they regard as unrealistic. Revise your budget on that basis. Then assume that your first jobs bring in 10 percent less than you assumed. Show how you would cut 10 percent out of your expenses.

If you are already married, prepare a budget outline (a list of all possible sources of income and of expenses) and ask three other couples to fill in the amounts that they feel they would need in order to live comfortably. Average their figures and compare them with your own budget. If you have not had a budget, prepare one before you survey the other couples. How does your budget compare with theirs? How do your figures compare with those in table 16.2? Where does it appear that you could make changes in your budget in order to enhance your financial well-being?

---

a private cache because her mother did so out of a lack of trust in her father's management of money. It can be very beneficial for spouses to discuss with each other and with their children the kinds of attitudes and practices surrounding money that they recall from their families of origin.

Financial conflict also can be minimized by regularly talking about financial matters. Such discussion should not be done only when there is a pressing need. In fact, the most helpful discussions occur when there are no financial decisions that have to be made. It isn't necessary, of course, to go into details with the children, but the children will benefit by having some broad idea of the family's financial situation and of a healthy decision-making process.

In addition to communication, certain financial practices tend to characterize couples who are stable and happily married. Treas (1993) found that husbands and wives who hold back money for themselves rather than add it to the common pot have lower expectations for their marriage continuing. Schaninger and Buss (1986) surveyed 140 couples over a ten-year period. Eighty-eight had divorced by the end of the period, while fifty-two of the couples were still (and happily) married. They found some important differences in financial practices between those who remained married and those who divorced. One difference was in the kinds of things the couples purchased. The happily

Parents need to teach children how to manage money.

married couples spent more than the divorced couples on such things as a home, the downpayment for the home, household appliances, and recreational vehicles. The divorced couples had spent more on stereos, color TVs, and living room furniture. As the researchers point out, the purchases of the divorced couples "tend to be worth as much after marital dissolution, and tend to be consistent with individual leisure enjoyment rather than family commitment" (Schaninger and Buss 1986:135).

PERSONAL
How I've Handled Our Money

Kay is a forty-two-year-old nurse who has been happily married for eighteen years. She and her husband, Don, have two children. Awareness and discussion of the meanings of money that developed in their families of origin have helped them minimize financial conflict. But they are still in the process of finding the most satisfying way to deal with finances:

Managing finances in our family has been a fairly easy process for us. The bottom line is that I have managed the finances. Part of this comes from my own background. My businessman father had my mother keep the books for his company. She also took care of the family records. I remember them talking about it when my father wanted to know how things stood or when he wanted to consider some new purchase or investment. I just assumed it was part of the woman's role to do it.

When I met Don, I soon learned that he had trouble making decisions about money. I sent him off one time to buy gro-

ceries for a dinner we were having for friends. He came back with only half the items. The prices were "so damned high," he said, that he just wouldn't pay them.

Shortly before our wedding, his mother took me aside and said that all the men in the family had trouble with money. She said they weren't cheap, just stubborn, and that I would have to help him out. She suggested that I follow her practice, which was to mention when I needed something and why I needed it. Don would say no, but I should just go out and get it anyway. Don would accept my decision and even be comfortable and happy with it. That's the way she handled Don's father, and it worked very well.

I was shocked at such a manipulative way of dealing with my husband and money. But I learned early on that Don has trouble spending. Like his father, he feels compelled to say no if I ask. So I didn't ask. I made the decisions. And he was satisfied with that. But I felt

cheated when my girlfriends talked about shopping with their husbands and planning together about spending and investing money.

Only recently, after all these years, has he started talking about our style of handling money. He was shocked one day when one of his colleagues told him about having separate checking accounts and buying a new car without even telling his wife about it. That gave us a chance to review our situation. Shortly after that, I decided to get my graduate degree. Now that I'm in school again, Don has taken over more of the home responsibilities, including some involvement in money matters. He is beginning to come to terms with his problem. For me, the sharing of responsibilities has been a breath of fresh air. Our marital relationship is much more fun-loving. I still write the checks, but Don does most of the shopping. He is making real progress in dealing with his money hang-ups.

Besides the differences in the kinds of things they purchased, the couples also handled their finances differently. Among the happily married, the wife or the husband and wife together tended to pay the bills. The husband tended to pay the bills among the divorced. Among the happily married, credit cards were in the husband's name or both names. About one out of six of the wives who divorced had credit cards in her own name (compared to none of the happily married wives). Happily married wives were more likely than those who got divorced to be responsible for the purchase of food, beverages, and groceries.

Overall, the researchers concluded, it appears that those who remained happily married had an early commitment to family life (as indicated by the kinds of purchases they made), to equity (as indicated by the number of things in which they made joint financial decisions), and to role specialization in which the wife had an important part in handling family finances.

TIME MANAGEMENT

In a marriage enrichment workshop, we asked the young couples to keep track of their communication patterns for a week. They were to write down the amount of time each day they talked and what they talked about. At the end of the week, a husband said, with a look of chagrin: "We found out that we do very little talking during the week. At least we don't talk about anything that's of any importance. We're just too busy. We try to cram seven days of communication into the weekend."

The challenge of effective time management is as important to family intimacy as that of effective financial management. In fact, many Americans believe that lack of time together is one of the greatest threats to the family today (Mellmann, Lazarus, and Rivlin 1990). A national survey reported that 69 percent of the respondents said they would like to slow down and live at a more relaxed pace (Castro 1991). Sixty-one percent of the respondents also felt that it is difficult to find time to enjoy life because of the demands of earning a living.

Time pressures, then, can be disruptive to intimacy. Connie, a divorced woman, tells about the time conflicts that disrupted her marriage:

> My husband and I couldn't agree on how to balance the time spent between working, doing household chores, being with the children, being together with just the two of us, and being with friends. We fought constantly. I remember once when we argued because I felt he didn't spend enough time with the children. He got a piece of paper and a pencil and threw them at me and told me to write out his daily schedule and show him when he would get the additional time.
>
> Our arguments eventually got to me. I started having health problems. That's when I decided that the marriage was destructive. We couldn't agree on what was important. Our schedules just wouldn't mesh with each other.

In an intimate relationship, then, it is important to agree on how to allocate time. It is important to have sufficient time to build intimacy, to construct a history of shared experiences. It is important for each of us to be able to remember what we did together with our spouses and our children rather than what we did not do together because we "didn't have the time."

How We Spend Our Time

For some people, the combination of work and sleep takes up the bulk of the day. For students, it may be the combination of classes, study, and sleep.

In addition, we spend a substantial amount of time eating. The rest is "free time." What do we do with our free time? The question is quite important, because the free time is crucial for building intimate relations. Meaningful communication and shared activities during free time can greatly enrich an intimate relationship.

One way to find out how people use free time is to ask them to keep time diaries, a record of what they do during a number of twenty-four-hour periods and the time consumed in each activity (Robinson and Godbey 1997). Such time diaries reveal what is a surprising finding to many Americans: we have *more* rather than less free time now than formerly. In fact, Americans have about five hours a week more free time today—that is, time not taken up with family care, personal care, paid work, or sleep—than they had in 1965. Nevertheless, people tend to *feel* pressured by time. In part, we create our own time pressure. Because we have so many options we try to cram as many activities as possible into the free time we have (Daly 1996). So there really "aren't enough hours in the day" to do all we need and want to do, not because we're spending more time working but because we have more and more things we want to do.

In addition to cramming more activities into the day, Americans feel pressured because the additional five hours of free time tends to be consumed by watching television. Watching television is not only the greatest consumer of each individual's free time, but is also the most time-consuming family activity. That is, families spend more of their time together watching television than any other activity.

When we look at the ways individuals spend their time, there are some gender differences. In order from the greatest to the least amount of time, American men who are employed outside the home spend their free time in:

Watching television.

Social activities (including outside entertainment and visiting friends and relatives).

Organizational activities (educational, religious, and voluntary organizations).

Reading (books, magazines, and newspapers).

Recreation.

Various other activities such as resting, corresponding, and listening to the radio.

Shared leisure activities enhance family intimacy.

Employed women differ from the men in that they spend less time in organizational activities than in reading and recreation. Also, they have less time for all of the activities mentioned because they spend more on housework. Interestingly, the children of mothers employed outside the home spend no more time on household work than do children of those not so employed (Key and Sanik 1990). Rather, the mother tends to add to the number of her daily working hours. Mothers employed outside the home spend about a half hour less per day caring for their children than do mothers who do not work outside, but they work 1.6 hours more per day and spend 2.1 hours more than their husbands per day in child care responsibilities (Sanik 1990).

Homemakers have more free time than either husbands or wives employed outside the home. And they spend more of it on recreation than either employed men or women, although television and social activities take up seven times as many minutes per day as recreation.

There are some racial and ethnic differences in the use of time (Robinson, Landry, and Rooks 1998). For instance, African Americans spend more time than other groups on religious activities. Whites spend more time than other groups on housework. Asians spend more time than others on education. And Hispanics spend more time than others in child care.

What the figures underscore is the fact that while the demands on our time frequently seem to be overwhelming, we usually have some discretion. Very few people are in the position of having more time than they know what to do with. Most of us sense a gnawing scarcity of hours. But while you cannot expand the hours you have in the day, you can learn to make the most efficient use of those you have. In a sense, then, you can increase the amount of time you have by becoming a better time manager.

How to Manage Your Time

Many articles and books are available to help people manage their time better (e.g., Lakein 1973). Obviously, time management is a problem for countless numbers of people. As with money management, time management begins by specifying your goals. How do you need or want to spend your time? What do you want to do with the free time? Do you want more quality time with your family? Do you want more time for personal development? Do you want more intimacy time with your spouse?

Second, list your goals on paper and then identify activities that will help you achieve those goals. Listing specific activities will help you to see exactly how much time you will need. Third, set up a priority list. Your priority list should include not only your goals for the additional free time but all of the demands on your time. Lakein (1973) suggests that you give letter values to each item, with "A" being the most important activity.

Fourth, take about ten minutes each morning to make up a "to-do list." The list is your schedule for the day. You do not have to include obvious things like bathing and eating but all other things that you have to do and want to do. You should prioritize your daily list by giving A, B, or C to each item. The items for a particular day can include everything from defrosting the freezer to getting the oil changed in the car to answering an ad for a new job to giving special attention to your spouse or children. If you can't do everything on the list, be sure to do those things first that you rated as A, then proceed to the B's and lastly the C's. You may decide, incidentally, that some of the C items aren't really important and could be delayed indefinitely or until you are less busy.

The to-do list may include items on some days that require the help of other members of the family. Those items should be discussed in the family before the day they appear on the list. For example, consider the task of cleaning the house. An employed mother might approach the family this way: "The house needs cleaning every week. How shall we handle it? What do you think each of us should do?"

Working our goals, priorities, and a daily to-do list is one of the most important parts of effective time management. In addition, however, there are numerous ways to save minutes each day. The following show the kinds of things that people do that help them make effective use of their time:

Plan weekly menus as a family instead of waiting until each day and letting one person make all the decisions.

Learn to do more than one thing at a time (such as ironing or writing a letter or exercising while watching television).

Bring your lunch from home and use the time you save for getting some personal things done.

Shop from catalogs instead of going to stores.

Make a list of daily chores for each family member and post it so everyone can help with the family work.

Carry a book with you to read when you are waiting for an appointment or a personal service.

We should add one caveat, however. As in the case of money management, time management should not become oppressive. If doing something else detracts from your enjoyment of watching television, you may need to find different ways of saving time. The purpose is not to detract from, but to enhance, the quality of your personal and family life. Time management, like money management, is successful only when it becomes an effective tool in our quest for intimacy.

MANAGING POWER AND CONFLICT

The addition of one or more children to the family makes issues of power and conflict an even greater challenge. Children raise the possibility of coalitions (see the discussion of triangulation that follows), the use of other people to aid in conflict and power struggles.

The Use and Misuse of Power

For those with an excessive need to exercise power, a child is, unfortunately, an easy victim. Psychiatrist Allen Wheelis (1973) has written about a time when he was eight years old. He came home from school the last day before the summer vacation and announced proudly to his parents that he had passed. He was looking forward to three months of fun with his friends. His father looked at the report card and asked about a "75" in conduct. Wheelis reluctantly admitted that he had probably talked and laughed too much, but he reminded his father that all the other grades were good. Then he asked if he could go over to a friend's house after dinner. "No," the father replied, "you have to work, son." What work? Wheelis wanted to know. The father, determined to teach his son a lesson that he wouldn't forget, pointed to several acres of tall grass in the back and told Wheelis he had to cut it. But he had to cut it with an old, straight-edge razor, carefully removing all the cut grass along with any rocks or sticks. Only when he was finished, his father told him, could he play baseball with his friends.

The outcome was that Wheelis spent all but the last two weeks of the summer doing nothing but cutting grass. By the time he finished, the grass he had first cut was long again and he had to begin all over. His father told him to remember that "whenever it

PERSPECTIVE
Wasting Time

We are a clock-conscious, some would say a clock-tyrannized, people. And it seems we have been so for most of our history. Indeed, we take seriously the advice of eighteenth-century sage Benjamin Franklin to use time well and avoid the horror of wasting time. What it means to waste time varies from generation to generation and person to person. Yet the practice is usually viewed with scorn or moral indignation. Moreover, those who feel that they are wasting time may experience guilt. Today, people define such things as excessive watching of television, gossiping with friends, and resting when one "should" be working as ways of wasting time. In the nineteenth century, some people argued that women's obsession with being fashionable in their dress and appearance was a way of wasting both time and money. In her book, *The Well-Dressed Woman: A Study in the Practical Application to Dress of the Laws of Health, Art, and Morals* (New York: Fowles & Wells Co., 1893, pp. 245–53), Helen Gilbert Ecob urged women to consider the folly of being consumed by fashion:

> What an amount of time, that precious material of which life is made, do women sacrifice to

love of dress! Shopping expeditions in search of the finest texture and the newest shade exhaust body and bewilder brain. Hours are consumed in matching ribbon, wool, and silk; hours are spent in consultation with the dressmaker, and in the fabrication of the wardrobe. The more personal details of the toilet, the frizzing of hair and the polishing of finger-nails, consume an appalling portion of time. One could solve a problem in Euclid while some women are adjusting hat, crimps, and veil. No one has better set forth the intellectual and spiritual loss which comes through this all absorbing passion for dress than Mrs. Phelps Ward: " 'I spent one hundred hours,' said an educated and cultivated lady recently—and she said it without a blush of shame or a tremor of self-depreciation—'I spent just one hundred hours in embroidering my winter suit . . .' One hundred hours! One could almost learn a language, or make the acquaintance of a science, or apprentice one's self to a business, or nurse a consumptive to the end of her sufferings, or save a soul, in one hundred well-selected hours. One—hundred—hours!" . . .

Waste of time goes hand in hand with waste of money. Extravagance in displays of dress is a sin common to rich and poor, and is not less pitiful in one than in the other . . . Time and money are nowhere more foolishly wasted than in gratifying the passion for dainty underclothing . . . Underclothing serves only the purposes of warmth and decency. Its ends are purely practical and utilitarian. To ornament the underclothing which regales only the eyes of the laundress is as idle as for a painter to ornament the back of his canvas. If reform were carried in this direction alone, what time might be secured for study, what money might be saved for books and art!

Clearly, Miss Ecob believed that time and money should be used more for self-improvement and helping others than for attending to one's appearance. The problem is, appearance is important in relationships. So how much of the time spent on appearance is wasted, and how much is helpful for relationships? The same question can be raised about activities today that are defined as a waste of time.

---

seems I'm being hard on you . . . it's because I love you" (Wheelis 1973:68).

When report cards came out the next year, Wheelis had a nearly perfect score in conduct. But, he wrote, he still feels the "steel fingers" of his father on him in his adult life. Wheelis' father illustrates the excessive use of parental power. He also illustrates the fact that we cannot construct healthy relationships when one party has nearly all of the power.

Systems Theory Applied

Power can also be misused when one family member uses another in a power struggle with a third member. This is a form of *"triangulation,"* a concept used by family therapists to identify certain problems in the family system (Bowen 1978). Triangulation can involve a parent and child against the other parent, two parents

COMPARISON
Who Runs the Family? The Case of Germans and Migrant Turks

In the United States, most people advocate a democratic family in which all members have a voice and each has some decision-making power. Many Americans believe that this arrangement contrasts sharply with that of other peoples—like Germans and Turks—who accept the male head of the house as the one who makes all important decisions.

Researchers who looked at the decision-making process in a sample of German and migrant Turkish families in Berlin, however, found that the question of "who wears the pants in the family" is not simple to answer. The researchers questioned both men and women in the families. They asked them how much influence various family members have on decisions made about fi-

nancial matters, children's issues, and family issues.

Basically, the husbands and wives from both groups agreed that there is a fair amount of equality in the decision-making process. However, the Turkish men had the dominant influence on family issues and the German women had the dominant influence on children's issues. The dominance of German women in the children's sphere is consistent with the pattern we noted in chapter 14 with regard to playground behavior—namely, the relative detachment of German fathers from their children.

And how much influence did the adolescent children have in the German and Turkish families? According to their parents, they have a good deal, depending on the issue. Turkish parents said their children

have a great deal of influence on matters specific to the children, much less on family issues, and still less on financial matters. German parents said their children have the most influence on family issues, slightly less on their own issues, and significantly less on financial matters. Overall, the Germans accorded their children a greater degree of influence than did the Turkish parents.

Thus, the answer to the question of who runs the family is: it all depends. It depends on what the issue is and on the family's nationality. For both the Germans and the Turks, however, there is no male dominance across all issues. Everyone in the family has influence in some things and little say in others (Schonpflug, Silbereisen, and Schulz 1990).

against the child, or siblings against a parent. For example, a mother can use a child in her struggles with her husband by reserving her affection for the child and by various subtle and not-so-subtle verbal assaults on her husband in front of the child. The mother may try to win the child's sympathy while simultaneously downgrading the father: "Your father never remembers our anniversary. But I've come to accept the fact that I live with a man who isn't thoughtful."

A parent might also engage in triangulation by using a child to win arguments. Thus, a father says to his son: "Listen to this, and then tell your mother who is right." Perhaps the worst use of triangulation occurs when the parents join together and blame the child for their problems. Rather than focusing on issues between them, the parents decide that the child is to blame for their lack of accord. The child becomes the family scapegoat. If the child was unwanted in the first place or in some way falls short of their expectations, the scapegoating is all the easier.

As the above suggests, healthy relationships require balanced power in the home. This doesn't mean that children have as much power as parents but rather that power is shared. No one should feel powerless. Beth, a fifty-year-old woman who owns her own clothing store, recalls how she learned the importance of sharing power in the family:

I could see as a child that power-sharing works well. My friends' parents were more conventional than mine. Most of them had fathers who were the breadwinners and sole decision makers in the home. They paid all the bills and doled out the money to their wife and kids. So the fathers had all the power. And I saw the difference in their mothers and my mother. My friends' mothers seemed sort of wimpy to me. When I was in their homes I heard some of them unable to answer even simple requests. They would tell their children to "wait until your father comes home and see what he says." They just didn't seem to have the vitality or strength that I saw in my mother who was truly a co-equal with my father.

One way to share power in the family is to have a regular family meeting. The meeting can be used to allocate family work, plan family recreation and activities, make decisions about various family matters, and air grievances. Power sharing in the family meeting does not mean that a majority vote wins. Parents must still be parents and not turn over their responsibilities to the vote of the group. But every family member should be heard equally. And all opinions should be respected. The listening skills, which we talked about earlier, are important in a family meeting. And it is an appropriate time for parents to teach children how to listen, both by modeling good listening and by explicit instruction.

Family meetings can be more appealing if the parents spend some time reminding everyone of the good things about the family or the achievements of particular family members. Family meetings should not degenerate into nothing but crisis-handling sessions. And children will find the meetings more appealing to the extent that they feel they have some influence over decisions. As the children grow, of course, their influence will increase.

Conflict and Family Well-Being

As in the case of marital conflict, conflict within the family can be both positive and negative. In her study of arguments between adolescent girls and their mothers, Apter (1990) concluded that the conflict was a sign of attachment rather than of separation. Whether mild or intense, the purpose of the argument was not to sever the relationship but to affirm it in the context of mutual acceptance. The underlying message was "see me as I am and love me for what I am." In spite of the typically high level of conflict during the adolescent years, Apter found, most of the girls affirmed their mothers as the person they loved the most and who gave them the most support.

On the negative side, whether the conflict is between parents, between parents and children, or both, it is likely to create problems for the children. Parents who have a highly conflicted relationship may be unable to give their children the kind of attention and warmth necessary for good parent-child relationships (Owen and Cox 1997; Harrist and Ainslie 1998). This can result in various kinds of personal and relational problems for the children.

The more hostile the conflict the more likely the children will have problems (Buehler et al. 1998). For example, children who experience a good deal of family conflict have more problems adjusting to school and more difficulties with their own emotional health (Kurdek and Sinclair 1988). A study of college students from conflicted homes reported that the conflict diminished students' confidence (Markland and Nelson 1993). And a study of adolescents who experienced family conflict found them to have higher levels of negative feelings about themselves and a greater number of self-destructive (suicidal) thoughts (Shagle and Barber 1993).

As we noted earlier, the conflict need not involve the children directly. Marital conflict can increase children's aggression, lead to conduct problems, raise anxiety levels, or result in self-isolation (Cummings 1994). A study of forty adolescents reported that those who perceived high levels of conflict between their parents had a variety of problems at school (Long et al. 1987), including:

Lower grade point average.
Lower cognitive competence rating by teachers.
Lower social competence rating by teachers.
More behavior problems reported by teachers.
Lower problem-solving skills.

Such results raise the question of whether children would be better off in a two-parent home that has a high level of conflict or a single-parent home with a lower level of conflict. James Peterson and Nicholas Zill (1986) addressed the question using a national sample of fourteen hundred children ages twelve to sixteen. The researchers looked at such things as rates of depression, antisocial behavior, and school problems among children in various kinds of home situations. They found that generally children who lived with both parents were the least depressed and withdrawn. But for those children in homes of high, persistent conflict, the levels of depression and withdrawal were even higher than for those who lived with just one of their biological parents. Antisocial behavior also tended to be higher among those in two-parent homes with high, persistent conflict. Thus, as painful as divorce is, remaining in an intact family with high and persistent conflict can be even more painful.

Both the intensity and kind of conflict in families vary depending on the family situation. For example, a study of 504 adolescents and their mothers investigated the effects of employment (Flanagan 1990). Adolescents in homes where the head of the household had been either laid off or demoted reported more frequent conflict with parents than those in families where the head of the household had stable employment.

It is clear that a healthy family has to manage conflict well in order to stay healthy. This does not mean to eliminate conflict. Conflict is a part of healthy relationships. Its absence may be a sign of problems rather than of well-being. In families without conflict, the members may be denying that they have differences, they may have a family norm against the overt expression of those differences, or they may not care sufficiently about each other to argue.

How, then, can families accept conflict and manage it well in order to maximize their well-being? Samuel Vuchinich (1985) videotaped dinner conversations in fifty-two families and analyzed their patterns of arguing. He found four ways in which a verbal attack by one member on another ended: withdrawal, submission, standoff, or compromise. In *withdrawal,* one of the participants simply withdraws from the conflict by either refusing to talk anymore or by leaving the room. The individual may even say "I don't want to talk about it anymore." Withdrawal often implies that the other person or persons in the conflict haven't played fair and that the withdrawing individual is too hurt or angry to continue.

Submission is giving in. It may occur when one family member recognizes that another is correct on a point of fact, when two or more family members convince another that he or she is wrong, or when parents intervene and require the bickering to stop. Submission may not be the end of the disagreement, however. It may just be the beginning of a cold war that will erupt at a later time if the winning party doesn't handle the situation well. Ways in which the situation is not handled well include the "winner" gloating over his or her "victory" and the "loser" submitting merely because he or she feels compelled to do so by pressure from other family members.

A *standoff* occurs when no progress is being made and the opponents simply drop the matter without resolving it. They may openly or tacitly agree to continue to disagree with each other. It may be that the issue is relatively trivial, or it may be that they realize that they will always have different perspectives. For instance, Karl and Sylvia, a professional couple known to the authors, have been married twenty-five years, but they still disagree over an incident that happened in the first year of their union. They were buying furniture and Karl, according to Sylvia, flirted openly with the beautiful young saleswoman. Karl insists that he was only being friendly, that he was much too much in love with Sylvia to flirt with anyone, much less to do so in front of her. They argued about it at the time and got nowhere. They laugh about it now, but they still disagree.

Finally, *compromise* occurs when one family member offers a concession to the other. If there is a reciprocal concession, and both agree, the conflict ends. Compromise can occur over ideas, attitudes, plans, responsibilities, and so on. Thus, two family members in a dispute may each modify positions about such things as which is the best political candidate, how the family should spend its money, who does the most work around the house, and the extent to which each member is a concerned and responsible member of society as well as of the family.

Each of the methods has implications for family intimacy. Withdrawal may alienate family members from each other. They may feel that they simply cannot get along or communicate effectively with each other. Vuchinich found withdrawal rarely used, however. Submission can lead to inequity, to dominance relations if the same member always tends to be the one to submit. Standoffs may maintain a sense of equality and may enable the participants to move on to other activities if the issue is defined as relatively trivial (as in the case of Karl and Sylvia). But if conflict is considered nontrivial and is frequent and standoffs occur regularly, the family members may find themselves getting increasingly frustrated and angry with each other.

Compromise, on the other hand, tends to build intimacy. The family members see that they are able to work through their disagreements. Unfortunately, less than 10 percent of the conflicts that Vuchinich studied ended in compromise. About a fourth ended with submission and the rest ended with a standoff. Family members, then, need to develop the ability to compromise. Recall that the willingness to compromise was one of the ways of "good fighting" discussed in chapter 12. The other principles identified there are as useful for family conflict as they are for marital conflict. The family that learns and uses good principles of conflict management is a family that is building meaningful intimate relationships.

PRINCIPLES FOR ENHANCING INTIMACY

1. Because money and what it can buy occupy so much of our attention and produces so many problems between people and anxieties within people, it is important that we learn to manage it wisely. And it is never too soon to start. Ideally, the process begins in childhood. When you become a parent, you can help your children develop the capacity for effective money management.

2. Before you marry, you will want to thoroughly discuss money matters—your combined incomes, expected expenses, handling of finances, and so forth. After you marry, regularly review your fiscal practices and modify them if necessary. Open discussion and prudent management will prevent money from being a threat to your intimate relationship.

3. Time, like money, often seems in short supply. Given the complexities and the increasing demands in most of our lives, it is essential for our physical and emotional well-being that we learn to manage our time well. Establish priorities and divide your day accordingly. Keep a calendar that schedules both the demands of your work as well as choices in your personal life. Remember: if you do not manage your time, someone else will.

4. Building an intimate relationship requires time together, yet all too often intimate moments are sacrificed to demands that seem more pressing. You can guard against this by scheduling a regular night out, a weekend away, or even a nightly thirty minutes of uninterrupted time with your special person.

5. If you want to minimize power conflicts in your family, create an atmosphere of love and respect. Where these coexist, each member of the family feels safe in expressing his or her feelings and concerns and is assured that problems will be worked out fairly.

SUMMARY

Most people feel that they need at least 25 percent more income than they are getting. We want more, because money brings many desirable benefits. Money means success, freedom, and power in American culture. Perceived financial well-being is an important part of satisfaction with family life. Those who perceive themselves as having financial problems are likely to worry, experience stress, have a lowered sense of security, have problems at school or work, and have more tension and conflict in the family.

Bankruptcy may ultimately result from serious financial problems. The overuse of credit is one of the major factors in bankruptcy. Many couples, however, learn sound money management practices after declaring bankruptcy.

More than half of all teenagers ages sixteen to nineteen are in the labor force. Benefits of working teenagers include the learning of valuable skills, financial responsibility, time management, and sharing in family support. Problems include the possibility of lower grades in school, the use of money for immediate personal gratification, and less involvement in family work.

Financial planning can help families cope with present financial responsibilities as well as plan for future security. Making a budget is an essential part of financial planning. Food, housing, and transportation will consume more than half of the average family's budget.

Financial conflict in the family can be minimized by certain measures, including open communication about money matters. In addition, happily married people make purchases that suggest a long-term commitment to each other, make joint financial decisions, and involve the wife in an important way in handling family finances.

Time management is as important to family intimacy as financial management. Work and sleep take up the bulk of our days. Watching television takes up a significant part of our free time. Thus, while time demands may appear overwhelming, we all have some discretion. Effective time management may require you to specify your goals, identify activities that will help you reach those goals, set up your priorities, and make a daily list of activities.

Both time and money get tangled up with power struggles and conflict in the family. Managing power and conflict is a third aspect, therefore, of effective family management. Power can be misused through such things as triangulation. Healthy relationships require balanced power in the home. Power can be shared through regular family councils or family meetings. Like power, conflict can be positive or negative. Intense, sustained conflict in the home tends to result in personal and school problems for children. Verbal conflict may end by withdrawal, submission, standoff, or compromise. Compromise tends to build intimacy.

INTERNET CONNECTION
Family Life as Management

The family is an economic unit as well as a social entity. As such, monetary concerns have a major impact on the quality of family life—especially on children. Education and money management are two key skill areas that can enhance economic well-being. To what degree have hardships and stresses in your family been due to money management style? Have other issues, such as lack of money or access to educational opportunity also been at play? What can we do to make the lives of poor or educationally deprived families more manageable? These are important questions to think about when examining the sites listed below.

www.mhhe
.com/lauer4

Institute for Research on Poverty

http://www.ssc.wisc.edu/irp/

This is a nonprofit organization looking at the measurement of and impact of poverty in the United States.

Family Resource Coalition for America

http://www.frca.org/

An organization devoted to innovative forms of social support for families.

Gateway to the Human Services
http://www.apwa.org/sites.html

A comprehensive meta-list of resources and statistics covering economic and policy issues related to welfare and the family.

Welfare Information Network
http://www.welfareinfo.org/

A website providing links to welfare policy, programs, and statistics with emphasis on welfare reform.

Use the websites above to answer the following questions:

1. What is poverty? How do you measure it? What kinds of families suffer from poverty? In your opinion, what is the impact of this poverty on children?
2. What is welfare reform? What is welfare-to-work? How will these policy initiatives impact poor families?
3. Describe the philosophy behind the so-called family support movement. Are advocates for this movement for or against welfare reform?
4. What evidence can you find at any of these websites, or any others you find, that financial management training is a feature of welfare reform? Should it, or can it, play a bigger role?

PART FIVE

CHALLENGES TO INTIMACY

A philosopher speculated that the family might one day become an obsolete institution. By contrast, an anthropologist speculated that if civilization were ever wiped out in a nuclear holocaust, the last man on earth would spend his dying days searching through the rubble for his family. We believe the anthropologist was closer to reality than was the philosopher. Most people try to maintain intimate relationships, especially family relationships, and they endure a great deal of suffering before they break such relationships.

In this final section, we will look at some of the crises that strain intimacy in the family. The crises can lead either to disruption or to an enhanced intimacy. Then we will discuss what happens when, in spite of the tendency to hang on, a decision is made to terminate the marital relationship. Finally, we will talk about the nature of and problems in the reconstituted family. The need for family intimacy is so strong that most divorced people try again to establish a meaningful family life. As the anthropologist suggested, in spite of the high rate of disruption in our society, people fundamentally value and strive to create and maintain families.

FAMILY CRISES

Learning Objectives

After reading chapter 17, you should be able to:
1. Explain how stressful events can result in a family crisis.
2. Discuss the various types of stressor events.
3. Define alcohol abuse and show how it affects the quality of family life.
4. Describe the extent and types of violence in families.
5. Define child abuse and incest and tell why these occur.
6. Explain the causes of spouse and parent abuse.
7. Discuss the consequences of abuse for families.
8. Relate the reasons that the same type of crisis can have different consequences in different families.
9. Show how denial, avoidance, and scapegoating are ineffective ways of coping with a crisis.
10. Discuss the five tools for effective coping with a crisis.

In his novel *The Mayor of Casterbridge,* Thomas Hardy told of a man who struggles throughout his life with his own passions. In the opening pages, Michael Henchard, the main character, gets drunk while attending a fair. Impetuously, he sells his wife and daughter to a sailor. For the rest of his life, Henchard is affected by his rash act. Years later, his wife comes back into his life, and for a brief time, Henchard once again has a family. But he cannot control himself. Ultimately, his self-destructive tendencies bring him to a tragic end.

In the novel, Hardy showed the disastrous consequences of one kind of family crisis—the inability of one member to control his or her impulses. For Henchard, the problem not only resulted in excessive drinking but also in suspicions and misattributions. As a result, his life was a series of crises. In this chapter, we will discuss some of the crises that come to families and threaten intimacy. We will look at greater length at two kinds of crises that are widespread: alcohol abuse and violence. These two problems involve severe trauma in the family. Finally, we will see how people deal with crises, including both successful and unsuccessful methods of coping.

SOURCES OF FAMILY CRISES

Have you ever experienced what you would call a family crisis? If so, what was the nature of that crisis? What caused it? If you posed these questions to other people, you might hear of some differing kinds of crises than you have experienced. In any case, crises are closely linked with stressful events and/or behavior.

Stress and Crisis

In their efforts to understand diverse family responses to stressful events, family scholars have used the ABCX model developed by Reuben Hill (1958). Hill (1949) began his work by studying the stress endured by families during war. He developed the ABCX family crisis model to try to account for differential success in coping. In essence, A is the stressor event and the hardships it produces. B is the management of the stress through coping resources that the family has. Since an important aspect of the impact of stress is *the way in which the stressful situation is defined,* C refers to the family's definition of the event. A, B, and C interact together to produce X, the crisis.

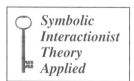
Symbolic Interactionist Theory Applied

For example, let us say that two families, the Smiths and the Joneses, face the stressor of unemployment (A). The Smiths define it as undesirable but also as a challenge (C), and they decide that each family member will try to find work and will do something to save money (B). The interaction of these three produces no serious crisis for them (X). The Joneses, on the other hand, define the event as a disaster (C). They expect the father to find a new job immediately and to do something to avoid any serious change in their life-style (B). The interaction of these three is a crisis (X).

The two examples are simplified, of course. In fact, the model itself is somewhat simplified, because there are other elements that may be important in the outcome of a stressor. Recognizing this, McCubbin and Patterson (1983) proposed a Double ABCX model. They relabeled the A factor, calling it *family demands.* There are three components to family demands. One is the stressor. The second is the hardships that accompany the stressor (such as increasing financial problems when a parent is unemployed). Third, there are "pile-ups,"

> the residuals of family tension that linger from unresolved prior stressors or that are inherent in ongoing family roles such as being a parent or spouse (McCubbin and Patterson 1983:279).

This model has been shown to explain the differential adaptation of women with severe physical disabilities (Florian and Dangoor 1994).

It is important to recognize the place of pile-ups or prior strains. A stressor does not occur in a vacuum but in the context of ongoing life. Suppose, for instance, that you learned more about the Smiths and the Joneses, the two families introduced in the preceding example. What if the unemployment of Mr. Smith occurred while there were few other strains, while that of Mr. Jones occurred in the midst of family illness and at a point when the oldest daughter was preparing to go to college? Clearly, we need to know something about what is going on in a family at the time of the stressor event to fully understand its response to that stressor.

Pauline Boss (1988), who has made extensive studies of family stress, concluded that many families in crisis are not sick families but are simply facing a greater volume of stress than they, or most other families, can handle. Boss (1988:10) claimed that families today are under more pressure than were those of the past:

> Some of the daily problems with which they must contend are traffic (unlike anything our grandparents ever saw); threats to life and property (few communities are free of potential or actual crimes); expectations for children (they must achieve in order to be accepted in the middle-class world); emancipated sons and daughters who move back home (because of unemployment or divorce); and both parents working outside the home (that's what it takes to keep up mortgage payments these days). Good child care has become a luxury that few working parents—especially single parents—can afford, so that work and family tensions are higher than ever before.

Most important, perhaps, is the loss of leisure; there is less and less time for couples to relax together or to spend time with people they care about. Family life has *not* gotten simpler for present generations; it is *more* complex and the pace is faster.

In other words, there are numerous commonplace tensions and strains in the lives of most of us. If some additional stressors in the form of unemployment, serious illness, or severe personal or interpersonal problems occur, their cumulative effect can lead to illness in the family (Bigbee 1992) or to some kind of crisis of well-being. Nearly all of us will experience such a crisis, if not a series of crises, because it is unlikely that you can live in a family for an extended period of time without encountering periods of severe stress.

Every family must deal with times of stress and crisis.

Stressor Events

As we discuss the stressor events that can bring about a family crisis, it is important to keep in mind that the events per se are not sufficient to cause serious problems. As the model indicates, the context in which the event occurs, the way that the family defines the event, and the resources the family has for dealing with it are all crucial to the outcome. Still, it is important to be aware of the kinds of events that are likely to cause a family crisis.

Types of Stressor Events　 What kinds of stressor events are most likely to result in a family crisis? Some of the common ones that you may face include the death of a family member, a serious illness or accident to a family member, unemploy-ment of a family member, an unwanted pregnancy, a miscarriage, a move to a new location, serious personal problems such as emotional illness or alcohol abuse by a family member, and serious inter-personal problems such as abuse, infidelity, or a child's broken engagement.

Boss (1988:40) has classified the various kinds of stressors in terms of a number of dimensions (table 17.1). Thus, the stressor may arise from within or outside the family. It can be an expected or an unpredictable event, controllable or uncontrollable. For instance, international and national shifts in the markets for agricultural products created economic hardship for American farmers in the 1980s, leading, in turn, to stress in many farm families and increased aggression and depression among farm children (Elder et al. 1992). We should note,

TABLE 17.1
Types of Stressor Events

Internal	External
Events that begin from someone inside the family, such as getting drunk, suicide, or running for election.	Events that begin from someone or something outside the family, such as earthquakes, terrorism, the inflation rate, or cultural attitudes toward women and minorities.
Normative	**Nonnormative**
Events that are expected over the family life cycle, such as birth, launching an adolescent, marriage, aging, or death.	Events that are unexpected, such as winning a lottery, getting a divorce, dying young, war, or being taken hostage. Often but not always disastrous.
Ambiguous	**Nonambiguous**
You can't get the facts surrounding the event. It's so unclear that you're not even sure that it's happening to you and your family.	Clear facts are available about the event: what is happening, when, how long, and to whom.
Volitional	**Nonvolitional**
Events that are wanted and sought out, such as a freely chosen job change, a college entrance, or a wanted pregnancy.	Events that are not sought out but just happen, such as being laid off or the sudden loss of someone loved.
Chronic	**Acute**
A situation that has long duration, such as diabetes, chemical addiction, or racial discrimination.	An event that lasts a short time but is severe, such as breaking a limb, losing a job, or flunking a test.
Cumulative	**Isolated**
Events that pile up, one right after the other, so that there is no resolution before the next one occurs. A dangerous situation in most cases.	An event that occurs alone, at least with no other events apparent at that time. It can be pinpointed easily.

From Pauline Boss, *Family Stress Management.* Copyright © 1988 Sage Publications, Inc., Newbury Park, CA. Reprinted by permission of Sage Publications, Inc.

however, that stressors are not always things that are imposed on us. Something that is freely chosen (the volitional category) may also turn out to be a stressor. As a businessman told us:

> I was excited about getting a new job in a new city. But for the first few months on that job, I was really distressed. I thought I had made the biggest mistake of my life.

Stressor Events and the Family Life Cycle   As you would expect, the kinds of things most likely to be important stressors vary somewhat over the family life cycle (Olson and McCubbin 1983:123f). Among young, recently wed couples, work-family and financial strains are most common. Changing jobs or careers, becoming dissatisfied with one's job or career, having problems with people on the job, and taking on additional responsibilities at work are all potential sources of stress for the young couple. There is a "contagion" of stress across work and family roles, such that stress in one area tends to spill over into the other (Bolger et al. 1989). In some cases, a self-perpetuating cycle can be set up: work stress is brought home, creating marital problems that make effective work problematic and cause further difficulty at work, aggravating the individual's stress, and so forth.

During the early childbearing years, financial strains are the most common. There are increased demands on the family's income for such things as food, clothing, and medical and dental care. Major purchases, such as homes and cars, are made, putting the family deeply into debt. The couple may have to take out additional loans or refinance their debt to cover the increased expenses of the growing family.

While financial pressures tend to lessen somewhat as the children grow, time demands generally increase. Additional stress can arise from the growing number of outside activities in which the children are involved. There is a sense that an increasing number of tasks around the home are simply not being done. These problems continue as the children grow into adolescence, at which point financial strains again may become severe.

By the time the couple has reached the empty-nest stage, time demands again are generally the prime source of stress with emphasis on chores that do not get done. In addition, difficulties with the sexual relationship, financial problems, decreasing satisfaction with work, and illness and death become more likely. Finally, in the retirement stage, financial problems once again become the most likely source of stress.

It is important to realize three things. First, some problems, such as financial strains, tend to be common at all stages. Second, the previous discussion does not include all the stressors that may occur but simply indicates the stressors most frequently named by people at various stages. Finally, as indicated by the nonnormative sources in table 17.1, such stressors as serious illness are unpredictable. Although serious illness is more likely to occur in the later years, it may happen at any time.

Not All Stressors Are Equal   What is the worst thing that could happen to you? You can probably think of some undesirable events that you could deal with relatively easily, others that would be much more difficult to cope with, and perhaps one or more that would make you feel like life was no longer worth living. In other words, the various stressors do not affect us equally. In fact, the same stressor may affect different people in different ways. Unemployment, for example, may be devastating to one person and a welcome break to another depending on their circumstances.

The death of a child is one of the most severe crises a family can face.

Caring for a chronically disabled family member, such as an Alzheimer's patient, is more or less difficult depending on such things as how close the caregiver feels to the patient and the extent to which the caregiver perceives that others understand what it is like to care for such a patient (Barber, Fisher, and Pasley 1990).

In spite of varying reactions, when we look at how large numbers of people respond to stressors, we can rank order the varied stressors in terms of severity. The Family Inventory of Life Events and Changes (FILE) is one effort to identify the severity (McCubbin and Patterson 1983). The researchers who developed FILE worked in the context of the Double ABCX model of stress. Thus, the instrument is an effort to measure the pile-ups in a family during the course of a year. It measures not only the number but the severity of stressors that accumulate and that can bring a family to the point of crisis.

FILE taps into nine important types of stressors in family life. Intrafamily strains include tensions between family members and the strains of parent-child relationships. The other types of stressors are: marital strains, pregnancy and childbearing strains, finance and business strains, work-family transitions and strains, illness and family care strains, family losses (loss of member or friend or a breakdown in the relationships), family transitions in and out (members of the family moving out or back into the home or engaging in a serious involvement of some kind outside the family), and family legal strains. The total of all these nine strains, weighted according to their severity, result in a "family pile-up" score. Given a sufficiently high score, most families are likely to experience difficulty in coping.

What are the most severe stressors? Ranked in terms of difficulty of adjusting, table 17.2 shows the fifteen most severe. At the lower end of the scale are such things as purchase of an automobile or other major item (19), increased strain on income for food, clothing, energy, and homecare (21), increased strain on income for children's education (22), and increased strain on income for medical and dental expenses (23). It is important to realize that the numbers, which are measures of relative severity, are averages for large numbers of people. The same event can have a quite different impact on different individuals, depending on a number of other factors. One factor is the time of life when the

TABLE 17.2
The 15 Most Severe Family Stressors
(numbers are a measure of relative severity)

Death of a child	99
Death of a spouse/parent	98
Separation or divorce of spouse/parent	79
Physical or sexual abuse or violence between family members	75
Family member becomes physically disabled or chronically ill	73
Spouse/parent has an affair	68
Family member jailed or sent to juvenile detention	68
Family member dependent on alcohol or drugs	66
Pregnancy of an unmarried family member	65
Family member runs away from home	61
Family member seems to have an emotional problem	58
Increased sexual problems in the marriage	58
Increased difficulty handling a disabled or chronically ill family member	58
Married child separates or gets a divorce	58
Family member picked up by police or arrested	57

From Hamilton I. McCubbin and Joan M. Patterson, "Stress: The Family Inventory of Life Events and Changes." In *Marriage and Family Assessment: A Sourcebook for Family Therapy*, pp. 285–286. Copyright © 1983 Erik Filsinger. Reprinted by permission of Erik Filsinger.

event occurs. For example, if a parent dies when you are a teenager, the impact is likely to be far more severe than when you are in your fifties or sixties.

Another factor is the nature of your relationship at the time of the event. If, for instance, your spouse has an affair in the context of years of conflict, you are less likely to be overwhelmed by it than if it occurs when you believe that the marriage is strong and meaningful to you both.

The impact of the various stressors, then, will vary somewhat from one individual to another depending on the circumstances. Yet their *relative* severity will generally reflect these numbers.

An interesting finding from the research using FILE relates to the amount of pile-up at various stages of the family life cycle. Again, keep in mind that the figures are averages for large numbers of families. You may or may not have the same experience in your own family. But looking at families generally, the researchers found that the highest amount of stress (pile-up) tends to occur during the time when the family is in the transition from having children in the home to the empty nest. During this "launching" stage, there tends to be more stressors than at any other time in the family life cycle. At this point, there is the stress of disrupting the home through children leaving for marriage or school and the likelihood of increased financial strain to cover the expenses of these events. It is also a time of life when one of the parents may be considering a change in jobs or career and when serious illness becomes more likely.

The lowest overall stress scores tend to occur in the retirement stage, and the second lowest are in the empty-nest stage of the family life cycle. It is not without some cause that the later years of life are sometimes termed the *golden* years. If grandmothers and grandfathers seem more relaxed and better able to flow with the events of life, it is in part because they are enjoying a time of life in which there are fewer stressor events with which they must cope.

ALCOHOL ABUSE IN THE FAMILY

Alcohol abuse ranks high on the list of family stressors. Some experts have even called alcohol abuse the nation's foremost health problem. When we look at the statistics, it is easy to see why they would make such a statement.

Extent of Alcohol Abuse

We will define **alcohol abuse** as the improper use of alcohol such that the consequences are detrimental to the user and the family. It is the abuse, not merely the use, of alcohol that creates problems. About two-thirds of the American population drink to some extent. But there are more than 14 million problem drinkers in the United States (Lauer 1998:95). About one in five Americans who drink every day or almost every day reports associated problems in the family as a result of the drinking.[1]

You may think of the skid-row derelict when you think of alcohol abuse, but more typically alcohol abusers are

> employed or employable, family-centered people. More than 70 percent of them live in respectable neighborhoods, with their husbands and wives, send

their children to school, belong to clubs, attend church, pay taxes, and continue to perform more or less effectively as businessmen, executives, housewives, farmers, salesmen, industrial workers, clerical workers, teachers, clergymen, and physicians (National Institute on Alcohol Abuse and Alcoholism 1975:15–16).

Alcohol abuse is far more common among men than women, though the proportion of women is increasing. Alcohol abuse is also more prevalent among whites than African Americans and among higher-income than lower-income people (Lauer 1995:94).

Alcohol Abuse and the Quality of Family Life

Alcohol abuse seriously detracts from the quality of family life. The consequences vary from relatively minor ones of more frequent arguments to the severe consequences of inadequate parenting, physical and emotional abuse, health problems that add stress to family life, marital and family disruption, and problem behavior on the part of the children (Roosa et al. 1993; Tubman 1993; Barnett and Fagan 1993; Deming, Chase, and Karesh 1996). The extent to which family life is disrupted may depend, in part, on whether the husband or the wife is the alcoholic. A study of forty-five couples in which one spouse was an alcoholic reported that, compared to the husband-alcoholic families, the wife-alcoholic couples had less disagreement, fewer communication problems, and more satisfaction with the marriage (Noel et al. 1991). In addition, alcoholic wives were more positive in behavior toward their husbands than were alcoholic husbands toward their wives.

Some families with an abuser seem to function fairly normally when the abuser is not drinking. The family can communicate with each other, enjoy family functions, carry on family work, and so forth. But when the abuser is drinking, the whole character of family life is likely to change. At the very least, the drinker is likely to become more negative and critical with his or her spouse while drinking (Jacob and Krahn 1988). At worst, the abuser of alcohol may become physically or emotionally abusive of his or her spouse. Looking at a national sample of over two thousand couples, Coleman and Straus (1983) found a positive link between alcohol

---

[1]*Gallup Report* no. 288, September 1989.

abuse and family violence. The more often a spouse was drunk during the year, the more often there was physical violence in the relationship. The exception occurred when the abuse was extreme. When the spouse was "almost always" drunk, violence was less likely than when the spouse was "often" or "very often" drunk. Still, more than one out of four males who were almost always drunk during the year of the survey engaged in violent behavior against their spouses.

In many families, particularly when the abuse is long-term, there are negative consequences whether or not the abuser is drinking. In fact, some research shows that couples with an alcoholic husband are like couples that are "maritally conflicted," that is, couples that have a high degree of dissatisfaction and a large number of disagreements (O'Farrell and Birchler 1987). In other words, the atmosphere in a family where there is an abuser of alcohol is likely to feature a great deal of tension, considerable dissatisfaction, and frequent conflict.

In addition, the spouses and children of the abusers may develop various physical and emotional problems. Wives of alcoholic men may become heavy drinkers themselves. In any case, they are likely to experience long-term marital problems, such as unsatisfactory sexual relations, abusive behavior, and high levels of tension in the home (Weinberg and Vogler 1990).

With regard to children, while the majority who come from a home with one or more alcoholics are not doomed to some kind of pathology, they are more vulnerable to a variety of behavioral and emotional problems (West and Prinz 1987; Rubio-Stipec et al. 1991; Easley and Epstein 1991; Jones and Houts 1992; Sher and Gershuny 1997). Among other things, children in such families are more likely than others to:

Blame themselves for their parents' problems.

Perceive less parental warmth and concern.

Have a conduct disorder or become delinquent.

Become an abuser of alcohol themselves.

Display higher rates of hyperactivity.

Have problems with school work.

Report higher rates of health problems.

Have higher rates of anxiety and depression.

The children of alcoholics also tend to describe their families as less cohesive and more conflict-ridden than do children from other families (Clair and Genest 1987). Nor do the negative consequences disappear quickly when the alcoholic parent stops drinking. A study that compared sons of recovering alcoholic and nonalcoholic fathers reported that the sons of the recovering alcoholics were more compulsive, insecure, fearful, subdued, and detached (Whipple and Noble 1991).

Many youths who have problems come from a home with one or two alcoholic parents.

INVOLVEMENT
Self-Help Groups

What can you do if you have a drinking problem or if you are in a family with someone who abuses alcohol? Alcoholics Anonymous is the best known and one of the most effective self-help organizations for alcoholics. Al-Anon and Alateen are organizations for the spouse and the children of the alcoholics. They help the individual cope with the difficulties of living with an alcoholic.

There are self-help groups today to deal with all kinds of problems that can create a crisis in a family, ranging from Alcoholics Anonymous (AA) to groups that help people with other kinds of addictions (gambling) to those that help people who have various kinds of emotional problems. There are groups for the overweight, the unemployed, and the abused.

Locate some kind of self-help group in your community (the telephone directory is a good place to begin), and get permission to visit a group meeting. Note the way that the group works to help each member to cope with problems. Ask one of the people attending if you can interview him or her for your class project. Tell the person that you are particularly interested in how his or her experience relates to family life—both the family of origin and the current family of which the individual is a part. Explore the following questions:

1. What kinds of experiences in the family of origin seemed to contribute to the problem, if any?

2. What kinds of experiences in the current family contributed to the problem, if any?
3. Did anyone else in the family or the family of origin have a similar problem?
4. How did the problem affect family life, including the marital relationship and relations with children?

If the entire class participates in this project, see if you can come up with any common factors in the family background of the people and any common consequences for family life. Do different kinds of problems seem to have different sources and consequences? Why or why not?

When the children become adults, their past experience in an alcoholic home can continue to trouble them. A group of Hispanic adult children of alcoholics reported more physical health problems than Hispanic adults from nonalcoholic homes (Harman and Arbona 1991). Other research shows that adult children of alcoholics have higher rates of anxiety and depression, lower levels of self-esteem, and higher rates of alcoholism themselves (Tweed and Ryff 1991; Domenico and Windle 1993; Schuckit and Smith 1996). Finally, when adult children of alcoholic parents marry, they have a greater probability than others of high levels of marital conflict and lower satisfaction with their children and their marriages, and are more likely to separate or divorce (Parker and Harford 1988; Kerr and Hill 1992; Domenico and Windle 1993). Clearly, the abuser is engaged not merely in a self-destructive process but in a process that may detract from both the immediate and long-term quality of life of other family members.

Family Problems and Alcohol Abuse

If alcohol abuse can lead to family problems, family problems can also lead to alcohol abuse. When there are disturbed relationships within the home, one of the family members may resort to heavy drinking in an effort to cope with the stress. Students who report more alcohol use also tend to report more stressor events in their lives, more daily hassles, and more conflict in their families (Baer et al. 1987). A husband or wife may resort to drinking because of serious marital problems. The drinking is an effort to cope with a frustrating, stressful situation. Like other inappropriate coping methods, it is counterproductive. It is a way of escape, rather than a way of confronting the problem and pursuing some constructive resolution.

If family problems result in a member becoming a problem drinker, the family may get caught in a vicious circle in which the problems and the abuse feed on and sustain each other. That is, the difficulties lead the member to drink, and the drinking intensifies the problems and creates additional ones. The added stress perpetuates the drinking, and the drinking continues to aggravate the problems. Once the pattern is established, it tends to be self-perpetuating.

Moreover, alcohol abuse can take its toll across a number of generations. Kayla, a graduate student in her thirties, has alcoholic grandparents on both sides of her family. Although neither of her parents abused alcohol, the effects of the grandparents' abuse have continued in the family:

> To this day, I see my mother struggling to establish her own identity and my father striving to free himself from the emotional tyranny of an alcoholic father. Growing up in alcoholic families, my parents didn't know how to deal with things like sickness, job loss, moving, or family conflict. Whenever they faced a crisis, they would lean on me as the oldest child to help resolve it. I grew up feeling overly responsible and quite inadequate.

Kayla married a man who was from an alcoholic family. She knows now that she looked to him to give her the nurturing she never got from her family, and he looked to her to be the capable and competent individual that he never had in his family. They were both wrong. Their marriage alternated between coldness and stormy passions and between self-blame and blaming the other. It eventually ended in divorce.

Kayla's experience is perhaps one of the more insidious consequences of alcohol abuse in a family. The inadequate parenting that results when there is an abuser can have negative effects through a number of subsequent generations.

VIOLENCE IN FAMILIES

Next to death, separation, and divorce, family violence is the most difficult experience people have to cope with (table 17.2). It is easy to understand the severity of the trauma. After all, we expect our families to be a source of comfort and support, a refuge from an often difficult world. For the refuge to become a violent battleground is, as one person told us, "like discovering that God is a malevolent tormentor rather than a loving Father."

We shall be looking primarily at physical abuse, but we should keep in mind that emotional abuse also occurs and always accompanies physical abuse. Emotional abuse includes such things as the threat of physical abuse and ridicule. Some victims report that the emotional abuse was more damaging to them than the physical abuse (Follingstad et al. 1990).

The Extent of Violence

If the bright side of intimate relationships is their potential for enhancing our well-being, the dark side is their potential for destruction because of physical and verbal abuse. Each year, nearly a million women aged twelve and over suffer violence from a current or former spouse, girlfriend, or boyfriend (Greenfeld et al. 1998:3). A national survey reported that nineteen parents per one thousand admitted using abusive violence against their children, and thirty per one thousand men acknowledged beating their wives (Gelles and Straus 1988). The figures are undoubtedly conservative, based only on the number of admitted cases. Even so, they indicate that millions of Americans experience violence in their homes. And the violence may be severe—data from the Bureau of Justice statistics show that 16 percent of murder victims were killed by a family member (Dawson and Langan 1994).

The rates of violence are even higher among African American than white families. In the national survey, African American wives were 1.2 times more likely to experience minor violence and 2.4 times more likely to experience severe violence than were white wives (Hamptom and Gelles 1994).

Child Abuse

If we define violence to include such mild forms as spanking, the majority of parents use some form of violence against their children. We are concerned here, however, with the more severe forms of violence, which range from depriving children of some of the necessities of life to severe physical injury (figure 17.1). When we look at cases of child maltreatment that are reported to the authorities, we find that nearly 40 percent of the victims are five years old or younger (U.S. Bureau of the Census 1997b:218). Females are somewhat more likely to be victims than are males. And the rates of maltreatment are proportionately higher among African Americans and Hispanics than among other racial groups.

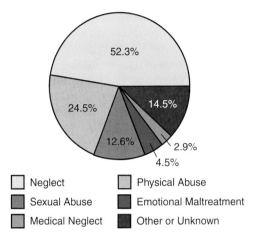

FIGURE 17.1   Types of Child Maltreatment
(*Source:* U.S. Bureau of the Census 1997b:274.)

A prototype of the abusive parent would be one who is single, is young (around thirty or less), has been married for fewer than ten years, had his or her first child before the age of eighteen, and is unemployed or employed part-time. Among the married, spouse abusers also are far more likely to be child abusers than are those who do not abuse their spouses (Ross 1996). And the more times someone has abused a spouse, the more likely that person is a child abuser as well. Women are slightly more likely to abuse children than are men, probably because women are more intensely involved with children (and the rates of child abuse are higher in single-parent, which for the most part means single-mother, families). Child abusers tend to have lower self-esteem than others, to define their children as more troublesome, to have serious financial problems, to have poorer mental health, and to have a large number of stressor events in their lives (Hamilton et al. 1987; Whipple and Webster-Stratton 1991; Kolko et al., 1993; Wolfner and Gelles 1993). Abusers are also more likely than nonabusers to have been abused themselves as children.

Obviously, child abuse is often associated with pile-up, a large number of stressors that overwhelms the parent or parents. What emerges is a portrait of a troubled, stressful home. Thus, in a survey of 1,770 undergraduates, 6.3 percent of whom said they had been physically abused by a parent, the researcher found that those abused were more likely to report a good deal of conflict in the home, parental drinking and drug problems, and one or both parents who were unsupportive, overly strict or overly permissive, angry, and depressed (Wright 1985).

Incest

Incest, a special form of child abuse, is any type of exploitive sexual contact between relatives in which the victim is under eighteen years of age. It is difficult to know exactly how many people are the victims of incest. It seems clear, however, that girls are much more likely than boys to be victims of incest. Overall, about one out of seven Americans reports that he or she was sexually abused as a child (Patterson and Kim 1991:125). Three-fourths of those abused are women. These figures are for sexual abuse generally, not just incest. Of girls who are sexually abused as children, about 4.5 percent are abused by their fathers (Russell 1986).

When father-daughter incest occurs, it usually begins when the daughter is between the ages of six and eleven, and the abuse lasts around two years on the average (Stark 1984). How could a father engage in sexual relationships with his daughter? The usual explanation is that such incest occurs when "the marital relationship has broken down, the mother is alienated from the roles of wife and mother, and the father makes an alliance with the oldest daughter that substitutes for the marital relationship and becomes sexual" (Finkelhor 1984:226).

Still, many men endure an alienated relationship with a wife without resorting to incest. Abusive fathers are like other abusive adults, troubled individuals who find it difficult to relate meaningfully and sexually with another adult. Indeed, some research has shown that incestuous fathers have personality problems and thus cannot seem to appropriately find the intimacy that they crave (Justice and Justice 1979). The incestuous father may feel alienated from the world generally, may view his daughter as his property, may be a tyrant in the home, or may be an abuser of alcohol. In any case, the father is also likely to be highly stressed, without a sexual relationship with his wife, and to nurture a fantasy about an ideal mother and wife that he lacks in his own wife and seeks in his daughter. At the same time, he is likely to justify the incest in terms of love and care and define himself as a considerate and fair person (Gilgun 1995).

A father may initiate sexual relations with his daughter by force or by intimidation. Some people believe that the mother colludes and that the daughter gets a certain amount of enjoyment out of the relationship. Yet the evidence suggests that incest is likely to be a horrifying experience to the victim, who, among other things, is likely to suffer from low self-esteem, conduct problems in school, and, when she grows up, problems of relating to men in a meaningful way and ongoing struggles with low self-esteem and depression (Jackson et al. 1990; Dadds et al. 1991).

Why doesn't the daughter rebel and refuse? We need to realize both how powerless and how responsible for family well-being girls tend to feel. For instance, Becky, an editor, is still "overwhelmed" as she discusses her experience. She remembers the intense conflict between her parents, and her mother finally being hospitalized for a period of time. She was about eleven years old, and "sex was not even the subject for jokes with my circle of friends. I hardly thought about it." When her father approached her for sex, she was passive. She "didn't react to the incest as a sexual act, but as a way to keep the family together." When Becky yielded to her father, things seemed better in the home. "I desperately wanted harmony in my family

and every other need became subordinate to that." When Becky's father asked her if she wanted him to return to her bedroom after each sexual encounter, she told him no. But she continued to allow him to use her. And she has spent the years since then trying to work through the agony of being betrayed by a man to whom she looked for support and unconditional love.

Mother-son incest seems to be quite rare. Other forms of incest, such as that between brother and sister and uncles and nieces and other relatives, occur, but we do not know how widespread they are. We do know, however, that most incestuous relationships are a betrayal of trust and lead to long-term problems for the victim. For example, a report on a small number of women who had experienced brother-sister incest noted that the women felt "isolation, secrecy, shame, anger, and poor communication" in their families (Canavan, Meyer, and Higgs 1992).

Spouse Abuse

The term *spouse abuse* is likely to conjure up the image of a man beating a woman. There are two things we need to keep in mind. First, "abuse" is more than physical. Verbal abuse can be as damaging as physical abuse. Using a national sample, Straus and Sweet (1992) found that three-fourths of

In recent years, spouse abuse has become both more openly acknowledged and less tolerated.

both men and women acknowledged verbal attacks on their partners during the year covered by the survey. The researchers defined verbal attacks as including such things as insulting, swearing at, and threatening the partner. They also included sulking and "stomping" away. Clearly, not everything defined as a verbal attack would inflict long-term damage on the partner or the relationship. Still, the amount of verbal aggression is quite high; the median number of attacks was between three and four. The attacks were more likely in homes where there was also alcohol and/or drug abuse.

Verbal aggression appears to be equally divided between men and women. There is some evidence that more women than men engage in physical aggression. In a national sample, women were slightly more likely than men to admit that they had hit, shoved, or thrown something at their spouse (Gelles and Straus 1988; Sorenson, Upchurch, and Shen 1996). However, men and women were equally likely to say that they had been the victims of abuse. Furthermore, women are likely to suffer greater physical injury from men than vice-versa. And women suffer more emotionally than men do from being victims of abuse (Umberson et al. 1998). Women who assault their husbands are likely to have been previously beaten by their husbands. Frequently a wife's violence is a form of self-defense.

What kind of man would beat his wife? Researchers have found that a male abuser tends to be young (between eighteen and twenty-four years); be unemployed or employed part-time; have lower levels of education; live at the poverty level; worry about finances; be dissatisfied with life; be married less than ten years; have been physically punished as a child; be insecure and jealous and have frequent conflict with his wife; and abuse alcohol or other drugs (Gelles and Straus 1988; Hotaling and Sugarman 1990; Sorenson, Upchurch, and Shen 1996; Straus and Yodanis 1996; Brookoff et al. 1997; Holtzworth-Munroe, Stuart, and Hutchinson 1997). He probably abuses his wife verbally as well as physically. He tends to view battered women in negative terms (Eisikovits et al. 1991) and to believe that the man should be the head of the family, but he lacks the resources to be dominant in his family. As Gelles and Straus put it:

> Perhaps the most telling of all attributes of the battering man is that he feels inadequate and sees violence

as a culturally acceptable way to be both dominant and powerful (1988:89).

As the preceding suggests, an egalitarian relationship is less likely to be marked by violence than one in which either the husband or the wife is striving to be dominant and the abuser believes in traditional male-female roles (Coleman and Straus 1986; Crossman, Stith, and Bender 1990). Those who are violent, whether women or men, may be using the violence as a way of establishing their dominance:

> Lurking beneath the surface of all intimate violence are the confrontations and controversies over power (Gelles and Straus 1988:92).

Why would a woman allow herself to be repeatedly beaten? Why does she stay in the relationship? In some cases, women lack (or believe that they lack) the economic means to leave. In an effort to retain some economic security or to make the relationship ultimately work out, they may be willing to tolerate abuse as long as it does not become too severe or involve their children.

In other cases, women have fallen into what Donald Dutton (1987:248) called a *social trap*. Thus, the abused woman begins her marriage with the same expectations as others—long-term happiness and fulfillment and her own heavy responsibility for such an outcome and for the emotional state of her husband. The violent episodes, which typically begin in the first year of marriage, are less severe at first and are likely to be followed by strong expressions of regret from the husband. She may therefore view the violence as an anomaly. At first, she does not expect the violence to continue. Eventually, she realizes that it will, but by that time, she has developed a strong commitment to the man. She is determined to make the relationship succeed. A "traumatic bonding" occurs, a bonding that is facilitated by the fact that the abuse occurs intermittently and may be followed by effusive apologies and promises to change.

In other words, women may have values and attitudes that override the physical and emotional damage they are enduring. Ferraro and Johnson (1983) interviewed over one hundred battered women and found that those who opted to remain in the relationship offered six different kinds of explanations. Some had a "salvation ethic." They saw

COMPARISON
Dowry Death in India

Many societies, as part of the marriage process, have had the custom of a dowry—the transfer of some kind of property (money, goods, land, etc.) from the family of the bride to the family of the groom. In India, the dowry has been not merely a social obligation but also a religious (Hindu) obligation as a symbol of the transfer of authority over a woman from her father to her husband.

The marriage celebration itself imposes a financial burden on many families, and the dowry can intensify that burden considerably. The problem is that the obligations of the dowry are not necessarily settled before the marriage takes place. Payments can continue for years after the marriage, and the family of

the groom can later request more than was originally agreed upon.

What if the bride's family simply refuses to give more? Indian families are well aware of the problem of dowry violence. Typically, when additional demands are not quickly met, the groom's family (in whose home the bride may be living) harasses and pressures the bride. The harassment can be so severe that the bride will commit suicide. Or the harassment can culminate in the murder of the bride, usually by burning her to death with kerosene.

An example of dowry death was a 25-year-old woman who, before she died of burns, told authorities that her husband's family had been harassing her on the grounds that she brought insufficient dowry.

During an argument, her husband held her while her mother-in-law poured kerosene over her clothes and set them on fire.

In an effort to deal with the problem of dowry death, the government passed the Dowry Prohibition Act in 1961. And "dowry death" is now a part of the Indian penal code. Unfortunately, the Act and the laws have not eliminated the practice. We do not know how many Indian women continue to endure physical violence or death over dowry disputes. But hundreds of brides die of third-degree burns each year in Delhi alone. And most of those responsible manage to escape prosecution. In India, as elsewhere in the world, domestic violence continues to take a toll (Van Willigen and Channa 1991).

their husbands as troubled or sick individuals who needed their wives to survive. Others said the problem was beyond the control of them or their husbands; the violence was due to some external factor, such as work pressure or loss of a job. A third group denied the injury; they said the beatings were tolerable and even normal. Fourth, some blamed themselves, saying the violence could be averted if only they were more passive and conciliatory. A small number of women continue to blame themselves even after they escape from the abusive relationship and presumably have a better perspective on it (Andrews and Brewin 1990). Fifth, some saw no options for themselves; they were too economically or emotionally dependent on their husbands. Finally, some of the women said that they lived by a "higher loyalty," such as a religious faith or commitment to a stable family life.

Parent Abuse

Although most of the attention has been focused on child and spouse abuse, researchers have discovered

that children also abuse their parents. Results from a national survey of 1,545 male, high school students reported that about one in ten admitted to a violent act against a parent, more often against the father than the mother (Peek, Fischer, and Kidwell 1985). A study of 445 white and Hispanic youth in California found that whites were somewhat more likely than Hispanics to hit a parent and that those who did assault parents were likely to be bored with school, have low self-esteem, and be less happy than others (Paulson, Coombs, and Landsverk 1990).

Abuse of elderly parents may also occur at the hands of their adult children (Pierce and Trotta 1986). The victims tend to be around seventy-five years of age or older. The most likely victim is a white female. The abuser is also likely to be a female (because women rather than men are generally the caregivers) and having some kind of personal crisis (alcohol or drug addiction, illness, or financial problems):

The combination of personal crisis and the new task of taking on the added responsibility of the aged parent created a situation which increased the likelihood of violence (Pierce and Trotta 1986:102).

Perhaps as many as a half- to a million elderly parents a year are victims of abuse.

Consequences of Abuse

In the short-term, of course, abuse involves serious physical and emotional damage. But abuse also tends to have serious long-term consequences. Let us look first at the consequences for children. The victims of incest may wind up in therapy as adults as they struggle with low self-esteem, guilt, depression, suicidal tendencies, other emotional problems, relationship problems, or drug or alcohol addiction, all of which may last for decades (Jehu, Gazan, and Klassen 1985; Roesler and McKenzie 1994).

Children who are physically abused are more likely than others to face a variety of physical and emotional problems that tend to remain with them when they become adults (Gelles and Straus 1988; Whipple and Webster-Stratton 1991; Holden and Ritchie 1991; Salzinger et al. 1993; DuCharme, Koverola, and Battle 1997; McCauley et al. 1997; Felitti et al. 1998; Garnefski and Arends 1998). About a third of them will grow up to be abusers, which means they are ten times more likely to become abusers than those who were not abused. Other effects include:

Behavior problems at home and at school.

Higher levels of anger and aggression.

Lower intellectual and academic development.

Emotional problems, including anxiety, depression, and thoughts of, and attempts at, suicide.

Abuse of alcohol and other drugs.

Problems of low self-esteem.

Health problems, including higher rates of chronic diseases.

Feelings of isolation, difficulty in trusting others, difficulty in forming meaningful intimate relationships, and lower levels of intimacy in the relationships.

Generalized unhappiness.

Interestingly, a study of sexually abused boys and girls found that the adverse consequences were greater for the boys than for the girls in terms of much higher rates of aggression, drug abuse, and

suicidal thoughts and behavior (Garnefski and Arends 1998). The reasons for the sex differences are unknown.

The consequences of spouse abuse for women (we know of no research on the consequences for male victims of spouse abuse) are serious problems with physical and mental health (Gelles and Straus 1988:136). Compared to those in nonviolent homes, women who are abused report more:

Headaches or pains in the head.

Nervousness and depression.

A sense of being overwhelmed by difficulties.

Feelings of worthlessness and hopelessness.

A sense of being unable to cope.

Suicidal thoughts and actual suicide attempts.

Verbal and physical abuse also depress women's marital satisfaction (Arias, Lyons, and Street 1997). The emotional damage is underscored by the fact that only about two women in one thousand think seriously about suicide in any one year, but about forty-six *abused* women in one thousand think about suicide frequently. One of the bitter ironies of the abusive relationship is that the woman's reaction to the abuse—for example, her depression—may be used to justify further beatings. In other words, the victim is blamed for the violence used against her.

We should note that *viewing* violence as well as being victimized by it has harmful consequences. Children who witness violence between their parents or between parents and siblings will suffer even if they are not themselves abused. Such children may suffer from both psychological and social maladjustment, and their problems may continue into adulthood (Henning et al. 1996). Thus, those who witness violence in their homes are more likely than others to:

Suffer from depression and other emotional problems and to have recurring problems of depression when they become adults (Carlson 1990; Kessler and Magee 1994; Graham-Germann and Levendosky 1998).

Have higher rates of delinquent activities and other behavior problems (Kruttschnitt and Dornfeld 1993; O'Keefe 1994).

Have more violence in their own relationships as adults (Carlson 1990; McNeal and Amato 1998).

It seems that children learn from watching their parents that those who love you also hit you and that this is an appropriate way to get your way and to deal with stress.

REACTING TO CRISES

As we have discussed, about one-third of abused children will grow up to become abusers; about two-thirds will not. Clearly, people react in different ways to family crises. The point we wish to stress in this section is that whatever the particular crisis you face, there are always alternative ways of dealing with it. You can't control all of the things that happen in your life, but you can control the way you respond to them. This doesn't mean that you can avoid the trauma of crises. It does mean, as

we will show in the final section of this chapter, that you can avoid long-term, adverse consequences. In fact, it is possible to turn the crisis into something that yields long-term, positive consequences (figure 17.2).

Whatever the type of crisis faced, different families will have somewhat different reactions. In some cases, an event may be a crisis for some families or some family members but not for others. Consider, for example, a perinatal loss (miscarriage, stillbirth, or infant death). To what extent is that a crisis? It varies, depending on the extent to which family members feel attachment:

Some family members will feel very strongly attached to an embryo, fetus, or newborn, even to the mere idea of a child. These people may grieve a perinatal loss quite intensely. Other people, even those who

FIGURE 17.2   Differing Outcomes of a Family Crisis

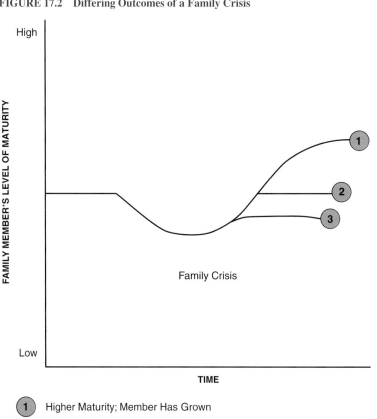

1   Higher Maturity; Member Has Grown

2   Same Level As Before; Member Has Coped

3   Lower Level; Member Has Long-Term Negative Reaction

PERSPECTIVE
Drinking and Fighting

We have seen that alcohol abuse may be associated with verbal and physical abuse as well. The problem is an old one. In June 1677, a case against Edmond Berry was heard in a Massachusetts court. Berry was fined for excessive drink and abusive behavior toward his wife. In the following account, which we have put into modern English from the old court record, Berry's wife accused him of intolerable abuse:

This honored Court knows of my woeful condition in living with my husband Edmond Berry, and of his most bitter, inhumane, and most ill-becoming behavior to me, as many of my neighbors can give testimony. I was compelled to go away from him and live where I could be safe. The honored Court, upon learning of this, compelled me—upon the penalty of five pounds—to live with him again, which as the Lord knows to my inexpressible sorrow has been now for about twelve months. If my testimony does not sufficiently speak for me and if the Court doesn't help me, what shall a poor woman do in this case? This is my situation: I have nothing of his nor have I ever had but a very small amount ever since I was his wife. For example, he had (and still has) an absurd manner in eating his victuals: he takes his meat out of the pickle and broils it upon the coals. And he tells me I must eat this or else I must fast. Therefore, if I had not re-

served something for myself to eat, I would have perished. Neither will he provide me with the absolute necessities to run a decent house, rather I am compelled to borrow from my neighbors. He has made it evident that he intends to do what he has previously reported: namely that he will have my estate or else he will make me weary of my life.

Now the honored Major Hathorne knows the contract that was made between us before marriage and acknowledged before him. However, in the hope of living more comfortably with him, I willingly brought into the house what I could. But he continued to bestow ill upon me. Please judge his behavior for yourself by this one more recent example. When I brought to him a cup of my own sugar and beer (for he will allow me nothing of his own) and drank a toast to him using these words: "Come husband let all former differences be buried and trod underfoot; why should we not live in love and unity as other folks do?" He replied to me, thus: "You old cheating rogue; the devil take thee if you don't bring me before this court." But such dire expressions towards me are not rare with him. Although this treatment was hard and very tedious to bear, I was willing to groan under it rather than to make a public display of his wicked and brutal behavior to me.

Yet he came before the Court and the grand jury had cog-

nizance of his impious behavior towards me. . . . It is reasonable that I should speak something before your honor in order to clear up of my own innocence; and also, since the matter has been brought before the court, I want to present my grievances before you—although God knows I preferred rather to have borne my affliction and waited upon Him who is the persuader of the heart, with my poor prayers to my good God in hopes of the work of His grace upon my husband's heart and soul, whereby he might be brought to see the evil of his ways and so to behave toward me as becomes an honest man to his wife. But the Lord in mercy look upon me, for I am now past hope of his changing, and the only wise God direct you in what to do with me in this my woeful case. For I am not only continually abused by my husband, with most vile, threatening, and opprobrious speeches, but also by his son who lives in the house with him. He has, in his father's presence, threatened to throw me headlong down the stairs. In addition, he has broken into my chest and taken away a part of that little which I had.

"Drinking and Fighting" from *America's Families* by Donald M. Scott and Bernard Wishy. Copyright © 1982 by Donald M. Scott and Bernard Wishy. Reprinted by permission of Harper-Collins Publishers, Inc.

consider an embryo, a fetus, or a newborn fully human, may feel relatively little attachment to it and grieve its loss little if at all (Rosenblatt and Burns 1986:237).

Among those who grieve after a perinatal loss, the reactions vary. Women are likely to experience depression for a year or more after a miscarriage (Robinson et al. 1994). In some cases of perinatal loss, the grief may continue for decades. A woman who lost a two-month-old son forty-two years previously told an interviewer that she still thinks about him every day (Rosenblatt and Burns 1986:243). She still has some feelings of sorrow, though she also has some pleasant memories. Overall, perhaps as many as one-fifth of those with a perinatal loss have long-term grief to some extent. The husband and wife may not feel the grief equally, and that can cause marital problems (Schwab 1992; Najman et al. 1993).

In contrast to perinatal loss, having a child die or succumb to a life-threatening illness like cancer is likely to be a crisis for every family. A study of thirty-one couples who had lost an infant reported that even after two years the couples reported less marital intimacy and significantly less sexual intimacy than they had before the loss (Gottlieb, Lang, and Amsel 1996). Many marriages do not survive the death of a child.

Life-threatening illnesses are also crises, though not as stressful as a child's death. A number of different reactions can be found to an illness like cancer. Alberta Koch (1985) interviewed the parents and siblings of thirty-two pediatric cancer patients and found five kinds of family responses, one or more of them being found in each family. Some family members had an increase in negative emotions after the diagnosis, particularly emotions of worry and grief. A second type of response was to develop rules prohibiting the display of such negative emotions as worry and anger. This was done to protect both the patient and other family members from further distress.

Third, some family members developed various health or behavioral problems or had existing problems intensify. Behavioral problems included drinking and affairs for parents and fighting and other disruptive behavior at school for children. Fourth, roles changed in some families, with the patient be-

coming the focal point of family concern and activities. Siblings in such families took on a caregiving role along with the parents. Finally, some families reported an increased closeness, a sense of greater cohesiveness as the family banded together to try to deal with the crisis.

To return to our earlier point, the families in Koch's sample could not control the event, the cancer, but they could and did react in various ways to it. Some of those ways were helpful and some were not. Specifically, then, what mechanisms and resources do families use to cope with a crisis? And which coping patterns are constructive? Which lead to the higher level of maturity of family members as indicated by path one in figure 17.2? That is our final topic.

COPING PATTERNS

Whatever you do in the face of a crisis is a coping pattern. Even if you do nothing, that is one way of trying to cope. Perhaps doing nothing is a way of saying there really is no crisis. Or perhaps it is based on the belief that time will heal all things, so that you need only hold on and wait it out. Unfortunately, "doing nothing" is not usually an effective coping pattern. Other patterns are also ineffective, and we need to be aware of them as well as of those that are more useful.

Ineffective Coping Patterns

"Ineffective" does not mean that a coping pattern does not work for an individual or family. Rather, ineffective means that it is not a pattern that typically will yield long-term, constructive outcomes. Those who use an ineffective coping pattern may follow path three in figure 17.2. The members of those families are functionally less capable after a crisis. They have not coped effectively, and, as a result, their growth as individuals and as a family is set back. What kinds of coping patterns are likely to result in path three?

Denial   Denial is perhaps the most common of the ineffective coping patterns. Denial is a defense mechanism in which people will not believe what they observe. For example, a woman may be married to an alcoholic but refuses to accept the fact that he has a drinking problem. She may believe that he will stop drinking as soon as his work stress eases, that he doesn't drink any more than most other men, or that the problem is exaggerated by others and not really as serious as they say. Whatever her rationale, she denies that he is an alcoholic and thereby delays a constructive confrontation with the problem.

We should note that denial is both normal and perhaps helpful in the initial stage of some crises (Boss 1988:87f). For example, denial is typically the initial response to the death of a loved one or to the news of a terminal illness. The denial may serve the useful purpose of giving the individual a chance to collect his or her thoughts and resources in order to deal with the problem constructively.

Where denial is a temporary measure that enables family members to mobilize their resources, it is useful. When denial becomes a long-term pattern of ignoring the problem, it is destructive. The family that continues to ignore the symptoms of illness in father or mother, the financial disaster that looms because of parental unemployment, or the abuse that father inflicts on his wife or the children is a family that will inevitably reap a bitter harvest of emotional and physical damage.

One of the ways to break out of denial is for some member of the family to openly admit that there is a problem. Parents may have to tell their children frankly about the difficulties they face because of unemployment. Children may have to talk frankly with their parents about problems of alcohol or physical abuse. Boss (1988:92) provides some examples:

> Dad, I love you, but I don't like the way you act when you're drunk. I would like you to stop because I care about you. If you don't stop, I won't hang around since it hurts me too much to see you that way.

> Mom, as your kid, I have to tell you that I can't stand watching you and Dad fight any more. If you don't call the cops the next time Dad hits you, I will.

> Grandpa, I know how sick you are. I just want you to know that I love you and that I will miss you when you die. Is there anything I can do for you now?

Once everyone admits that there is a problem, the family can begin to work together to find the best way to deal with it.

Avoidance Admitting the existence of a problem is not sufficient, however. Sometimes people acknowledge that the problem exists, but they avoid confronting and dealing with it. Avoidance occurred, for instance, among those parents we noted in the previous section, who reacted to their child's cancer by drinking excessively or having an affair. They didn't deny the cancer, but they didn't act in a way to deal constructively with their own and their family's distress.

Avoidance can be used in any kind of crisis. Children of alcoholic fathers have been found to use avoidance behaviors to some extent. Compared with other children, they deal with their distress by such things as sleeping more than usual or trying to make themselves feel better by drinking or smoking (Clair and Genest 1987).

Like denial, avoidance is not always a dysfunctional way of coping. There may be times when avoidance is necessary in order to give the family time to mobilize their resources. If, in other words, avoidance means a temporary delay in confronting the problem, it may be useful. If avoidance means long-term refusal to deal with the problem, it can have the same disastrous results as denial.

Scapegoating Sometimes people admit a problem but feel that they have to find someone or something to blame. They select a family scapegoat to bear the brunt of the responsibility for the problem. A young woman who experienced a miscarriage told us that her suffering was intensified by the queries of some family members and acquaintances, who asked such things as whether she overexerted or took proper care of herself. In other words, they suggested that her own behavior was to blame for the loss.

Scapegoating is an insidious way to respond to crisis. It boils down to selecting one of the victims of the crisis and further victimizing that person. We offered an example of this earlier when we pointed out that a man often uses the reaction of his beaten wife as an excuse for further beating.

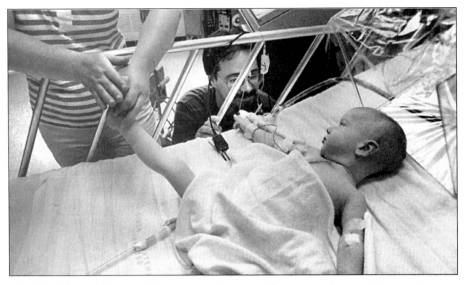

A family crisis can bring disruption or increased closeness, depending on how members react.

Scapegoating, unlike denial and avoidance, is not even useful in the short run. Rather, it is a way of shifting responsibility so that one does not have to feel guilt or personal responsibility for resolving the crisis. Thus, if the family blames the father's unemployment on his own inept work habits, then other members of the family do not have to sacrifice or worry about the family's financial problems. On the other hand, if father blames the kids for draining his energies so that he could not do his work properly, then he has shifted the responsibility to the rest of the family.

The Foundation of Effective Coping

If a crisis occurs in a family that is not functioning well to begin with, the family may not be able to marshall the resources necessary to deal effectively with the crisis. To put the matter another way, a family is most likely to cope effectively with problems or crises when the members have worked together to develop certain family strengths. The strengths become a foundation on which the family can stand together and deal with crises.

The family that has developed strengths is likely to be a **resilient family,** one that can resist disruption in the face of change and cope effectively with crises. What are the strengths that help make a fam-

ily resilient? Hamilton and Marilyn McCubbin (1988) have identified eleven, some of which are important at all stages of the family life cycle and all of which are important at one or more stages. The strengths are:

Accord, or relationships that foster problem-solving and manage conflict well.

Celebrations, including birthdays, religious days, and other special events.

Communication, including both beliefs and emotions.

Good financial management.

Hardiness, which includes commitment to the family, the belief that family members have control over their lives, and a sense that the family can deal with all changes.

Health, both physical and emotional.

Shared leisure activities.

Acceptance of each member's personality and behavior.

A social support network of relatives and friends.

Sharing routines such as family meals and chores.

Traditions that carry over from one generation to another.

Families that have worked at developing the above strengths will be in a position to deal effectively with stressors and with crises.

Tools for Effective Coping

In our research on how people master life's unpredictable crises (Lauer and Lauer 1988), we found a number of tools that people use to deal with everything from divorce to abuse to serious illness. We were particularly interested in how people deal with a crisis in a way to follow path one in figure 17.2, rather than paths two or three. The following are "path one" tools, those that enable people to confront a crisis and eventually emerge at a higher level of functioning. For any particular crisis, one or a number of these tools may be useful.

Take Responsibility   In contrast to denial, avoidance, and scapegoating, effective coping begins when you take responsibility for yourself and your family. Taking responsibility means not only that you will not deny or avoid the problem or blame others, but also that you will not play the victim game. That is, even though you may have been victimized by something or someone, you will not continue to act as a victim—hurt, oppressed, exploited, in pain, and helpless.

If the crisis is some kind of family disruption, such as death or divorce, taking responsibility means charting a new course as an alternative to playing the victim game. For example, Amy, a Mormon woman, felt victimized by her husband of twenty-four years when he abruptly told her he wanted a divorce. After her initial shock and grief, she decided to accept the responsibility for her own life:

> My first step was to resolve not to become a woman wrapped up in her past, clinging to it like a life raft. I wanted to be able to move beyond the hurt and pain and make something special out of my life. I began by taking a real-estate course and getting my license.

In some cases, taking responsibility may mean a willingness to disengage from your family. One of the ways that children of alcoholic parents avoid becoming problem drinkers themselves is to distance themselves to some extent from their families (Bennett et al. 1987). If the alcoholic family is unwilling to take responsibility as a group and con-

front the problem, then an individual member may escape the negative impact by disengaging. Similarly, an abused wife may find that the only way she can maintain her own well-being is to leave the abusive situation.

Affirm Your Own and Your Family's Worth
Crises assault people's self-esteem. This makes it more difficult to deal with the crisis. It is important to believe in yourself and in your ability to deal with difficult situations in order to be effective in a crisis. In a crisis, you may have to remind yourself that you and your family are people with strengths and the capacity to cope effectively.

A woman who stayed in an abusive relationship for years told us that one of her problems was her sense of being a worthless individual. The husband who abused her suggested that there was something about her that made him violent, something defective or deficient in her that made her deserve to be beaten. Her ability to deal with the critical situation began one day when she decided to stop viewing herself as somehow deserving the abuse. She had seen some information about abusive relationships and realized that she was a victim rather than a worthless person. She affirmed her own worth, which meant that being beaten was no longer tolerable. She left her husband and began a new life in another state.

Balance Self-Concern with Other-Concern   We have said that you must take responsibility for your own well-being. That doesn't mean to ignore the  well-being of others. The totally self-focused life is as self-destructive as the totally other-focused life. Someone who stays in an abusive relationship because "my spouse needs me" may be too other-focused. Still, someone who leaves a spouse simply because "I want my space so I can grow" may be too self-focused.

A crisis tends not only to attack our self-esteem but also to throw us into self-absorption. Some people get so enmeshed in the crisis that they seem to neither listen to nor care about others in the family. If all family members become self-absorbed, the situation can become hazardous to both marital and familial well-being. Each may *perceive inequity,*

Exchange Theory Applied

for each may be expecting the others to give support and, finding none, may feel abandoned by the family—a sense of "I've put a lot into this family and now, when I need help, I'm getting nothing in return." Dealing effectively with a crisis requires a healthy amount of both self-concern and other-concern on the part of at least some, and ideally all, family members.

In a study of families in which a child had died of cancer two to nine years earlier, the researchers found that families that handled the crisis best were those in which the individual family members were aware of the grieving of other members and made efforts to empathize and support them (Davies et al. 1986). Families with a poorer adjustment, on the other hand, tended to have members who focused on their own personal grief without relating that grief to other family members:

> It seemed as if each person was carrying the burden of grief all alone and there seemed to be a lack of empathy for how the other members were doing (Davies et al. 1986:302).

In some cases, even when the researchers asked people about how others in the family were doing, the person would respond in terms of his or her personal feelings. For example, when a father was asked about how his wife and daughter were dealing with the situation, he said he didn't know what to do about them. Rather than indicating an understanding of their feelings, he simply talked about his own sense of helplessness. In families that dealt more effectively with the loss, members knew and talked spontaneously about each other as well as about themselves.

Learn the Art of Reframing   Reframing, or redefining the meaning of something, is a way of changing your perspective on a situation. It isn't the situation that is changed but the way that you look at it. In essence, you learn to look at something that you had defined as troublesome and redefine it as adaptive and useful. The technique can help you overcome a variety of problems (Easley and Epstein 1991).

Reframing is not denial. It is based on the fact that people can look at any situation in various ways. You can see a crisis as an intruder that has robbed you of a measure of peace and happiness, or

you can define the crisis as an obstacle that will ultimately lead to your growth as you overcome it.

Celia, an undergraduate student, had a crisis situation in her family when she was still in high school. Her father had begun to drink heavily. He was having problems at his work. The drinking, of course, only exacerbated the problems and put his job in jeopardy. Celia was preparing to go to college and feared that she could not go if her father lost his job. Then one day her mother sat down with her and helped her reframe the situation:

> "This may mean that you won't go to college when you thought," her mother said. "But it doesn't mean you won't go. At the most, it means you will have to wait for a year or so. But you *will* go. Furthermore, I want you to see this for what it is. It isn't a disaster. In fact, it may be the best lesson you ever learn, in school or out of school. Your father picked the wrong way to deal with the problem. But if we just condemn him, we will also pick the wrong way to deal with it. He needs us to help him now. We're going to do that."

Celia, as the oldest child, worked with her mother to firmly help her father cut back on his drinking. They gave him extra attention and support. Eventually, his work stress eased, and the family made it through the crisis. Celia went to college as she had planned. In good part, it was her mother's reframing of the situation that made the difference.

Find and Use Available Resources   Every family has numerous internal and external resources to which it can turn in a time of crisis. Family members themselves are internal resources. That is, family members can be a source of emotional support for each other. Most of the respondents in one study reported that a child's cancer had strengthened the cohesion of the family and that spouses were the most important source of support (Barbarin, Hughes, and Chesler 1985). Internal resources also include all of the family strengths we identified earlier. Recall that one of the strengths was open communication of both beliefs and feelings. Another characteristic of those families that handled the crisis well in which a child had died of cancer was openness,

> free discussion about the deceased child, his illness, death, and the family's responses since the time of the death (Davies et al. 1986:302).

PERSONAL
"Things Were Terribly Still"

Kim is in her early twenties. She has been married for five years. Phil, her husband, works as an electronics engineer. Their daughter was four years old when Kim got pregnant again. Kim and Phil were very happy. Both wanted a large family. However, the "blessed event" turned into a crisis for them, a crisis for which they needed some outside help:

I was so happy when I got pregnant that I prepared a nursery in rainbow colors for the baby. Phil and I were really excited as the due date approached. He loved to put his hand on my stomach and feel the baby moving. He wanted a boy so he could go fishing with him. And our daughter looked forward to a baby brother or sister.

A few weeks before the baby was due, I felt sick to my stomach. The doctor thought I had a virus and needed to get more rest. But a few days later, I suddenly realized that things were terribly still inside me. I went to the doctor immediately. She decided to induce labor. Phil was with me when I delivered a still-born baby boy. An autopsy showed that our son had a chromosomal disorder.

We were devastated. We spent forty-five minutes with our son, holding and touching him. We said goodbye to him, and the nurse asked if we wanted her to take a picture. We said no, but I regret it now. It would mean a lot to me to have a picture of that child.

I left the hospital the next morning. Phil got a week off from work. Our son's name was to be Bradley. We had him cremated and held a memorial service at the beach. We scattered his ashes in the Pacific Ocean.

The first week, we spent most of our time talking and crying about it. When Phil went back to work, he tried to act macho about it all. He told everyone that we were fine and that everything was going to be all right. But I was upset all the time. I began to feel depressed and guilty. We went for genetic tests. But we are not at high risk for genetic defects. Phil didn't want to talk about it any more. He reminded me that we could have more children.

Phil and I were really close before Bradley's death. Even right afterward. But as time went on, we grew apart. We couldn't seem to communicate. And we didn't have much sex. I spent most of my time with our daughter, and Phil spent more time at work and watching television.

We talked about another child, but I don't think either of us wanted to take the risk. I talked about it with my doctor one day, and she suggested that before we try to have another child we should attend Healing Hearts, a self-help group for people who have had a child die. Phil refused to go at first. He told me to go, that he was fine and didn't need it. So I went alone. It helped me a lot. I kept asking Phil and he finally agreed to go. Toward the end of his first meeting, he broke down and cried for several minutes. He finally began to open up and talk about how he really felt.

It's been five months now since Bradley died. We still go to Healing Hearts. We're also working on our relationship with each other. We're beginning to feel intimate with each other again. Some day we will try to have another child. We're still scared, but we're working at it. We're a lot more mature, and I think we have a new kind of respect for each other.

For many families, religious beliefs are an important resource (Weigel and Weigel 1987). Religious beliefs can be a basis for reframing crises. Religious beliefs also provide family members with hope for an acceptable outcome and with strength for enduring the trauma until the crisis is resolved.

External resources include such things as the extended family, friends, books, self-help groups, and therapists. There are resources in all large communities that are designed to help people through crises of every kind.

Using the available resources along with other coping strategies we have discussed can enable a family to emerge from a crisis at a higher level of functioning than it had before the crisis. Indeed, the very meaning of effective coping is that the individual will achieve a new level of maturity and that the family will attain a new level of intimacy.

PRINCIPLES FOR ENHANCING INTIMACY

1. When you or your family are undergoing major stress, avoid deliberately adding on other sources of pressure. Multiple stresses can be a lethal combination that can threaten any individual or intimate relationship. If you should lose your job, for example, it is probably a bad time to buy a new car or go on a diet. Or if your marriage is undergoing difficulties of one sort or another, it is not a good time to make a major career change or decide to have a baby.

2. Keep your economic house in order. Financial difficulties are a continuing source of stress throughout the family life cycle. By maintaining realistic expectations, careful budgeting, and avoiding the excessive use of credit, families can reduce financial strains and enhance their well-being and stability.

3. Alcohol abuse is difficult to cope with alone. If you are an abuser, organizations like AA can provide needed assistance. If someone in your family abuses alcohol, you also can benefit from a support group like Al-Anon.

4. Family violence—whatever its form and whoever its victim—results in serious physical and emotional damage. If the damage is to be minimized, family violence must be acknowledged and then dealt with as quickly and effectively as possible. It is not possible to have true intimacy in the context of violence.

5. Remember that you can cope with a crisis in your family. Even the most difficult situation offers the possibility of long-term, positive consequences. Indeed, by using effective coping strategies, you can transform the crisis into an opportunity for personal growth and enhanced intimacy.

SUMMARY

Family crises are associated with various kinds of stressful events and/or behavior. A family in crisis is not necessarily a sick family but may be a family overwhelmed by a stressor or piled-up stressors in accord with the ABCX and Double ABCX models. Some of the common stressor events are death, serious illness, accidents, loss of work, an unwanted pregnancy, moving, alcohol abuse, and interpersonal problems, such as abuse and infidelity.

The kinds of stressors people face vary over the family life cycle. The highest amount of stress tends to occur during the time when the family is in the transition from having children in the home to the empty nest. Not all stressors are equally severe; rather, they range in severity from such highly stressful events as a death in the family to the mildly stressful event of a major purchase.

Alcohol abuse ranks high on the list of family stressors. About one in five Americans who drinks daily or nearly every day has alcohol-associated problems in the family. Some families function fairly normally when the abuser is not drinking. But

during the times of heavy drinking, the character of family life is likely to change and may even become violent. When the abuse is long-term, negative consequences tend to result whether or not the abuser is drinking. The family life of a long-term abuser tends to be filled with tension, dissatisfaction, and frequent conflict. Spouses and children of abusers may develop various physical and emotional problems.

Family problems can contribute to, as well as result from, alcohol abuse. In this way, the family can get caught in a vicious circle. In fact, the abuse may take its toll across a number of generations.

Next to death, separation, and divorce, family violence is the most difficult experience people confront. Millions of American adults and children endure violence in their homes. A substantial proportion of abused children are five years old or younger, with females slightly more likely than males to be abused. The typical abusive parent is single, is young (around thirty or under), has been married for less than ten years, had his or her first child before the age of eighteen, and is unemployed or employed part-time. Abusers tend to have low self-esteem, to have many stressors in their lives, and to have been victims of abuse themselves. Women are slightly more likely to abuse children than are men. Child abuse is proportionately higher among African Americans and Hispanics than whites.

Incest is a form of abuse more likely to happen to girls than boys. Incest usually begins when the child is between six and eleven and lasts around two years on the average. Father-daughter incest is the most common form, tending to occur in families where the marital relationship has broken down and the father has many stressors and a problem relating meaningfully and sexually with an adult.

Spouse abuse may involve either husband or wife being the victim, but the damage is likely to be more severe for abused wives. The typical wife-beater tends to be young (between eighteen and twenty-four years); be unemployed or employed part-time; have lower levels of education; live at the poverty level; worry about finances; be dissatisfied with life; be married less than ten years; have been physically punished as a child; be insecure and jealous and have frequent conflict with his wife; and abuse alcohol or other drugs. Various values and attitudes can lead a woman to remain in an abusive relationship in spite of the physical and emotional damage she suffers.

Parent abuse also occurs. There is a certain amount of abuse by adolescent children, particularly of fathers. There is also some abuse of elderly parents by their adult children.

Abuse results in short-term physical and emotional damage. It also tends to have serious long-term consequences. Victims may have to undergo therapy to work through their trauma. Viewing abuse as well as enduring it can perpetuate violence in family life.

People react to crises in different ways. We cannot control the events that occur in our lives, but we can control the way we respond to them. Ineffective coping patterns are ways of response that leave people at a lower level of functioning after a crisis. Denial, avoidance, and scapegoating are ineffective coping patterns. Effective coping is facilitated by developing family strengths. It involves such things as taking responsibility, affirming individual and family worth, balancing self-concern with other-concern, learning the art of reframing, and finding and using available resources.

INTERNET CONNECTION
Family Crisis

As society becomes increasingly complex, and economic as well as personal challenges grow, so does the potential for stress and crisis. Increases in poverty lead to increased levels of drug abuse, violence, and sexual abuse which all dramatically impact the way people cope in families. How will you be better able to address issues of violence or abuse your friends or family encounter after examining the websites below?

The National Coalition Against Domestic Violence
http://www.ncadv.org/

(NCADV) is dedicated to the empowerment of battered women and their children and to the elimination of personal and societal violence in the lives of women and their children.

Men and Domestic Violence Index
http://www.vix.com/pub/men/domestic-index.html

An online resource for abused men, as well as selected web references to statistics and issues concerning husband abuse.

www.mhhe
.com/lauer4

Violence at Home
http://www.sacbee.com/news/projects/violence/index.html

This website chronicles articles on the issue of domestic violence in the *Sacramento Bee,* which focused on the issue for one year. Statistical resources, police logs, and other additional material is included at the site.

1. How does the view of the family violence issue portrayed at the NCADV site differ from the perspectives offered at the Men and Domestic Violence index?
2. What are some of the myths about domestic violence? Realities? How can we use these websites to deal with these myths and realities?
3. Describe the forms of family abuse portrayed in articles at the Violence at Home website. How do these articles change your view on who can be victims of domestic violence?

SEPARATION AND DIVORCE

Learning Objectives

After reading chapter 18, you should be able to:

1. Relate the trends in the rate of and grounds for divorce in American society.
2. Explain the four periods in marital dissolution.
3. Identify the six "stations" that people often experience when they divorce.
4. Discuss the sociodemographic factors that contribute to the failure of a marriage.
5. Summarize the interpersonal factors that lead to divorce.
6. Describe the positive and negative effects of divorce for adults.
7. Discuss the impact of divorce on children.
8. Contrast and compare the differing reaction of boys and girls to the divorce of their parents.
9. Review the prevailing pattern of custody arrangements and show how it has changed over time.
10. Identify the ways in which parents and children can best cope with divorce.

Is divorce ever good for you? Is it ever good for children? In the short run, the answer to both questions is "no" for most people. In the long run, the answer varies. In other words, neither question has a simple answer.

For example, consider one student's account of her parents' divorce:

> My most painful experience when I was growing up was when my parents got a divorce. My greatest pain wasn't the actual breakup. That was the best thing to happen. They had always fought. And so getting a divorce made all of our lives easier. The pain I experienced was deciding whom to live with.

Another undergraduate told us that the stress in her life was dramatically reduced when her parents divorced and, as a result, the quality of her life greatly improved. But others talk about the pain, the loss, the emptiness. Disrupting an intimate relationship is never easy, even when the relationship is defined as a destructive one (recall that people tend to stay in abusive relationships for long periods of time).

In this chapter, we will look closely at what has become a common experience for Americans: the disruption of an intimate relationship through separation and/or divorce. We will examine first the trends in divorce. Then we will discuss the process of "uncoupling." We will talk about some of the causes and correlates of divorce, the effects on spouses, parents, and children, and, finally, how people work through the issues raised by the disruption.

DIVORCE TRENDS

Should a divorce be easier or more difficult to obtain? Nearly half of Americans who were asked that question in a national poll said that a divorce should be more difficult to secure.[1] Twenty-two percent said it should stay as it is, and another 22 percent said it should be easier to obtain.

A great many Americans are concerned today about the numbers of people divorcing and about the relative ease with which people dissolve their marriages. To be sure, both the numbers and the relative ease are in contrast with the past, though, as we shall see in the following discussion, they are not inconsistent with long-term trends.

Divorce Rates

Since 1860, the number of divorces per one thousand population has generally increased. However, the rate rose significantly during World War II, peaked at the conclusion of the war (1945–1947), and then began to decline. The rate remained fairly stable during the 1950s and early 1960s, then increased rapidly again after 1965 (figure 18.1). By the mid-1970s, the United States had the highest divorce rate in the Western world. In 1974, for the first time in our history, more marriages ended through divorce than through death of a spouse.

Although many people believe that the high rates of the 1970s represented a striking break with tradition, Andrew Cherlin (1981:25) pointed out that there has been a fairly regular trend over the past century or so, a trend represented by a rising curve. There are variations, of course: Those who married during the 1950s have lower-than-expected rates of

---

[1]Reported in *The American Enterprise,* July/August 1995, p. 103.

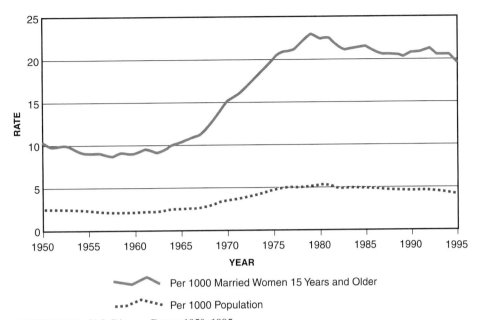

FIGURE 18.1   U.S. Divorce Rates: 1950–1995
(*Sources:* U.S. Bureau of the Census 1975:64; 1994:104; 1997b:105.)

TABLE 18.1
Divorces: 1950 to 1995

Divorces	1950	1955	1960	1965	1970	1975	1980	1985	1990	1995
Total (1,000)	385	377	393	479	708	1026	1189	1190	1182	1169
Rate per 1,000 population	2.6	2.3	2.2	2.5	3.5	4.8	5.2	5.0	4.7	4.4
Rate per 1,000 married women, 15 yrs and over	10.3	9.3	9.2	10.6	14.9	20.3	22.6	21.7	20.9	19.8
Percent divorced, 18 yrs and over:										
Male	1.8	1.9	2.0	2.5	2.5	3.7	5.2	7.6	7.2	8.0
Female	2.3	2.4	2.9	3.3	3.9	5.3	7.1	10.1	9.3	10.3

Source: U.S. Bureau of the Census 1980:81; 1989:41; 1997b:55, 105.

divorce, while those who married during the 1960s and 1970s have higher-than-expected rates (where "expected" means the rate we would have according to the long-term trend line). However, the high rates of the 1970s are modest rather than dramatic deviations from the long-term trend.

After 1981, the rates tended to decline. By 1995, they had gone down to 4.4 per one thousand people (table 18.1), a number lower than any since the early 1970s. Of course, the figures for a particular year do not tell us how many people have ever been separated or divorced. Some of those who are reported as divorced in a particular year will be married in an-

other year and vice versa. Overall, marriages ending in divorce last an average of 9.8 years, and the likelihood of new marriages ending in divorce was 43 percent as of 1988 (National Center for Health Statistics 1998). Divorce rates have declined since 1988, and if they continue to decline, of course, your chances of breakup will also decline.

Changing Grounds for Divorce

For what legal reasons can you attain a divorce? State rather than federal laws answer that question. In the past, the states provided many different answers. For example, in the nineteenth century, South Carolina did not allow divorce at all, while New York allowed it only on the grounds of adultery (Degler 1980:167). Some states permitted more lenient grounds than others. As a result, people often established temporary residency in order to make use of a state's more liberal divorce laws. At one time or another, Pennsylvania, Ohio, South Dakota, North Dakota, and Nevada, among others, made it relatively easy for people to establish residency and obtain a divorce (Day and Hook 1987). However, only middle- and upper-class people could typically afford to pursue a divorce under such conditions.

In response to the increase in divorces, states have changed divorce laws. The changes reflect a different perspective on divorce—that it is essentially an individual rather than a government-controlled decision. Because it is viewed as an individual decision, states have abandoned the adversarial approach to divorce, an approach that assumes one of the spouses is at fault. In the past, "fault" could have been such things as adultery, insanity, imprisonment, or cruelty. In any case, the plaintiff had to provide evidence to show that the partner was at fault. When both spouses wanted the divorce, they might agree to lie or present false evidence in order to comply with the law.

In the 1970s, California and New York began the trend toward no-fault divorce, which is now practiced in all states. In no-fault divorce, no proof for divorce is needed. Neither spouse accuses the other of impropriety or immorality. Rather, the marriage is deemed to be unworkable and therefore is dissolved. Some states allow either spouse to initiate the divorce unilaterally, while others require mutual consent.

The purpose of no-fault divorce laws was to remove some of the acrimony and pain from the process. In many cases, they have achieved that aim. However, the laws have generated controversy and opposition (Gallagher and Whitehead 1997). Opponents point out that they make divorce easier to obtain at a time when there is a need to save marriages rather than foster divorce. Moreover, no-fault laws empower the spouse who wishes to leave but make the other spouse relatively helpless; some people, therefore, advocate a five-year waiting period when the no-fault divorce is contested by one of the spouses.

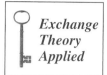

Exchange Theory Applied

On the other hand, proponents argue that the laws not only remove acrimony but also *make divorce a more equitable process,* and Americans strongly believe in *equity.* The process is more equitable because settlements are not to be made on the basis of someone having been wronged but on the basis of need. The settlement does not presume that the man should continue to support the woman nor that the woman should assume total care of any children. As we shall see, this aspect of the law has turned out to be detrimental for women, who have suffered economically under the no-fault system.

THE PROCESS OF UNCOUPLING

What happens in a family that is in the process of breaking up? What stages bring an intimate relationship to the point of disruption? What is the meaning of the disruption? Researchers have identified a number of features in the process that are common to most divorcing couples.

Typically, divorce is an emotionally devastating experience.

Toward Marital Dissolution

While few if any of those who "fall in love" expect to fall out of it, many do. They may experience disaffection, which is:

> the gradual loss of emotional attachment, including a decline in caring about the partner, an emotional estrangement, and an increasing sense of apathy and indifference toward one's spouse (Kayser 1993:6).

Dissolution may follow such disaffection. Not all disaffected people divorce, and not all divorces involve disaffection. When people do divorce, for whatever reason, four phases tend to mark the process: recognition, discussion, action, and post-dissolution (Ponzetti and Cate 1986).

Recognition   Recognition begins when one or both spouses become aware of serious problems. A spouse may feel discontent or dissatisfaction and realize that the feeling is sufficiently strong to call the relationship into question. Frequently, recognition occurs when marital stress and open conflict are followed by a period of cold war between the spouses.

However, the period of recognition may occur very early. In her interviews with disaffected people who divorced, Kayser (1993:29) concluded that "the ink is barely dry on the marriage license when doubts and disillusionment about marriage and the partner can begin to set in." Forty percent of her respondents said that doubts occurred within the first six months, and 60 percent had doubts within the first year.

What caused such doubts? The most frequent causes given by Kayser's respondents were the spouse's controlling behavior, lack of responsibility, and lack of emotional support. Controlling behavior involves such things as making decisions without consulting the spouse or taking into account the spouse's opinion. Lack of responsibility refers to such things as driving while drunk, getting fired from a job for just cause, spending excessive amounts of time with friends, and leaving children unattended. Lack of emotional support involves behavior that suggests a lack of concern and care for the spouse, particularly during such stressful times as pregnancy, childbirth, or death of a family member.

These early doubts intensified when the troubling behavior continued, leading to anger, hurt, and disillusionment. The offended spouse became

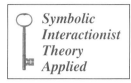 *Symbolic Interactionist Theory Applied*

deeply aware of his or her partner's flaws and recognized that the marriage had taken an unexpected and undesirable turn. In some cases, the offended spouse believed that the partner had changed after the marriage. What had mainly changed, Kayser (1993:33) notes, was not the partner "but the *respondent's perception*" of his or her partner. The changed perception led to a definition of the marriage as moving in a very different direction than expected, and than could be tolerated.

Discussion   Discussion is the period at which one or both spouses begin to share the marital problems with others—friends, relatives, a counselor, and often the spouse. The discussion is not merely a sharing of information but an opportunity to redefine the relationship. The partner may be defined in negative terms, and the history of the relationship may be reconstructed as a series of negative experiences. Gratifying experiences also may be redefined: "Yes, we had a good time on that trip but that was only because we were with friends."

Discussion with the partner involves the breaking down of the pretense that all is well with the marriage. The initiator, the partner who first feels but doesn't openly acknowledge discontent, finally discloses that discontent and does so with sufficient force and clarity that the partner cannot deny the fact that the marriage is in serious trouble. With such a confrontation, conflict increases significantly in the discussion period (Ponzetti and Cate 1986). One of the functions of such conflict is to maintain the relationship for a time. Conflict at least means that there is interaction. But the conflict also serves to underscore that there are problems in the relationship.

During the discussion period, the discontented spouse will find a "transitional person," someone who can help him or her to move from the old life to a new one. The transitional person may be a temporary lover but may also be a friend who can provide emotional support. The problem with the relationship has now become a public matter.

Some effort may be made to save the marriage during this period. Once the confrontation has taken place and the problem is openly acknowledged, the noninitiating partner may ask for an opportunity to try to save the relationship. The initiator feels that he or she has already tried but may be willing to give the partner a chance to try also. Yet in many cases, the odds are against any change for the better. The initiator has been making the transition to a new life for a period of time. The initiator is already a somewhat different person, with a new ideology, perhaps new friends, and new commitments. Many initiators tell their partners during this period, "You don't know me anymore." If the initiator has gone far enough in the process of transition to a new life, he or she may allow the partner to try to save the relationship but will not allow the partner to succeed. Letting the noninitiating partner try but fail can be a way of getting him or her to agree that the intimate bond has been severed irreparably.

Action   In the period of action, one of the spouses secures a lawyer in order to legally dissolve the marriage. Many are already preparing for independence by such things as paying their own bills and not relying on their partner for emotional support or companionship (Kayser 1993). Separation also is likely in this period and may occur before or after a lawyer is consulted. The amount of time involved can vary considerably. A study of 199 California women reported that they took from sixty-five days or less to as much as several years to move from the decision to end their marriage to actually separate and file a petition for divorce (Melichar and Chiriboga 1985). The women who moved very quickly tended to be a few years older (mean age 36.5 years) than the others, to have married at a later age, and to have somewhat less education than those who moved more slowly through the process.

Separation, of course, does not always lead to divorce. An estimated one of every six couples separates for at least two days at some time in their relationship (Kitson 1985). The separation can be a cooling-off period that allows couples to deal more rationally with their differences and effect a reconciliation. Other couples get involved in a long-term, unresolved separation; nonwhites and those with lower incomes are more likely to fall into this category (Morgan 1988).

Difficulties mount once a lawyer is secured and the divorce petition is filed. At this point in the process, couples frequently struggle over such things as division of property and child custody. Moreover, they often are anxious about the separation and have lingering uncertainties about whether dissolution is really in their best interests.

This period can also last much longer than people anticipate if there are disagreements about the settlement. For example, community property laws do not make financial settlements an automatic matter. Thus, there can be considerable wrangling over the division of property and intense bitterness about the outcome.

Postdissolution   The postdissolution period begins when both spouses accept the fact that the marriage has ended. During this period, the spouses probably will think about reasons for the divorce and construct some acceptable rationale for what has happened. Many people do not accept completely the fact that the marriage has ended until the former spouse is coupled with a new partner.

The Six Stations of Divorce

Paul Bohannan (1970) discussed divorce in terms of six "stations" or six different experiences that people are likely to have. Marriage, he pointed out, makes us feel good in part because, out of all those available, we have been selected by someone to be an intimate partner. Divorce, by contrast, makes you feel "so awful," in part, because "you have been de-selected" (Bohannan 1970:33). To some extent, deselection occurs in each of the six different stations of divorce.

The *emotional* divorce involves a loss of trust, respect, and affection for each other. Rather than supporting each other, the spouses act in ways to hurt, to frustrate, to lower self-esteem. The spouses grate on each other. Each is visible evidence to the other of failure and rejection.

The *legal* divorce, in which a court officially brings the marriage to an end, is the only one of the six stations that provides a tangible benefit to the partners: relief from the legal responsibilities of the marriage and the right to remarry. The legal divorce can also help partners to feel free of other kinds of obligations, such as that of caring for a sick partner. Legal divorce may follow a period of separation, but increasingly couples opt directly for divorce rather than a trial separation.

The *economic* divorce involves settlement of the property. The division of property is rarely an easy matter. Actually, economic settlements were easier under the adversary system, where one of the parties was at fault and therefore "owed" the other compensation. The economic divorce is likely to be painful for at least three reasons. First, there are never enough assets for each partner to feel that he or she is getting all that is needed to continue living at a comfortable level. Second, there can be considerable acrimony over who gets what—the condo, silver, favorite painting, and so forth. And third, there is likely to be a sense of loss as each partner realizes that he or she must live in the future without some familiar and cherished possessions.

The *co-parental* divorce is experienced by those with children—about two-thirds of all couples. Decisions must be made about who will have custody, visitation rights, and continuing responsibilities of each parent. This is perhaps the most tragic part of the divorce (see the discussion on the consequences of divorce for children later in the chapter), particularly when the parents use their children as weapons against each other or even fail to protect them from the conflict and bitterness of the struggle.

The *community* divorce means that each of the partners leaves one community of friends and relations and enters another. A newly divorced person may feel uncomfortable with some of the friends he or she shared with the former spouse, especially if there is a feeling that the friends were more sympathetic with the former spouse. Relationships with former in-laws may cease or become minimal and strained. The process of changing from one community of relationships to another is likely to be difficult and frequently leaves the individual feeling lonely and isolated for a period of time.

Finally, the *psychic* divorce is the central separation that occurs—the individual must accept the disruption of the relationship and regain a sense of being an individual rather than a part of an intimate couple. Eventually, as the healing process takes place, the individual will begin to feel whole again. But he or she can only feel whole to the extent that the psychic divorce is final; that is, to the extent that there is a distancing from both the positive and negative aspects of the broken relationship.

CAUSES AND CORRELATES OF DIVORCE

In recent decades, the proportion of people who say their marriage is "very happy" declined somewhat (Glenn 1991). That decline occurred in the context of high rates of divorce. Compared to the past, then, fewer marriages brought high levels of satisfaction and more broke up. What factors make it more or less likely that someday you may be involved in a divorce?

Sociodemographic Factors

If a couple files for divorce, you might wonder what the spouses did to bring about the breakup. Social scientists have found that it is not just what people do that helps account for the failure of a marriage, but such things as their socioeconomic status, race, religion, and other sociodemographic factors also play a role.

Socioeconomic Status An inverse relationship exists between socioeconomic status and divorce rates. That is, the higher your status, the less likely you are to divorce. Higher status, of course, means higher income and vice versa. Thus, when the wife works but has a low income, or when the wife is not working and the husband has a low income, the chances of marital disruption are higher (Ono 1998). Undoubtedly, the financial pressures on those in lower income brackets add to the instability of their marriages. The pressures are so severe, in fact, that couples with children who live below the poverty line are nearly twice as likely as those above the poverty line to divorce within two years (Hernandez 1993).

Age at Marriage In earlier chapters, we pointed out that one's age at marriage is related to marital stability. The younger you are when you marry, the greater are your chances of divorce, particularly during the first five years of marriage (Booth et al. 1986; Bumpass, Castro-Martin, and Sweet 1991; Amato and Rogers 1997). In part, younger age at marriage is associated with higher rates of breakup because early marriage is detrimental to high educational attainment (South 1995). And that, of course, means lower income levels are likely. The effects of age are not the same for all races, however. Whites

INVOLVEMENT
Divorce Court

Attend a local divorce court for a day. Write down your observations of what is happening. Note the expressions on the faces of the couples, lawyers, and judge. To what extent can you sense the trauma of divorce from the proceedings of the court? Note the outcomes of the various cases. What are the similarities and differences? If possible, see if you can obtain court records from a time when divorce was an adversarial process. Compare some of the proceedings with those you have observed. What differences are there? Which system do you think works best?

Finally, find someone who has recently been through a divorce. Discuss that person's recollections of the court proceedings. How did the person feel during the court session? How does the person feel about the legal aspects of divorce generally? How would that person change the legal system to make divorce more equitable or less painful for people? Do you agree or dis-agree with the divorced person's position? Why?

If divorce court proceedings in your locale are not available, an alternative option would be to write the history of a divorce you are familiar with. It might be the divorce of your parents or another relative, a friend, or even your own. The four periods—recognition, discussion, action, and postdissolution—of divorce may provide a useful device for organizing your account.

who marry after age twenty-six have more stable unions, but African Americans and Hispanics who wait to marry until after age twenty-six are more likely than those who marry earlier to divorce (Heaton 1991). Unfortunately, we do not know the reason for these racial differences.

Race   African Americans are more likely both to separate and to divorce than are whites. In fact, African Americans have higher rates than any other racial group in the United States (Glenn and Supancic 1984). The greatest differences between African Americans and others occur in the lower socioeconomic levels, but they exist at all levels. Some scholars have suggested that because of their experience of low income, job instability, and high unemployment rates, African Americans have learned to depend less on marriage and more on the extended kin network for support (Cherlin 1981:108). This may have established a cultural tradition in which marriage is less central and in which there is thus less commitment to the marital relationship. An alternative explanation is that African Americans still have to deal with overt and covert discrimination and rejection, leading them to be more likely to have a pile-up of stressor events in their lives. The pile-up, in turn, places greater strains on their marriages than on those of other races.

Social Integration   **Social integration** is a state of relative harmony and cohesion in a group. People who are members of an integrated group have an important source of support, a buffer against stress. We would expect, then, that social integration would help to minimize the divorce rates. Evidence exists to support that conclusion.

Religious groups provide one source of social integration. In addition, religion places great value on the family. It is reasonable to expect, therefore, that the more religious people are, the less likely they are to divorce. Indeed, people who are members of churches and who attend services are less likely to divorce than are nonmembers (Breault and Kposowa 1987; Krishnan 1994; Amato and Rogers 1997). Moreover, there are striking differences in the rates of divorce and separation among people depending on their frequency of attendance at religious services (figure 18.2). Differences also exist between various denominations. Jewish couples are least likely to divorce. Protestants have the highest rates. And among Protestants, the rates of the more conservative groups, such as Pentecostals and Baptists, tend to be higher than those of the more liberal groups, such as Presbyterians and Episcopalians (Glenn and Supancic 1984:567).

The variations among denominations reflect, to some extent, socioeconomic differences. Episcopalians and Presbyterians tend to have a higher-status

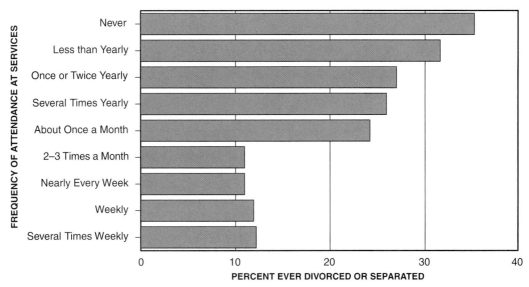

FIGURE 18.2 Divorce and Religious Activity
(*Source:* Data from N. D. Glenn and M. Supancic, *Journal of Marriage and the Family,* 46:567, 1984.)

Religious people are less likely to have their marriages end in divorce.

membership than do Pentecostals and Baptists. But the rates of divorce among the conservative groups are still substantially lower than among those with no religion at all.

Social integration occurs in more than religious groups, of course. Using data from a national survey, three researchers found that "normative integration" (measured by the number of nondivorced people who are significant to the individual) is as-

sociated with lower divorce rates and that "communicative integration" (measured by the number of friends and organizational memberships the individual has) is associated with a slightly lower divorce rate among those married seven years or less (Booth, Edwards, and Johnson 1991).

Children can also be an integrating factor. Marital stability tends to grow with increasing family size up to the third child but declines when family size is five or more children (Heaton 1990). Perhaps the strains of a large number of children outweigh the tendency for children to integrate a family. The integrating power of children may also vary by their gender. Using national data, Katzev, Warner, and Acock (1994) found that mothers with at least one son reported a significantly lower propensity to divorce than mothers who only had girls.

If social integration tends to minimize divorce, the lack of integration should be associated with higher rates of divorce. It is not surprising, then, that childless couples are more prone to divorce (Weinberg 1990). People also get into a situation with less integration when they move to a new community. There they are likely to be cut off from friends and family and may not become an integral part of religious or other community organizations for some time. Thus, there is an association between residential mobility and divorce rates (Shelton 1987). In regions of the nation where there is a high rate of residential movement, such as the West, there are higher rates of divorce (Glenn and Shelton 1985). And it is probably this same phenomenon—the higher rate of mobility and lower likelihood of integration—that accounts for higher rates of divorce in urban areas (Breault and Kposowa 1987).

Changing Norms and Roles   Divorce has become more acceptable over time. And it has become more acceptable even in nations such as Japan where, until recent years, divorced persons were stigmatized (Sakurai 1997). In the context of a long tradition of self-sacrifice and family stability, the Japanese are now divorcing in increasing numbers (see COMPARISON).

In the United States, we have a "divorce culture" that is rooted in our individualism and insistence on personal happiness (Whitehead 1997). Individual happiness takes priority over couple well-being. In a national survey, nearly half the respondents agreed that divorce is usually the best solution when couples can't seem to work out their problems. In addition, over two-thirds disagreed with the idea that people who don't get along should stay in a marriage for the sake of the children (Jacques 1998). Because Americans marry in order to be happy, they opt for divorce and look for happiness in a new relationship if their present marriage does not fulfill their expectations. Earlier in our history, a successful marriage was one that lasted and produced offspring. Now, a successful marriage is one that facilitates the happiness and well-being of both partners.

In addition, the changing roles of women are associated with higher divorce rates. Women are more likely than men to initiate divorce, and they do so in England, Wales, and Canada as well as in the United States (Buckle, Gallup, and Rodd 1996). Both the higher rates and the tendency of women to initiate divorce are associated with the increasing economic independence of women. An analysis of national data found that those couples in which wives earned between half and three-fourths of the household income were significantly more likely to separate or divorce than were other couples (Heckert, Nowak, and Snyder 1998). The financial independence women gain by working allows those in unhappy marriages to free themselves. In addition,

women have varied ideologies about their roles, and only those with nontraditional gender ideologies show a positive relationship between number of work hours and divorce rate (Greenstein 1995).

One other way in which roles relate to marital breakup involves premarital sexual relations: Women who are sexually active before marriage have a considerably higher rate of divorce than those who are virgins (Kahn and London 1991). This may reflect differing norms about roles, the fact that

> women who continue to hold traditional attitudes about marriage are less likely than other women to consider both premarital sex and divorce as acceptable options for themselves (Kahn and London 1991:853).

Interpersonal Factors

These various sociodemographic factors are important, of course, because they have a bearing on the way that people interact. Ultimately, however, it is the interaction that leads to disruption. If we focus on the interaction itself, rather than on the sociodemographic variables that underlie the interaction, what do we find?

Complaints   In a review of nine studies of the reasons people give for their divorces, Kitson, Babri, and Roach (1985) found that eight mentioned extramarital sex. Since infidelity may grow out of, as well as cause, marital unhappiness, we can't be sure whether the infidelity was the last straw in a deteriorating relationship or the beginning of the deterioration. Four of the studies reported personality and financial problems as important; most of the rest of the complaints involved such interpersonal problems as the lack of communication, feeling unloved, too little family life, and conflict over roles.

A national survey reported that the top ten reasons Americans give for why they were divorced are communication problems, infidelity, constant conflict, emotional abuse, falling out of love, unsatisfactory sex, spouse had insufficient income, physical abuse, falling in love with someone else, and boredom (Patterson and Kim 1991:93). The reasons are listed in the order of the frequency with which people gave them (they could give as many reasons as they wanted), from 64 percent naming communi-

PERSPECTIVE
The Roaring Twenties and Divorce

Historians debate just how roaring the 1920s actually were. But from the perspective of many contemporary observers it was truly a revolutionary decade in the United States. This is the picture that Frederick Lewis Allen portrayed in his 1930s book, *Only Yesterday: An Informal History of the Nineteen-Twenties.* Allen described a "first-class revolt against the accepted American order" in the years following the First World War. The revolt, he said, was the product of a variety of influences—"post-war disillusion, the new status of women, the Freudian gospel, the automobile, prohibition, the sex and confession magazines, and the movies."

Although the revolt began among young people, it spread rapidly and affected the "manners and morals" of "men and women of every age in every part of the country." Nothing seemed sacred, as fashions, pastime activities, dating customs, and sexual behavior underwent a radical transformation. Allen wrote that:

There was an unmistakable and rapid trend away from the old American code toward a philosophy of sex relations and of marriage wholly new to the country: toward a feeling that the virtues of chastity and fidelity had been rated too highly.

As for the amount of outright infidelity among married couples, one is . . . without reliable data, the private relations of men and women being happily beyond the reach of the statistician. The divorce rate, however, continued its steady increase. . . . There was a corresponding decline in the amount of disgrace accompanying divorce. In the urban communities men and women who had been divorced were now socially accepted without question; indeed, there was often about the divorced person just enough of an air of unconventionality, just enough of a touch of scarlet, to be considered rather dashing and desirable. Many young women probably felt as did the New York girl who said, toward the end of the decade, that she was thinking of marrying Henry, although she didn't care very much for him, because even if they didn't get along she could get a divorce and "it would be much more exciting to be a divorcee than to be an old maid" (Frederick Lewis Allen, *Only Yesterday: An Informal History of the Nineteen-Twenties* [New York: Blue Ribbon Books, Inc., 1931], pp. 88, 103, 115–17).

cation problems to 22 percent citing boredom. Finally, another national survey added the problems of spending money foolishly, drinking or drug use or both, jealousy, and irritating habits to the common complaints already noted (Amato and Rogers 1997).

Conflict   Some marriages are characterized by intense conflict. The conflict is pervasive; the couple argues over nearly everything. About one-half of divorcing couples indicate that they had frequent and intense conflict (Kelly 1988:121). The conflict may involve both severe (infidelity) and trivial (who takes the garbage out) issues.

Few, if any, people are comfortable and happy living in a situation of continual conflict. The situation may be compounded by a lack of conflict management skills. That is, the partners may get into a vicious circle in which the inability to resolve early conflicts acceptably only exacerbates subsequent conflicts. Thus, a conflict that may begin over a trivial issue may be an opportunity to bring back a severe issue that is still unresolved.

Changed Feelings and Perspectives   Although many divorced couples had a great deal of conflict in their marriage, many did not. A fourth or more of couples who divorce report little or no conflict in the two years before they separate (Kelly 1988:121). The marital bond eroded from decay, not from war. The marriage ended because feelings changed—the couple no longer loved each other, no longer had respect for each other, or no longer enjoyed being together.

One of the possible reasons for the slow, nonconflicted erosion of a marriage is changed perspectives. We all change throughout our lives. Two people who begin a marriage with similar perspectives

COMPARISON
Divorce, Japanese Style

Divorce rates have tended to go up throughout the world and have risen faster in some countries than they have in the United States. In Japan, as in the United States, divorce rates soared in the second half of the 1960s. The number of divorces per year was double in 1996 what it was in 1970, and about one in three marriages now ends in divorce in Japan. A writer who interviewed divorced Japanese couples identified three causes: a greater acceptance of divorce in Japanese society, greater opportunities for women outside the home, and women's changing attitudes. In the selection below, the writer talks about the changing attitudes of women:

Women are no longer satisfied with being glorified housemaids and cooks. They want to live more rewarding lives now that they can expect to live longer ones. . . . Even more important, however, may be the changing character of these divorces. There has been a rapid increase in divorces among middle-aged couples and among couples with children. No longer are children the bond that keeps a marriage going. . . .

Another change in the character of divorce is relatively new: They are initiated by the wife. For a long time it was assumed that only the husband had the prerogative to make such a selfish demand. In the Edo period (1603–1868), a husband could easily get rid of his wife by handing her a letter of divorce called a *mikudarihan* (three and a half lines). Today, however, 60 percent of the divorce cases that are brought to the family courts come from wives. Japanese men, accustomed to being lord of the manor, are having difficulty adjusting to this new fact of life.

Socioeconomic change has not only changed the nature of divorce in Japan; it has created certain types of divorce that may be unique to this country. One of these is the nondivorce divorce, which happens to couples who have grown miles apart in heart and mind and yet continue to live under the same roof, appearing to be a normal married couple to the outside world but barely on speaking terms within their own home. . . .

If the husband's fear of social stigma has created the nondivorce, the wife's capacity for submission has created the retirement divorce. Mr. and Ms. B divorced when he was 57, she, 49. They had been married 28 years and had a son, 26, and a daughter, 24. Ms. B decided to get a divorce some 10 years before she finally carried it out. She waited so long because she wanted to see her children through college and felt that she should continue fulfilling her role as wife as long as her husband was working. . . . Once she had set a target date, Ms. B began to save money in small amounts. Since she would be the one asking for a divorce, she had no intention of demanding a settlement from her husband. Not that she wasn't entitled. Having sacrificed most of her life to this man, it would not be strange to demand at least half of his hefty retirement pay. But that wouldn't be honorable, she thought.

Yamashita Katsutoshi. Reprinted by permission.

may find themselves changing in ways that make them less compatible. Their perspectives diverge. They no longer enjoy doing the same things. They are no longer the same two people who were married, and unfortunately, neither likes very much the way that the other has changed.

For example, Marie and Don were married as teenagers. He was in engineering school, and she was preparing to be a teacher. A few years later, Don realized that he didn't like engineering. He was restless, and decided that having a child might make his life more meaningful. Although they had always talked about having a family, Marie was happy with her teaching and decided she didn't want children yet. She worked with children all day and felt that they fulfilled whatever maternal instincts she had. She began to wonder if she would ever want children of her own. Don resented Marie's changed perspective. In his restlessness, he quit his job and went back to school to study social work. Marie felt uncomfortable with his new aspirations. She resented the fact that he would probably work for less money than he got as an engineer. They agreed to a trial separation. Within six months, Marie filed for divorce. They never argued much. They simply watched each other change, and neither liked the changes of the other.

Emotional Problems One of the consequences of divorce is likely to be an increase in emotional problems. But not all problems are the result of the divorce. Some exist before and contribute to the deterioration of the relationship. Recall the *principle of circularity* in systems theory—for many things it is not a case of *a* causing *b*, but of *a* causing *b* causing more *a* causing more *b*, etc. Thus, emotional problems can cause a marriage to deteriorate and as the marriage grows troublesome the emotional problems intensify, causing the marriage to deteriorate even more.

Two researchers looked at a sample of men over a five-year period, dividing them into those who were married throughout, those divorced or separated at the beginning and still so at the end, and a third group who had a separation or divorce during the five years (Erbes and Hedderson 1984). They found that the men who were separated or divorced during the period had lower psychological well-being scores at the beginning of the study than did those who were married throughout. Of course, it is possible that marital problems were already contributing to the lower scores, but the separation or divorce itself did not seem to be a factor.

Additional studies also suggest that at least some divorces are the result of emotional problems in one or both of the spouses (Kitson, Babri, and Roach 1985:275). Furthermore, research indicates that people who have been divorced more than once also tend to show some signs of emotional disorder (Brody, Neubaum, and Forehand 1988:212).

EFFECTS OF DIVORCE ON SPOUSES/PARENTS

We began the chapter with the question, is divorce ever good for you? The answer, we suggested, is "yes" and "no." There will probably be short-term negative effects. There may be long-term positive effects. The intensity of the effects depends on such things as gender and whether the individual is the initiator or the one left. Generally, initiators are likely to be more positive about the divorce than the ones left, and females adjust better to a divorce than do males (Black et al. 1991; Diedrick 1991). Most studies focus on the negative consequences of divorce, but there are positive ones as well. We will look at the latter first.

Positive Outcomes

Buehler and Langenbrunner (1987) collected data from eighty people whose divorces had been finalized six to twelve months earlier. They asked their respondents to indicate which of 140 things they had experienced since their separation. Table 18.2 shows the most common experiences, those identified by at least 85 percent of the sample. Note that the five most common are all positive. Keep in mind that these were people who were still working through the aftermath of the divorce. Although troubled by anger, insecurity, and depression, they had some positive experiences as well.

In the longer run, most people will view the divorce as a positive turning point, perhaps even a necessary step in their own well-being. For instance, Heather, who runs an art gallery, believes

TABLE 18.2
Most Frequent Experiences of 80 Divorced Individuals

	Percentage Experiencing
I have felt worthwhile as a person.	96
I have experienced personal growth and maturity.	94
I have felt relieved.	92
I have felt closer to my children.	89
I have felt competent.	89
The cost of maintaining the household has been difficult.	87
I have felt angry toward my former spouse.	87
I have felt insecure.	86
My leisure activities have increased.	86
I have been depressed.	86
Household routines and daily patterns have changed.	85

From Cheryl Buehler and Mary Langenbrunner, "Divorce-Related stressors: Occurrence, Disruptiveness, and Area of Life Change" in *Journal of Divorce*, 11:35. Copyright © 1987 Haworth Press, Inc., New York, NY. Reprinted by permission.

that her divorce set her on the road to autonomy for the first time in her life (Lauer and Lauer 1988:129). She had not established her independence before getting married:

> I switched from parental control to marital control. At the age of thirty, I began to gain autonomy. At thirty-two, I rebelled. At forty, I finally became a person. I mean I finally became me, Heather, an independent human being.

She became that "independent human being" by leaving a marriage with a domineering man. She says that she feared being on her own and hesitated leaving him, but she "had to yank that safety net of marriage in order to realize that I can survive without it."

Not everyone is equally likely to have such a positive outcome. Veevers (1991) searched the literature to identify factors associated with divorce being a personality enhancing or growth experience. In summary, divorce is more likely to be positive for females, particularly those with a high level of education; those who are relatively young; those in a relatively short-lived marriage; those who define the divorce as normal rather than an abnormal failure; those with adequate income; and those holding to more nontraditional gender and marital roles. In addition, a positive outcome is more likely for those with good social support (Garvin, Kalter, and Hansell 1993).

Health Problems

Not all outcomes are positive, even in the long run. Problems with physical and emotional health are common among people who are in the process of divorcing. Moreover, sometimes these problems last for years or even decades after the divorce is final. Physical health problems occur because the stress of the divorce tends to suppress the functioning of the body's immune system (Gottman 1994:3).

Although some emotional difficulties may be present before and contribute to a divorce, the process is sufficiently stressful to create such problems. Divorced people have higher rates of suicide, accidents, physical and mental health problems (including anxiety and depression), and alcoholism (Kurdek 1990; Wasserman 1990; Hetherington 1993; Richards, Hardy, and Wadsworth 1997). Divorced people also

report themselves as less happy than do married people (Weingarten 1985; Kurdek 1991).

The stress of a divorce is great because it involves the disruption of an intimate relationship. There is a sense of loss. There are uncertainties about the future, about the individual's network of relationships, and perhaps about the decision to divorce. The prospect of such a radical change in one's life tends to create a certain amount of anger, depression, and guilt. Interestingly, such feelings are likely to occur to those who initiate the divorce as well as to their partners. The difference is that the initiators are likely to experience the negative emotions earlier in the process (Buehler 1987).

How long do such negative emotions last? Typically, it takes anywhere from two to four years to work through a divorce. However, if the individual does not cope well, the problems may go on for decades or even a lifetime (Lauer and Lauer 1988:122). In a long-term study of sixty families disrupted by divorce, the researchers found that a fourth of the mothers and a fifth of the fathers were still struggling ten years after their divorces (Wallerstein and Blakeslee 1989). The researchers discovered something else of importance: The parents tended to be chronically disorganized and had difficulty meeting the demands of parenting. Other research supports that conclusion. A study of 45 toddlers concluded that the divorced mothers provided their children with less stimulation than did married mothers (Poehlmann and Fiese 1994). Older children may even find their divorced parents leaning on them for support; the children, in effect, become parents to their own parents (Wallerstein and Blakeslee 1989).

Financial Problems

Although no-fault divorce laws were supposed to make marital disruption a more equitable process, we may speak of "his" divorce and "her" divorce. And her divorce usually involves a more severe financial crisis than does his. Lenore Weitzman (1985) conducted research over a ten-year period, looking at twenty-five hundred California court records and interviewing lawyers, judges, and divorced men and women. Among other things, an updated analysis of her data shows that, within a year after the divorce was finalized, men experience

Financial problems increase the stress of single mothers.

about a 10 percent improvement in their standard of living, while women's standard of living drops about 27 percent.

Of course, not every woman's standard of living goes down, or down that dramatically, nor does every man's standard rise. But women generally tend to be penalized financially by the no-fault divorce procedure.

Weitzman recognized that no-fault divorce relieves some of the conflict of the old adversarial system. She argued that no-fault procedures have weakened the bargaining position of women with the result that divorced women and their children tend to be systematically impoverished. The primary reason for this is that the new laws require husbands and wives to be treated equally. Yet the division of labor in the family, along with the experiences and special skills of each partner, mean that men and women are unequal in terms of their resources and opportunities. Because the law no longer presumes that the husband is responsible for supporting the family after the divorce, men tend to benefit and women, particularly those with children, tend to suffer from no-fault laws.

Other research supports the conclusion that women suffer financially under no-fault divorce laws. Arendell (1986) interviewed sixty middle-class, divorced mothers. Only six of the women received alimony. More than half got no or sporadic and insufficient child support. The women all lived in California, but the community property law did not take into account their contributions to their husbands' education and earning power. Nine out of ten said that their incomes had dropped close to or below the poverty line after their divorces. In addition, the women found themselves facing all kinds of difficult problems—finding and coping with work, the conflict between working and caring for the children, getting food stamps, dealing with welfare agencies, selling jewelry or furniture or renting out rooms to make ends meet, and dealing with feelings of loneliness and isolation.

Another longitudinal study reported that eleven years after divorce, 18 percent of divorced mothers, 10 percent of remarried mothers, and 2 percent of nondivorced mothers in a comparison group had been on public assistance at some time (Hetherington 1993). National data show that the economic problems of divorced women occur for African Americans and Hispanics as well as for whites (Smock 1994). The disadvantage endured by women is largely related to two factors. One is the likelihood for the woman to remain the primary child caretaker. The other is the fact that many if not most divorced fathers seldom or never make contributions of any kind—financial, moral, social, or emotional—to their children (Teachman 1991).

Interaction Between Former Spouses

A divorce doesn't necessarily end interaction between former spouses. If children are involved in the divorce, of course, at least some contact between the ex-spouses is likely, although having children also means the contact probably will be less friendly and involve more quarreling than contact between the childless (Masheter 1991). According to a study of eighty couples, about one of five had a relatively high degree of coparental interaction a year after the divorce and another 59 percent reported a moderate amount of interaction (Ahrons and Wallisch 1987). By three years after the divorce, however, only one in ten of the respondents reported a continuingly high degree of interaction. Among other things, the couples said that they interacted to share major decisions about the children, discuss children's personal, school, and medical problems, discuss children's progress and accomplishments, and talk about child-rearing problems generally. Nearly half of the ex-spouses spent time together with their children for the first year after divorce, but the number dropped to 30 percent two years later.

On matters other than parenting, the ex-spouses had less interaction. Still, after one year, about a fourth continued to interact with each other every few months. They talked about such things as new experiences, their families (other than the children), old friends, personal problems, and finances. For many people, then, the relationship continues, at least to some extent, even after divorce.

Of course, the quality of the interaction between ex-spouses varies considerably. Psychologist Constance Ahrons found four types of relationships between ninety-eight pairs of ex-spouses: fiery foes, angry associates, cooperative colleagues, and perfect pals (Stark 1986a). About a fourth were fiery foes, those who had minimal contact with each other and who became bitter and angry when they did interact. Fiery foes try to avoid each other. Another fourth were angry associates, those who could tolerate being in the same place with the ex-spouse but who still feel so angry and bitter that they cannot interact pleasantly.

The largest group, 38 percent, were cooperative colleagues. They have a moderate amount of interaction and can mutually support each other. They strive to get along for the children's sake. Finally, the perfect pals comprised 12 percent of the sample. Like cooperative colleagues, they are child-centered and try to put the interests of their children above any anger or frustration they still have. But perfect pals are much more involved with each other than are cooperative colleagues. Neither partner has remarried. They enjoy each other's company. They may telephone to share exciting news with each other. They maintain a fairly active involvement in each other's life even though they are not trying to reestablish the marriage.

EFFECTS OF DIVORCE ON CHILDREN

One of the reasons given by some people for remaining in an unhappy marriage is to protect their children. Most people are aware that divorce can be a very painful experience for children. Still, is it always better for children if their parents' marriage is intact? Just how painful is divorce for the children? These questions take on increasing importance in an age when the number of children affected by divorce is enormous. In 1993, 17.9 million children, representing over a fourth of all children, and 57 percent of African American children, lived with one parent; of those living with one parent, 37 percent (6.6 million children) were in a home broken by divorce (Saluter 1994:xi–xii).

Short-Term Effects

In the short term, children are likely to suffer a variety of physical and emotional problems when their parents divorce. In some cases, such as a family in which there was abuse or intense and constant conflict, the separation and divorce may be a relief rather than a traumatic experience. Most of the time, however, the short-term effects will be negative. In fact, parental separation is likely to create a crisis for the child but one that will diminish within the first six to twelve months (Kelly 1988:122).

Among the negative consequences identified by researchers are:

Initial reactions to parental separation may include intense anger, self-blame, fears about the future, and loyalty conflicts as the child is pressured to take sides in the parental battle

PERSONAL
"My Whole World Was Lost"

Divorce is generally painful but particularly so when one of the partners doesn't expect it. In some cases, the "secret" is so well kept that a spouse is stunned by the announcement that the marriage is over. Craig, a forty-year-old salesman, had that experience. He describes his feelings:

Even though we had been having a few problems and seeing a marriage counselor, I was really caught by surprise. I came home from work one day to discover that my wife and children were gone. I felt like hell and nearly powerless to change the situation. They were gone, and what was I to do? I made several attempts to get my wife to return, but she wouldn't consider it. Two days later, I was served with divorce papers.

I had to deal with the reality. It was over. I blamed myself. I blamed her mother. I even blamed the marriage counselor that we had visited. I reached for anything that would take the pain away. I was hurt and I wanted my family back.

I kept hoping things would get better. But they didn't. I wanted to see my children as often as I could, but that became an impossibility. Then one day I thought of a way that I might at least see them. My wife had moved in with her mother, and across from their house was a school with a track. I started jogging at the school so that I could be near my children and maybe even get a glimpse of them at times. But I was jogging too early in the morning. I decided to join the YMCA, which was just a block from their house. I could jog there any time of the day.

The jogging track at the Y had piped in music, and everyday I would hear the same song about how somebody had done somebody else wrong. I was not only running to the music but living its harsh message. I hurt in places deep in my soul. Sometimes I cried. My whole world was lost, and I couldn't get it back. I returned to the only place that I could remember that left me feeling good about myself—my church.

The court date finally arrived, and the judge gave custody to my ex-wife. However, I was awarded liberal visitation rights. My ex-wife sometimes tried to make excuses and keep me from picking up the children on weekends. That went on for fourteen years. It was only recently that I finally forgave her for the pain and suffering I have endured. I have remarried, and my new wife is helping me with her love and patience. I am finally beginning to trust people again.

(Bonkowski, Boomhower, and Bequette 1985; Healy, Stewart, and Copeland 1993; Hetherington 1993).

Physical health ratings of children from divorced families are lower than those from intact families (Guidubaldi and Cleminshaw 1985).

Children from divorced families rate themselves lower in social competence, and, in fact, are likely to be less sociable and less responsive at home, school, and play (Devall, Stoneman, and Brody 1986; Baker, Barthelemy, and Kurdek 1993; Peretti and di Vitorrio 1993).

Children from divorced families are more likely to be anxious, depressed, and withdrawn than those in intact families (Peterson and Zill 1986; Dawson 1991).

Children from divorced families are more likely to have eating problems and disorders (Wynn and Bowering 1990).

Children from divorced families tend to receive less maternal warmth and empathy (the conflict and pain of most divorces leave little energy for nurturing children), which contributes to various emotional and behavior problems (Kline, Johnston, and Tschann 1991).

Intact-family children have fewer absences at school; higher popularity ratings; higher IQ, reading, spelling, and math scores; and fewer behavioral problems at school than do children from divorced families (Kinard and Reinherz 1986; Dawson 1991; Downey 1994).

Adolescents from divorced families tend to have higher rates of drug use (including alcohol) and premarital sexual activity; poorer academic performance; and higher rates of dropout from school (Flewelling and Bauman 1990; Needle, Su, and Doherty 1990; Foxcraft and Lowe 1991; Doherty and Needle 1991; Zimiles and Lee 1991; Sandefur, McLanahan and Wojtkiewicz 1992, Hoffmann and Johnson 1998).

The various consequences are understandable. Disruptions in intimate relationships are very stressful for all of us. Children are likely to be even more stressed because they have no control over what is happening to them and see no long-term benefits to the disruption. Thus, they react with anger, depression, and anxiety, and this emotional turbulence interferes with other aspects of their lives.

Long-Term Effects

Fortunately, the picture is not as bleak when we look at longer-term consequences. There may be some positive outcomes for the children (Demo and Acock 1988: 626–27). For example, children in single-parent homes are more likely to be androgynous in their behavior. The pressures toward traditional gender roles do not seem to be as prevalent in single-parent as they are in two-parent homes. In addition, adolescents in single-parent homes tend to be more mature and to have a greater sense of their own efficacy. This is probably due to the fact that they take more responsibility for family life, doing some things that might otherwise be done by the absent parent.

In those cases in which family life was marked by intense conflict, the children are likely to be better off in both the short and long run. Rates of depression, withdrawal, and other problems are higher for those who live in a home of persistent conflict and unhappiness than those in single-parent homes (Peterson and Zill 1986; Amato and Booth 1991; Jekielek 1998). Based on their twelve-year longitudinal study, three researchers sum up the relationship between parental conflict, divorce, and the long-term well-being of the children as follows (Amato, Loomis, and Booth 1995). Where the level of parental conflict is high, children have higher levels of well-being as young adults if the parents divorce. Where the level of parental conflict is low,

the children are better off if the parents stay together. If the parents do not divorce, the more their conflict the lower the level of well-being of the children as young adults.

If some of the effects are positive, others are neutral; that is, in the long run, no differences exist between those who come from intact and those who come from disrupted homes. For example, there are no variations in self-esteem (Amato 1988a; Demo and Acock 1988; Slater and Calhoun 1988). Moreover, children from divorced families appear to be as competent in social situations as those from intact families (Long et al. 1987). And using a sample of 313 volunteers, we found no differences in the quality of intimate relationships of those from intact, death-disrupted, and divorce-disrupted families (Lauer and Lauer 1991).

However, there may be some negative long-term consequences. The severity of the consequences depends on a number of factors. In both the short and the long run, children will adjust better if the custodial parent functions well, the children have regular contact with the noncustodial parent, and the children's exposure to conflict between the parents has been minimal (Furstenberg and Cherlin 1991). Some of the possible consequences of poor adjustment include:

Compared to those from intact homes, adults whose parents divorced tend to have lower levels of: psychological well-being (higher levels of depression and lower life satisfaction), family well-being (lower marital quality and higher chances of divorce), socioeconomic well-being (lower educational attainment, income, and occupational prestige), and physical health (Amato 1991; Amato and Keith 1991a; Kessler and Magee 1993; Powell and Parcel 1997; Couch and Lillard 1997). The lower socioeconomic well-being applies to white males, white females, black females, and, to a somewhat lesser extent, Hispanic females but not to black or Hispanic males (Amato and Keith 1991b). Higher levels of depression are more likely among African Americans than whites whose parents divorced but not among Hispanics, perhaps because of the close-knit extended Hispanic family (Amato 1991). Researchers have also found long-term negative effects on emotional health in

Children are likely to have more behavioral problems at school after their parents divorce.

a longitudinal study of people in Britain (Cherlin, Chase-Lansdale, and McRae 1998), a survey of 1,656 Finnish subjects (Palosaari, Aro, and Laippala 1996), and interviews with 12,537 Australians (Rodgers, Power, and Hope 1997). The negative impact of divorce on children's well-being may be independent of culture.

College students from divorced families have significantly more sexual partners and more negative attitudes toward marriage than students from intact families (Gabardi and Rosen 1991).

Compared to those from intact families, adults from divorced families have less sense of personal power, view their families of origin in more negative terms, and are more likely to have poor relationships with parents and particularly with their fathers (Zill, Morrison, and Coiro 1993; Booth and Amato 1994; Cooney 1994; Aquilino 1994a; White 1994). The negative impact on parent-child relations also occurs if the divorce takes place after the children are already adults (Aquilino 1994b).

Divorce tends not to reduce attachment to the custodial parent but does reduce it with the noncustodial parent (White, Brinkerhoff, and Booth 1985; Cooney and Uhlenberg 1990); nearly half of the children in a national survey had not seen their nonresident fathers in the past year (Furstenberg and Nord 1985), although frequency of visitation and the closeness of the relationship with the father revealed no consistent influence on the child's academic difficulty, problem behavior, and psychological distress (Furstenberg, Morgan, and Allison 1987:695).

When the noncustodial parent is perceived as "lost," the adult child is likely to be depressed (Drill 1986).

Those from disrupted homes report themselves as less happy than those from intact homes (Glenn and Kramer 1985).

Women from disrupted homes are less likely to marry than are women from intact homes (Goldscheider and Waite 1986).

Those from disrupted homes have lower levels of trust and altruistic love in their intimate relationships, which can both hinder the development of intimacy and jeopardize the continuation and well-being of a relationship (Southworth and Schwarz 1987; Johnston and Thomas 1996; Sprague and Kinney 1997). They also have more relationship difficulties as young adults than do those who come from intact homes (McCabe 1997).

A long-term study reported that two-thirds of young women from disrupted homes developed anxiety as young adults, feared betrayal in intimate relationships, and had problems committing themselves to a relationship, while 40 percent of young men from disrupted homes had, as young adults, no set goals and a sense of having limited control over their lives (Wallerstein and Blakeslee 1989).

Those from disrupted homes have a higher risk of premature mortality across the life span (Tucker et al. 1997). A long-term study found that adult children of divorced parents have a one-third greater chance of dying earlier than those whose parents remained married until they were at least 21 years old (Friedman et al. 1995). The predicted median age at death for men was 76 years for those from divorced homes and 80 years for those from intact homes; the predicted median age for women was 82 years for those from divorced homes and 86 years for those from intact homes.

Gender Differences

Will you handle the divorce of your parents better if you are a girl or a boy? One of the interesting conclusions to emerge from research is that girls tend to adjust more easily to divorce than do boys. Boys from divorced homes exhibit significantly more problematic behavior than do boys from intact homes; no such differences are found among girls (Demo and Acock 1988; Hetherington 1993). Boys who live with a divorced mother have even higher levels of depression and withdrawal than boys who live in an intact family with high, persistent conflict (Peterson and Zill 1986). Boys also take a longer time to adjust than do girls. Boys' problems are less, however, if the conflict between their divorced parents is relatively low (Amato and Rezac 1994).

There are various reasons boys have more difficulty adjusting to divorce. One factor is that boys tend to be more aggressive than girls at all ages. Both boys and girls from divorced families tend to be more aggressive than those from intact families, but the increase may "push the boy's behavior past acceptable limits while an increase in a girl's aggressive behavior might still not be labeled problematic behavior" (Lowery and Settle 1985:458).

A number of researchers have suggested that the main problem of boys may be the lack of a same-sex parent. Most boys live with their mother. The need for a father seems to intensify during adolescence (Wallerstein 1987), when the boy, unlike the girl, has no same-sex role model in the home. Evidence from national data, however, shows no benefits for either boys or girls living in a same-sex rather than an opposite-sex home (Downey and Powell 1993).

CHILD CUSTODY

At the beginning of this chapter, we quoted the undergraduate student who said that the most painful part of her parents' divorce was deciding with whom to live. She was forced to make a decision that could only hurt regardless of who she chose:

> I was daddy's girl but mother's baby. My sister wanted to live with mom and so did I. But my dad wanted me to live with him. I didn't want to be apart from my sister and my mom. So one day all four of us sat down to legalize where we'd live. My dad asked me who I wanted to live with. I didn't want to answer. It just killed me. I was only ten years old. When I finally answered, it was awful. My dad broke down and began to cry. That was the first time I'd ever seen him cry. It was devastating to me to have my dad feel so disappointed with me.

Custody arrangements can be very painful for both the parents and the children. Interestingly, the arrangements have changed over time. Until relatively recently, the only arrangement was **sole custody,** in which one of the parents is given the responsibility for the care and raising of the child. Before the early part of this century, the parent who got such custody was the father. Fathers were the economic head of the family and were presumed to be in a better position to care for the needs of the children. Increasingly in the twentieth century, however, mothers were granted custody under the "tender years" doctrine, the notion that the child's well-being is maximized by the mother's care. By 1925, the phrase "best interests of the child" was incorporated into state laws. Until the mid-1960s, then, mothers were generally given custody, and they won custody in more than 90 percent of contested cases (Ihinger-Tallman and Pasley 1987:80).

Unless a father could show that his former wife was unstable or unable to provide proper care, the courts routinely gave custody to the mother. The role of the father was reduced to providing financial support and to some visitation rights. Then fathers began to ask for more. After the mid-1960s, an increasing number of fathers won the right to sole custody. A study of 509 cases in Michigan found that fathers were more likely to get custody when the children are older (especially if the oldest child is male) and the father is the plaintiff (Fox and Kelly 1995). As the examples of the student quoted above and the experience of Craig (PERSONAL) illustrate, fathers as well as mothers may find the separation from their children to be extremely painful. Indeed, divorced fathers who have custody of their children are less depressed, less anxious, and have fewer problems of adjustment than those without custody (Stewart, Schwebel, and Fine 1986).

Why not, then, find another alternative, one that allows both parents to continue to be involved in some way in their children's lives? **Joint custody,** an arrangement in which both parents continue to share the responsibility for the care and raising of the children, is an attempt to provide a better solution. In 1980, California adopted a joint custody arrangement. Other states soon followed suit.

A number of states now award joint custody unless there is some compelling reason to do otherwise. The way in which joint custody actually works out in daily life varies somewhat (Ihinger-Tallman and Pasley 1987:81). The children may spend some time each day at two different homes, various amounts of time during the week at two dif-

ferent homes, differing periods of the time in each of two homes, or alternate years in each of the two homes. In other cases, joint custody does not even require shared living arrangements but is rather joint legal custody where both parents are involved in important decisions in their child's life.

Does joint custody resolve the problems? Does it provide the ideal way, or even a better way, to deal with the issues? There are differences of opinion (Ferreiro 1990). Basically, joint custody has some advantages and some drawbacks.

Joint custody may be more satisfying to the parents. A study of fathers found that those with joint custody had more contact with their children and more satisfaction with the arrangement than the noncustodial fathers (Arditti 1992). Joint custody is more likely to lead to compliance with obligations of financial support—a major cause, as we have noted, of women's financial stress—and to eliminate the problem of visitation denial (Seltzer 1991; Bender 1994).

Joint custody also appears to be more satisfying to the children (Kelly 1988; Bender 1994). Joint custody children can avoid the struggle with the sense of loss that afflicts children in sole-custody arrangements. Joint-custody boys are as well-adjusted overall as boys in intact families.

In large part, the adjustment of the children to a joint-custody arrangement depends on the way in which the parents relate to them and to each other (Maccoby and Mnookin 1992). Joint custody, of course, means that the ex-spouses will continue to interact more than they would have under sole custody. If their interaction is one of ongoing conflict, the joint custody arrangement may be worse for the child than sole custody. If the parents can relate to each other without anger and conflict, the children will usually prefer joint custody. They find the benefits of maintaining intimate contact with both parents worth the hassles of living alternately in two homes.

Of course, there may be some disadvantages to joint custody even if the parents get along. Basically, it is too early to know of any long-term consequences. What, for example, will be the effect on children of not having a single, stable environment in which to grow up? What is the effect on their peer relationships? What if they have diverse and contrary experiences with the two parents? In the

Children adjust to a divorce better if their parents can be cordial to each other.

future we may be able to answer such questions. Meanwhile, joint custody seems to be a considerable improvement over sole custody for most parents and their children.

COPING WITH THE DISRUPTION

How can both parents and children cope effectively with the disruption of their intimate relationships? How can they maximize their chances of eventually turning the divorce into something positive for themselves?

For children, adjustment depends in part on the behavior of their parents (Kelly 1988). Children adjust better when the custodial parent is well adjusted (Silitsky 1996). The mother is particularly important in the child's adjustment, even when she does not have sole custody (Buchanan, Maccoby, and Dornbusch 1996). Whatever else happens, one of the prime needs of the children is a stable home and a loving, supportive mother. The children also

need to understand what the disruption is about (so that they don't, among other things, blame themselves), and the parents need to beware of becoming so preoccupied with their own concerns that they are unaware of their children's concerns— which are likely to be different from their own (Stewart et al. 1997).

As you would expect from our discussion about parental conflict, children adjust better to the extent that the divorce reduces the conflict between the parents. Under a sole-custody arrangement, children's adjustment is better if there is frequent contact with the noncustodial parent and if the custodial parent is satisfied with the noncustodial parent's relationship with the children. Obviously, children benefit when their parents grow beyond the anger and bitterness of the divorce and establish cordial relations.

How can parents cope with divorce and develop a relationship that is helpful to their children? To begin with, ex-spouses need to be open about their feelings and work through the anger, guilt, and anxiety that attend the disruption of an intimate relationship. Such feelings should not be repressed or denied; that only delays adjustment. Blaming someone for the disruption is generally unprofitable. Neither self-blame nor other-blame pays off in terms of adjusting well. Initially, of course, condemning the ex-spouse may be a part of venting one's anger. But eventually each of the partners must get beyond blaming and get on with the business of constructing a new life with new intimate relationships.

Divorced parents will also help their children adjust to the extent that they have a sense of control over their child-rearing responsibilities. A study of fifty-eight divorced mothers found that those who perceived themselves as being in control had children with higher self-esteem and fewer physical and psychological problems than mothers who perceived less control (Machida and Holloway 1991). Parents who have problems with such control can find help in various books and classes on parenting.

Finally, the parents will adjust well to a divorce, and thereby help their children to adjust, to the extent that they are able to define it as an opportunity for growth. We need to understand that "both marriage and divorce can generate adult unfolding or, conversely, block individual development, depending on a multitude of factors" (Rice and Rice 1986:71). We have seen examples of how divorce can block growth, leading to long-term stagnation as the individual persists in anger, bitterness, and depression. But divorce can also be an opportunity. In our study of watersheds in people's lives, we found that those who successfully coped with a divorce came to a point where they defined the disruption as an important step in their growth (Lauer and Lauer 1988:125). For instance, a number of women told about how divorce allowed them for the first time in their lives to test their capacity for self-sustained living. The discovery of their capacity for independence was an exhilarating experience. The pain of disruption eventually led to the excitement of self-discovery. For many people, then, a divorce becomes the beginning of a new journey into fulfillment, a journey that includes both personal growth and meaningful intimate relationships.

PRINCIPLES FOR ENHANCING INTIMACY

Although divorce can have a potentially damaging impact on children, the following principles suggest some ways in which parents can help their offspring and maximize the probability of maintaining meaningful, intimate relations.

1. Be open and straightforward when discussing the divorce with children. Children sometimes blame themselves for a parental divorce. Don't deny the marital difficulties that led to the divorce; rather, help your children to see the situation as clearly as possible.

2. Avoid blaming anyone for the divorce. Make sure the children know they are not to blame. But don't heap blame on the other spouse. The children probably want to continue to love and interact with both parents. Don't make that difficult for them.

3. Help the children to understand that neither parent is divorcing them. Don't ask them to choose the parent with whom they want to live. Let them know that both parents continue to love them even though the family will no longer be living together.

4. Let the children vent their emotions, including any anger, fear, and guilt they feel. Being open about their feelings will help them work through the disruption.

5. Avoid unnecessary changes. Children will usually benefit by staying in the same neighborhood and school in the period immediately following a divorce.

SUMMARY

Since 1860, there has been a general increase in the divorce rate. The rate peaked just after World War II and again in the 1970s. Overall, less than a third of Americans who have ever been married have also been divorced. The grounds for divorce are set by the states, all of which now have no-fault laws.

The process of uncoupling is marked by four time periods: recognition, discussion, action, and postdissolution. In the recognition period, one partner senses that the relationship is deteriorating but may not openly confront the other. In the discussion period, the marital problems may be shared with outsiders as well as the spouse. The history of the relationship may be redefined in terms of a series of negative experiences. The initiator is making the transition to a new life. The action period involves legal steps to formally dissolve the marriage. This is a difficult period, involving the struggle over such things as division of property, child custody, and ambivalent feelings. The postdissolution period begins when both spouses accept the fact that the marriage is over.

Bohannan has identified six experiences that people are likely to have in divorce. Divorce involves an emotional, legal, community, and psychic separation, and an economic and co-parental (for those with children) settlement.

Divorce is more likely for those of lower socioeconomic status, those married at a younger or later age, African Americans, and those who lack membership in an integrated group, such as a religious group. Changed laws and attitudes and the changing roles of women are associated with higher divorce rates. At an interpersonal level, divorce is associated with various complaints, such as infidelity and conflict over personalities and finances. Some divorces are the result of changed feelings about the partner, and some result from a spouse's emotional problems.

Divorce can have positive as well as negative outcomes. For some, a divorce is a positive turning point in personal well-being. But numerous negative outcomes are likely, including short-term and in some cases long-term health problems and, particularly for women, financial problems. Divorce doesn't necessarily end interaction between the spouses, though the quality of the interaction varies considerably.

Divorce has both short-term and long-term effects on children. In the short run, children are likely to suffer various physical, behavioral, and emotional problems. Over the long run, there may be positive outcomes for children, especially if the home was marked by intense and continual conflict. In some ways, children from disrupted homes are no different than those from intact homes in the long run. But there can also be some long-term negative consequences, including lower levels of educational and occupational achievement, problematic relationships with the noncustodial parent, problems with trust, and depression.

Girls tend to adjust more easily to divorce than do boys. Boys from disrupted homes have significantly more problematic behavior. The main problem for boys may be the lack of a same-sex parent.

Child custody arrangements can be painful for both parents and children. Sole custody is giving way to joint custody in many states. The type of custody can affect the child's adjustment to the divorce. Some evidence exists that joint custody, while not solving all the problems, does have benefits for both the children and the parents.

Children's adjustment to the divorce depends in part on the behavior of the parents. If the divorce reduces conflict significantly, children adjust better. The parents will adjust better to the extent that they work through their feelings and are able to define the divorce as an opportunity to grow.

INTERNET CONNECTION
Separation and Divorce

Divorce has become a commonplace experience in American society. This is, in part, an outcome of the supremacy of individual values and choices over governmental regulation, social roles and social norms. Economic factors however, as well as issues related to social status, are as important to the issue of divorce as is personal choice.

Divorce.com

http://www.divorcing.com/

A very comprehensive website with links to resources concerning all aspects of divorce.

1. What resources exist at this website to help people negotiate divorces without legal assistance? In your opinion is the material you find at the divorce websites geared toward lower income or upper income people?

2. This website includes a section on divorce and bankruptcy. Who is the audience for these sites?

3. How can the resources available through Divorcing.com help families cope with the uncoupling process?

CHAPTER 19

REMARRIAGE AND STEPFAMILIES

Learning Objectives

After reading chapter 19, you should be able to:

1. Classify the various types of remarriage.
2. Relate the demographic characteristics of remarriages and stepfamilies.
3. Evaluate the prospects for those who remarry.
4. Discuss the processes of courting and choosing a partner for those who remarry.
5. Summarize the reasons that people choose to remarry.
6. Explain the myths and the challenges of remarriage.
7. Contrast and compare the general quality of remarriages to first marriages.
8. Describe the complexities and difficulties that confront stepfamilies.
9. Discuss the stepparent-stepchild relationship.
10. Summarize the ways in which a stepfamily can cope with its difficulties and foster satisfying relationships.

There is a song that says that love is better the "second time around." If this is true, millions of Americans are living out the ecstasy of a loving relationship in second marriages. A more cynical view was expressed by the eighteenth-century writer Samuel Johnson, who called remarriage the "triumph of hope over experience." If this is true, millions of Americans are living in the disillusionment of a second marriage.

The actual experiences of those who remarry, as we shall see, are somewhere between these two extremes. Remarriage has its own unique potential and its own unique problems. In this chapter, we will look at the extent of remarriage, the experiences and hopes that lead up to it, and the prospects and pitfalls involved in it. We will look in some detail at the various issues raised by **stepfamilies**—remarriages involving children. Finally, we will examine some ways in which people can maximize the probability of a positive outcome when they remarry and live in a stepfamily.

TYPES AND NUMBER OF REMARRIAGES AND STEPFAMILIES

How many people do you know who have remarried or who are living in a stepfamily? The chances are good that either you or someone you know has had such an experience. When we discuss remarriages and stepfamilies, we are talking about a significant proportion of the American population. But considerable diversity exists among the remarried. We will look first at the various types and then at some related statistics.

Types of Remarried Couples

There are many ways to classify remarried couples. For instance, men and women come to remarriage from a variety of situations (Sager et al. 1983:64). At the time of remarriage, the man and woman each were in one of five different conditions: single, divorced or widowed with no children, divorced or widowed with custody of children, divorced or widowed without custody of children, or divorced or widowed with custody of some children but not others. Such a classification yields twenty-four different types of remarriages (the number is twenty-four rather than twenty-five because two single people do not constitute a remarriage).

The possible combinations could be further multiplied if we added those who have adult children no longer living at home and those who have had more than one divorce. The important point here is that each combination is likely to produce different outcomes. As we shall see, the prospects for a stable and satisfying union are quite different for a single woman who marries a divorced man who has custody of his children versus those for a marriage between two divorced people without children versus those for the marriage between two divorced parents, each of whom has custody.

As may already be clear, remarried life, and especially stepfamily life, can become incredibly complicated. The network of relationships expands enormously. Consider the problems of a divorced woman who has custody of her children marrying a divorced man who has custody of his children. There may be ex-spouses to deal with, grandparents who are still very attached to the children, other relatives of the ex-spouses with whom there were close relationships, new stepparent relationships, and new stepsibling relations to work through. It is likely to be a difficult process at best.

Stepfamilies are increasingly common.

Demographics of Remarriage and Stepfamilies

Of the more than 2 million Americans who divorce each year, the majority will eventually remarry. Around 46 percent of marriages involves one or both partners in a remarriage (U.S. Bureau of the Census 1997b:105). Among those who divorce, about one of six remarry within a year after the divorce, and half marry within five years (U.S. Bureau of the Census 1997b:107).

The probability of remarriage varies by a number of factors (Bumpass, Sweet, and Castro-Martin 1990). For women, remarriage is less likely when they have children and when they are older at the time of separation. Mothers who receive child support and those who get above-average amounts of child support are less likely to remarry (Folk, Graham, and Beller 1992). Remarriage is also less likely for African Americans than for whites.

Many remarriages do involve children, of course. Of all families with two parents in the home, 76.1 percent have both biological parents, 16 percent have a stepparent, and 1.4 percent have adoptive parents (U.S. Bureau of the Census 1994:65). That translates into more than 7.25 million children under the age of eighteen living in stepfamilies. The proportion varies by racial/ethnic group (figure 19.1), but overall about one in six American children lives in a stepfamily.

What are the prospects for those who remarry? In general, the rate of divorce for remarrieds is slightly higher than that for first marriages. However, the higher rate may hold true only in the early years of the remarriage; a second marriage that lasts 15 years or more has the same probability of breakup as a first marriage of the same duration (Clarke and Wilson 1994). In other words, remarriages are only more fragile than first marriages in the first 15 years.

Children also are an important factor in the stability of a remarriage. Studying national data, White and Booth (1985) concluded that when one spouse was remarried and the other had been single, the chances for divorce were not significantly greater than they were for unions in which both partners were in a first marriage. But the chances increased 50 percent if both partners were previously married but without children and another 50 percent if both partners were previously married and one or both brought stepchildren into the marriage. The presence of stepchildren is particularly destabilizing for remarriages. If the remarried couple has children of their own, however, the second marriage is less likely to break up (Wineberg 1992).

One other type of remarriage that is unstable is that involving an individual who is in a serial-marriage pattern. **Serial marriage** refers to three or more marriages that occur as a result of repeated

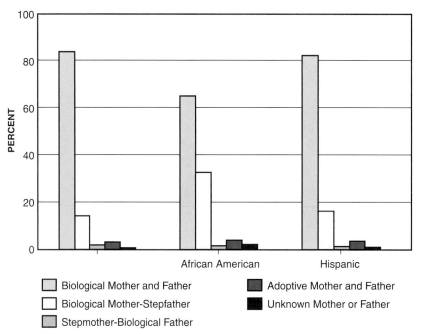

FIGURE 19.1   **Children Living with Biological, Step, and Adoptive Parents**
(*Sources:* U.S. Bureau of the Census 1994:66.)

divorces. At least 2 percent (more than 2 million people) of the ever-married population has been married three times or more (Brody, Neubaum, and Forehand 1988). The duration of each marriage tends to be shorter than the previous one.

DÉJÀ VU: DATING AND MATE SELECTION REVISITED

Those who remarry must go through the processes of dating and mate selection again. Although we think of dating and mate selection as something that occurs mainly in adolescence and the twenties, millions of Americans repeat the process at other times in their lives.

How is dating at forty or fifty or sixty different from what it was in youth? As we pointed out in chapter 6, the reasons that older people date as well as some of their experiences are the same as those of younger people. Whatever your age, you are likely to date because you want to establish an intimate relationship, generally one that will culminate in marriage.

Is it any easier to date when you are older? Perhaps not. As a divorced man of fifty put it: "I felt like

a kid again. The same anxiety. The same awkwardness whenever the conversation stopped. The same questions about what I should or shouldn't do." The man was experiencing only one of the problems that the divorced face in dating. There may be problems of children and limited money because of alimony and/or child support as well as a sense of impatience to establish a new relationship and a reluctance to waste time on one that is going nowhere.

Most divorced people, as we have noted, intend to remarry eventually. And dating is instrumental toward that end. Therapists suggest that there may be an optimum time between the breakup of a first marriage and the initiation of a second one (Sager et al. 1983:63). If dating, courtship, and remarriage occur too quickly after a breakup, the individual may not have had sufficient time to work through his or her pain and disappointment, completely sever ties with the ex-spouse, or learn from the failed relationship. The popular notion of avoiding a "rebound" marriage is sound because an old relationship can adversely affect a new one. Yet if the time between marriages is too long, problems also can develop. For example, in a remarriage where one participant has had long-time custody of a child, it may be difficult for a new spouse to break into the existing parent-child relationship. Unfortunately, many parents do not discuss dating issues with their children (Sumner 1997). They may proceed with a relationship that will eventually be stressed or disrupted because they will be forced to choose who will get priority in their lives—a child or a new mate.

While there is no set amount of time that is ideal in every situation, in general a period of from three to five years before remarriage seems optimal. This should allow the divorced individual sufficient time to work through the emotional pain and to experience a number of relationships.

Many people do not wait three to five years. As noted in the first section, a substantial number remarry within a year of the divorce. Those who remarry also tend to spend less time in the dating and engagement periods. A study involving 248 volunteers reported that before their first marriage, respondents spent a median of twelve months dating and five months being engaged (O'Flaherty and Eells 1988). Before remarriage, they spent a median of seven months dating and two months being engaged. In other words, the second marriages occurred in about half the dating and courtship time as the first marriages. Because courtship time tends to be related to marital success, this could be a factor in the greater instability of remarriages.

What do the divorced do to prepare for remarriage? Knowing the vulnerability of marriages, what steps do they take to minimize the possibility of a second breakup? Not a great deal, according to the little evidence we have. Ganong and Coleman (1989) asked 100 men and 105 women about their preparation for a second marriage. The majority (59 percent) simply lived together. They tested their capacity to be a family through a period of cohabitation. About a fourth of the men and 38 percent of the women received counseling. A little over half of the men and 72 percent of the women sought advice from written materials (such as self-help books) and from friends.

An important way of preparing for any marriage, including a second one, is for the couple to discuss significant issues and potential problems. The researchers found that the couples in their study did not discuss many of the issues regarded as important by stepfamily experts (Ganong and Coleman 1989:30). Children from a previous marriage, the most frequently mentioned issue, were discussed by 56 percent of the couples. Less than a fourth said they talked about the next most frequently named topic—finances. Thirteen percent said they didn't seriously discuss any issues:

> Responses to other questions seemed to reinforce the sense that these couples were either overly optimistic or naive (Ganong and Coleman 1989:30).

If these results are generally true, then people are not taking the necessary steps to ensure stability and satisfaction in their second marriages.

WHY REMARRY?

People remarry for many of the same reasons that they married the first time. In particular, people wish to establish an intimate relationship:

> We find the promise of a caring and loving relationship to be the prime motivation for remarriage (Sager et al. 1983:61).

The most frequently given reason of 205 men and women, that "it was time," probably reflects the felt need for intimacy (figure 19.2). As figure 19.2 shows, those who remarry also have some reasons that are different from those in first marriages. Thus, parents with custody of their children may be motivated by the desire to find a suitable co-parent.

In chapter 10 we discussed private contracts, assumptions, and expectations that each partner has

While some couples prepare for remarriage by discussing important issues, most do not.

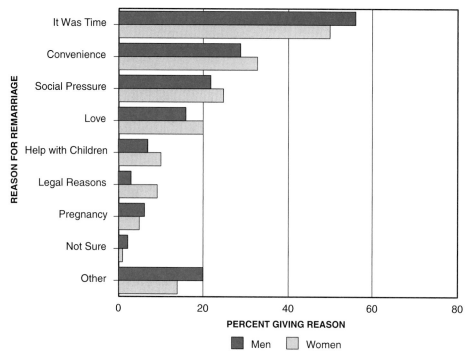

FIGURE 19.2 **Reasons for Remarriage Offered by 205 Men and Women**
(*Source:* Data from L. H. Ganong and M. Coleman, *Family Relations,* 38:30,1989.)

for the other in the marital relationship. People also bring their private contracts to remarriage. Based on clinical experience, Clifford Sager and his associates (1983:67–68) have identified some of the common expectations in remarriage. Those who remarry tend to assume and expect that the new spouse will:

1. Be loyal, devoted, and faithful, providing a kind of romantic love and intimacy that occurred when the first marriage was at its best (or that was lacking altogether in the first marriage).
2. Help nurture and discipline the children.
3. Provide companionship and relief from the loneliness of being single.
4. Help deal with problems and stresses and gain, or regain, the order and stability of a two-parent family.
5. Be committed to making this marriage last.

Depending on age and circumstances, those who remarry may also expect to have shared children (even if one or both bring children to the marriage).

In some cases, the private contract may be unrealistic. It may in essence say to the other: "I expect you to do everything for me that my former spouse didn't. I expect this to be the marriage 'made in heaven' that I didn't have before." Ideally, however, those who remarry will be more realistic, avoiding fanciful illusions and maintaining flexibility about roles in order to maximize the chances of success (Kvanli and Jennings 1986).

ISSUES IN RECOUPLING

What is it like to remarry? What are the problems and prospects the second time around? Is it just as demanding? Does it ever get any easier? Remarriage, like marriage for the first time, requires insight and effort if it is to succeed. Unfortunately, many people enter a second marriage holding on to certain mythical beliefs that can be detrimental.

The Myths of Remarriage

We act on what we believe, not necessarily on what is true or appropriate or helpful. As in the case of first marriages, those who remarry may act on the basis of myths. Coleman and Ganong (1985) have

INVOLVEMENT
Toward Remarriage

Little research has been done on how people move toward a second marriage. What is it like to date? How has the experience of divorce affected dating and courtship patterns and preparatory steps toward marriage? What kind of expectations do people have for their second marriage?

Interview someone in your family or someone you know who has been divorced and remarried. Write an account of the person's remarriage experience, beginning with the time immediately after the divorce. Ask the following questions:

1. After the divorce, how did you feel about the prospect of dating or getting involved in a new relationship?
2. When, why, and how did you start dating again?
3. What problems did you encounter with dating again? How did your feelings and behavior on dates compare with those before your first marriage?
4. What made you decide to get remarried?
5. What did you do to try to make sure that the second marriage would work out better than the first?
6. What did you learn from the first marriage that you think will help you in the second one?
7. Looking back on it now, what would you do differently if you could do it all over?
8. What are you doing now, in this marriage, that is different from your first marriage?
9. What advice would you give to young men and women who are looking toward their first marriage?

If the entire class participates in this project, see if there are any common elements in the answers. In what ways, if any, do your findings differ from those presented in the text?

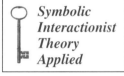

Symbolic Interactionist Theory Applied

identified a number of remarriage myths that can detract from the quality of the new union. These myths may be held by those in the legal system, churches, and helping professions, as well as friends and family members. They also appear in the popular media.

Things Must Work Out   People in first marriages tend to believe this also, but there may be a quality of desperation in those who are remarrying. They insist on "getting it right" the second time. Or they believe that everything will work out because this time it is *really* love. But if insistence or confidence were sufficient, second marriages would not break up at a slightly higher rate than first marriages.

Consider Other People First   In remarriage, an individual may believe that success this time demands that he or she put personal needs secondary to those of spouse or children. But trying to fulfill everyone's needs is frustrating, stressful, and probably impossible. The problems of remarriage are not resolved by either partner denying his or her own needs.

Be an Individual First and a Couple Second
This is the opposite of the myth of always considering others first. It is held by those who felt that they suffered in the first marriage because they didn't care for their own needs. They believe that they must "look out for number one" regardless of what that means for the marital relationship.

Focus on the Positive and Forget Criticism
Some people who remarry believe that if they had followed this rule in their first marriage, it might have succeeded. They may be determined to follow it in the second marriage. As a result, they may

> "walk on eggs" rather than confront, challenge, or argue with other family members. Pseudomutuality may lead to unhappiness and feelings of powerlessness and alienation rather than unity (Coleman and Ganong 1985:117).

Avoid Mistakes of the Past   When things are not going well in the second marriage, some believe that they need to remember mistakes made in the first marriage and avoid repeating them. But, again, this may be a way of avoiding the realities of the present. It is an effort to keep working at the past relationship rather than an attempt to build a new and unique relationship in the present.

Marriage Makes People Happier   Of course, it is true that the married tend to be happier than the unmarried. But remarriage, like marriage, is not a magic elixir that guarantees happiness or your money back. For some who remarry, happiness becomes even more of an imperative in the second than the first marriage, an aspect of the notion that this time it *has* to work out. A related myth is the idea that if the couple is happy, everyone else will be happy. But friends, grandparents, ex-spouses, and children may react very differently to the remarriage, and the happiness of the spouses cannot be separated from those reactions.

The Challenges of Remarriage

Those who remarry are likely to differ from those in a first marriage in a number of ways. They may be older and, therefore, in a different phase of their life cycle than those marrying for the first time. They may have different ideas about the meaning of love. They have experience in marriage. They know the pain of divorce. In addition, they must face issues that are unique to remarriage.

Complex Kin Relations and Ambiguous Roles
The acquisition of a whole new set of kin relationships, including steprelations, combined with ambiguity about many of the roles, can create considerable uncertainty and confusion for those involved in a remarriage (Bernstein and Collins 1985; Hobart 1991). Many a stepparent has had to deal with the retort: "You aren't my *real* parent." And many a spouse in a remarriage has had to contend with a partner's continuing relationship with an ex-spouse. No social norms exist for such relationships. What is appropriate? What is expected?

Consider the following case reported by Sager and his associates (1983:64). Mrs. Prince was single when she met Mr. Prince, who was divorced and the father of two school-age children who lived with their mother. Problems began early in Mr. Prince's second marriage. He felt that his wife resented his children and the time and money he spent on them. She complained that he talked constantly on the telephone with his ex-wife, as often

as several times during a day. She also resented the fact that they couldn't be with her parents on holidays because his parents wanted to see his children. The problems seemed monumental, and the couple eventually went to a therapist to try and work out the difficulties resulting from their complex family situation.

Unresolved Emotional Issues Related to the First Marriage   In addition to problematic relationships, there may be unresolved emotional issues from the first marriage and the divorce that continue to nag people and to affect their relationships. Whether positive (lingering desire for the ex-spouse) or negative (anger, etc.) feelings are involved, emotional attachment to the divorced spouse diminishes the intimacy in the remarriage (Gold, Bubenzer, and West 1993). The emotional attachment comes out in various ways. For example, a husband may react to something his wife says or does because it reminds him of a problem or situation in his first marriage. He may shout at wife number two, but he is really still battling with wife number one. A woman, who had the habit of shrugging at either of two acceptable options for recreation, decided to change her behavior because her husband's first wife had done that to show her contempt for him. To the second wife, her shrug meant "I don't care. I'll be happy doing either as long as I'm with you." To him, however, it had been a sign of scorn in the past, and he still found himself reacting angrily.

Another example of how unresolved emotional issues continue to affect people is the difficulty that some have in developing trust in the remarriage (Kvanli and Jennings 1986). Trust is crucial to the well-being of an intimate relationship, but the failure of a first marriage is frequently a crisis of trust for people. Having found their trust in the first spouse betrayed, they must work hard to learn to trust a second spouse.

Adjustment of Children   As we noted earlier, children pose perhaps the biggest problem to a remarriage. In the past, remarriage generally meant a spouse had died. Now, the children are more likely to have continuing relationships with both biological parents as well as a stepparent. The problems can be severe; we shall discuss them in detail shortly.

Financial Issues   Next to children, financial issues are likely to loom large as a source of stress in
remarriages (Hobart 1991). Fi-

*Exchange
Theory
Applied*

nancial problems can be complex and painful because of
obligations to ex-spouses and
children (PERSONAL). Plus,
questions arise of the inheri-
tance rights of children and stepchildren. Such
problems raise the issue of *equity, and if partners
do not feel that the financial arrangements are equitable, the marriage will be severely strained.*

How, then, can family finances be managed in a
way that is equitable? Should the couple have only
separate accounts, only joint accounts, or a combination of separate and joint accounts? If everything
is in a joint account, for example, the spouses put
their total income (including any alimony and child
support) into the account and allocate it among
family members according to need instead of according to who earned what. The use of separate
accounts suggests a safeguarding of resources for
personal use and one's own children.

For example, one couple, Sheila and Harry, have
separate accounts. Sheila has three sons and Harry
has a daughter. The daughter does not live with them.
Harry gives Sheila money each week for his share of
food and household expenses. Sheila adds a much
larger amount that she gets in child support and uses
the total to run the home and pay for her sons' expenses. Harry pays fixed expenses, such as the mortgage and utilities. He also supports his own child.

Which arrangement, then, works best? Exchange
theory suggests that, because of diverse circumstances, different couples will need different
arrangements in order to feel equity. In other words,
none of the arrangements is intrinsically superior to
the others. A study of 91 remarried couples supports
that conclusion (Pasley, Sandras, and Edmondson
1994). The researchers reported no differences in
satisfaction or happiness between couples using one
or the other of the three types of arrangements.

Legal Issues   Although the biological children and
the ex-spouse may all have legal rights, what of
stepchildren? There are no laws specific to stepparent-stepchild relationships. Some couples, therefore,
may opt for a premarital agreement that takes into
account what each has brought to the marriage and

protects each spouse as well as the children of each
and any children they may have in common (Bernstein and Collins 1985). This may require negotiation
and a rather complex agreement. But the complexity
of the arrangement is a reflection of the intricacies of
the multiple relationships of remarriage.

The Quality of Remarried Life

What can you anticipate in a second marriage in
terms of the quality of marital life? First, the same
factors that lead to satisfaction in a first marriage
are also important in any subsequent marriage
(Leigh et al. 1985). Such things as companionship,
general feelings for the other, and satisfaction with
parenting are crucial to remarital as well as to marital satisfaction.

Second, failure in a first marriage has no necessary bearing on the quality of a second marriage
(Johnson and Booth 1998). In a sense a second
marriage is a fresh start. It, too, can fail. But it can
also be a much better marriage, one that lasts and is
fulfilling to both spouses.

Third, people who remarry have high levels of
intimacy and a high-quality relationship in terms of
such things as amount of interaction, amount of tension in the relationship, number of disagreements,
and level of happiness (White and Booth 1985). In
general, the quality of remarried life is as high as
that of first marriages.

In at least one way, however, the quality of remarried life differs: the remarried are more divorce-
prone in the sense that they think more about divorce, talk more about their marital problems with
others, and are more likely to report a decline in
marital quality in the first eight years (Booth and
Edwards 1992). The decline in marital quality is not
dramatic, but it may take less to bring about a divorce among those who have experienced a previous decline and divorce. Those in remarriages also
tend to have less interaction with parents and in-
laws (Booth and Edwards 1992). Thus, they are less
likely to have an important support group when
problems arise.

Finally, remarried couples may not deal with conflict as effectively as the first-married. Remarriage
and stepchildren do not produce more marital conflict than occurs in a first marriage (MacDonald and
DeMaris 1995). But the remarried may not handle

COMPARISON
Remarrying in Canada and Japan

About one of every three marriages in Canada involves one or both partners in a remarriage. Canadians are more likely to remarry after a divorce when they define the remarriage as rewarding in some way and when there is a pool of desirable marriage partners available. Women are more likely to remarry if they married the first time at a relatively young age; the longer the first marriage lasts, however, the less likely they are to remarry.

The likelihood of Canadian men remarrying is not affected by such factors. Education affects the probability of remarriage for men, however, with those who have more education likelier to remarry than those with less.

As in the United States, Canadian women with children are less likely to remarry than the childless. This is not true for men, probably because most men do not have sole custody of their children.

Finally, religious beliefs are a factor in remarriage. Because of the Catholic Church's prohibition of divorce and remarriage, Canadian Catholics are less likely to remarry than are Protestants. In Japan, marriage tends to occur at a later age, and divorce rates, while increasing considerably, have remained lower than those in the United States. Among those who divorce, men are more likely to remarry than women, a pattern that is also true in the United States. However, the difference between male and female rates of remarriage is greater in Japan than in the United States. And at every age category, Japanese women are less likely than American women to remarry. Until the age of forty, a divorced Japanese woman is about 15 percent more likely than her American counterpart to remain single, but the figure increases to 25 percent at age forty-five and 65 percent at age fifty-one.

One factor of importance is that many divorced Japanese women report that they do not want to remarry. In one survey, nearly half of the divorced women in their twenties and two-thirds of those in their thirties said they did not wish to remarry. Thus, while the majority of Americans usually reach a point where they want to try marriage again, the same cannot be said of people everywhere (Cornell 1989 and Wu 1994).

---

the conflict as well (which could have been a factor in the breakup of the first marriage also). In a comparative study of thirty-three first-married and thirty-three remarried couples, Larson and Allgood (1987) reported that the remarried were more likely to use unproductive problem-solving strategies, such as shouting and anger, during conflict. The researchers suggested that the less effective conflict management may be due to the greater number of challenges and problems faced by remarried couples, incompatibility resulting from patterns established and remaining from the first marriage, or the lack of social norms for problem solving in remarriage.

If there are special challenges, there may also be unique strengths in second marriages. Some evidence exists that those who remarry have a better balance between self-interest and the other's interest than they had in their first marriages (Smith et al. 1991). The husbands have learned to focus more on the interests of their wives, while the wives have learned something about the importance of caring for their own interests as well as those of their hus-

bands. Thus, remarrieds may be somewhat more nontraditional in their gender-role orientation. This would explain, at least in part, why husbands in remarried families contribute significantly more than husbands in first marriages to the household tasks of cooking, meal clean-up, shopping, laundry, and housecleaning (Ishii-Kuntz and Coltrane 1992; Sullivan 1997).

What about relationships with ex-spouses? How do they affect the remarriage? Contrary to what some think, complete isolation from ex-spouses is not necessarily the best arrangement. Of course, such contact can cause disruption in the remarriage if not handled properly. Nevertheless, women who have friendly contact with their ex-husbands, particularly where children are involved, express more satisfaction with the remarriage than do others (Hobart 1990; Weston and Macklin 1990).

In sum, the marital relationship of the remarried can be as satisfying as that of the first-married. By the same token, second marriages break down for the same reasons as first marriages. However, the

PERSONAL
"My Husband's First Wife is Straining My Marriage"

Judy, an ebullient young woman in her early thirties, fell in love with and married Kurt, a divorced man with a teenaged daughter by his first wife, Eve. Judy and Kurt have a child of their own and are expecting a second. They are caught up in conflict between their relationships and the legal system, and as a result, their marriage is strained:

Kurt has been divorced for over ten years. During most of that time he paid Eve three hundred dollars a month for Sharon's child support and half of the costs for her dance lessons and other activities. He also has had to pay all of her medical and dental expenses. A year ago, Sharon decided to move in with us. That meant that Kurt would no longer have to pay child sup-

port to Eve. Because of Kurt's and my salaries, however, Eve wouldn't have to contribute to Sharon's support while she lived with us.

Six months after she moved in, Sharon decided to go back and live with her mother. Eve told Kurt that she had a letter from a therapist recommending that she not work due to stress-related illnesses. She would continue to work until Sharon moved back, but at that time, she would have to quit. She implied that she would need more child support because of not being able to work.

I went to a lawyer to see if I had any rights about my salary not being used to help support Sharon. And what I found out was not encouraging. The law

says that Kurt's first responsibility is to Eve and Sharon. Because of my salary, more of Kurt's can be used to support Sharon. But this is going to cause a good deal of financial strain for us.

I feel like I'm being punished for being successful. The law is letting Eve steal from us. I don't blame Sharon. In fact, we're pretty good friends. But Kurt and I suspect that Eve's so-called problems are just a way of making things difficult for us and easy for herself. We're both angry, and we find ourselves getting irritable with each other at times. Eve is straining our marriage. The law supports her. And we don't quite know how to handle it at this point.

remarried are more likely than the first-married to divorce. The reason, as we have noted, is likely to be found in the total family system, particularly in the relationships with children and stepchildren. We need, then, to look closely at the problems encountered in stepfamilies.

LIVING IN A STEPFAMILY

What exactly is it about stepfamilies that makes them more vulnerable to breaking up than others? In the first place, a stepfamily is built upon loss— the loss of the earlier family with its unique identity, history, and shared expectations (Lauer and Lauer 1999a). Stepfamilies also present people with numerous adjustments, with loyalty conflicts (e.g., between one's spouse and one's children or between one's stepparent and one's biological parent), and with problems of resources (a stepfather, e.g., may pay child support for his biological children, which puts a financial strain on the stepfamily). In

this section, we will look at the challenges posed by the stepfamily life cycle, by the structure of the stepfamily, and by the troublesome stepparent-stepchild relationship.

The Stepfamily Life Cycle

In a nine-year study of over 200 stepfather families, Bray and Kelly (1998) found three phases in the first ten years of stepfamily life. The first phase involves the "turbulent first two years." Even stepfamilies that turn out to be satisfying in the future tend to experience a good deal of turmoil and conflict in the first two years.

An important source of trouble in the first phase is the unrealistic expectations that people bring to the stepfamily. We call them "fantasy expectations," expectations that reflect our love of fairy-story endings—"they all lived happily ever after" (Lauer and Lauer 1999a). They include such things as: "we will be a normal family again"; "we will all love each other from the start"; and "we won't have the problems that other stepfamilies have because we all get along well." But in point of fact, a stepfamily is not like a biological family. It is built on loss, as we noted earlier. It involves complicated and troublesome relationships that grow out of the loss. And even when people seem to get along well before the parent and stepparent marry, unanticipated struggles and problems can emerge once the stepfamily is formed.

In the second phase, from the third to the fifth year, stepfamilies are in the "golden period" (Bray and Kelly 1998). The challenges and problems of the first two years have been addressed or at least are no longer as troublesome as they were (if the family is still together). In this phase, stepfamily life seems finally to become the circle of intimacy that family members had hoped for. One thing that facilitates the relative harmony in this phase is the fact that stepchildren are frequently in the period of latency (between the ages of eight and eleven), which is one of the calmest periods of childhood. Also, the family members have now had a chance to work through some of the many issues (meal times, bed times, who has the right to discipline, how much time shall be given to the marriage vs. time given to parenting, etc.) that have to be negotiated in stepfamily life.

Unfortunately, the tranquil phase doesn't last. From about the sixth year on, the stepfamily enters the phase of "singing in the rain" (Bray and Kelly 1998). It's a time when some things (like the marital relationship) continue to get better, while other matters (like stepparenting) become troublesome again, particularly if the stepchildren are now entering their teen years. A danger at this point is that the couple may attribute their difficulties to the fact of being a stepfamily rather than to the typical problems of all families with teenagers (Lauer and Lauer 1999a). In spite of some renewed difficulties, however, most stepfamilies now have the stability and strengths to keep the family intact.

The Structure of the Stepfamily

Stepfamilies function somewhat differently than other families because of certain structural differences (Peek et al. 1988). These structural differences make the stepfamily a greater challenge to the quest for intimacy.

Complexity Stepfamilies are more complex because of the increased number of relationships. Thus, greater interpersonal skills are necessary in the stepfamily as people must deal with ex-spouses, the parents of ex-spouses (who are also grandparents), and various new steprelations. An additional point to keep in mind is that the complexity is there from the start. The spouses in a stepfamily have no child-free period of time in which to adjust to each other and build their marital relationship. Rather, they are immediately beset with an intricate and potentially troublesome set of relationships that can put considerable strain on their marriage.

The children, too, face a complex situation. Satir (1972:175) wrote of an adolescent girl who was acting "alternately crazy and depressed." The girl lived with her mother and stepfather but alternated weekends with her father and his fiancée, her maternal grandparents, and her paternal grandparents. At each place, she was asked to tell about what went on at the other places and told to keep quiet about what was discussed "here." The girl became the unwitting victim of a network of jealous and angry people.

Ambiguous Family Boundaries **Family boundary** is a concept from family systems theory that

Systems Theory Applied

refers to rules about who is a member of the family and how much each member participates in family life. Family boundaries are not likely to be as clear-cut in the stepfamily. Family therapists have found that boundary ambiguity tends to be associated with stress and various problems in family functioning (Pasley and Ihinger-Tallman 1989). In the stepfamily, considerable ambiguity may exist.

For instance, in her study of sixty adolescents whose parents had divorced, Gross (1986) found four ways of defining family. A third of the adolescents defined family in terms of *retention*. They named both biological parents as part of the family but did not include a stepparent. They considered stepparents mainly as outsiders who "just weren't related." Thirteen percent defined their families in terms of *substitution*. They excluded the missing biological parent and included the stepparent as a family member. However, they did not completely regard the stepparent as a parent. The stepparent was a family member but not a total replacement for a parent.

A fourth of the adolescents chose a third category, *reduction,* in which they defined the family in terms of the biological parents with whom they were living. Some were living with a stepparent but didn't include that person, while others were living with a single parent and excluded the nonresidential parent. Finally, 28 percent of the adolescents defined family in terms of *augmentation,* identifying both biological parents and any stepparent as a family member. They saw the stepparent as an addition to the family. Those who fell into this category tended to move freely between the homes of their biological parents and reported little hostility between the parents.

There are, then, differences in the way that the children of divorce define the boundaries of their family. Parents may also have vague ideas of exactly who is and who isn't a part of "our family." The problem may be compounded by pressures to make the boundaries more open than family members prefer (Ihinger-Tallman and Pasley 1987:55). For example, there may be pressure to allow a nonresidential child to visit whenever he or she wants. Life in such a stepfamily really gets complicated if the child's biological parent views the child as a family member who should be able to enter freely into the home and other family members view the nonresidential child as an outsider who needs permission to enter the home.

Normative Ambiguity Fewer cultural norms exist to deal with life in the stepfamily than in the intact family. This means that there must be a good deal more negotiation. What, precisely, is the role of a stepparent? What if the stepparent and the nonresidential biological parent differ on appropriate behavior for the child? What do stepparents and stepchildren call each other? How much interaction with an ex-spouse is appropriate? What obligations remain to relatives of an ex-spouse with whom one has had close ties in the past?

All such questions must be worked out by each stepfamily. No cultural norms prescribe the behavior. Unfortunately, there may be as many different ideas about ways to answer the question as there are people in the stepfamily.

Stepparents and Stepchildren

What do the terms *stepparent* and *stepchild* mean to you? Is your initial reaction positive, neutral, or negative? As increasing numbers of people experience stepparenting, attitudes may be improving (Keshet 1990). But students generally tend to react negatively to the very terms *stepparent* and *stepchild* (Bryan et al. 1986). They believe that stepparents are both less obligated and less likely than either biological or adoptive parents to be supportive in various situations requiring parent-child interaction (Schwebel, Fine, and Renner 1991). And students from step-families, single-parent families, and intact families all share the less positive perceptions of stepparents (Fine 1986).

These negative perceptions may be rooted, at least in part, in experience. Analysis of data from a national survey showed the stepparents report significantly fewer activities with and positive responses to children than do biological parents (Thomson, McLanahan, and Curtin 1992). Stepfathers are likely to engage in less play, private talks, and projects with children than are biological fathers (Marsiglio 1991). Nevertheless, stereotyping the stepfamily in negative terms does not help members adjust easily to each other. Children are being pulled into something that they have learned to think of as negative. It would not be surprising, then, if many children entered the stepfamily with pessimism and the expectation of problems.

Older children may pose more problems for a stepparent than younger children. Some evidence exists that stepparents have less positive relationships with older than with younger stepchildren (Hobart 1987). Even the adult children of those who remarry may create problems for a couple. A forty-five-year-old woman whose sixty-nine-year-old mother remarried some years after being widowed admitted that she had problems accepting her stepfather:

> One reason I got so upset was that I felt like Mom's new husband was just after her money—Dad's money. Her new husband gave his house to his son and then moved in with Mom. I remember Dad saying that he didn't mind dying because he knew that his grandchildren and his great-grandchildren would be running around that house just like I did when I was little. But he left the house to Mom. If she dies first,

I'm afraid her new husband will get everything and my children and grandchildren will lose what my dad expected them to have.

Whatever their age, stepchildren can resent and resist a stepparent coming into the family.

Stepfathering   Because of custody arrangements over the past few decades, stepfathering with custody of the child has been more common than stepmothering with custody. How do stepfathers regard their performance? Apparently not very well. They tend to see themselves as less competent than either their wives or their stepchildren see them. They feel more inadequate in maintaining close physical and emotional contact with stepchildren than do biological fathers with their own children (Weingarten 1980). Still, Marsiglio (1992) found, in a national survey, that over half of stepfathers disagree that it is harder to love stepchildren than one's own children. The survey also showed that stepfathers who have both stepchildren and their own children in the same household and who have a happy relationship with their partner are more likely to say that they feel "fatherlike" toward the stepchildren and report better relationships with their stepchildren.

     Stepchildren themselves report less support, control, and punishment from stepfathers than do children from biological fathers (Amato 1987). However, from the stepchild's point of view, the relationship tends to improve over time and become more like that with a biological father. In addition, the mothers in stepfather families may have a more positive view of what is going on than do the stepfathers themselves. Using a small American sample, Kurdek and Fine (1991) reported that wives (mothers), compared to their husbands (stepfathers), were more optimistic about stepfamily life, less likely to believe in myths about stepfamilies, and more satisfied with their husbands' relationships with the children.

     The difficulties notwithstanding, many stepfathers are satisfied with their roles and experience a positive parenting experience. This is more likely to happen when (Ihinger-Tallman and Pasley 1987; Fine, Ganong, and Coleman 1997; Everett 1998):

- They have prior, involved parenting experience with their natural children.

Disciplining is one of the more problematic tasks for a stepfather.

- They frequently engage in parenting behavior and view their parenting as their right and their responsibility.
- They communicate often and well with their stepchildren.
- Their wives support them in their involvement with and discipline of stepchildren.

     Discipline of stepchildren is a particularly problematic area (Newman 1994; Lauer and Lauer 1999a). The child may resent discipline from a stepfather and/or the mother may disagree with her husband about that discipline. If either or both of these situations exist, they can be disruptive to the marriage and the family. A study of fifty stepfather families reported that stepfather-adolescent relationships were best when both the stepfather and the adolescents perceived stepfather-mother agreement about parenting of the adolescents (Skopin, Newman, and McKenry 1993).

     In spite of the stepfathers' perceptions and the problems that can arise, a number of studies have reported no significant differences between stepfather and intact families in such things as perceptions of family conflict and the quality of family relationships (Ganong and Coleman 1988). The majority of stepchildren say that they like their stepparents and get along well with them. Adults who were raised in stepfamilies seem to get along as well in family relationships as those raised in intact families.

Some gender differences have been found in the experiences of children in stepfather families, however. Although boys have a harder time adjusting to divorce than do girls, they seem to have an easier time adjusting to stepfamily life than do girls (Peterson and Zill 1986). Boys have warmer relationships with stepfathers than do girls. As noted earlier, one of the main problems boys seem to have with divorce is adjusting to living without a same-sex parent. The stepfather apparently fills that void for most boys.

Stepmothering   In a study of stepfamilies, mothers reported themselves responding as positively to their stepchildren as to their biological children (Fine, Voydanoff, and Donnelly 1993). Nevertheless, the family with a stepmother is the most likely to be conflicted and poorly adjusted (Ganong and Coleman 1994:77).

A survey of 104 undergraduates reported that those in stepmother families perceived less relationship quality, less support, and more conflict with their stepmother than those who lived with their biological mothers (Pruett, Calsyn, and Jensen 1993). Hobart (1987) found that stepmothers in 232 Canadian families had fewer positive relationships with stepchildren than did the stepfathers. The challenge of stepmothering is not helped by the fact that there is a long cultural tradition of the "wicked stepmother" (PERSPECTIVE). In addition, there are abundant illustrations of disastrous efforts at stepmothering. A woman whose marriage broke up because of stepchildren tells about the agony:

> I was in my early twenties when I married a man with two kids, one eight and one twelve. He had joint custody with his wife. I tried from the first to be their friend. Eventually the boy and I developed a good relationship. But the girl would have none of it. She never would look at me or talk to me directly if she could avoid it. I remember one time I suggested we all go camping on the next weekend. I thought it would be a good family activity. She turned to her father and said, "Does *she* have to go along?" He told her yes, because "she's my wife." They were talking about me as if I wasn't even in the room. My husband never tried to get her to change her behavior towards me. He was afraid she might stop spending time with us. I didn't want to make him choose between me and his daughter. So I left him.

Stepmothering isn't necessarily a painful experience (Ambert 1986). Some stepmothers report very close relationships with their stepchildren, and the majority of stepchildren report satisfying relationships with stepmothers. But stepmothering does seem to be more troublesome than stepfathering. Perhaps one factor in this is that stepmothering is more likely than stepfathering to involve a noncustodial relationship. When the stepchild is in the home, the stepmother rather than the child's father is likely to have the extra work of cleaning and cooking. The stepmother is called on to assume a burden that will have little or no emotional benefit to her. Not only is the stepchild not hers but she may feel left out because the father is involving his ex-wife more than her in the parenting process.

Stepchildren and the Marital Relationship   Stepparents are more likely than biological parents to perceive strains on their marriage from the parenting experience. White and Booth (1985:695–96) reported that those with stepchildren in their homes are more likely than others to prefer living apart from the children and to perceive the children as giving them problems. They are also less likely to be satisfied with their spouse's relationship with their children. Finally, they are more prone to see the marriage as having a negative effect on the children and more likely to say that if they could do it all over, they would not have married. In fact, 15 percent of those with stepchildren said they wouldn't have married, compared with only 6 percent of those without stepchildren. Not surprisingly, those with stepchildren reported somewhat less marital happiness than others.

Wives are more likely to see their marital relationship affected by the husband's relationships with the children (his children, her children, or their children) than vice versa (Hobart and Brown 1988). Marital satisfaction is also affected by the type of family. Satisfaction is significantly lower when both spouses bring children to the marriage than when only one had children by a previous marriage (Clingempeel 1981). Satisfaction also is significantly affected by the living arrangements of the stepchildren. Stepmothers who have the least amount of difficulty and report the highest amount of marital satisfaction are those who have live-in stepchildren rather than stepchildren who visit the

PERSPECTIVE
The Unacceptable Stepmother

As noted in the text, the very word *stepparent* tends to have negative connotations for us. In part, this is because stepparents are portrayed in very negative terms in literature. Consider the wicked stepfather in Shakespeare's *Hamlet* and Dickens's *David Copperfield* or the wicked stepmother in such children's stories as "Snow White," "Hansel and Gretel," and "Cinderella." The following ballad, part of a collection of Missouri folklore, tells the reaction of a blind girl to the news of her father's remarriage. The girl cannot accept the notion of a stepmother in the home. Her grief over the situation eventually leads to her death:

> "They tell me, father, that tonight
> You wed another bride,
> And that you'll clasp her in your arms
> Where my poor mother died.
>
> They say her name is Mary, too,
> The name my mother bore.
> Oh, tell me, is she kind and true
> As the one you loved before?
>
> "And is her step so soft and low,

her voice so sweet and mild,
And do you think that she will love
Your blind and only child?

"Please, father, do not bid me come
To greet your loving bride.
I could not meet her in the room
Where my poor mother died.

"Her picture's hanging on the wall,
Her books are lying near;
And there's the harp her fingers touched;
And there's her vacant chair—

"The chair whereby I've often knelt
To say my evening prayer
Oh! father, it would break my heart.
I could not meet her there.

"I love you but I long to go
To yon bright world so fair
Where God is true, and I am sure
There'll be no blind ones there.

"Now let me kneel down by your side

And to our Savior pray
That God's right hand may shield you both
Through life's long dreary way.

"My prayers are ended now, dear pa,
I'm tired now," she said.
He picked her up all in his arms
And laid her on the bed.

And as he turned to leave the room
A joyful cry was given.
He heard, and caught the last sweet smile—
His blind child was in heaven.

They laid her by her mother's side
And raised a marble fair,
And but engraved these simple words:
"There'll be no blind ones there."

William Tyler, *The Blind Girl.* Reprinted from *Ballads and Songs* by H. M. Belden, by permission of the University of Missouri Press. Copyright 1973 by the Curators of the University of Missouri.

home (Ambert 1986). While a live-in stepchild is not necessarily an easy situation, stepmothers apparently find it easier to develop a close relationship with the live-in child. Thus, the greater frequency of problems with stepmothers than stepfathers may be rooted in the fact that most stepmothers do not have live-in stepchildren.

There are a variety of reasons stepchildren can adversely affect the marital relationship (Sager et al. 1980; Lauer and Lauer 1999a). The stepfamily is an instant creation rather than a gradual process of pregnancy, birth, and intimate relationships from the beginning of the child's life. Coming into an instant family and dealing with the challenges and is-

sues of that stage of the family life cycle may not be fully compatible with the stepparent's individual stage of life. As one stepmother put it:

> I do my best. I really like my stepdaughter. But I find myself still thinking about the fact that I'm raising another woman's child. And meanwhile, I'm trying to establish my career. It's not quite fair. But I remind myself that I do like her and that she is my husband's child.

Another factor that complicates the stepfamily is that the ex-spouse and his or her parents may continue to have input into the children's lives. This can contribute to divided loyalties. The stepchild may like the stepparent but get conflicting guidance from the stepparent and the absent biological parent or may simply feel that liking the stepparent too much is disloyalty to the absent biological parent.

In addition, the stepchild may still be suffering from the emotional trauma of loss of the absent parent. In such cases, the stepchild may act out his or her anger against the stepparent. Even when the child is consulted about the remarriage, the child may feel resentment. The biological parent, then, is torn between loyalty to the child and loyalty to the new spouse.

Adjustment of Stepchildren   In spite of the problems that can arise, not only are the majority of children in stepfamilies satisfied with their stepparents but they also have no more negative attitudes toward themselves or others than do children in intact families (Ganong and Coleman 1993). Children in stepfamilies do exhibit more behavior problems of various kinds (Hetherington 1993; Thomson, Hanson, and McLanahan 1994). But these children are not lower in self-esteem, psychological functioning, or academic achievement than those in intact families (Ihinger-Tallman and Pasley 1987; Thomson, Hanson, and McLanahan 1994). When children in stepfamilies do perform lower academically, it is rooted more in a lack of resources (parental education and income) than in living in a stepfamily per se

(Downey 1995). The psychological functioning of children may vary by type of stepfamily. One study found that sixth- and seventh-grade students living with stepfathers had higher self-esteem and reported fewer problems than those living with stepmothers (Fine and Kurdek 1992).

What about longer-term consequences? Surveys carried out by the national opinion research center asked respondents about their living arrangements at the age of sixteen. Beer (1988) pooled results from a twelve-year period and found some interesting differences depending on whether the respondents lived with both biological parents, a father and a stepmother, or a mother and stepfather (table 19.1). Males from intact families scored better than those from stepfamilies on seven out of ten of the measures, while females from intact families scored better than others on five of the measures. A close examination of table 19.1 shows that no simple conclusions can be drawn. In some things, people from stepfamilies scored better than those from intact families. Overall, both males and females from intact families had somewhat better emotional adjustment (as defined by the five items in the survey) than did those from stepfamilies. And males from intact families had better social adjustment. But an intact family yielded little or no advantage to female social adjustment or to the familial adjustment of males or females.

In spite of many problems, most children in stepfamilies are satisfied with their stepparents.

TABLE 19.1
Long-Term Adjustment by Type of Family Background

	Males at Age Sixteen, Lived with:			Females at Age Sixteen, Lived with:		
	Mother and Father	Father and Stepmother	Mother and Stepfather	Mother and Father	Father and Stepmother	Mother and Stepfather
Emotional Adjustment	Percent					
Say they are very happy	34	38	23	39	24	34
Believe most people try to be helpful	51	41	43	60	56	57
Believe most people try to be fair	63	66	54	69	66	60
Believe most people can be trusted	51	41	41	46	44	42
Find life exciting	50	34	44	44	32	49
Social Adjustment						
Very satisfied with job	50	43	41	51	48	50
Get a very great deal of satisfaction from friendships	29	27	24	35	25	37
Respond "no" when asked if they drink more than they should	52	49	48	69	73	55
Familial Adjustment						
Very happy married	70	65	66	67	57	67
Get a very great deal of satisfaction from family life	42	43	36	47	30	49

Source: William Beer, "New Family Ties: How Well Are We Coping?" *Public Opinion,* March/April 1988:15. Copyright © 1988 American Enterprise Institute. Reprinted with the permission of the American Enterprise Institute for Public Policy Research.

Another interesting finding in table 19.1 is the differences between the backgrounds of stepfathers and stepmothers. In spite of the research that shows that stepmothers have more problems with children, only the females from stepmother families reported less adjustment than those from stepfather families. For males, those from stepmother families scored higher than those from stepfather families on six of the ten measures. Finally, note that males from stepfather families and females from stepmother families were much less likely than others to say that they are very happy and had the lowest scores on a majority of the ten measures. It may be, then, that the most difficult time for children occurs when the stepparent is the same sex as the stepchild.

Family Functioning

Apart from the stepparent-stepchild relationship, how do people see the stepfamily as a whole? How well does the stepfamily function? A study of 631 college students reported that those from stepfamilies perceived less cohesion and more stress in family life than did those from intact families (Kennedy 1985). Using a smaller sample of twenty-eight intact and twenty-eight stepfamilies, Pink and Wampler (1985) obtained ratings from both parents and adolescent children and also found lower levels of cohesion in the stepfamilies. In addition, the stepfamily respondents reported lower levels of adaptability, the family's ability to successfully deal with differing problems and situations.

Thus, stepfamilies tend to have less closeness between members and less ability to change when confronted with stress than do intact families. The same results, plus some additional findings, were reported by four researchers who compared 106 intact with 108 stepfamilies (Peek et al. 1988). The stepfamilies scored lower not only on cohesion and adaptability but also on expressiveness (the extent to which people feel free to express their feelings to other family members), ability to manage conflict effectively, problem-solving skills, openness of communication, and the quality of relationships.

Again, it is important to emphasize that these results do not mean that stepfamilies are all in trouble. Lower scores do not mean pathological scores. The point is not that life in a stepfamily is miserable. The point is that stepfamilies tend to function at a somewhat lower level than intact families. You will probably not be damaged by living in a stepfamily; you may not, however, have the same experience of family closeness and flexibility as someone who grows up in an intact family.

On the other hand, stepfamilies have a number of potential strengths (Coleman, Ganong, and Gingrich 1985). The divorced parent may feel less harassed by financial problems and child-rearing responsibilities when he or she remarries. The children of divorce may benefit more from the stepfamily than the single-parent experience. In fact, children from stepfamilies are more like those from intact families than are children from single-parent families.

In stepfamilies, new people with new ideas and skills are encountered—sources of new opportunities for children. Children also once again have a model of marriage and of adult intimacy. Having seen one marriage break up, they may benefit by a second marriage that shows them that adults can have a stable and happy relationship.

The merging of two families in the stepfamily means that children come into a situation that requires a good deal of negotiation and flexibility. They may learn much about how, and how not, to cope effectively with other people in situations that require the working out of differences. As a result, stepchildren can be more accommodating and adaptable in their adult relationships.

In sum, stepfamily life has both advantages and disadvantages. Overall, your chances of growing up in a stable and healthy environment are somewhat less in a stepfamily than in an intact family. But in those stepfamilies that function well, the outcome will be similar to the well-functioning intact family. In fact, Bray and Kelly (1998) found that the great majority of the children they studied were functioning well academically, personally, and socially after ten years in a stepfamily.

MAKING IT WORK

Tanya is a thirty-four-year-old secretary who is expecting her first child. She is in her second marriage. At the age of twenty, she married her high school sweetheart. The union lasted six years. "It was a clear example of the conflict-habituated marriage," she recalls. "We were both pulling our own way and expecting the other to 'prove how much you love me.'" At one point, they moved to a different state, hoping the move would give their marriage a fresh start. When it didn't, her husband moved back, but Tanya remained where she was. They divorced. She met another man and remarried a year later. She is delighted: "It was, and continues to be, six and one-half years later, wonderful to have someone with whom I can truly share my life. With him, I have found the intimacy that is so important for well-being and growth."

Clearly, not everyone who remarries will have Tanya's experience. But second marriages, including those involving stepfamilies, can work out well and be stable and satisfying. In our study of long-term marriages, about 10 percent of the couples involved a remarriage (Lauer and Lauer 1986). What factors are at work in those second marriages and stepfamilies that succeed?

First, as far as the marriage itself is concerned, the same factors that make a first marriage work well also apply to a second marriage. For example, we have talked about the importance of communication. A therapist told us that some remarried couples make the mistake of giving priority to the needs of their children over their needs as a couple. He suggests, however, that parents in a remarriage should set aside a minimum amount of time each day and some special times on weekends when they can be alone. One of the best things a couple can do for their children, he notes, is to show them that their parent and stepparent care about each other and need to spend time together to enrich their marriage. It is also one of the best things they can do for their relationship as husband and wife. Second marriages, like first marriages, need careful nurturing.

Furthermore, stepfamilies will work well to the extent that they confront and adequately respond to a number of challenges and tasks (Lauer and Lauer 1999a), including:

- Help each other deal with feelings of loss that arise out of the disruption of the previous families.

- Replace fantasy expectations with realistic ones.
- Develop a sense of family identity, including the sense that "we are a family" rather than "we are a stepfamily."
- Assist each other work through such loyalty conflicts as when children are torn between a desire to maintain a close relationship with the natural parent while still developing one with the stepparent.
- Resolve any lingering issues with ex-spouses.
- Develop stepparenting rules and behaviors that are acceptable to everyone.

- Be aware of, and responsive to, the feelings and needs of each members of the stepfamily.
- Nurture a strong marital relationship.

In sum, remarriage and the stepfamily represent another effort to create meaningful intimate relationships after the first effort has failed. The task is no easier the second time. On the contrary, it is more difficult. But millions of Americans have already shown that it can be done. A failed quest for intimacy does not mean that the quest is fruitless. With patience, understanding, and hard work, fulfilling intimate relationships are within the grasp of each of us.

PRINCIPLES FOR ENHANCING INTIMACY

The following suggestions, published by the U.S Department of Health, Education, and Welfare (1978), are very useful principles for dealing with the special problems of being a stepparent:

1. Let the relationship with stepchildren develop gradually. Don't force it. Remember that both stepparents and stepchildren need time to adjust.
2. Don't try to replace the lost parent. Try to be an additional parent to the child.
3. Expect a confusion of various feelings in each member of the stepfamily. Anxiety, ambivalence, feelings of divided loyalties, love, caring, and other feelings will all be mixed together over the course of creating the new family unit.
4. Be prepared for comparisons with the absent parent. Work out with your spouse what is best for you and the stepchildren and stand by it.
5. You will need support from your spouse in rearing the children. It is important that the two of you agree. Raising children is a difficult task; raising someone else's children can be even harder.
6. Make every effort to be open and fair and honest with both stepchildren and children. Openly acknowledge good relations between stepsiblings.
7. Try to recognize and admit your need for help if the situation becomes too difficult for you. We all need help at times. Numerous counselors and organizations are available to help people with the difficult task of stepparenting.

SUMMARY

People may enter a remarriage from one of five different situations. One partner may have been single. And one or both partners may have been divorced or widowed with no children, divorced or widowed with custody of children, divorced or widowed without custody of children, or divorced or widowed with custody of some children but not others. Most of the more than 2 million Americans who divorce each year will remarry, and many of the remarriages will involve children. The divorce rate is slightly higher among second than first marriages when both partners were married previously and are even higher when one or both partners bring children to the marriage.

Second marriages fare better if there is a period of three to five years of dating after the divorce. But a substantial number of those who remarry do so within the first year after the divorce. Those who remarry tend to spend less time in dating and engagement to second spouses. They also do little to prepare for a second marriage other than living together, though some get counseling or seek advice from friends or books. People remarry for the same reasons they marry the first time; in addition, some may be looking for suitable stepparents for their children.

Some myths about remarriage can be detrimental to the relationship. There are also challenges and issues that are peculiar to remarriage. The kin relations are complex and the roles may be ambiguous. There may be unresolved emotional issues from the first marriage. Issues of children and finances and legal matters also arise.

The quality of remarried life depends on such things as companionship, feelings, and satisfaction with parenting. Remarried people tend to report as satisfying relationships as those in first marriages.

Life in a stepfamily typically involves a phase of turmoil, followed by a phase of relative harmony, then by another phase of difficulties. Stepfamilies are unique because of their complexity (the large number of relationships involved), ambiguous family boundaries, and normative ambiguity. The very term *stepfamily* has negative connotations for many people.

Stepfathers tend to feel inadequate. Their stepchildren report less support, control, and punishment from them than do children of biological fathers. Yet the relationship tends to improve over time and become more like that with a biological father. Discipline is a particularly problematic area. However, the majority of stepchildren say they like stepparents and get along well with them, though boys have an easier time than girls in adjusting to stepfamily life.

Stepmothers have less positive relationships with stepchildren than do stepfathers. Still a majority of their stepchildren report satisfying relationships. One of the reasons stepmothering poses more problems than stepfathering is it is more likely to involve a noncustodial relationship.

Stepparents are more likely than biological parents to perceive strains on the marriage from the parenting experience, and satisfaction is significantly lower when both spouses bring children to the marriage. Noncustodial stepchildren tend to create more problems than those who live in the stepfamily.

In spite of the problems, the majority of children in stepfamilies are satisfied with their stepparents and seem to have no greater incidence of problems than children in intact families. In the long run, however, both males and females from intact families have somewhat better emotional adjustment and males have somewhat better social adjustment than those who grow up in stepfamilies. There tends to be less cohesion, less adaptability, and more stress in stepfamilies. Stepfamilies also have strengths, particularly compared with single-parent families.

The same factors that make a first marriage work well also apply to the second marriage. For the stepfamily to work well, the various members must work together through a set of challenges and tasks that range from clearing away unrealistic expectations to forming a family identity.

INTERNET CONNECTION
Remarriage and Stepfamilies

If you have experienced remarriage in your personal life as a marriage partner, stepchild, or grandparent, you know that the challenges associated with remarriage are many. As the statistics at the divorce rates web site below indicate, the United States is not the only country dealing with divorce and remarriage.

www.mhhe
.com/lauer4

International Comparison of Divorce rates

http://www.jinjapan.org/stat/stats/02VIT33.html

Step by Step: Helping Stepfamilies in Southern Australia

http://www.terra.net.au/~jscott/

A website devoted to remarriage issues in Southern Australia

Stepfamily Foundation

http://www.stepfamily.org/

A U.S. based organization devoted to helping stepfamilies

1. Search the internet for information on divorce and remarriage in the following countries: Italy, the United Kingdom, Japan, Germany, India. What can you find? How do your efforts differ when conducting a similar search for divorce in America? Explain the difference (i.e., government agencies, nonprofit organizations, other public and private groups).

2. Given what you know about the countries cited at the International Comparison website, why are the rates of divorce for the other countries lower? Do you believe the rates of divorce will increase in developed countries. Why or why not?

3. Based on your examination of the two stepfamily websites above, what are the challenges facing U.S. stepfamilies versus those of Australian stepfamilies? Do you imagine the challenges are similar in other developed countries? How about in third-world nations?

GLOSSARY

abortion expulsion of the fetus from the uterus

alcohol abuse improper use of alcohol such that the consequences are detrimental to the user and the family

androgyny possession of both traditional masculine (instrumental) and traditional feminine (expressive) traits

artificial insemination injection of sperm into a woman's vagina

assortative mating marriage between people who are similar on one or more characteristics

authoritarian parenting a style of parenting with strong control, minimal affection, and the expectation of unquestioning obedience

authoritative parenting a style of parenting with warmth and acceptance in the context of clear rules and boundaries on what is acceptable behavior

birth rate number of births per one thousand women in the childbearing years (15–44 years of age)

bundling two people sleeping on the same bed without undressing

celibacy abstaining from sexual relations

cohabitation living with someone in an intimate, sexual relationship without being legally married

commuter marriage a dual-career marriage in which the spouses live in different areas

companionate love affection for, and commitment to, someone with whom one is deeply involved

contraception use of devices or techniques to prevent fertilization

cunnilingus oral stimulation of the female genitals

death rate the number of deaths per one thousand population

definition of the situation if a situation is defined as real, it will have real consequences

dual-career family a family in which both spouses are in careers and have a commitment to work that has a long-term pattern of mobility

dual-earner family a family in which both spouses are involved in paid work outside the home, and one or both view the work only as a job rather than a career

ejaculation discharge of semen from the penis during orgasm

endometriosis a disease in which the tissue that lines the inside of the uterus grows outside as well

equity fairness, in the sense that people are rewarded in proportion to their contributions

expressive traits those traits, associated with the traditional female gender role, that facilitate good relationships

extended family a group of three or more generations formed as an outgrowth of the parent-child relationship

familism a value on family living

family a group united by marriage, blood, and/or adoption in order to satisfy intimacy needs and/or bear and socialize children

family boundary a systems theory concept, referring to rules about who is a member of the family and how each member participates in family life

family of origin the family into which one is born

fellatio oral stimulation of the male genitalia

gay   a male homosexual

gender   social male or female, as distinguished from the biological male or female

gender role   behavior associated with the status of being male or female

gender-role orientation conception of the self as having some combination of masculine and feminine traits

group marriage   a form of marriage in which members of a group are each married to every other opposite-sex member of the group

heterogamy   marriage between people who are dissimilar in social and demographic characteristics

homogamy   marriage between people who are similar in social and demographic characteristics

homophobia   an irrational fear of homosexuality

hypergamy   marriage with someone who is from a higher socioeconomic background

impotence   inability of a male to get or sustain an erection

incest   any type of exploitive sexual contact between relatives in which the victim is under 18 years of age

infertility   failure to conceive after one year of unprotected intercourse

institution   a collective, regularized solution to a problem of social life, such as economic or family arrangements

instrumental traits   those traits, associated with the traditional male gender role, that facilitate goal achievement

integration   the state of being a significant and meaningful part of some group

intimacy   a relationship characterized by mutual commitment, affection, and sharing

in vitro fertilization   removal of eggs from a woman's body, fertilizing them with sperm in a laboratory, and implanting the resulting embryo in the woman's uterus

jealousy   a negative emotional reaction to a real or imagined threat to a love relationship

joint custody   an arrangement in which both divorced parents continue to share responsibility for the care and raising of their children

lesbian   a female homosexual

loneliness   a feeling of isolation from desired relationships

marriage rate   the proportion of unmarried women, ages 15 and above, who get married during a year

matrilineal   descent is traced through the female line

misattribution of arousal   attributing the wrong emotion to physical arousal

monogamy   marriage to one person at a time

network family   a support group of nonkin others

nonverbal cues   facial expressions, body position, gestures, and paralanguage (inflection, rate, and loudness of speaking, etc.) that communicate meaning

norm   an expected pattern of behavior

nuclear family   a group composed of husband, wife, and children, if any

orgasm   third phase of the sexual response cycle in which there is a sudden discharge of sexual tension

ovulation   release of an egg from the ovary

passionate love   a preoccupation with and intense longing for union with a particular other

patrilineal   descent is traced through the male line

penis   male sex organ

permissive parenting   a style of parenting with little or no guidance or control

polyandry   the marriage of a woman to two or more husbands

polygamy   the marriage of one person to two or more people of the opposite sex

polygyny   the marriage of a man to two or more wives

power   ability to get someone to think, feel, or act in a way that he or she would not have done spontaneously

promiscuity   frequent and indiscriminate sexual relations with many partners

propinquity   nearness in place

rape   attempted or actual sexual intercourse by the use of force or the threat of force

rapport   a harmonious and comfortable relationship with someone

reactance theory   resistance to coercion even when the behavior is consistent with the person's attitudes

refractory period   period of time after ejaculation by the male during which he cannot have another orgasm

reframe   redefine the meaning of something in order to make it more acceptable

resilient family   a family that can resist disruption in the face of change and cope effectively with crises

resource theory   the balance of power in a marriage that reflects the relative resources of each spouse

rite of passage   a ceremony that recognizes a significant time of change in an individual's life

self-concept   the totality of an individual's beliefs and attitudes about himself or herself

self-disclosure   the honest revealing of oneself to another

semen   the fluid that carries the sperm and is ejaculated during orgasm

serial marriage   three or more marriages as a result of repeated divorces

sex ratio   the number of males per 100 females

sexual dysfunction   impairment of the physical responses in sexual activity

social class a social group consisting of people with similar income, education, and occupational prestige

social integration a state of relative harmony and cohesion in a group

socialization the process of learning to function effectively in a group

sole custody an arrangement in which the responsibility for the care and raising of children after a divorce is given to one of the parents

static interference of some kind with accurate communication

status the prestige attached to a particular position in society

stepfamily a remarriage in which one or both of the spouses has children from a previous marriage

stereotype a standardized image of something or someone that exists among a group of people

sterilization a surgical procedure that prevents fertilization

testes the male reproductive glands that hang in the scrotum

undifferentiated perception of one's self as low on both masculine and feminine traits

vagina the canal leading from the uterus to the vulva (the exterior part of the female genitals); it is the passage for menstrual flow, for giving birth, and for receiving the penis during heterosexual intercourse

REFERENCES

Abbey, Antonia. 1982. "Sex Differences in Attributions for Friendly Behavior: Do Males Misperceive Females' Friendliness?" *Journal of Personality and Social Psychology* 42:830–38.

Abbey, Antonia, Frank M. Andrews, and L. Jill Halman. 1992. "Infertility and Subjective Well-Being: The Mediating Roles of Self-Esteem, Internal Control, and Interpersonal Conflict." *Journal of Marriage and the Family* 54:408–17.

Abloff, Richard, and Jay Hewitt. 1985. "Attraction to Men and Women Varying in Self-Esteem." *Psychological Reports* 56:615–18.

Abma, Joyce, Anne Driscoll, and Kristin Moore. 1998. "Young Women's Degree of Control Over First Intercourse." *Family Planning Perspectives* 30:12–18.

Abma, Joyce C., et al. 1997. "Fertility, Family Planning, and Women's Health." *Vital and Health Statistics,* Series 23: No. 19 (May).

Adams, Jeffrey M., and Warren H. Jones. 1997. "The Conceptualization of Marital Commitment: An Integrative Analysis." *Journal of Personality and Social Psychology* 72:1177–96.

Adams, Susan, Janet Kuebli, Patricia A. Boyle, and Robyn Fivush. 1995. "Gender Differences in Parent-Child Conversations about Past Emotions." *Sex Roles* 33:309–23.

Ahrons, Constance R., and Lynn S. Wallisch. 1987. "The Relationship Between Former Spouses." In D. Perlman and S. Duck, eds., *Intimate Relationships: Development, Dynamics, and Deterioration.* Beverly Hills, Calif.: Sage.

Alba, Richard D., and Reid M. Golden. 1986. "Patterns of Ethnic Marriage in the United States." *Social Forces* 65:202–23.

Albers, Lawrence J., Jeri A. Doane, and Jim Mintz. 1986. "Social Competence and Family Environment: 15-Year Follow-Up of Disturbed Adolescents." *Family Process* 25:379–89.

Aldous, Joan. 1987. "New Views on the Family Life of the Elderly and the Near-Elderly." *Journal of Marriage and the Family* 49:227–34.

Alessandri, Steven M. 1992. "Effects of Maternal Work Status in Single-Parent Families on Children's Perception of Self and Family and School Achievement." *Journal of Experimental Child Psychology* 54:417–33.

Alford-Cooper, Finnegan. 1998. *For Keeps: Marriages That Last a Lifetime.* Armonk, New York: M. E. Sharpe.

Allen, Agaitha, and Teresa Thompson. 1984. "Agreement, Understanding, Realization, and Feeling Understood As Predictors of Communicative Satisfaction in Marital Dyads." *Journal of Marriage and the Family* 46:915–21.

Allen, Katherine R., and Robert S. Pickett. 1987. "Forgotten Streams in the Family Life Course: Utilization of Qualitative Retrospective Interviews in the Analysis of Lifelong Single Women's Family Careers." *Journal of Marriage and the Family* 49:517–26.

Allport, Gordon. 1961. *Pattern and Growth in Personality.* New York: Holt, Rinehart and Winston.

Alpert, Dona, and Amy Culbertson. 1987. "Daily Hassles and Coping Strategies of Dual-Earner and Nondual-Earner Women." *Psychology of Women Quarterly* 11:359–66.

Altman, I., and J. Ginat. 1996. *Polygamous Families in Contemporary Societies.* Cambridge, MA: Cambridge University Press.

Amato, Paul R. 1986. "Marital Conflict, the Parent-Child Relationship and Child Self-Esteem." *Family Relations* 35:403–10.

———. 1987. "Family Processes in One-Parent, Step-parent, and Intact Families: The Child's Point of View." *Journal of Marriage and the Family* 49:327–37.

———. 1988. "Long-Term Implications of Parental Divorce for Adult Self-Concept." *Journal of Family Issues* 9:201–13.

———. 1991. "Parental Absence During Childhood and Depression in Later Life." *The Sociological Quarterly* 32:543–56.

———. 1994. "Father-Child Relations, Mother-Child Relations, and Offspring Psychological Well-Being in Early Adulthood." *Journal of Marriage and the Family* 56:1031–42.

Amato, Paul R., and Alan Booth. 1991. "Consequences of Parental Divorce and Marital Unhappiness for Adult Well-Being." *Social Forces* 69:895–914.

———. 1995. "Changes in Gender Role Attitudes and Perceived Marital Quality." *American Sociological Review* 60:58–66.

Amato, Paul R., and Bruce Keith. 1991a. "Parental Divorce and Adult Well-Being: A Meta-Analysis." *Journal of Marriage and the Family* 53:43–58.

———. 1991b. "Separation from a Parent During Childhood and Adult Socioeconomic Attainment." *Social Forces* 70:187–206.

Amato, Paul R., Laura Spencer Loomis, and Alan Booth. 1995. "Parental Divorce, Marital Conflict, and Off-spring Well-Being During Early Adulthood." *Social Forces* 73:895–915.

Amato, Paul R., and Sandra J. Rezac. 1994. "Contact with Nonresident Parents, Interparental Conflict, and Children's Behavior." *Journal of Family Issues* 15:191–207.

Amato, Paul R., and Stacy J. Rogers. 1997. "A Longitudinal Study of Marital Problems and Subsequent Divorce." *Journal of Marriage and the Family* 59:612–24.

Ambert, Anne-Marie. 1982. "Differences in Children's Behavior Toward Custodial Mothers and Custodial Fathers." *Journal of Marriage and the Family* 44:73–86.

Ambert, Anne-Marie. 1986. "Being a Stepparent: Live-in and Visiting Stepchildren." *Journal of Marriage and the Family* 48:795–804.

Ambry, Margaret K. 1993. "Receipts from a Marriage." *American Demographics,* February, pp. 30–37.

American Indian Law Center. 1986. *Indian Family Law and Child Welfare.* Albuquerque, N.M.: American Indian Law Center.

Ammon, Richard Albright. 1985. "When There's No Wedding, How Do You Know You're Married? The Development and Characteristics of Bonding in Long-Term Gay Male Relationships." Unpublished Ph.D. Dissertation. San Diego: U.S. International University.

Anderson, Elaine A., and Leigh A. Leslie. 1991. "Coping with Employment and Family Stress: Employment Arrangement and Gender Differences." *Sex Roles* 24:223–37.

Anderson, Stephen A., Candyce S. Russell, and Walter R. Schumm. 1983. "Perceived Marital Quality and Family Life-Cycle Categories: A Further Analysis." *Journal of Marriage and the Family* 45:127–39.

Andrews, Bernice, and Chris R. Brewin. 1990. "Attributions of Blame for Marital Violence: A Study of Antecedents and Consequences." *Journal of Marriage and the Family* 52:757–67.

Anonymous. 1878. "Some Plain Answers." *The Shaker Manifesto* 9:223–24.

Antonucci, Toni C., and Hiroko Akiyama. 1987. "An Examination of Sex Differences in Social Support Among Older Men and Women." *Sex Roles* 17:737–48.

Apter, Terri. 1990. *Altered Loves: Mothers and Daughters During Adolescence.* New York: St. Martin's Press.

Aquilino, William S. 1994a. "Impact of Childhood Family Disruption on Young Adults' Relationships with Parents." *Journal of Marriage and the Family* 56:295–313.

———. 1994b. "Later Life Parental Divorce and Widowhood: Impact on Young Adults' Assessment of Parent-Child Relations." *Journal of Marriage and the Family* 56:908–22.

———. 1996. "The Life Course of Children Born to Unmarried Mothers: Childhood Living Arrangements and Young Adult Outcomes." *Journal of Marriage and the Family* 58:293–310.

———. 1997. "From Adolescent to Young Adult: A Prospective Study of Parent-Child Relations During the Transition to Adulthood." *Journal of Marriage and the Family* 59:670–86.

Aquilino, William S., and Khalil R. Supple. 1991. "Parent-Child Relations and Parent's Satisfaction with Living Arrangements When Adult Children Live at

Home." *Journal of Marriage and the Family* 53:13–27.

Archer, Richard L., and Christie E. Cook. 1986. "Personalistic Self-Disclosure and Attraction: Basis for Relationship or Scarce Resource." *Social Psychology Quarterly* 49:268–72.

Arditti, Joyce A. 1992. "Differences Between Fathers with Joint Custody and Noncustodial Fathers." *American Journal of Ortho-Psychiatry* 62:186–95.

Arendell, Terry. 1986. *Mothers and Divorce: Legal, Economic, and Social Dilemmas.* Berkeley and Los Angeles: University of California Press.

Arias, Ileana, Carolyn M. Lyons, and Amy E. Street. 1997. "Individual and Marital Consequences of Victimization." *Journal of Family Violence* 12:193–210.

Armistead, Lisa, Michelle Wierson, and Rex Forehand. 1990. "Parent Work and Early Adolescent Development." *Journal of Early Adolescence* 10:260–78.

Arnstein, Helene S. 1985. *Between Mothers-In-Law and Daughters-In-Law.* New York: Dodd, Mead.

Aschenbrenner, Joyce, and Carolyn Hameedah Carr. 1980. "Conjugal Relationships in the Context of the Extended Black Family." *Alternative Lifestyles* 3:463–84.

Association of American Colleges. 1982. *The Classroom Climate: A Chilly One for Women?* Washington, D.C.: Association of American Colleges.

Atkinson, Maxine P., and Becky L. Glass. 1985. "Marital Age Heterogamy and Homogamy." *Journal of Marriage and the Family* 47:685–91.

Bachrach, Christine A., Kathryn A. London, and Penelope L. Maza. 1991. "On the Path to Adoption: Adoption Seeking in the United States, 1988."*Journal of Marriage and the Family* 53:705–18.

Bachrach, Christine A., Kathy Shepherd Stolley, and Kathryn A. London. 1992. "Relinquishment of Premarital Births: Evidence from National Survey Data." *Family Planning Perspectives* 24:27–32.

Bachu, Amara. 1993. "Fertility of American Women: June 1992." In U.S. Bureau of the Census, *Current Population Reports, series P20, no. 470.* Washington, D.C.: Government Printing Office.

———. 1998. "Trends in Marital Status of U.S. Women At First Birth: 1930 to 1994." *Population Division Working Paper No. 20.* Washington, D.C.: Government Printing Office.

Backman, Carl W. 1981. "Attraction in Interpersonal Relationships." In M. Rosenberg and R. H. Turner, eds., *Social Psychology: Sociological Perspectives.* New York: Basic Books.

Baer, Paul E., Lisa-Berg Garmezy, Robert J. McLaughlin, Alex D. Pokorny, and Mark J. Wernick. 1987. "Stress, Coping, Family Conflict, and Adolescent Al-

cohol Use." *Journal of Behavioral Medicine* 10:449–66.

Bagarozzi, Dennis A. 1990. "Marital Power Discrepancies and Symptom Development in Spouses: An Empirical Investigation." *American Journal of Family Therapy* 18:51–64.

Bahr, Kathleen S. 1994. "The Strengths of Apache Grandmothers: Observations on Commitment, Culture, and Caretaking." *Journal of Comparative Family Studies* 25:233–48.

Bailey, J. Michael, David Bobrow, Marily Wolfe, and Sarah Mikach. 1995. "Sexual Orientation of Adult Sons of Gay Fathers." *Developmental Psychology* 31:124–29.

Bailey, William C., Clyde Hendrick, and Susan S. Hendrick. 1987. "Relation of Sex and Gender Role to Love, Sexual Attitudes, and Self-Esteem." *Sex Roles* 16:637–48.

Baker, Angela K., Kimberly J. Barthelemy, and Lawrence A. Kurdek. 1993. "The Relation Between Fifth and Sixth Graders' Peer-Rated Classroom Social Status and Their Perceptions of Family and Neighborhood Factors." *Journal of Applied Developmental Psychology* 14:547–56.

Bales, Alba. 1929. "A Course in Home Economics for College Men." *Journal of Home Economics* 21:427–28.

Ball, F. L., Philip Cowan, and Carolyn Pape Cowan. 1995. "Who's Got the Power? Gender Differences in Partners' Perceptions of Influence During Marital Problem-Solving Discussions." *Family Process* 34:303–21.

Barbarin, Oscar A., Diane Hughes, and Mark A. Chesler. 1985. "Stress, Coping, and Marital Functioning Among Parents of Children with Cancer." *Journal of Marriage and the Family* 47:473–80.

Barber, Brian K. 1994. "Cultural, Family, and Personal Contexts of Parent-Adolescent Conflict." *Journal of Marriage and the Family* 56:375–86.

Barber, Brian K., Bruce A. Chadwick, and Rolf Oerter. 1992. "Parental Behaviors and Adolescent Self-Esteem in the United States and Germany." *Journal of Marriage and the Family* 54:128–41.

Barber, Clifton E., Barbara L. Fisher, and Kay Pasley. 1990. "Family Care of Alzheimer's Disease Patients: Predictors of Subjective and Objective Burden." *Family Perspective* 24:289–309.

Barber, Jennifer S., and William G. Axinn. 1998. "Gender Role Attitudes and Marriage Among Young Women." *The Sociological Quarterly* 39:11–31.

Bardwell, Jill R., Samuel W. Cochran, and Sharon Walker. 1986. "Relationship of Parental Education,

Race, and Gender to Sex Role Stereotyping in Five-Year-Old Kindergartners." *Sex Roles* 15:275–81.

Barker, Kathleen. 1993. "Changing Assumptions and Contingent Solutions: The Costs and Benefits of Women Working Full- and Part-Time." *Sex Roles* 28:47–71.

Barnes, Gordon E., Leonard Greenwood, and Reena Sommer. 1991. "Courtship Violence in a Canadian Sample of Male College Students." *Family Relations* 40:37–44.

Barnett, Ola W., and Ronald W. Fagan. 1993. "Alcohol Use in Male Spouse Abusers and Their Female Partners." *Journal of Family Violence* 8:1–25.

Barnett, Rosalind C. 1994. "Home-to-Work Spillover Revisited: A Study of Full-Time Employed Women in Dual-Earner Couples." *Journal of Marriage and the Family* 56:647–56.

Barnett, Rosalind C., Robert T. Brennan, and Nancy L. Marshall. 1994. "Gender and the Relationship Between Parent Role Quality and Psychological Distress." *Journal of Family Issues* 15:229–52.

Barnett, Rosalind C., Nancy L. Marshall, Stephen W. Raudenbush, and Robert T. Brennan. 1993. "Gender and the Relationship Between Job Experiences and Psychological Distress: A Study of Dual-Earner Couples." *Journal of Personality and Social Psychology* 64:794–806.

Barnett, Rosalind C., and Caryl Rivers. 1996. *She Works/He Works: How Two-Income Families are Happier, Healthier, and Better-Off.* San Francisco, CA: Harper San Francisco.

Barnett, Rosalind C., and Yu-Chu Shen. 1997. "Gender, High- and Low-Schedule-Control Housework Tasks, and Psychological Distress." *Journal of Family Issues* 18:403–28.

Barranti, Chrystal C. Ramirez. 1985. "The Grandparent/Grandchild Relationship: Family Resource in an Era of Voluntary Bonds." *Family Relations* 34:343–52.

Barret, Robert L., and Bryan E. Robinson. 1990. *Gay Fathers.* Lexington, MA.: D.C. Heath.

Bart, Pauline M. 1971. "Depression in Middle-Aged Women." In V. Gornick and B. K. Moran, eds., *Woman in Sexist Society.* New York: Mentor.

Basting, Louis. 1887. "Reply." *The Manifesto* 16:91.

Baumrind, D. 1967. "Child Care Practices Anteceding Three Patterns of Preschool Behavior." *Genetic Psychology Monographs* 75:43–88.

Beach, Steven R. H., and Abraham Tesser. 1993. "Decision-Making Power and Marital Satisfaction: A Self-Evaluation Maintenance Perspective." *Journal of Social and Clinical Psychology* 12:471–94.

Beauvais, Frederick. 1996. "Trends in Drug Use Among American Indian Students and Dropouts, 1975 to 1994." *American Journal of Public Health* 86:1594–98.

Beauvais, Fred, and Bernard Segal. 1992. "Drug Use Patterns Among American Indian and Alaskan Native Youth." *Drugs and Society* 7:77–94.

Beck, Aaron T. 1988. *Love Is Never Enough.* New York: Harper & Row.

Beckett, Joyce O. 1976. "Working Wives: A Racial Comparison." *Social Work* 21:463–71.

Beer, William. 1988. "New Family Ties: How Well Are We Coping?" *Public Opinion,* March/April, pp. 14–15, 57.

Bell, Alan, and Martin Weinberg. 1978. *Homosexualities: A Study of Diversity Among Men and Women.* New York: Simon & Schuster.

Bell, Grad. 1993. "Emotional Loneliness and the Perceived Similarity of One's Ideas and Interests." *Journal of Social Behavior and Personality* 8:273–80.

Bellah, Robert N., Richard Madsen, William M. Sullivan, Ann Swidler, and Steven M. Tipton. 1985. *Habits of the Heart: Individualism and Commitment in American Life.* New York: Harper & Row.

Bellamy, Edward. 1960. *Looking Backward.* New York: Signet.

Belsky, Jay, and John Kelly. 1994. *The Transition to Parenthood.* New York: Delacorte Press.

Belsky, Jay, and Michael Rovine. 1990. "Patterns of Marital Change Across the Transition to Parenthood: Pregnancy to Three Years Postpartum." *Journal of Marriage and the Family* 52:5–19.

Bem, Sandra L. 1974. "The Measurement of Psychological Androgyny." *Journal of Consulting and Clinical Psychology* 42:155–62.

Bender, William N. 1994. "Joint Custody: The Option of Choice." *Journal of Divorce and Remarriage* 21:115–31.

Benin, Mary Holland, and Joan Agostinelli. 1988. "Husbands' and Wives' Satisfaction with the Division of Labor." *Journal of Marriage and the Family* 50:349–61.

Benin, Mary Holland, and Barbara Cable Nienstedt. 1985. "Happiness in Single- and Dual-Earner Families: The Effects of Marital Happiness, Job Satisfaction, and Life Cycle." *Journal of Marriage and the Family* 47:975–84.

Bennett, Linda A., Steven J. Wolin, David Reiss, and Martha A. Teitelbaum. 1987. "Couples at Risk for Transmission of Alcoholism: Protective Influences." *Family Process* 26:111–29.

Bennett, Neil G., Ann Klimas Blanc, and David E. Bloom. 1988. "Commitment and the Modern Union: Assessing the Link Between Premarital Cohabitation and Subsequent Marital Stability." *American Sociological Review* 53:127–38.

Bereczkei, Tamas. 1996. "Mate Choice, Marital Success, and Reproduction in a Modern Society." *Ethology and Sociobiology* 17:17–35.

Berelson, Bernard. 1979. "The Value of Children: A Taxonomical Essay." In J. G. Wells, ed., *Current Issues in Marriage and the Family.* 2d ed. New York: Macmillan.

Berg, John H., and Ronald D. McQuinn. 1986. "Attraction and Exchange in Continuing and Noncontinuing Dating Relationships." *Journal of Personality and Social Psychology* 50:942–52.

Bernard, Jessie. 1972. *The Future of Marriage.* New York: World.

———. 1974. *The Future of Motherhood.* New York: Dial Press.

———. 1975. "Note on Changing Life Styles, 1970–1974." *Journal of Marriage and the Family* 37:582–93.

———. 1981. "The Good Provider Role: Its Rise and Fall." *American Psychologist* 36:1–12.

Bernstein, Barton E., and Sheila K. Collins. 1985. "Remarriage Counseling: Lawyer and Therapist's Help with the Second Time Around." *Family Relations* 34:387–91.

Berscheid, Ellen, and Elaine Walster. 1974. "A Little Bit About Love." In T. L. Huston, ed., *Foundations of Interpersonal Attraction.* New York: Academic Press.

Berscheid, Ellen, and Elaine Walster. 1978. *Interpersonal Attraction.* Reading, Mass.: Addison-Wesley.

Berthiaume, Marc, Helene David, Jean Francois Saucier, and Francois Borgeat. 1996. "Correlates of Gender Role Orientation During Pregnancy and the Postpartum. *Sex Roles* 35:781–800.

Best, Deborah L., Amy S. House, Anne E. Barnard, and Brenda S. Spicker. 1994. "Parent-Child Interactions in France, Germany, and Italy." *Journal of Cross-Cultural Psychology* 25:181–93.

Bienvenu, Millard J., Sr. 1978. *A Counselor's Guide to Accompany a Marital Communications Inventory.* Saluda, N.C.: Family Life.

Bigbee, Jeri L. 1992. "Family Stress, Hardiness, and Illness: A Pilot Study." *Family Relations* 41:212–17.

Bigner, Jerry J., and R. Brooke Jacobsen. 1989. "Parenting Behaviors of Homosexual and Heterosexual Fathers." *Journal of Homosexuality* 18:173–86.

Biller, Henry B. 1993. *Fathers and Families: Paternal Factors in Child Development.* Westport, Conn.: Auburn House.

Binion, Victoria Jackson. 1990. "Psychological Androgyny: A Black Female Perspective." *Sex Roles* 22:487–507.

Bird, Chloe E. 1997. "Gender Differences in the Social and Economic Burdens of Parenting and Psychological Distress." *Journal of Marriage and the Family* 59:809–23.

Bischoping, Katherine. 1993. "Gender Differences in Conversation Topics, 1922–1990." *Sex Roles* 28:1–18.

Bitter, Robert G. 1986. "Late Marriage and Marital Instability: The Effects of Heterogeneity and Inflexibility." *Journal of Marriage and the Family* 48:631–40.

Black, Leora E., Michael M. Eastwood, Douglas H. Sprenkle, and Elaine Smith. 1991. "An Exploratory Analysis of the Construct of Leavers Versus Left As It Relates to Levinger's Social Exchange Theory of Attractions, Barriers, and Alternative Attractions." *Journal of Divorce and Remarriage* 15:127–39.

Blair, Sampson Lee. 1993. "Employment, Family, and Perceptions of Marital Quality Among Husbands and Wives." *Journal of Family Issues* 14:189–212.

Blair, Sampson Lee, and Daniel T. Lichter. 1991. "Measuring the Division of Household Labor." *Journal of Family Issues* 12:91–113.

Blair, Sampson Lee, and Zhenchao Qian. 1998. "Family and Asian Students' Educational Performance." *Journal of Family Issues* 19:355–74.

Blood, Robert O., Jr., and Donald M. Wolfe. 1960. *Husbands and Wives.* New York: Free Press.

Blum, Deborah. 1998. "Face It!" *Psychology Today,* September/October, pp. 32–39.

Blumstein, Philip, and Pepper Schwartz. 1983. *American Couples: Money, Work, Sex.* New York: William Morrow.

Blyth, Dale A., and Frederick S. Foster-Clark. 1987. "Gender Differences in Perceived Intimacy with Different Members of Adolescents' Social Networks." *Sex Roles* 17:689–718.

Bograd, Ruth, and Bernard Spilka. 1996. "Self-Disclosure and Marital Satisfaction in Mid-Life and Late-Life Remarriages." *International Journal of Aging & Human Development* 42:161–72.

Bohannan, Paul. 1970. *Divorce and After.* New York: Doubleday.

———. 1985. *All the Happy Families: Exploring the Varieties of Family Life.* New York: McGraw-Hill.

Bolger, Niall, Anita DeLongis, Ronald C. Kessler, and Elaine Wethington. 1989. "The Contagion of Stress Across Multiple Roles." *Journal of Marriage and the Family* 51:175–83.

Bolton, Frank, Jr. 1980. *The Pregnant Adolescent.* Beverly Hills, Calif.: Sage.

Bonkowski, Sara E., Sara J. Boomhower, and Shelly Q. Bequette. 1985. "What You Don't Know *Can* Hurt You: Unexpressed Fears and Feelings of Children from Divorcing Families." *Journal of Divorce* 91:33–45.

Boon, Susan D., and Mariana J. Brussoni. 1996. "Young Adults' Relationships with Their 'Closest' Grandparents: Examining Emotional Closeness." *Journal of Social Behavior and Personality* 11:439–58.

Booth, Alan, and Paul R. Amato. 1994. "Parental Marital Quality, Parental Divorce, and Relations with Parents." *Journal of Marriage and the Family* 56:21–34.

Booth, Alan, David B. Brinkerhoff, and Lynn K. White. 1984. "The Impact of Parental Divorce on Courtship." *Journal of Marriage and the Family* 46:85–94.

Booth, Alan, and John N. Edwards. 1992. "Starting Over: Why Remarriages Are More Unstable." *Journal of Family Issues* 13:179–94.

Booth, Alan, John N. Edwards, and David R. Johnson. 1991. "Social Integration and Divorce." *Social Forces* 70:207–24.

Booth, Alan, David R. Johnson, Lynn White, and John N. Edwards. 1984. "Women, Outside Employment, and Marital Instability." *American Journal of Sociology* 90:567–83.

———. 1986. "Divorce and Marital Instability over the Life Course." *Journal of Family Issues* 7:421–42.

Booth, Richard, and Marshall Jung. 1998. *Romancing the Net: A "Tell-All" Guide to Love Online.* Rocklin, Calif.: Prima.

Borders, L. DiAnne, Lynda K. Black, and B. Kay Pasley. 1998. "Are Adopted Children and Their Parents at Greater Risk for Negative Outcomes?" *Family Relations* 47:237–41.

Borland, Delores. 1982. "A Cohort Analysis Approach to the Empty-Nest Syndrome Among Three Ethnic Groups of Women: A Theoretical Position." *Journal of Marriage and the Family* 44:117–29.

Boss, Pauline. 1988. *Family Stress Management.* Beverly Hills, Calif.: Sage.

Botwin, Michael D., David M. Buss, and Todd K. Shackelford. 1997. "Personality and Mate Preferences." *Journal of Personality* 65:107–36.

Bowen, Gary L. 1987. "Changing Gender-Role Preferences and Marital Adjustment: Implications for Clinical Practice." *Family Therapy* 14:17–29.

Bowen, Murray. 1978. *Family Therapy in Clinical Practice.* New York: Jason Aronson.

Boyd, Lenore Anglin, and Arthur J. Roach. 1977. "Interpersonal Communication Skills Differentiating More Satisfying from Less Satisfying Marital Relationships." *Journal of Counseling Psychology* 24:540–42.

Boyer, Debra, and David Fine. 1992. "Sexual Abuse As a Factor in Adolescent Pregnancy and Child Maltreatment." *Family Planning Perspectives* 24:4–11.

Boyes, Michael C., and Sandra G. Allen. 1993. "Styles of Parent-Child Interaction and Moral Reasoning in Adolescence." *Merrill Palmer Quarterly* 39:551–70.

Boyle, Jacquelynn. 1995. "Survey Indicates Most Women Want to Work But to Work Less." *The San Diego Union-Tribune,* May 13.

Bozett, Frederick W. 1989. "Gay Fathers: A Review of the Literature." *Journal of Homosexuality* 18:137–62.

Brannon, Robert. 1976. "The Male Sex Role: Our Culture's Blueprint for Manhood, What It's Done for Us Lately." In D. David and R. Brannon, eds., *The Forty-Nine Percent Majority: The Male Sex Role.* Reading, Mass.: Addison-Wesley.

Bray, James, and John Kelly. 1998. *Stepfamilies.* New York: Broadway Books.

Brayfield, April. 1995. "Juggling Jobs and Kids: The Impact of Employment Schedules on Fathers' Caring for Children." *Journal of Marriage and the Family* 57:321–32.

Breault, K. D., and Augustine J. Kposowa. 1987. "Explaining Divorce in the United States: A Study of 3,111 Counties, 1980." *Journal of Marriage and the Family* 49:549–58.

Brehm, Jack W. 1966. *A Theory of Psychological Reactance.* New York: Academic Press.

Bremer, Fredrika. 1853. *The Homes of the New World: Impressions of America,* trans. by Mary Howitt. New York: Harper & Brothers.

Bretschneider, Judy G., and Norma L. McCoy. 1988. "Sexual Interest and Behavior in Healthy 80- to 102-Year-Olds." *Archives of Sexual Behavior* 17:109–29.

Brewer, Richard. 1997. "Living on Both Sides of the Fence: Gay Male Couples with Children." *Progress: Family Systems Research and Therapy* 6:137–50.

Brillinger, Margaret E. 1985. "Marital Satisfaction and Planned Change." *Family Perspective* 19:35–43.

Broderick, Carlfred B. 1993. *Understanding Family Process: Basics of Family Systems Theory.* Newbury Park, Calif.: Sage.

Brody, Gene H., Eileen Neubaum, and Rex Forehand. 1988. "Serial Marriage: A Heuristic Analysis of an Emerging Family Form." *Psychological Bulletin* 103:211–22.

Brody, Robert. 1985. "New Research Dispels Myths About Unhappy Retirements." *San Diego Union,* December 20.

Brodzinsky, D. M., D. E. Schechter, A. M. Braff, and L. M. Singer. 1984. "Psychological and Academic Adjustment in Adopted Children." *Journal of Consulting and Clinical Psychology* 52:582–90.

Broman, Clifford L. 1988a. "Household Work and Family Life Satisfaction of Blacks." *Journal of Marriage and the Family* 50:743–48.

———. 1988b. "Satisfaction Among Blacks: The Significance of Marriage and Parenthood." *Journal of Marriage and the Family* 50:45–51.

———. 1991. "Gender, Work-Family Roles, and Psychological Well-Being of Blacks." *Journal of Marriage and the Family* 53:509–20.

———. 1993. "Race Differences in Marital Well-Being." *Journal of Marriage and the Family* 55:724–32.

Bromberger, Joyce T., and Karen A. Matthews. 1994. "Employment Status and Depressive Symptoms in Middle-Aged Women." *American Journal of Public Health* 84:202–06.

Bronstein, Phyllis et al. 1996. "Family and Parenting Behaviors Predicting Middle School Adjustment." *Family Relations* 45:415–26.

Brookoff, Daniel, Kimberly O'Brien, Charles S. Cook, and Terry D. Thompson. 1997. "Characteristics of Participants in Domestic Violence." *Journal of the American Medical Association* 277:1369–73.

Brophy, Beth. 1997. "Saturday Night and You're All Alone?" *U.S. News & World Report,* February 17.

Brown, George W., and Tirril Harris. 1978. *Social Origins of Depression.* New York: Free Press.

Brown, Larry K., Ralph J. DiClemente, and Teron Park. 1992. "Predictors of Condom Use in Sexually Active Adolescents." *Journal of Adolescent Health* 13:651–57.

Brown, Philip M. 1995. *The Death of Intimacy: Barriers to Meaningful Interpersonal Relationships.* New York: Haworth.

Brown, Susan L., and Alan Booth. 1996. "Cohabitation Versus Marriage: A Comparison of Relationship Quality." *Journal of Marriage and the Family* 58:668–78.

Bryan, Linda R., Marilyn Coleman, Lawrence Ganong, and S. Hugh Bryan. 1986. "Person Perception: Family Structure As a Cue for Stereotyping." *Journal of Marriage and the Family* 48:169–74.

Bryson, Ken, and Lynne Casper. 1998. "Household and Family Characteristics: March 1997." In *Current Population Reports.* Washington, D.C.: Government Printing Office.

Buchanan, Christy M., Eleanor Maccoby, and Sanford M. Dornbusch. 1996. *Adolescents After Divorce.* Cambridge, Mass.: Harvard University Press.

Buckle, Leslie, Gordon G. Gallup, Jr., and Zachary A. Rodd. 1996. "Marriage As a Reproductive Contract." *Ethology and Sociobiology* 17:363–77.

Buehler, Cheryl. 1987. "Initiator Status and the Divorce Transition." *Family Relations* 36:82–86.

Buehler, Cheryl, and Mary Langenbrunner. 1987. "Divorce-Related Stressors: Occurrence, Disruptiveness, and Area of Life Change." *Journal of Divorce* 11:25–50.

Buehler, Cheryl et al. 1998. "Interpersonal Conflict Styles and Youth Problem Behaviors: A Two-Sample Replication Study." *Journal of Marriage and the Family* 60:119–32.

Buhrmester, Duane, and Wyndol Furman. 1987. "The Development of Companionship and Intimacy." *Child Development* 58:1101–13.

Bulcroft, Kris, and Margaret O'Connor. 1986. "The Importance of Dating Relationships on Quality of Life for Older Persons." *Family Relations* 35:397–401.

Bulcroft, Kris, and Margaret O'Conner-Roden. 1986. "Never Too Late." *Psychology Today,* June, pp. 66–69.

Bulcroft, Richard A., and Kris A. Bulcroft. 1993. "Race Differences in Attitudinal and Motivational Factors in the Decision to Marry." *Journal of Marriage and the Family* 55:338–55.

Bumpass, Larry L., Teresa Castro-Martin, and James A. Sweet. 1991. "The Impact of Family Background and Early Marital Factors on Marital Disruption." *Journal of Family Issues* 12:22–42.

Bumpass, Larry L., and James A. Sweet. 1989. "National Estimates of Cohabitation." *Demography* 26:615–26.

Bumpass, Larry, James Sweet, and Andrew Cherlin. 1991. "The Role of Cohabitation in Declining Rates of Marriage." *Journal of Marriage and the Family* 53:913–27.

Bumpass, Larry L., James A. Sweet, and Teresa Castro-Martin. 1990. "Changing Patterns of Remarriage." *Journal of Marriage and the Family* 52:747–56.

Bunker, Barbara B., Josephine M. Zubek, Virginia J. Vanderslice, and Robert W. Rice. 1992. "Quality of Life in Dual-Career Families: Commuting Versus Single-Residence Couples." *Journal of Marriage and the Family* 54:399–407.

Burden, Dianne S. 1986. "Single Parents and the Work Setting: The Impact of Multiple Job and Homelife Responsibilities." *Family Relations* 35:37–43.

Burford, Heather C., Linda A. Foley, Patricia G. Rollins, and Kemberly S. Rosario. 1996. "Gender Differences in Preschoolers' Sharing Behavior." *Journal of Social Behavior and Personality* 11:17–25.

Burger, Jerry M., and Linda Burns. 1988. "The Illusion of Unique Invulnerability and the Use of Effective Contraception." *Personality and Social Psychology Bulletin* 14:264–70.

Burgess, Ernest W., and Leonard S. Cottress. 1939. *Predicting Success or Failure in Marriage.* Englewood Cliffs, N.J.: Prentice-Hall.

Burgess, Ernest, and Paul Wallin. 1943. "Homogamy in Social Characteristics." *American Journal of Sociology* 49:109–24.

———. 1953. *Engagement and Marriage.* Philadelphia: Lippincott.

Burley-Allen, Madelyn. 1982. *Listening: The Forgotten Skill.* New York: John Wiley & Sons.

Burnett, Paul C., and Wayne J. Demnar. 1996. "The Relationship Between Closeness to Significant Others and Self-Esteem." *Journal of Family Studies* 2:121–29.

Buss, David M. 1985. "Human Mate Selection." *American Scientist* 73:47–51.

Buss, David M., and Michael Barnes. 1986. "Preferences in Human Mate Selection." *Journal of Personality and Social Psychology* 50:559–70.

Buss, David M. et al., 1990. "International Preferences in Selecting Mates: A Study of 37 Cultures." *Journal of Cross-Cultural Psychology* 21:5–47.

Butler, Robert N., and Myrna Lewis. 1981. *Aging and Mental Health.* St. Louis, Mo.: Mosby.

Buunk, Bram, and Robert G. Bringle. 1987. "Jealousy in Love Relationships." In D. Perlman and S. Duck, eds., *Intimate Relationships: Development, Dynamics, and Deterioration.* Beverly Hills, Calif.: Sage.

Cabot, Tracy. 1984. *How to Make a Man Fall in Love with You.* New York: St. Martin's.

Callan, Victor J. 1986a. "The Impact of the First Birth: Married and Single Women Preferring Childlessness, One Child, or Two Children." *Journal of Marriage and the Family* 48:261–69.

Callan, Victor J. 1986b. "Single Women, Voluntary Childlessness and Perceptions About Life and Marriage." *Journal of Biosocial Science* 18:479–87.

Callan, Victor J. 1987. "The Personal and Marital Adjustment of Mothers and of Voluntarily and Involuntarily Childless Wives." *Journal of Marriage and the Family* 49:847–56.

Canavan, Margaret M., Walter J. Meyer, III, and Deborah C. Higgs. 1992. "The Female Experience of Sibling Incest." *Journal of Marital and Family Therapy* 18:129–42.

Cancian, Francesca M. 1985. "Gender Politics: Love and Power in the Private and Public Sphere." In A. Rossi, ed., *Gender and the Life Course.* New York: Aldine.

Caplow, Theodore, Howard M. Bahr, Bruce A. Chadwick, Reuben Hill, and Margaret Holmes Williamson. 1982. *Middletown Families: Fifty Years of Change and Continuity.* Minneapolis: University of Minnesota Press.

Cardoza, Desdemona. 1991. "College Attendance and Persistence Among Hispanic Women: An Examina-tion of Some Contributing Factors." *Sex Roles* 24:133–47.

Cargan, Leonard, and Matthew Melko. 1982. *Singles: Myths and Realities.* Beverly Hills, Calif.: Sage.

Carlson, Bonnie E. 1990. "Adolescent Observers of Marital Violence." *Journal of Family Violence* 5:285–99.

Carstensen, Laura L., John M. Gottman, and Robert W. Levenson. 1995. "Emotional Behavior in Long-Term Marriage." *Psychology and Aging* 10:140–49.

Carter, Elizabeth A., and Monica McGoldrick. 1980. *The Family Life Cycle.* New York: Gardner Press.

Carver, Karen Price, and Jay D. Teachman. 1993. "Female Employment and First Union Dissolution in Puerto Rico." *Journal of Marriage and the Family* 55:686–98.

Caspar, Lynne. 1997. "My Daddy Takes Care of Me! Fathers As Care Providers." *Current Population Reports,* September, pp. 70–90.

Caspi, Avshalom, Bradley R. Entner Wright, Terrie E. Moffitt, and Phil A. Silva. 1998. "Early Failure in the Labor Market: Childhood and Adolescent Predictors of Unemployment in the Transition to Adulthood." *American Sociological Review* 63:424–51.

Cassidy, Margaret L., and Bruce O. Warren. 1996. "Family Employment Status and Gender Role Attitudes." *Gender & Society* 10:312–29.

Castaneda, Donna M. 1993. "The Meaning of Romantic Love Among Mexican-Americans." *Journal of Social Behavior and Personality* 8:257–72.

Castro, Janice. 1991. "The Simple Life." *Time,* April 8, pp. 58–63.

Cate, Rodney, and Alan I. Sugawara. 1986. "Sex Role Orientation and Dimensions of Self-Esteem Among Middle Adolescents." *Sex Roles* 15:145–58.

Centers for Disease Control. 1997a. "Assisted Reproductive Technology Success Rates." CDC website.

———. 1997b. "Infertility. CDC website.

———. 1998. "Primary and Secondary Syphilis—United States, 1997. *Morbidity and Mortality Weekly Report,* June 26.

Chafetz, Janet Saltzman. 1974. *Masculine/Feminine or Human?* Itaska, Ill.: F. E. Peacock.

Chan, Cheryl-Jean, and Gayla Margolin. 1994. "The Relationship Between Dual-Earner Couples' Daily Work Mood and Home Affect." *Journal of Social and Personal Relationships* 11:573–86.

Chandra, Anjani, and Elizabeth Hervey Stephen. 1998. "Impaired Fecundity in the United States: 1982–1995." *Family Planning Perspectives* 30:34–42.

Charny, I. W., and S. Parnass. 1995. "The Impact of Extramarital Relationships on the Continuation of Marriages." *Journal of Sex and Marital Therapy* 21:100–15.

Chassin, Laurie, Antonette Zeiss, Kristina Cooper, and Judith Reaven. 1985. "Role Perceptions, Self-Role Congruence and Marital Satisfaction in Dual-Worker Couples with Preschool Children." *Social Psychology Quarterly* 48:301–11.

Chelune, Gordon J., Lawrence B. Rosenfeld, and E. M. Waring. 1985. "Spouse Disclosure Patterns in Distressed and Nondistressed Couples." *The American Journal of Family Therapy* 13:24–32.

Cherlin, Andrew J. 1980. "Postponing Marriage: The Influence of Young Women's Work Expectations." *Journal of Marriage and the Family* 42:355–65.

———. 1981. *Marriage, Divorce, Remarriage.* Cambridge: Harvard University Press.

Cherlin, Andrew J., P. Lindsay Chase-Lansdale, and Christine McRae. 1998. "Effects of Parental Divorce on Mental Health Throughout the Life Course." *American Sociological Review* 63:239–49.

Cherlin, Andrew J., Frank F. Furstenberg, Jr., P. Lindsay Chase-Lansdale, Kathleen E. Kiernan, Philip K. Robins, Donna Ruane Morrison, and Julien O. Teitler. 1991. "Longitudinal Studies of Effects of Divorce on Children in Great Britain and the United States." *Science* 252:1386–88.

Chevan, Albert. 1996. "As Cheaply As One: Cohabitation in the Older Population." *Journal of Marriage and the Family* 58:656–67.

Choo, Patricia, Timothy Levine, and Elaine Hatfield. 1996. "Gender, Love Schemas, and Reactions to Romantic Break-Ups." *Journal of Social Behavior and Personality* 5:143–60.

Chowdhury, Fakhrul I., and Frank Trovato. 1994. "The Role and Status of Women and the Timing of Marriage in Five Asian Countries." *Journal of Comparative Family Studies* 25:143–57.

Cicerello, Antoinette, and Eugene P. Sheehan. 1995. "Personal Advertisements: A Content Analysis." *Journal of Social Behavior and Personality* 10:751–56.

Clair, David, and Myles Genest. 1987. "Variables Associated with the Adjustment of Offspring of Alcoholic Fathers." *Journal of Studies on Alcohol* 48:345–55.

Clanton, Gordon, and L. G. Smith. 1977. *Jealousy.* Englewood Cliffs, N.J.: Prentice-Hall.

Clark, Richard D., and Glenn Shields. 1997. "Family Communication and Delinquency." *Adolescence* 32:81–92.

Clarkberg, Marin, Ross M. Stolzenberg, and Linda J. Waite. 1995. "Attitudes, Values, and Entrance into Cohabitational Versus Marital Unions." *Social Forces* 74:609–34.

Clark-Nicolas, Patricia, and Bernadette Gray-Little. 1991. "Effect of Economic Resources on Marital Quality in Black Married Couples." *Journal of Marriage and the Family* 53:645–55.

Clarke, Sally Cunningham, and Barbara Foley Wilson. 1994. "The Relative Stability of Remarriages." *Family Relations* 43:305–10.

Clemens, Audra W., and Leland J. Axelson. 1985. "The Not-So-Empty-Nest: The Return of the Fledgling Adult." *Family Relations* 34:259–64.

Clements, Mark. 1994. "Sex in America Today." *Parade Magazine,* August 7, pp. 4–6.

Clingempeel, W. Glenn. 1981. "Quasi-Kin Relationships and Marital Quality in Stepfather Families." *Journal of Personality and Social Psychology* 41:890–901.

Cobliner, W. Godfrey. 1988. "The Exclusion of Intimacy in the Sexuality of the Contemporary College-Age Population." *Adolescence* 23:99–113.

Cockrum, Janet, and Priscilla White. 1985. "Influences on the Life Satisfaction of Never-Married Men and Women." *Family Relations* 34:551–56.

Cohen, Laurie L., and R. Lance Shotland. 1996. "Timing of First Sexual Intercourse in a Relationship." *Journal of Sex Research* 33:291–99.

Coleman, Diane Hoshall, and Murray A. Straus. 1983. "Alcohol Abuse and Family Violence." In E. Gottheil, K. A. Druley, T. E. Skoloda, and H. M. Waxman, eds., *Alcohol, Drug Abuse, and Aggression.* Springfield, Ill.: Charles C. Thomas.

Coleman, Diane H., and Murray A. Strauss. 1986. "Marital Power, Conflict, and Violence in a Nationally Representative Sample of American Couples." *Violence and Victims* 1:141–57.

Coleman, Marilyn, and Lawrence H. Ganong. 1985. "Remarriage Myths: Implications for the Helping Professions." *Journal of Counseling and Development* 64:116–20.

Coleman, Marilyn, Lawrence H. Ganong, and Ronald Gingrich. 1985. "Stepfamily Strengths: A Review of Popular Literature." *Family Relations* 34:583–89.

Collins, LaVerne Vines. 1997a. "Facts for Asian and Pacific Islander American Heritage Month. *Census Bureau Fact Sheet.* U.S. Bureau of the Census website.

———. 1997b. "Facts for Father's Day." *Census Bureau Fact Sheet.* U.S. Bureau of the Census website.

———. 1997c. "Facts for Hispanic Heritage Month." *Census Bureau Fact Sheet.* U.S. Bureau of the Census website.

———. 1997d. "Facts for Native American Month." *Census Bureau Fact Sheet.* U.S. Bureau of the Census website.

Condon, Richard G., and Pamela R. Stern. 1993. "Gender-Role Preference, Gender Identity, and Gender Socialization Among Contemporary Inuit Youth." *Ethos* 21:384–416.

Conger, Rand D., Xiaojia Ge, Glen H. Elder, and Frederick O. Lorenz. 1994. "Economic Stress, Coercive Family Process, and Developmental Problems of Adolescents." *Child Development* 65:541–61.

Cooney, Teresa M. 1994. "Young Adults' Relations with Parents: The Influence of Recent Parental Divorce." *Journal of Marriage and the Family* 56:45–56.

Cooney, Teresa M., Frank A. Pedersen, Samuel Indelicato, and Rob Palkovitz. 1993. "Timing of Fatherhood: Is 'On-Time' Optimal?" *Journal of Marriage and the Family* 55:205–15.

Cooney, Teresa M., and Peter Uhlenberg. 1990. "The Role of Divorce in Men's Relations with Their Adult Children After Midlife." *Journal of Marriage and the Family* 52:677–88.

Coontz, Stephanie. 1992. *The Way We Never Were: American Families and the Nostalgia Trap.* New York: Basic Books.

———. 1997. *The Way We Really Are: Coming To Terms With America's Changing Families.* New York: Basic Books.

Coopersmith, Stanley. 1967. *The Antecedents of Self-Esteem.* San Francisco: Freeman.

Cornell, Laurel L. 1989. "Gender Differences in Remarriage After Divorce in Japan and the United States." *Journal of Marriage and the Family* 41:457–63.

Cortez, Katharine. 1996. "My Two Moms: Issues and Concerns of Lesbian Couples Raising Sons." *Progress: Family Systems Research and Therapy* 5:37–50.

Coser, Lewis. 1956. *The Functions of Social Conflict.* New York: Free Press.

Couch, Kenneth A., and Dean R. Lillard. 1997. "Divorce, Educational Attainment, and the Earnings Mobility of Sons." *Journal of Family and Economic Issues* 18:231–45.

Craddock, Alan E. 1980. "Marital Problem-Solving as a Function of Couples' Marital Power Expectations and Marital Value Systems." *Journal of Marriage and the Family* 42:185–92.

Crawley, Brenda. 1988. "Black Families in a Neo-Conservative Era." *Family Relations* 37:415–19.

Crnic, Keith A., and Cathryn L. Booth. 1991. "Mothers' and Fathers' Perceptions of Daily Hassles of Parenting Across Early Childhood." *Journal of Marriage and the Family* 53:1042–50.

Crnic, Keith A., and Mark T. Greenberg. 1990. "Minor Parenting Stresses with Young Children." *Child Development* 61:1628–37.

Crohan, Susan E. 1992. "Marital Happiness and Spousal Consensus on Beliefs About Marital Conflict: A Longitudinal Investigation." *Journal of Social and Personal Relationships* 9:89–102.

———. 1996. "Marital Quality and Conflict Across the Transition to Parenthood in African American and White Couples." *Journal of Marriage and the Family* 58:933–44.

Crosby, John F. 1991. *Illusion and Disillusion: The Self in Love and Marriage.* 4th ed. Belmont, Calif.: Wadsworth.

Crossman, Rita K., Sandra M. Stith, and Mary M. Bender. 1990. "Sex Role Egalitarianism and Marital Violence." *Sex Roles* 22:293–304.

Crowley, M. Sue. 1998. "Men's Self-Perceived Adequacy as the Family Breadwinner: Implications for Their Psychological, Marital, and Work-Family Well-Being." *Journal of Family and Economic Issues* 19:7–23.

Cummings, E. Mark. 1994. "Marital Conflict and Children's Functioning." *Social Development* 3:16–36.

Cunningham, John D., Harriet Braiker, and Harold H. Kelley. 1982. "Marital Status and Sex Differences in Problems Reported by Married and Cohabiting Couples." *Psychology of Women Quarterly* 6:415–27.

Curtin, Richard. 1980. "Facing Adversity with a Smile." *Public Opinion,* April/May, pp. 17–19.

Dadds, Mark, Michelle Smith, Yvonne Webber, and Anthony Robinson. "An Exploration of Family and Individual Profiles Following Father-Daughter Incest." *Child Abuse and Neglect* 15:575–86.

Dalton, Sandra T. 1992. "Lived Experience of Never-Married Women." *Issues in Mental Health Nursing* 13:69–80.

Daly, Kerry J. 1996. *Families & Time: Keeping Pace in a Hurried Culture.* Thousand Oaks, Calif.: Sage.

Davidson, Bernard. 1984. "A Test of Equity Theory for Marital Adjustment." *Social Psychology Quarterly* 47:36–42.

Davidson, Sara. 1970. "Open Land: Getting Back to the Commercial Garden." *Harper's Magazine* 240:95.

Davies, Betty, John Spinetta, Ida Martinson, Sandra McClowry, and Emily Kulenkamp. 1986. "Manifestations of Levels of Functioning in Grieving Families." *Journal of Family Issues* 7:297–313.

Davis, Alan G., and Philip M. Strong. 1977. "Working Without a Net: The Bachelor As a Social Problem." *Sociological Review* 25:109–29.

Davis, Keith E. 1985. "Near and Dear: Friendship and Love Compared." *Psychology Today* 19:22–28.

Davis-Brown, Karen, Sonya Salamon, and Catherine A. Surra. 1987. "Economic and Social Factors in Mate Selection: An Ethnographic Analysis of an Agricultural Community." *Journal of Marriage and the Family* 49:41–55.

Dawson, Deborah A. 1991. "Family Structure and Children's Health and Well-Being: Data from the 1988

National Health Interview Survey on Child Health." *Journal of Marriage and the Family* 53:573–84.

Dawson, John M., and Patrick A. Langan. 1994. "Murder in Families." *Bureau of Justice Statistics: Special Report,* July.

Day, Jennifer, and Andrea Curry. 1998: "Educational Attainment in the United States." *Current Population Reports.* Washington, D.C.: Government Printing Office.

Day, Randal D., and Daniel Hook. 1987. "A Short History of Divorce: Jumping the Broom—and Back Again." *Journal of Divorce* 10:57–73.

Dean-Church, Linda, and Faith D. Gilroy. 1993. "Relation of Sex-Role Orientation to Life Satisfaction in a Healthy Elderly Sample." *Journal of Social Behavior and Personality* 8:133–40.

de Anda, Diana, Rosina M. Becerra, and Eve Fielder. 1990. "In Their Own Words: The Life Experiences of Mexican-American and White Pregnant Adolescents and Adolescent Mothers." *Child and Adolescent Social Work Journal* 7:301–18.

DeBruyn, Lemyra M., Carol C. Lujan, and Philip A. May. 1992. "A Comparative Study of Abused and Neglected American Indian Children in the Southwest." *Social Science and Medicine* 35:305–15.

Degler, Carl N. 1980. *At Odds: Women and the Family in America from the Revolution to the Present.* New York: Oxford University Press.

del Castillo, Richard G. 1984. *La Familia: Chicano Families in the Urban Southwest, 1848 to the Present.* Notre Dame, IN.: University of Notre Dame Press.

Delgado-Gaitan, Concha. 1993. "Parenting in Two Generations of Mexican American Families." *International Journal of Behavioral Development* 16:409–27.

De Luccie, Mary F., and Albert J. Davis. 1991. "Do Men's Adult Life Concerns Affect Their Fathering Orientations?" *Journal of Psychology* 125:175–88.

DeMaris, Alfred, and Geoffrey L. Greif. 1992. "The Relationship Between Family Structure and Parent-Child Relationship Problems in Single-Family Households." *Journal of Divorce and Remarriage* 18:55–77.

DeMaris, Alfred, and K. Vaninadha Rao. 1992. "Premarital Cohabitation and Subsequent Marital Stability in the United States: A Reassessment." *Journal of Marriage and the Family* 54:178–90.

Demb, Janet. 1990. "Black, Inner-City, Female Adolescents and Condoms: What the Girls Say." *Family Systems Medicine* 8:401–6.

DeMeis, Debra K., and H. Wesley Perkins. 1996. " 'Supermoms' of the Nineties: Homemaker and Employed Mothers' Performance and Perceptions of the Motherhood Role." *Journal of Family Issues* 17:777–92.

Deming, Mary P., Nancy D. Chase, and David Karesh. 1996. "Parental Alcoholism and Perceived Levels of Family Health Among College Freshmen." *Alcoholism Treatment Quarterly* 14:47–57.

Demo, David H., and Alan C. Acock. 1988. "The Impact of Divorce on Children." *Journal of Marriage and the Family* 50:619–48.

Demos, John. 1968. "Families in Colonial Bristol, Rhode Island: An Exercise in Historical Demography." *William and Mary Quarterly* 25:34–61.

DePaulo, Bella M., Julie I. Stone, and G. Daniel Lassiter. 1985. "Telling Ingratiating Lies: Effects of Target Sex and Target Attractiveness on Verbal and Nonverbal Deceptive Success." *Journal of Personality and Social Psychology* 48:1191–1203.

Derlega, Valerian J., Sandra Metts, Sandra Petronio, and Stephen T. Margulis. 1993. *Self-Disclosure.* Newbury Park, Calif.: Sage.

Devall, Esther, Zolinda Stoneman, and Gene Brody. 1986. "The Impact of Divorce and Maternal Employment on Preadolescent Children." *Family Relations* 35:153–59.

Deveraux, Lara, and Ann Jackoway Hammerman. 1998. *Infertility and Identity.* San Francisco, Calif.: Jossey-Bass.

De Vita, Carol J. 1996. "The United States at Mid-Decade." *Population Bulletin* 50 (no. 4): March.

Diedrick, Patricia. 1991. "Gender Differences in Divorce Adjustment." *Journal of Divorce and Remarriage* 14:33–45.

Diener, Ed, Marissa Diener, and Carol Diener. 1995. "Factors Predicting the Subjective Well-Being of Nations." *Journal of Personality and Social Psychology* 69:851–64.

Dion, Karen K., and Kenneth L. Dion. 1985. "Personality, Gender, and the Phenomenology of Romantic Love." In P. Shaver, ed., *Self, Situations, and Social Behavior.* Beverly Hills, Calif.: Sage.

———. 1991. "Psychological Individualism and Romantic Love." *Journal of Social Behavior and Personality* 6:17–33.

Dion, Kenneth L., and Karen K. Dion. 1993. "Gender and Ethnocultural Comparisons in Styles of Love." *Psychology of Women Quarterly* 17:463–73.

DiTommaso, Enrico, and Barry Spinner. 1997. "Social and Emotional Loneliness." *Personality & Individual Differences* 22:417–27.

Doherty, William J., and Richard H. Needle. 1991. "Psychological Adjustment and Substance Use Among Adolescents Before and After a Parental Divorce." *Child Development* 62:328–37.

Dolcini, M. Margaret et al. 1996. Cognitive and Emotional Assessments of Perceived Risk for HIV Among

Unmarried Heterosexuals." *AIDS Education & Prevention* 8:294–307.

Domenico, Donna, and Michael Windle. 1993. "Intrapersonal and Interpersonal Functioning Among Middle-Aged Female Adult Children of Alcoholics." *Journal of Consulting and Clinical Psychology* 61:659–66.

Donoghue, William E. 1987. *William E. Donoghue's Lifetime Financial Planner.* New York: Harper & Row.

Dorius, Guy L., Tim B. Heaton, and Patrick Steffen. 1993. "Adolescent Life Events and Their Association with the Onset of Sexual Intercourse." *Youth and Society* 25:3–23.

Dornbusch, Sanford M., et al. 1981. "Sexual Development, Age, and Dating: A Comparison of Biological and Social Influences Upon One Set of Behaviors." *Child Development* 52:179–85.

Dornbusch, Sanford M., J. Merrill Carlsmith, Herbert Leiderman, Albert H. Hastorf, Ruth T. Gross, and Philip L. Ritter. 1984. "Black Control of Adolescent Dating." *Sociological Perspectives* 27:301–23.

Downey, Douglas B. 1994. "The School Performance of Children from Single-Mother and Single-Father Families: Economic or Interpersonal Deprivation?" *Journal of Family Issues* 15:129–47.

———. 1995. "Understanding Academic Achievement Among Children in Stephouseholds." *Social Forces* 73:875–94.

Downey, Douglas B., Pamela Braboy Jackson, and Brian Powell. 1994. "Sons Versus Daughters: Sex Composition of Children and Maternal Views on Socialization." *Sociological Quarterly* 35:33–50.

Downey, Douglas B., and Brian Powell. 1993. "Do Children in Single-Parent Households Fare Better Living with Same-Sex Parents?" *Journal of Marriage and the Family* 55:55–71.

Draper, Thomas W., and Tom Gordon. 1986. "Men's Perceptions of Nurturing Behavior in Other Men." *Psychological Reports* 59:11–18.

Drass, Kriss A. 1986. "The Effect of Gender Identity on Conversation." *Social Psychology Quarterly* 49:294–301.

Dreman, Solly, and Hagar Ronen-Eliav. 1997. "The Relation of Divorced Mothers' Perceptions of Family Cohesion and Adaptability to Behavior Problems in Children." *Journal of Marriage and the Family* 59:324–31.

Drill, Rebecca L. 1986. "Young Adult Children of Divorced Parents: Depression and the Perception of Loss." *Journal of Divorce* 10:169–78.

DuCharme, Jennifer, Catherine Koverola, and Paula Battle. 1997. "Intimacy Development: The Influence of Abuse and Gender." *Journal of Interpersonal Violence* 12:590–99.

Duck, Steve. 1994. *Meaningful Relationships: Talking Sense, and Relating.* Newbury Park, Calif.: Sage.

Dudley, Margaret G., and Frederick A. Kosinski, Jr. 1990. "Religiosity and Marital Satisfaction: A Research Note." *Review of Religious Research* 32:78–86.

Durant, Robert H., Robert Pendergast, and Carolyn Seymore. 1990. "Sexual Behavior Among Hispanic Female Adolescents in the United States." *Pediatrics* 85:1051–58.

Durant, Will. 1954. *Our Oriental Heritage.* New York: Simon & Schuster.

Durbin, Denise L., Nancy Darling, Laurence Steinberg, and Bradford B. Brown. 1993. "Parenting Style and Peer Group Membership Among European-American Adolescents." *Journal of Research on Adolescence* 3:87–100.

Durkheim, Emile. 1933. *The Division of Labor in Society.* Translated by George Simpson. New York: Free Press.

Dutton, Donald G. 1987. "Wife Assault: Social Psychological Contributions to Criminal Justice Policy." In S. Oskamp, ed., *Family Processes and Problems: Social Psychological Aspects.* Beverly Hills, Calif.: Sage.

Duvall, Evelyn M. 1954. *In-Laws: Pro & Con.* New York: Association Press.

———. 1977. *Marriage and Family Development.* 5th ed. Philadelphia: J. B. Lippincott.

Dwyer, Kathleen M. 1990. "Characteristics of Eighth-Grade Students Who Initiate Self-Care in Elementary and Junior High School." *Pediatrics* 86:448–54.

Dyk, Patricia A. H. 1987. "Graduate Student Management of Family and Academic Roles." *Family Relations* 36:329–32.

Eagly, Alice H. 1978. "Sex Differences in Influenceability." *Psychological Bulletin* 85:86–116.

Earle, Alice Morse. 1893. *Customs and Fashions in Old New England.* London: David Nutt.

Easley, Margaret J., and Norman Epstein. 1991. "Coping with Stress in a Family with an Alcoholic Parent." *Family Relations* 40:218–24.

East, Patricia L., Marianne E. Felice, and Maria C. Morgan. 1993. "Sisters' and Girlfriends' Sexual and Childbearing Behavior: Effects on Early Adolescent Girls' Sexual Outcomes." *Journal of Marriage and the Family* 55:953–63.

Eccles, Jacquelynne S., Janis E. Jacobs, and Rena D. Harold. 1990. "Gender Role Stereotypes, Expectancy Effects, and Parents' Socialization of Gender Differences." *Journal of Social Issues* 46:183–201.

Eggebeen, David, Anastasia R. Snyder, and Wendy D. Manning. 1996. "Children in Single-Father Families in Demographic Perspective." *Journal of Family Issues* 17:441–64.

Eisenman, Russell. 1985. "Marijuana Use and Attraction: Support for Byrne's Similarity-Attraction Concept." *Perceptual and Motor Skills* 61:582.

Eisikovits, Zvi C., Jeffrey L. Edleson, Edna Guttmann, and Michal Sela-Amit. 1991. "Cognitive Styles and Socialized Attitudes of Men Who Batter: Where Should We Intervene?" *Family Relations* 40:72–77.

Elder, Glen H., Jr. 1974. *Children of the Great Depression.* Chicago: University of Chicago Press.

Elder, Glen H., Jr., Rand D. Conger, E. Michael Foster, and Monika Ardelt. 1992. "Families Under Economic Pressure." *Journal of Family Issues* 13:5–37.

Elliott, Marta. 1996. "Impact of Work, Family, and Welfare Receipt on Women's Self-Esteem in Young Adulthood." *Social Psychology Quarterly* 59:80–95.

Ellison, Christopher G. 1990. "Family Ties, Friendships, and Subjective Well-Being Among Black Americans." *Journal of Marriage and the Family* 52:298–310.

Erbes, Janine Twomey, and John J. Cunneen Hedderson. 1984. "A Longitudinal Examination of the Separation/Divorce Process." *Journal of Marriage and the Family* 46:937–41.

Erickson, P. I., and A. J. Rapkin. 1991. "Unwanted Sexual Experience Among Middle and High School Youth." *Journal of Adolescent Health* 12:319–25.

Erickson, Rebecca J. 1993. "Reconceptualizing Family Work: The Effect of Emotion Work on Perceptions of Marital Quality." *Journal of Marriage and the Family* 55:888–900.

Erikson, Erik H. 1952. *Childhood and Society.* New York: W. W. Norton.

Espenshade, Thomas J., and Wenzhen Ye. 1994. "Differential Fertility Within an Ethnic Minority: The Effect of 'Trying Harder' Among Chinese-American Women." *Social Problems* 41:97–106.

Etaugh, Claire, and Joanne Stern. 1984. "Person Perception: Effects of Sex, Marital Status, and Sex-Typed Occupation." *Sex Roles* 11:413–24.

Everett, Lou Whichard. 1998. "Factors That Contribute to Satisfaction or Dissatisfaction in Stepfather-Stepchild Relationships." *Perspectives in Psychiatric Care* 34:25–36.

Falk, Dennis R., and Pat Noonan Wagner. 1985. "Intimacy of Self-Disclosure and Response Processes As Factors Affecting the Development of Interpersonal Relationships." *Journal of Social Psychology* 125:557–70.

Farber, Naomi. 1990. "The Significance of Race and Class in Marital Decisions Among Unmarried Adolescent Mothers." *Social Problems* 37:51–63.

Faulkenberry, J. Ron, Murray Vincent, Arnold James, and Wayne Johnson. 1987. "Coital Behaviors, Attitudes, and Knowledge of Students Who Experience Early Coitus." *Adolescence* 22:321–32.

Fausto-Sterling, Anne. 1985. *Myths of Gender: Biological Theories About Women and Men.* New York: Basic Books.

Feigelman, William. 1997. "Adopted Adults: Comparisons with Persons Raised in Conventional Families." *Marriage and Family Review* 25:199–23.

Feingold, Alan. 1990. "Gender Differences in Effects of Physical Attractiveness on Romantic Attraction: A Comparison Across Five Research Paradigms." *Journal of Personality and Social Psychology* 59:981–93.

Felitti, Vincent J. et al. 1998. "Relationship of Childhood Abuse and Household Dysfunction to Many of the Leading Causes of Death in Adults." *American Journal of Preventive Medicine* 14:245–58.

Felmlee, Diane, Susan Sprecher, and Edward Bassin. 1990. "The Dissolution of Intimate Relationships: A Hazard Model. *Social Psychology Quarterly* 53:13–30.

Fenell, David L. 1993. "Characteristics of Long-Term First Marriages." *Journal of Mental Health Counseling* 15:446–60.

Ferraro, Kathleen, and John M. Johnson. 1983. "How Women Experience Battering: The Process of Victimization." *Social Problems* 30:325–39.

Ferreiro, Beverly Webster. 1990. "Presumption of Joint Custody: A Family Policy Dilemma." *Family Relations* 39:420–26.

Festinger, Leon, Stanley Schachter, and Kurt Back. 1950. *Social Pressures in Informal Groups.* New York: Harper & Row.

Fiebert, Martin S., and Lisa M. Tucci. 1998 "Sexual Coercion: Men Victimized by Women." *The Journal of Men's Studies* 6:127–33.

Fiese, Barbara H., Karen H. Hooker, Lisa Kotary, and Janet Schwagler. 1993. "Family Rituals in the Early Stages of Parenthood." *Journal of Marriage and the Family* 55:633–42.

Fine, Mark A. 1986. "Perceptions of Stepparents: Variation in Stereotypes As a Function of Current Family Structure." *Journal of Marriage and the Family* 48:537–43.

Fine, Mark A., Brenda W. Donnelly, and Patricia Voydanoff. 1986. "Adjustment and Satisfaction of Parents." *Journal of Family Issues* 7:391–404.

Fine, Mark A., Lawrence H. Ganong, and Marilyn Coleman. 1997. "The Relation Between Role Constructions and Adjustment Among Stepfathers." *Journal of Family Issues* 18:503–25.

Fine, Mark A., and Lawrence A. Kurdek. 1992. "The Adjustment of Adolescents in Stepfather and Stepmother Families." *Journal of Marriage and the Family* 54:725–36.

Fine, Mark A., Patrick C. McKenry, and Hyunsook Chung. 1992. "Post-Divorce Adjustment of Black and White Single Parents." *Journal of Divorce and Remarriage* 17:121–34.

Fine, Mark A., Patrick C. McKenry, Brenda W. Donnelly, and Patricia Voydanoff. 1992. "Perceived Adjustment of Parents and Children: Variations by Family Structure, Race, and Gender." *Journal of Marriage and the Family* 54:118–27.

Fine, Mark A., and Andrew I. Schwebel. 1987. "An Emergent Explanation of Differing Racial Reactions to Single Parenthood." *Journal of Divorce* 11:1–15.

Fine, Mark A., Patricia Voydanoff, and Brenda W. Donnelly. 1993. "Relations Between Parental Control and Warmth and Child Well-Being in Stepfamilies." *Journal of Family Psychology* 7:222–32.

Finkelhor, David. 1984. *Child Sexual Abuse: New Theory and Research.* New York: Free Press.

Finkelson, Laura. 1995. "College Date Rape." *Psychological Reports* 77:526.

Fiorentine, Robert. 1988. "Increasing Similarity in the Values and Life Plans of Male and Female College Students? Evidence and Implications." *Sex Roles* 18:143–58.

Fisher, Celia B., James D. Reid, and Marjorie Melendez. 1989. "Conflict in Families and Friendships of Later Life." *Family Relations* 38:83–89.

Fitchen, Janet M., and Orna Cohen. "Divorced Fathers Raise Their Children By Themselves." *Journal of Divorce & Remarriage* 23:55–73.

Fitzpatrick, Mary Anne. 1988. *Between Husbands & Wives: Communication in Marriage.* Beverly Hills, Calif.: Sage.

Flanagan, Constance A. 1990. "Change in Family Work Status: Effects on Parent-Adolescent Decision Making." *Child Development* 61:163–77.

Flaste, Richard. 1991. "Sidelined by Loneliness." *New York Times Magazine,* April 28.

Fleming, Douglas T. et al. 1997. "Herpes Simplex Virus Type 2 in the United States, 1976 to 1994." *New England Journal of Medicine* 337:1105–11.

Flewelling, Robert L., and Karl E. Bauman. 1990. "Family Structure As a Predictor of Initial Substance Use and Sexual Intercourse in Early Adolescence." *Journal of Marriage and the Family* 52:171–81.

Florian, Victor, and Nira Dangoor. 1994. "Personal and Familial Adaptation of Women with Severe Physical Disabilities." *Journal of Marriage and the Family* 56:735–46.

Fluehr-Lobban, Carolyn, and Lois Bardsley-Sirois. 1990. "Obedience (TA'A) in Muslim Marriage: Religious Interpretation and Applied Law in Egypt." *Journal of Comparative Family Studies* 21:39–53.

Folk, Karen Fox, John W. Graham, and Andrea H. Beller. 1992. "Child Support and Remarriage." *Journal of Family Issues* 13:142–57.

Follingstad, Diane R., Larry L. Rutledge, Barbara J. Berg, and Elizabeth S. Hause. 1990. "The Role of Emotional Abuse in Physically Abusive Relationships." *Journal of Family Violence* 5:107–20.

Fong, Margaret L., and Ellen S. Amatea. 1992. "Stress and Single Professional Women." *Journal of Mental Health Counseling* 14:20–29.

Ford, Clellan S., and Frank A. Beach. 1951. *Patterns of Sexual Behavior.* New York: Harper Torchbooks.

Forehand, Rex, and Sarah Nousianinen. 1993. "Maternal and Paternal Parenting: Critical Dimensions in Adolescent Functioning." *Journal of Family Psychology* 7:213–21.

Forrest, Jacqueline Darroch, and Susheela Singh. 1990. "The Sexual and Reproductive Behavior of American Women, 1982–1988." *Family Planning Perspectives* 22:206–14.

Fossett, Mark A., and K. Jill Kiecolt. 1990. "Mate Availability, Family Formation, and Family Structure Among Black Americans in Nonmetropolitan Louisiana: 1970–1980." *Rural Sociology* 55:305–27.

Fossett, Mark A., and K. Jill Kiecolt. 1993. "Mate Availability and Family Structure Among African Americans in U.S. Metropolitan Areas." *Journal of Marriage and the Family* 55:288–302.

Foubert, John D., and Barbara K. Sholley. 1996. "Effects of Gender, Gender Role, and Individualized Trust on Self-Disclosure." *Journal of Social Behavior and Personality* 11:277–88.

Fowers, Blaine J. 1991. "His and Her Marriage: A Multivariate Study of Gender and Marital Satisfaction." *Sex Roles* 24:209–21.

———. 1996. "Predicting Marital Success for Premarital Couple Types Based on PREPARE." *Journal of Marital and Family Therapy* 22:103–19.

Fowers, Blaine J., and David H. Olson. 1986. "Predicting Marital Success with PREPARE: A Predictive Validity Study." *Journal of Marital and Family Therapy* 12:403–13.

Fox, Greer Litton, and Robert F. Kelly. 1995. "Determinants of Child Custody Arrangements at Divorce." *Journal of Marriage and the Family* 57:693–708.

Foxcraft, David R., and Geoff Lowe. 1991. "Adolescent Drinking Behavior and Family Socialization Factors: A Meta-Analysis." *Journal of Adolescence* 14:255–73.

Franklin, Donna L., Susan E. Smith, and William E. P. McMiller. 1995. "Correlates of Marital Status Among African American Mothers in Chicago Neighborhoods of Concentrated Poverty." *Journal of Marriage and the Family* 57:141–52.

Frazier, Patricia, Nancy Arikian, Sonja Benson, and Ann Losoff. 1996. "Desire for Marriage and Life Satisfaction Among Unmarried Heterosexual Adults." *Journal of Social and Personal Relationships* 13:225–39.

Freud, Sigmund. 1949. *Three Essays on the Theory of Sexuality.* Translated by James Strachey. London: Imago Publishing Co.

Freudenberger, Herbert J. 1987. "Today's Troubled Men." *Psychology Today,* December, pp. 46–47.

Friedman, Howard S. et al. 1995. "Psychosocial and Behavioral Predictors of Longevity." *American Psychologist* 50:69–78.

Frieze, Irene H., Jacquelynne E. Parsons, Paula B. Johnson, Diane N. Ruble, and Gail L. Zellman. 1978. *Women and Sex Roles.* New York: W. W. Norton.

Fromm, Erich. 1956. *The Art of Loving.* New York: Bantam.

Furstenberg, Frank F., Jr., J. Brooks-Gunn, and S. Philip Morgan. 1987. *Adolescent Mothers in Later Life.* Cambridge University Press.

Furstenberg, Frank, Jr., and Andrew J. Cherlin. 1991. *Divided Families: What Happens to Children When Parents Part.* Cambridge, Mass.: Harvard University Press.

Furstenberg, Frank F., Jr., S. Philip Morgan, and Paul D. Allison. 1987. "Paternal Participation and Children's Well-Being After Marital Dissolution." *American Sociological Review* 52:695–701.

Furstenberg, Frank F., Jr., and Christine Winquist Nord. 1985. "Parenting Apart: Patterns of Childrearing After Marital Disruption." *Journal of Marriage and the Family* 47:893–904.

Gabardi, Lisa, and Lee A. Rosen. 1991. "Differences Between College Students from Divorced and Intact Families." *Journal of Divorce and Remarriage* 15:175–91.

Gadberry, James H., and Richard A. Dodder. 1993. "Educational Homogamy in Interracial Marriages: An Update." *Journal of Social Behavior and Personality* 8:155–63.

Gaelick, Lisa, Galen V. Bodenhausen, and Robert S. Wyer, Jr. 1985. "Emotional Communication in Close Relationships." *Journal of Personality and Social Psychology* 49:1246–65.

Galambos, Nancy L., David M. Almeida, and Anne C. Petersen. 1990. "Masculinity, Femininity, and Sex Role Attitudes in Early Adolescence: Exploring Gender Intensification." *Child Development* 61:1905–14.

Gallagher, Maggie, and Barbara Dafoe Whitehead. 1997. "End No-Fault Divorce?" *First Things,* August/September. p. 24.

Gallup, George, Jr., and Frank Newport. 1990. "Virtually All Adults Want Children, But Many of the Reasons Are Intangible." *The Gallup Poll Monthly,* no. 297, June, pp. 8–14.

Gallup, George, Jr., and Frank Newport. 1991. "For First Time, More Americans Approve of Interracial Marriage Than Disapprove." *The Gallup Poll Monthly,* no. 311, August, pp. 60–66.

Gallup Organization. 1997. "Family Values Differ Sharply Around the World." *International Gallup Poll.* Gallup Organization website.

Ganong, Lawrence H., and Marilyn Coleman. 1987. "Sex, Sex Roles, and Familial Love." *Journal of Genetic Psychology* 148:45–52.

———. 1988. "Do Mutual Children Cement Bonds in Stepfamilies?" *Journal of Marriage and the Family* 50:687–98.

———. 1989. "Preparing for Remarriage: Anticipating the Issues, Seeking Solutions." *Family Relations* 38:28–33.

———. 1992. "Gender Differences in Expectations of Self and Future Partner." *Journal of Family Issues* 13:55–64.

———. 1993. "A Meta-Analytic Comparison of the Self-Esteem and Behavior Problems of Stepchildren to Children in Other Family Structures." *Journal of Divorce and Remarriage* 19:143–63.

———. 1994. *Remarried Family Relationships.* Thousand Oaks, Calif.: Sage.

Garbarino, James. 1982. *Children and Families in the Social Environment.* New York: Aldine.

Gardner, Rick M., Randy G. Sorter, and Brenda N. Friedman. 1997. "Developmental Changes in Children's Body Images." *Journal of Social Behavior and Personality* 12:1019–1036.

Garnefski, Nadia, and Ellen Arends. 1998. "Sexual Abuse and Adolescent Maladjustment." *Journal of Adolescence* 21:99–107.

Garnefski, Nadia, and Rene F. W. Diekstra. 1997. "Adolescents from One Parent, Stepparent and Intact Families: Emotional Problems and Suicide Attempts." *Journal of Adolescence* 20:201–208.

Garner, Pamela W., Shanon Robertson, and Gail Smith. 1997. "Preschool Children's Emotional Expressions with Peers: The Roles of Gender and Emotion Socialization." *Sex Roles* 36:675–91.

Garrett, William R. 1982. *Seasons of Marriage and Family Life.* New York: Holt, Rinehart & Winston.

Garrison, M. C. Betsy, Lydia B. Blalock, John J. Zarski, and Penny B. Merritt. 1997. "Delayed Parenthood: An

Exploratory Study of Family Functioning." *Family Relations* 46:281–90.

Garvin, Vicki, Neil Kalter, and James Hansell. 1993. "Divorced Women: Factors Contributing to Resiliency and Vulnerability." *Journal of Divorce and Remarriage* 21:21–39.

Gazmararian, J. A., S. A. James, and J. M. Lepkowski. 1995. "Depression in Black and White Women: The Role of Marriage and Socioeconomic Status." *Annals of Epidemiology* 5:455–63.

Gecas, Victor, and Michael L. Schwalbe. 1986. "Parental Behavior and Adolescent Self-Esteem." *Journal of Marriage and the Family* 48:37–46.

Gehring, Thomas M., Kathryn R. Wentzel, Shirley S. Feldman, and Jeffrey Munson. 1990. "Conflict in Families of Adolescents: The Impact on Cohesion and Power Structures." *Journal of Family Psychology* 3:290–309.

Geiss, Susan K., and K. Daniel O'Leary. 1981. "Therapist Ratings of Frequency and Severity of Marital Problems: Implications for Research." *Journal of Marital and Family Therapy* 7:515–20.

Gelles, Richard J., and Murray A. Straus. 1988. *Intimate Violence.* New York: Simon & Schuster.

George, Kenneth D., and Andrew E. Behrendt. 1987. "Therapy for Male Couples Experiencing Relationship Problems and Sexual Problems." *Journal of Homosexuality* 14:77–88.

Gerson, Mary-Joan. 1986. "The Prospect of Parenthood for Women and Men." *Psychology of Women Quarterly* 10:49–62.

Gerstel, Naomi, and Harriet Gross. 1984. *Commuter Marriage.* New York: Guilford Press.

Gibbons, Judith L., Maria Lynn, and Deborah A. Stiles. 1997. "Cross-National Gender Differences in Adolescents' Preferences for Free-Time Activities." *Cross-Cultural Research* 31:55–69.

Gigy, Lynn L. 1980. "Self-Concept of Single Women." *Psychology of Women Quarterly* 5:321–40.

Gilbert, Lucia Albino. 1993. *Two Careers/One Family.* Newbury Park, Calif.: Sage.

Gilbert, Lucia Albino, and Vicki Rachlin. 1987. "Mental Health and Psychological Functioning of Dual-Career Families." *The Counseling Psychologist* 15:7–49.

Gilbert, Susan. 1998. "Raising Grandchildren, Rising Stress." *The New York Times,* August 3.

Gilford, Rosalie. 1984. "Contrasts in Marital Satisfaction Throughout Old Age: An Exchange Theory Analysis." *Journal of Gerontology* 39:325–33.

Gilgun, Jane F. 1995. "We Shared Something Special: The Moral Discourse of Incest Perpetrators." *Journal of Marriage and the Family* 57:265–81.

Gillis, Yvonne. 1993. "New Methods of Birth Control." *San Diego Family Press,* November, pp. 62–63.

Gladstone, James, and Anne Westhues. 1998. "Adoption Reunions: A New Side of Intergenerational Family Relationships." *Family Relations* 47:177–84.

Glasser, William. 1984. *Control Theory.* New York: Harper & Row.

Glenn, Norval D. 1982. "Interreligious Marriage in the United States: Patterns and Recent Trends. *Journal of Marriage and the Family* 44:555–66.

———. 1987. "Social Trends in the United States: Evidence from Sample Surveys." *Public Opinion Quarterly* 51:S109–S126.

———. 1991. "The Recent Trend in Marital Success in the United States." *Journal of Marriage and the Family* 53:261–70.

———. 1992. "What Does Family Mean?" *American Demographics,* June, pp. 30–37.

Glenn, Norval D., and Kathryn B. Kramer. 1985. "The Psychological Well-Being of Adult Children of Divorce." *Journal of Marriage and the Family* 47:905–12.

Glenn, Norval D., and Beth Ann Shelton. 1985. "Regional Differences in Divorce in the United States." *Journal of Marriage and the Family* 47:641–49.

Glenn, Norval D., and Michael Supancic. 1984. "The Social and Demographic Correlates of Divorce and Separation in the United States: An Update and Reconsideration." *Journal of Marriage and the Family* 46:563–75.

Glenn, Norval D., and Charles N. Weaver. 1988. "The Changing Relationship of Marital Status to Reported Happiness." *Journal of Marriage and the Family* 50:317–24.

Glick, Paul C. 1984. "Marriage, Divorce, and Living Arrangements: Prospective Changes." *Journal of Family Issues* 5:7–26.

———. 1988. "Demographic Pictures of Black Families." In H. P. McAdoo, *Black Families.* 2d ed. Beverly Hills, Calif.: Sage.

———. 1997. "Demographic Pictures of African American Families." In Harriette Pipes McAdoo, ed., *Black Families.* 3rd ed. Thousand Oaks, Calif.: Sage.

Goetting, Ann. 1986. "The Developmental Tasks of Siblingship over the Life Cycle." *Journal of Marriage and the Family* 48:703–14.

Goetting, Ann. 1986. "Parental Satisfaction: A Review of Research." *Journal of Family Issues* 7:83–109.

Goetting, Ann. 1990. "Patterns of Support Among In-Laws in the United States." *Journal of Family Issues* 11:67–90.

Gold, Joel A., Richard M. Ryckman, and Norman R. Mosley. 1984. "Romantic Mood Induction and Attraction to a Dissimilar Other: Is Love Blind?" *Personality and Social Psychology Bulletin* 10:358–68.

Gold, Joshua M., Donald L. Bubenzer, and John D. West. 1993. "Differentiation from Ex-Spouses and Stepfamily Marital Intimacy." *Journal of Divorce and Remarriage* 19:83–95.

Gold, Steven J. 1993. "Migration and Family Adjustment: Continuity and Change Among Vietnamese in the United States." In H. P. McAdoo, ed., *Family Ethnicity: Strength in Diversity.* Newbury Park, Calif.: Sage.

Goldberg, J. J. 1997. "Interfaith Marriage: The Real Story." *The New York Times,* August 3.

Goldberg, Martin. 1987. "Patterns of Disagreement in Marriage." *Medical Aspects of Human Sexuality* 21:42–52.

Goldberg, Wendy A., Ellen Greenberger, Sharon Hamill, and Robin O'Neil. 1992. "Role Demands in the Lives of Employed Single Mothers with Preschoolers." *Journal of Family Issues* 13:312–33.

Goldberg, Wendy A., Gerald Y. Michaels, and Michael E. Lamb. 1985. "Husbands' and Wives' Adjustment to Pregnancy and First Parenthood." *Journal of Family Issues* 6:483–503.

Goldman, Noreen. 1993. "The Perils of Single Life in Contemporary Japan." *Journal of Marriage and the Family* 55:191–204.

Goldscheider, Calvin, and William D. Mosher. 1991. "Patterns of Contraceptive Use in the United States: The Importance of Religious Factors." *Studies in Family Planning* 22:102–15.

Goldscheider, Frances. 1997. "Recent Changes in U.S. Young Adult Living Arrangements in Comparative Perspective." *Journal of Family Issues* 18:708–24.

Goldscheider, Frances K., and Calvin Goldscheider. 1991. "The Intergenerational Flow of Income: Family Structure and the Status of Black Americans." *Journal of Marriage and the Family* 53:499–508.

Goldscheider, Frances K., and Calvin Goldscheider. 1993. *Leaving Home Before Marriage: Ethnicity, Familism, and Generational Relationships.* Madison, Wis.: University of Wisconsin Press.

Goldscheider, Frances Kobrin, and Linda J. Waite. 1986. "Sex Differences in the Entry into Marriage." *American Journal of Sociology* 92:91–109.

Goleman, Daniel. 1985. "Talk Leads to a Good Marriage." *San Diego Union,* April 17.

Goleman, Daniel. 1986. "Two Views of Marriage Explored: His and Hers." *New York Times,* April 1.

Golombok, Susan, and Fiona Tasker. 1996. "Do Parents Influence the Sexual Orientation of Their Children?" *Developmental Psychology* 32:3–11.

Googins, Bradley K. 1991. *Work/Family Conflicts: Private Lives—Public Responses.* New York: Auburn House.

Gottlieb, Laurie N., Ariella Lang, and Rhonda Amsel. 1996. "The Long-Term Effects of Grief on Marital Intimacy Following an Infant's Death." *Omega* 33:1–19.

Gottman, John Mordechai. 1994. *What Predicts Divorce?* Hillsdale, N.J.: Lawrence Erlbaum Associates.

Gottman, John M., James Coan, Sybil Carrere, and Catherine Swanson. 1998. "Predicting Marital Happiness and Stability from Newlywed Interactions." *Journal of Marriage and the Family* 60:5–22.

Gottman, John M., and Lowell J. Krokoff. 1989. "Marital Interaction and Satisfaction: A Longitudinal View." *Journal of Consulting and Clinical Psychology* 57:47–52.

Graham-Bermann, Sandra A., and Alytia A. Levendosky. 1998. "Traumatic Stress Symptoms in Children of Battered Women." *Journal of Interpersonal Violence* 13:111–28.

Gray-Little, Bernadette. 1982. "Marital Quality and Power Processes Among Black Couples." *Journal of Marriage and the Family* 44:633–46.

Gray-Little, Bernadette, Donald H. Baucom, and Sherry L. Hamby. 1996. "Marital Power, Marital Adjustment, and Therapy Outcome." *Journal of Family Psychology* 10:292–303.

Greenberger, Ellen, Laurence D. Steinberg, Alan Vaus, and Sharon McAuliffe. 1980. "Adolescents Who Work: Effects of Part-Time Employment on Family and Peer Relations." *Journal of Youth and Adolescence* 9:189–202.

Greenfield, Lawrence A. et al. 1998. *Violence by Intimates.* Washington, D.C.: Government Printing Office.

Greenglass, Esther R. 1985. "A Social-Psychological View of Marriage for Women." *International Journal of Women's Studies* 8:24–31.

Greenstein, Theodore N. 1993. "Maternal Employment and Child Behavioral Outcomes." *Journal of Family Issues* 14:323–54.

———. 1995. "Gender Ideology, Marital Disruption and the Employment of Married Women." *Journal of Marriage and the Family* 57:31–42.

Greif, Geoffrey L. 1985. *Single Fathers.* Lexington, Mass.: Lexington Books.

Gringlas, Marcy, and Marsha Weinraub. 1995. "The More Things Change . . . Single Parenting Revisited." *Journal of Family Issues* 16:29–52.

Groller, Ingrid. 1987. "Family Ties." *Parents Magazine,* December, p. 27.

Gross, Penny. 1986. "Defining Post-Divorce Remarriage Families: A Typology Based on the Subjective Perceptions of Children." *Journal of Divorce* 10:205–17.

Grosskopf, D. 1983. *Sex and the Married Woman.* New York: Simon & Schuster.

Grossman, Michele, and Wendy Wood. 1993. "Sex Differences in Intensity of Emotional Experience." *Journal of Personality and Social Psychology* 65:1010–22.

Grotevant, H. I. et al. 1994. "Adoptive Family System Dynamics: Variations by Level of Openness in the Adoption." *Family Process* 33:125–46.

Groves, Melissa M., and Diane M. Horm-Wingerd. 1991. "Commuter Marriages: Personal, Family and Career Issues." *Sociology and Social Research* 75:212–17.

Guidubaldi, John, and Helen Cleminshaw. 1985. "Divorce, Family Health, and Child Adjustment." *Family Relations* 34:35–41.

Gunter, Nancy C., and B. G. Gunter. 1990. "Domestic Division of Labor Among Working Couples: Does Androgyny Make a Difference?" *Psychology of Women Quarterly* 14:355–70.

Gwanfogbe, Philomina N., Walter R. Schumm, Meredith Smith, and James L. Furrow. 1997. "Polygyny and Marital Life Satisfaction." *Journal of Comparative Family Studies* 28:55–71.

Gwartney-Gibbs, Patricia A. 1986. "The Institutionalization of Premarital Cohabitation: Estimates from Marriage License Applications, 1970 and 1980." *Journal of Marriage and the Family* 48:423–34.

Gwinnell, Esther. 1998. *Online Seductions: Falling in Love with Strangers on the Internet.* New York: Kodansha.

Hagestad, Gunhild O. 1988. "Demographic Change and the Life Course: Some Emerging Trends in the Family Realm." *Family Relations* 37:405–10.

Hahn, Jennifer, and Thomas Blass. 1997. "Dating Partner Preferences." *Journal of Social Behavior and Personality* 12:595–610.

Halford, W. Kim, Kurt Hahlweg, and Michael Dunne. 1990. "The Cross-Cultural Consistency of Marital Communication Associated with Marital Distress." *Journal of Marriage and the Family* 52:487–500.

Hamilton, Amy, William B. Stiles, Fred Melowsky, and Donald G. Beal. 1987. "A Multilevel Comparison of Child Abusers with Nonabusers." *Journal of Family Violence* 2:215–25.

Hamilton, Beatrice. 1996. "Ethnicity and the Family Life Cycle: The Chinese-American Family." *Family Therapy* 23:199–212.

Hampson, Robert B., Robert W. Beavers, and Yosaf Hulgus. 1990. "Cross-Ethnic Family Differences: Interactional Assessment of White, Black, and Mexican-American Families." *Journal of Marital and Family Therapy* 16:307–19.

Hamptom, Robert L., and Richard J. Gelles. 1994. "Violence Toward Black Women in a Nationally Representative Sample of Black Families." *Journal of Comparative Family Studies* 25:105–19.

Hansen, Gary L. 1985a. "Dating Jealousy Among College Students." *Sex Roles* 12:713–19.

Hansen, Gary L. 1985b. "Perceived Threats and Marital Jealousy." *Social Psychology Quarterly* 48:262–68.

Hansen, Jeffrey E., and W. John Schuldt. 1984. "Marital Self-Disclosure and Marital Satisfaction." *Journal of Marriage and the Family* 46:923–26.

Hanson, Sandra L., David E. Myers, and Alan L. Ginsburg. 1987. "The Role of Responsibility and Knowledge in Reducing Teenage Out-of-Wedlock Childbearing." *Journal of Marriage and the Family* 49:241–56.

Hanson, Sandra L., and Theodora Ooms. 1991. "The Economic Costs and Rewards of Two-Earner, Two-Parent Families." *Journal of Marriage and the Family* 53:622–34.

Hanson, Shirley M. 1986. "Healthy Single Parent Families." *Family Relations* 35:125–32.

Hanson, Shirley M. H., and Frederick W. Bozett. 1987. "Fatherhood: A Review and Resources." *Family Relations* 36:333–40.

Hansson, Robert O., and Jacqueline H. Remondet. 1987. "Relationships and the Aging Family: A Social Psychological Analysis." In S. Oskamp, ed., *Family Processes and Problems: Social Psychological Aspects.* Beverly Hills, Calif.: Sage.

Harman, M. J., and C. Arbona. 1991. "Psychological Adjustment Among Hispanic Adult Children of Alcoholics: An Exploratory Study." *Hispanic Journal of Behavioral Sciences* 13:105–12.

Harpster, Paula, and Elizabeth Monk-Turner. 1998. "Why Men Do Housework: A Test of Gender Production and the Relative Resources Model." *Sociological Focus* 31:45–59.

Harriman, Linda Cooper. 1986. "Marital Adjustment As Related to Personal and Marital Changes Accompanying Parenthood." *Family Relations* 35:233–39.

Harris, Ian M. 1995. *Messages Men Hear: Constructing Masculinities.* Bristol, PA: Taylor & Francis.

Harris, Kathleen Mullan, and S. Philip Morgan. 1991. "Fathers, Sons, and Daughters: Differential Paternal Involvement in Parenting." *Journal of Marriage and the Family* 53:531–44.

Harris, Mary B., Cynthia Begay, and Polly Page. 1989. "Activities, Family Relationships, and Feelings About Aging in a Multicultural Elderly Sample." *Interna-*

tional Journal of Aging and Human Development 29:103–17.

Harris, Mary B., and Pauline H. Turner. 1985/86. "Gay and Lesbian Parents." *Journal of Homosexuality* 12:101–13.

Harris, Thomas L., and Reiko Schwab. 1990. "Sex-Role Orientation and Personal Adjustment." *Journal of Social Behavior and Personality* 5:473–79.

Harrist, Amanda W., and Ricardo C. Ainslie. 1998. "Marital Discord and Child Behavior Problems." *Journal of Family Issues* 19:140–63.

Harry, Joseph. 1982. "Decision Making and Age Differences Among Gay Couples." *Journal of Homosexuality* 2:9–21.

Hatchett, Shirley J., and James S. Jackson. 1993. "African American Extended Kin Systems." In H. P. McAdoo, ed., *Family Ethnicity: Strength in Diversity.* Newbury Park, Calif.: Sage.

Hatfield, Elaine, and Richard L. Rapson. 1993. "Historical and Cross-Cultural Perspectives on Passionate Love and Sexual Desire." *Annual Review of Sex Research* 4:67–97.

Hatfield, Elaine, and Susan Sprecher. 1986. "Measuring Passionate Love in Intimate Relationships." *Journal of Adolescence* 9:383–410.

Haub, C. 1992. "The Late 1980s Baby Boomlet: Delayed Childbearing or Not?" *Population Today* 20:3.

Haveman, Robert, and Barbara L. Wolfe. 1994. *Succeeding Generations.* New York: Russell Sage Foundation.

Hawton, Keith, Dennis Gath, and Ann Day. 1994. "Sexual Function in a Community Sample of Middle-Aged Women with Partners: Effects of Age, Marital, Socioeconomic, Psychiatric, Gynecological, and Menopausal Factors." *Archives of Sexual Behavior* 23:375–95.

Healy, Joseph M., Abigail J. Stewart, and Anne P. Copeland. 1993. "The Role of Self-Blame in Children's Adjustment to Parental Separation." *Personality and Social Psychology Bulletin* 19:279–89.

Heaton, Tim B. 1990. "Marital Stability Throughout the Child-Rearing Years." *Demography* 27:55–63.

Heaton, Tim B. 1991. "Time-Related Determinants of Marital Dissolution." *Journal of Marriage and the Family* 53:285–95.

Heaton, Tim B., and Stan L. Albrecht. 1991. "Stable Unhappy Marriages." *Journal of Marriage and the Family* 53:747–58.

Heaton, Tim B., and Edith L. Pratt. 1990. "The Effects of Religious Homogamy on Marital Satisfaction and Stability." *Journal of Family Issues* 11:191–207.

Hecht, Michael L., Peter J. Marston, and Linda Kathryn Larkey. 1994. "Love Ways and Relationship Quality

in Heterosexual Relationships." *Journal of Social and Personal Relationships* 11:25–43.

Heckert, D. Alex, Thomas C. Nowak, and Kay A. Snyder. 1998. "The Impact of Husbands' and Wives' Relative Earnings on Marital Disruption." *Journal of Marriage and the Family* 60:690–703.

Heidemann, Bridget, Olga Suhomlinova, and Angela M. O'Rand. 1998. "Economic Independence, Economic Status, and Empty Nest in Midlife Marital Disruption." *Journal of Marriage and the Family* 60:219–31.

Hein, Carol, and John H. Lewko. 1994. "Gender Differences in Factors Related to Parenting Style: A Study of High Performing Science Students." *Journal of Adolescent Research* 9:262–81.

Heiss, Jerold. 1988. "Women's Values Regarding Marriage and the Family." In H. P. McAdoo, ed., *Black Families.* 2d ed. Beverly Hills, Calif.: Sage.

Helson, Ravenna, Teresa Elliott, and Janet Leigh. 1990. "Number and Quality of Roles: A Longitudinal Personality View." *Psychology of Women Quarterly* 14:83–101.

Henderson-King, Donna H., and Joseph Veroff. 1994. "Sexual Satisfaction and Marital Well-Being in the First Years of Marriage." *Journal of Social and Personal Relationships* 11:509–34.

Hendrick, Clyde, and Susan S. Hendrick. 1988. "Lovers Wear Rose Colored Glasses." *Journal of Social and Personal Relationships* 5:161–83.

Hendrick, Susan S., and Clyde Hendrick. 1987. "Love and Sex Attitudes and Religious Beliefs." *Journal of Social and Clinical Psychology* 5:391–98.

Hendrick, Susan S., and Clyde Hendrick. 1992. *Romantic Love.* Newbury Park, Calif.: Sage.

Hendrick, Susan S., Clyde Hendrick, and Nancy L. Adler. 1988. "Romantic Relationships: Love, Satisfaction, and Staying Together." *Journal of Personality and Social Psychology* 54:980–88.

Hendrix, Lewellyn. 1997. "Quality and Equality in Marriage: A Cross-Cultural View." *Cross-Cultural Research* 31:201–25.

Henning, Kris, Harold Leitenberg, Patricia Coffey, and Tonia Turner. 1996. "Long-Term Psychological and Social Impact of Witnessing Physical Conflict Between Parents." *Journal of Interpersonal Violence* 11:35–51.

Hensley, Wayne E. 1996. "The Effect of a Ludus Love Style on Sexual Experience." *Social Behavior and Personality* 24:205–12.

Hernandez, Donald J. 1993. "When Families Break Up." In *U.S. Bureau of the Census,* Current Population Reports, series P20, no. 478. Washington, D.C.: Government Printing Office.

Herring, Cedric, and Karen Rose Wilson-Sadberry. 1993. "Preference or Necessity? Changing Work Roles of Black and White Women, 1973–1990." *Journal of Marriage and the Family* 55:314–25.

Hertz, Rosanna. 1986. *More Equal Than Others: Women and Men in Dual-Career Marriages.* Berkeley: University of California.

Hesse-Biber, Sharlene. 1996. *Am I Thin Enough Yet? The Cult of Thinness and the Commercialization of Identity.* New York: Oxford University Press.

Hester, Colleen. 1996. "The Relationship of Personality, Gender, and Age to Adjective Check List Profiles of the Ideal Romantic Partner." *Journal of Psychological Type* 36:28–35.

Hetherington, E. Mavis. 1993. "An Overview of the Virginia Longitudinal Study of Divorce and Remarriage with a Focus on Early Adolescence." *Journal of Family Psychology* 7:39–56.

Higgins, Christopher, Linda Duxbury, and Catherine Lee. 1994. "Impact of Life-Cycle Stage and Gender on the Ability to Balance Work and Family Responsibilities." *Family Relations* 43:144–50.

Hightower, Eugene. 1990. "Adolescent Interpersonal and Familial Precursors of Positive Mental Health at Midlife." *Journal of Youth and Adolescence* 19:257–76.

Hill, Reuben. 1949. *Families Under Stress.* New York: Harper & Row.

———. 1958. "Generic Features of Families Under Stress." *Social Casework* 49:139–50.

Hiller, Dana V., and William W. Philliber. 1986. "The Division of Labor in Contemporary Marriage: Expectations, Perceptions, and Performance." *Social Problems* 33:191–201.

Hira, Tahira K., and Olive M. Mugenda. 1987. "Families' Perception of the Bankruptcy Process." *Family Perspective* 21:59–67.

Hobart, Charles. 1987. "Parent-Child Relations in Remarried Families." *Journal of Family Issues* 8:259–77.

———. 1990. "Relationships Between the Formerly Married." *Journal of Comparative Family Studies* 21:81–97.

———. 1991. "Conflict in Remarriages." *Journal of Divorce and Remarriage* 15:69–86.

Hobart, Charles, and David Brown. 1988. "Effects of Prior Marriage Children on Adjustment in Remarriage: A Canadian Study." *Journal of Comparative Family Studies* 19:381–96.

Hochschild, Arlie Russell. 1997. *The Time Bind: When Work Becomes Home and Home Becomes Work.* New York: Metropolitan Books.

Hoffmann, John P., and Robert A. Johnson. 1998. "A National Portrait of Family Structure and Adolescent Drug Use." *Journal of Marriage and the Family* 60:633–45.

Holden, George W., and Kathy L. Ritchie. 1991. "Linking Extreme Marital Discord, Child Rearing, and Child Behavior Problems: Evidence from Battered Women." *Child Development* 62:311–27.

Holman, Thomas B., and Gregory W. Brock. 1986. "Implications for Therapy in the Study of Communication and Marital Quality." *Family Perspective* 20:85–94.

Holman, Thomas B., and Wesley R. Burr. 1980. "Beyond the Beyond: The Growth of Family Theories in the 1970s." *Journal of Marriage and the Family* 42:729–41.

Holman, Thomas B., and Bing Dao Li. 1997. "Premarital Factors Influencing Perceived Readiness for Marriage." *Journal of Family Issues* 18:124–44.

Holmbeck, Grayson N., Karen A. Waters, and Richard R. Brookman. 1990. "Psychosocial Correlates of Sexually Transmitted Diseases and Sexual Activity in Black Adolescent Females." *Journal of Adolescent Research* 5:431–48.

Holtzworth-Munroe, Amy, Gregory L. Stuart, and Glenn Hutchinson. 1997. Violent Versus Nonviolent Husbands." *Journal of Family Psychology* 11:314–31.

Hong, Lawrence K., and Robert W. Duff. 1997. "Relative Importance of Spouses, Children, and Friends in the Life Satisfaction of Retirement Community Residents." *Journal of Clinical Geropsychology* 3:275–82.

Horowitz, Leonard M. 1979. "Cognitive Structure of Interpersonal Problems Treated in Psychotherapy." *Journal of Consulting and Clinical Psychology* 47:453–58.

Horowitz, Allan V., Helene Raskin White, and Sandra Howell-White. 1996. "Becoming Married and Mental Health: A Longitudinal Study of a Cohort of Young Adults." *Journal of Marriage and the Family* 58:895–907.

Hossain, Ziarat, and Jaipaul L. Roopnarine. 1993. "Division of Household Labor and Child Care in Dual-Earner African American Families with Infants." *Sex Roles* 29:571–83.

Hotaling, Gerald T., and David B. Sugarman. 1990. "A Risk Marker Analysis of Assaulted Wives." *Journal of Family Violence* 5:1–13.

Houseknecht, Sharon K., Suzanne Vaughan, and Anne Statham. 1987. "The Impact of Singlehood on the Career Patterns of Professional Women." *Journal of Marriage and the Family* 49:353–66.

Houts, Renate M., Elliot Robins, and Ted L. Huston. 1996. "Compatibility and the Development of Premarital Relationships." *Journal of Marriage and the Family* 58:7–20.

Hovell, Mel et al. 1994. "Family Influences on Latino and Anglo Adolescent Sexual Behavior." *Journal of Marriage and the Family* 56:973–86.

Howard, Judith A., Philip Blumstein, and Pepper Schwartz. 1986. "Sex, Power, and Influence Tactics in Intimate Relationships." *Journal of Personality and Social Psychology* 51:102–109.

Hugick, Larry, and Jennifer Leonard. 1991. "Sex in America." *The Gallup Poll Monthly,* no. 313, October, pp. 60–73.

Hunt, Morton. 1974. *Sexual Behavior in the 1970s.* Chicago: Playboy Press.

Huntley, Debra K., Randy E. Phelps, and Lynn P. Rehm. 1986. "Depression in Children from Single-Parent Families." *Journal of Divorce* 10:153–62.

Huppe, Micheline, and Mirielle Cyr. 1997. "Division of Household Labor and Marital Satisfaction of Dual Income Couples According to Family Life Cycle." *Canadian Journal of Counselling* 31:145–62.

Hurtz, Wilhelm, and Kevin Durkin. 1997. "Gender Role Stereotyping in Australian Radio Commercials." *Sex Roles* 36:103–13.

Huston, Ted L., Susan M. McHale, and Ann C. Crouter. 1986. "When the Honeymoon's Over: Changes in the Marriage Relationship Over the First Year." In R. Gilmour and S. Duck, eds., *The Emerging Field of Personal Relationships.* Hillsdale, N.J.: Lawrence Erlbaum Associates.

Hutchison, Ray, and Miles McNall. 1994. "Early Marriage in a Hmong Cohort." *Journal of Marriage and the Family* 56:579–90.

Huxley, Aldous. 1932. *Brave New World.* New York: Bantam.

Hyde, Janet Shibley. 1986. *Understanding Human Sexuality.* 3d ed. New York: McGraw-Hill.

Idle, Tracey, Ellen Wood, and Serge Desmarais. 1993. "Gender Role Socialization in Toy Play Situations." *Sex Roles* 28:679–91.

Ihinger-Tallman, Marilyn, and Kay Pasley. 1987. *Remarriage.* Beverly Hills, Calif.: Sage.

Inderbitzen-Pisaruk, Heidi, M. L. Clark, and Cecilia H. Solano. 1992. "Correlates of Loneliness in Midadolescence." *Journal of Youth and Adolescence* 21:151–67.

Inman-Amos, Jill, Susan S. Hendrick, and Clyde Hendrick. 1994. "Love Attitudes: Similarities Between Parents and Between Parents and Children." *Family Relations* 43:456–61.

Isaacs, Marla Beth, and George H. Leon. 1988. "Remarriage and Its Alternatives Following Divorce: Mother and Child Adjustment." *Journal of Marital and Family Therapy* 14:163–73.

Ishii-Kuntz, Masako, and Scott Coltrane. 1992. "Remarriage, Stepparenting, and Household Labor." *Journal of Family Issues* 13:215–33.

Jackson, Joan L., Karen S. Calhoun, Angelynne E. Amick, Heather M. Maddever, and Valerie L. Habif. 1990. "Young Adult Women Who Report Childhood Intrafamilial Sexual Abuse: Subsequent Adjustment." *Archives of Sexual Behavior* 19:211–21.

Jackson, Pamela Braboy. 1992. "Specifying the Buffer Hypothesis: Support, Strain, and Depression." *Social Psychology Quarterly* 55:363–78.

Jacob, Theodore, and Gloria L. Krahn. 1988. "Marital Interactions of Alcoholic Couples: Comparison with Depressed and Nondistressed Couples." *Journal of Counseling and Clinical Psychology* 56:73–79.

Jacobs, Ruth Harriet, and Barbara H. Vinick. 1981. *Re-Engagement in Later Life.* Stamford, Conn.: Greylock.

Jacobsen, R. Brooke, and Jerry J. Binger. 1991. "Black Versus White Single Parents and the Value of Children." *Journal of Black Studies* 21:302–12.

Jacoby, Susan. 1987. "The Private Life of the American Family." *Family Circle,* October 20, pp. 12–14.

Jacques, Jeffrey M. 1998. "Changing Marital and Family Patterns." *Sociological Perspectives* 41:381–411.

Javaid, Ghazala A. 1993. "The Children of Homosexual and Heterosexual Single Mothers." *Child Psychiatry and Human Development* 23:235–48.

Jehu, Derek, Marjorie Gazan, and Carole Klassen. 1985. "Common Therapeutic Targets Among Women Who Were Sexually Abused in Childhood." *Journal of Social Work and Human Sexuality* 3:25–45.

Jekielek, Susan M. 1998. "Parental Conflict, Marital Disruption, and Children's Emotional Well-Being." *Social Forces* 76:905–35.

Jendrek, Margaret Platt. 1993. "Grandparents Who Parent Their Grandchildren: Effects on Lifestyle." *Journal of Marriage and the Family* 55:609–21.

———. 1994. "Grandparents Who Parent Their Grandchildren: Circumstances and Decisions." *Gerontologist* 34:206–16.

Jennerson-Madden, Dolores, Peter Ebersole, and Ana Maria Romero. 1992. "Personal Life Meaning of Mexicans." *Journal of Social Behavior and Personality* 7:151–61.

Jensen, Larry, Rea J. Newell, and Tom Holman. 1990. "Sexual Behavior, Church Attendance, and Permissive Beliefs Among Unmarried Young Men and Women." *Journal for the Scientific Study of Religion* 29:113–117.

Jezl, David R., Christian E. Molidor, and Tracy L. Wright. 1996. "Physical, Sexual and Psychological Abuse in High School Dating Relationships." *Child & Adolescent Social Work Journal* 13:69–87.

Joebgen, Alicia M, and Maryse H. Richards. 1990. "Maternal Education and Employment: Mediating Maternal and Adolescent Emotional Adjustment." *Journal of Early Adolescence* 10:329–43.

Joesch, Jutta M. 1998. "Where Are the Children? Extent and Determinants of Preschoolers' Child Care Time." *Journal of Family and Economic Issues* 19:75–99.

John, Daphne. 1996. "Women's Reports of Men's Childcare Participation." *The Journal of Men's Studies* 5:13–30.

John, R., 1988. "The Native American Family." In C. H. Mindel, R. W. Habenstein, and R. Wright, Jr., eds., *Ethnic Families in America.* 3d ed. New York: Elsevier.

Johnson, Bette Magyar, Shmuel Shulman, and W. Andrew Collins. 1991. "Systemic Patterns of Parenting As Reported by Adolescents." *Journal of Adolescent Research* 6:235–52.

Johnson, David R., and Alan Booth. 1998. Marital Quality: A Product of the Dyadic Environment or Individual Factors?" *Social Force* 76:883–905.

Johnson, Ronald C., and Craig T. Nagoshi. 1986. "The Adjustment of Offspring of Within-Group and Interracial/Intercultural Marriages: A Comparison of Personality Factor Scores." *Journal of Marriage and the Family* 48:279–84.

Johnson, Susan. 1994. "Love: The Immutable Longing for Contact." *Psychology Today,* March/April, pp. 32–37.

Johnston, Stacy Glaser, and Amanda McCombs Thomas. 1996. "Divorce Versus Intact Parental Marriage and Perceived Risk and Dyadic Trust in Present Heterosexual Relationships." *Psychological Reports* 78:387–90.

Johnston, Thomas. 1990. "Retirement: What Happens to the Marriage." *Issues in Mental Health Nursing* 11:347–59.

Jones, Diane C., Nancy Bloys, and Marie Wood. 1990. "Sex Roles and Friendship Patterns." *Sex Roles* 23:133–145.

Jones, Diane Carlson, and Renate Houts. 1992. "Parental Drinking, Parent-Child Communication, and Social Skills in Young Adults." *Journal of Studies on Alcohol* 53:48–56.

Jones, Elise F., and Jacqueline Darroch Forrest. 1992. "Contraceptive Failure Rates Based on the 1988 NSFG." *Family Planning Perspectives* 24:12–19.

Jones, Warren H. 1982. "Loneliness and Social Behavior." In L. A. Peplau and D. Perlman, eds., *Loneliness: A Sourcebook of Current Theory, Research and Therapy.* New York: Wiley-Interscience.

Jorgensen, Stephen R., and Janis C. Gaudy. 1980. "Self-Disclosure and Satisfaction in Marriage: The Relation Examined." *Family Relations* 29:281–87.

Jose, Paul E., and William J. McCarthy. 1988. "Perceived Agentic and Communal Behavior in Mixed-Sex Group Interactions." *Personality and Social Psychology Bulletin* 14:57–67.

Judd, Eleanore Parelman. 1990. "Intermarriage and the Maintenance of Religio-Ethnic Identity. A Case Study: The Denver Jewish Community." *Journal of Comparative Family Studies* 21:251–68.

Julian, Teresa W., Patrick C. McKenry, and Mary W. McKelvey. 1994. "Cultural Variations in Parenting." *Family Relations* 43:30–37.

Juliusdottir, Sigrun. "An Icelandic Study of Five Parental Life Styles." *Journal of Divorced Remarriage* 26:87–103.

Justice, Blair, and Rita Justice. 1979. *The Broken Taboo: Incest.* New York: Human Sciences Press.

Kaczmarek, Peggy, Barbara Backlund, and Paul Biemer. 1990. "The Dynamics of Ending a Romantic Relationship: An Empirical Assessment of Grief in College Students." *Journal of College Student Development* 31:319–24.

Kahn, Arnold S. 1984. *Social Psychology.* Dubuque, Iowa: Wm. C. Brown.

Kahn, Joan R., and Kathryn A. London. 1991. "Premarital Sex and the Risk of Divorce." *Journal of Marriage and the Family* 53:845–55.

Kalb, Claudia. 1997. "How Old Is Too Old?" *Newsweek,* May 5.

Kalick, Michael S., and Thomas E. Hamilton. 1986. "The Matching Hypothesis Re-examined." *Journal of Personality and Social Psychology* 51:673–82.

Kalmijn, Matthijs. 1991a. "Shifting Boundaries: Trends in Religious and Educational Homogamy." *American Sociological Review* 56:786–800.

Kalmijn, Matthijs. 1994. "Mother's Occupational Status and Children's Schooling." *American Sociological Review* 59:257–75.

Kamo, Yoshinori, and Min Zhou. 1994. "Living Arrangements of Elderly Chinese and Japanese in the United States." *Journal of Marriage and the Family* 56:544–58.

Kanter, Rosabeth Moss. 1978. "Work in a New America." *Daedalus* 107:47–78.

Kantor, David, and William Lehr. 1975. *Inside the Family.* San Francisco: Jossey-Bass.

Kao, Erika M., Donnal K. Nagata, and Christopher Peterson. 1997. "Explanatory Style, Family Expressiveness, and Self-Esteem Among Asian American and European American College Students." *Journal of Social Psychology* 137:435–44.

Kasian, Marilyn, and Susan L. Painter. 1992. "Frequency and Severity of Psychological Abuse in a Dating Population." *Journal of Interpersonal Violence* 7:350–64.

Kate, Nancy Ten. 1998. "Two Careers, One Marriage." *American Demographics,* April.

Katzev, Aphra R., Rebecca L. Warner, and Alan C. Acock. 1994. "Girls or Boys? Relationship of Child Gender to Marital Instability." *Journal of Marriage and the Family* 56:89–100.

Kawakami, Norito, R. E. Roberts, E. S. Lee, and S. Araki. 1995. "Changes in Rates of Depressive Symptoms in a Japanese Working Population." *Psychological Medicine* 25:1181–90.

Kayser, Karen. 1993. *When Love Dies: The Process of Marital Disaffection.* New York: Guilford.

Keith, Pat M. 1985. "Work, Retirement, and Well-Being Among Unmarried Men and Women." The *Gerontologist* 25:410–16.

Keith, Pat M. 1986. "Isolation of the Unmarried in Later Life." *Family Relations* 35:389–95.

Keith, Pat M., Rita Braito, and Michael Breci. 1990. "Rethinking Isolation Among the Married and the Unmarried." *American Journal of Orthopsychiatry* 60:289–97.

Keith, Pat M., and Andre Nauta. 1988. "Old and Single in the City and in the Country: Activities of the Unmarried." *Family Relations* 37:79–83.

Keith, Verna M. 1997. "Life Stress and Psychological Well-Being Among Married and Unmarried Blacks." In Robert Joseph Taylor, James S. Jackson, and Linda M. Chatters, eds., *Family Life in Black America.* Thousand Oaks, Calif.: Sage.

Keller, Warren D., Katherine A. Hildebrandt, and Mary E. Richards. 1985. "Effects of Extended Father-Infant Contact During the Newborn Period." *Infant Behavior and Development* 8:337–50.

Kelley, Jane E., Mark A. Lumley, and James C. Leisen. 1997. "Health Effects of Emotional Disclosure in Rheumatoid Arthritis Patients." *Health Psychology* 16:331–40.

Kelly, Joan B. 1988. "Longer-Term Adjustment in Children of Divorce: Converging Findings and Implications for Practice." *Journal of Family Psychology* 2:119–40.

Kennedy, Gregory E. 1985. "Family Relationships as Perceived by College Students from Single-Parent, Blended, and Intact Families." *Family Perspective* 19:117–26.

Kennedy, Gregory E. 1991. "Grandchildren's Reasons for Closeness with Grandparents." *Journal of Social Behavior and Personality* 6:697–712.

Kephart, William M. 1967. "Some Correlates of Romantic Love." *Journal of Marriage and the Family* 29:470–74.

Kerr, Allen S., and Wayne E. Hill. 1992. "An Exploratory Study Comparing ACoAs to Non-ACoAs on Current

Family Relationships." *Alcoholism Treatment Quarterly* 9:23–38.

Keshet, Jamie Kelem. 1990. "Cognitive Remodeling of the Family: How Remarried People View Stepfamilies." *American Journal of Orthopsychiatry* 60:196–203.

Kessler, Ronald C. et al. 1997. "The Epidemiology of DSM-III-R Bipolar I Disorder in a General Population Survey." *Psychological Medicine* 27:1079–89.

Kessler, Ronald C., and William J. Magee. 1993. "Childhood Adversities and Adult Depression: Basic Patterns of Association in a U.S. National Survey." *Psychological Medicine* 23:679–90.

———. 1994. "Childhood Family Violence and Adult Recurrent Depression." *Journal of Health and Social Behavior* 35:13–27.

Key, Rosemary J., and Margaret Mietus Sanik. 1990. "The Effect of Homemaker's Employment Status on Children's Time Allocation in Single- and Two-Parent Families." *Lifestyles* 11:71–88.

Kibria, Nazli. 1993. *Family Tightrope: The Changing Lives of Vietnamese Americans.* Princeton: Princeton University Press.

———. 1994. "Household Structure and Family Ideologies: The Dynamics of Immigrant Economic Adaptation Among Vietnamese Refugees." *Social Problems* 41:81–95.

Kiernan, John E., Vincent L. Taylor. 1990. "Coercive Sexual Behavior Among Mexican-American College Students." *Journal of Sex and Marital Therapy* 16:44–50.

Kim, Oksoo. 1997. "Loneliness: A Predictor of Health Perceptions Among Older Korean Immigrants." *Psychological Reports* 81:591–94.

Kimble, Charles E., and Frank R. Kardes. 1987. "Information Patterns, Attribution and Attraction." *Social Psychology Quarterly* 50:338–44.

Kinard, E. Milling, and Helen Reinherz. 1986. "Effects of Marital Disruption on Children's School Aptitude and Achievement." *Journal of Marriage and the Family* 48:285–93.

King, Jeff, Janette Beals, Spero M. Manson, and Joseph E. Trimble. 1992. "A Structural Equation Model of Factors Related to Substance Abuse Among American Indian Adolescents." *Drugs and Society* 6:253–68.

King, Laura A. 1993. "Emotional Expression, Ambivalence over Expression, and Marital Satisfaction." *Journal of Social and Personal Relationships.* 10:601–07.

King, Lynda A., and Daniel W. King. 1985. "Sex-Role Egalitarianism: Biographical and Personality Correlates." *Psychological Reports* 57:787–92.

King, Valarie, and Glen H. Elder, Jr. 1997. "The Legacy of Grandparenting: Childhood Experiences with Grandparents and Current Involvement with Grandchildren." *Journal of Marriage and the Family* 59:848–59.

Kinsey, A. C., W. B. Pomeroy, and C. E. Martin. 1948. *Sexual Behavior in the Human Male.* Philadelphia: Saunders.

Kinsey, A. C., W. B. Pomeroy, C. E. Martin, and P. H. Gebhard. 1953. *Sexual Behavior in the Human Female.* Philadelphia: Saunders.

Kitano, Harry H. L., and Roger Daniels. 1988. *Asian Americans: Emerging Minorities.* Englewood Cliffs, N.J.: Prentice-Hall.

Kitson, Gay C. 1985. "Marital Discord and Marital Separation: A County Survey." *Journal of Marriage and the Family* 47:693–700.

Kitson, Gay C., Karen Benson Babri, and Mary Joan Roach. 1985. "Who Divorces and Why: A Review." *Journal of Family Issues* 6:255–93.

Kivett, Vira R. 1991. "The Grandparent-Grandchild Connection." *Marriage and Family Review* 16:267–90.

Kleinke, Chris L., Frederick B. Meeker, and Richard A. Staneski. 1986. "Preference for Opening Lines: Comparing Ratings by Men and Women." *Sex Roles* 15:585–600.

Kleinplatz, Peggy, Michael McCarrey, and Claude Kateb. 1992. "The Impact of Gender-Role Identity on Women's Self-Esteem, Lifestyle Satisfaction and Conflict." *Canadian Journal of Behavioural Science* 24:333–47.

Klerman, Lorraine V. 1993. "The Relationship Between Adolescent Parenthood and Inadequate Parenting." *Children and Youth Services Review* 15:309–20.

Kline, Marsha, Janet R. Johnston, and Jeanne M. Tschann. 1991. "The Long Shadow of Marital Conflict: A Model of Children's Post-Divorce Adjustment." *Journal of Marriage and the Family* 53:297–309.

Koch, Alberta. 1985. " 'If Only It Could Be Me': The Families of Pediatric Cancer Patients." *Family Relations* 34:63–70.

Kohn, Alfie. 1988. "Girl Talk, Guy Talk." *Psychology Today,* February, pp. 65–66.

Kolata, G. 1983. "Math Genius May Have Hormonal Basis." *Science* 222:1312.

Kolko, David J., Alan E. Kazdin, Amanda M. Thomas, and Brian Day. 1993. "Heightened Child Physical Abuse Potential: Child, Parent, and Family Dysfunction." *Journal of Interpersonal Violence* 8:169–92.

Kollock, Peter, Philip Blumstein, and Pepper Schwartz. 1994. "The Judgment of Equity in Intimate Relationships." *Social Psychology Quarterly* 57:340–51.

Konner, Melvin. 1982. "She & He." *Science* 82:54–61.

Kopelman, Richard E., and Dorothy Lang. 1985. "Alliteration in Mate Selection: Does Barbara Marry Barry?" *Psychological Reports* 56:791–96.

Kornhaber, Arthur, and Kenneth L. Woodward. 1981. *Grandparents/Grandchildren: The Vital Connection.* Garden City, N.Y.: Anchor.

Kortenhaus, Carole M., and Jack Demarest. 1993. "Gender-Role Stereotyping in Children's Literature." *Sex Roles* 28:219–32.

Kotsopoulous, S. et al. 1988. "Psychiatric Disorders in Adopted Children." *American Journal of Orthopsychiatry* 58:608–12.

Kotva, H. J., and H. G. Schneider. 1990. "Those 'Talks'—General and Sexual Communication Between Mothers and Daughters." *Journal of Social Behavior and Personality* 5:603–13.

Kouri, Kristyan M., and Marcia Lasswell. 1993. "Black-White Marriages: Social Change and Intergenerational Mobility." *Marriage and Family Review* 19:241–55.

Krishnan, Vijaya. 1994. "The Impact of Wives' Employment on Attitude Toward Divorce." *Journal of Divorce and Remarriage* 22:87–101.

Kruttschnitt, Candace, and Maude Dornfeld. 1993. "Exposure to Family Violence: A Partial Explanation for Initial and Subsequent Levels of Delinquency?" *Criminal Behavior and Mental Health* 3:61–75.

Kurdek, Lawrence A. 1990. "Divorce History and Self-Reported Psychological Distress in Husbands and Wives." *Journal of Marriage and the Family* 52:701–08.

Kurdek, Lawrence A. 1991. "The Relations Between Reported Well-Being and Divorce History, Availability of a Proximate Adult, and Gender." *Journal of Marriage and the Family* 53:71–78.

Kurdek, Lawrence A. 1993. "The Allocation of Household Labor in Gay, Lesbian, and Heterosexual Married Couples." *Journal of Social Issues* 49:127–39.

———. 1994. "Areas of Conflict for Gay, Lesbian, and Heterosexual Couples: What Couples Argue About Influences Relationship Satisfaction." *Journal of Marriage and the Family* 56:923–34.

———. 1995. "Predicting Change in Marital Satisfaction from Husbands' and Wives' Conflict Resolution Styles." *Journal of Marriage and the Family* 57:153–64.

Kurdek, Lawrence A., and Mark A. Fine. 1991. "Cognitive Correlates of Satisfaction for Mothers and Stepfathers in Stepfather Families." *Journal of Marriage and the Family* 53:565–72.

Kurdek, Lawrence A., and Mark A. Fine. 1993. "The Relation Between Family Structure and Young Adolescents' Appraisals of Family Climate and Parenting Behavior." *Journal of Family Issues* 14:279–90.

Kurdek, Lawrence A., and J. Patrick Schmitt. 1986. "Early Development of Relationship Quality in Heterosexual Married, Heterosexual Cohabiting, Gay, and Lesbian Couples." *Developmental Psychology* 22:305–9.

Kurdek, Lawrence A., and J. Patrick Schmitt. 1987. "Perceived Emotional Support from Family and Friends in Members of Homosexual, Married, and Heterosexual Cohabiting Couples." *Journal of Homosexuality* 14:57–68.

Kurdek, Lawrence A., and Ronald J. Sinclair. 1988. "Adjustment of Young Adolescents in Two-Parent Nuclear, Stepfather, and Mother-Custody Families." *Journal of Consulting and Clinical Psychology* 56:91–96.

Kvanli, Judith A., and Glen Jennings. 1986. "Recoupling: Development and Establishment of the Spousal Subsystem in Remarriage." *Journal of Divorce* 10:189–203.

Ladewig, Becky Heath, and Gail W. McGee. 1986. "Occupational Commitment, a Supportive Family Environment, and Marital Adjustment: Development and Estimation of a Model." *Journal of Marriage and the Family* 48:821–29.

Lakein, Alan. 1973. *How to Get Control of Your Time and Your Life.* New York: Signet.

Lamb, Michael E., ed. 1997. *The Role of the Father in Child Development.* 3rd ed. New York: John Wiley & Sons.

Lamm, Helmut, and Ulrich Wiesmann. 1997. "Subjective Attributes of Attraction." *Personal Relationships* 4:271–84.

Landale, Nancy S., and Katherine Fennelly. 1992. "Informal Unions Among Puerto Ricans: Cohabitation or an Alternative to Legal Marriage." *Journal of Marriage and the Family* 54:269–81.

Laner, Mary Riege, and Jeanine Thompson. 1982. "Abuse and Aggression in Courting Couples." *Deviant Behavior* 3:229–44.

Lang-Takac, Esther, and Zahava Osterweil. 1992. "Separateness and Connectedness: Differences Between the Genders." *Sex Roles* 27:277–89.

Lanz, Jean B. 1995. "Psychological, Behavioral, and Social Characteristics Associated with Early Forced Sexual Intercourse Among Pregnant Adolescents." *Journal of Interpersonal Violence* 10:188–200.

Larson, Jeffry H. 1988. "The Marriage Quiz: College Students' Beliefs in Selected Myths About Marriage." *Family Relations* 37:3–11.

Larson, Jeffry H., and Scot M. Allgood. 1987. "A Comparison of Intimacy in First-Married and Remarried Couples." *Journal of Family Issues* 8:319–31.

Larson, Jeffry H., and Thomas B. Holman. 1994. "Premarital Predictors of Marital Quality and Stability." *Family Relations* 43:228–37.

Larson, Reed W. 1990. "The Solitary Side of Life: An Examination of the Time People Spend Alone from Childhood to Old Age." *Developmental Review* 10:155–83.

Laslett, Peter. 1977. *Family Life and Illicit Love in Earlier Generations.* Cambridge: Cambridge University Press.

Lasswell, Marcia. 1985. "Illusions Regarding Marital Happiness." *Medical Aspects of Human Sexuality* 19:144–58.

Lauer, Jeanette C., and Robert H. Lauer. 1986. '*Til Death Do Us Part: How Couples Stay Together.* New York: Haworth.

———. 1993. *No Secrets? How Much Honesty Is Good for Your Marriage?* Grand Rapids, Mich.: Zondervan.

———. 1999a. *Becoming Family: How to Build a Stepfamily That Really Works.* Minneapolis, Minn.: Augsburg.

———. 1999b. *The Empty Nest.* Oakland, Calif.: New Harbinger.

Lauer, Robert H. 1998. *Social Problems and the Quality of Life.* 7th ed. Dubuque, Ia.: Wm. C. Brown.

Lauer, Robert H., and Jeanette C. Lauer. 1983. *The Spirit and the Flesh: Sex in Utopian Communities.* Metuchen, N.J.: The Scarecrow Press, Inc.

———. 1988. *Watersheds: Mastering Life's Unpredictable Crises.* New York: Little, Brown.

———. 1991. "The Long-Term Consequences of Problematic Family Backgrounds." *Family Relations* 40:286–90.

Lauer, Robert H., Jeanette C. Lauer, and Sarah T. Kerr. 1990. "The Long-Term Marriage: Perceptions of Stability and Satisfaction." *International Journal of Aging and Human Development* 31:189–95.

Lauer, Robert H., and Warren H. Handel. 1983. *Social Psychology: The Theory and Application of Symbolic Interactionism.* 2nd ed. Englewood Cliffs, N.J.: Prentice-Hall.

Laumann, Edward O., Robert T. Michael, John H. Gagnon, and Stuart Michaels. 1994. *The Social Organization of Sexuality.* Chicago: University of Chicago Press.

Lavee, Yoav, Shlomo Sharlin, and Ruth Katz. 1996. "The Effect of Parenting Stress on Marital Quality." *Journal of Family Issues* 17:114–35.

Leary, Mark R., and William E. Snell, Jr. 1988. "The Relationship of Instrumentality and Expressiveness to Sexual Behavior in Males and Females." *Sex Roles* 18:509–22.

Lederer, William J., and Don D. Jackson. 1968. *The Mirages of Marriage.* New York: W. W. Norton.

Lee, Gary R., and Larry R. Petersen. 1983. "Conjugal Power and Spousal Resources in Patriarchal Cultures." *Journal of Comparative Family Studies* 14:23–38.

Lee, Gary R., Karen Seccombe, and Constance L. Shehan. 1991. "Marital Status and Personal Happiness: An Analysis of Trend Data." *Journal of Marriage and the Family* 53:839–44.

Lee, Gary R., and Lorene H. Stone. 1980. "Mate-Selection Systems and Criteria: Variation According to Family Structure." *Journal of Marriage and the Family* 42:319–26.

Lee, John Alan. 1973. *The Colors of Love: An Exploration of the Ways of Loving.* Don Mills, Ontario: New Press.

Lee, Sharon M., and Keiko Yamanaka. 1990. "Patterns of Asian-American Intermarriages and Marital Assimilation." *Journal of Comparative Family Studies* 21:287–305.

Leiblum, Sandra R. 1993. "The Impact of Infertility on Sexual and Marital Satisfaction." *Annual Review of Sex Research* 4:99–120.

Leigh, Barbara C., Mark T. Temple, and Karen F. Trocki. 1993. "The Sexual Behavior of U.S. Adults: Results from a National Survey." *American Journal of Public Health* 83:1400–08.

Leigh, Geoffrey K., Glenda S. Ladehoff, Andrea Trost Howie, and Donna L. Christians. 1985. "Correlates of Marital Satisfaction Among Men and Women in Intact First Marriage and Remarriage." *Family Perspective* 19:139–49.

Lennon, Mary Clare, and Sarah Rosenfield. 1994. "Relative Fairness and the Division of Housework: The Importance of Options." *American Journal of Sociology* 100:506–31.

Levant, Ronald, and Gini Kopecky. 1994. *Masculinity Reconstructed: Changing the Rules of Manhood at Work, in Relationships, and in Family Life.* New York: Dutton.

Leve, Leslie D., and Beverly I. Fagot. 1997. "Gender-Role Socialization and Discipline Processes in One- and Two-Parent Families." *Sex Roles* 36:1–21.

Levenson, Robert W., Laura L. Carstensen, and John M. Gottman. 1993. "Long-Term Marriage: Age, Gender, and Satisfaction." *Psychology and Aging* 8:301–13.

Levin, Ira, and Joseph P. Stokes. 1986. "An Examination of the Relation of Individual Difference Variables to Loneliness." *Journal of Personality* 54:727–33.

Levinger, George. 1965. "Marital Cohesiveness and Dissolution: An Integrative Review." *Journal of Marriage and the Family* 27:19–28.

Levinson, Daniel J., Charlotte N. Darrow, Edward B. Klein, Maria H. Levinson, and Braxton McKee. 1978. *The Seasons of a Man's Life.* New York: Alfred A. Knopf.

Levy-Skiff, Rachel. 1994. "Individual and Contextual Correlates of Marital Change Across the Transition to Parenthood." *Developmental Psychology* 30:591–601.

Lewis, C. S. 1960. *The Four Loves.* New York: Harcourt Brace Jovanovich.

Lewis, Karen Gail, and Sidney Moon. 1997. "Always Single and Single Again Women." *Journal of Marital and Family Therapy* 23:115–34.

Lewis, Robert A., and Graham B. Spanier. 1979. "Theorizing About the Quality and Stability of Marriage." In W. R. Burr, R. Hill, F. I. Nye, and I. L. Reiss, eds., *Contemporary Theories About the Family.* Vol. 1. New York: Free Press.

Li, Jiang Hong, and Roger A. Wojtkiewicz. 1994. "Childhood Family Structure and Entry into First Marriage." *The Sociological Quarterly* 35:247–68.

Liberman, Robert P., Eugenie G. Wheeler, Louis A. J. M. de Visser, Julie Kuehnel, and Timothy Kuehnel. 1980. *Handbook of Marital Therapy.* New York: Plenum Press.

Libman, Gary. 1991. "At a Crossroads." *Los Angeles Times,* August 6.

Lichter, Daniel T. Robert N. Anderson, and Mark D. Hayward. 1995. "Marriage Markets and Marital Choice." *Journal of Family Issues* 16:412–31.

Lichter, Daniel T., Felicia B. LeClere, and Diane McLaughlin. 1991. "Local Marriage Markets and the Marital Behavior of Black and White Women." *American Journal of Sociology* 96:843–67.

Lichter, Daniel T., Diane K. McLaughlin, George Kephart, and David J. Landry. 1992. "Race and the Retreat from Marriage: A Shortage of Marriageable Men?" *American Sociological Review* 57:781–99.

Liebowitz, Michael. 1983. *The Chemistry of Love.* Boston: Little, Brown.

Lightbody, Pauline, Gerda Siann, Ruth Stocks, and David Walsh. 1996. "Motivation and Attribution at Secondary School: The Role of Gender." *Educational Studies* 22:13–25.

Liker, Jeffrey K., and Glen H. Elder, Jr. 1983. "Economic Hardship and Marital Relations in the 1930s." *American Sociological Review* 48:343–59.

Lin, Chien, and William T. Liu. 1993. "Intergenerational Relationships Among Chinese Immigrant Families from Taiwan." In H. P. McAdoo, ed., *Family Ethnicity: Strength in Diversity.* Newbury Park, Calif.: Sage.

Lin, Yuan-Huei W., and Caryl E. Rusbult. 1995. "Commitment to Dating Relationships and Cross-Sex Friendships in America and China." *Journal of Social and Personal Relationships* 12:7–26.

Litovsky, Viviana G., and Jeromie B. Dusek. 1985. "Perceptions of Child Rearing and Self-Concept Development During the Early Adolescent Years." *Journal of Youth and Adolescence* 14:373–87.

Lloyd, Kim M., and Scott J. South. 1996. "Contextual Influences on Young Men's Transition to First Marriage." *Social Forces* 74:1097–1119.

Lloyd, Sally A. 1991. "The Darkside of Courtship: Violence and Sexual Exploitation." *Family Relations* 40:14–20.

Lloyd, Sally A., Rodney M. Cate, and June M. Henton. 1984. "Predicting Premarital Relationship Stability: A Methodological Refinement." *Journal of Marriage and the Family* 46:71–76.

Lobdell, Judith, and Daniel Perlman. 1986. "The Intergenerational Transmission of Loneliness: A Study of College Females and Their Parents." *Journal of Marriage and the Family* 48:589–95.

Loewenstein, Sophie Freud, Natalie Ebin Bloch, Jennifer Campion, Jane Sproule Epstein, Peggy Gale, and Maggie Salvatore. 1981. "A Study of Satisfactions and Stresses of Single Women in Midlife." *Sex Roles* 7:1127–41.

Logan, John R., and Glenna D. Spitze. 1996. *Family Ties: Enduring Relations Between Parents and Their Grown Children.* Philadelphia, Penn.: Temple University Press.

Long, Barbara H. 1987. "Perceptions of Parental Discord and Parental Separations in the United States: Effects on Daughters' Attitudes Toward Marriage and Courtship Progress." *Journal of Social Psychology* 127:573–82.

Long, Nicholas, Rex Forehand, Robert Fauber, and Gene H. Brody. 1987. "Self-Perceived and Independently Observed Competence of Young Adolescents as a Function of Parental Marital Conflict and Recent Divorce." *Journal of Abnormal Child Psychology* 15:15–27.

Long, Vonda Olson. 1986. "Relationship of Masculinity to Self-Esteem and Self-Acceptance in Female Professionals, College Students, Clients, and Victims of Domestic Violence." *Journal of Consulting and Clinical Psychology* 54:323–27.

Longman, Phillip J. 1998. "The Cost of Children." *U.S. News and World Report,* March 27.

Loomis, Laura Spencer, and Nancy S. Landale. 1994. "Nonmarital Cohabitation and Childbearing Among Black and White American Women." *Journal of Marriage and the Family* 56:949–62.

Lopez, Linda C., and Minami Hamilton. 1997. "Comparison of the Role of Mexican-American and Euro-American Family Members in the Socialization of Children." *Psychology Reports* 80:283–88.

Lorence, Jon. 1987. "A Test of 'Gender' and 'Job' Models of Sex Differences in Job Involvement." *Social Forces* 66:121–42.

Lowery, Carol R., and Shirley A. Settle. 1985. "Effects of Divorce on Children: Differential Impact of Custody and Visitation Patterns." *Family Relations* 34:455–63.

Lugaila, Terry. 1998. "Marital Status and Living Arrangements: March 1997 (Update)." *Current Population Survey Reports,* U.S. Bureau of the Census website.

Lum, Casey Man Kong. 1991. "Communication and Cultural Insularity: The Chinese Immigrant Experience." *Critical Studies in Mass Communication* 8:91–101.

Luster, Tom, and Stephen A. Small. 1994. "Factors Associated with Sexual Risk-Taking Behaviors Among Adolescents." *Journal of Marriage and the Family* 56:622–32.

Lye, Diane N., and Timothy J. Biblarz. 1993. "The Effects of Attitudes Toward Family Life and Gender Roles on Marital Satisfaction." *Journal of Family Issues* 14:157–88.

Lykken, David T., and Auke Tellegen. 1993. "Is Human Mating Adventitious or the Result of Lawful Choice? A Twin Study of Mate Selection." *Journal of Personality and Social Psychology* 65:56–68.

McAdams, Dan P., and Fred B. Bryant. 1987. "Intimacy Motivation and Subjective Mental Health in a Nationwide Sample." *Journal of Personality* 55:395–413.

McAdoo, John. 1985/86. "Black Perspective on the Father's Role in Child Development." *Marriage and Family Review* 9:117–33.

McAdoo, John Lewis. 1993. "Decision Making and Marital Satisfaction in African American Families." In H. P. McAdoo, ed., *Family Ethnicity: Strength in Diversity.* Newbury Park, Calif.: Sage.

McCabe, Kristen M. 1997. "Sex Differences in the Long-Term Effects of Divorce on Children." *Journal of Divorce and Remarriage* 27:123–35.

McCabe, Marita P. 1987. "Desired and Experienced Levels of Premarital Affection and Sexual Intercourse During Dating." *The Journal of Sex Research* 23:23–33.

McCabe, Marita P., Robert A. Cummins, and Yolanda Romeo. 1996. "Relationships Status, Relationship Quality, and Health." *Journal of Family Studies* 2:109–20.

McCall, Mary E., and Nancy J. Struthers. 1994. "Sex, Sex-Role Orientation and Self-Esteem As Predictors of Coping Style." *Journal of Social Behavior and Personality* 9:801–10.

McCauley, Jeanne et al. 1997. "Clinical Characteristics of Women With a History of Childhood Abuse." *Journal of the American Medical Association* 277:1362–69.

Maccoby, Eleanor E., and Robert Mnookin. 1992. *Dividing the Child: Social and Legal Dimensions of Custody.* Cambridge, Mass.: Harvard University Press.

McCrae, Robert R., and Paul T. Costa, Jr. 1988. "Recalled Parent-Child Relations and Adult Personality." *Journal of Personality* 56:417–34.

McCubbin, Hamilton I., and Joan M. Patterson. 1983. "Stress: The Family Inventory of Life Events and Changes." In E. E. Filsinger, ed., *Marriage and Family Assessment: A Sourcebook for Family Therapy.* Beverly Hills, Calif.: Sage.

McCubbin, Hamilton I., and Marilyn A. McCubbin. 1988. "Typologies of Resilient Families: Emerging Roles of Social Class and Ethnicity." *Family Relations* 37:247–54.

McDermott, John F., Jr., and Chantis Fukunaga. 1977. "Intercultural Family Interaction Patterns." In W. Tseng, J. F. McDermott, Jr., and T. W. Maretzki, eds., *Adjustment in Intercultural Marriage.* Honolulu: University Press of Hawaii.

MacDonald, William L., and Alfred DeMaris. 1995. "Remarriage, Stepchildren, and Marital Conflict: Challenges to the Incomplete Institutionalization Hypothesis." *Journal of Marriage and the Family* 57:387–98.

McGoldrick, Monica. 1980. "The Joining of Families Through Marriage: The New Couple." In E. A. Carter and M. McGoldrick, eds., *The Family Life Cycle: A Framework for Family Therapy.* New York: Gardner Press.

McHale, Susan M., and Ted L. Huston. 1985. "The Effect of the Transition to Parenthood on the Marriage Relationship." *Journal of Family Issues* 6:409–33.

McKenry, Patrick C., Kevin D. Arnold, Teresa W. Julian, and James Kuo. 1987. "Interpersonal Influences on the Well-Being of Men at Mid-Life." *Family Perspective* 21:224–33.

McKenry, Patrick C., and Mark A. Fine. 1993. "Parenting Following Divorce: A Comparison of Black and White Single Mothers." *Journal of Comparative Family Studies* 24:99–111.

Mackey, Richard A., and Bernard A. O'Brien. 1995. *Lasting Marriages: Men and Women Growing Together.* Westport, Conn.: Praeger.

McLanahan, Sara, and Gary Sandefur. 1994. *Growing Up with a Single Parent: What Hurts, What Helps.* Cambridge, Mass.: Harvard University Press.

McLaughlin, Mike, L. Sherilyn Cormier, and William H. Cormier. 1988. "Relation Between Coping Strategies and Distress, Stress, and Marital Adjustment of Multiple-Role Women." *Journal of Counseling Psychology* 35:187–93.

McLeod, Beverly. 1986. "Rx for Health: A Dose of Self-Confidence." *Psychology Today,* October, pp. 46–49.

McLeod, Jane D. 1995. "Social and Psychological Bases of Homogamy for Common Psychiatric Disorders." *Journal of Marriage and the Family* 57:201–14.

McLloyd, Vonnie C. 1990. "The Impact of Economic Hardship on Black Families and Children: Psychological Distress, Parenting, and Socioemotional Development." *Child Development* 61:311–46.

McLloyd, Vonnie C., Toby Epstein Jayaratne, Rosario Ceballo, and Julio Borquez. 1994. "Unemployment and Work Interruption Among African American Single Mothers: Effects on Parenting and Adolescent Socioemotional Functioning." *Child Development* 65:562–89.

McMahon, Martha. 1995. *Engendering Motherhood: Identity and Self-Transformation in Women's Lives.* New York: Guildford Press.

McNally, James W., and William D. Mosher. 1991. "AIDS-Related Knowledge and Behavior Among Women 15–44 Years of Age: United States, 1988." *Advance Data,* No. 200, May 14.

McNeal, Cosandra, and Paul R. Amato. 1998. "Parents' Marital Violence: Long-Term Consequences for Children. *Journal of Family Issues* 19:123–39.

McWhirter, David P., and Andrew M. Mattison. 1984. *The Male Couple.* Englewood Cliffs, N.J.: Prentice-Hall.

MacDermid, Shelley M., Ted L. Huston, and Susan M. McHale. 1990. "Changes in Marriage Associated with the Transition to Parenthood: Individual Differences As a Function of Sex-Role Attitudes and Changes in the Division of Household Labor." *Journal of Marriage and the Family* 52:475–86.

Machida, Sandra, and Susan D. Holloway. 1991. "The Relationship Between Divorced Mothers' Perceived Control over Child Rearing and Children's Post-Divorce Development." *Family Relations* 40:272–78.

Madanes, Cloe. 1994. *The Secret Meaning of Money.* San Francisco, Calif.: Jossey-Bass.

Madden, Margaret E. 1987. "Perceived Control and Power in Marriage: A Study of Marital Decision Making and Task Performance." *Personality and Social Psychology Bulletin* 13:73–82.

Mahon, Noreen E., Adela Yarcheski, and Thomas J. Yarcheski. 1993. "Health Consequences of Loneliness in Adolescents." *Research in Nursing and Health* 16:23–31.

Mainemer, Henry, Lorraine C. Gilman, and Elinor W. Ames. 1998. "Parenting Stress in Families Adopting Children from Romanian Orphanages." *Journal of Family Issues* 19:164–80.

Makepeace, James M. 1986. "Gender Differences in Courtship Violence Victimization." *Family Relations* 35:383–88.

Malandro, Loretta A., and Larry Barker. 1983. *Nonverbal Communication.* Reading, Mass.: Addison-Wesley.

Malinowski, Bronislaw. 1932. *The Sexual Life of Savages in Northwestern Melanesia.* London: George Routledge.

Maneker, Jerry S., and Robert P. Rankin. 1993. "Religious Homogamy and Marital Duration Among Those Who File for Divorce in California." *Journal of Divorce and Remarriage* 19:233–47.

Manning, Wendy D. 1990. "Parenting Employed Teenagers." *Youth and Society* 22:184–200.

Manning, Wendy D. 1993. "Marriage and Cohabitation Following Premarital Conception." *Journal of Marriage and the Family* 55:839–50.

Manusov, Valerie, Kory Floyd, and Jeff Kerssen-Griep. 1997. "Yours, Mine, and Ours: Mutual Attributions for Nonverbal Behaviors in Couples' Interactions." *Communication Research* 24:234–60.

Mare, Robert D. 1991. "Five Decades of Educational Assortative Mating." *American Sociological Review* 56:15–32.

Markides, Kyriakos S., and Sue Keir Hoppe. 1985. "Marital Satisfaction in Three Generations of Mexican Americans." *Social Science Quarterly* 66:147–54.

Markland, Stacy R., and Eileen S. Nelson. 1993. "The Relationship Between Familial Conflict and the Identity of Young Adults." *Journal of Divorce and Remarriage* 20:193–209.

Markman, Howard, Scott Stanley, and Susan L. Blumberg. 1994. *Fighting for Your Marriage.* San Francisco, Calif.: Jossey-Bass.

Marks, Gary, Jean L. Richardson, and Norma Maldonado. 1991. "Self-Disclosure of HIV Infection to Sexual Partners." *American Journal of Public Health* 81:1321–23.

Marks, Nadine F. 1996. "Caregiving Across the Lifespan: National Prevalence and Predictors." *Family Relations* 45:27–36.

Marks, Nadine F., and Sara S. McLanahan. 1993. "Gender, Family Structure, and Social Support Among Parents." *Journal of Marriage and the Family* 55:481–93.

Markstrom-Adams, Carol. 1989. "Androgyny and Its Relation to Adolescent Psychosocial Well-Being: A Review of the Literature." *Sex Roles* 5/6:325–40.

Marshall, Linda L., and Patricia Rose. 1990. "Premarital Violence: The Impact of Family of Origin Violence, Stress, and Reciprocity." *Violence and Victims* 6:51–64.

Marsiglio, William. 1991. "Paternal Engagement Activities with Minor Children." *Journal of Marriage and the Family* 53:973–86.

Marsiglio, William. 1992. "Stepfathers with Minor Children Living at Home." *Journal of Family Issues* 13:195–214.

Martin, Carol Lynn, and Jane K. Little. 1990. "The Reaction of Gender Understanding to Children's Sex-Typed Preferences and Gender Stereotypes." *Child Development* 61:1427–39.

Martin, Karin A. 1998. "Becoming a Gendered Body: Practices of Preschools." *American Sociological Review* 63:494–511.

Martinez, Estella A. 1993. "Parenting Young Children in Mexican American/Chicago Families." In H. P. McAdoo, ed., *Family Ethnicity: Strength in Diversity.* Newbury Park, Calif.: Sage.

Mashal, Meeda M. S. 1985. "Marital Power, Role Expectations, and Marital Satisfaction." *International Journal of Women's Studies* 8:40–46.

Masheter, Carol. 1991. "Postdivorce Relationships Between Ex-Spouses: The Roles of Attachment and Interpersonal Conflict." *Journal of Marriage and the Family* 53:103–10.

Mason, Jerald W. 1992. "Meaning of Money." *American Behavioral Scientist* 35:771–80.

Mastekaasa, Arne. 1994. "Marital Status, Distress, and Well-Being: An International Comparison." *Journal of Comparative Family Studies* 25:183–205.

Masters, William H., Virginia E. Johnson, and Robert C. Kolodny. 1988. *Human Sexuality,* 3rd ed. Glenview, Ill.: Scott, Foresman and Company.

Matthews, Lisa S., Rand D. Conger, and K. A. S. Wickrama. 1996. "Work-Family Conflict and Marital Quality." *Social Psychology Quarterly* 59:62–79.

Mead, Margaret. 1969. *Sex and Temperament in Three Primitive Societies.* New York: Dell.

Mednick, Martha T. 1987. "Single Mothers: A Review and Critique of Current Research." In S. Oskamp, ed., *Family Processes and Problems: Social Psychological Aspects.* Beverly Hills, Calif.: Sage.

Mehren, Elizabeth. 1988. "New Study Downplays the Effects of Menopause." *Los Angeles Times,* June 14, 1988.

Melichar, Joseph, and David A. Chiriboga. 1985. "Timetables in the Divorce Process." *Journal of Marriage and the Family* 47:701–708.

Mellman, Mark, Edward Lazarus, and Allan Rivlin. 1990. "Family Time, Family Values." In D. Blankenhorn, S. Bayme, and J. B. Elshtain, eds., *Rebuilding the Nest: A New Commitment to the American Family.* Milwaukee, Wis.: Family Service America.

Melson, Gail F., and Alan Fogel. 1988. "Learning To Care." *Psychology Today,* January, pp. 39–45.

Menninger, Karl. 1942. *Love Against Hate.* New York: Harcourt, Brace, and Co.

Meredith, Dennis. 1986. "Day-Care: The Nine-to-Five Dilemma." *Psychology Today,* February, pp. 36–44.

Meyer, Cynthia J. 1987. "Stress: There's No Place Like a First Home." *Family Relations* 36:198–203.

Mickelson, Kristin D., Ronald C. Kessler, and Phillip R. Shaver. 1997. "Adult Attachment in a Nationally Representative Sample." *Journal of Personality and Social Psychology* 73:1092–1106.

Mikulincer, Mario. 1998. "Attachment Working Models and Sense of Trust." *Journal of Personality and Social Psychology* 74:1209–24.

Miller, Brent C., J. Kelly McCoy, Terrance D. Olson, and Christopher M. Wallace. 1986. "Parental Discipline and Control Attempts in Relation to Adolescent Sexual Attitudes and Behavior." *Journal of Marriage and the Family* 48:503–12.

Miller, Brent C., and Terrance D. Olson. 1988. "Sexual Attitudes and Behavior of High School Students in Relation to Background and Contextual Factors." *The Journal of Sex Research* 24:194–200.

Miller, Louisa. 1993. "Marriage, Divorce, and Remarriage." In U.S. Bureau of the Census. Current Population Reports, series P23, no. 185. *Population Profile of the United States: 1993.* Washington, D.C.: Government Printing Office.

Miller, Nancy B., Virginia L. Smerglia, D. Scott Gaudet, and Gay C. Kitson. 1998. "Stressful Life Events, Social Support, and the Distress of Widowed and Divorced Women." *Journal of Family Issues* 19:181–203.

Millman, Marcia. 1991. *Warm Hearts and Cold Cash: The Intimate Dynamics of Families and Money.* New York: Free Press.

Mills, Randy, and Ryan Mills. 1996. "Adolescents' Attitudes Toward Female Gender Roles." *Adolescence* 31:735–45.

Mills, Robert John, Harold G. Grasmick, Carolyn Stout Morgan, and DeeAnn Wenk. 1992. "The Effects of Gender, Family Satisfaction, and Economic Strain on Psychological Well-Being." *Family Relations* 41:440–45.

Minton, Carmelle, and Kay Pasley. 1996. "Fathers' Parenting Role Identity and Father Involvement." *Journal of Family Issues* 17:26–45.

Mintz, Steven, and Susan Kellogg. 1988. *Domestic Revolutions: A Social History of American Family Life.* New York: Free Press.

Mitchell, Susan. 1993. "Who Says Abortion Is Murder?" *American Demographics,* February, p. 21.

Mitka, Mike. 1998. "Viagra Leads As Rivals Are Moving Up." *Journal of the American Medical Association* 280 (July 8):119.

Moen, Phyllis, Mary Ann Erickson, and Donna Dempster-McClain. 1997. "Their Mother's Daughters? The Intergenerational Transmission of Gender Attitudes in a World of Changing Roles." *Journal of Marriage and the Family* 59:281–93.

Monk, Timothy H., Marilyn J. Essex, Nancy A. Snider, and Marjorie H. Klein. 1996. "The Impact of the Birth of a Baby on the Time Structure and Social Mixture of a Couple's Daily Life and Its Consequences for Well-Being." *Journal of Applied Social Psychology* 26:1237–58.

Montgomery, Barbara M. 1981. "The Form and Function of Quality Communication in Marriage." *Family Relations* 30:21–30.

Montgomery, Marilyn J., and Gwendolyn T. Sorell. 1997. "Differences in Love Attitudes Across Family Life Stages." *Family Relations* 46:55–61.

Moore, Kristin A., James L. Peterson, and Frank F. Furstenberg. 1986. "Parental Attitudes and the Occurrence of Early Sexual Activity." *Journal of Marriage and the Family* 48:777–82.

Morgan, Edmund S. 1944. *The Puritan Family.* New York: Harper Torchbooks.

Morgan, Leslie A. 1988. "Outcomes of Marital Separation: A Longitudinal Test of Predictors." *Journal of Marriage and the Family* 50:493–98.

Morley, Rebecca. 1994. "Wife Beating and Modernization: The Case of Papua New Guinea." *Journal of Comparative Family Studies* 25:25–52.

Morokoff, Patrician J., and Ruth Gillilland. 1993. "Stress, Sexual Functioning, and Marital Satisfaction." *Journal of Sex Research* 30:43–53.

Morris, Monica. 1988. *Last-Chance Children: Growing Up with Older Parents.* New York: Columbia University Press.

Morrison-Beedy, Dianne. 1997. "Correlates of HIV Risk Appraisal in Women." *Annals of Behavioral Medicine* 19:36–41.

Mosher, William D. 1990. "Contraceptive Practice in the United States, 1982–1988." *Family Planning Perspectives* 22:198–205.

Mosher, William D., and James W. McNally. 1991. "Contraceptive Use at First Premarital Intercourse: United States, 1965–1988." *Family Planning Perspectives* 23:108–16.

Moss, Barry F., and Andrew I. Schwebel. 1993. "Defining Intimacy in Romantic Relationships." *Family Relations* 42:31–37.

Muehlenhard, Charlene L. 1988. "Misinterpreted Dating Behaviors and the Risk of Date Rape." *Journal of Social and Clinical Psychology* 6:20–37.

Muehlenhard, Charlene L., and Stephen W. Cook. 1988. "Men's Self-Reports of Unwanted Sexual Activity." *The Journal of Sex Research* 24:58–72.

Muehlenhard, Charlene L., and Lisa C. Hollabaugh. 1988. "Do Women Sometimes Say No When They Mean Yes? The Prevalence and Correlates of Women's Token Resistance to Sex." *Journal of Personality and Social Psychology* 54:872–79.

Muehlenhard, Charlene L., and Melaney A. Linton. 1987. "Date Rape and Sexual Aggression in Dating Situations: Incidence and Risk Factors." *Journal of Counseling Psychology* 34:186–96.

Muehlenhard, Charlene L., Mary A. Koralewski, Sandra L. Andrews, and Cynthia A. Burdick. 1986. "Verbal and Nonverbal Cues That Convey Interest in Dating: Two Studies." *Behavior Therapy* 17:404–19.

Muehlenhard, Charlene L., and Teresa J. Scardino. 1985. "What Will He Think? Men's Impressions of Women Who Initiate Dates and Achieve Academically." *Journal of Counseling Psychology* 32:560–69.

Mueller, Daniel P., and Philip W. Cooper. 1986. "Children of Single Parent Families: How They Fare as Young Adults." *Family Relations* 35:169–76.

Muller, Chandra. 1995. "Maternal Employment, Parent Involvement, and Mathematics Achievement Among Adolescents." *Journal of Marriage and the Family* 57:85–100.

Munch, Allison, J. Miller McPherson, and Lynn Smith-Lovin. 1997. "Gender, Children, and Social Contact: The Effects of Childrearing for Men and Women." *American Sociological Review* 62:509–20.

Murphy, Mike, Karen Glaser, and Emily Grundy. 1997. "Marital Status and Long-Term Illness in Great Britain." *Journal of Marriage and the Family* 59:156–64.

Murphy, Patricia Ann. 1986/1987. "Parental Death in Childhood and Loneliness in Young Adults." *Omega* 17:219–28.

Murstein, Bernard I. 1974. *Love, Sex, and Marriage Through the Ages.* New York: Springer.

Murstein, Bernard, and Robert G. Brust. 1985. "Humor and Interpersonal Attraction." *Journal of Personality Assessment* 49:637–40.

Najman, Jake M., John C. Vance, Fran Boyle, and Gary Embleton. 1993. "The Impact of a Child's Death on Marital Adjustment." *Social Science and Medicine* 37:1005–10.

Nakkab, Sylvain. 1997. "Adolescent Sexual Activity." *International Journal of Mental Health* 26:23–34.

National Cancer Institute. 1998. "Fertility Drugs As a Risk Factor for Ovarian Cancer." NCI website.

National Center for Health Statistics. 1998a. "Teen Birth Rates Down in All States." Press Release, NCHS website.

————. 1998b. "Marriage." NCHS website.

National Institute on Alcohol Abuse and Alcoholism. 1975. *Facts About Alcohol and Alcoholism.* Rockville, Md.: National Institute on Alcohol Abuse and Alcoholism.

National Institute of Mental Health. 1982. *Television and Behavior: Ten Years of Scientific Progress and Implications for the Eighties.* Vol. 1, Summary Report. Washington, D.C.: Government Printing Office.

Needle, Richard H., S. Susan Su, and William J. Doherty. 1990. "Divorce, Remarriage, and Adolescent Substance Use: A Prospective and Longitudinal Study." *Journal of Marriage and the Family* 52:157–69.

Neimeyer, R. A., and K. A. Mitchell. 1988. "Similarity and Attraction: A Longitudinal Study." *Journal of Social and Personal Relationships* 5:131–48.

Neugarten, Bernice L., and Karol K. Weinstein. 1968. "The Changing American Grandparent." In B. L. Neugarten, ed., *Middle Age and Aging.* Chicago: University of Chicago Press.

Nevid, Jeffrey S. 1984. "Sex Differences in Factors of Romantic Attraction." *Sex Roles* 11:401–11.

Newcomb, Michael D. 1986. "Sexual Behavior of Cohabitors: A Comparison of Three Independent Samples." *Journal of Sex Research* 22:492–513.

Newman, Margaret. 1994. *Stepfamily Realities.* Oakland, Calif.: New Harbinger Publications.

Nezu, Arthur M., and Christine M. Nezu. 1987. "Psychological Distress, Problem Solving, and Coping Reactions: Sex Role Differences." *Sex Roles* 16:205–14.

Nieto, Daniel S. 1990. "The Custodial Single Father: Who Does He Think He Is?" *Journal of Divorce* 13:27–43.

Niraula, Bhanu B. 1994. "Marriage Changes in the Central Nepali Hills." *Journal of Asian and African Studies* 29:91–109.

Nock, Steven L. 1987. "The Symbolic Meaning of Childbearing." *Journal of Family Issues* 8:373–93.

Nock, Steven L. 1995. "A Comparison of Marriages and Cohabiting Relationships." *Journal of Family Issues* 16:53–76.

Noel, Nora E., Barbara S. McCrady, Robert L. Stout, and Hilary Fisher-Nelson. 1991. "Gender Differences in Marital Functioning of Male and Female Alcoholics." *Family Dynamics of Addiction Quarterly* 1:31–38.

Noller, Patricia, Judith A. Feeney, Denise Bonnell, and Victor J. Callan. 1994. "A Longitudinal Study of Conflict in Early Marriage." *Journal of Social and Personal Relationships* 11:233–52.

Nye, F. Ivan. 1988. "Fifty Years of Family Research, 1937–1987." *Journal of Marriage and the Family* 50:305–16.

Oakley, Ann. 1974. *Sociology of Housework.* New York: Pantheon.

Obeidallah, Dawn A., Susan M. McHale, and Rainer K. Silbereisen. 1996. "Gender Role Socialization and Adolescents' Reports of Depression: Why Some Girls and Not Others? *Journal of Youth & Adolescence* 25:775–85.

O'Connell, Ann. 1993. "Voices from the Heart: The Developmental Impact of a Mother's Lesbianism on Her Adolescent Children." *Smith College Studies in Social Work* 63:281–99.

Oetting, E. R., and Fred Beauvais. 1990. "Adolescent Drug Use: Findings of National and Local Surveys." *Journal of Consulting and Clinical Psychology* 58:385–94.

O'Farrell, Timothy J., and Gary R. Birchler. 1987. "Marital Relationships of Alcoholic, Conflicted, and Nonconflicted Couples." *Journal of Marital and Family Therapy* 13:259–74.

O'Flaherty, Kathleen M., and Laura Workman Eells. 1988. "Courtship Behavior of the Remarried." *Journal of Marriage and the Family* 50:499–506.

Oggins, Jean, Joseph Veroff, and Douglas Leber. 1993. "Perceptions of Marital Interaction Among Black and White Newlyweds." *Journal of Personality and Social Psychology* 65:494–511.

O'Keefe, Maura. 1994. "Linking Marital Violence, Mother-Child/Father-Child Aggression, and Child Behavior Problems." *Journal of Family Violence* 9:63–78.

———. 1997. "Predictors of Dating Violence Among High School Students." *Journal of Interpersonal Violence* 12:546–68.

Oliver, Mary B., and Janet S. Hyde. 1993. "Gender Differences in Sexuality: A Meta-Analysis." *Psychological Bulletin* 114:29–51.

Oliver, Mary Beth, and Constantine Sedikides. 1992. "Effects of Sexual Permissiveness on Desirability of Partner As a Function of Low and High Commitment to Relationship." *Social Psychology Quarterly* 55:321–33.

Olmstead, R. E., S. M. Guy, P. M. O'Malley, and P. M. Bentler. 1991. "Longitudinal Assessment of the Relationship Between Self-Esteem, Fatalism, Loneliness, and Substance Use." *Journal of Social Behavior and Personality* 6:749–70.

Olson, David H., and Hamilton I. McCubbin. 1983. *Families: What Makes Them Work.* Beverly Hills, Calif.: Sage.

Olson, Josephine E., Irene H. Frieze, and Ellen G. Detlefsen. 1990. "Having It All? Combining Work and Family in a Male and a Female Profession." *Sex Roles* 23:515–33.

Olson, Myrna R., and Judith A. Haynes. 1993. "Successful Single Parents." *Families in Society* 74:259–67.

Olson, Sheryl L., and Victoria Banyard. 1993. "Stop the World So I Can Get Off for a While: Sources of Daily Stress in the Lives of Low-Income Single Mothers of Young Children." *Family Relations* 42:50–56.

Ono, Hiromi. 1998. "Husbands' and Wives' Resources and Marital Dissolution." *Journal of Marriage and the Family* 60:674–89.

Orbuch, Terri L., and Lindsay Custer. 1995. "The Social Context of Married Women's Work and Its Impact on Black Husbands and White Husbands." *Journal of Marriage and the Family* 57:333–45.

Orbuch, Terri L., James S. House, Richard P. Mero, and Paula S. Webster. 1996. "Marital Quality over the Life Course." *Social Psychology Quarterly* 59:162–71.

Oropesa, R. S. 1997. "Development and Marital Power in Mexico." *Social Forces* 75:1291–1317.

Orosan, Pamela G., and Karen M. Schilling. 1992. "Gender Differences in College Students' Definitions and Perceptions of Intimacy." *Women and Therapy* 12:201–12.

Orthner, Dennis K. 1990. "Parental Work and Early Adolescence: Issues for Research and Practice." *Journal of Early Adolescence* 10:246–59.

Oskamp, Stuart, Karen Kaufman, and Lianna Atchison Wolterbeek. 1996. "Gender Role Portrayals in Preschool Picture Books." *Journal of Social Behavior and Personality* 11:27–39.

O'Sullivan, Lucia F., and E. Sandra Byers. 1992. "College Students' Incorporation of Initiator and Restrictor Roles in Sexual Dating Interactions." *The Journal of Sex Research* 29:435–46.

Ou, Young-Shi, and Harriette Pipes McAdoo. 1993. "Socialization of Chinese American Children." In H.P. McAdoo, ed., *Family Ethnicity: Strength in Diversity.* Newbury Park, Calif.: Sage.

Owen, Margaret Tresch, and Martha J. Cox. 1997. "Marital Conflict and the Development of Infant-Parent Attachment Relationships." *Journal of Family Psychology* 11:152–64.

Padgett, Deborah L. 1997. "The Contribution of Support Networks to Household Labor in African American Families." *Journal of Family Issues* 18:227–50.

Page, Randy M., and Galen E. Cole. 1991. "Demographic Predictors of Self-Reported Loneliness in Adults." *Psychological Reports* 68:939–45.

Palisi, Bartolomeo J., and Claire Canning. 1983. "Urbanism and Social Psychological Well-Being: A Cross-Cultural Test of Three Theories." *The Sociological Quarterly* 24:527–43.

Palosaari, U., H. Aro, and P. Laippala. 1996. "Parental Divorce and Depression in Young Adulthood." *Acta Psychiatrica Scandinavica* 93:20–26.

Paludi, Michele A., and Dominic F. Gullo. 1986. "The Effect of Sex Labels on Adults' Knowledge of Infant Development." *Sex Roles* 16:19–30.

Parcel, Toby L., and Elizabeth G. Menaghan. 1994. *Parents' Jobs and Children's Lives*. New York: Aldine De Gruyter.

Parke, Ross D., and Douglas B. Sawin. 1977. "Fathering: It's a Major Role." *Psychology Today*. November, pp. 109–12.

Parker, Ben L., and Susan J. Drummond. 1993. "The Death of a Dyad: Relational Autopsy, Analysis, and Aftermath." *Journal of Divorce and Remarriage* 21:95–119.

Parker, Douglas A., and Thomas C. Harford. 1988. "Alcohol-Related Problems, Marital Disruption and Depressive Symptoms Among Adult Children of Alcohol Abusers in the United States." *Journal of Studies on Alcohol* 49:306–19.

Parkes, Colin M. 1985. "Bereavement." *British Journal of Psychiatry* 146:11–17.

Pasley, B. Kay, and Marilyn Ihinger-Tallman. 1989. "Boundary Ambiguity in Remarriage: Does Ambiguity Differentiate Degree of Marital Adjustment and Integration?" *Family Relations* 38:46–52.

Pasley, Kay, Eric Sandras, and Mary Ellen Edmondson. 1994. "The Effects of Financial Management Strategies on Quality of Family Life in Remarriage." *Journal of Family and Economic Issues* 15:53–70.

Patterson, Charlotte J. 1995. "Families of the Baby Boom: Parents' Division of Labor and Children's Adjustment." *Developmental Psychology* 31:115–23.

Patterson, James, and Peter Kim. 1991. *The Day America Told the Truth*. New York: Prentice-Hall.

Patton, David, and E. M. Waring. 1985. "Sex and Marital Intimacy." *Journal of Sex and Marital Therapy* 11:176–84.

Paulson, Morris J., Robert H. Coombs, and John Landsverk. "Youth Who Physically Assault Their Parents." *Journal of Family Violence* 5:121–33.

Paulson, Sharon E., Joseph J. Koman, and John P. Hill. 1990. "Maternal Employment and Parent-Child Relations in Families of Seventh Graders." *Journal of Early Adolescence* 10:279–95.

Payne, Frank D. 1987. " 'Masculinity,' 'Femininity,' and the Complex Construct of Adjustment." *Sex Roles* 17:359–72.

Paz, Juan J. 1993. "Support of Hispanic Elderly." In H. P. McAdoo, ed., *Family Ethnicity: Strength in Diversity*. Newbury Park, Calif.: Sage.

Pedersen, Darhl M. 1997. "Psychological Functions of Privacy." *Journal of Environmental Psychology* 17:147–56.

Pedersen, Darhl M., and Barbara L. Bond. 1985. "Shifts in Sex Role After a Decade of Cultural Change." *Psychological Reports* 57:43–48.

Peek, Charles W., Nancy J. Bell, Terry Waldren, and Gwendolyn T. Sorrell. 1988. "Patterns of Functioning in Families of Remarried and First-Married Couples." *Journal of Marriage and the Family* 50:699–708.

Peek, Charles W., Judith L. Fischer, and Jeannie S. Kidwell. 1985. "Teenage Violence Toward Parents: A Neglected Dimension of Family Violence." *Journal of Marriage and the Family* 47:1051–73.

Peele, Stanton, and Aaron Brodsky. 1976. *Love and Addiction*. New York: New American Library.

Pepe, Margaret V., and T. Jean Byrne. 1991. "Women's Perceptions of Immediate and Long-Term Effects of Failed Infertility Treatment on Marital and Sexual Satisfaction." *Family Relations* 40:303–309.

Peplau, Letitia Anne. 1981. "What Homosexuals Want." *Psychology Today*, March, pp. 28–37.

Peplau, Letitia Anne, and S. Cochran. 1981. "Value Orientations in the Intimate Relationships of Gay Men." *Journal of Homosexuality* 6:1–19.

Peretti, Peter O., and Anthony di Vitorrio. 1993. "Effect of Loss of Father Through Divorce on Personality of the Preschool Child." *Social Behavior and Personality* 21:33–38.

Peretti, Peter O., and Bernard C. Pudowski. 1997. "Influence of Jealousy on Male and Female College Daters." *Social Behavior and Personality* 25:155–60.

Perlman, Daniel, and Beverley Fehr. 1987. "The Development of Intimate Relationships." In D. Perlman and S. Duck, eds., *Intimate Relationships: Development, Dynamics, and Deterioration*. Beverly Hills, Calif.: Sage.

Perry-Jenkins, Maureen, and Karen Folk. 1994. "Class, Couples, and Conflict: Effects of the Division of Labor on Assessments of Marriage in Dual-Earner Families." *Journal of Marriage and the Family* 56:165–80.

Pestrak, Victor A., Don Martin, and Maggie Martin. 1985. "Extramarital Sex: An Examination of the Literature." *International Journal of Family Therapy* 7:107–15.

Peters, John F. 1987. "Yanomama Mate Selection and Marriage." *Journal of Comparative Family Studies* 18:79–98.

Petersen, Larry R., and Gregory V. Donnenwerth. 1997. "Secularization and the Influence of Religion on Beliefs About Premarital Sex." *Social Forces* 75:1071–90.

Peterson, James L., and Nicholas Zill. 1986. "Marital Disruption, Parent-Child Relationships, and Behavior Problems in Children." *Journal of Marriage and the Family* 48:295–307.

Petronio, Sandra, and Thomas Endres. 1985/86. "Dating and the Single Parent: Communication in the Social Network." *Journal of Divorce* 9:83–105.

Pettijohn, Terry F. 1996. "Perceived Happiness of College Students Measured by Maslow's Hierarchy of Needs." *Psychological Reports* 79:759–62.

Pierce, Robert Lee, and Rosilee Trotta. 1986. "Abused Parents: A Hidden Family Problem." *Journal of Family Violence* 1:99–110.

Pietromonaco, Paula R., Jean Manis, and Hazel Markus. 1987. "The Relationship of Employment to Self-Perception and Well-Being in Women: A Cognitive Analysis." *Sex Roles* 17:467–77.

Pillemer, Karl, and J. Jill Suitor. 1991. " 'Will I Ever Escape My Child's Problems?' Effects of Adult Children's Problems on Elderly Parents." *Journal of Marriage and the Family* 53:585–94.

Pilon, Marc. 1994. "Types of Marriage and Marital Stability: The Case of the Moba-Gurma of North Togo." In C. Bledsoe and G. Pison, eds., *Nuptiality in Sub-Saharan Africa*. Oxford, England: Clarendon Press.

Pines, Ayala, and Elliot Aronson. 1983. "Antecedents, Correlates, and Consequences of Sexual Jealousy. *Journal of Personality* 51:108–35.

Pingree, Suzanne, and Margret E. Thompson. 1990. "The Family in Daytime Serials." In J. Bryant, ed., *Television and the American Family*. Hillsdale, N.J.: Lawrence Erlbaum.

Pink, Jo Ellen Theresa, and Karen Smith Wampler. 1985. "Problem Areas in Stepfamilies: Cohesion, Adaptability, and the Stepfather-Adolescent Relationship." *Family Relations* 34:327–35.

Pittman, Frank. 1993. "Beyond Betrayal: Life After Infidelity." *Psychology Today,* May/June, pp. 33–38.

Pneuman, Roy W., and Margaret E. Bruehl. 1982. *Managing Conflict.* Englewood Cliffs, N.J.: Prentice-Hall.

Poehlmann, Julie A., and Barbara H. Fiese. 1994. "The Effects of Divorce, Maternal Employment, and Maternal Social Support on Toddlers' Home Environments." *Journal of Divorce and Remarriage* 22:121–31.

Pollock, Alann D., Ann H. Die, and Richard G. Marriott. 1990. "Relationship of Communication Style to Egalitarian Marital Role Expectations." *Journal of Social Psychology* 130:619–24.

Pomerleau, Andree, Daniel Bolduc, Gerard Malcuit, and Louise Cossette. 1990. "Pink or Blue: Environmental Gender Stereotypes in the First Two Years of Life." *Sex Roles* 22:359–67.

Pomeroy, H. S. 1888. *The Ethics of Marriage.* New York: Funk & Wagnalls.

Ponzetti, James J., Jr., and Rodney M. Cate. 1986. "The Developmental Course of Conflict in the Marital Dissolution Process." *Journal of Divorce* 10:1–15.

Popenoe, David. 1990. "Family Decline in America." In D. Blankenhorn, S. Bayme, and J. B. Elshtain, eds., *Rebuilding the Nest: A New Commitment to the American Family.* Milwaukee, Wis.: Family Service America.

Porterfield, Ernest. 1982. "Black-American Intermarriages in the United States." In G. Crester and J. J. Leon, eds., *Intermarriages in the United States.* New York: Haworth.

Potts, Marilyn K. 1997. "Social Support and Depression Among Older Adults Living Alone." *Social Work* 42:348–62.

Powell, Mary Ann, and Toby L. Parcel. 1997. "Effects of Family Structure on the Earnings Attainment Process: Differences by Gender." *Journal of Marriage and the Family* 59:419–33.

Prather, Jane E. 1990. " 'It's Just As Easy to Marry a Rich Man As a Poor One.' Students' Accounts of Parental Messages About Marital Partners." *Mid-American Review of Sociology* 14:151–62.

Presser, Harriet B. 1994. "Employment Schedules Among Dual-Earner Spouses and the Division of Household Labor By Gender." *American Sociological Review* 59:348–64.

Propst, L. Rebecca, Ann Pardington, Richard Ostrom, and Philip Watkins. 1986. "Predictors of Coping in Divorced Single Mothers." *Journal of Divorce* 9:33–53.

Pruett, Cheryl L., Robert J. Calsyn, and Fred M. Jensen. 1993. "Social Support Received by Children in Stepmother, Stepfather, and Intact Families." *Journal of Divorce and Remarriage* 19:165–79.

Qian, Zhenchao, and Samuel H. Preston. 1993. "Changes in American Marriage, 1972 to 1987: Availability and Forces of Attraction by Age and Education." *American Sociological Review* 58:482–95.

Quackenbush, Robert L. 1990. "Sex Roles and Social-Sexual Effectiveness." *Social Behavior and Personality* 18:35–39.

Queen, Stuart A., Robert W. Habenstein, and Jill Sobel Quadagno. 1985. *The Family in Various Cultures.* 5th ed. New York: Harper & Row.

Quinn, Naomi. 1982. " 'Commitment' in American Marriage: A Cultural Analysis." *American Ethnologist* 9:775–98.

Quinn, William H., Neal A. Newfield, and Howard O. Protinsky. 1985. "Rites of Passage in Families with Adolescents." *Family Process* 24:101–11.

Quinsey, Vernon L. et al. 1996. "Adult Attachment Style and Partner Choice." *Personal Relationships* 3:117–36.

Ragone, Helena. 1994. *Surrogate Motherhood: Conception in the Heart.* Boulder, Colo.: Westview.

Raley, R. Kelly. 1995. "Black-White Differences in Kin Contact and Exchange Among Never Married Adults." *Journal of Family Issues* 16:77–103.

Ramu, G. N., and Nicholas Tavuchis. 1986. "The Valuation of Children and Parenthood Among the Voluntarily Childless and Parental Couples in Canada." *Journal of Comparative Family Studies* 17:99–116.

Rankin, Robert P., and Jerry S. Maneker. 1987. "Correlates of Marital Duration and Black-White Intermarriage in California." *Journal of Divorce* 11:51–67.

Raty, Hannu, and Leila Snellman. 1997. "Children's Images of an Intelligent Person." *Journal of Social Behavior and Personality* 12:773–84.

Raven, Bertram H., Richard Centers, and Aroldo Rodrigues. 1975. "The Bases of Conjugal Power." In R. Cromwell and D. Olson, eds., *Power in Families.* New York: Halstead Press.

Ray, JoAnn. 1990. "Interactional Patterns and Marital Satisfaction Among Dual-Career Couples." *Journal of Independent Social Work* 4:61–73.

Reis, Harry T. 1984. "Social Interaction and Well-Being." In S. Duck, ed., *Personal Relationships: Repairing Personal Relationships.* London: Academic Press.

Reis, Harry T. 1986. "Gender Effects in Social Participation: Intimacy, Loneliness, and the Conduct of Social Interaction." In R. Gilmour and S. Duck, eds., *The Emerging Field of Personal Relationships.* Hillsdale, N.J.: Lawrence Erlbaum Associates.

Reiss, Ira L. 1960. "Toward a Sociology of the Heterosexual Love Relationship." *Marriage and Family Living* 26:139–45.

Reiss, Ira L., and Gary R. Lee. 1988. *Family Systems in America.* 4th ed. New York: Holt, Rinehart & Winston.

Rempel, Judith. 1985. "Childless Elderly: What Are They Missing?" *Journal of Marriage and the Family* 47:343–59.

Rexroat, Cynthia, and Constance Shehan. 1987. "The Family Life Cycle and Spouses' Time in Housework." *Journal of Marriage and the Family* 49:737–50.

Rice, David G. 1979. *Dual-Career Marriage: Conflict and Treatment.* New York: The Free Press.

Rice, Joy K., and David G. Rice. 1986. *Living Through Divorce: A Developmental Approach to Divorce Therapy.* New York: Guilford Press.

Rice, Roselyn J., Pacita L. Roberts, H. Hunter Handsfield, and King K. Holmes. 1991. "Sociodemographic Distribution of Gonorrhea Incidence: Implications for Prevention and Behavioral Research." *American Journal of Public Health* 81:1252–58.

Rich, Alexander R., and Martha Scovel. 1987. "Causes of Depression in College Students: A Cross-Lagged Panel Correlational Analysis." *Psychological Reports* 60:27–30.

Richards, Leslie, N., and Cynthia J. Schmiege. 1993. "Problems and Strengths of Single-Parent Families: Implications for Practice and Policy." *Family Relations* 42:277–85.

Richards, Marcus, R. Hardy, and M. Wadsworth. 1997. "The Effects of Divorce and Separation on Mental Health in a National U.K. Birth Cohort." *Psychological Medicine* 27:1121–28.

Richardson, Laurel. 1986. "Another World." *Psychology Today,* February, pp. 22–27.

Richardson, Rhonda A., Nancy L. Galambos, John E. Schulenberg, and Anne C. Petersen. 1984. "Young Adolescents' Perceptions of the Family Environment." *Journal of Early Adolescence* 4:131–53.

Richmond, Virginia P. 1995. "Amount of Communication in Marital Dyads as a Function of Dyad and Individual Marital Satisfaction." *Communication Research Reports* 12:152–59.

Ricks, Shirley S. 1985. "Father-Infant Interactions: A Review of Empirical Research." *Family Relations* 34:505–11.

Ridley, Carl, Dan J. Peterman, and Arthur W. Avery. 1978. "Cohabitation: Does It Make for a Better Marriage?" *Family Coordinator* 27:129–36.

Riedmann, A. 1995. "Lesbian and Gay Male Families." *Primis* 4:66–83.

Rieker, Patricia Perri, and Elaine Carmen. 1986. "The Victim-to-Patient Process: The Disconfirmation and Transformation of Abuse." *American Journal of Orthopsychiatry* 56:361–62.

Rieves, Laura, and Thomas F. Cash. 1996. "Social Developmental Factors and Women's Body-Image Attitudes." *Journal of Social Behavior and Personality* 11:63–78.

Riggs, David S. 1993. "Relationship Problems and Dating Aggression: A Potential Treatment Target." *Journal of Interpersonal Violence* 8:18–35.

Riggs, David S., and Marie B. Caulfield. 1997. "Expected Consequences of Male Violence Against Their

Female Dating Partners." *Journal of Interpersonal Violence* 12:229–40.

Risman, Barbara J. 1986. "Can Men 'Mother'? Life As a Single Father." *Family Relations* 35:95–102.

Roberts, Robert E. L., and Vern L. Bengtson. 1993. "Relationships with Parents, Self-Esteem, and Psychological Well-Being in Young Adulthood." *Social Psychology Quarterly* 56:263–77.

———. 1996. "Affective Ties to Parents in Early Adulthood and Self-Esteem Across 20 Years." *Social Psychology Quarterly* 59:96–106.

Robinson, Elizabeth A., and Diane R. Follingstad. 1985. "Development and Validation of a Behavioral Sex-Role Inventory." *Sex Roles* 13:691–713.

Robinson, Gail Erlick, Ruth Stirtzinger, Donna E. Stewart, and Elizabeth Ralevski. 1994. "Psychological Reactions in Women Followed for 1 Year After Miscarriage." *Journal of Reproductive and Infant Psychology* 12:31–36.

Robinson, John, and Geoffrey Godbey. 1997. *Time for Life: The Surprising Way Americans Use Their Time*. University Park: The Pennsylvania State University Press.

———. 1998. "No Sex, Please . . . We're College Graduates." *American Demographics*, February.

Robinson, John, Bart Landry, and Ronica Rooks. 1998. "Time and the Melting Pot." *American Demographics*, June.

Robinson, Linda C., and Priscilla W. Blanton. 1993. "Marital Strengths in Enduring Marriages." *Family Relations* 42:38–45.

Rodgers, Bryan, Chris Power, and Steven Hope. 1997. "Parental Divorce and Adult Psychological Distress." *Journal of Child Psychology and Psychiatry* 38:867–72.

Roesler, Thomas A., and Nancy McKenzie. 1994. "Effects of Childhood Trauma on Psychological Functioning in Adults Sexually Abused As Children." *Journal of Nervous and Mental Disease* 182:145–50.

Rogers, Stacy J., and Lynn K. White. 1998. "Satisfaction with Parenting: The Role of Marital Happiness, Family Structure, and Parents' Gender." *Journal of Marriage and the Family* 60:293–308.

Rogler, Lloyd H., and Mary E. Procidano. 1989. "Egalitarian Spouse Relations and Wives' Marital Satisfaction in Intergenerationally Linked Puerto Rican Families." *Journal of Marriage and the Family* 51:37–39.

Rokach, Ami, and Monika Sharma. 1996. "The Loneliness Experience in Cultural Context." *Journal of Social Behavior and Personality* 11:827–39.

Rolison, Garry L. 1992. "Black, Single Female-Headed Family Formation in Large U.S. Cities." *The Sociological Quarterly* 33:473–81.

Rollins, Judy. 1986. "Single Men and Women: Differences and Similarities." *Family Perspective* 20:117–25.

Romero-Daza, Nancy. 1994. "Multiple Sexual Partners, Migrant Labor, and the Makings for an Epidemic: Knowledge and Beliefs About AIDS Among Women in Highland Lesotho." *Human Organization* 53:192–205.

Ronfeldt, Heidi M., Rachel Kimerling, and Ileana Arias. 1998. "Satisfaction with Relationship Power and the Perpetration of Dating Violence." *Journal of Marriage and the Family* 60:70–78.

Roosa, Mark W. et al. 1993. "Mothers' Parenting Behavior and Child Mental Health in Families with a Problem Drinking Parent." *Journal of Marriage and the Family* 55:107–18.

Roosa, Mark W., Jenn-Yun Tien, Cindy Reinholtz, and Patricia Jo Angelini. 1997. "The Relationship of Childhood Sexual Abuse to Teenage Pregnancy." *Journal of Marriage and the Family* 59:119–30.

Roper, Burns W., and Edward B. Keller. 1988. "Thoughts of Youth." *Public Opinion*, March/April, pp. 16–17, 58–59.

Roschelle, Anne R. 1997. *No More Kin: Exploring Race, Class, and Gender in Family Networks*. Thousand Oaks, Calif.: Sage.

Roscoe, Bruce, Mark S. Diana, and Richard H. Brooks, II. 1987. "Early, Middle, and Late Adolescents' Views on Dating and Factors Influencing Partner Selection." *Adolescence* 22:59–68.

Roscoe, Bruce, Donna Kennedy, and Tony Pope. 1987. "Adolescents' Views of Intimacy: Distinguishing Intimate from Nonintimate Relationships." *Adolescence* 22:511–16.

Rose, Phyllis. 1983. *Parallel Lives: Five Victorian Marriages*. New York: Vintage.

Rosen, Margery D. 1990. "The American Mother: A Landmark Survey for the 1990s." *Ladies' Home Journal*, May, pp. 132–36.

Rosenberg, Morris. 1965. *Society and the Adolescent Self-Image*. Princeton: Princeton University Press.

Rosenblatt, Paul C., and Linda Hammer Burns. 1986. "Long-Term Effects of Perinatal Loss." *Journal of Family Issues* 7:237–53.

Rosenblatt, Paul C., Terri A. Karis, and Richard D. Powell. 1995. *Multiracial Couples: Black & White Voices*. Thousand Oaks, Calif.: Sage.

Rosenbluth, Susan C., Janice M. Steil, and Juliet H. Whitcomb. 1998. "Marital Equality: What Does It Mean?" *Journal of Family Issues* 19:227–44.

Rosenfeld, Lawrence B., and Gary L. Bowen. 1991. "Marital Disclosure and Marital Satisfaction: Direct-Effect Versus Interaction-Effect Models." *Western Journal of Speech Communication* 55:69–84.

Rosin, Hazel M., and Karen Korabik. 1990. "Marital and Family Correlates of Women Managers' Attrition from Organizations." *Journal of Vocational Behavior* 37:104–20.

Ross, Catherine E. 1991. "Marriage and the Sense of Control." *Journal of Marriage and the Family* 53:831–38.

Ross, Catherine E., and John Mirowsky. 1992. "Households, Employment, and the Sense of Control." *Social Psychology Quarterly* 55:217–35.

Ross, Catherine E., John Mirowsky, and Joan Huber. 1983. "Dividing Work, Sharing Work, and In-Between: Marriage Patterns and Depression." *American Sociological Review* 48:809–23.

Ross, Catherine E., and Marieke Van Willigen. 1996. "Gender, Parenthood, and Anger." *Journal of Marriage and the Family* 58:572–84.

Ross, Louie E., and A. Clarke Davis. 1996. "Black-White College Student Attitudes and Expectations in Paying for Dates." *Sex Roles* 35:43–56.

Ross, Susan M. 1996. "Risk of Physical Abuse to Children of Spouse Abusing Parents." *Child Abuse and Neglect* 10:589–98.

Rossi, Alice S., and Peter H. Rossi. 1990. *Of Human Bonding: Parent-Child Relations Across the Life Course.* New York: Aldine de Gruyter.

Rotenberg, Ken J., and Susan Korol. 1995. "The Role of Loneliness and Gender in Individuals' Love Styles." *Journal of Social Behavior and Personality* 10:537–46.

Rotkin, Mark. 1983. "Sex Roles Among Married and Unmarried Couples." *Sex Roles* 9:975–85.

Rubenstein, Carin. 1981. "Money and Self-Esteem, Relationships, Secrecy, Envy, Satisfaction." *Psychology Today,* May, pp. 29–44.

———. 1983. "The Modern Art of Courtly Love." *Psychology Today,* July, pp. 40–49.

———. 1988. "Is There Sex After Baby?" *Utne Reader,* September/October, pp. 66–67.

Rubenstein, Carin, and Phillip Shaver. 1982. *In Search of Intimacy.* New York: Delacorte Press.

Rubin, Zick. 1970. "Measure of Romantic Love." *Journal of Personality and Social Psychology* 16:265–73.

Rubin, Zick, Charles T. Hill, Letitia Anne Peplau, and Christine Dunkel-Schetter. 1980. "Self-Disclosure in Dating Couples: Sex Roles and the Ethic of Openness." *Journal of Marriage and the Family* 42:305–17.

Rubin, Zick, Letitia Anne Peplau, and Charles T. Hill. 1981. "Loving and Leaving: Sex Differences in Romantic Attachments." *Sex Roles* 7:821–34.

Rubinsky, Hillel J., David A. Eckerman, Elizabeth W. Rubinsky, and Chip R. Hoover. 1987. "Early-Phase Physiological Response Patterns to Psychosexual Stimuli: Comparison of Male and Female Patterns." *Archives of Sexual Behavior* 16:45–56.

Rubenstein, Robert L. 1994. "Culture, Caregiving, and the Frail Elderly on Malo, Vanuatu." *Journal of Cross-Cultural Gerontology* 9:355–68.

———. 1986. *Singular Paths: Old Men Living Alone.* New York: Columbia University Press.

Rubio-Stipec, Maritza, Hector Bird, Glorisa Canino, Milagros Bravo, and Margarita Alegria. 1991. "Children of Alcoholic Parents in the Community." *Journal of Studies on Alcohol* 52:78–88.

Rueter, Martha A., and Rand D. Conger. 1995. "Antecedents of Parent-Adolescent Disagreements." *Journal of Marriage and the Family* 57:435–48.

Rusbult, Caryl E. 1987. "Responses to Dissatisfaction in Close Relationships." In D. Perlman and S. Duck, eds., *Intimate Relationships: Development, Dynamics, and Deterioration.* Beverly Hills, Calif.: Sage.

Russek, Linda G., and Gary E. Schwartz. 1997. "Feelings of Parental Caring Predict Health Status in Midlife: A 35-Year Follow-Up of the Harvard Mastery of Stress Study." *Journal of Behavioral Medicine* 20:1–13.

Russell, Diana E. H. 1986. *The Secret Trauma: Incest in the Lives of Girls and Women.* New York: Basic Books.

Saad, Lydia. 1997. "Majority of American Not Fazed by Ellen's Coming Out Episode." *The Gallup Poll.* Gallup Organization Website.

Sabatelli, Ronald M., and Erin F. Cecil-Pigo. 1985. "Relational Interdependence and Commitment in Marriage." *Journal of Marriage and the Family* 47:931–37.

Sabatelli, Ronald M., Richard L. Meth, and Stephen M. Gavazzi. 1988. "Factors Mediating the Adjustment to Involuntary Childlessness." *Family Relations* 37:338–43.

Sack, William H., Morton Beiser, Gloria Baker-Brown, and Roy Redshirt. 1994. "Depressive and Suicidal Symptoms in Indian School Children: Findings From the Flower of Two Soils." *American Indian and Alaska Native Mental Health Research* 4:81–96.

Sadalla, Edward K., Douglas T. Kenrick, and Beth Vershure. 1987. "Dominance and Heterosexual Attraction." *Journal of Personality and Social Psychology* 52:730–38.

Safilios-Rothschild, Constantina. 1970. "The Study of Family Power Structure: A Review 1960–1969." *Journal of Marriage and the Family* 32:539–43.

Sager, Clifford J., and Bernice Hunt. 1979. *Intimate Partners: Hidden Patterns in Love Relationships.* New York: McGraw-Hill.

Sager, Clifford J., Hollis Steer Brown, Helen Crohn, Tamara Engel, Evelyn Rodstein, and Libby Walker.

1983. *Treating the Remarried Family.* New York: Brunner/Mazel.

Sager, Clifford J., Hollis Steer, Helen Crohn, Evelyn Rodstein, and Elizabeth Walker. 1980. "Remarriage Revisited." *Family and Child Mental Health Journal* 6:19–33.

Sakurai, Joji. 1997. "Divorce Gains New Acceptance in Japan." *The San Diego Union-Tribune,* December 28.

Salovey, Peter, and Judith Rodin. 1985. "The Heart of Jealousy." *Psychology Today* 19: 22–29.

Saluter, Arlene F. 1994. "Marital Status and Living Arrangements: March 1993." In *U.S. Bureau of the Census, Current Population Reports,* series P20, no. 478. Washington, D.C.: Government Printing Office.

Salzinger, Suzanne, Richard S. Feldman, Muriel Hamer, and Margaret Rosario. 1993. "The Effects of Physical Abuse on Children's Social Relationships." *Child Development* 64:169–87.

Sanchez, Laura. 1994. "Gender, Labor Allocations, and the Psychology of Entitlement within the Home." *Social Forces* 73:533–53.

Sandefur, Gary D., Sara McLanahan, and Roger A. Wojtkiewicz. 1992. "The Effects of Parental Marital Status During Adolescence on High School Graduation." *Social Forces* 71:103–21.

Sanders, Gordon F., David A. Dosser, Jr., Ann K. Mullis, and Carol Bidon. 1987. "Life Satisfaction of Older Couples: The Contribution of Affective Self-Disclosure." *Family Perspective* 21:107–17.

Sanders, L. L., Jr. 1986. "Treatment of Sexually Transmitted Chlamydial Infections." *Journal of the American Medical Association* 255:1750–56.

Sandven, Kari, and Michael D. Resnick. 1990. "Informal Adoption Among Black Adolescent Mothers." *American Journal of Ortho-psychiatry* 60:210–24.

Sanik, Margaret Mietus. 1990. "Parent's Time Use: A 1967–1986 Comparison." *Lifestyles* 11:299–316.

Sanik, Margaret Mietus, and Teresa Mauldin. 1986. "Single Versus Two Parent Families: A Comparison of Mothers' Time." *Family Relations* 35:53–56.

Santi, Lawrence L. 1987. "Change in the Structure and Size of American Households: 1970 to 1985." *Journal of Marriage and the Family* 49:833–37.

Sapp, Stephen G., Wendy J. Harrod, and LiJun Zhao. 1996. "Leadership Emergence in Task Groups with Egalitarian Gender-Role Expectations." *Sex Roles* 34:65–80.

Satir, Virginia. 1972. *Peoplemaking.* Palo Alto, Calif.: Science and Behavior Books, Inc.

Sauer, Mark. 1995. "Abortions Are Down But Reasons Vary." *San Diego Union-Tribune,* January 12.

Sawyer, Robin G., and Donald J. Moss. 1993. "Sexually Transmitted Diseases in College Men." *Journal of American College Health* 42:111–15.

Scanzoni, John. 1970. *Opportunity and the Family.* New York: Free Press.

Scarf, Maggie. 1987. *Intimate Partners: Patterns in Love and Marriage.* New York: Ballantine.

Schachter, Stanley, and Jerome E. Singer. 1962. "Cognitive, Social, and Physiological Determinants of Emotional State." *Psychological Review* 69:379–99.

Schaninger, Charles M., and W. Christian Buss. 1986. "A Longitudinal Comparison of Consumption and Finance Handling Between Happily Married and Divorced Couples." *Journal of Marriage and the Family* 48:129–36.

Schneider, Danielle S., Paul A. Sledge, Stephen R. Shuchter, and Sidney Zisook. 1996. "Dating and Remarriage over the First Two Years of Widowhood." *Annals of Clinical Psychiatry* 8:51–57.

Schonpflug, Ute, Rainer K. Silbereisen, and Jorg Schulz. 1990. "Perceived Decision-Making Influence in Turkish Migrant Workers' and German Workers' Families." *Journal of Cross-Cultural Psychology* 21:261–82.

Schrader, David. 1990. "A Refined Measure of Interpersonal Communication Competence: The Inventory of Communicator Characteristics." *Journal of Social Behavior and Personality* 5:343–55.

Schuckit, Marc A., and Tom L. Smith. 1996. "An 8-Year Followup of 450 Sons of Alcoholic and Control Subjects." *Archives of General Psychiatry* 53:202–10.

Schulenburg, Joy. 1985. *Gay Parenting.* New York: Anchor Press.

Schwab, Reiko. 1992. "Effects of a Child's Death on the Marital Relationship." *Death Studies* 16:141–54.

Schwartz, Joe. 1987. "Family Traditions." *American Demographics* 9:58–60.

Schwartz, Richard S., and Jacqueline Olds. 1997. "Loneliness." *Harvard Review of Psychiatry* 5:94–98.

Schwebel, Andrew I., Mark A. Fine, and Maureena A. Renner. 1991. "A Study of Perceptions of the Stepparent Role." *Journal of Family Issues* 12:43–57.

Seccombe, Karen. 1991. "Assessing the Costs and Benefits of Children: Gender Comparisons Among Childfree Husbands and Wives." *Journal of Marriage and the Family* 53:191–202.

Secord, Paul F., and Kenneth Ghee. 1986. "Implications of the Black Marriage Market for Marital Conflict." *Journal of Family Issues* 7:21–30.

Seidman, Stuart N., and Ronald O. Rieder. "A Review of Sexual Behavior in the United States." *American Journal of Psychiatry* 151:330–41.

Seltzer, Judith A. 1991. "Legal Custody Arrangements and Children's Economic Welfare." *American Journal of Sociology* 96:895–929.

Shagle, Shobha C., and Brian K. Barber. 1993. "Effects of Family, Marital, and Parent-Child Conflict on Adolescent Self-Derogation and Suicidal Ideation." *Journal of Marriage and the Family* 55:964–74.

Shanas, Ethel. 1980. "Older People and Their Families." *Journal of Marriage and the Family* 42:9–15.

Shapiro, Brenda L., and J. Conrad Chwarz. 1995. "Date Rape: Its Relationship to Trauma Symptoms and Sexual Self-Esteem." *Journal of Interpersonal Violence* 12:407–19.

Shapiro, Jerrold Lee. 1987. "The Expectant Father." *Psychology Today,* January, pp. 36–42.

Sharlin, Shlomo A. 1996. "Long-Term Successful Marriages in Israel." *Contemporary Family Therapy* 18:225–42.

Sharpsteen, Don J., and Lee A. Kirkpatrick. 1997. "Romantic Jealousy and Adult Romantic Attachment." *Journal of Personality and Social Psychology* 72:627–40.

Sheehy, Gail. 1976. *Passages: Predictable Crises of Adult Life.* New York: Bantam Books.

Shehan, Constance L., Felix M. Berardo, Hernan Vera, and Sylvia Marion Carley. 1991. "Women in Age-Discrepant Marriages." *Journal of Family Issues* 12:291–305.

Shehan, Constance L., E. Wilbur Bock, and Gary R. Lee. 1990. "Religious Heterogamy, Religiosity, and Marital Happiness: The Case of Catholics." *Journal of Marriage and the Family* 52:73–79.

Shehan, Constance L., Mary Ann Burg, and Cynthia A. Rexroat. 1986. "Depression and the Social Dimensions of the Full-Time Housewife Role." *The Sociological Quarterly* 27:403–21.

Shelton, Beth Anne. 1987. "Variations in Divorce Rates by Community Size: A Test of the Social Integration Explanation." *Journal of Marriage and the Family* 49:827–32.

Shelton, Beth Anne, and Daphne John. 1993. "Does Marital Status Make a Difference?" *Journal of Family Issues* 14:401–20.

Sher, Geoffrey, Virginia Marriage Davis, Jean Stoess, and Virginia A. Marriage. *In Vitro Fertilization: The A.R.T. of Making Babies.* New York: Facts on File, Inc.

Sher, Kenneth J., and Beth S. Gershuny. 1997. "The Role of Childhood Stressors in the Intergenerational Transmission of Alcohol Use Disorders." *Journal of Studies on Alcohol* 58:414–27.

Shinagawa, Larry Hajime, and Gin Yong Pang. 1988. "Intraethnic and Interracial Marriages Among Asian Americans in California, 1980." *Berkeley Journal of Sociology* 33:95–114.

Shute, Rosalie, and Dennis Howitt. 1990. "Unravelling Paradoxes in Loneliness: Research and Elements of a Social Theory of Loneliness." *Social Behavior* 5:169–84.

Siegel, Judith M. 1995. "Looking for Mr. Right? Older Single Women Who Become Mothers." *Journal of Family Issues* 16:194–211.

Silitsky, Daniel. 1996. "Correlates of Psychosocial Adjustment in Adolescents from Divorced Families." *Journal of Divorce and Remarriage* 26:151–69.

Sills, Judith. 1984. *How to Stop Looking for Someone Perfect and Find Someone to Love.* New York: St. Martin's Press.

Simenauer, Jacqueline, and David Carroll. 1982. *Singles: The New Americans.* New York: Simon & Schuster.

Simon, Barbara Levy. 1987. *Never Married Women.* Philadelphia: Temple University Press.

Simons, Ronald L., Christine Johnson, and Rand D. Conger. 1994. "Harsh Corporal Punishment Versus Quality of Parental Involvement As an Explanation of Adolescent Maladjustment." *Journal of Marriage and the Family* 56:591–607.

Simons, Ronald L., Kuei-Hsiu Lin, and Leslie C. Gordon. 1998. "Socialization in the Family of Origin and Male Dating Violence." *Journal of Marriage and the Family* 60:467–78.

Simpson, Jeffry A. 1987. "The Dissolution of Romantic Relationships: Factors Involved in Relationship Stability and Emotional Distress." *Journal of Personality and Social Psychology* 53:683–92.

Simpson, Jeffry A. 1990. "Influence of Attachment Styles on Romantic Relationships." *Journal of Personality and Social Psychology* 59:971–80.

Simpson, Jeffry A., Bruce Campbell, and Ellen Berscheid. 1986. "The Association Between Romantic Love and Marriage: Kephart (1967) Twice Revisited." *Personality and Social Psychology Bulletin* 12:363–72.

Skopin, Ann R., Barbara M. Newman, and Patrick McKenry. 1993. "Influences on the Quality of Stepfather-Adolescent Relationships." *Journal of Divorce and Remarriage* 19:181–96.

Skurnick, Joan H., Robert L. Johnson, Mark A. Quinones, and James D. Foster. 1991. "New Jersey High School Students' Knowledge, Attitudes and Behavior Regarding AIDS." *AIDS Education and Prevention* 3:21–30.

Slade, P., H. Raval, P. Buck, and B. E. Lieberman. 1992. "A 3-Year Follow-Up of Emotional, Marital and Sexual Functioning in Couples Who Were Infertile."

Journal of Reproductive and Infant Psychology 10:233–43.

Slater, Elisa J., and Karen S. Calhoun. 1988. "Familial Conflict and Marital Dissolution: Effects on the Social Functioning of College Students." *Journal of Social and Clinical Psychology* 6:118–26.

Small, Stephen A., and Donell Kerns. 1993. "Unwanted Sexual Activity Among Peers During Early and Middle Adolescence: Incidence and Risk Factors." *Journal of Marriage and the Family* 55:941–52.

Small, Stephen A., and Tom Luster. 1994. "Adolescent Sexual Activity: An Ecological, Risk-Factor Approach." *Journal of Marriage and the Family* 56:181–92.

Smith, Drake S. 1985. "Wife Employment and Marital Adjustment: A Cumulation of Results." *Family Relations* 34:483–90.

Smith, John P., and Janice G. Williams. 1992. "From Abusive Household to Dating Violence." *Journal of Family Violence* 7:153–65.

Smith, Rebecca M., Mary Anne Goslen, Anne Justice Byrd, and Linda Reece. 1991. "Self-Other Orientation and Sex-Role Orientation of Men and Women Who Remarry." *Journal of Divorce and Remarriage* 14:3–32.

Smock, Pamela J. 1994. "Gender and Short-Run Economic Consequences of Marital Disruption." *Social Forces* 73:243–62.

Snell, William E., Jr., Sharyn S. Belk, Amy Flowers, and James Warren. 1988. "Women's and Men's Willingness to Self-Disclose to Therapists and Friends: The Moderating Influence of Instrumental, Expressive, Masculine, and Feminine Topics." *Sex Roles* 18:769–76.

Snell, William E., Jr., Rowland S. Miller, and Sharyn S. Belk. 1988. "Development of the Emotional Self-Disclosure Scale." *Sex Roles* 18:59–73.

Snyder, Douglas K. 1979. "Multidimensional Assessment of Marital Satisfaction." *Journal of Marriage and the Family* 41:813–23.

Solie, Linda J., and Lois J. Fielder. 1987/88. "The Relationship Between Sex Role Identity and a Widow's Adjustment to the Loss of a Spouse." *Omega* 18:33–40.

Sommers-Flanagan, Rita, John Sommers-Flanagan, and Britta Davis. 1993. "What's Happening on Music Television? A Gender Role Content Analysis." *Sex Roles* 28:745–53.

Sonenstein, Freya L., Joseph H. Pleck, and Leighton C. Ku. 1991. "Levels of Sexual Activity Among Adolescent Males in the United States." *Family Planning Perspectives* 22:162–67.

Sorenson, Kelly A., Shauna M. Russell, Daniel J. Harkness, and John H. Harvey. 1993. "Account-Making, Confiding, and Coping with the Ending of a Close Relationship." *Journal of Social Behavior and Personality* 8:73–86.

Sorenson, Susan B., Dawn M. Upchurch, and Haikang Shen. 1996. "Violence and Injury in Marital Arguments." *American Journal of Public Health* 86:35–40.

South, Scott J. 1985. "Economic Conditions and the Divorce Rate: A Time-Series Analysis of the Postwar United States." *Journal of Marriage and the Family* 47:31–41.

———. 1988. "Sex Ratios, Economic Power, and Women's Roles: A Theoretical Extension and Empirical Test." *Journal of Marriage and the Family* 50:19–31.

———. 1991. "Sociodemographic Differentials in Mate Selection Preferences." *Journal of Marriage and the Family* 53:928–40.

———. 1993. "Racial and Ethnic Differences in the Desire to Marry." *Journal of Marriage and the Family* 55:357–70.

———. 1995. "Do You Need to Shop Around? Age at Marriage, Spousal Alternatives, and Marital Dissolution." *Journal of Family Issues* 16:432–49.

South, Scott J., and Kim M. Lloyd. 1992. "Marriage Opportunities and Family Formation: Further Implications of Imbalanced Sex Ratios." *Journal of Marriage and the Family* 54:440–51.

South, Scott J., and Glenna Spitze. 1994. "Housework in Marital and Nonmarital Households." *American Sociological Review* 59:327–47.

Southworth, Suzanne, and J. Conrad Schwarz. 1987. "Post-Divorce Contact, Relationship with Father, and Heterosexual Trust in Female College Students." *American Journal of Orthopsychiatry* 57:371–82.

Spain, Daphne, and Suzanne M. Bianchi. 1996. *Balancing Act: Motherhood, Marriage, and Employment Among American Women.* New York: Russell Sage Foundation.

Speckhard, Anne C., and Vincent M. Rue. 1992. "Postabortion Syndrome: An Emerging Public Health Concern." *Journal of Social Issues* 48:95–119.

Spence, Janet T., and Robert L. Helmreich. 1978. *Masculinity and Femininity: Their Psychological Dimensions, Correlates, and Antecedents.* Austin, Tex.: University of Texas Press.

Sprague, Heather E., and Jennifer M. Kinney. 1997. "The Effects of Interparental Divorce and Conflict on College Students' Romantic Relationships." *Journal of Divorce and Remarriage* 27:85–104.

Sprecher, Susan. 1996. "College Virgins: How Men and Women Perceive Their Sexual Status." *Journal of Sex Research* 33:3–15.

Sprecher, Susan, and Kathleen McKinney. 1993. *Sexuality.* Newbury Park, Calif.: Sage.

Sprecher, Susan, Quintin Sullivan, and Elaine Hatfield. 1994. "Mate Selection Preferences: Gender Differences Examined in a National Sample." *Journal of Personality and Social Psychology* 66:1074–80.

Sroufe, L. Alan. 1978. "Attachment and the Roots of Competence." *Human Nature,* October, pp. 50–57.

Stack, Steven, and J. Ross Eshleman. 1998. "Marital Status and Happiness: A 17-Nation Study." *Journal of Marriage and the Family* 60:527–36.

Stack, Steven, and Ira Wasserman. 1993. "Marital Status, Alcohol Consumption, and Suicide: An Analysis of National Data." *Journal of Marriage and the Family* 55:1018–24.

———. 1995. "The Effect of Marriage, Family, and Religious Ties on African American Suicide Ideology." *Journal of Marriage and the Family* 57:215–22.

Staines, Graham L., Kathleen J. Pottick, and Deborah A. Fudge. 1986. "Wives' Employment and Husbands' Attitudes Toward Work and Life." *Journal of Applied Psychology* 71:118–28.

Stake, Jayne E. 1992. "Gender Differences and Similarities in Self-Concept within Everyday Life Contexts." *Psychology of Women Quarterly* 16:349–63.

Stanley, Sandra C., Janet G. Hunt, and Larry L. Hunt. 1986. "The Relative Deprivation of Husbands in Dual-Earner Households." *Journal of Family Issues* 7:3–20.

Stapen, Candyce H. 1987. "Marriage Loneliness." *Parents* 26:87–91.

Staples, Robert. 1981. *The World of Black Singles: Changing Patterns of Male/Female Relations.* Westport, Conn.: Greenwood Press.

Staples, Robert. 1988. "The Emerging Majority: Resources for Nonwhite Families in the United States." *Family Relations* 37:348–54.

Staples, Robert, and Alfredo Mirande. 1980. "Racial and Cultural Variations Among American Families: A Decennial Review of the Literature on Minority Families." *Journal of Marriage and the Family* 42:887–903.

Stark, Elizabeth. 1984. "The Unspeakable Family Secret." *Psychology Today,* May, pp. 39–46.

Stark, Elizabeth. 1986. "Friends Through It All." *Psychology Today,* May, pp. 54–60.

Starrels, Marjorie E. 1994. "Gender Differences in Parent-Child Relations." *Journal of Family Issues* 15:148–65.

Starrels, Marjorie E., Berit Ingersoll-Dayton, David W. Dowler, and Margaret B. Neal. 1997. "The Stress of Caring for a Parent: Effects of the Elder's Impairment on an Employed, Adult Child." *Journal of Marriage and the Family* 59:860–72.

Steil, Janice, and Karen Weltman. 1991. "Marital Inequality: The Importance of Resources, Personal Attributes, and Social Norms on Career Valuing and the Allocation of Domestic Responsibilities." *Sex Roles* 24:161–79.

Stein, Peter J. 1976. *Single.* Englewood Cliffs, N.J.: Prentice-Hall.

Steinbeck, John. 1962. *Travels with Charley.* New York: Penguin.

Steinberg, Laurence D. 1987. "Family Processes at Adolescence: A Developmental Perspective." *Family Therapy* 14:77–86.

Steinberg, Laurence, Nina S. Mounts, Susie D. Lamborn, and Sanford M. Dornbusch. 1991. "Authoritative Parenting and Adolescent Adjustment Across Varied Ecological Niches." *Journal of Research on Adolescence* 1:19–36.

Steinberg, Laurence, and Susan B. Silverberg. 1987. "Influences on Marital Satisfaction During the Middle Stages of the Family Life Cycle." *Journal of Marriage and the Family* 49:751–60.

Stephen, Timothy D. 1985. "Fixed-Sequence and Circular-Causal Models of Relationship Development: Divergent Views on the Role of Communication in Intimacy." *Journal of Marriage and the Family* 47:955–63.

Sternberg, Robert J. 1987. "Liking Versus Loving: A Comparative Evaluation of Theories." *Psychological Bulletin* 102:331–45.

Sternberg, Robert J., and Diane M. Dobson. 1987. "Resolving Interpersonal Conflicts: An Analysis of Stylistic Consistency." *Journal of Personality and Social Psychology* 52:794–812.

Stets, Jan E. 1991. "Cohabiting and Marital Aggression: The Role of Social Isolation." *Journal of Marriage and the Family* 53:669–80.

Stets, Jan E. 1993. "The Link Between Past and Present Intimate Relationships." *Journal of Family Issues* 14:236–60.

Stets, Jan E., and Maureen A. Pirog-Good. 1987. "Violence in Dating Relationships." *Social Psychology Quarterly* 50:237–46.

Stevens, Gillian, and Robert Schoen. 1988. "Linguistic Intermarriage in the United States." *Journal of Marriage and the Family* 50:267–79.

Stevens, Michael J., Mary Beth Rice, and James J. Johnson. 1986. "Effect of Eye Gaze on Self-Disclosure." *Perceptual and Motor Skills* 62:939–42.

Stewart, A. J., A. P. Copeland, N. L. Chester, J. E. Malley, and N. C. Barenbaum. 1997. *Separating Together: How Divorce Transforms Families.* New York: Guilford.

Stewart, James R., Andrew I. Schwebel, and Mark A. Fine. 1986. "The Impact of Custodial Arrangement on the Adjustment of Recently Divorced Fathers." *Journal of Divorce* 9:55–65.

Stiffman, Arlene Rubin, Felton Earls, Lee N. Robins, Kenneth G. Jung, and Pamela Kulbok. 1987. "Adolescent Sexual Activity and Pregnancy: Socioenvironmental Problems, Physical Health, and Mental Health." *Journal of Youth and Adolescence* 16:497–509.

Stiles, Deborah A., Judith L. Gibbons, and Jo De La Garza Schnellmann. 1990. "Opposite-Sex Ideal in the U.S.A. and Mexico As Perceived by Young Adolescents." *Journal of Cross-Cultural Psychology* 21:180–99.

Stiles, Henry Reed. 1871. *Bundling: Its Origin, Progress and Decline in America.* New York: Book Collectors Association.

Stinson, Kandi M., Judith N. Lasker, Janet Lohmann, and Lori J. Toedter. 1992. "Parents' Grief Following Pregnancy Loss: A Comparison of Mothers and Fathers." *Family Relations* 41:218–23.

Stockard, Jean, Alphons J. C. Van De Kragt, and Patricia J. Dodge. 1988. "Gender Roles and Behavior in Social Dilemmas: Are There Sex Differences in Cooperation and in Its Justification?" *Social Psychology Quarterly* 51:154–63.

Stohs, Joanne Hoven. 1995. "Predictors of Conflict over the Household Division of Labor Among Women Employed Full-Time." *Sex Roles* 33:257–76.

Stoppard, Janet M., and Kim J. Paisley. 1987. "Masculinity, Femininity, Life Stress, and Depression." *Sex Roles* 16:489–96.

Straus, Murray A., and Stephen Sweet. 1992. "Verbal Aggression in Couples: Incidence Rates and Relationships to Personal Characteristics." *Journal of Marriage and the Family* 54:346–57.

Straus, Murray A., and Carrie L. Yodanis. 1996. "Corporal Punishment in Adolescence and Physical Assaults on Spouses in Later Life." *Journal of Marriage and the Family* 58:825–41.

Street, Sue, Ellen B. Kimmel, and Jeffery D. Kromrey. 1995. "Revisiting University Student Gender Role Perceptions." *Sex Roles* 33:183–202.

Strom, Robert, Dianne Griswold, Shirley Strom, Pat Collinsworth, and Jesse Schmid. 1990. "Perceptions of Parenting Success by Black Mothers and Their Preadolescent Children." *Journal of Negro Education* 59:611–22.

Strouse, Jeremiah S. 1987. "College Bars as Social Settings for Heterosexual Contacts." *The Journal of Sex Research* 23:374–82.

Stuart, Freida M., D. Corydon Hammond, and Marjorie A. Pett. 1987. "Inhibited Sexual Desire in Women." *Archives of Sexual Behavior* 16:91–106.

Studer, Marlena, and Arland Thornton. 1987. "Adolescent Religiosity and Contraceptive Use." *Journal of Marriage and the Family* 49:117–28.

Stull, Donald E., and Annemarie Scarisbrick-Hauser. 1989. "Never-Married Elderly: A Reassessment with Implications for Long-Term Care Policy." *Research on Aging* 11:124–39.

Sugar, Martha Hahn. 1994. *When Mothers Work, Who Pays?* New York: Greenwood.

Suitor, J. Jill. 1991. "Marital Quality and Satisfaction with the Division of Household Labor Across the Family Life Cycle." *Journal of Marriage and the Family* 53:221–30.

Suitor, J. Jill, and Karl Pillemer. 1987. "The Presence of Adult Children: A Source of Stress for Elderly Couples' Marriages?" *Journal of Marriage and the Family* 49:717–25.

Sullivan, Oriel. 1997. "The Division of Housework Among 'Remarried' Couples." *Journal of Family Issues* 18:205–23.

Suman, H. C. 1992. "Towards Choosing a Mate: Perceived Dimensions of Mate Selection." *Journal of Personality and Clinical Studies* 8:143–46.

Sumner, William C. 1997. "The Effects of Parental Dating on Latency Children Living with One Custodial Parent." *Journal of Divorce and Remarriage* 27:137–57.

Sung, Betty Lee. 1990. "Chinese American Intermarriage." *Journal of Comparative Family Studies* 21:337–52.

Surra, Catherine A., and Debra K. Hughes. 1997. "Commitment Processes in Accounts of the Development of Premarital Relationships." *Journal of Marriage and the Family* 59:5–21.

Swanson, Janice M., and Carole W. Chentiz. 1993. "Regaining a Valued Self: The Process of Adaptation to Living with Genital Herpes." *Qualitative Health Research* 3:270–97.

Swensen, Clifford H., and Geir Trahaug. 1985. "Commitment and the Long-Term Marriage." *Journal of Marriage and the Family* 47:939–45.

Takaki, Ronald. 1989. *Strangers from a Different Shore: A History of Asian-Americans.* Boston: Little, Brown.

Takeuchi, David T., David R. Williams, and Russell K. Adair. 1991. "Economic Stress in the Family and Children's Emotional and Behavioral Problems." *Journal of Marriage and the Family* 53:1031–41.

Talbot, Margaret. 1998. "Attachment Theory: The Ultimate Experiment." *The New York Times Magazine,* May 24.

Tanfer, Koray. 1987. "Patterns of Premarital Cohabitation Among Never-Married Women in the United States." *Journal of Marriage and the Family* 49:483–97.

Tannen, Deborah. 1990. *You Just Don't Understand: Women and Men in Conversation.* New York: William Morrow.

Tasker, Fiona, and Susan Golombok. 1997. "Young People's Attitudes Toward Living in a Lesbian Family: A Longitudinal Study of Children Raised by Post-Divorce Lesbian Mothers." *Journal of Divorce and Remarriage* 28:183–202.

Teachman, Jay D. 1991. "Contributions to Children by Divorced Fathers." *Social Problems* 38:358–71.

Thomas, Jeanne L. 1990. "The Grandparent Role: A Double Bind." *International Journal of Aging and Human Development* 31:169–77.

Thomas, Sandra, Kay Albrecht, and Priscilla White. 1984. "Determinants of Marital Quality in Dual-Career Couples." *Family Relations* 33:513–21.

Thomas, Veronica G. 1990. "Determinants of Global Life Happiness and Marital Happiness in Dual-Career Black Couples." *Family Relations* 39:174–78.

Thompson, Anthony P. 1983. "Extramarital Sex: A Review of the Research Literature." *The Journal of Sex Research* 19:1–22.

Thompson, Edward H., Christopher Grisanti, and Joseph H. Pleck. 1985. "Attitudes Toward the Male Role and Their Correlates." *Sex Roles* 13:413–27.

Thomsett, Michael C. 1987. *Homeowners Money Management.* Emmaus, Penn.: Rodale Press.

Thomson, Elizabeth, and Ugo Colella. 1992. "Cohabitation and Marital Stability: Quality or Commitment." *Journal of Marriage and the Family* 54:259–68.

Thomson, Elizabeth, Thomas L. Hanson, and Sara S. McLanahan. 1994. "Family Structure and Child Well-Being: Economic Resources Vs. Parental Behaviors." *Social Forces* 73:221–42.

Thomson, Elizabeth, Sara S. McLanahan, and Roberta Braun Curtin. 1992. "Family Structure, Gender, and Parental Socialization." *Journal of Marriage and the Family* 54:368–78.

Thornton, Arland. 1991. "Influence of the Marital History of Parents on the Marital and Cohabitational Experiences of Children." *American Journal of Sociology* 96:868–94.

Thornton, Arland, William G. Axinn, and Daniel H. Hill. 1992. "Reciprocal Effects of Religiosity, Cohabitation, and Marriage." *American Journal of Sociology* 98:628–51.

Tidwell, Marie-Cecile O., Harry T. Reis, and Phillip R. Shaver. 1996. "Attachment, Attractiveness, and Social Interaction." *Journal of Personality and Social Psychology* 71:729–45.

Treas, Judith. 1993. "Money in the Bank: Transaction Costs and the Economic Organization of Marriage." *American Sociological Review* 58:723–34.

Trent, Katherine, and Kyle Crowder. 1997. "Adolescent Birth Intentions, Social Disadvantage, and Behavioral Outcomes." *Journal of Marriage and the Family* 59:523–35.

Trovato, Frank. 1988. "A Macrosociological Analysis of Change in the Marriage Rate: Canadian Women, 1921–25 to 1981–85." *Journal of Marriage and the Family* 50:507–21.

Truman, Dana M., David M. Tokar, and Ann R. Fischer. 1996. "Dimensions of Masculinity: Relations to Date Rape Supportive Attitudes and Sexual Aggression in Dating Situations." *Journal of Counseling & Development* 74:555–62.

Tubman, Jonathan G. 1993. "Family Risk Factors, Parental Alcohol Use, and Problem Behaviors Among School-Age Children." *Family Relations* 42:81–86.

Tucker, Joan S., Howard S. Friedman, Joseph E. Schwartz, and Michael H. Criqui. "Parental Divorce: Effects on Individual Behavior and Longevity." *Journal of Personality and Social Psychology* 73:381–91.

Tucker, M. Belinda, and Claudia Mitchell-Kernan. 1990. "New Trends in Black American Interracial Marriage: The Social Structural Context." *Journal of Marriage and the Family* 52:209–18.

Tucker, Paula, and Arthur Aron. 1993. "Passionate Love and Marital Satisfaction at Key Transition Points in the Family Life Cycle." *Journal of Social and Clinical Psychology* 12:135–47.

Turner, Barbara F., and Catherine G. Adams. 1988. "Reported Change in Preferred Sexual Activity over the Adult Years." *The Journal of Sex Research* 25:289–303.

Turner, Pauline H., Lynn Scadden, and Mary B. Harris. 1990. "Parenting in Gay and Lesbian Families." *Journal of Gay and Lesbian Psychotherapy* 1:55–66.

Tweed, S. H., and C. D. Ryff. 1991. "Adult Children of Alcoholics: Profiles of Wellness Amidst Distress." *Journal of Studies on Alcohol* 52:133–41.

Tzeng, Meei-Shenn. 1992. "The Effects of Socioeconomic Heterogamy and Changes on Marital Dissolution for First Marriages." *Journal of Marriage and the Family* 54:609–19.

Uchitelle, Louis. 1998. "Still Married to the Job." *The New York Times,* April 20.

Ulbrich, Patricia M., Andrea Tremaglio Coyle, and Maria M. Llabre. 1990. "Involuntary Childlessness and Marital Adjustment: His and Hers." *Journal of Sex and Marital Therapy* 16:147–58.

Ulrichson, Ardys M., and Tahira K. Hira. 1985. "The Impact of Financial Problems on Family Relationships." *Family Perspective* 19:177–87.

Umberson, Debra, Kristin Anderson, Jennifer Glick, and Adam Shapiro. 1998. "Domestic Violence, Personal Control, and Gender." *Journal of Marriage and the Family* 60:442–52.

U.S. Bureau of the Census. 1975. *Historical Statistics of the United States, Colonial Times to 1970.* Washington, D.C.: Government Printing Office.

———. 1980. *Statistical Abstract of the United States, 1980.* Washington, D.C.: Government Printing Office.

———. 1987a. "Population Profile of the United States: 1984–85," *Current Population Reports,* series P-23, no. 150. Washington, D.C.: Government Printing Office.

———. 1987b. *Statistical Abstract of the United States, 1987.* Washington, D.C.: Government Printing Office.

———. 1988. *Statistical Abstract of the United States, 1988.* Washington, D.C.: Government Printing Office.

———. 1989. *Statistical Abstract of the United States, 1989.* Washington, D.C.: Government Printing Office.

———. 1990. *Statistical Abstract of the United States, 1990.* Washington, D.C.: Government Printing Office.

———. 1994. *Statistical Abstract of the United States, 1994.* Washington, D.C.: Government Printing Office.

———. 1997a. "Selected Characteristics of the Population by Race: March 1997. In *Current Population Survey.* Washington, D.C.: Government Printing Office.

———. 1997b. *Statistical Abstract of the United States, 1997.* Washington, D.C.: Government Printing Office.

———. 1998. "Grandparents Day 1998." Press release. U.S. Bureau of the Census website.

U.S. Department of Health and Human Services. 1994. "Annual Summary of Births, Marriages, Divorces, and Deaths: United States, 1993." *Monthly Vital Statistics Report* 42 (October 11).

U.S. Department of Health, Education, and Welfare. 1978. *Yours, Mine, and Ours: Tips for Stepparents.* Washington, D.C.: Government Printing Office.

Vaillant, Caroline O., and George E. Vaillant. 1993. "Is the U-Curve of Marital Satisfaction an Illusion? A 40-Year Study of Marriage." *Journal of Marriage and the Family* 55:230–39.

Vangelisti, Anita, and Mary A. Banski. 1993. "Couples' Debriefing Conversations: The Impact of Gender, Occupation, and Demographic Characteristics." *Family Relations* 42:149–57.

Van Willigen, John, and V. C. Channa. 1991. "Law, Custom, and Crimes Against Women: The Problem of Dowry Death in India." *Human Organization* 50:369–78.

Veevers, Jean E. 1991. "Traumas Versus Stress: A Paradigm of Positive Versus Negative Divorce Outcomes." *Journal of Divorce and Remarriage* 15:99–126.

Vega, William A., Thomas Patterson, James Sallis, Philip Nader, Catherine Atkins, and Ian Abramson. 1986. "Cohesion and Adaptability in Mexican-American and Anglo Families." *Journal of Marriage and the Family* 48:857–67.

Ventura, Jacqueline N. 1987. "The Stresses of Parenthood Reexamined." *Family Relations* 36:26–29.

Vera, Hernan, Donna H. Berardo, and Felix M. Berardo. 1985. "Age Heterogamy in Marriage." *Journal of Marriage and the Family* 47:553–66.

Vera, Hernan, Felix M. Berardo, and Joseph S. Vandiver. 1990. "Age Irrelevancy in Society: The Test of Mate Selection." *Journal of Aging Studies* 4:91–95.

Verbrugge, Lois M., and Jennifer H. Madans. 1985. "Women's Roles and Health." *American Demographics* 8:35–39.

Vinokur, Amiram D., Richard H. Price, and Robert D. Caplan. 1996. "Hard Times and Hurtful Partners: How Financial Strain Affects Depression and Relationship Satisfaction of Unemployed Persons and Their Spouses." *Journal of Personality and Social Psychology* 71:166–79.

Violet, Darlene, T. Neal Garland, and Brian F. Pendleton. 1986. "High School Students' Marital Lifestyle Preferences: A Test of Reference Group Theory." *Human Relations* 39:1053–66.

Volling, Brenda L., and Jay Belsky. 1993. "Parent, Infant, and Contextual Characteristics Related to Maternal Employment Decisions in the First Year of Infancy." *Family Relations* 42:4–12.

Vuchinich, Samuel. 1985. "Arguments, Family Style." *Psychology Today,* October, pp. 40–46.

Waehler, Charles. 1995. "Relationship Patterns of Never-Married Men and Their Implications for Psychotherapy." *Psychotherapy* 32:248–57.

Wagner, Roland M. 1987. "Changes in Extended Family Relationships for Mexican American and Anglo Single Mothers." *Journal of Divorce* 11:69–87.

Waite, Linda J., Frances Korbrin Goldscheider, and Christina Witsberger. 1986. "Nonfamily Living and the Erosion of Traditional Family Orientations Among Young Adults." *American Sociological Review* 51:541–54.

Waite, Linda J., and Lee A. Lillard. 1991. "Children and Marital Disruption." *American Journal of Sociology* 96:930–53.

Walker, Alexis J. 1996. "Couples Watching Television: Gender, Power, and the Remote Control." *Journal of Marriage and the Family* 58:813–23.

Waller, Willard. 1951. *The Family.* Revised by Reuben Hill. New York: Dryden Press.

Wallerstein, Judith S. 1987. "Children of Divorce: Report of a Ten-Year Follow-Up of Early Latency-Age Children." *American Journal of Orthopsychiatry* 57:199–211.

———. 1994. "The Early Psychological Tasks of Marriage." *American Journal of Orthopsychiatry* 64:640–50.

Wallerstein, Judith S., and Sandra Blakeslee. 1989. *Second Chances: Men, Women and Children a Decade After Divorce.* New York: Ticknor & Fields.

Walsh, Debra G., and Jay Hewitt. 1985. "Giving Men the Come-On: Effect of Eye Contact and Smiling in a Bar Environment." *Perceptual and Motor Skills* 61:873–74.

Walster, Elaine, and G. William Walster. 1978. *A New Look at Love.* Reading, Mass.: Addison-Wesley.

Walster, Elaine, G. W. Walster, and Ellen Berscheid. 1978. *Equity: Theory and Research.* Boston: Allyn & Bacon.

Walster, Elaine, G. W. Walster, and Jane Traupmann. 1978. "Equity and Premarital Sex." *Journal of Personality and Social Psychology* 36:82–92.

Walzer, Susan. 1996. "Thinking About the Baby: Gender and Divisions of Infant Care." *Social Problems* 43:219–34.

Ward, Russell A. 1981. "The Never-Married in Later Life." In P. J. Stein, ed., *Single Life: Unmarried Adults in Social Context.* New York: St. Martin's.

Ward, Russell A. 1993. "Marital Happiness and Household Equity in Later Life." *Journal of Marriage and the Family* 55:427–38.

Waring, E. M., and Gordon J. Chelune. 1983. "Marital Intimacy and Self-Disclosure." *Journal of Clinical Psychology* 39:183–90.

Waris, Robert G. 1997. "Age and Occupation in Selection of Human Mates." *Psychological Reports* 80:1223–26.

Wasserheit, Judith. 1997. "Chlamydia Trachomatis Genital Infections—United States, 1995." *Morbidity and Mortality Weekly Report,* March 7.

Wasserman, Ira M. 1990. "The Impact of Divorce on Suicide in the United States: 1970–1983." *Family Perspective* 24:61–68.

Weber, Barbara, Arlene Metha, and Edward Nelsen. 1997. "Relationships Among Multiple Suicide Ideation Risk Factors in College Students." *Journal of College Student Psychotherapy* 11:49–64.

Weigel, Randy R., and Daniel J. Weigel. 1987. "Identifying Stressors and Coping Strategies in Two-Generation Farm Families." *Family Relations* 36:379–84.

Weinberg, Howard. 1990. "Delayed Childbearing, Childlessness and Marital Disruption." *Journal of Comparative Family Studies* 21:99–110.

Weinberg, Thomas S., and Conrad C. Vogler. 1990. "Wives of Alcoholics: Stigma Management and Adjustments to Husband-Wife Interaction." *Deviant Behavior* 11:331–43.

Weingarten, Helen R. 1980. "Remarriage and Well-Being: National Survey Evidence of Social and Psychological Effects." *Journal of Family Issues* 1:533–59.

Weingarten, Helen R. 1985. "Marital Status and Well-Being: A National Study Comparing First-Married, Currently Divorced, and Remarried Adults." *Journal of Marriage and the Family* 47:653–62.

Weiss, Miriam Strauss. 1969. *A Lively Corpse.* South Brunswick and New York: A. S. Barnes.

Weiss, R. S. 1973. *Loneliness: The Experience of Emotional and Social Isolation.* Cambridge: MIT Press.

Weiss, Robert. 1979. *Going It Alone.* New York: Basic Books.

Weitzman, Lenore J. 1985. *The Divorce Revolution: The Unexpected Social and Economic Consequences for Women and Children in America.* New York: Free Press.

West, James. 1945. *Plainville, U.S.A.* New York: Columbia University Press.

West, Melissa Owings, and Ronald J. Prinz. 1987. "Parental Alcoholism and Childhood Psychopathology." *Psychological Bulletin* 102:204–18.

Weston, Carolyn A., and Eleanor D. Macklin. 1990. "The Relationship Between Former-Spousal Contact and Remarital Satisfaction in Stepfather Families." *Journal of Divorce and Remarriage* 14:25–47.

Wheelis, Allen. 1973. *How People Change.* New York: Harper & Row.

Whipple, Ellen E., and Carolyn Webster-Stratton. 1991. "The Role of Parental Stress in Physically Abusive Families." *Child Abuse and Neglect* 15:279–91.

Whipple, S. C., and E. P. Noble. 1991. "Personality Characteristics of Alcoholic Fathers and Their Sons." *Journal of Studies on Alcohol* 52:331–37.

Whisman, Mark A., and Neil S. Jacobson. 1990. "Power, Marital Satisfaction, and Response to Marital Therapy." *Journal of Family Psychology* 4:202–12.

Whitbeck, Les B., Rand D. Conger, and Meei-Ying Kao. 1993. "The Influence of Parental Support, Depressed Affect, and Peers on the Sexual Behaviors of Adolescent Girls." *Journal of Family Issues* 14:261–78.

Whitbeck, Les B., Rand D. Conger, Ronald L. Simons, and Meei-Ying Kao. 1993. "Minor Deviant Behaviors and Adolescent Sexual Activity." *Youth and Society* 25:24–37.

White, Gregory, Sanford Fishbein, and Jeffrey Rutstein. 1981. "Passionate Love and the Misattribution of Arousal." *Journal of Personality and Social Psychology* 41:56–62.

White, James M. 1987. "Marital Perceived Agreement and Actual Agreement Over the Family Life Cycle." *Journal of Comparative Family Studies* 18:47–59.

White, James M. 1989. "Reply to Comment by Trussell and Rao: A Reanalysis of the Data." *Journal of Marriage and the Family* 51:540–44.

White, Kathleen M., Joseph C. Speisman, Doris Jackson, Scott Bartis, and Daryl Costos. 1986. "Intimacy Maturity and Its Correlates in Young Married Couples." *Journal of Personality and Social Psychology* 50:152–62.

White, Lynn. 1994. "Growing Up with Single Parents and Stepparents: Long-Term Effects on Family Solidarity." *Journal of Marriage and the Family* 56:935–48.

White, Lynn K., and Alan Booth. 1985. "Stepchildren in Remarriages." *American Sociological Review* 50:689–98.

White, Lynn K., Alan Booth, and John N. Edwards. 1986. "Children and Marital Happiness: Why the Negative Correlation?" *Journal of Family Issues* 7:131–47.

White, Lynn K., David B. Brinkerhoff, and Alan Booth. 1985. "The Effect of Marital Disruption on Child's Attachment to Parents." *Journal of Family Issues* 6:5–22.

Whitehead, Barbara Dafoe. 1997. *The Divorce Culture.* New York: Alfred A. Knopf.

Whitley, Bernard E. 1990. "College Student Contraceptive Use: A Multivariate Analysis." *Journal of Sex Research* 27:305–13.

Whyte, Martin King. 1990. *Dating, Mating, and Marriage.* New York: Aldine de Gruyt.

Wickrama, K. A. S., Frederick O. Lorenz, Rand D. Conger, and Glen H. Elder, Jr. 1997. "Marital Quality and Physical Illness: A Latent Growth Curve Analysis." *Journal of Marriage and the Family* 59:143–55.

Widmer, Eric D. 1997. "Influence of Older Siblings on Initiation of Sexual Intercourse." *Journal of Marriage and the Family* 59:928–38.

Wiederman, Michael W. 1998. "Attractiveness Still Key to Dating Activity." *USA Today* 126:6.

Wiederman, Michael W., and Elizabeth Rice Allgeier. 1996. "Expectations and Attributions Regarding Extramarital Sex Among Young Married Individuals." *Journal of Psychology & Human Sexuality* 8:21–35.

Wilcoxon, S. Allen, and Alan J. Hovestadt. 1985. "Perceived Similarity in Family-of-Origin Experiences and Dyadic Adjustment: A Comparison Across Years of Marriage." *Family Therapy* 12:165–74.

Wilkie, Jane Riblett. 1991. "The Decline in Men's Labor Force Participation and Income and the Changing Structure of Family Economic Support." *Journal of Marriage and the Family* 53:111–22.

Wilkie, Jane Riblett, Myra Marx Ferree, and Kathryn Strother Ratcliff. 1998. "Gender and Fairness: Marital Satisfaction in Two-Earner Couples." *Journal of Marriage and the Family* 60:577–94.

Willi, Jurg. 1997. "The Significance of Romantic Love for Marriage." *Family Process* 36:171–82.

Williams, Dale E., and Joseph D. D'Alessandro. 1994. "A Comparison of Three Measures of Androgyny and Their Relationship to Psychological Adjustment." *Journal of Social Behavior and Personality* 9:469–80.

Williams, David R., David T. Takeuchi, and Russell K. Adair. 1992. "Marital Status and Psychiatric Disorders Among Blacks and Whites." *Journal of Health and Social Behavior* 33:140–57.

Williams, Flora L., and Susan S. Prohofsky. 1986. "Teenagers' Perception of Agreement over Family Expenditures, Employment, and Family Life." *Journal of Youth and Adolescence* 15:243–57.

Williams, Norma. 1990. *The Mexican American Family: Tradition and Change.* New York: General Hall, Inc.

Willis, Frank N., and Roger A. Carlson. 1993. "Singles Ads: Gender, Social Class, and Time." *Sex Roles* 29:387–404.

Wilmot, Joyce Hocker, and William W. Wilmot. 1978. *Interpersonal Conflict.* Dubuque, Iowa: Wm. C. Brown.

Wilson, Melvin N., Timothy F. Tolson, Ivora D. Hinton, and Michael Kiernan. 1990. "Flexibility and Sharing of Childcare Duties in Black Families." *Sex Roles* 22:409–25.

Wilson, Michele D., Mariana Kastrinakis, Lawrence J. D'Angelo, and Pamela Getson. 1994. "Attitudes, Knowledge, and Behavior Regarding Condom Use in Urban Black Adolescent Males." *Adolescence* 29:13–26.

Wilson, Stephan M., and Nilvfer P. Madora. 1990. "Gender Comparisons of College Students' Attitudes Toward Sexual Behavior." *Adolescence* 25:615–27.

Wineberg, Howard. 1992. "Childbearing and Dissolution of the Second Marriage." *Journal of Marriage and the Family* 54:879–87.

Winkler, Karen J. 1985. "Scholars Diagnose 'Cancerous' Individualism in the Character of American Citizens." *Chronicle of Higher Education,* April 24, p. 8.

Wolfner, Glenn D., and Richard J. Gelles. 1993. "A Profile of Violence Toward Children." *Child Abuse and Neglect* 17:197–212.

Wright, David W., and Robert Young. 1998. "The Effects of Family Structure and Maternal Employment on the Development of Gender-Related Attitudes among Men and Women." *Journal of Family Issues* 19:300–14.

Wright, Loyd S. 1985. "Correlates of Perceived Child Abuse Among College Undergraduates." *Family Perspective* 19:171–88.

Wu, Zheng. 1994. "Remarriage in Canada: A Social Exchange Perspective." *Journal of Divorce and Remarriage* 21:191–219.

Wynn, Ruth L., and Jean Bowering. 1990. "Homemaking Practices and Evening Meals in Married and Separated Families with Young Children." *Journal of Divorce and Remarriage* 14:107–23.

Wynne, Lyman C., and Adele R. Wynne. 1986. "The Quest for Intimacy." *Journal of Marital and Family Therapy* 12:383–94.

Yamaguchi, Kazuo, and Linda R. Ferguson. 1995. "The Stopping and Spacing of Childbirths and Their Birth-History Predictors." *American Sociological Review* 60:272–98.

Yax, Laura K. 1998. "Hispanic Population of the United States: Current Population Survey—March 1997." U.S. Bureau of the Census website.

Ybarra, Lea. 1982. "When Wives Work: The Impact on the Chicano Family." *Journal of Marriage and the Family* 44:169–98.

Yee, Barbara W. K. 1990. "Gender and Family Issues in Minority Groups." *Generations: Gender and Aging* 14:39–42.

Yelsma, Paul. 1986. "Marriage vs. Cohabitation: Couples' Communication Practices and Satisfaction." *Journal of Communication* 36:94–102.

Yelsma, Paul, and Charles T. Brown. 1985. "Gender Roles, Biological Sex, and Predisposition to Conflict Management." *Sex Roles* 12:731–47.

Youngblut, JoAnne M., Carol J. Loveland-Cherry, and Mary Horan. 1993. "Maternal Employment, Family Functioning, and Preterm Infant Development at 9 and 12 Months." *Research in Nursing and Health* 16:33–43.

Zablocki, Benjamin. 1980. *Alienation and Charisma.* New York: Free Press.

Zajonc, Robert B. 1968. "Attitudinal Effects of Mere Exposure." *Journal of Personality and Social Psychology* 9:1–17.

Zammuner, Vanda L., and Agneta H. Fischer. 1995. "The Social Regulation of Emotions in Jealousy Situations: A Comparison Between Italy and the Netherlands." *Journal of Cross-Cultural Psychology* 26:189–208.

Zick, Cathleen D., and W. Keith Bryant. 1996. "A New Look at Parents' Time Spent in Child Care: Primary and Secondary Time Use." *Social Science Research* 25:260–80.

Zietlow, Paul H., and Alan L. Sillars. 1988. "Life-Stage Differences in Communication During Marital Conflicts." *Journal of Social and Personal Relationships* 5:223–45.

Zill, Nicholas, Donna R. Morrison, and Mary J. Coiro. 1993. "Long-Term Effects of Parental Divorce on Parent-Child Relationships, Adjustment, and Achievements in Young Adulthood." *Journal of Family Psychology* 7:91–103.

Zill, Nicholas, and Charlotte A. Schoenborn. 1990. "Developmental, Learning and Emotional Problems: Health of Our Nation's Children, United States, 1988." Advance Data, No. 190, *Vital and Health Statistics of the National Center for Health Statistics.*

Zillmann, Dolf, James B. Weaver, Norbert Mundorf, and Charles F. Aust. 1986. "Effects of an Opposite-Gender Companion's Affect to Horror on Distress, Delight, and Attraction." *Journal of Personality and Social Psychology* 51:586–94.

Zimiles, Herbert, and Valerie E. Lee. 1991. "Adolescent Family Structure and Educational Progress." *Developmental Psychology* 27:314–20.

Zollar, Ann Creighton, and J. Sherwood Williams. 1987. "The Contribution of Marriage to the Life Satisfaction of Black Adults." *Journal of Marriage and the Family* 49:87–92.

PHOTO CREDITS

Chapter 9

Opener: © Myrleen Ferguson/Photo Edit; 1: p.204: © Jean Claude Lejeune; 2: p.207: © Alan Carey/The Image Works; 3: p.213: © David Young Wolff/Photo Edit; 4: p.215: © Robert Brenner/Photo Edit

Chapter 10

Opener: © Jean Claude Lejeune; 1: p.225: © Amy C. Etra/Photo Edit; 2: p.230: © David Young Wolff/Photo Edit; 3: p.233: © Bill Aron/Photo Edit

Chapter 11

Opener: © David Frazier Photolibrary; 1: p.244: © M. Antman/The Image Works; 2: p.249: © Brian Yarvin/The Image Works; 3: p.255: © Vic Bider/Photo Edit; 4: p.258: © Wil and Deni McIntyre/Photo Researchers, Inc.

Chapter 12

Opener: © Mary Kate Denny/Photo Edit; 1: p.266: © Jeff Greenberg/Photo Researchers, Inc. 2: p.268: © M. Ferguson/Photo Edit; 3: p.275: © Esbin/Anders/The Image Works; 4: p.279: © Scott Witte/The Picture Cube; 5: p.282: © Walter Gans/The Image Works

Chapter 13

Opener: © Blair Seitz/Photo Researchers, Inc.; 1: p.289: © Laima Druskis/Photo Researchers, Inc.; 2: p.296: © Robert Brenner/Photo Edit; 3: p.298: © Mark Richards 4: p.302: © Spencer Grant/Photo Edit

Chapter 14

Opener: © 1: p.315: © David Frazier Photolibrary; 2: p.320: © Wil and Deni McIntyre/Photo Researchers, Inc.; 3: p.324: © James L. Shaffer; 4: p.328: © Alan Carey/The Image Works; 5: p.333: © Michael Siluk

Chapter 15

Opener: © Karen Preuss/The Image Works; 1: p.341: © Bob Daemmrich/The Image Works; 2: p.347: © Everton/The Image Works; 3: p.352: © David Young Wolff/Photo Edit; 4: p.355: © Tony Freeman/Photo Edit

Chapter 16

Opener: © Bill Bachmann/The Image Works; 1: p.369: © M. Schwarz/The Image Works; 2: p.371: © Rhoda Sidney/Photo Edit; 3: p.374: © Michael Newman/Photo Edit

Chapter 17

Opener: © Dennis MacDonald/Photo Edit; 1: p.387: © Michael Newman/Photo Edit; 2: p.389: © Tony Freeman/Photo Edit; 3: p.392: © James L. Shaffer; 4: p.396: © T. Shumsky/The Image Works; 5: p.404: © Norman R. Rowan/The Image Works

Chapter 18

Opener: Novastock/Photo Edit; 1: p.414: © Robert Ginn/Photo Edit; 2: p.419: © David Young Wolff/Photo Edit; 3: p.425: © Ursula Markus/Photo Researchers, Inc.; 4: p.429: © Marilyn Nolt; 5: p.432: © Paul Gerda/Leo de Wys

Chapter 19

Opener: © Michael Siluk; 1: p.439: © Jeff Greenberg/Photo Researchers, Inc.; 2: p.441: © Michael Siluk; 3: p.450: © Ellen B. Senise/The Image Works; 4: p.453: © Jean Claude Lejeune

NAME INDEX

Abbey, Antonia, 124, 319
Abloff, Richard, 128
Abma, Joyce, 8, 9, 86, 88, 94, 98, 316, 320
Acock, Alan C., 419, 428, 430
Adair, Russell K., 209, 366
Adams, Abigail, 331
Adams, Catherine G., 100
Adams, Charles Francis, 331
Adams, John Quincy, 331
Adams, Susan, 72, 237
Adler, Nancy J., 170
Agostinelli, Joan, 298
Ahrons, Constance R., 426
Ainslie, Ricardo C., 378
Akiyama, Hiriko, 357
Alba, Richard D., 184
Albers, Lawrence J., 272
Albrecht, Kay, 303
Albrecht, Stan L., 20
Aldous, Joan, 356
Alessandri, Steven M., 34
Alford-Cooper, Finnegan, 273, 275, 281, 327
Allen, Frederick Lewis, 421
Allen, Katherine R., 204, 207, 208, 254, 332
Allgeier, Elizabeth Rice, 102
Allgood, Scot M., 446
Allison, Paul D., 429
Allport, Gordon, 124
Almeida, David M., 69
Alpert, Dona, 298
Altman, I., 28
Amatea, Ellen S., 209
Amato, Paul R., 34, 36, 77, 272, 332, 399, 417, 418, 421, 428, 429, 430, 450
Ambert, Anne-Marie, 35, 451, 452
Ambry, Margaret K., 370
Ames, Elinor W., 327
Ammon, Richard Allbright, 50, 53, 54
Amsel, Rhonda, 402
Anderson, Elaine A., 295

Anderson, Robert N., 223
Anderson, Stephen A., 340
Andrews, Bernice, 398
Andrews, Frank M., 319
Antonucci, Toni C., 357
Apter, Terri, 378
Aquilino, William S., 350, 357, 429
Arbona, C., 393
Archer, Richard L., 131
Arditti, Joyce A., 431
Arendell, Terry, 425
Arends, Ellen, 399
Arias, Ileanna, 142, 399
Aristotle, 157
Armistead, Lisa, 300
Arnold, Kevin D., 348
Arnstein, Helene S., 235
Aro, H., 429
Aron, Arthur, 165
Aronson, Elliot, 171, 173
Aschenbrenner, Joyce, 43
Atkinson, Maxine P., 184
Avery, Arthur W., 146
Axelson, Leland J., 357
Axinn, William G., 144, 223

Babri, Karen Benson, 420, 423
Bachrach, Christine A., 323
Bachu, Amara, 8
Back, Kurt, 128
Backlund, Barbara, 148
Backman, Carl W., 128, 132
Baer, Paul E., 393
Bagarozzi, Dennis A., 267
Bahr, Kathleen S., 48
Bailey, J. Michael, 52, 77
Baker, Angela K., 427
Bales, Alba, 179n
Banski, Mary A., 254
Banyard, Victoria, 32
Barbarin, Oscar A., 406
Barber, Brian K., 333, 346, 378, 390
Barber, Jennifer S., 223
Bardsley-Sirois, Lois, 267
Bardwell, Jill R., 69

Barker, Kathleen, 243, 295
Barnes, Gordon E., 188
Barnes, Michael, 181
Barnett, Rosalind C., 18, 298, 299, 305, 325, 391
Barranti, Chrystal C. Ramirez, 352, 353
Barret, Robert L., 52
Bart, Pauline M., 351
Barthelmy, Kimberly J., 427
Bartis, Scott, 120
Basler, Roy P., 193
Bassin, Esward, 149
Basting, Louis, 15
Battle, Paula, 399
Baucom, Donald H., 234
Bauman, Karl E., 428
Baumrind, D., 331
Beach, Steven R. H., 85, 266
Beauvais, Frederick, 47
Beavers, Robert W., 44
Becerra, Rosina M., 90
Beck, Aaron T., 252
Beckett, Joyce O., 43
Beer, William, 453, 454
Begay, Cynthia, 48
Behrendt, Andrew E., 51
Belden, H. M., 452
Belk, Sharyn S., 131
Bell, Alan, 53
Bellah, Robert N., 19
Bellamy, Edward, 12–13
Beller, Andrea H., 439
Belsky, Jay, 290, 326
Bem, Sandra, 69
Bender, Mary M., 397
Bender, William N., 431
Benedict, Ruth, 224
Bengtson, Vern L., 333
Benin, Mary Holland, 298, 305, 345
Bennett, Linda A., 405
Bequette, Shelley Q., 427
Bereczkei, Tamas, 183, 184
Berelson, Bernard, 315, 316
Berg, John H., 131

Bernard, Jessie, 210, 233–234, 297, 316, 328
Bernardo, Felix M., 184
Bernstein, Barton E., 444, 445
Berry, Edmund, 401
Berscheid, Ellen, 98, 126, 127, 160
Berthiaume, Marc, 77
Best, Deborah L., 330
Bianchi, Suzanne M., 67, 289
Biblarz, Timothy J., 77
Biemer, Paul, 148
Bienvenu, Millard J., 254
Bigbee, Jeri L., 387
Bigner, Jerry J., 42, 51
Biller, Henry H., 329
Binion, Victoria Jackson, 75
Birchler, Gary R., 392
Bird, Chloe E., 324, 329
Bischoping, Katherine, 252
Bitter, Robert G., 190
Black, Laura E., 328, 423
Blair, Sampson Lee, 45, 46, 2 90, 303
Blakeslee, Sandra, 424, 430
Blanton, Priscilla W., 21
Blass, Thomas, 137, 188
Blood, Robert O., Jr., 265, 266, 268, 272
Bloys, Nancy, 77
Blum, Deborah, 124
Blumberg, Susan L., 271, 282
Blumstein, Philip, 50, 51, 76, 121, 147, 148, 268, 269
Blyth, D. A., 64
Bock, E. Wilbur, 187
Bodenhausen, G. V., 246, 247
Bogard, Ruth, 255
Bohannan, Peul, 35
Bolger, Niall, 389
Bolton, Frank, Jr., 91
Bond, Barbara L., 75
Bonkowski, Sara E., 427
Boomhower, Sara J., 427
Boon, Susan D., 353

Booth, Alan, 77, 137, 140–141, 147, 302, 325, 327, 417, 419, 428, 429, 439, 445, 451
Borders, L. DiAnne, 328
Borland, Delores, 43
Boss, Pauline, 387, 388, 403
Botwin, Michael D., 188
Bowen, Gary L., 77, 255, 350, 376
Bowen, Murray, 22
Bowering, Jean, 427
Boyd, Lenore Anglin, 256
Boyer, Debra, 90
Boyes, Michael C., 332
Boyle, Jacquelynn, 291
Bozett, Frederick W., 52, 330
Braiker, H., 273
Braito, Rita, 208
Brannon, Robert, 66
Bray, James, 447, 448, 455
Brayfield, April, 290
Breault, K. D., 418, 420
Breci, Michael, 208
Brehm, Jack W., 271
Bremer, Fredrika, 16
Brennan, Robert T., 325
Brewer, Richard, 51
Brewin, Chris R., 398
Brillinger, Margaret E., 338
Bringle, Robert G., 173
Brinkerhoff, David B., 140–141, 429
Brock, Gregory W., 255
Broderick, Carlfred B., 325, 348
Brodsky, Aaron, 161
Brody, Gene, 427
Brody, Robert, 355, 423, 440
Brodzinsky, D. M., 328
Broman, Clifford I., 42
Bromberger, Joyce T., 305
Bronstein, Phyllis, 332
Brookman, Richard R., 88
Brookoff, Daniel, 397
Brooks, Richard H.,II, 138
Brooks-Gunn, J., 91
Brophy, Beth, 137
Brown, Charles T., 75, 280
Brown, David, 451
Brown, George W., 120
Brown, Larry L., 104
Brown, Louise, 321
Brown, Philip M., 69, 269
Brown, Susan I., 147
Bruehl, Margaret E., 245
Brussoni, Mariana J., 353
Brust, Robert G., 188
Bryan, Linda R., 449
Bryant, Fred B., 120
Bryant, W. Keith, 329
Bryson, Ken, 9, 17
Bubenzer, Donald L., 444
Buchanan, Christy M., 432
Buckle, Leslie, 420
Buehler, Cheryl, 378, 423, 424
Buhrmester, Duane, 119, 131
Bulcroft, Kris, 40, 138, 208
Bumpass, Larry L., 146, 148, 417, 439
Bunker, Barbara B., 294
Burden, Dianne S., 37
Burford, Heather C., 64
Burg, Mary Ann, 305
Burger, Jerry M., 94
Burgess, Ernest W., 144
Burley-Allen, Madelyn, 247, 248

Burnett, Paul C., 119
Burns, Linda, 94
Burns, Linda Hammer, 402
Burr, Wesley R., 22
Buss, David M., 181, 182, 183, 188, 371
Butler, Robert N., 355
Butler, Samuel, 125
Buunk, Bram, 173
Byers, E. Sandra, 84
Byrne, T. Jean, 320

Cabot, Tracy, 157
Calhoun, Karen S., 428
Callan, Victor J., 212, 317, 319
Calsyn, Robert J., 451
Canavan, Margaret M., 396
Cancian, Francesca M., 158
Canning, Claire, 120
Caplan, Robert D., 365
Caplow, Theodore, 287
Cardoza, Desdemonna, 75
Cargan, Leonard, 200, 201, 206, 207, 209, 215
Carlson, Bonnie E., 137, 399
Carmen, Elaine, 120
Carr, Caroline Hameedah, 43
Carroll, David, 198, 201, 203, 205, 208, 212, 214, 215
Carroll, Lewis, 242
Carstensen, Laura L., 281, 351
Carter, Elizabeth A., 338–339
Carver, Karen Price, 301
Cash, Thomas F., 72
Caspar, Lynne, 9, 17, 298
Caspi, Avshalom, 34
Cassidy, Margaret L., 72
Castaneda, Donna M., 160
Castillo, Richard del, 45
Castro, Janice, 373
Castro-Martin, Teresa, 417, 439
Cate, Rodney, 76, 139, 415
Caulfield, Marie B., 142
Cecil-Pigo, Erin F., 238
Centers, Richard, 269–270
Chadwick, Bruce A., 333
Chafetz, Janet Saltzman, 70
Chan, Cheryl-Jean, 299
Chandra, Anjani, 318
Channa, V. C., 398
Charny, I. W., 102
Chase, Nancy D., 391
Chase-Lansdale, P. Lindsay, 429
Chassin, Laurie, 302
Chelune, Gordon J., 119, 131, 255, 256
Cherlin, Andrew J., 4, 146, 201, 412, 428, 429
Chesler, Mark A., 406
Chiriboga, David A., 416
Choo, Patricia, 150
Chung, Hyuindook, 43
Chwarz, J. Conrad, 143
Cicerello, Antoinette, 137
Clair, David, 40, 392
Clanton, Gordon, 171
Clark, M. I., 117
Clark, Richard D., 346
Clarkberg, Marin, 146
Clarke, Sally Cunningham, 439
Clark-Nicolas, Patricia, 365
Clemens, Audra W., 357
Clements, Mark, 88, 105, 106

Cleminshaw, Helen, 427
Clingempeel, W. Glenn, 451
Cobliner, W. Godfrey, 88
Cochran, Samuel W., 53, 69
Cockrum, Janet, 212
Cohen, Laurie L., 98
Coiro, Mary J., 429
Cole, Galen E., 208
Colella, Ugo, 148
Coleman, Diane Hoshall, 77, 232, 391, 441, 442–443, 450, 451, 453, 455
Collins, LaVerne Vines, 44, 45, 47, 444, 445
Collins, W. Andrew, 332
Coltrane, Scott, 446
Condon, Richard G., 73
Conger, Rand D., 89, 299, 332, 346
Cook, Christie, 131
Cook, S. W., 86, 87
Coombs, Robert H., 398
Cooney, Teresa M., 334, 429
Coontz, Stephanie, 4, 287
Cooper, Philip W., 34
Coopersmith, Stanley, 333
Copeland, Anne P., 427
Cormier, Sherilyn, 306
Cormier, William H., 306
Cornell, Laurel L., 446
Cortez, Katherine, 51
Coser, Lewis, 272
Costa, Paul T., Jr, 331
Costos, Daryl, 120
Cotton, John, 200
Couch, Kenneth A., 428
Cowan, John, 165, 291
Cox, Martha J., 378
Coyle, Andrea Tremaglio, 320
Craddock, Alan E., 193
Crawley, Brenda, 41
Crnic, Keith A., 325
Crohan, Susan E., 278, 326
Crosby, John F., 22, 163
Crossman, Rita K., 397
Crouter, Ann C., 236
Crowder, Kyle, 89–90
Crowley, M. Sue, 75
Culbertson, Amy, 298
Cummings, F. Mark, 378
Cummings, Robert A., 209
Cunningham, John D., 273
Curry, Andrea, 40, 45
Curtin, Richard, 365, 449
Custer, Lindsay, 303
Cyr, Mirielle, 234, 290

Dadds, Mark, 396
D'Alessandro, Joseph D., 76
Dalton, Sandra T., 203
Daly, Kerry J., 373
Dangoor, Nira, 387
Daniels, Roger, 45
Davidson, Bernard, 190
Davidson, Sara, 15
Davies, Betty, 406
Davis, A. Clarke, 139
Davis, Alan G., 210
Davis, Albert J., 330
Davis, Britta, 74
Davis, Keith, 167
Davis-Brown, Karen, 184, 189
Dawson, Deborah A., 394, 427
Day, Ann, 355

Day, Jennifer, 40, 45, 414
Dean-Church, Linda, 77
De Anda, Diana, 90
DeBruyn, Lemyra, 47
Degler, Carl N., 286, 287, 414
Delgado-Gaitan, Concha, 44
De Luccie, Mary F., 330
Demarest, Jack, 72
DeMaris, Alfred, 35, 148, 445
Demb, Janet, 88
DeMeis, Debra K., 295
Deming, Mary P., 391
Demo, David H., 428, 430
Demos, John, 8
Dempster-McLain, Donna, 72
Denmar, Wayne J., 119
DePaulo, Bella M., 127
Derlega, Valerian J., 131, 255
Desmarais, Serge, 72
Detlefsen, Ellen G., 294
Devall, Esther, 427
Devereaux, Lara, 319
De Vita, Carol J., 7
DeWitt, 137
Diana, Mark S., 138
Dickens, Charles, 452
DiClemente, Ralph J., 104
Die, Ann H., 254
Diedrick, Patricia, 423
Diekstra, F. W., 33
Diener, Carol, 365
Diener, Ed, 365
Diener, Marissa, 365
Dion, Karen K., 160, 169
Dion, Kenneth I., 160, 169
DiTommaso, Enrico, 114
Doane, Jeri A., 272
Dobson, Diane M., 277
Dodder, Richard H., 187
Dodge, Patricia J., 61
Doherty, William J., 428
Dolcini, M. Margaret, 105
Domenico, Donna, 393
Donnelly, Brenda W., 32, 36, 451
Donnenwerth, Gregory V., 97–98
Donoghue, William F., 368, 370
Dorius, Guy L., 88
Dornbusch, Sanford M., 136, 141, 432
Dornfeld, Candace, 399
Dornfeld, Maude, 399
Douglass, Frederick, 49
Downey, Douglas B., 33, 300, 427, 430, 453
Draper, Thomas W., 66
Drass, Kriss A., 75
Dreman, Sally, 34
Driscoll, Anne, 86
Drummond-Reeves, Susan J., 274
DuCharme, Jennifer, 399
Duck, Steve, 130
Dudley Margaret G., 187
Duff, Robert W., 211
Dunne, Michael, 256
Durant, Robert H., 98
Durant, Will, 28
Durbin, Denise L., 332
Durkheim, Emile, 115–117
Durkin, Kevin, 74
Dusek, Jerome B., 333
Dutton, Donald G., 397
Duvall, Evelyn M., 235, 338
Duxbury, Linda, 299

Dwyer, Kathleen M., 301
Dyk, Patricia A. H., 234

Eagly, Alice H., 61
Earle, Alice Morse, 200
Earls, Felton, 90
Easley, Margaret J., 392, 406
East, Patricia L., 99
Ebersole, Peter, 44
Eccles, Jacquelynne, 7
Ecob, Helen Gilbert, 376
Edmondson, Mary Ellen, 445
Edwards, John N., 327, 419, 445
Edwards, Robert, 321
Eells, Laura Workman, 441
Eisenman, Russell, 127
Eisikovits, Zvi C., 397
Elder, Glen H. Jr., 274, 352, 388
Elliott, Marta, 295
Ellison, Christopher G., 38
Endres, Thomas, 36
Epstein, Norman, 392, 406
Erbes, Janine Twoomey, 423
Erickson, Mary Ann, 72
Erickson, P. L., 86
Erickson, Rebecca J., 192
Erikson, Erik, 120–121
Eshleman, J. Ross, 18
Espenshade, Thomas J., 46
Etaugh, Claire, 198
Everett, Lou Whichard, 450

Fagan, Ronald W., 391
Fagot, Beverly I., 72
Falk, Dennis R., 131
Farber, Naomi, 42
Faulkenberry, J. Ron, 95
Fausto-Sterling, Anne, 69–70
Fehr, Beverley, 119
Feigelman, William, 328
Feingold, Alan, 182
Felice, Marianne E., 99
Felitti, Vincent J., 399
Felmlee, Diane, 149
Fenell, David L., 21
Fennelly, Katherine, 148
Ferraro, Kathleen, 397
Ferree, Myra Marx, 302
Ferreiro, Beverly Webster, 431
Festinger, Leon, 128
Fiebert, Martin S., 143
Fielder, Eve, 90
Fielder, Lois J., 77
Fiese, Barbara H., 345, 424
Fine, Mark A., 32, 33, 36, 42, 43, 90,
    332, 431, 449, 450, 451, 453
Finkelhor, David, 395
Finkelson, Laura, 142
Fiorentine, Robert, 74, 75
Fischer, Agneta H., 172
Fischer, Ann R., 143
Fischer, Judith L., 398
Fishbein, Sanford, 160
Fisher, Barbara L., 390
Fisher, Celia B., 356
Fitzpatrick, Mary Anne, 255, 271
Flanagan, Constance A., 379
Flaste, Richard, 119
Fleming, Douglas T., 103
Flewelling, Robert L., 428
Florian, Victor, 387
Floyd, Kory, 244
Fluehr-Lobban, Carolyn, 267

Fogel, Alan, 70
Folk, Karen Fox, 191, 439
Follingstad, Diance R., 66
Fong, Margaret L., 209
Ford, Clellan S., 85
Forehand, Rex, 300, 332, 423, 440
Forrest, Jacqueline Darroch, 8, 89
Fossett, Mark A., 41, 205
Foster-Clark, F.S., 64
Foubert, John D., 131
Fournier, David, 193
Fowers, Blaine J., 193, 233–234
Fox, Greer Litton, 431
Foxcraft, David R., 428
Franklin, Benjamin, 376
Franklin, Donna J., 32
Frazier, Patricia, 201
Freud, Sigmund, 13, 304–305
Freudenberger, Herbert J., 205
Friedman, Brenda N., 71
Frieze, Irene H., 264, 294
Fromm, Erich, 169
Fudge, Deborah A., 305
Fukunaga, Chantis, 49, 50
Furman, Wydol, 119, 131
Furstenberg, Frank F. Jr., 91, 99,
    428, 429

Gabardi, Lisa, 429
Gadberry, James H., 187
Gaelick, L., 246–247
Galambos, Nancy L., 69
Gallagher, Maggie, 414
Gallup, George, Jr., 315, 325, 420
Ganong, Lawrence J., 77, 232, 441,
    442–443, 450, 451, 453, 455
Garbarino, James, 274
Gardner, Rick M., 71
Garland, T. N., 226, 228
Garnefski, Nadia, 33, 399
Garner, Pamela W., 72
Garrett, William R., 233
Garrison, M. C. Betsy, 334
Garvin, Vicki, 424
Gath, Dennis, 355
Gaudy, Janies C., 131
Gavazzi, Stephen M., 320
Gazan, Marjorie, 399
Gazmararian, J. A., 41
Gecas, Victor, 333
Gehring, Thomas M., 272
Geiss, Susan K., 273, 274
Gelles, Richard J., 42, 394, 395,
    397, 399
Genest, Myles, 392, 403
George, Kenneth D., 51
Gershuny, Beth S., 392
Gerson, Mary-Joan, 315, 316
Gerstel, Naomi, 294
Ghee, Kenneth, 41
Gibbons, Judith L., 62, 126
Gigy, Lynn L., 204
Gilbert, Lucia Albino, 291, 293, 296,
    297, 353
Gilford, Rosalie, 355, 356
Gilgun, Jane F., 396
Gilliland, Ruth, 106
Gillis, Yvonne, 91
Gilman, Lorraine C., 327
Gilroy, Faith D., 77
Ginat, J., 28
Gingrich, Ronald, 455
Ginsberg, Alan L., 90

Gladstone, James, 323
Glaser, Karen, 18
Glass, Becky L., 184
Glasser, William, 119
Glenn, Norval D., 16, 17, 186, 187,
    417, 418, 419, 420, 429
Glick, Paul C., 40, 48, 202
Godbey, Geoffrey, 99, 289, 373
Goetting, Ann, 236, 327, 357
Gold, Joel A., 160
Gold, Joshua M., 444
Gold, Steven J., 46
Goldberg, J. J., 187
Goldberg, Martin, 276, 277
Goldberg, Wendy A., 32, 327
Golden, Reid M., 184
Goldman, Noreen, 210
Goldscheider, Calvin, 42, 350
Goldscheider, Frances Korbrin, 16,
    42, 95, 350, 430
Goleman, Daniel, 192, 234
Golombok, Susan, 52
Googins, Bradley K., 295
Gordon, Leslie C., 142
Gordon, Tom, 66
Gottlieb, Laurie N., 402
Gottman, John Mordechai, 250, 271,
    272, 281, 282, 351, 424
Graham, John W., 439
Graham-Bermann, Sandra A., 399
Grasmick, Harold G., 18
Gray-Little, Bernadette, 234, 365
Greenberg, Mark T., 325
Greenberger, Ellen, 367
Greenfield, Lawrence A., 394
Greenglass,, Esther R., 203
Greenstein, Theodore N., 300, 420
Greenwald, Anthony, 60
Greif, Geoffrey L., 32, 35
Gringlas, Marcy, 33
Grisanti, Christopher, 66
Groiler, Ingrid, 18
Gross, Penny, 294, 448
Grosskopf, D., 102
Grossman, Michele, 70
Grotevant, H. I., 323
Groves, Melissa M., 294
Grundy, Emily, 18
Guidobaldi, John, 427
Gullo, Dominic F., 74
Gunter, B. G., 298
Gunter, Nancy C., 298
Gwanfogbe, Philomena N., 29
Gwartny-Gibbs, Patricia A., 144
Gwinnell, Esther, 137

Habenstein, Robert W., 28, 30, 47
Hagestad, Gunhild O., 342
Hahlweg, Kurt, 256
Hahn, Jennifer, 137, 188
Halford, W. Kim, 256
Halman, L. Jill, 319
Hamby, Sherry L., 234
Hamilton, Beatrice, 45
Hamilton, Thomas E., 130
Hammerman, Ann Jackoway, 319
Hammond, D. Corydon, 106
Hampson, Robert B., 44
Hampton, Robert L., 42, 395
Hamsell, James, 424
Handel, Warren H., 23, 242, 301
Hansen, Gary L., 172, 173
Hansen, Jeffrey E., 255

Hanson, Sandra L., 90, 290, 330, 453
Hanson, Shirley M., 36
Hanson, Thomas L., 32
Hansson, Robert O., 358
Hardy, R., 424
Hardy, Thomas, 386
Harford, Thomas C., 393
Harman, M. J., 393
Harold, Rena D., 72
Harpster, Paula, 290
Harriman, Linda Cooper, 6, 327
Harris, Ian M., 66
Harris, Kathleen Mullan, 330
Harris, Mary B., 48, 51
Harris, Thomas L., 76
Harris, Tirril, 120
Harrist, Amanda W., 378
Harrod, Wendy J., 62
Harry, Joseph, 53
Hatchett, Shirley J., 43
Hatfield, Elaine, 150, 163, 164, 181
Haub, C., 313
Haveman, Robert, 300
Hawton, Keith, 355
Hayes, Mark D., 223
Haynes, Judith A., 38
Hayward, Mark D., 223
Healy, Joseph M., 427
Heaton, Tim B., 20, 89, 187,
    418, 419
Hecht, Michael L., 166
Heckert, D. Alex, 420
Hedderson, John J. Cunneen, 423
Heidemann, Bridget, 350
Hein, Carol, 332
Heiss, Jerold, 38
Helmreich, Robert L., 68
Helson, Ravenna, 295
Henderson-King, Donna H., 100
Hendrick, Clyde, 77, 157, 169,
    170, 171
Hendrick, Susan S., 77, 157, 169,
    170, 171
Hendrix, Lewellyn, 292
Henning, Kris, 399
Hensley, Wayne E., 169
Henton, June M., 139
Hernandez, Donald ., 417
Herring, Cedric, 291
Hertz, Rosanna, 292
Hesse-Biber, Sharlene, 71
Hester, Colleen, 127
Hetherington, E. Mavis, 424, 425,
    427, 430, 453
Hewitt, Jay, 124, 128
Higgins, Christopher, 299
Higgs, Deborah C., 396
Hightower, Eugene, 119
Hildebrandt, Katherine A., 330
Hill, Daniel H., 144
Hill, John P., 301
Hill, Reuben, 160, 386
Hiller, Dana V., 231, 232
Hira, Tahira K., 275, 367
Hobart, Charles, 445, 446, 449, 451
Hochschild, Arlic Russell, 299
Hoffmann, John P., 428
Holden, George W., 399
Hollabaugh, Lisa C., 84
Holloway, Susan D., 433
Holman, Thomas B., 22, 98, 190, 255
Holmbeck, Grayson N., 88
Holtzworth-Munroe, Amy, 397
Hong, Lawrence K., 211

Hook, Daniel, 414
Hope, Steven, 429
Hoppe, Sue Keir, 44
Horan, Mary, 300
Horm-Wingerd, Diane M., 294
Horowitz, Allen V., 18
Horowitz, Leonard M., 119
Hossain, Ziarat, 41
Hotaling, Gerald T., 397
Houseknecht, Sharon K., 201
Houts, Renate M., 188, 392
Hovell, Mel, 99
Hovestadt, Alan J., 344
Howard, Judith A., 76
Howell-White, Sandra, 18
Howitt, Dennis, 114
Huber, Joan, 306
Hughes, Diane, 406
Hughes, Ted K., 237
Hugick, Larry, 18, 97, 105
Hulgus, Yosuf, 44
Hunt, Morton, 99, 229, 231, 305
Huntley, Debra K., 33
Huppe, Micheline, 234, 290
Hurtz, Wilhelm, 74
Huston, Ted L., 188, 236, 327
Hutchinson, Glen, 397
Hutchison, Ray, 46
Huxley, Aldous, 13
Hyde, Janet Shibley, 84, 97,
   98, 165

Idle, Tracey, 72
Ihinger-Tallman, Marilyn, 431, 448,
   449, 450, 453
Inderbitzen-Pisaruk, Heidi, 117
Inman-Amos, Jill, 170
Isaacs, Maria Beth, 147
Ishii-Kuntz, Masako, 446

Jackson, Don D., 6, 163, 259
Jackson, Doris, 120
Jackson, James S., 43
Jackson, Joan L., 396
Jackson, Pamela Braboy, 18, 300
Jacob, Theodore, 391
Jacobs, Janice F., 72
Jacobs, Ruth Harriet, 358
Jacobsen, R. Brooke, 42, 51
Jacobson, Neil S., 267
Jacoby, Susan, 181
Jacques, Jeffrey M., 420
James, S. A., 41
Javaid, Ghazala A., 52
Jehu, Derek, 399
Jekielek, Susan M., 428
Jendrek, Margaret Platt, 353
Jenerson-Madden, Dolores, 44
Jennings, Glenn, 442, 444
Jensen, Larry, 98, 451
Jezl, David R., 142
Joebgen, Alicia M., 300
Joesch, Julia M., 300
John, Daphne, 43, 148
John, R., 48
Johnson, Bette Magyar, 332
Johnson, David R., 419, 445
Johnson, John M., 397
Johnson, Robert A., 428
Johnson, Ronald C., 49
Johnson, Susan, 163, 164
Johnson, Virginia E., 82–83, 104,
   105, 206, 319, 321

Johnston, Janet R., 272, 427
Johnston, Stacy Glaser, 430
Johnston, Thomas, 354
Jones, Diane Carlson, 77, 392
Jones, Elise F., 89
Jones, Warren H., 114, 237
Jorgensen, Stephen R., 131
Jose, Paul E., 75
Judd, Eleanor Parelman, 187
Julian, Teresa W., 45, 348
Juliusdottir, Sigrun, 33
Jung, Kenneth G., 90
Jung, Marshall, 137
Justice, Blair, 395
Justice, Rita, 395

Kaczmarek, Peggy, 148
Kahn, Arnold S., 61, 62, 63, 65
Kahn, Joan R., 420
Kalb, Claudia, 334
Kalick, Michael S., 130
Kalmijn, Matthijs, 186, 187, 300
Kalter, Neil, 424
Kamo, Yoshinori, 46
Kanter, Rosabeth Moss, 305
Kantor, David, 226, 228
Kao, Erika M., 45, 89
Kardes, Frank R., 128
Karesh, David, 391
Karis, Terri A., 48
Kasian, Marilyn, 142
Kate, Nancy Ten, 294
Kateb, Claude, 76
Katsutoshi, Yamashita, 522
Katz, Ruth, 326
Katzev, Aphra R., 419
Kaufman, Karen, 72
Kawakami, Norito, 18
Kayser, Karen, 415, 416
Keith, Bruce, 428
Keith, Pat M., 208
Keith, Verna M., 38
Keller, Warren D., 330, 348
Kelley, Jane E., 256
Kellogg, Susan, 17
Kelly, H. H., 273
Kelly, Joan B., 326, 421, 426, 431,
   432, 447, 448, 455
Kennedy, Donna, 121
Kennedy, Gregory E., 36, 353, 454
Kenrick, Douglas T., 66
Kephart, William M., 161
Kerns, Donell, 86
Kerr, Allen S., 21
Kerssen-Griep, Jeff, 244
Keshet, Jamie Kelem, 449
Kessler, Ronald C., 18, 164,
   399, 428
Key, Rosemary J., 374
Kibria, Nazli, 46
Kidwell, Jeannie S., 398
Kiecolt, K. Jill, 41, 205
Kiernan, John F., 143
Kim, Oksoo, 115
Kim, Peter, 143, 395, 420
Kimble, Charles E., 128
Kimerling, Rachel, 142
Kimmel, Ellen B., 75
Kinard, E. Milling, 427
King, Daniel W., 75
King, Jeff, 47
King, Laura A., 255
King, Lynda A., 75

King, Valerie, 352
Kinney, Jennifer M., 430
Kinsey, Alfred C., 98, 99
Kirkpatrick, Lee A., 173
Kitano, Harry H. L., 45
Kitson, Gay C., 416, 420, 423
Klassen, Carole, 399
Kleinke, Chris L., 125
Kleinplatz, Peggy, 76
Klerman, Lorraine V., 91
Kline, Marsha, 272, 427
Koch, Alberta, 402
Kohn, Alfie, 64
Kolata, G., 69
Kolko, David J., 395
Kollock, Peter, 121
Kolodny, Robert C., 82, 104, 105,
   206, 319, 321
Koman, Joseph J., 301
Konner, Melvin, 62
Kopecky, Gini, 70
Kopelman, Richard E., 188
Korabik, Karen, 294
Kornhaber, Arthur, 353
Korol, Susan, 170
Kortenhaus, Carole M., 72
Kosinski, Frederick A., Jr., 187
Kotsopoulous, S., 328
Kotva, H. J., 95
Kouri, Kristyan M., 48
Koverola, Catherine, 399
Kposowa, Augustine J., 418, 420
Krahn, Gloria, 391
Kramer, Kathryn B., 429
Krishman, Vijaya, 418
Krokoff, Lowell J., 272
Kromrey, Jeffrey D., 75
Krutchsnitt, Candace, 399
Ku, Leighton C., 8
Kulbok, Pamela, 90
Kuo, James, 348
Kurdek, Lawrence A., 52, 53,
   147, 271, 332, 378, 424, 427,
   450, 453
Kvanli, Judith A., 442, 444

Ladewig, Becky Heath, 302
Laippala, P., 429
Lakein, Alan, 374, 375
Lamb, Michael E., 327, 332
Lamm, Helmut, 160
Landale, Nancy S., 146, 148
Landry, Bart, 374
Landsverk, John, 398
Laner, Mary Riege, 142
Lang, Ariella, 402
Lang, Dorothy, 188
Langan, Patrick A., 394
Langenbrunner, Mary, 423
Lang-Takac, Esther, 63
Lanz, Jean B., 87
Larkey, Linda Kathryn, 166
Larson, Jeffrey H., 6, 190, 446
Larson, Reed W., 114
Laslett, Peter, 5
Lassiter, G. Daniel, 127
Lasswell, Marcia, 48, 275
Lauer, Jeanette C., 6, 13, 14, 18, 20,
   21, 84, 85, 100, 101, 120, 169,
   211, 229, 235, 238, 257, 281,
   350, 351, 405, 424, 428, 433,
   447, 448, 450, 452, 455

Lauer, Robert H., 6, 13, 14, 18, 20,
   21, 23, 39, 84, 85, 100, 101,
   120, 169, 210, 211, 229, 235,
   238, 242, 257, 281, 301, 305,
   350, 351, 405, 424, 428, 433,
   447, 448, 450, 452, 455
Laumann, Edward O., 85, 99
Lavee, Yoav, 326
Lazarus, Edward, 373
Leary, Mark R., 85
Leber, Douglas, 42
Lederer, William J., 6, 163, 259
Lee, Catherine, 299
Lee, Gary R., 18, 30, 158, 163, 178,
   187, 268
Lee, John Alan, 169, 170
Lee, Sharon M., 186
Lee, Valerie E., 428
Lehr, William, 226, 228
Leiblum, Sandra R., 319
Leigh, Barbara C., 101
Leigh, Geoffrey K., 445
Leisen, James C., 256
Lennon, Mary Clare, 290
Leon, George H., 147
Leonard, Jennifer, 18, 97, 105
Lepowski, J. M., 41
Leslie, Leigh A., 295
Levant, Ronald, 70
Leve, Leslie D., 72
Levendosky, Alytia A., 399
Levenson, Robert W., 281, 351
Levin, Ira, 115, 150
Levinger, George, 20
Levinson, Daniel J., 347, 348
Levy-Skiff, Rachel, 327, 345
Lewis, C. S., 156, 157
Lewis, Karen Gail, 213
Lewis, Myrna, 355
Lewis, Robert A., 326
Lewko, John H., 332
Li, Jiang Hong, 190
Liberman, Robert P., 250
Libman, Gary, 186
Lichter, Daniel T., 223, 290
Liebowitz, Michael, 163
Lightbody, Pauline, 62
Liker, Jeffrey K, 274
Lillard, Dean R., 428
Lillard, Lee A., 326
Lin, Chien, 46
Lin, Kuei-Hsiu, 142
Lin, Yuan-Huei, 140
Lincoln, Abraham, 193
Linton, Melaney A., 142
Litovsky, Vivianna G., 333
Little, Jane K., 69
Liu, William T., 46
Llabre, Maria M., 320
Lloyd, Kim M., 142, 204, 223
Lloyd, Sally A., 139
Lobdell, Judith, 117
Loewenstein, Sophie Freud, 211, 212
Logan, John R., 350
London, Kathryn A., 323, 420
Long, Barbara H., 205
Long, Nicholas, 378, 428
Long, Vonda Olson, 76
Longman, Phillip J., 317
Loomis, Laura Spencer, 146, 428
Lopez, Linda C., 45
Lorence, Jon, 62
Loveland-Cherry, Carol J., 300

Lowe, Geoff, 428
Lowery, Carol R., 430
Lujan, Carol C., 47
Lumley, Mark A., 256
Luster, Tom, 95, 99
Lye, Diane N., 77
Lynn, Maria, 62
Lyons, Carolyn M., 399

Maccoby, Eleanor E., 431, 432
MacDermid, Shelley M., 327
MacDonald, William L., 445
Machida, Sandra, 433
Mackey, Richard A., 252, 254
Macklin, Eleanor D., 446
Madanes, Cloe, 305, 364
Madden, Margaret E., 267
Madora, Nilvfer P., 98
Magee, William J., 399, 428
Mahon, Noreen E., 115
Mainemer, Henry, 327
Makepeace, James M., 142
Malandro, Loretta, 243
Maldonado, Norma, 105
Malinowski, Bronislaw, 85
Maneker, Jerry S., 48, 187
Manis, Jean, 305
Manning, Wendy D., 146, 368
Manusov, Valerie, 244
Mare, Robert D., 187
Margolin, Gayla, 299
Markides, Kyriakos S., 44
Markland, Stacy R., 378
Markman, Howard, 271, 282
Marks, Gary, 105, 328, 346
Markstrom-Adams, Carol, 76
Markus, Hazel, 305
Marriott, Richard G., 254
Marshall, Linda L., 142
Marshall, Nancy L., 325
Marsiglio, William, 449, 450
Marston, Peter J., 166
Martin, C. E., 99
Martin, Carol Lynn, 69
Martin, Don, 102
Martin, Karin A., 72
Martin, Maggie, 102
Martinez, Estella A., 45
Mashal, Meeda M. S., 267
Masheter, Carol, 426
Mason, Jerald W., 364
Mason, Karen Oppenheim, 227
Mastekaasa, Arne, 209
Masters, William H., 82–83, 104, 105, 206, 319, 321
Matthews, Lisa S., 299, 305
Mattison, Andrew M., 53, 54
Mauldin, Teresa, 32
May, Philip A., 47
Maza, Penelope L., 323
McAdams, Dan P., 120
McAdoo, John, 41, 43, 45
McCabe, Marita P., 88, 209, 430
McCall, Mary E., 63
McCarrey, Michael, 76
McCarthy, William J., 75
McCauley, Jeanne, 399
McCrae, Robert R., 331
McCubbin, Hamilton I., 343, 344, 346, 348, 386–387, 389, 390, 404
McCubbin, Marilyn A., 404
McDermott, John F. Jr., 49, 50

McGee, Gail W., 302
McGoldrick, Monica, 338–339, 344
McHale, Susan M., 76, 236, 327
McKelvey, Mary W., 45
McKenry, Patrick C., 42, 43, 45, 348, 450
McKenzie, Nancy, 399
McKinney, Kathleen, 87, 137, 139
McLanahan, Sara S., 32, 34, 328, 428, 449, 453
McLaughlin, Mike I., 306
McLeod, Beverly, 188, 266
McLloyd, Vonnie C., 34, 42
McMahon, Martha, 329
McMiller, William E. P., 32
McNally, James W., 46, 105
McNeal, Cosandra, 399
McPherson, J. Miller, 329
McQuinn, Ronald D., 131
McRae, Christine, 429
McWhirter, David P., 53, 54
Mead, Margaret, 70
Mednick, Martha T., 35, 37, 38
Meeker, Fredrick B., 125
Melendez, Marjorie, 356
Melichur, Joseph, 416
Melko, Matthew, 200, 201, 206, 207, 209, 215
Mellmann, Mark, 373
Melson, Gail F., 70
Menaghan, Elizabeth G., 300, 301
Menninger, Karl, 247
Meredith, Dennis, 300
Meth, Richard L., 320
Metha, Arlene, 115
Meyer, Cynthia J., 275
Meyer, Walter J., III, 396
Michaels, Gerald Y., 327
Mickelson, Kristin D., 164
Mikulincer, Mario, 164
Mill, John Stuart, 190
Miller, Brent C., 88, 99
Miller, Louisa, 7, 222
Miller, Nancy B., 357
Miller, Rowland S., 131
Millman, Marcia, 365
Mills, Randy, 75
Mills, Robert John, 18
Mills, Ryan, 75
Minton, Carmelle, 330
Mintz, Jim, 272
Mintz, Steven, 17
Mirande, Alfredo, 44
Mirowsky, John, 291, 306
Mitchell, Susan, 95, 127
Mitchell-Kernan, Claudia, 48
Mitka, Mike, 106
Mnookin, Robert, 431
Moen, Phyllis, 72
Molidor, Christian F., 142
Monk, Timothy H., 326
Monk-Turner, Elizabeth, 290
Montgomery, Barbara M., 259
Montgomery, Marilyn J., 169
Moon, Sidney, 213
Moore, Kristin A., 86, 99
More, Thomas, 13, 203, 222
Morgan, Carolyn Stout, 18
Morgan, Edmund S., 200
Morgan, Leslie A., 416
Morgan, Maria C., 99
Morgan, S. Philip, 91, 330, 429
Morley, Rebecca, 172

Morokoff, Patrician J., 106
Morris, Monica, 333, 334
Morrison, Donna R., 429
Morrison-Beedy, Dianne, 105
Mosher, William D., 95, 105
Mosley, Norman R., 160
Moss, Barry F., 105, 121
Muehlenhard, Charlene L., 84, 86, 87, 140, 142, 143
Mueller, Daniel P., 34
Mugenda, Olive M., 367
Munch, Allison, 329
Murphy, Mike, 18
Murphy, Patricia Ann, 117
Murstein, Bernard I., 178, 188
Myers, David E., 90

Nagoshi, Craig T., 49
Najman, Jake M., 402
Nakkab, Sylvain, 89
Nauta, Andre, 208
Needle, Richard H., 428
Negata, Donnal K., 45
Neimeyer, R. A., 127
Nelsen, Edward, 115
Nelson, Eileen S., 378
Neubaum, Eileen, 423, 440
Neugarten, Bernice L., 352
Nevid, Jeffrey S., 138
Newcomb, Michael D., 144
Newell, Rea J., 98
Newfield, Neal A., 348, 349
Newman, Margaret, 450
Newport, Frank, 315, 325
Nezu, Arthur M., 76
Nezu, Christine M., 76
Nienstedt, Barbara Cable, 305, 345
Nieto, Daniel S., 37
Nightingale, Florence, 291
Nock, Steven L., 147, 317
Noel, Nora E., 391
Noble, E. P., 392
Noller, Patricia, 272
Nord, Christine Winquist, 429
Nousianinen, 332
Nowak, Thomas C., 420
Noyes, John Humphrey, 14
Nye, F. Ivan, 22

Oakley, Ann, 286
Obeidallah, Dawn A., 76
O'Brien, Bernard A., 252, 254
O'Connell, Ann, 52
O'Connor, Margaret, 138
O'Connor-Roden, Margaret, 208
Oerter, Rolf, 333
Oetting, F. R., 47
O'Farrell, Timothy J., 392
O'Flaherty, Kathleen M., 441
Oggins, Jean, 42
O'Keefe, Maura, 142, 399
Olds, Jacqueline, 115
O'Leary, K. Daniel, 273, 274
Oliver, Mary Beth, 84, 96
Olmstead, R. E., 117
Olson, David H., 193, 343, 344, 346, 348, 389
Olson, Josephine E., 294
Olson, Myrna R., 38
Olson, Sheryl L., 32
Olson, Terrance D., 88
Ono, Hiromi, 417
Ooms, Theodora, 290

O'Rand, Angela M., 350
Orbuch, Terri L., 303
Oropesa, R. S., 268
Orosan, Pamela G., 63
Orthner, Dennis K., 300
Oskamp, Stuart, 72
Osterwell, Zahava, 63
O'Sullivan, Lucia F., 84
Ou, Young-Shi, 45
Owen, Margaret Tresch, 378

Padgett, Deborah L., 42
Page, Polly, 48
Page, Randy M., 208
Painter, Susan L., 142
Paisely, Kim J., 77
Palisi, Bartolomeo J., 120
Palosaari, U., 429
Paludi, Michele A., 74
Pang, Gin Yong, 48
Parcel, Toby L., 300, 301, 428
Park, Teron, 105
Parke, Ross D., 332
Parker, Ben L., 274
Parker, Douglas A., 393
Parkes, Colin M., 357
Parnass, S., 102
Pasley, Kay, 328, 330, 390, 431, 445, 448, 449, 450, 453
Patterson, Charlotte J., 53
Patterson, James, 143, 395, 420
Patterson, Joan M., 386–387, 390
Patton, David, 100
Paulson, Morris J., 398
Paulson, Sharon E., 301
Payne, Frank D., 77
Paz, Juan J., 45
Pedersen, Darhl M., 75, 114
Peek, Charles W., 398, 448
Peele, Stanton, 161
Pendergast, Robert, 98
Pendleton, B. F., 226, 228
Pepe, Margaret V., 320
Peplau, Letitia Anne, 52, 53, 160
Peretti, Peter O., 173, 427
Perkins, H. Wesley, 295
Perlman, Daniel, 117, 119
Perry-Jenkins, Maureen, 191
Pestrak, Victor A., 102
Peterman, Dan J., 146
Peters, John F., 180
Peters, Samuel, 145
Petersen, Anne C., 69
Petersen, Larry R., 97, 268
Peterson, Christopher, 45
Peterson, James L., 99, 378, 427, 428, 430, 451
Petronio, Sandra, 35–36
Pett, Marjorie A., 106
Pettijohn, Terry F., 156
Phelps, Randy E., 33
Philliber, William V., 231, 232
Pickett, Robert S., 204, 207, 208
Pierce, Robert Lee, 399
Pietromonaco, Paula R., 305
Pillemer, Karl, 276, 326
Pilon, Marc, 229
Pines, Ayala, 171, 173
Pingree, Suzanne, 4
Pink, Jo Ellen Theresa, 454
Pirog-Good, Maureen A., 142
Pittman, Frank, 102
Plato, 13

Pleck, Joseph H., 8, 66
Pneumann, Roy W., 245
Poehlmann, Julie A., 424
Pollock, Alann D., 254
Polo, Marco, 28
Pomerleau, Andree, 72
Pomeroy, H. S., 67
Pomeroy, W. B., 99
Ponzetti, James J., Jr., 415
Pope, Tony, 121
Popenoe, David, 17
Porterfield, Ernest, 48
Pottick, Kathleen J., 305
Potts, Marilyn K., 211
Powell, Brian, 300
Powell, Mary Ann, 428, 430
Powell, Richard D., 48
Power, Chris, 429
Prather, Jane E., 189
Pratt, Edith L., 187
Presser, Harriet B., 290
Preston, Samuel H., 184, 187
Price, Richard H., 365
Prinz, Ronald J., 392
Procidano, Mary E., 44
Prokofsky, Susan S., 368
Propst, L. Rebecca, 32
Protinsky, Howard O., 348, 349
Pruett, Cheryl D., 451
Pudowski, Bernard C., 173

Qian, Zhenchao, 45, 46, 184, 187
Quackenbush, Robert L., 77
Quadagno, Jill Sobel, 28, 30, 47
Queen, Stuart A., 28, 30, 47
Quinn, Naomi, 236, 348, 349
Quinsey, Vernon L., 188

Rachlin, Vicki, 294, 296, 297
Ragone, Helena, 322
Raley, R. Kelly, 43
Ramu, G. N., 316, 317
Rankin, Robert P., 48, 187
Rao, K. Vaninadha, 148
Rapkin, A. J., 86
Rapson, Richard L., 163
Ratcliff, Kathryn Strother, 302
Raty, Hannu, 62
Raven, Bertram H., 269–270
Ray, JoAnn, 292
Rehm, Lynn P., 33
Reid, James D., 356
Reider, Ronald O., 84
Reinherz, Helen, 427
Reis, Harry T., 63, 120, 165
Reiss, Ira L., 30, 158, 163
Remondet, Jacqueline H., 358
Rempel, Judith, 327
Renner, Maureen A., 449
Resnick, Michael D., 323
Rexroat, Cynthia A., 305, 351, 355
Rezac, Sandra J., 430
Rice, David G., 294, 295, 433
Rice, Joy K., 433
Rice, Roselyn J., 103
Rich, Alexander R., 115
Richards, Leslie N., 35, 36
Richards, Marcus, 424
Richards, Mary E., 330
Richards, Maryse H., 300
Richardson, Jean L., 105
Richardson, Laurel, 211–212
Richardson, Rhonda A., 348

Richmond, Virginia P., 254
Ricks, Shirley S., 330
Ridley, Carl, 146
Riedmann, A., 53
Rieker, Patricia Perri, 120
Rieves, Laura, 72
Riggs, David S., 142
Risman, Barbara J., 37
Ritchie, Kathy L., 399
Rivers, Caryl, 298, 305
Rivlin, Allan, 373
Roach, Arthur J., 256
Roach, Mary Joan, 420, 423
Roberts, Robert E. L., 333
Robertson, Sharon, 72
Robins, Elliot, 188
Robins, Lee N., 90
Robinson, Bryan E., 52
Robinson, Elizabeth A., 66
Robinson, Gail Erlick, 402
Robinson, John, 99, 289, 373, 374
Robinson, Linda C., 21
Rodd, Zachary A., 420
Rodgers, Bryan, 429
Rodin, Judith, 172
Rodrigues, Aroldo, 269–270
Roesler, Thomas A., 399
Rogers, Stacy J., 327, 417, 418, 421
Rogler, Lloyd H., 44
Rokach, Ami, 115
Rolison, Garry L., 41
Rollins, Judy, 201, 214
Romeo, Yolanda, 209
Romero, Anna Maria, 44
Romero-Daza, Nancy, 107
Ronen-Eliav, Hagar, 34
Ronfeldt, Heidi M., 142
Rooks, Ronica, 374
Roopnarine, Jaipaul L., 41
Roosa, Mark W., 89, 391
Roper, Burns W., 348
Roschelle, Anne R., 42
Roscoe, Bruce, 121, 138
Rose, Phyllis, 105, 142, 190
Rosen, Margery D., 329, 429
Rosenberg, Morris, 333
Rosenblatt, Paul C., 48, 402
Rosenbluth, Susan C., 290, 292, 293
Rosenfeld, Lawrence B., 255, 256
Rosenfield, Sarah, 290
Rosin, Hazel M., 294
Ross, Catherine E., 234, 291, 306, 329
Ross, Louie E., 139
Ross, Susan M., 395
Rossi, Alice S., 327, 330
Rossi, Peter H., 327, 330
Rotenberg, Ken J., 170
Rotkin, Mark, 147
Rovine, Michael, 326
Rubenstein, Carin, 10, 115, 116, 119, 156, 158, 364
Rubin, Zick, 131, 160, 166
Rubinsky, Hillel J., 61
Rubinstein, Robert L., 206, 356
Rubo-Stipec, Maritza, 392
Rue, Vincent M., 96
Rueter, Martha, 346
Ruskin, John, 105, 264
Russek, Linda G., 331
Russell, Candyce S., 340
Russell, Diana E. H., 395

Rutstein, Jeffrey, 160
Ryckman, Richard M., 160
Ryff, C. D., 393

Saad, Lydia, 50
Sabatelli, Ronald M., 236, 320
Sack, William H., 47
Sadalla, Edward K., 66
Safilios-Rothschild, Constantina, 266
Sager, Clifford J., 229, 231, 438, 440, 441, 442, 452
Sakurai, Joji, 420
Salamon, Sonya, 184, 189
Salovey, Peter, 172
Saluter, Arlene F., 426
Salzinger, Suzanne, 399
Sanchez, Laura, 290
Sandefur, Gary D., 34, 428
Sanders, Gordon F., 255
Sandras, Eric, 445
Sandven, Kari, 323
Sanger, William W., 103
Sanik, Margaret Mietus, 32, 374
Santi, Lawrence J., 9
Sapp, Stephen G., 62
Sargent, Dudley, 60
Satir, Virginia, 258, 259, 448
Sauer, Mark, 95
Sawin, Douglas B., 332
Sawyer, Robin G., 105
Scadden, Lynn, 51
Scanzoni, John, 272
Scardino, Teresa J., 140
Scarf, Maggie, 102
Scarisbrick-Hauser, Annemarie, 208
Schachter, Stanley, 128, 160
Schaninger, Charles M., 371
Schilling, Karen M., 63
Schmiege, Cynthia J., 35, 36
Schmitt, J. Patrick, 52, 147
Schneider, Danielle S., 95
Schnellmann, Jo De La Garza, 126
Schoen, Robert, 188
Schoenborn, Charlotte A., 33
Schonpflug, Ute, 377
Schrader, David, 254
Schuckit, Marc A., 393
Schuldt, W. John, 255
Schulenburg, Joy, 50
Schulz, Jorg, 377
Schumm, Walter R., 340
Schwab, Reiko, 76, 402
Schwartz, Gary F., 331
Schwartz, Joe, 18
Schwartz, Pepper, 50, 51, 76, 121, 147, 148, 268, 269
Schwartz, Richard S., 115
Schwarz, J. Conrad, 430
Schwebel, Andrew L., 33, 42, 43, 121, 431, 449
Scovel, Martha, 115
Seccombe, Karen, 18, 316
Seccord, Paul F., 41
Sedikides, Constantine, 96
Segal, Bernard, 47
Seidman, Stuart N., 84
Seltzer, Judith A., 431
Settle, Shirley A., 430
Seymore, Carolyn, 98
Shackelford, Todd K., 188
Shagle, Shobha C., 378
Shakespeare, William, 130, 189, 452
Shanas, Ethel, 342

Shapiro, Brenda L., 143
Shapiro, Jerold Lee, 329
Sharlin, Shlomo A., 21, 326
Sharma, Monika, 115
Sharpsteen, Don J., 173
Shaver, Phillip, 115, 116, 119, 164, 165
Sheehan, Eugene P., 137
Sheehy, Gail, 214, 225, 348
Shehan, Constance L., 18, 41, 187, 305, 351, 355
Shelton, Beth Anne, 148, 419–420
Shen, Haikang, 397
Shen, Yu-Chu, 299
Sher, Geoffrey, 321, 392
Shields, Glenn, 346
Shinagawa, Larry Hajime, 48
Sholley, Barbara K., 131
Shotland, R. Lance, 98
Shulman, Shmuel, 332
Shute, Rosalie, 114
Silbereisen, Rainer K., 76, 377
Silitsky, Daniel, 432
Sillars, A. L., 340
Silverberg, Susan B., 348
Simenauer, Jacqueline, 198, 201, 203, 205, 208, 212, 214, 215
Simon, Barbara Levy, 203, 208, 211
Simons, Ronald L., 89, 142, 332
Simpson, Jeffry A., 148, 161, 164
Sinclair, Ronald J., 378
Singer, Jerome E., 160
Singh, Susheela, 8
Skopin, Ann R., 450
Skurnick, Joan H., 104
Slade, P., 319
Slater, Elisa J., 428
Small, Stephen A., 86, 95, 99
Smith, Drake S., 302
Smith, Gail, 72
Smith, I. G., 171
Smith, John P., 142
Smith, Rebecca M., 446
Smith, Susan F., 32
Smith, Tom I., 393
Smith-Lovin, Lynn, 329
Smock, Pamela J., 425
Snell, William E. Jr., 64, 85, 131
Snellman, Leila, 62
Snyder, Douglas K., 6
Snyder, Kay A., 420
Solano, Cecilia H., 117
Solie, Linda J., 77
Sommers-Flanagan, John, 74
Sommers-Flanagan, Rita, 74
Sonenstein, Freya L., 8
Sorell, Gwendolyn T., 170
Sorenson, Kelly A., 149
Sorenson, Susan B., 397
Sorter, Randy G., 71
South, Scott J., 40, 43, 75, 182, 204, 223, 366, 417
Southworth, Suzanne, 430
Spain, Daphne, 67, 289
Spanier, Graham B., 326
Speckhard, Anne C., 96
Speisman, Joseph C., 120
Spence, Janet T., 68
Spilka, Bernard, 255
Spinner, Barry, 114
Spitze, Glenna D., 75, 350
Sprague, Heather F., 430

Sprecher, Susan, 87, 137, 139, 149, 163, 164, 181
Sroufe, L. Alan, 332
Stack, Steven, 18
Staines, Graham L., 305
Stake, Jayne F., 62
Stanley, Sandra C., 305
Stanley, Scott, 271, 282
Stanseki, Richard A., 125
Stanton, Elizabeth Cady, 270
Staples, Robert, 44, 47, 204
Stark, Elizabeth, 395, 426
Starrels, Marjorie E., 330, 347
Statham, Anne, 201
Steffen, Patrick, 89
Steil, Janice M., 290, 292, 293
Stein, Peter J., 200
Steinbeck, John, 114
Steinberg, Laurance D., 332, 345, 347, 348
Stephen, Timothy D., 143, 318
Steptoe, Patrick, 321
Stern, Joanne, 198
Stern, Pamela R., 73
Sternberg, Robert J., 167, 168, 170, 277
Stets, Jan E., 142, 148
Stevens, Gillian, 188
Stewart, Alfred J., 427
Stewart, James R., 431, 432
Stiffman, Arlene Rubin, 90
Stiles, Deborah A., 62, 126, 145
Stinson, Kandi M., 315
Stith, Sandra M., 397
Stockard, Jean, 61
Stohs, Joanne Hoven, 292
Stokes, Joseph P., 115
Stolley, Kathy Shepherd, 323
Stolzenberg, Ross M., 146
Stone, Julie I., 127
Stone, Lorene H., 178
Stoneman, Zolinda, 427
Stoppard, Janet M., 77
Straus, Murray A., 391, 394, 396, 397, 399
Street, Amy E., 399
Street, Sue, 75
Strom, Robert, 327
Strong, Philip M., 210
Strouse, Jeremiah S., 136
Struthers, Nancy J., 63
Stuart, Freida M., 106
Stuart, Gregory I., 397
Studer, Marlena, 95
Stull, Donald E., 208
Su, Susan, 428
Sugar, Martha Hahn, 301
Sugarman, David B., 397
Sugawara, Alan I., 76
Suhomlinova, Olga, 350
Suitor, J. Hill, 191, 276, 326
Sullivan, Oriel, 181, 446
Suman, H. C., 182
Sumner, William C., 441
Sung, Betty Lee, 186
Supancic, M., 418, 419
Supple, Khalil R., 357
Surra, Catherine A., 184, 189, 236
Swanson, Janice M., 104

Sweet, James A., 146, 148, 417, 439
Sweet, Stephen, 396
Swenson, Clifford H., 236

Takaki, Ronald, 46
Takeuchi, David T., 209, 366
Talbot, Margaret, 327
Tanfer, Koray, 146, 148
Tannen, Deborah, 252
Tasker, Fiona, 52
Tavuchis, Nicholas, 316, 317
Taylor, Vincent L., 143
Teachman, Jay D., 301, 425
Temple, Mark T., 101
Tesser, Abraham, 266
Thomas, Amanda McCombs, 430
Thomas, J., 353
Thomas, Jeanne L., 38
Thomas, Sandra, 303
Thompson, Anthony P., 102
Thompson, Edward H., 45
Thompson, Jeanine, 142
Thompson, Margaret E., 4
Thompson, Teresa, 254
Thomsett, Michael C., 368
Thomson, Elizabeth, 32, 148, 449, 453
Thornton, Arland, 95, 144
Tidwell, Marie-Ceciles O., 165
Tokar, David M., 143
Tolstoy, Leo, 4
Trahaug, Geir, 238
Traupmann, J., 98, 121, 122
Treas, Judith, 371
Trent, Katherine, 89–90
Trocki, Karen F., 101
Trotta, Rosilee, 399
Truman, Dana Ann, 143
Tschann, Jeanne M., 272, 427
Tubman, Jonathan G., 391
Tucci, Lisa M., 143
Tucker, Belinda M., 48
Tucker, Joan S., 430
Tucker, Paula, 165
Turner, Barbara F., 100
Turner, Pauline H., 51
Tweed, S. H., 393
Tyler, William, 452
Tzeng, Meei-Shann, 187

Uchitelle, Louis, 290
Uhlenberg, Peter, 429
Ulbrich, Patricia M., 320
Ulrichson, Ardys M., 275
Umberson, Debra, 397
Upchurch, Dawn M., 397

Vaillant, Caroline O., 326
Valentine, Ruth, 224
Van de Kragt, J. C., 61
Vandiver, Joseph S., 184
Vangelesti, Anita, 254
Van Willigen, John, 398
Van Willigen, Maricke, 329
Vaughan, Suzanne, 201
Veevers, Jean E., 424
Vega, William A., 38
Ventura, Jacqueline N., 325
Vera, Herman, 184

Verbrugge, Lois M., 305
Veroff, Joseph, 42, 100
Vershure, Beth, 66
Vinick, Barbara H., 358
Vinokur, Amiram D., 365
Violet, Darlene, 226, 228
Vitorrio, Anthony di, 427
Vogler, Conrad C., 392
Volling, Brenda L., 290
Voydanoff, Patricia, 32, 36, 451
Vuchinich, Samuel, 379

Wachler, Charles, 205
Wadsworth, M., 424
Wagner, Roland M., 44, 131
Waite, Linda J., 16, 146, 326, 430
Walker, Alexis J., 266
Walker, Sharon, 69
Wallerstein, Judith S., 344, 424, 430
Wallin, Paul, 144, 186
Wallisch, Lynn S., 426
Walsh, Debra G., 124, 354, 356
Walster, Elaine, 98, 121, 122, 126, 127, 160
Walster, G. William, 121, 122, 160
Walzer, Susan, 329
Wampler, Karen Smith, 454
Ward, Mrs. Phelps, 376
Ward, Russell A., 191, 215
Waring, E. M., 100, 119, 131, 255, 256
Waris, Robert G., 182
Warner, Rebecca L., 419
Warren, Bruce O., 72
Wasserheit, Judith, 104
Wasserman, Ira M., 18, 424
Waters, Karen A., 88
Weaver, Charles N., 17
Weber, Barbara, 115
Webster-Stratton, Carolyn, 395, 399
Weigel, Daniel J., 407
Weigel, Randy R., 407
Weinberg, Howard, 419
Weinberg, Martin, 53
Weinberg, Thomas S., 392
Weingarten, Helen R., 424, 450
Weinraub, Marsha, 33
Weinstein, Karol K., 352
Weiss, Miriam Strauss, 179
Weiss, R. S., 114
Weiss, Robert, 32
Weitzman, Lenore J., 424
Weltman, Karen, 292
Wenk, DeeAnn, 18
West, James, 96
West, John D., 444
West, Melissa Owings, 392
Westhues, Anne, 323
Weston, Carolyn A., 446
Wheelis, Allen, 375–376
Whipple, Ellen E., 395, 399
Whipple, S. C., 392
Whisman, Mark A., 267
Whitbeck, Les B., 89
Whitcomb, Juliet H., 290, 292, 293
White, Gregory, 160
White, Helene Raskin, 18
White, James M., 148, 345
White, Kathleen M., 120

White, Lynn K., 140–141, 327, 429, 439, 445, 451
White, Priscilla, 212, 303
Whitehead, Barbara Dafoe, 414, 420
Whitehead, Mary Beth, 322
Whitley, Bernard E., 95
Whyte, Martin King, 42, 190
Wickrama, K. A. S., 18, 299
Widmer, Eric D., 99
Wiedermann, Michael W., 102, 127
Wierson, Michelle, 300
Wiesmann, Ulrich, 160
Wilcoxon, S. Allen, 344
Wilkie, Jane Riblett, 287, 302
Willi, Jurg, 156
Williams, Dale E., 76
Williams, David R., 209, 366
Williams, Flora L., 367
Williams, J. Sherwood, 38
Williams, Janice G., 142
Williams, Norma, 44, 45
Willis, Frank N., 137
Wilmot, Joyce Hocker, 277
Wilson, Barbara Foley, 439
Wilson, Stephan M., 98
Wilson-Sadberry, Karen Rose, 291
Windle, Michael, 393
Wineberg, Howard, 439
Winkler, Karen J., 117
Winslow, Edward, 200
Witsberger, Christina, 16
Wojtkiewicz, Roger O., 428
Wolfe, Donald M., 265, 266, 268, 272, 300
Wolfner, Glenn D., 395
Wolterbeck, Lianna Atchison, 72
Wood, Ellen, 72
Wood, Marie, 77
Wood, Wendy, 70
Woodward, Kenneth L., 353
Wright, David W., 72
Wright, Lloyd S., 395
Wright, Tracy I., 142
Wu, Zheng, 446
Wyer, R. S., Jr., 246–247
Wynn, Ruth L., 427
Wynne, Lyman C., 123

Yamanaka, Keiko, 186
Yarcheski, Adela, 115
Yarcheski, Thomas J., 115
Ye, Wenzhen, 46
Yee, Barbara W. K., 47, 48
Yelsma, Paul, 75, 147, 280
Yodanis, Carrie L., 397
Young, Robert, 72
Youngblut, JoAnne M., 300

Zablocki, Benjamin, 15
Zajonc, Robert B., 128
Zammuner, Vanda L., 172
Zhao, LiJun, 62
Zhou, Min, 46
Zick, Cathleen D., 329
Zietlow, Paul H., 340
Zill, Nicholas, 33, 378, 427, 428, 429, 430, 451
Zillman, Dolf, 67
Zimiles, Herbert, 428
Zollar, Ann Creighton, 38

SUBJECT INDEX

ABCX family crisis model, 386–387
Ability, gender differences, 62
Abortion, 95–96
  extent of, 96
  psychological consequences,
    95–96
Accommodation, 278–279
Additive adjustment, 50
Adolescents
  in dual-earner families, 300
  and grandparents, 353
  needs of, 345–346
  parental midlife concerns,
    346–348
  and parental midlife satisfaction,
    348–349
  problems with parents, 346
  self-esteem, 333–334
  in stepfamilies, 448–449
  working, 367–368
Adoption, 322–324
  children's problems from, 328
Adoption agencies, 323
Adult children
  source of stress, 325–326
  strains with aging parents, 357
Adultery; *see* Extramarital sex
Affairs, 212
African American families
  demographics of, 38–39
  divorce among, 418
  general characteristics, 38
  life in, 41–44
  median income, 40
  social institutions, 39–41
Agape, 157
Agapic lover, 169
Age factor in mate selection,
  183–184
Age heterogamy, 184
Age homogamy, 184
Aggression, gender differences,
  62–63

Aging family
  death of spouse, 357–358
  marital relations, 355–356
  retirement, 354–355
  social relationships, 356–357
AIDS, 23, 51, 88, 103, 104, 105, 107
Alcohol abuse
  extent of, 391
  as family problem, 393–394
  fighting, 401
  and quality of family life, 391–393
  self-help, 393
Alcoholics Anonymous, 393
Alternative life-style marriage, 226
Altruism, 87
Ambiguous family boundaries,
  448–449
Analytic remarks, 342
Analyzing, 251
Anatomy is destiny, 69
Androgyny, 69
  and intimacy, 77
  and mental health, 76–77
Anna Karenina (Tolstoy), 4
Anorgasmia, 106
Anxious/ambivalent lovers, 163–165
Appearance
  at first impression, 123–124
  importance to women, 71–72
  of life partner, 180
Arguments, frequency of, 278
Arranged marriages, 178
Artificial insemination, 321
Asian American families, 45–46
Assortative mating, 183, 188–189
As the World Turns, 170
Attachment to social
  environment, 348
Attraction
  in mating, 189
  powers of, 125–128
Augmentation, 449
Authoritarian parenting, 331, 332

Authoritative parenting, 331–332
Autocracy, 76
Avoidance, 278, 403
Avoidant lovers, 163–165

Bankruptcy, 367
Bargaining, 76
Behavior
  biological/social components, 70
  high-risk, 104–105
  importance of roles, 70
  sloppy, impulsive, or careless, 273
  Type A, 66
Beliefs, 130
Birth control
  abortion, 95–96
  contraception, 91–95
  methods, 92–93
Birth rates, 10, 312–313
Blamer, 259
Blending stage, 53, 147
Bob Newhart Show, 286
Body language, 124
Boys, in single-parent homes, 35
Brave New World (Huxley), 13
Breaking up, 148–150
Brideservice marriage, 229
Bridewealth marriage, 229
Budgeting expenses, 369–370, 372
Building stage, 54
Bullying, 76
Bundling, 145
Bureau of the Census, 10–11, 208
Business ability, 180

Canada, 446
Careers, 288–298
  instead of children, 317
  of singles, 201–203
CBS/*New York Times* poll, 95
Celibacy, 13–14, 15
Centers for Disease Control, 103, 318
Character, 179

Chemistry, personal, 128
Child abuse
  and alcohol, 391
  consequences of, 399–400
  extent of, 394–395
  incest, 395–396
Childbearing
  birthrates, 312–313
  changing patterns, 312–315
  decision, 315–317
  early, 89–91
  preference of sex of children
  preference of size of family,
    313–315
Child betrothal, 229
Child care, 326–327
  father's experience, 320–330
  mother's experience, 328–329
Child custody, 430–432
  and stepfather, 450
Children
  adjustment in remarriage, 444
  adjustments to parental
    behavior, 332
  adoption of, 322–324
  in African American homes, 42–43
  of alcoholics, 392–393
  coping with disruption from
    divorce, 432–433
  costs of both parents working,
    299–301
  death rates, 342
  desire for, 225
  detraction form marital
    relationship, 317
  in dual-career families, 294–295
  economic costs, 317
  effects of divorce, 426–430
  families by number of, 313
  families with young, 344–345
  gender difference in response to
    divorce, 430
  giving status, 316

Children—*Cont.*
  of Hispanic origin, 41
  in homosexual families, 51–52
  impact on sex in marriage, 101
  as integration factor, 419
  and marital satisfaction, 326–327
  out-of-wedlock, 8
  parental preference for sex of,
    313–315
  parental response to loss of, 402
  parenting and well-being of,
    330–334
  as personal/family legacy, 316
  as personal fulfillment, 315–316
  problems from adoption, 328
  and quality of life, 324–328
  reasons for wanting, 315–316
  religion as basis for having, 316
  satisfaction in marriage, 6
  satisfaction of raising, 327–328
  self-esteem, 333–334
  of single parents, 33–36
  of single women, 212
  and social expectations, 316
  in stepfamilies, 439, 448
  strains with aging parents, 357
  stress from raising, 324–326
  of teen parents, 89–91
Chinatowns, 46
Chinese Americans, 46
Chlamydial infection, 104
Cinderella, 452
Closed-type family, 226–227
Clothing, as nonverbal cue, 243
Clustering, 129
Cohabitation, 144–148
  blending stage, 147
  compared to marriage, 147–148
  heterosexual or homosexual, 147
  and jealousy, 172
  maintaining stage, 147
  patterns of, 146–147
  preferred to marriage, 148
  types of individuals, 144–146
Collaboration, 279
Commitment, 321
  building, 238
  meaning of, 237–238
  role of, 238
  by women to work, 291
Communication
  destructive messages, 250–252
  discussion about sex, 245
  and gender-role orientation, 75–76
  exerting power, 271
  of feelings, 246–247
  gender differences, 252
  impediments to, 250–254
  importance of listening, 247–250
  as interaction process, 244–247
  lack of in marriage, 252–254
  and marital satisfaction, 192–193,
    254–257
  about money matters, 370–371
  nature of, 242–244
  nonverbal, 243–244
  nonverbal behavior, 64–65
  nonverbal cues, 124
  opening lines, 124–125
  between parents and children, 346
  satisfying, 254
  silent marriage, 250

Communication—*Cont.*
  uninterrupted, 281–282
  verbal, 242
Communication skills
  practice and exercise, 258–260
  rules for, 258
Communication static, 245–246
Community divorce, 417
Commuter marriages, 293–294
Companionship, dating for, 138
Compassionate love, 161–162
  and intimacy, 168
  from passionate love, 165–166
Competition, 278
Competitive symmetry, 271
Complaints, divorce communication
    problems, 420–421
Complementary adjustment, 50
Complementary conversation, 271
Complementary interaction, 271
Complexity, of stepfamily, 448
Compromise, 130, 279, 282, 379
Computer personality, 259
Conciliatory remarks, 342
Conflict
  in aging family, 356–357
  to attack problems, 282
  avoiding festering resentment, 281
  categories of, 273
  communicating without ceasing,
    281–282
  and family well-being, 378–380
  flexibility and compromise, 282
  frequency of arguments, 278
  functions of, 271–272
  good fighting, 280–282
  grandparent-grandchild
    relations, 353
  issues and areas of, 272–274
  and lack of rites of passage,
    348–349
  leading to divorce, 421
  loving while fighting, 282
  maintaining perspective, 280
  in marriage, 271–282
  in money management, 370–372
  positive use, 272
  sensitivity to timing, 281
  sources of tension, 274–277
  styles in family life cycle, 341–342
  styles in, 277–280
  tension outlets, 281
  between work and family, 299
Conflict theory
  and abortion, 95–96
  and African American families,
    39–40
  children and marital
    satisfaction, 326
  definition, 23
  destructive messages, 251–252
  his/her marriage, 233–234
  jealousy, 173
  nonverbal behavior, 65
  parent-adolescent problems, 346
  power in marriage, 254
  and premarital sex, 96–97
  race of life partner, 186
  status attainment, 139
Confrontational remarks, 342
Consensus in marriage, 234–235
Consummate love, 168–169

Contraception, 91–95
Contraceptives
  age differences in use, 94–95
  amount and kinds of use, 94
  and religion, 95
Contracts, 229–231
Control/autonomy, 333
Convenience relationship, 146
Conversation
  competitive symmetry, 271
  symmetrical, 271
Co-parental divorce, 417
Coping
  by affirming family's worth, 405
  by avoidance, 403
  balancing self with other-concern,
    405–406
  by denial, 402–403
  with disruption from divorce,
    432–433
  by reframing, 406
  by scapegoating, 403–404
  by taking responsibility, 405
  using available resources, 406–407
Coping patterns
  dual-earner families, 306
  effective, 404–405
  ineffective, 402–404
Costs, 23
Courtship; *see* Dating; Falling in
    love; Mate selection
Cunnilingus, 99

Dai people, 85
Date rape, 142–143
Dating, 136–143
  changing patterns of, 138
  after divorce, 440–441
  finding a date, 136–137
  functions of, 138–139
  for intimacy and
    companionship, 138
  for mate selection, 139
  moving beyond, 143–144
  and parents' marriage, 141
  patterns of, 139–141
  problems in, 141–143
  for recreation, 138
  selecting a partner, 137–138
  by single parents, 35–36
  for socialization, 139
  status attainment, 139
  US-Taiwan comparisons, 140
  violence in, 142
David Copperfield (Dickens), 452
Days of Our Lives, 170
Death of spouse, 357–358
Death rates, 342
Decision conflicts, 273
De-escalating conflict, 281–282
Definition of the situation, 23
Demographics
  of African American families,
    38–39
  of Native American families, 47
  of remarriage, 430–440
Denial, 319, 340–342, 402–403
Dependence on partner, 273
Dependent listeners, 247
Depo-Provera, 92–93
Depression, 319
Destructive messages, 250–252

Deterioration of relationships,
    149–150
Differences in style, 277
DINS (double-income, no sex),
    100–101
Discussion, 340
Disengagement, 76
Disposition, 180
Distant-figure grandparent, 353
Distractor, 258
Division and fulfillment of
    responsibility, 273
Divorce
  causes and correlates, 417–423
  from changed feelings, 421–423
  changing grounds for, 413–414
  changing norms and roles, 420
  and child custody, 430–432
  child response to, 430
  coping with disruption from,
    432–433
  dating after, 440–441
  effects on children, 426–430
  effects on parents, 423–426
  and extramarital sex, 102
  financial problems from, 424–425
  and health problems, 424
  interaction between former
    spouses, 426
  interpersonal factors, 420–423
  in Japan, 422
  positive outcomes, 423–424
  and race, 418
  and remarriage, 417–418, 438–440
  in Roaring Twenties, 421
  six stations of, 416–417
  and social integration, 418–420
  sociodemographic factors,
    417–420
  and socioeconomic status, 417
Divorce court, 418
Divorce culture, 420
Divorce rate, 8, 11–12, 412–413
Divorce trends, 412–414
Dobu people, 224
Domesticity, 180
Double standard, 96–97
Dual-career families, 289, 291–297
  challenges faced by, 294–296
  child-free option, 317
  with children, 294–295
  commuter marriages, 293–294
  high- versus low-quality, 303
  level of equity in, 292–293
  marital roles, 293
  relations with other people, 295
  satisfactions of, 296–297
  time management, 294
  types of, 293–296
Dual-career wife, 295–296
Dual-earner families, 289
  challenges of, 297–304
  coping strategies, 306
  costs of both parents working,
    299–301
  and divorce, 301
  family work, 297–298
  home versus workplace, 299
  marital satisfaction, 302–304
  role negotiation, 301–302
  stress, intimacy, and family life,
    298–301

Early childbearing, 89–91
Economic costs of children, 317
Economic divorce, 417
Economic status of women, 314
Economy
    as cause of conflict, 274–275
    and working women, 290
Education
    of life partner, 180
    single-parent children, 34
    after teen pregnancy, 90
Education factor, 187
Egalitarian marriage, 226
Egypt, 267
Ejaculation, 82
Ejaculation dysfunction, 105–106
Elder abuse, 398–399
Emancipation, 146
Emotional divorce, 416
Emotional loneliness, 114, 115
Emotional overload, 32
Emotional problems, from divorce,
    423
Emotional support, 191–192
Empathy, 340
Employed mothers/women, 10–11
    child-free option, 317
    coping strategies, 306
    and household tasks, 289–290
    impact on children, 299–301
    jobs or careers, 288–298
    marital and family status, 288
    mental/physical health, 305–306
    reasons for working, 290–291
    in workforce 1990-1996, 287
Empty-nest stage, 349–354
    becoming a couple again, 350–352
    grandparenthood, 352–353
Empty-shell marriage, 20
Endometriosis, 319
Energy, 179
Engagement, 144
Equality
    in African American homes, 43
    in Hispanic families, 44
Equity
    in dual-career families, 292–293
    and intimacy, 121–122
    in marriage, 234–235
    in mate selection, 190–192
    and premarital sex, 98
    in remarriage, 445
    sense of, 290
Erection dysfunction, 105–106
Eros, 157
Erotic lover, 169
Ethnicity
    in mate selection, 184–185
    and sexual disease, 103–104
Everyday conversation, 254–255
Exchange theory
    definition, 22–23
    and divorce, 414
    equity/consensus in marriage,
        234–235
    financial issues in remarriage, 445
    intimacy and equity, 121–122
    on life partner, 182
    and premarital sex, 98
    self-concern *versus* other-concern,
        405–406
    self-disclosure, 255–256
    sense of equity, 290

Excitement stage, 82
Exit, 149
Expectant fathers, 329
Expectations from marriage,
    228–236
Experimenters, 206
Expressive individualism, 19
Expressive traits, 67–68
Extended family, 5
Extramarital sex, 101–103
    consequences of, 102–103
    reasons for, 102

Facial expressions, 243
Failure to give attention/reward, 273
Fake listeners, 247
Falling in love
    knowing when, 160–161
    love-prone people, 158
    male/female differences, 158–160
    misattribution of arousal, 160–161
    process, 157–160
    tests of love, 161
Familism, 19
Family background
    and premarital sex, 98–99
    of singles, 205
Family Circle, 181
Family crisis
    ABCX model, 386–387
    alcohol abuse, 391–394
    coping patterns, 402–407
    differing outcomes, 400
    reaction to, 400–402
    sources of, 386–391
    stressor events, 388–391
    violence, 394–400
Family crisis and stress, 386–387
Family/Families; *see also*
        Homosexual families
    with adolescents, 345–349
    affirming worth of, 405
    aging, 354–358
    anthropological definitions, 30
    Asian American, 45–46
    changes in traditional
        arrangements, 15–17
    childbearing decision, 315–317
    child-free option, 316–317
    children and marital satisfaction,
        326–327
    with children under, 351
    closed-type, 226–27
    in colonial America, 29–30
    conflict and well-being, 378–380
    conflicting evidence on, 18–19
    defense of, 17–18
    DINS (double-income, no sex),
        100–101
    dual-career, 291–297
    dual-earner, 298-301
    economic resources, 72
    extended/nuclear, 5
    happiness for children, 315
    Hispanic, 44–45
    household size, 10
    ideal, 12–15
    interracial, 48–50
    involuntary childlessness, 317–320
    managing power and conflict,
        375–380
    money management, 364–372
    Native American, 46–48

Family/Families—*Cont.*
    newly married, 343–344
    nonwhite, 38–50
    and number of children, 313
    open system, 227–228
    options for the infertile, 320–321
    preference for size of, 313–315
    prospects for, 19–21
    quality of life with children,
        324–328
    random system, 228
    resilient, 404
    rites of passage, 348–349
    role in socialization, 72
    satisfaction of raising children,
        327–328
    single-parent, 30–38
    slave, 49
    social science theories, 22–23
    time management, 372–375
    uncoupling process, 414–417
    in utopian communities, 13–15
    in utopian writings, 13
    with young children, 344–345
Family Inventory of Life-Events and
    Changes, 390
Family legacy, children as, 316
Family life
    dual-earner families, 298–301
    and mass media, 4–5
    myths about, 4–7
    and soap operas, 4–5
    variability in, 28–30
Family life cycle
    aging family 354–358
    changes in, 340–342
    conflict styles, 341
    empty-nest stage, 349–354
    families with young children,
        344–345
    family with adolescents, 345–349
    meaning of, 338–340
    newly married couples, 343–344
    19th-century, 343
    parental midlife concerns,
        346–348
    satisfaction at midlife, 348–349
    social changes, 342–343
    stages in, 339
    stepfamily, 447–448
    stressor events, 389
Family of origin, 4
Family pressures/traditions, 189
Family relations, of singles, 207–208
Family rituals, 349
Family work, 297–298
Farm, The, 15
Father-daughter incest, 395–396
Fatherhood, 329–330
Fatuous love, 168
Feelings, 246–247
Fellatio, 99
Feminine traits, 70–71
Femininity, and mental health, 76–77
Fertility clinics, 321
Fertility rates, 10
Festering resentment, 281
Fidelity, 277
Fighting, in marriage, 280–282
Financial conflict, 370–371
Financial issues, in remarriage, 445
Financial planning
    making a budget, 369–370, 372

Financial planning—*Cont.*
    nature of, 368–369
Financial problems, 365–366
    after divorce, 424–425
Financial well-being, 365
First impressions, 124–125
    general appearance, 123–124
    nonverbal cues, 124
First-year-changes in marriage, 236
Fixed expenses, 369
Flexibility, 282
Formal grandparent, 352
Friendship
    eight qualities of, 167
    and love, 167–168
Full-shell marriage, 20

Gallup poll, 18, 313–314
Gay fathers, 52
Gays, 50; *see also* Homosexual
        families
    long-term relationship, 53–55
Gender, 65
Gender differences, 65
    in ability, 62
    in aggression, 62–63
    in communicating feelings, 247
    in communication, 252
    interaction, 63–64
    nonverbal behavior, 64–65
Gender-role orientation, 65, 67–69
    changing patterns, 74–75
    and communication, 75–76
    essence of, 60–65
    family role, 72
    and intimacy, 77–81
    learned from family, 7
    lingering traditionalism, 75
    media role, 73–74
    of men in midlife, 347–348
    and mental health, 76–77
    school role, 72–73
    and self-concept, 76
    and sexual activity, 84–85
    significance of, 75–766
    and socialization, 71–74
Gender roles, 65
    biological basis, 69–70
    changing patterns, 74–75
    consequences of tradition, 66–67
    deviation form tradition, 70
    importance of nurture, 70–71
    nature-nurture controversy, 69–74
    and sexual activity, 84–85
    traditional, 65–66
General appearance, 123–124
Genital herpes, 104
Gonorrhea, 103, 104
Grandparenthood, 342, 352–353
Grandparents
    function of, 353
    types of, 352–353
Great Depression, 204, 274–275
Grief, 319–320
Group marriage, 14
Group norms, 130
Guilt, 319

Half-shell marriage, 20
Hamlet (Shakespeare), 452
Hansel and Gretel, 452
Health, 180
    and divorce, 424

Health—*Cont.*
of singles, 209–210
and work, 306
Heterogamous, 48
Heterogamy, 183
High-quality dual-career
marriage, 303
High-risk behavior, 104–105
Hispanic families, 44–45
Hispanics, and sexual disease,
103–104
Historian-grandparent, 353
HIV, 104, 107
Hmong, 46
Home responsibilities, 191
Home-workplace priorities, 299
Homogamy, 48, 183
Homophobia, 51
Homosexual cohabitation, 147
Homosexual families, 50–55
intimacy in, 52–53
long-term relationships, 35–55
problems in, 51–52
Homosexual marriage, 227
Honesty, 179
Households
expenditures, 370
money income, 366
by race, 39
size of, 10
Housewife, 286–287
and dual-career wife, 295–296
House work, 289–290
How to Make a Man Fall in Love
with You (Cabot), 157
Husband-dominant marriage, 265
Husbands
child care experience, 320–330
effects of divorce, 423–426
in successful marriages, 20–21
at work, 286–287
Hypergamy, 183

Iceland, 33
I Love Lucy, 286
Impotence, 106
Incest, 395–396
Individual happiness, 420
Industrialization, 286–287
Inexperience, 87
Infatuation, 168
Infertility
and adoption, 322–324
artificial insemination, 321
coping with, 319–320
nature of, 318–319
options for, 320–324
and surrogate motherhood, 322
in vitro fertilization, 321
Influence, tactics in, 76
Inhibited sexual desire, 106
In-law relationships, 235–236, 237
Institution of marriage, 224
Instrumental traits, 67–68
Integration, 115–117
Intellectual listener, 248
Intelligence, 179
Interpersonal skills, of females, 64
Interaction
by communication, 244–247
complementary, 271
gender differences, 63–64
loneliness in, 114–115

Interaction—*Cont.*
of mothers with children, 332
power and control, 276
in power struggle, 271
Interdependence, 321
Interfaith marriages, 186
Internet, meeting people via, 137
Interracial families, 48–50
Interrogating, 251
Interrupters, 247–248
Intimacy, 4, 168
in aging family, 355–356
in closed-type family, 226–227
and communication, 254–257
dating for, 138
developing, 130–132
dual-earner families, 298–301
and equity, 121–122
fulfillment through, 119–120
and gender-role orientation, 77–78
in homosexual families, 52–53
meaning of, 120–121
nature of, 120–123
need for, 119
perils of, 120
and privacy, 276–277
search for, 118
as self-sustaining, 122–123
and sex, 82
sex and search for, 89
and singles, 210–212
and well-being, 119–120
Intimate relationships
attractive qualities of others,
125–128
birth, life, and death of, 151
breaking up, 148–150
changing patterns of, 7–12
cohabitation, 144–148
commitment, 321
components, 120–121
dating, 136–143
developing intimacy, 130–132
developmental stages, 128–133
engagement, 144
enhancing quality of, 4
in family life cycle, 340–342
first impressions, 123–125
initial meeting and awareness,
128–129
initiating, 123–128
interdependence, 321
maintaining or dissolving, 132
mate selection, 178–182
moving beyond dating, 143–144
responding to deterioration,
149–150
selection process, 129–130
and sex, 87–88
for singles, 211
Inuit, 73
In vitro fertilization, 321
Involuntary retirement, 355
Irreverent remarks, 342

Japan
divorce in, 422
remarriage in, 446
singles in, 210
Jealousy, 170–173
consequences of, 173
ethnic comparisons, 172
gender differences, 171–172

Jealousy—*Cont.*
situations that provoke, 173
Jen, 111
Jobs, 288–298
Joint custody, 431–432
Journal of Sex Research, 87

Keristar, 15

Labor force, 287–290
Ladies Home Journal, 100
La Leche League, 324
Lecturing, 251
Legal divorce, 416
Legal issues, in remarriage, 445
Leisure, of singles, 206–207
Lesbian mothers, 52
Lesbians, 50
Lesotho, 107
Leviratic marriage, 229
Life partner
age factor, 183–184
assortative mating, 188–189
education factor, 187
ethnic factor, 184–185
exchange and equity, 182
expectations of, 179–181
as intimate relationship, 178–182
most valued qualities, 181
personality factor, 187
predictors of marital satisfaction,
190–193
race factor, 185–186
religion factor, 186–187
selection as filtering process,
182–183
Life satisfaction
factors in, 21–213
for singles, 212–216
from work, 305
Liking, 166–168
Linus-blanket type, 146
Listener
dependent, 247
fakers, 247
intellectual, 248
interrupter, 247–248
poor, 247–248
self-conscious, 248
Listening skills, 248–250
Living arrangement, of singles, 206
Loneliness
definition, 114
downward spiral, 116
effects of, 115
emotional, 114
in interaction, 114–115
and search for intimacy, 118
of singles, 208–209
sources of, 115–119
symptoms, 115
Looking Backward (Bellamy), 12–13
Love
and friendship, 167–168
Fromm's view, 87
and jealousy, 170–173
marriage for, 5–56
meanings of, 156–157
19th-century view, 165
passionate versus compassionate,
161–166
Rubin's scale, 166–167
and soap operas, 170

Love—*Cont.*
tests of, 161
triangular theory, 168
types of, 168
Love Plan, 157
Love-prone people, 158
Lovers, types of, 169–170
Loving
implications of differences, 170
and liking, 166–168
styles, 169–170
Low-quality dual-career
marriage, 303
Low sperm counts, 319
Loyalty, 149, 179
Ludic lover, 169
Ludus, 169, 170

Maintaining stage, 53–54, 147
Male/female ratios, 183
Male infertility, 319
Mandatory retirement, 355
Mangaians, 85
Mania, 169
Manic lover, 169
Manipulation, 76
Marital Communication
Inventory, 254
Marital disruption, 342
Marital dissolution; *see also* Divorce
action stage, 416
discussion stage, 415–416
postdissolution, 416
recognition stage, 415
Marital life style choices, 228
Marital power relationships, 265
Marital preferences, 227
Marital satisfaction
and children, 326–327
communication factor, 254–257
dual-earner families, 302–304
everyday conversation, 254–255
self-disclosure, 255–256
strains from young children, 345
Marital satisfaction predictors
communication, 192–193
equity, 190–192
timing, 190
uncertainty of, 194–195
Marital status of populations,
222–223
Marital system, 344
Marriage; *see also* Remarriage
adjusting to, 233–236
arranged, 178
Asian women, 9
changing personal contracts, 232
and children, 6
classified by alternative
life-styles, 226
classified by relationship structure,
226–228
closed-type, 226–227
cohabitation as path to, 144
in colonial America, 29–30
commitment in, 237–238
compared to cohabitation,
147–148
conflict in, 271–282
defense of, 17–18
desire for children, 225
destructive messages, 250–252
educational combinations, 187

Marriage—Cont.
    ending in divorce, 8
    equity/consensus in, 234–235
    expectations from, 228–236
    first-year changes, 236
    good fighting, 280–282
    good sex life, 7–8
    group marriage, 14
    his and her work, 286–287
    his/her marriage, 233–234
    ingredients for success, 20–21
    in-law relationships, 235–236, 237
    interfaith, 186
    lack of communication, 252–254
    life-span changes, 100–101
    for love, 5–56
    mixed-race couples, 187
    open system, 227–228
    and personal fulfillment, 225
    postponed by black men, 40–41
    power in, 264–270
    power struggle in, 270–271
    as practical solution, 226
    preparation for, 192–194
    private contracts, 229–231
    prospects for, 19–21
    random system, 228
    reasons for, 223–226
    by reimbursement, 229
    role expectations, 231–232
    serial marriage, 439–440
    sexual activity, 99–101
    sexual practices, 99
    sexual satisfaction n, 100
    silent, 250
    social expectations, 224
    and social ideals, 225
    social science theories, 22–23
    starting with two strikes, 234
    after teen pregnancy, 91
    in Togo, 229
    traditional, 230
    types of power n, 269–270
Marriage by abduction, 229
Marriage by exchange, 229
Marriage contract
    characteristics, 229–231
    clarifying expectations, 232–233
    clauses for, 233
    negotiating change, 232
Marriage questionnaire, 227
Marriage rate, 222–223
Marriage squeeze, 204–205
Masculine traits, 70–71
Masculinity, and mental health,
    76–77
Mass media, 4–5
    role in socialization, 73–74
Matchmakers, 178
Mate selection, 139
    after divorce, 440–441
    filtering process, 182–189
    means of, 178–182
    most valued qualities, 181
    predictors of marital satisfaction,
        190–193
Matrilineal descent, 47
Mayor of Casterbridge (Hardy), 386
Median income
    African American families, 40
    Asian American families, 45
    Hispanic families, 44

Media static, 245–246
Men
    benefits of marriage, 234
    careers as singles, 201–203
    commonalties with women, 60–61
    in empty-nest stage, 350–351
    falling in love, 158–160
    gender-role orientation, 60–65
    gender roles, 66–67
    ideal life partner, 179–180
    impotence, 106
    and jealousy, 171–172
    and personal freedom, 203
    sexual dysfunctions, 105–106
Mental health
    and gender-role orientation, 76–77
    and work, 306–306
Mentor-grandparent, 353
Mexican American families, 44–45
Mexican Americans, and sexual
    disease, 103–104
Midlife crisis, 347
Midlife parental concerns, 346–348
Midlife satisfaction, 348–349
Misattribution of arousal, 160–161
Miscarriage, 95
Mixed-race couples, 187
Moba-Gurma people, 229
Money
    and family well-being, 365–367
    meaning of, 364–365
Money income, 366
Money management, 364–372
    bankruptcy, 367
    financial planning, 368–370
    financial problems, 365–366
    minimizing conflict, 370–372
    and working teens, 367–368
Monogamy, 13
Monterey Park, California, 46
Moralizing, 251
Mormons, 28–29
    encouragement of large
        families, 316
Motherhood, 331
Mothers
    child care experience, 328–329
    interaction with children, 332
Mother-son incest, 396
Mutual dependency, 158
My Fair Lady, 252

National Center for Health
    Statistics, 33
National Institute of Mental
    Health, 73
National Survey of Families and
    Households, 42–43
Native American families, 46–48
Nature-nurture controversy, 69–74
Need for differentiation, 350
Needs, sharing, 130
Neglect, 149
Nesting stage, 53
Network family, 211
Neutralized symmetry, 271
Newly married couples, 343–344
No-fault divorce, 414, 425
Noncommittal remarks, 342
Nonverbal communication
    functions of, 243–244
    gender differences, 64–65

Nonverbal communication—Cont.
    kinds of, 243
Nonverbal cues, 124, 140
    as complementing words, 243
    as contradictions, 243
    as regulating communication, 244
    as repetition, 244
    as substitutes for words, 244
    triggering emotions, 244
Nonwhite families, 38–50
Normative ambiguity, 449
Normative integration, 419
Norms, 130
    changing, 420
Norplant, 92–93
No-shell marriage, 20
Nuclear family, 5
Nurturance, 276
Nurturer/great parent, 353
Nurture, importance of, 70–71

Old age, of singles, 208
Oneida Community, 15
Only Yesterday (Allen), 421
Open adoption, 323
Opening lines, 124–125
Open-type families, 227–228
Oral sex, 85, 99
Ordering, 251
Orgasm, 83–84
Other-concern, 405–406
Out-of-wedlock births, 8
Ovulation, improper, 319

Painful intercourse, 106
Papua New Guinea, 172
Parent abuse, 398–399
Parental behavior
    and age of parents, 334
    children's adjustments to, 332
    control/autonomy, 333
    and self-esteem, 333–334
Parent-child interaction, 331–332
Parenting
    doubts about skills, 317
    father's experience, 320–330
    styles of, 331–332
    and well-being of children,
        330–334
    wife's experience, 328–329
Parenting stress, 324–326
Parents
    in African American homes, 42–43
    coping with disruption from
        divorce, 432–433
    and dating patterns, 141
    death rates, 342
    effects of divorce on, 423–426
    homosexual, 51–52
    midlife concerns, 346–348
    and premarital sex, 99
    problems with adolescents, 346
    satisfaction at midlife, 348–349
    of singles, 207–208
    teaching gender roles, 72
Parents magazine, 18
Parents Without Partners, 324
Participant dual-career family, 293
Passion, 168
Passionate love, 161–166
    to compassionate love, 165–166
    emergence of, 162–163

Passionate love—Cont.
    experience of, 163–165
    kinds of lovers, 163–165
    measuring, 163
Passionate love scale, 164
Patrilineal descent, 47
Penis, 82
Penis envy, 69
Perceived inequity, 405–406
Perinatal loss, 402
Personal Attributes Questionnaire,
    67–68
Personal chemistry, 128
Personal contracts, 232
Personal freedom of singles, 203
Personal fulfillment, 225
    children as, 315–316
    by not having children, 316–317
Personality factor, 187
Personal legacy, children as, 316
Personal qualities
    physical attractiveness, 126
    similar or opposite, 127–128
Personal status, from having
    children, 316
Philia, 156
Physical aspects of sex, 82–89
Physical attractiveness, 126
    and dating, 137–138
Placator, 259
Polyandry, 28–29
Polygamy, 28–29
Polygyny, 28–29
Population, marital status, 222–223
Postdissolution, 416
Poverty level, 32
Power
    definition, 264–265
    importance of, 26–267
    inequities in, 270
    in marriage, 264–270
    measuring, 265–266
    resource theory, 268–269
    sources of, 268–270
    types in marriage, 269–270
Power and control interaction, 276
Power-management, 375–378
Power struggle
    in marriage, 270–271
    reactance theory, 270–271
    types of interaction, 271
Pragma, 169
Pragmatic lover, 169
Pregnancy
    options for the infertile, 320–321
    unwanted, 89–91
Premarital sex, 8
    changing attitudes, 97–98
    changing behavior, 98–99
    double standard, 96–97
    extent of, 98
    and social background, 98–99
    survey on, 97
PREPARE, 193–194
Principle of circularity, 423
Private contracts, 229–231
Problem drinker, 393–394
Promiscuity, 53, 88
Propinquity, 128, 188–189
Protestants, and premarital sex,
    97–98
Providing solutions, 251

Psychic divorce, 417
Psychological Abstracts, 87
Psychology Today, 156, 158, 172, 173
Puerto Rico, 301

Race
  and divorce, 418
  in selecting life partner, 185–186
  and sexual disease, 103–104
Random-type families, 228
Rape, 143
Rapport, 158
Reactance theory, 270–271
Receiver static, 246
Recreational dating, 138
Reduction, 449
Refractory period, 84
Reframing, 406
Regard, 340
Relationship orientation, of females, 63–64
Releasing stage, 54
Religion
  basis for having children, 316
  and contraceptives, 95
  and premarital sex, 98
  and social integration, 418–419
Religion factor, 186–187
Resilient family, 404
Reluctance, 87
Remarriage, 342
  adjustment of children, 444
  ambiguous roles, 449
  in Canada and Japan, 446
  challenges in, 444–445
  complex kin relations, 449
  demographics of, 49–440
  after divorce, 425
  financial issues, 445
  issues from first marriage, 444
  legal issues, 445
  making it work, 455–456
  myths on, 442–444
  quality of life, 445–447
  reasons for, 441–442
  types and number of, 438–440
Remarried couples, 438
Renewing stage, 54
Resentment, 281
Reservoir of family wisdom, 353
Resolution, 84, 320
Resource theory, 268–269
Response cycle, 82–89
Responsibility overload, 32
Retention, 448–449
Retirement, 354–355
  for singles, 208
Rewards, 23
Ridiculing, 251
Rites of passage, 348–349
Roaring Twenties, 421
Roe v. Wade, 95
Role expectations in marriage, 231–232
Role-making, 301
Role model grandparent, 353
Role negotiation, 301–302
Role-sharing, 293
Roles in shaping behavior, 70
Roman Catholic church
  encouragement of large families, 316

Roman Catholic church—*Cont.*
  on premarital sex, 97–98
Romantic love, 168
Romeo and Juliet (Shakespeare), 130, 189
Rubin's love scale, 166–167

Safe sex, 106–107
Salvation ethic, 397–398
Sandwich generation, 346
Scapegoating, 403–404
School, socialization role, 72–73
Second National Family Violence survey, 42
Secular lovers, 163–165
Seekers, 206
Selection process, 129–130
Self-awareness, sharing, 130
Self-care, coping strategies, 306
Self-concept, and gender-role orientation, 76
Self-concern, 405–406
Self-conscious listener, 248
Self-disclosure, 129–130, 158, 340
  and marital satisfaction, 255–256
Self-esteem, 76
  and parental behavior, 333–334
Semen, 84
Sender static, 245–246
Separateness, 348
Separation
  and divorce, 416
  moves toward, 415–416
Serial marriage, 439–440
Sex
  availability for singles, 203
  meaning of, 82–87
  physical aspects, 82–89
  social aspects, 84–87
  and society, 87
Sex hormones, 69–70
Sex purity, 179
Sex ratio, 204–205
Sexual activity
  affairs, 212
  in aging family, 355–356
  and contraception, 91–95
  and disease, 104–105
  experimenters, 206
  extramarital, 101–103
  gender roles, 84–85
  and intimate relationships, 87–88
  life-span changes, 100–101
  in marriage, 7–8, 99–101
  premarital, 8, 96–99
  safe and unsafe, 106–107
  and search for intimacy, 89
  seekers, 206
  of singles, 206
  among teenagers, 88–91
  traditionalist, 206
  unwanted, 85–87
  variations in, 85
Sexual desire, inhibited, 106
Sexual dysfunction, 51
  prevalence of, 106
  types of, 105–106
Sexually transmitted disease
  incidence of, 103–104
  and behavior, 104–105
  major types, 104
Sexual satisfaction, in marriage, 100
Sexual standards, 30

Shakers, 13–14, 15
Sharing emotions, needs, thoughts, and beliefs, 130
Silent marriage, 250
Silent treatment, 242
Single life style, 205–208
  family relations, 207–208
  leisure, 206–207
  living arrangements, 206
  old age, 208
  social activity, 206
Single-parent families, 30–38, 212
  births by race/ethnicity, 213
  challenges of, 32
  children of, 33–36
  by choice, 37
  dating by, 35–36
  in Iceland, 33
  marriage choice, 192
  parent-children problems, 35–36
  success of, 36–38
Singles
  availability of sex, 203
  awfulness of being unmarried, 200
  careers of, 201–203
  by choice, 214
  community activities, 209
  family background, 205
  health of, 209–210
  in Japan, 210
  life satisfaction, 212–216
  and loneliness, 208–209
  myths about, 198–201
  network family, 211
  number of, 198
  personal characteristics, 105
  personal growth, 203–204
  personal freedom, 203
  and question of children, 212
  reasons for status, 201–205
  sexual intimacy, 210–212
  social conditions, 204–205
  stigma on, 30
  types of, 201
  voluntary/involuntary, 201
Slave family, 49
Sloppy, impulsive, or careless behavior, 273
Snow White, 452
Soap operas, 4–5
  and love, 170
Social aspects of sex, 84–87
Social background, and premarital sex, 98–99
Social change, 276
  and family life cycle, 342–343
Social class, 129
  and mate selection, 189
Social creatures, 114–120
Social definitional changes, 345
Social environment, 348
Social expectations
  for having children, 316
  from marriage, 223–225
Social ideals, 225
Social illusions, 275–276
Social institutions, African American families, 39–41
Social integration
  from children, 419
  and divorce, 418–420
Socialization, 70
  dating for, 139

Socialization—*Cont.*
  and gender-role orientation, 71–74
Social relationships, caring for, 356
Social Science Index, 87
Social science theories, 22–23
Social sources of tension, 274–276
Social trap, 397
Societies
  differences between, 28–29
  variations within, 29–30
Society, and sex, 87
Sociodemographic factors in divorce, 417–420
Socioeconomic status
  and divorce, 417
  single-parent homes, 34
Sole custody, 420–431
Spontaneous abortion, 95
Spousal abuse
  and alcohol, 391
  characteristics, 396–398
  consequences of, 399–400
Spouse, death of, 357–358
Standoff, 379
State divorce laws, 413–414
Static, in communication, 245–246
Status
  dating for, 139
  from having children, 316
  and money, 365
Stepchildren, 449–454
  adjustments of, 453–454
  and marital relationship, 451–453
Stepfamilies
  demographics of, 439–440
  family functioning, 454–455
  life cycle, 447–448
  living in, 447–455
  making it work, 455–456
  structure of, 448–449
  types and number of, 438–440
Stepfathering, 450–451
Stepmother, unacceptable, 452
Stepmothering, 451
Step parents, 449–454
Stereotype, 123
Sterilization, 94
Storge, 156, 170
Storgic lover, 169
Stress
  from adult children, 325–326
  from divorce, 424
  dual-earner families, 298–301
  and family crisis, 386–387
  of raising children, 324–326
  from unemployment, 305
  work-induced, 305
Stressor events
  family life cycle and, 389
  most severe, 390
  types of, 388–389
  inequality of, 389–390
Student marriages, 234
Submission, 379
Submissive symmetry, 271
Substitution, 448–449
Success, and money, 365
Supplication, 76
Surrogate motherhood, 322
Surrogate parents, 352
Swinging marriage, 226
Symbolic interaction theory
  definition, 23

Symbolic interaction theory—*Cont.*
  developing intimacy, 130–131
  gay relationships, 53
  importance of power, 266–267
  marital dissolution, 415
  marriage role expectations,
    231–232
  meaning of love, 157
  and nurture, 70
  personal freedom, 203
  on remarriage, 443
  role negotiation, 301–302
  and self-concept, 76
  and sexual activity, 85
  strains from young children, 345
  verbal communication, 242
  violence in dating, 142
Symmetrical conversation, 271
Sympathy, 179
Syphilis, 103, 104
Systems theory
  ambiguous family boundaries,
    448–449
  Asian American children, 46
  definition, 22
  and divorce, 423
  dual-earner families, 298–299
  empty-nest stage, 350
  and nurture, 70
  parenting stress, 325–326
  power management, 376–377
  reaction to mate selection, 189
  and self-disclosure, 130

Taiwan, 140
Taking responsibility, 405
Task overload, 32
Tchambuli people, 70
Teenage sex, 88–91
  early childbearing, 89–91
  extent of, 88–89
  unwanted pregnancy, 89–91
Teen parents, difficulties of, 334
Teen pregnancy
  consequences of, 90–91
  reasons for, 89–90

Television, and gender-role
    orientation, 73
Tension
  interpersonal/personal sources,
    276–277
  social sources, 274–276
  sources of, 274–277
Tension outlets, 281
Term marriage, 226
Testes, 83–84
Testing relationships, 146
Testosterone, 69
Theory, 22
Thoughts, sharing, 130
Threatening, 251
Through the Looking Glass
    (Carroll), 242
Time management, 372–375
  coping strategies, 306
  dual-career families, 294
Time-wasting, 376
Timing
  of conflict, 281
  in mate selection, 190
Togo, 229
Touching, 243
Traditional dual-career family, 293
Traditionalism, in gender
    orientation, 75
Traditionalist, 206
Traditional marriages, 230
Traumatic bonding, 397
Triangular theory of love, 168
Triangulation, 376–377
Trobriand Islanders, 85
Trust, 277
Type A behavior, 66

Undetermined lovers, 163–165
Undifferentiated traits, 69
Unemployment, 274–275, 305
Unsafe sex, 107
Unselfishness, 179
Unwanted sex, 85–87
Utilitarian individualism, 19
Utopia (More), 13, 23

Utopian communities, 13–15, 16
Utopian writings, 12–13, 16

Vaginal lubrication, 82
Vaginismus, 106
Variable expenses, 369–370
Venereal disease; *see* Sexually
    transmitted disease
Verbal aggression, 397
Verbal communicate, 242
Viagra, 106
Vietnamese, 46
Violence
  in African American families, 42
  and alcohol abuse, 391
  child abuse, 394–395
  consequences of, 399–400
  in dating, 142
  extent of, 394
  incest, 395–396
  by men, 62–63
  parent abuse, 398–399
  spousal abuse, 396–398
Voice, 149
Voluntary childlessness, 316–317

Way of All Flesh (Butler), 125
Well-being
  of children, 330–334
  consequences of jealousy, 173
  and family conflict, 378–380
  financial, 365–367
  of infertile women, 319–320
  and intimacy, 119–120
  and work, 304–305
Well-Dressed Woman (Ecob), 376
Widow, 357
Widower, 357
Wife-dominant marriage, 265
Withdrawal, 379
Wives
  in African American families, 42
  dual-career, 295–296
  effects of divorce, 423–426
  employed mothers, 10–11
  parenting experience, 328–329

Wives—*Cont.*
  in successful marriages, 20–21
  at work, 286–287
Wizard grandparent, 353
Women; *see also* Dual-career
    families; Dual-earner families;
    Employed women
  Asian marriage age, 9
  benefits of marriage, 234
  careers as singles, 201–203
  commitment to work, 291
  commonalties with men, 60–61
  divorce rates and social roles, 420
  in empty-nest stage, 351
  falling in love, 158–160
  financial problems after
    divorce, 425
  gender-role orientation, 60–65
  gender roles, 66–67
  ideal life partner, 180–181
  importance of appearance, 71–72
  and jealousy, 171–172
  midlife issues, 348
  and no-fault divorce, 425
  occupations held by, 63
  after perinatal loss, 402
  and personal freedom, 203
  reasons for wanting to work,
    290–291
  sexual dysfunctions, 106
  sexual need, 103
  social/economic
    characteristics, 314
  and spousal abuse, 496–398
  in traditional gender roles, 66
  use of contraceptives, 94–95
Work
  changing patterns of, 287–290
  and life satisfaction, 305
  mental/physical health and, 306
  and well-being, 304–305
  women in labor force, 287–290
Work-family conflict, 299
Working-wife marriage, 226